ELEVENTH EDITION

Strategies for Teaching Learners with Special Needs

EDWARD A. POLLOWAY
Rosel H. Schewel Chair of Education, Lynchburg College

JAMES R. PATTON
University of Texas at Austin

LORETTA SERNA
University of New Mexico

JENEVIE W. BAILEY-JOSEPH
Lynchburg College in St. Lucia

330 Hudson Street, NY, NY 10013

Director and Portfolio Manager: Kevin M. Davis
Content Producer: Janelle Rogers
Development Editor: Jill Ross
Content Project Manager: Pamela D. Bennett
Media Project Manager: Lauren Carlson
Portfolio Management Assistant: Anne McAlpine
Executive Field Marketing Manager: Krista Clark
Executive Product Marketing Manager: Christopher Barry

Procurement Specialist: Carol Melville
Cover Designer: Carie Keller
Cover Photo: Getty Images/Wealan Pollard
Full-Service Project Management: Cenveo® Publisher Services
Composition: Cenveo® Publisher Services
Printer/Binder: LSC Communications/Willard
Cover Printer: Phoenix Color/Hagerstown
Text Font: Sabon LT Pro Roman

Cataloging-in-Publication Data is on file at the Library of Congress

1 17

ISBN 13: 978-0-13-457579-7
ISBN 10:   0-13-457579-2

In Memory of
Ruth Ann Payne and
James E. Smith, Jr.
Dedicated professionals, great friends, and co-authors

In Honor of
Jim Payne, mentor, friend and magician

We are pleased to present the 11th edition of *Strategies for Teaching Learners with Special Needs*. It is our honor to share this book with preservice and in-service professional educators. We trust that the information contained in this textbook will complement your knowledge and skills for working with students with disabilities and other learning challenges.

Strategies for Teaching Learners with Special Needs has been published since 1977, by Merrill, Prentice Hall, and now Pearson. When a textbook goes through multiple revisions, it develops its own stories. In 1975, Dr. Jim Payne, teacher extraordinaire and mentor, mentioned to James (Smitty) Smith and me that he had an offer from Merrill Publishing to develop a methods book in special education. Smitty and I assured him that the two of us would gladly share the work of getting the book written. The 1st edition, with fourth author Ruth Ann Payne moved forward.

Several years later, we lost Smitty, a wonderful colleague and most special friend still missed by all. The book moved into its 3rd edition in 1985 with the addition of Jim Patton as the fourth author. Subsequently we lost Ruth Ann Payne, a person who had taught us so much.

For the 5th and 6th editions, Jim Patton and I served as co-authors of the text. Then we invited Loretta Serna to join us as co-author of the 7th edition. Loretta brought to the book numerous important additional areas of expertise. Beginning with the 10th edition, we were pleased that Wendy Bailey-Joseph joined us to further enhance the text. Their work continues to make the 11th edition what we believe to be a unique contribution to the special education literature, in part because of the breadth of coverage that is presented within the book.

Our hope is that *Strategies for Teaching Learners with Special Needs* (11e) will enhance your skills as you take on the world's most important work—that of teacher and particularly that of teacher of individuals with special needs.

ORGANIZATION OF THE TEXT

Although many of the core content topics remain consistent with that of previous editions, we have made some significant organizational and content changes in the 11th edition. The chapters in Part I, Teaching Learners with Special Needs, serve as a foundation for the later chapters in the text. In Part I we discuss:

- Special Education: An Introduction to Teaching Students with Special Needs (Chapter 1)
- Foundations of Effective Instruction (Chapter 2)
- Teaching and Differentiating Instruction in a Multi-Tiered System of Education (Chapter 3)
- Strategies for Classroom Management and Positive Behavioral Support (Chapter 4)

In Part II, Content Areas, we discuss strategies for specific content areas:

- Spoken Language (Chapter 5)
- Reading: Word Recognition (Chapter 6)
- Reading: Comprehension (Chapter 7)
- Written Language (Chapter 8)
- Mathematics Instruction (Chapter 9)
- Social Studies (Chapter 10)
- Science (Chapter 11)

In Part III, Critical Skills, we discuss additional strategies that complement the core content areas:

- Study Skills (Chapter 12)
- Social Competence and Self-Determination Skills (Chapter 13)
- Applied Academics (Chapter 14)
- Career Development and Transition across School Levels (Chapter 15)

FEATURES OF STRATEGIES 11TH EDITION

The focus of *Strategies for Teaching Learners with Special Needs* (11e) is on effective teaching strategies for students being taught in any setting. This increased emphasis on successful strategies—in the text and in your teaching—will enable students with special needs to be successful in inclusive classrooms. The following special features provide important complements to the core textual material:

- **Learning Outcomes**—Within each chapter, the chapter learning outcomes focus the reader on key information that will be presented.
- **Student Understanding Checks**—Corresponding with each learning outcome and major section within each respective chapter, students can access questions that serve as a check for understanding and can receive feedback on their responses.
- **Teaching Tips**—Two Teacher Tips features are included in the content-area chapters—one that relates to an elementary classroom and one that relates to a secondary school classroom.
- **Culturally Responsive Classrooms**—Throughout the text we have included diversity box features that relate specifically to chapter content and give readers a broader understanding of today's classroom.
- **Classroom Activities**—Ideas are presented on how concepts discussed in the chapter can be incorporated and/or applied to daily classroom activities and routines.
- **Video links**—Within each chapter, multiple links are included that lead the reader to brief videos that illustrate and/or further explain specific strategies discussed in text.
- **Learning Modules**—Throughout the text, a series of learning modules expand on key concepts and strategies noted in text.
- **Key Terms**—In this text key terms have been boldfaced to highlight their importance to understanding strategies for teaching students with special needs.

INSTRUCTOR SUPPLEMENTS

- **Test Bank**—Each chapter of the Test Bank contains the following: a test bank with answer key (multiple choice, true/false, short answer, and essay).
- **Online PowerPoint® Presentation**—Every lecture presentation (in PowerPoint) highlights the key concepts and content for each chapter.

Both the Test Bank and the PowerPoint Presentations are available online. To access these resources, go to www.pearsonhighered.com and click on My Instructor Resource Center to log in or register for user name and password to download the textbook supplement files directly to your computer.

The Instructor Resource Center opens the door to a variety of media resources in downloadable, digital format.

ACKNOWLEDGMENTS

We recognize the great contributions of several key persons to the development of the 11 editions of this text. Of particular note are the multiple-edition contributions of chapters by Rosel Schewel, Glenn Buck, Lynda Miller, John Hoover, and Ginger Blalock. John's and Lynda's contributions continue in the Study Skills and Spoken Language chapters, respectively, within this edition. Special thanks go to Jacqueline Lubin and Andrew Bruce for their new contributions to the Reading: Word Recognition and Mathematics chapters, respectively. Special thanks also to Jacqueline Lubin for serving as author of the embedded student assessment protocols. Thank you also to the various professionals cited within the book for their contributions of diversity boxes and teacher tips.

In addition, a number of other persons helped with the book or with individual chapters; we have recognized their contributions throughout previous editions and regret that they are too numerous to note here. At Pearson, we have been assisted greatly by Kevin Davis, Janelle Rogers, Jill Ross and Anne McAlpine, who have provided everything we have needed and coaxed us along, by Ann Davis who has been our editor on multiple editions of the book and Julie Peters on the 11th edition, and by Kathy Smith at Cenveo. Also, we appreciate the support at Lynchburg College of Maryleen Auguste, Antonia Charles, and Delia Peters for assistance across multiple phases of the production of this book. We also appreciate the resources from the IRIS Center/Vanderbilt University that have enhanced this edition of the book.

We also thank Nicole Dobbins, University of North Carolina–Greensboro; Elizabeth M. French, Lebanon Valley College; Heather Garrison, East Stroudsburg University of Pennsylvania; Maryann Gromoll, Daytona State College; and Lisa Tritschler, Northeastern State University for their most helpful reviews that guided the revision of the 11th edition.

EAP for JRP, LS, & JWB-J

Brief Contents

Contents

Edward A. Polloway is the Rosel H. Schewel Distinguished Chair of Education at Lynchburg College. He completed his bachelor's degree at Dickinson College and his graduate degrees at the University of Virginia. He is the author of over 100 professional articles on special education with particular emphases in the areas of intellectual disability and learning disabilities. In addition to co-authoring the prior ten editions of this textbook, he also is the co-author of *Teaching Students with Special Needs in Inclusive Settings* (sixth edition), *Language Instruction for Students with Disabilities* (fourth edition), *Attention-Deficit/Hyperactivity Disorder in the Classroom, Children and Adults with Learning Disabilities*, and *Language Arts: Teaching Exceptional Students*, and served as co-editor of the Conquest of Mental Retardation and editor of *The Death Penalty and Intellectual Disability*. He also served for six years as the editor of the journal *Remedial and Special Education*. He has been honored as the 2007 Distinguished Alumnus of the Curry School of Education at the University of Virginia, the Burton Blatt Humanitarian Award from the Division on Autism and Developmental Disabilities of the Council for Exceptional Children, Lynchburg College's James A. Huston award for scholarship and as a Fellow of the American Association on Intellectual and Developmental Disabilities.

James R. Patton is educational consultant and adjunct associate professor at the University of Texas at Austin. He received his master's and doctoral degree from the University of Virginia after completing his bachelor's degree at Notre Dame. He is a former high school biology teacher and elementary-level special education resource teacher. He has also taught students who were gifted and those who were gifted/learning disabled. His professional interests include transition, life skills instruction, adult issues related to individuals with special needs, behavioral intervention planning, study skills, and classroom accommodations. He has served on the national boards of the Division on Autism and Developmental Disabilities, the Council for Learning Disabilities, and the National Joint Committee on Learning Disabilities.

Loretta Serna is professor of special education at the University of New Mexico. She completed her doctoral degree in special education and developmental and child psychology at the University of Kansas. In addition to her work on multiple versions of this textbook, Dr. Serna also was the principal investigator of the Self-Determination in Integrated Settings project. She has significant experience working with adolescents in both individual and group work as well as with families of adolescents who are at risk for failure. Her research interests include social and self-determination skills for youth at risk, teacher preparation, and curriculum and program development.

Jenevie Wendy Bailey-Joseph completed her doctoral degree in leadership studies at Lynchburg College. She also holds bachelor's and master's degrees in special education from Lynchburg College and a master's degree in Language and Communication impairments from the University of Sheffield (United Kingdom). Dr. Bailey was both a high school special education and literacy teacher and former kindergarten teacher in St. Lucia. She also served in the capacity as special education resource person, conducting in-service trainings with early childhood practitioners and general education teachers at both the elementary and high school level throughout that nation. She currently directs Lynchburg College's undergraduate and graduate programs in St. Lucia. Her professional interests include early childhood education, the effects of culture on self-determination, transition, and post school outcomes for students with high incidence disabilities.

1

Special Education: An Introduction to Teaching Students with Special Needs

LEARNING OUTCOMES

Upon completion of this chapter, the reader should be able to:

1.1 Identify the populations of students with disabilities that are the primary focus of the text and summarize information concerning categories of exceptionality, prevalence, and educational environments for these students.

1.2 Identify and discuss significant educational program considerations for students with special needs.

1.3 Demonstrate an understanding of how considerations of professionalism frame the responsibilities of educators.

Special education was established to ensure that students with disabilities were provided opportunities to reach their learning and post-school potentials. Over 40 years have passed since the initial passage of the Education for All Handicapped Children Act (EHA; Public Law [P.L.] 94-142), later re-named the Individuals with Disabilities Education Act (IDEA). The key focus was to provide a free, appropriate education to students who, in many instances, had not received such opportunities in the past.

Special education is different today from the earlier days after P.L. 94-142 in a number of ways. The majority of students with special needs receive most or all of their education in the general education classroom. Standards-based education often now drives what schools do and how teachers function. It is related to the parallel emphasis on federal and state initiatives that most students with special needs should have access to the general education curriculum. As special education has changed, so also has the role of the special education professional.

This text focuses on effective teaching methods with an emphasis on evidence-based practices. The strategies presented seek to provide teachers with an opportunity to extend and refine their repertoire of knowledge and skills.

This first chapter introduces a number of key concepts and considerations that will then become the foundation of subsequent chapters. It is framed by the key questions that relate to the provision of special education.

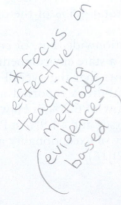
focus on effective teaching methods (evidence-based)

Therefore, the chapter begins with a discussion of the question of *who?*, the target populations for whom the topics addressed in the text are most appropriate. Next, we address the question of *through what?*, briefly considering the concept of individualized educational programs for students with special needs. Subsequently, we briefly address the question of *where?*, with attention to the assumption of inclusion of students with special needs in general education classrooms as well as attending to some introductory information related to collaboration. Then we look at the question of *what?*, which relates to the curriculum for students, focusing in particular on students having access to the general education curriculum, including content commonly based on state standards or the common core of education. The focus then is on *how?*, with a discussion of evidence-based practices to enhance the learning of these students. Then brief consideration is given to *with whom?*, the collaborative partnerships with families that are important to successful programs in special education. Following this, we address the question of *toward what?*, looking specifically at school completion and transition. The chapter concludes with a discussion of professionalism.

Collectively, these concepts and considerations lay the foundation for much of the subsequent detailed discussion in this textbook and frame key aspects of the roles of special education professionals in schools. A final section of the chapter briefly highlights the structure of the book.

STUDENTS WITH DISABILITIES

The primary focus of this text is on strategies for teaching students who experience learning difficulties. Included in this generic category are subgroups of students who may have been formally identified by schools in a variety of ways, using terms such as *learning disabled, intellectually disabled, emotionally disturbed*, and *behaviorally disordered*. The particular terms vary on a state-by-state basis but, taken collectively, represent individuals who have often been referred to as constituting high-incidence disabilities or the more common term *mild disabilities*. However, the latter term frequently understates the significant learning needs of these students and thus inadvertently could be used to question their real need for specialized

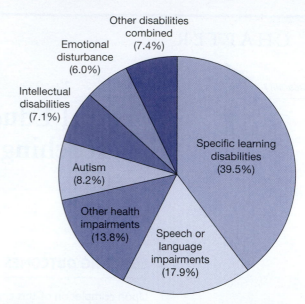

FIGURE I–I Percentages of Students Ages 6 to 21 by Disability Category

Source: 37th annual report to Congress on the implementation of IDEA (p. 36), by the U.S. Department of Education, 2015, Washington, DC: Author. (Note: Data from 2013)

instruction. Based on data from the U.S. Department of Education (2016), three key groups of students (those with learning disabilities, intellectual disabilities, and emotional and behavioral disorders) make up 52.1% of individuals served under IDEA (see also Figure 1-1). Percentages across key disability groups are highlighted in the figure.

Table 1-1 extends this analysis of prevalence by providing comparative data indicating the percentage of the school population with these selected disabilities in 2003 and 2014, respectively. As can be noted in the table, this decade shows an overall reduction in the number of students being identified and also parallel trends of lower prevalence for learning disabilities, intellectual disabilities, and emotional disturbance. Nevertheless, these three groups of students total 4.5% of the overall school population.

The above data are nationwide, but, of course, educators function within a state environment. It is therefore interesting to note that the overall number of students with disabilities reported across the states ranged from a low of 6.2% in Hawaii to highs of 11.7% in New Jersey and 14.9% in Puerto Rico. Variance by category of exceptionality also is quite common (USDOE, 2016).

TABLE 1–1 Percentage of school population with selected disabilities (ages 6 to 21)

Disability Area	2016 Report (2014 Data) of School Population	2003 Data
Specific learning disabilities	3.4%	4.3%
Intellectual disabilities	0.6%	0.9%
Emotional disturbance	0.5%	0.7%
All disabilities	8.6%	8.9%

Source: Adapted from *38th annual report to Congress on the implementation of IDEA* (p. 38), by the U.S. Department of Education, 2016, Washington, DC: Author.

Because federal and state legislation provide for special education based on certain eligibility standards within particular disability categories, we have begun our discussion of populations of students with disabilities from a categorical perspective. However, teachers are encouraged to consider several related caveats when attempting to match curriculum design and instructional methods to students' needs.

First, the population associated with specific categorical groups is continually influenced by public policy decisions and both research-informed and non–research-based professional decisions. Additionally, efforts to revise definitions and terminology regularly bring about regulatory changes that further alter those served under the labels of learning disabilities, emotional or behavioral disorders, intellectual disability, or other disability designations.

Second, categorical labels convey little about curriculum design and specific teaching strategies that should be used. Such labels at face value indicate only that a student has met a set of diagnostic criteria established by a state for a specific disability. Furthermore, these labels often indicate only that students so classified have experienced difficulty learning through traditional means or within traditionally organized general education classroom environments to such an extent that schools recognize and identify them. Ultimately, these students are likely to require more direct, intensive, extensive, or highly individualized instruction to reach their learning potential and also require specific accommodations to existing curriculum and/or instruction.

Third, in a related vein, it is important that teachers view students with disabilities as students first and then address the needs that these students have for modifications in instruction and curriculum. Again, categorical labels do not yield specific prescriptions in terms of educational interventions.

Fourth, the strategies highlighted in this text have applicability for individuals with a variety of learning problems, regardless of whether they have been labeled as disabled or merely set apart from others in the classroom due to their difficulties. A large number of students who can be considered at risk for having academic, social, or behavioral difficulties will not meet eligibility criteria for special education yet may benefit greatly from the teaching methods presented in this text. This would include students who are identified with attention-deficit/hyperactivity disorder (ADHD). Ultimately, an analysis of an individual's learning needs is necessary to determine the relevance of any particular curricular orientation or any specific instructional procedure.

 Check Your Understanding 1.1 Click here to gauge your understanding of the concepts in this section.

EDUCATIONAL PROGRAM CONSIDERATIONS

Individualized Education Program

All students identified as having a disability under IDEA must have an **individualized education program** (IEP). The IEP is a written document summarizing a student's learning program. The major purposes of an IEP are to establish learning goals for an individual student, to determine the educational services the schools must provide to meet those learning goals, and to enhance communication among parents and other professionals about a student's program.

The IEP includes attention to the student's participation in general education, levels of performance, annual goals, the special education and related services and supplementary aids to be provided, and the program adaptations or supports for school personnel that will be provided to the child. Further, the IEP addresses the ways in which the student's disability is affecting his or her progress within the general curriculum. The IEP should explain the extent, if any, to which the student will not participate with students who are non-disabled. Statements related to the student's participation or lack of participation in statewide and districtwide assessments must also be included in the IEP. Critical considerations in the IEP should provide the basis for determining and implementing evidence-based educational practices. Significant detail on the development and implementation of individualized educational programs is provided in Chapter 3.

School Inclusion

The most consistent theme in special education over the past 50 years has been the increasing commitment to and the importance of providing persons with disabilities the opportunity to have a place in school and society. Schools seek to educate children with disabilities—to as great an extent as possible—with their peers who are non-disabled. The least restrictive environment (LRE) principle provided the initial impetus for students to attend school in the most inclusive setting possible, which is now most often defined as the general education setting (i.e., regular classroom).

Figure 1-2 provides a summative graphic of educational placement for students with disabilities based on data collected in 2013. Table 1-2 then provides a comparative analysis of these data across selected groups of students with disabilities. For both the figure and the table, the data reflect students with disabilities placed, respectively, more than 80% of the day in the general education classroom, between 40% and 79% of the time in the general education classroom (with the assumption that the remainder of the time is typically in resource rooms or self-contained classes), and less than 40% of the school day in the general education classroom (i.e., in special education classes) and enrolled in other environments (defined as special separate schools, residential facilities, homebound or hospitalization programs, correctional facilities, or parentally placed in private schools). The clear trend over the past several decades has been an increased percentage of students spending the majority of their time in general education classes with support from special education teachers.

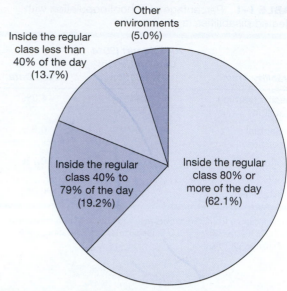

FIGURE 1–2 Percentage of Students Served under IDEA by Educational Environment

Source: 37th annual report to Congress on the implementation of IDEA (p. 45), by the U.S. Department of Education, 2015, Washington, DC: Author. (Note: Data from 2013)

As noted in the table, the educational placement percentages vary across disability group. The expectation is that primary services for students with disabilities will clearly be in general education programs for students that are taught for all or a significant percentage of the school day. However, for some disability groups, especially for students identified as having intellectual disabilities and emotional/behavioral disorders, there remains a greater likelihood of educational placement being in settings for a smaller percentage of the school day and, particularly in the case of students with emotional and behavioral disorders, in other environments.

In the discussion above concerning prevalence, it was noted that there are significant differences between states; this is certainly true in terms of educational environments as well. For example, the variance in terms of placement in the general education classroom at least 80% of the time ranges from 83.7% of all students with disabilities in Alabama to 35.8% in Hawaii. In terms of students spending less than 40% of the time in the special classroom, the range was from a high of 22.2% in California to a low of 5.4% in South Dakota (U.S. Department of Education, 2014).

TABLE 1–2 Percentage of students with selected disabilities in variant educational environments (ages 6 to 21) (2014)

Disability Area	>80% in General Education	40% to 79% in General Education	<40% in General Education	Other Environments
Specific learning disabilities	69.2%	23.0%	5.8%	2.0%
Intellectual disabilities	16.9%	26.3%	49.2%	7.6%
Emotional disturbance	46.2%	17.6%	18.8%	17.5%
All disabilities	62.6%	18.6%	13.5%	5.3%

Source: Adapted from *38th annual report to Congress on the implementation of IDEA* (p. 50), by the U.S. Department of Education, 2016, Washington, DC: Author.

Teachers must carefully consider their role in providing effective instruction that facilitates the successful inclusion of students with disabilities in general education and in evaluating the efficacy of these efforts. The term *supported education* is an important complement to the term (and the process of) *inclusion* (Smith, Polloway, Doughty, Patton, & Dowdy, 2015). It emphasizes that successful inclusion hinges on the provision of appropriate supports in the general education classroom as a basis for establishing a successful learning environment, particularly for students with special needs. The most critical supports for these students will come from highly effective special education teachers. While inclusive environments are now most often the "home" for the majority of students with disabilities, the premise of special education is still that their educational program is to be individualized.

Thus, the emphasis in education is teaching the clear majority of students within the general education classroom. Increasingly, this is a reflection of the application of the three-tiered model for education (see Chapter 2 for a full discussion). Successful educational programs in general require that a collaborative environment be established within the school environment. Consequently, all special educators should presume that their ability to effectively collaborate with others is a significant part of their responsibilities. Special educators must operate as part of a team in many aspects of their roles, including screening, making assessments, planning individual programs, developing placement options, providing direct instruction and instructional supports, and monitoring success. Teachers must work with others to operationalize the required aspects of all initiatives or changes in effect within the instructional program. *School collaboration* considerations are addressed in Chapter 3.

ENHANCEDetext
video example 1.1
Watch this video for further discussion concerning placement issues and students with disabilities.

Curriculum

The core of educational programs is the curriculum. It is the essential "what" question for education. For individuals with special needs, there is a long history of variance in terms of the nature of curricular emphases for the students. The brief discussion here focuses on the contemporary emphasis on access to the general education curriculum with some additional discussion on functional curriculum considerations. This section essentially provides an overview of the chapters that follow, which address the areas of the curriculum relevant to students with disabilities.

The general curriculum is the same curriculum as that afforded to students without disabilities. It is the explicit curriculum (i.e., clearly identified by the district or state) for the majority of students in the school, as defined by standards that states have identified. Access to the general education curriculum is an overriding theme of special education service delivery. It underscores the focus of the

IEP that must be developed for each student with a disability (see the prior section on IEPs). A critical goal of special education is to help students gain those skills and acquire the knowledge that will allow them to access—and be successful in—the curriculum afforded to students who are not disabled.

Standards-based education refers to the curriculum in which what is taught is tied to the state-derived content and performance standards in the core subject areas of reading/language arts/English, mathematics, social studies, and science (either based in individual state standards or tied to the common core federal standards). The intent of developing standards is to have a common set of goals and mileposts. Although a number of ways exist for classifying standards, the most common distinction is between content standards that reflect the knowledge and skills that students are accountable for in academic subjects and performance standards that focus on achievement levels that they must meet to confirm proficiency. Most students with disabilities must meet a challenging set of standards and participate in the state testing process.

The trend toward standards-based education is reflected in development of the *common core state standards*. Developed in 2009 and based on collaborative research begun in 2007 and released in 2010, the common core standards have been adopted by 45 states. The Common Core State Standards Initiative (CCSSI) (2010) indicates that the standards are "research and evidence-based; clear, understandable, and consistent; aligned with college and career expectation; based on rigorous content in the application of knowledge through higher-order thinking skills; built upon the strengths and lessons of current state standards; and informed by other top-performing countries to prepare all students for success in our global economy and society" (para. 1).

The importance of standards (and the high-stakes testing that accompanies them) is a central fact of contemporary public education. The focal question now is not whether students with special needs will participate in a standards-based system but rather, more appropriately, how well students with special needs will do in this new system.

A curricular dilemma facing professionals in special education, particularly for teachers at the secondary school level, is finding the balance between addressing the content and performance standards of the general education curriculum (within which most students with disabilities must show progress) while ensuring that the current and future needs of their students are addressed. Making curriculum and instruction more life relevant requires knowledge, skills, and effort. A functional curriculum is particularly relevant in considerations of special education programs for students with intellectual disabilities. Particularly for this population, the functional focus in curriculum reflects its potential merits for successful post-school outcomes. In spite of the attention given to the possible role of functional curricula, Bouck and Satsangi (2014) found a limited body of research on such a focus. An extensive discussion of functional curriculum considerations is provided in Chapter 14.

Achievement Assessment. The advent of placing students with special needs in inclusive classrooms that followed the establishment of state standards has been accompanied by a parallel emphasis on student evaluation, typically by means of high-stakes testing. As Zumeta (2015) noted, "The inclusion of students with disabilities in the National Assessment of Educational Progress [reports], as well as in states' and districts' high stakes assessments . . . brought much-needed attention to the poor achievement of students with disabilities" (p. 84).

Most students with disabilities are expected to take the regular districtwide or statewide tests; some who take these tests receive some type of accommodation or modification. In the U.S. Department of Education (2014) report, for example, data indicated that a range of 38.9% to 45.8% of all students with disabilities (grades 3 to 8) participated in regular assessments based on grade-level academic standards with accommodations, while an additional 29.9% to 39.3% participated without accommodations. The comparable numbers in reading with accommodations was 37.4% to 41.5% and without accommodations 33.1% to 41.5%.

Some students with more significant needs will be exempt from taking a regular standards-based test and will be administered an alternative assessment. According to the U.S. Department of Education (2014), the percentage of students with disabilities who participated in assessments with modified standards (i.e., assessments that measure the achievement of students who access the grade-level curriculum but whose disabilities preclude them from achieving grade-level proficiency) across the above curricular areas and grade levels ranged from 5.2% to 15.1%, and those who participated in assessments with alternate standards (i.e., assessments designed to measure the achievement of students with significant cognitive disabilities) ranged from 9.0% to 10.0%.

The major challenge is to determine appropriate ways for students with diverse needs to access the general curriculum. For most students at this time, instruction will occur increasingly within the context of inclusive classrooms.

Universal Design. In order to facilitate successful programs for students with special needs in the general education classroom, these programs should reflect features commonly associated with the concept of universal design for learning, which is built on classrooms that welcome all students, promote positive interactions, provide opportunities for students to demonstrate knowledge and skills through multiple means, provide flexibility in the presentation of information as well as in the ways in which students may demonstrate their skills or knowledge, accommodate learning differences with supports, and use technology (King-Sears, 2015; Rao, Wook & Bryant, 2014). Universal design for learning is discussed in greater detail in Chapter 3.

Evidence-Based Practices

The principles of science have been incorporated into general and special education through teachers using interventions that have empirical support indicating that that they work with the populations of students with whom they are being used. The genesis for the concept of **evidence-based practice** in special education comes from the assumption that education should be scientifically based. Appropriate educational programs are to be based on empirical assessments on the use of particular practices with students.

Cook, Tankersley, and Landrum (2009) defined an educational intervention as evidence-based practice (EBP) "when a sufficient quantity of high-quality research studies that demonstrate experimental content have been conducted and show that student outcomes are improved as a result of using the practice" (p. 70). Zirkel (2008) broadened the definition to include interventions validated by empirical research complemented by "documented

results of continuous progress monitoring, teacher or other professional reports, and professional testimony" (p. 2). Given the fact that the latter definition might invite non-validated practices under the evidence-based practice umbrella, the central, most relevant concept is that evidence-based practices are those "shown to be effective by credible research" (Cook et al., 2009, p. 70).

Cook et al. (2015) further defined evidence-based practices as interventions that were supported, for example, by at least "two methodologically sound group comparison studies with random assignments to groups, with positive effects, and at least 60 participants across studies; four methodologically sound group comparison studies with non-random assignments and at least 120 participants across studies; or five methodologically sound single-subject studies with positive effects and at least 20 total participants across studies" (p. 230). They also offered further qualifiers for evidence-based practice and potential evidence-based practice.

Historically, translating research into practice in education has lagged. As a result, difficulty exists in separating validated from non-validated interventions. To illustrate the concept, specific examples of evidence-based practices that are discussed in subsequent chapters include using data-based decision making; direct instruction of basic skills, such as in terms of instruction in decoding in reading; teaching to mastery in the development of automaticity; using mnemonic strategies; assisting students in acquiring cognitive strategies to enhance independence in the learning process; using reading comprehension strategies; and implementing the concrete, semi-concrete, and abstract (CSA) model in mathematics.

Periodic reviews of instructional practices used by special education teachers show mixed results in terms of teachers relying on interventions that have empirical support. For example, Burns and Ysseldyke (2009) reported high levels of reliance on direct instruction (evidence-based practice is discussed further below) while also finding a significant number of teachers indicating regular reliance on modality instruction and perceptual motor training, both of which lack empirical support.

Effective Instruction. An overriding consideration regarding evidence-based practice for students with special needs is that effective instruction for students with disabilities consistently is found to be systematic and explicit. *Systematic instruction* requires that teachers focus on instruction of a carefully selected and useful set of skills and that those skills are organized into a logical sequence for instruction. Students consequently know what is expected and why it is important. It requires a planned and ordered process to be followed.

Explicit instruction provides a clear purpose for learning accompanied by clear and understandable directions and explanations. Explicit instruction focuses on the skills and strategies that are needed by students. Further, it includes a process that addresses the importance of modeling and demonstration, guided practice, independent practice, maintenance activities, and provisions for generalization.

Explicit and systematic instruction includes direct teacher modeling or explanation, frequent student responding reflective of high engagement and verified learning, direct and immediate feedback to student responses, and precise sequencing of content to be presented. Little and Delisio (2015) noted that "explicit instruction . . . refer(s) to instruction that incorporates the following teaching behaviors: logical sequencing (i.e., lessons build on one another), review of previous content, teacher-directed presentation and modeling, guided and repeated practice with specific feedback, independent practice by learners, curriculum-based assessments, and periodic review" (p. 1).

ENHANCEDetext
video example 1.2
Watch this video to learn more about explicit instruction.

A third concept of importance is *intensive instruction*, which suggests that sufficient time is allocated to comprehension. Moreover, intensive instruction includes a broad scope and sequence, incorporating the active participation of the student in the lessons. Lessons should include many opportunities for the students to try out what they have learned and should also include ample feedback for the students.

In sum, teachers should anticipate the need to provide complete explicit, systematic, intensive instruction to increase the likelihood that skills and strategies will be acquired.

Cautions.   There are several cautions concerning adopting appropriate educational practices. First, evidence-based research requires a quantity of research studies across settings and teachers with replication. Relatively few educational interventions have received the degree of research attention and validation to fully achieve the gold standard as discussed above. Given the challenges in achieving such a goal, the teacher should integrate the best available body of research evidence complemented by professional expertise. In this regard, one might consider "levels of assurance" in terms of the validity of specific strategies for teaching with a continuum that would range from intuition, observation, and expert endorsements to research based and evidence based or scientifically validated.

Second, it is important to consider the observations of Fuchs and Deshler (2007), who noted, "When we say an instructional approach is 'scientifically validated,' we mean it's a 'good bet' for many. It should be considered seriously for adoption, but it comes with no guarantees. No program is valid for all students or for all time. The [programs] must be implemented and evaluated by practitioners" (p. 132).

Third, in a field traditionally beset with new and too often unproven ideas, teachers must also be cautious in adopting treatments that, at a minimum, threaten the availability of precious instructional time or financial resources. For example, Worrall (1990), in a classic treatise on health care interventions, provided a series of helpful suggestions that also are relevant to special education interventions:

- If it sounds too good to be true, it probably is.
- Be wary of any treatment or product offering a "cure." . . . Cures are actually few and far between.
- Be cautious when "complete," "immediate," "effortless," "safe," or "guaranteed" results are promised.
- Legitimate . . . researchers do not use words such as "amazing," "secret," "exclusive," "miracle," and "special" in describing treatments. (p. 212)

The clear call, both professionally and in legislation, is for reliance on instructional practices that have a research base if they are to be used with students with special needs. The use of evidence-based practices in instructional programs will subsequently provide a strong foundation for successful school and life transitions that are critical for students with special needs. Effective instruction is discussed in greater detail in Chapter 2.

Partnerships with Families

Since the advent of P.L. 94-142 in 1975, parents have always been encouraged to participate in the special education process. However, the amount and quality of this participation has varied greatly. Parents must consent to the evaluation of a student's educational abilities and needs, the determination of necessary services, and the actual placement of a child in any type of special program. Parents have the right to obtain an independent educational evaluation of their child. Some parents engage the process fully, whereas others participate minimally for a variety of reasons. Parental partnerships are detailed in Chapter 3.

Transitions

Research consistently has illustrated the challenges faced by students with disabilities after the completion of secondary school (e.g., National Longitudinal Transition Study-2; Newman, Wagner, Cameto, & Knokey, 2009). Therefore, programs, services, and supports for individual children and youth cannot be focused solely on their needs at the present time. Rather, an attitude typified by concurrent concern for students' success in the future must be adopted. Regardless of the population being served or the setting in which services are being delivered, teachers must be cognizant of how their current instructional and curricular efforts ultimately will impact students' transitions into the school and community environments that lie ahead; such outcomes-focused and results-oriented thinking should be at the core of educational efforts for students with disabilities. Because students are guaranteed the right to an appropriate education, they should also be assisted in benefiting from it—both during their school years and on completion of K–12 education. This commitment is a major tenet of this text.

Students face a number of significant transitions: those from early intervention (Part C of IDEA) to early childhood programs (Part B, for young children who are eligible for early childhood special education programs), from preschool

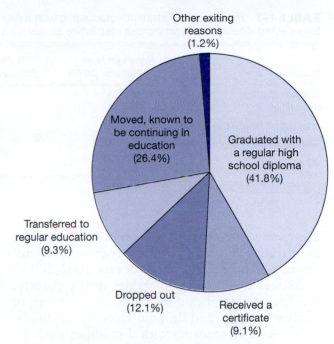

FIGURE 1–3 Percentage of Students Ages 14 to 21 by Reason of Exit from School

Source: Adapted from *38th annual report to Congress on the implementation of IDEA* (p. 38), by the U.S. Department of Education, 2016, Washington, DC: Author. (Note: Data from 2012–2013)

to kindergarten, from elementary to middle school, from middle school to secondary school, and from high school to post-school settings, including post-secondary education and independent living in the community. Each of these transitions can be crucial to an individual's positive quality of life. The specific transition that has received the most attention has been that from school to post-school settings, certainly in large part because young adults with disabilities are disproportionately underrepresented in the nation's workforce as well as in many educational, training, and employment programs.

An initial key consideration that impacts successful transition is school completion. Students with disabilities are overrepresented in the ranks of school dropouts and underrepresented among those receiving diplomas (see Figure 1-3) (U.S. Department of Education, 2015).

Table 1-3 provides data specifically on graduation and dropout rates for selected disability groups. As reflected in this table, the trend data are increasingly positive for each disability group and for students with special needs overall, with a significant increase in the percentage of students receiving high school diplomas and a parallel

TABLE 1–3 Percentage of students graduating with a regular high school diploma and dropping out of school for selected disability groups (across respective annual idea reports)

Disability Area	% Received High School Diploma (2016)	% Received High School Diploma (2003)	% Dropped Out (2016)	% Dropped Out (2003)
Specific learning disabilities	70.8%	57.7%	18.1%	31.4%
Intellectual disabilities	40.8%	37.8%	16.8%	29.3%
Emotional disturbance	54.7%	35.6%	35.2%	55.9%
All disabilities	66.1%	52.5%	18.5%	33.6%

Source: Adapted from *38th annual report to Congress on the implementation of IDEA* (p. 63, 65), by the U.S. Department of Education, 2016, Washington, DC: Author.

decrease in the dropout rates noted between the most recent data from the U.S. Department of Education as contrasted to those data for 2002–2003.

As was noted for prior tables in the chapter, there is also significant state variance in terms of graduation rates and dropout rates. For example, in terms of all students with disabilities graduating with a high school diploma, the range across states is from 88.3% in Minnesota to 27.8% in Mississippi. For dropout rates for all students with disabilities, the range is from a high of 46.2% in South Carolina to a low of 7.3% in Tennessee.

IDEA reflects a commitment to **transition planning** for students. The transition process involves the efforts of students, their families, school personnel, and potentially an array of adult service providers. Transition services are intended to reflect a coordinated set of activities for students, promoting movement from school to post-school activities, including postsecondary education, vocational training, integrated employment, continuing and adult education, adult services, independent living, or community participation. These activities should be based on the individual student's needs, taking into account the student's preferences and interests, and should include instruction, community experiences, the development of employment and other post-school adult living objectives, and, as appropriate, acquisition of daily living skills and functional vocational evaluation. Consistent with federal law, transition planning and services must begin prior to a student reaching age 16. Transition is discussed in detail in Chapter 15.

 Check Your Understanding 1.2 Click here to gauge your understanding of the concepts in this section.

PROFESSIONALISM

Beyond the demands of a teacher's role as discussed throughout this section, effective special educators also must display a high degree of personal determination to positively influence the education and acceptance of persons with special needs. Bateman's (1971) historical challenge half a century ago still has significant merit: Teachers must have a personal philosophy of education, have a willingness to be agents of social change, be accountable for services provided, possess and continue to develop personal and professional competencies and a comprehensive knowledge base, and care deeply about all human beings, including themselves. These professional attributes serve as the foundation for advocacy crucial to the welfare of students.

The role of special educators as change agents requires them to question whether their own and others' actions best benefit students. Accepting minimal levels of professional conduct or acquiescing to administrative practices contrary to students' basic interests threatens those core aspects of special education for all students with unique learning needs. Assuming a professional role thus requires the commitment of an advocate as well as effectiveness in instruction.

In addition to the importance of using teaching strategies that are empirically supported, it is also important to consider the qualitative aspects of teaching. Effective teachers develop positive relationships with students that become critical contributors to achievement and to retention in school, particularly for those students experiencing difficulties. The above admonitions certainly hold for teachers in general given the significant trend toward including students with disabilities and regular classrooms. Successful education for all students requires a professional commitment to collaboration.

Professionalism also requires teachers to commit to continuing development (e.g., credit courses, workshops, conferences, and regular reviews of professional research). Unlike some professions (e.g., speech and language pathology) that have comprehensive and regulated requirements for continuing education, teaching (and special education) unfortunately is far less prescriptive and consequently may in practice be much looser concerning this important area. Nevertheless, all teachers—and certainly those who work with the most challenging students in education—need to remain current of new developments and practices in the field.

Good teachers are, above all, effective; they nurture learning and their students, use evidence-based practices, and constantly evaluate their teaching programs. A teacher who remains energetic, enthusiastic, and positive and who works hard, embraces effective teaching competencies, remains committed to further professional development, and develops a broad repertoire of skills, ideas, and instructional activities can achieve teaching excellence.

 Check Your Understanding 1.3 Click here to gauge your understanding of the concepts in this section.

ORGANIZATION OF THE TEXT

The chapters in this book address a range of instructional strategies associated with teaching students with disabilities. Chapters 2 and 3 focus on the curricular and instructional aspects that constitute the foundation of specialized education. The organization and management of a classroom is initially discussed in Chapter 4. Topics include various classroom arrangements, behavior change, grouping, scheduling, homework materials selection, grading, and record keeping.

Chapters 5 to 11 present strategies for instruction within seven core curricular areas: oral language/reading, word recognition, reading comprehension, written language, mathematics, science, and social studies, respectively. Each chapter includes information on assessment, general and specific approaches to instruction, and suggested teaching activities.

Additional important topical areas for students with special learning needs are covered in the final four chapters. Chapter 12 discusses the critical area of study skills. Chapter 13 focuses on social competence and self-determination, both frequently overlooked within the general education curriculum. Chapter 14 discusses functional academics. Chapter 15 focuses on career development and transition.

Foundations of Effective Instruction

LEARNING OUTCOMES

Upon completion of this chapter, the reader should be able to:

2.1 Discuss the basic concepts and model for delivering effective instruction.

2.2 Design instructionally meaningful IEPs.

2.3 Understand various issues related to curriculum.

2.4 Discuss and apply effective instructional practices.

Critical issues and questions have in the past pervaded education and continue to do so. Two of the most significant questions facing school personnel are the question of curriculum (what to teach) and instruction (how to teach). Effective school programs begin with considerations of what information students need to learn (typically decided by state agencies and local school boards), how best to teach that information deemed necessary, and, ultimately, how student learning can be measured accurately, effectively, and reasonably (i.e., high-stakes testing).

In addition to the topics noted above, it is also important to recognize that teachers who will be working with students with special learning needs must be highly knowledgeable about and competent in developing appropriate individualized education programs (IEPs) for students who have qualified for special education under the Individuals with Disabilities Education Act (IDEA).

This chapter introduces a general model for conceptualizing the key components of effective instruction. Furthermore, the chapter provides an overview of the topics just mentioned, as they are critical issues in providing appropriate education to students with special needs and are referred to in other chapters throughout the book.

MODEL FOR DELIVERING EFFECTIVE INSTRUCTION

Teacher effectiveness is a function of two dimensions: the learning the student achieves and the instructionally relevant behaviors that contribute to this learning (e.g., time and effort). It is often the case that the more a student learns, the more effective the teacher or the learning climate is likely to have been. If students learn more quickly from one teacher than from another, the more efficient teacher logically also will be judged to be the more effective.

Rosenshine and Stevens (1986) developed a general model of effective instruction highlighting six specific teaching activities validated from research as associated with student achievement. These principles remain relevant today:

- A review or check of the previous day's work (re-teaching if necessary)
- Presentation of new content or skills
- Guided student practice (with verification for understanding)
- Feedback and correction (re-teaching if necessary)
- Independent student practice
- Weekly and monthly reviews

Englert (1983) contributed to the thinking on effective instruction by identifying four teacher behaviors that are associated with direct instruction and are linked to achievement: maintaining a high level of content coverage, providing successful practice activities for students, providing feedback to signal the beginning and the conclusion of individual learning trials, and maintaining a high level of student task involvement.

Englert and her colleagues (Englert, Mariage, Garmon, & Tarrant, 1998; Englert, Tarrant, & Mariage, 1992) identified four complementary elements that derive from a constructivist approach to teaching: embedding instruction in meaningful activities, promoting dialogue for self-regulated learning, demonstrating instructional responsiveness, and establishing classroom learning communities.

Marzano, Pickering, and Pollock (2001) identified nine research-based strategies that led to increased levels of student achievement. These strategies relate closely to those that were identified previously. The nine areas are identifying similarities and differences, summarizing and note taking, reinforcing effort in providing recognition, homework and practice, cooperative learning, non-linguistic representations (graphic representations), setting objectives and providing feedback, generating and testing hypotheses, and cues, questions, and advanced organizers.

Mastropieri and Scruggs (2002) introduced the idea of SCREAM variables as a way to guide effective instruction. These variables are described below:

Structure

Clarity

Redundancy (i.e., review)

Enthusiasm

Appropriate rate

Maximized engagement

The What Works Clearinghouse (http://ies.ed.gov/ncee/wwc) identifies resources that have been proven to be effective with various populations. Online sources such as this website now offer teachers a convenient way to verify the appropriateness of various instructional strategies.

A substantial database exists indicating what elements of teaching constitute effective instructional practice. Figure 2-1 presents a model of effective educational practice. The model is predicated on a division of key elements of the instructional process into a focus on three major time-related aspects: (a) activities and events that precede teaching, (b) various activities associated with the actual instructional process, and (c) actions that are performed subsequent to instruction. Furthermore, the model reflects interactivity across the three areas. For example, various evaluative activities will have an effect on management dimensions or instructional practices. The comprehensive nature of delivering effective instruction is evident from examination of the entries in the model. Consistent with the purposes of this book, the elements of this model are discussed throughout the book.

 Check Your Understanding 2.1 Click here to gauge your understanding of the concepts in this section.

PLANNING CONSIDERATIONS: DEVELOPING AN INSTRUCTIONALLY MEANINGFUL IEP

The passage of P.L. 94-142 in 1975 incorporated the IEP into routine pedagogical practice. Reauthorization of this law in 1990 (P.L. 101-476) and in 1997 (P.L. 105-17), along with the 2004 amendments to IDEA (IDEIA), added many new features to the law. Some of the most noteworthy changes that resulted from amendments to the original legislation include the requirement that plans for transition services be part of the IEP for all students no later than age 16 and the requirement of functional behavioral assessment/behavior intervention plans for certain students.

Management Considerations		Instructional Practices		Evaluative and Collaborative Activities
	↔		↔	

Management Considerations ↔ **Instructional Practices** ↔ **Evaluative and Collaborative Activities**

Physical management:
 classroom arrangements
 environmental factors

Psychosocial management:
 student factors
 teacher factors
 school factors
 peer factors
 family factors

Procedural management:
 classroom rules
 classroom procedures

Behavior management:
 increasing desirable
  behaviors
 decreasing undesirable
  behaviors
 generalizing and maintaining
  behaviors

Instructional management:
 assessment of instructional
  needs
 direct, daily measurement
  of learning
 individual program planning
 grouping
 scheduling
 materials acquisition
 record keeping

Personnel management:
 professional
 nonprofessional

Time management:
 work environment
 personal applications

General instructional orientations:
 teacher-directed instruction
 student-directed learning
 peer-mediated learning

Fundamental practices:
 student understanding of
  teacher expectations
  and task requirements
 student motivation
 active engagement
 demonstration-guided
  practice-independent
  practice paradigm
 clear presentation of
  instruction
 immediate feedback

Adaptation:
 specialized use of successful
  constructivist practices
 curricular adaptation
 instructional adaptation
 product adaptations

Assistive technology:
 services and support
 specific devices

Ongoing monitoring of progress:
 data management
 data analysis
 decision making
 program review
 data-based planning

Student evaluation:
 instructional performance
 grades
 high-stakes assessments
  analysis of instructional
  environment

Communication with families

Collaboration with teachers
 and other professionals

FIGURE 2–1 Dimensions of Effective Educational Practice

The IEP is the primary document that outlines specific plans for services, placement, transitional planning, and now other assurances. This document serves as the driving force in the delivery of an appropriate education for students who qualify for special education. This document should be a valuable asset for all students.

Initially, a student is determined eligible for special education if he or she meets various eligibility criteria. This process is based on a comprehensive assessment. The data gathered for the eligibility process and any further information collected by multidisciplinary specialists and by both special and general education teachers can assist with the development of the IEP. However, in almost all situations, special education teachers will have to conduct further curriculum-related assessments to gather the type of instructionally useful data to be able to develop appropriate annual goals and to know where to begin instruction.

Although IEPs can serve a number of purposes, three stand out from the rest. First, IEPs should provide instructional direction. Effective written goal setting can help remedy a so-called cookbook approach (i.e., pulling together isolated or marginally related instructional exercises in the name of good teaching). Second, IEPs function as the basis for evaluation. Formally established annual goals that are measurable for students help determine the effectiveness and efficiency of instruction, although this form of accountability is not intended to become the basis for evaluating teacher effectiveness per se. A third use of IEPs is improved communication. IEPs can facilitate contact across teachers and parents and ideally between teachers and students. Parental involvement, in particular, has resulted in increased mutual support and cooperation between home and school.

IEP Team

The identified members of the IEP team, as specified in the most recent reauthorization of IDEA, reflect key emphases of the new law: parent involvement, coordination with the general education curriculum, and involvement in the general education settings. The members include parents of the student; special education teacher; one or more general education teachers; local education agency representative (i.e., a person with authority to commit necessary resources); a person who can interpret the evaluation results; the student, when appropriate; and other knowledgeable persons whom the parents or school may choose to invite.

The team needs to function with the best interests of the student in mind during all meetings and other actions. It is also critical to remember that the parents are equal members of the team, a fact that is sometimes overlooked.

ENHANCEDetext
video example 2.1
Watch this video to learn more about related parent rights and due process.

Key Elements of the IEP

Individualized education programs are intended to serve as the guiding document for the provision of an appropriate education. Moreover, IEPs function as an integral link between assessment and instruction; thus, the development of the IEP follows from the initial and ongoing collection of assessment data. The IEP also details the least restrictive, most appropriate placement and outlines the instructional program. The IEP must be evaluated and then rewritten annually as long as services are still necessary.

IDEA requires that each IEP that is developed contain certain components. These mandated components include the following:

- Statement of the child's present level of academic achievement and functional performance
- Statement of measurable annual goals, including benchmarks, or short-term objectives when applicable
- Statement of the special education and related services and supplementary aids and services to be provided to the child
- Statement of the program modifications or supports for school personnel that will be provided to the child
- Explanation of the extent, if any, to which the child will not participate with non-disabled children in the regular class
- Statement of any individual modifications in the administration of statewide or districtwide assessments of student achievement
- Projected date for the beginning of the services and modifications
- Anticipated frequency, location, and duration of those services and modifications
- Statement of how the child's progress toward the annual goals will be measured
- Statement of how the child's parents will be regularly informed of their child's progress toward the annual goals

Two other components of the IEP will be necessary for older students:

- By age 16, appropriate measurable postsecondary goals must be set and a statement of transition services (including courses of study) determined.
- Beginning at least 1 year before a student reaches the age of majority under state law, the IEP must include a statement that the student has been informed of his or her rights that will transfer on reaching the age of majority.

ENHANCEDetext
video example 2.2
Watch this video to learn
more about the components
of an IEP.

Focus on Key Instructional Components of the IEP

From an instructional perspective, certain components of the IEP are particularly noteworthy. These components, if developed appropriately and thoroughly, provide a picture of the critical areas that need attention and how to address them. These areas are the parts of the IEP that general education teachers need to review if the student with an IEP is in their classrooms.

Present Levels of Academic Achievement and Functional Performance.

A summary of a student's current functioning provides a basis for subsequent goal setting. **Performance levels** should be determined for all areas needing special instruction—in both academic and functional areas. Depending on the individual, relevant information could be gathered for academic skills, behavioral patterns, self-help skills, vocational talents, or communication abilities.

Performance levels should be viewed as summaries of an individual's strengths and weaknesses. We suggest that these statements emphasize the positive aspects of the student (i.e., what the student can do) while clearly indicating what needs to be addressed.

Although performance statements can take a variety of forms, including formal test scores, informal test results, behavioral descriptions, a listing of specific abilities relative to a sequence of skills in a given area, and self-report data obtained from the student, descriptions that are instructionally relevant are warranted. Gibb and Dyches (2016) recommended that present levels of educational performance include the following three elements:

- Statement of how the disability affects the student's involvement and progress in the general curriculum
- Description of the student's performance levels in the skill areas affected by the disability
- Logical cues for writing the accompanying goals for improvement

Hoover and Patton (in press) recommend that teachers use the acronym SCIN when developing present levels of performance. SCIN involves the following:

Sufficient detail

Current data/information

Informal assessment techniques

Needs and accomplishments

These four guidelines will contribute to the generation of useful present levels on which appropriate measurable annual goals can be identified.

Measurable Annual Goals.

The next key instructional-related component of an IEP is listing measurable annual goals. As the name implies, these goals predict long-term gains that can be evaluated clearly during the school year. The annual goals should reflect the educator's (and the parents') best guess of what the student can reasonably achieve within the school year. The following features can help determine realistic expectations: chronological age, past learning profile, and recent learning history and response to instruction. Teachers can conceptualize annual goals, which may range from outcomes that might be considered the most optimistic to the most pessimistic. Against these parameters, reasonable estimates can be derived.

Annual goals should include four major elements. IDEA 1997 lists four characteristics of an annual goal:

- It must be measurable.
- It must tell what the student can reasonably accomplish in a year.
- It must relate to helping the student be successful in the general education curriculum or address other educational needs resulting from the disability.
- It must be accompanied by benchmarks or short-term objectives. (Gibb & Dyches, 2014)

Betty (in press) recommends the use of the SMART acronym for developing appropriate goals. The key features of a SMART goal include the following:

Specific

Measurable

Attainable

Relevant

Time limited

The SMART guidelines highlight the essential elements of appropriate goals and provide a basis for being able to evaluate a student. Statements should use precise behavioral terms that denote action and can therefore be operationally defined (e.g., *pronounce*, *write*, or *identify motorically*) rather than vague, general language that confounds evaluation and observer agreement (e.g., *know*, *understand*, *improve*, or *appreciate*). For example, "will correctly identify all initial consonant sounds" is more appropriate than the unmeasurable "will improve reading skills."

Goals that are positive provide an appropriate direction for instruction. Avoiding negative goals creates an atmosphere that is helpful in communicating with parents as well as in charting student progress. The goal "will respond verbally to teacher questions" gives the student something to strive for, as opposed to "will learn to keep mouth closed," which negatively emphasizes something to avoid.

Goals should also be oriented to the student. Developing students' skills is the intent, and the only measure of effectiveness should be what is learned, not what is taught. Thus, "will verbally respond to questions with two-word phrases" is preferable to "will be given oral language readiness materials."

Finally, goals must be relevant to the individual student's current and future needs across a range of academic, personal/social, and daily living domains. Unfortunately, research indicates that IEPs frequently do not meet this criterion.

 ENHANCEDetext
video example 2.3
Watch these videos to learn more about IEP Goals Parts 1 and 2.

Supplemental Aids and Services. These aids and services are intended to assist the student with disabilities in successfully performing in the general education setting. According to Gibb and Dyches (2014), these aids, services, and other supports are "provided in regular education classes or other educational-related settings to enable students with disabilities to be educated with non-disabled students to the maximum extent appropriate" (p. 70).

The IEP team may recommend that adjustments be made in one or more of the following areas:

- The way teachers present information
- The ways students complete tasks
- The ways teachers assess student learning
- The ways teachers structure the environment

Many suggestions for supporting a student in general education settings are discussed in detail in the next chapter when the topic of differentiating instruction is covered. In addition to specific techniques that are student focused, this IEP requirement also may require that teachers, parents, and other school personnel receive specific training on various topics that are related to the student in question.

 Check Your Understanding 2.2 Click here to gauge your understanding of the concepts in this section.

CURRICULAR CONSIDERATIONS

The core component of educational programs for individuals with disabilities is the curriculum. Regardless of teaching effectiveness and efficiency, questions related to the value of education must properly address the issue of what is taught. This section addresses four topics related to curricular issues: access to the general education curriculum, the relationship of standards to what is taught to students with special needs, types of curricula, and the concept of a comprehensive curriculum.

Access to the General Education Curriculum

The reauthorization of IDEA (2004) clearly emphasized that all students with disabilities must have access to the general education curriculum. This feature of the law, bolstered by a strong movement toward standards-based education, now ensures that these students are being given more access to the general education curriculum. Nearly all states have instituted standards to ensure that students develop a common set of knowledge and skills during their school experience. With such changes come a host of issues that have to be recognized and addressed.

It is helpful to begin by considering the various applications of the term *curriculum*. This term can refer strictly to the courses taught in school or, more literally, to a document that includes a design that others have developed and that teachers implement in the classroom. Using a broader conceptualization of "curriculum," Hoover and Patton (2004a) referred to curriculum as planned and guided learning experiences under the direction of the school with intended educational outcomes.

One of the primary concerns of the curriculum is its "functionality" in meeting the needs of the individual student. For our purposes, curriculum functionality is defined as the degree to which the curriculum prepares students for the environments in which they will live, work, play, and learn when formal schooling ends. At the same time, careful attention must be given to how students' needs can be met within the context of the general education curriculum while placed in inclusive settings.

Relationship of Standards to Curriculum Taught to Students with Special Needs

It is important for teachers who work with students with special learning needs to be able to relate what they are teaching to standards and conversely be able to interpret the functionality of grade-level standards. At face value, many content and performance standards (i.e., Common Core) do not seem to be functionally relevant to many students with special needs. However, on the contrary, most standards have functional value and can be interpreted in functionally relevant ways.

An example of how a standard can be made functionally significant would be within a secondary level standard that may include a focus on vocabulary development. For such an example, a teacher could choose to focus on "occupational" vocabulary or perhaps some other type of functional vocabulary that will be needed in life, thus addressing a vocabulary standard with a functional focus. Patton and Trainor (2002) have provided an extensive analysis of the relationship between functional content and standards along with a number of examples; this source can be consulted for additional examples.

Curriculum Types

Hoover and Patton (2004a) pointed out that curriculum needs to be conceptualized on the basis of what is taught and what is not taught but should be. The three types of curricula that are frequently mentioned are explicit, hidden, and absent (e.g., Schubert, 1993). These are defined as follows:

- **Explicit curriculum**—the formal and stated curriculum that teachers and students are expected to follow
- **Hidden curriculum**—the actual curriculum implemented in the classroom
- **Absent curriculum**—the curriculum that, for whatever reason, is not included in school

Other terminology is also used to describe types of curricula. In general, the various perspectives highlight the same points; however, some subtle differences exist. As Hoover and Patton (2004a) stressed, elements from all three types of curricula operate continually in classrooms, sometimes in complementary ways and other times in a conflicting fashion.

The *explicit curriculum* (intended curriculum) can be found in a state's standards and thus is typically reflected in a school district's curriculum guides. This type of curriculum includes the specific goals and objectives for subject areas across grade levels that articulate with a state's content and performance standards. With the increased attention to and pressure of these standards and school accountability, a heightened interest in ensuring that this content is covered pervades instruction today.

The *hidden curriculum* (taught curriculum) is what students are exposed to on a daily basis. It will include much of the explicit curriculum as well as lessons on topics other than those stated in curriculum guides. The hidden curriculum includes interpretations of the explicit curricula related to implementation procedures and the emphasis that different explicit curriculum aspects receive. It also includes the insertion of content that the teacher chooses to cover, either by necessity based on student needs (e.g., study skills instructions) or by personal interest (enrichment). It should be pointed out that often teachers may have to teach skills and content that they were not expecting to teach. For example, if two students are not interacting appropriately in a small-group setting, the teacher may have to teach certain interpersonal skills (i.e., social skills) to one or more of the students.

The *absent curriculum* represents content that is not covered. Sometimes, this is because certain content is not part of the explicit curriculum. Other times, it is a choice made by teachers. Examples of topics that are important for students with special needs but often absent from the curriculum are social skills instruction and the development of self-determination skills (see Chapter 13) or study skills (see Chapter 12).

Comprehensive Curriculum

When educational programs are designed for students who have various types of disabilities, the importance of a **comprehensive curriculum** should be apparent because the primary goal is to develop an outcome focus consistent with their diverse yet specific needs. A comprehensive curriculum refers to a program of study guided by the reality that each student is in school on a time-limited basis. Moreover, the real test of the value of the curriculum is how students fare once they exit the program (i.e., how what was taught affects adult outcomes).

Thus, educators must consider what lies ahead for their students; this requires a perspective that is sensitive to the environments in which students will need to adapt and function in the future. Hence, curriculum design should be influenced not only by the stated standards and individual needs of the students but also by a "subsequent environments" (Polloway, Patton, Smith, & Roderique, 1992). A subsequent environment perspective requires school personnel to consider the demands of the likely settings to which an individual will be moving in the near and more distant future. The central attributes of a comprehensive curriculum include the following:

- Responding to the needs of an individual at the current time
- Accommodating the concurrent needs so that students can truly have access to the general education curriculum in a meaningful and effective way
- Attending to crucial needs that are absent from the general education curriculum
- Striving for maximum interaction with peers
- Developing curriculum from a realistic appraisal of potential adult outcomes of individuals
- Ensuring consistency with each individual's transitional needs across levels of schooling and life span

- Remaining sensitive to graduation goals and specific diploma track requirements

The importance of comprehensive curriculum at the secondary level relates closely to the basic elements of the transition process that will be covered in Chapter 15. The value of a comprehensive curriculum for students with special needs is further warranted based on the following realities:

- Many individuals are not being prepared for the complex demands of adulthood that they will face on a daily basis.
- Many students who have special needs do not find the school experience valuable and may drop out.
- The educational programs of many students with special needs do not meet their current academic, social, and emotional needs.
- The opportunities for continuing educational options for adults with special needs on their exiting of high school are limited but nonetheless critical.

The recurring need is for relevant curricula that address these concerns and features. However, although a careful analysis of secondary programs is essential, consideration of curricular design must begin at the elementary level to overcome the problems that otherwise may be recognized at the secondary or postsecondary level.

 Check Your Understanding 2.3 Click here to gauge your understanding of the concepts in this section.

EFFECTIVE INSTRUCTIONAL PRACTICES

Classrooms in most public schools today are comprised of a diverse group of students, and, as a result, the challenges for teaching are significant. Students represent diverse cultural backgrounds or may be learning English. In many inclusive classrooms, special education supports are provided to an increased number of students. Students at varying academic levels are being served by one teacher. Consequently, there has not been a time when the use of effective instructional and differentiated methodologies has been of greater significance. Consistent with IDEA (2004), effective instruction has been defined as those practices that are research based and empirically validated (Boardman, Arguelles, Vaughn, Hughes, & Klingnerr, 2005; Cook et al., 2015; Stanovich & Stanovich, 2003).

Special education brings to the challenge of inclusion a wealth of instructional strategies that will be discussed throughout this text. As Lloyd and Hallahan (2005) noted, the field of learning disabilities in particular has been one of the "foremost sources for empirically founded practices—practices that are proven valuable for a wide spectrum of students, not just those with learning disabilities. Reasonably informed people interested in learning disabilities . . . argue strongly for explicit, systematic instruction that focuses on teaching students strategies for completing academic tasks and that includes monitoring of progress so instruction can be adjusted to maximize progress" (p. 135).

In an important article focused on effectiveness in special education, Heward (2003) identified six dimensions of practice that characterize positive features of instruction. These dimensions and features are provided in Table 2-1. The dimensions provide a strong foundation for the focus of effective teaching of students with special needs.

This section describes teaching approaches consistent with the effective instruction model presented in Figure 2-1 and the ideas featured in Table 2-1. An overview and description of the following effective teaching practices is presented: culturally responsive instruction, teacher-directed instruction, cooperative teaching, grouping for instruction, scaffolding, student-directed and self-regulated learning, peer-mediated instruction, the use of technology, and the concept of universal design for learning.

TABLE 2–1   Dimensions and defining features of special education instruction

Dimension	Defining Features
Individually planned	• Learning goals and objectives selected for each student based on assessment results and input from parents and student • Teaching methods and instructional materials selected and/or adapted for each student • Setting(s) where instruction will occur determined relative to opportunities for student to learn and use targeted skills
Specialized	• Sometimes involves unique or adapted teaching procedures seldom used in general education (e.g., constant time delay, token reinforcement, self-monitoring) • Incorporates a variety of instructional materials and support—both natural and contrived—to help student acquire and use targeted learning objectives • Related services (e.g., audiology, physical therapy) provided as needed • Assistive technology (e.g., adapted cup holder, head-operated switch to select communication symbols) provided as needed
Intensive	• Instruction presented with attention to detail, precision, structure, clarity, and repeated practice • "Relentless, urgent" instruction (Zigmond & Baker, 1995) • Efforts made to provide incidental, naturalistic opportunities for student to use targeted knowledge and skills
Goal-directed	• Purposeful instruction intended to help student achieve the greatest possible personal self-sufficiency and success in present and future environments • Value/goodness of instruction determined by student's attainment of learning outcomes
Research-based methods	• Recognition that not all teaching approaches are equally effective • Instructional programs and teaching procedures selected on basis of research support
Guided by student performance	• Systematic, ongoing monitoring of student progress • Results of frequent and direct measures of student learning used to inform modifications in instruction

Source: Adapted from Heward, William L., *Exceptional Children: An Introduction to Special Education* (7th ed.) © 2003, pp. 40–41. Reprinted by permission of Pearson Education, Inc., Upper Saddle River, NJ.

Culturally Responsive Instruction

Given the diversity present in classrooms, it is essential that teachers adopt a philosophy and modus of operandi that reflects an attitude of openness, sensitivity, and responsiveness to the particular needs and backgrounds of the students with whom they work. To do this, teachers must become culturally knowledgeable and provide instruction that is culturally responsive. Smith and Tyler (2014) defined culturally responsive instruction (CRI) as instruction that "teaches to the strengths of each student while validating and affirming their cultures" (p. 66). They stated that CRI

- acknowledges and legitimizes different cultural heritages;
- connects the meaning between home and school experiences;
- uses a wide variety of instructional techniques that account for varied learning needs, preferences, and communication styles;
- teaches students to understand and appreciate their own and others' cultural heritages; and
- incorporates multicultural knowledge, resources, and materials in all new subjects. (p. 66)

ENHANCEDetext
video example 2.4
Watch this video to learn more about cultural considerations.

Teacher-Directed Instruction

With **teacher-directed instruction**, the teacher plays a direct and active role in the teaching process. This role varies depending on the objectives of the lesson or subject area. Students with learning problems often require special services and instructional supports because they are not dealing well with traditional methods and materials. These students must be provided with lessons in which teachers proceed systematically, sequence within and between lessons, pace instruction appropriately, question students differentially, and involve them actively.

A key aspect of successful instruction is the intensity of the instruction provided. As Deshler (2005) noted, to be effective for students with special needs, instruction must be highly intensive:

Intensive instruction involves helping students maintain a high degree of attention and response during instructional sessions that are scheduled as frequently and consistently as possible. In other words, a key factor affecting learning is both the amount of time and instruction and how effectively each instructional moment is used to engage students in activities that contribute to their learning. Intensity during instruction is achieved by progressive pacing, frequent question-answer interactions, and frequent activities that require a physical response (e.g., pointing, writing, raising hands, repeating). Intensity can also be achieved through reflective or open-ended questions if the activities are focused on a process that engages interest and maintains the student's attention. For adolescents who are far behind, all of these elements must define the instructional dynamic. (pp. 123–124)

One of the most widely used instructional methods is the use of **direct instruction**. Although there are many versions of direct instruction, it typically includes the essential elements of explaining the skill, modeling the skill, practicing the skill, and giving feedback on the skill performance.

Teachers engaging in direct instruction present lessons that provide students with opportunities to respond and receive feedback on how they respond to the lesson that is being presented. They are shown how a skill is performed and are then given ample time to perform the new skill in a guided practice situation. Teachers engage all students by providing positive as well as constructive feedback while they are practicing, the ultimate goal being mastery of the skill. Typically, such lessons follow a pattern so that students can predict the structure of the lesson and the learning environment.

Kauffman (2002) stressed the importance of direct instruction in stating:

Nothing is gained by keeping students guessing about what it is they are supposed to learn. In all or nearly all of the education programs in which the majority of students can be demonstrated to be highly successful in learning the facts and skills they need, these . . . are taught directly rather than indirectly. That is, the teacher is in control of instruction, not the student, and information is given to students. Giving information doesn't mean that the instruction is dull, and it doesn't mean that students don't learn to apply their knowledge and skills to everyday problems. Neither does it mean that students have nothing to say about their education. But it does mean that students don't waste time and effort trying to figure out what they're to learn. It also means that students aren't allowed to learn misrules—learn the wrong thing or a faulty application so that their learning can be described as false, misleading, or useless. (p. 236)

An example of a systematic instructional approach, referred to as **PURPOSE**, provides teachers with a way to remember direct instruction procedures as well as to employ generalization procedures so that students can perform the skill in other settings outside of the classroom where the skill is learned initially. The procedure is divided into seven steps. The following discussion describes how this teaching format can be implemented during instructional periods.

Prepare the student to learn the skill—The step requires that the teacher prepare the students to learn the skill and know why it is important to learn. The teacher asks the students to (a) define the skill to be learned, (b) state why it is an important skill, and (c) explain where they can use this skill once learned. It is important that the teacher incorporate an interactive dialogue with the students and listen to their answers.

Understand the skill steps—The second step requires the teacher to help the student understand the skill components to be learned. The teacher reviews each component of the skill's task analysis by presenting each skill component individually, asking students to state what it is and why it is needed to execute the skill. If the students are unable to do this, the teacher should explain the skill component, give an example of it, and state why it is an essential component of the skill. Again, the teacher should involve the students in the discussion.

This step also builds on task analysis of the skill so that each step is easy to grasp. Task analysis allows the teacher to determine whether the skill is too difficult for a student and at what point the student is having trouble. By analyzing the steps associated with each skill, teachers are able to modify the skill to best meet the needs of the students.

Rehearse the skill—Once students have a clear understanding of each skill component, teachers rehearse the skill for and with the students. The teacher begins by modeling the skill as it should be performed. If the skill is interactive, the teacher can model the skill through a role-play

situation, and the students then perform the skill exactly as the teacher modeled it.

If the skill is cognitive, the teacher can model it by "talking through" each step of the skill. The importance of having the students hear and see what the teacher is thinking is also underscored. Students will see and hear how a person thinks through a cognitive problem and can perform the skill.

After the modeling, the teacher should seek feedback by asking the students about each skill step and requiring them to provide some details about the skill component that was just modeled. The teacher should praise the students for their correct answers and refresh their memories when they cannot remember what happened during the performance of a skill step.

The teacher then should require the students to learn each of the skill components before they are asked to perform the skill. This task can be accomplished through strategies dependent on the age and cognitive ability of the student, such as (a) memorization of the skill steps through verbal rehearsal, (b) development and utilization of a mnemonic, or (c) use of flash cards or pictures. When the students are able to verbally state each step of the skill, they should try to perform the skill under guided practice. Mastery of the skill should be achieved during this step.

Rehearsal focuses on the importance of developing proficiency in a particular skill and then maintaining it once mastered. To provide further elaboration on concepts related to rehearsal and practice, Hardman and Drew (2005) identified the following types of practice that result in enhanced learning: massed practice (e.g., cramming before an examination), distributed practice (holding daily practice sessions that may be shorter in duration but regularly occurring and may reflect varied context), and naturally distributed practice (e.g., practicing the skills in the context of where that skill will be most importantly used; naturally distributed practice relates directly to the importance of generalization, which is discussed in the following text).

Perform a skill check—After a mastery rehearsal, the teacher and student perform a self-check of the skill performance. It involves an evaluation of each skill component. When the student thinks that mastery of the skill has been accomplished, he or she should ask the teacher to evaluate the performance for accuracy. This outside check will confirm the students' perceptions of their own performance.

Overcome any performance barrier—As with the acquisition of any skill, there may be difficulties in obtaining performance at targeted levels, and thus teachers will need to help students overcome any performance problems.

When these situations occur, the teacher must pinpoint where the problem lies in order to help the student overcome the problem and to develop an appropriate instructional intervention. The teacher may need to develop supplemental materials or provide extra practice to accomplish the desired goal of learning the skill to mastery.

Select other situations where the skill can be performed—As the student achieves mastery over the skill, the teacher and student must select other situations where the skill can be used. During this step, the teacher focuses on generalizing a skill mastered in the classroom to other situations. This emphasis on generalization provides a foundation for showing students how they can apply knowledge or skills to new tasks, problems, or situations and acquire a set of rules to solve problems of a similar nature in the future (Smith, Polloway, Doughty, Patton, & Dowdy, 2016).

Together, the student and teacher decide where or with whom the skill can be used and determine when the student will use the skill. They might talk about how the skill will be performed and the importance of using the skill in the selected situation. Once a specific situation is selected, the student and teacher agree that the student will perform the skill as soon as the occasion arises and that the student will report the outcome of the performance as soon as possible. This generalization step requires students to use the skill where it is most meaningful to them. Further, generalization can be promoted by teaching the skill in multiple contexts, providing reinforcement for the successful generalization of the skill behavior, and reminding students when it is appropriate to apply the skill that they have learned in a new situation (Smith, Polloway, Patton, & Dowdy, 2008).

Evaluate skill performance—The last component is to evaluate the skill performance in the generalized situation. Once the situation has occurred, students must assess the effectiveness of their performance and determine the outcome. If possible, students should be encouraged to use a checklist to evaluate how well each skill component was executed. If all the skill components were executed successfully, the student must then determine whether the performance of the skill accomplished the desired goal. If the student did not perform the skill correctly, the teacher and the student should determine why it was not performed correctly and develop a procedure that would help the student the next time the performance of the skill is necessary. If problems persist, the teacher engages in additional practice of the skill with the student or problem solves with the child to ensure that a similar situation outside the classroom might be met with more favorable results in the future.

Instructional Collaboration: Co-Teaching

Co-teaching (or **cooperative teaching**) represents an attractive way of providing general education class support not only for students with disabilities but also for other students who are experiencing learning difficulties in the class. Hourcade and Bauwens (2003) described cooperative teaching as occurring when "two educators combine their complementary sets of professional knowledge and skills and work simultaneously in general education classrooms" (p. xiii).

It is sufficient to note here that cooperative teaching involves a team approach to supporting students within the general education classroom, combining the content expertise of the classroom teacher with the pedagogical skills of the special education teacher (Smith et al., 2016). It is a logical outgrowth of collaboration between teachers that includes consultative arrangements, additional help given by special educators to students not identified as eligible for special services, and the sharing of teaching assistants, especially to accompany students who require certain supports in the general education classroom.

Thousand, Villa, and Nevin (2007) have identified four different approaches to the delivery of co-teaching: supported teaching, parallel teaching, complementary teaching, and team teaching. The supported teaching approach is where one co-teacher is the lead teacher and the other teacher circulates around the room during instruction. The parallel teaching approach is best explained as a situation where both co-teachers are leading separate groups. The complementary teaching approach is where one co-teacher typically has expertise and the other co-teacher complements the instruction of the lead teacher. The team teaching approach is best characterized as a situation where both co-teachers are equally engaged in the delivery of instruction.

ENHANCEDetext
video example 2.5
Watch this video to learn more about team teaching.

Hourcade and Bauwens (2003) noted that the essential philosophy of cooperative teaching is a simple one: *sharing*, especially of responsibilities and accountability. They suggested that true cooperative teaching emerges when five key elements are operative:

- **Cooperative presence**—initial stage is related to mere proximity.
- **Cooperative planning**—regular meetings occur where various planning-related activities are done collaboratively; as a way to facilitate effecting cooperative, joint lesson planning is useful.
- **Cooperative presenting**—teachers present simultaneously and are actively involved for a sustained period of time.
- **Cooperative processing**—teachers determine how monitoring and evaluation will occur.
- **Cooperative problem solving**—teachers devote time to solving inevitable problems that arise when implementing a cooperative teaching arrangement.

Hoover and Patton (in press) describe five co-teaching principles. The first principle is that teachers are teaching together in a co-working climate. The second principle is that implementation occurs in the classroom at the same time with all students.

The third principle is that planning and implementation occur collaboratively with both teachers actively engaged. The fourth principle is that assessment of student learning is conducted by both co-teachers. The last principle is that co-teachers provide each other with constructive feedback and support and decide about future adjustments together.

LEARNING MODULE 2.1 Click here to learn more about co-teaching.

The trend toward co-teaching warrants careful attention. The existing studies reflected a moderate level of success for co-teaching. Mastropieri et al. (2005) reported that success was influenced in particular by the compatibility of the two teachers based on mutual trust and respect and on shared commitment to effective teaching behaviors (i.e., "structure, clarity, enthusiasm, maximizing student engagement, and motivational strategies" [p. 269]).

Instructional Grouping

A key consideration that is integral to the planning and instructional process is how students are grouped for instruction. Vaughn and Schumm (1997) provided a detailed analysis of the grouping practices typically used by general and special education teachers. For the former, the most commonly used strategy was whole-class grouping with students of mixed ability combined within the group. General educators tend to use smaller groups for practice and reinforcement activities but not for teacher-led instruction.

On the other hand, special educators reported that they were much more likely to use groups of similar ability. Further, they reported that they had greater autonomy in making decisions about how students were grouped. Consequently, the traditional pattern of homogeneously set-up groupings appeared more common with this group of teachers. To the extent that students need work on specific skills, large-group instruction with mixed-ability groups would likely not be an effective instructional practice.

Although there is much benefit in the use of skills-based grouping for students with special needs, too often such groups have remained static. Student grouping tends to remain the same due to an emphasis on achievement level being the primary determinant of group placement. Teachers are encouraged to consider options that periodically introduce change and flexibility into grouping procedures.

Grouping that is based on various interests and non-academic factors should be considered and implemented on a regular basis. Interest groups can be formed around a common theme (e.g., sports) regardless of achievement level. The teacher can assign trade book material at levels appropriate for each student, with questions and activities suitable for the group. In skill groups, students periodically meet with the teacher to work on a specific skill deficit. Here again, students of varying levels of achievement work together on a common problem.

Scaffolding

The concept of **scaffolding** describes interactions between teachers and students that facilitate the learning process. Stone (1998) described the scaffolding metaphor as follows:

> In providing temporary assistance to children as they strive to accomplish a task just out of their competency, adults are said to be providing a scaffold, much like that used by builders in erecting a building. [Scaffolding] connotes a custom-made support for the "construction" of new skills, a support that can be easily disassembled when no longer needed. It also connotes a structure that allows for accomplishment of some goal that would otherwise be either unattainable or quite cumbersome to complete. (p. 344)

In scaffolding instruction, teachers model a learning-related process by thinking aloud or talking through the steps they follow to reach a specific conclusion. As students begin to understand the process, they gradually take over this talking-through procedure, and the teacher acts as a coach, providing prompts when needed.

An example of a scaffolding procedure is seen in this exercise, which focuses student attention on story grammar. The teacher begins by modeling the scaffolding steps, thinking aloud by saying to the students after they have read to a designated point in the story, "I see a problem." The teacher states the problem and writes it on a note sheet for students. The teacher then describes the attempts in the story to solve the problem or conflict and gives an analysis of the events that led to the solution of the problem. After the teacher models these steps, the students begin to talk themselves through a story following the same steps (Gersten & Dimino, 1990). This strategy leads students into being active participants in the reading process, and, when used, students' responses to both lower- and higher-level questions are likely to improve.

Student-Directed Learning

A major goal of education is to develop students so that they become independent learners, able to direct their own behavior in ways that assist in maximizing the amount of time engaged in learning (i.e., **student-directed learning**) or displaying appropriate behaviors. Many students with special needs have significant difficulty in this area, which can limit their success in general education where self-regulated actions are expected—but often not directly taught (Marzano, 2003). This relates to the notion of hidden curriculum that was discussed earlier in the chapter where some skills/behaviors may have to be taught in addition to the explicit curriculum.

Teachers need to assist students in becoming independent learners and to be in control of their behaviors. To accomplish this goal, teachers need to structure the classroom environment in ways that assist students in developing self-regulation strategies. Self-directed learners typically demonstrate competence in a range of skills associated with self-regulation, as shown in Figure 2-2. When students become competent in using these skills, they will be able to navigate their current learning environment—both academically and behaviorally. Moreover, these skills will contribute to success in areas such as action planning and goal setting and planning now and in the future.

Key Components of Self-Regulation. Special attention needs to be given to students to not display self-directed behaviors. Initially taught by teachers, these skill sets must be learned and eventually used by students without much effort. Figure 2-2 identified the four subcomponents of self-regulation: self-monitoring, self-instruction, self-evaluation, and self-reinforcement. Each of these skill areas must be evaluated and taught when students show deficiencies in these areas. These four areas are described as follows:

- **Self-monitoring**—skills associated with monitoring one's own behavior

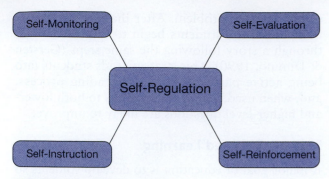

FIGURE 2–2 Self-Regulation

- **Self-instruction**—skills associated with talking oneself through a task using overt or covert verbalizations
- **Self-evaluation**—skills associated with the ability to analyze one's performance and make necessary corrections
- **Self-reinforcement**—skills associated with rewarding oneself for correct behavior or successfully accomplishing a task

Problem-Based Learning. Problem-based learning consists of a series of stages in which the students become investigators of a real problem or topic. First, students are guided, through different activities, to *explore many topics, issues, and areas* into which they may delve more deeply. Teachers must assess the interests of the student and explore several avenues, as students may not know what they would like to learn about.

The second major stage is *choosing a topic* and determining certain goals and objectives that are to be accomplished to develop the chosen content into an interesting project. Teachers can help students determine these goals and objectives by working with them to decide what is to be accomplished.

The third stage is *developing a project management plan*. This plan includes creating timelines, getting started, and finalizing product ideas. After the plan is outlined, the student begins to research the ideas and produce the products based on research and guidance from the teacher.

The final stage of this process is guiding students through the process of independent or small-group study to help them evaluate what they have accomplished. Students and teachers can develop evaluation plans that best suit their needs.

Peer-Mediated Instruction

The primary purpose for using **peer-mediated strategies** is to promote learning within the context of collaborative interactions among students. Although the development of *self-directed* learners is desirable, students also need to be able to work *interdependently* with other students in their classes and ultimately with co-workers in the future. Students benefit not only from being able to direct their own learning activities but also from knowing how to work with others in joint talks or how to seek assistance from others when needed. This section discusses ways in which students with learning-related problems can engage along with their fellow students. The primary focus is on peer tutoring and cooperative learning.

Peer Tutoring. **Peer tutoring** typically but not always involves the pairing of a more skilled student with a student who is less proficient in a particular behavioral or academic area. Peer tutoring procedures have been used to teach academic skills and develop social behaviors with regard to classroom discipline, peer relations, and appropriate interaction behaviors. The effectiveness of peer tutoring has been demonstrated across ages, settings, and types of students.

Cooke, Heron, and Heward (1983) summarized the advantages of peer tutoring as follows: (a) children can effectively teach each other skills when tutors emphasize repetition, mastery, and a review system; (b) tutors are able to learn from teaching others; (c) tutors can individualize content material to meet the needs of each student; (d) students can engage in one-to-one instruction without requiring a full class lesson; (e) one-to-one teaching greatly increases the opportunity for correct responses by the tutee; and (f) tutors and tutees gain in self-esteem, self-respect, and ability to interact with each other on a constructive and appropriate basis.

When selecting tutors, teachers must ensure that the students are individuals who can help in the teaching process. These students should be enthusiastic about being peer tutors and willing to learn the procedures necessary to work with another student. Figure 2-3 outlines a direct instructional procedure using the PURPOSE format, described earlier in the chapter, that a teacher can use when preparing students to become peer tutors.

A Systematic Procedure for Teaching Peers to Be Tutors

- **P**repare the students to learn about peer tutoring:

    ____ Ask the students if they know the *definition* of a "tutor."

    ____ Ask the students why it is *important* to be a tutor.

    ____ Ask the students for *examples* of what subjects they might tutor.

- Help the student to **U**nderstand and learn the steps to being a tutor.

    ____ *Outline* the steps tutors must exhibit in order to tutor a peer in a designated subject area.

    ____ *Explain* each step to the tutors and ask them to tell you why that step is important.

- **R**ehearse the skill by watching a model and then practicing the lesson with someone else.

    ____ *Show or model* how you would like the tutors to execute the lesson when tutoring another student in a particular subject area.

    ____ Have the students *rehearse* the lesson with you role-playing the tutee.

    ____ *Give feedback* to the tutors after each role-play situation.

- **P**erform a self-check to ensure that the lesson was performed correctly.

    ____ Once the tutors have role-played the lesson, have them *evaluate* whether they performed each step needed to teach the lesson.

- **O**vercome any performance problems to produce the desired outcomes.

    ____ If a tutor is not exhibiting all of the steps needed to correctly teach the lesson, *work with the tutor* until he/she is able to execute it appropriately.

- **S**elect or recognize other situations where the skill can be performed.

    ____ Pair the tutors with other students and have them *begin tutoring* the students.

- **E**valuate the performances of the tutor and the tutee during the lesson.

    ____ Evaluate whether the tutor executed the lesson appropriately and if the tutee's skill level improved.

FIGURE 2–3   Teaching Peers How to Be Tutors

An example of a successful peer tutoring approach is Peer-Assisted Learning Strategies (PALS; see also Chapter 6). With PALS, groups as varied as beginning readers or middle school math students (Kroeger & Kouche, 2006) are assisted in learning through paired instruction. Each member of the pair takes turns serving as a coach and a reader with the first coach being the reader at a higher achievement level who listens to, comments on, and reinforces the other student before the roles are reversed. Mathes and Torgesen (1998) reported that PALS enhanced students' learning by promoting careful attention to saying and hearing sounds, sounding out words, and reading stories. They recommended using the approach three times a week for approximately 16 weeks with each session lasting 35 minutes. In addition, Fuchs, Fuchs,

Mathes, and Martinez (2002) reported that participation in PALS resulted in enhanced social acceptance for students with learning disabilities and that these students had similar social standing when compared to their peers who were not disabled.

Kroeger and Kouche (2006) similarly provided an example of a successful application of PALS to middle school students in math. As they noted, the benefits reflected in "a world of students discussing and talking through math problems, regardless of ability levels or past experiences in math classes. . . . PALS is an effective intervention to increase engagement and opportunities to respond for all students" (p. 12).

Another approach for using students as instructors is classwide peer tutoring (CWPT). Maheady,

Harper, and Mallette (2001) identified the four primary components of CWPT as follows: "competing teams; a highly structured tutoring procedure; daily point earning and public posting of people performance; and direct practice in the implementation of instructional activities. In using CWPT, the teacher's role changes from primary 'deliverer' of instruction to facilitator and monitor of peer-teaching activities" (p. 1).

CWPT is intended to be a reciprocal tutoring approach. That is, students assume roles as both tutors and tutees during individual instructional sessions. Further, the sessions are highly structured by the teacher to ensure that students are on task and focused on key instructional content.

To enhance the impact of any peer tutoring program, students can be taught to enlist the help of their peers by teaching them strategies to get assistance. Wolford, Heward, and Alber (2001) demonstrated that teaching simple phrases (e.g., "Can you help me?" or "How am I doing so far?") had a positive impact on the rate at which feedback was received or students' accuracy and productivity on classroom tasks.

Cooperative Learning. Cooperative learning (CL) also can be employed to enlist the support of students while simultaneously promoting the learning of academic and behavioral skills. According to Schniedewind and Salend (1987), teachers can structure their class lessons so that students work together to achieve a shared academic goal. They stated, "Cooperative learning is especially worthwhile for a heterogeneous student population, because it encourages liking and learning among students of various academic abilities, [disabilities], and racial and ethnic backgrounds" (p. 22).

When planning a CL lesson, teachers should consider four elements: (a) positive interdependence, (b) individual accountability, (c) collaborative skills, and (d) processing. Within a lesson, *positive interdependence* is structured by having each student group agree on the answer to the task and the process for solving each problem.

Individual accountability is determined if group members have mastered the process of solving the problem or demonstrate the skills necessary for accomplishing the task. The element of individual accountability is structured by having the teacher randomly score a group's work and determine whether the correct answer has been written on their answer sheet. If the answer is correct, the teacher then asks a student to explain how to solve each problem.

Collaborative skills emphasize student support for one another (e.g., praising and offering help), enthusiasm for group work, and contributions to the group's efforts. These collaborative skills are necessary for the appropriate behaviors to occur within a group.

Finally, *problem-solving processing* requires that the group members evaluate how well they worked together and what they could do in the future to be an even more effective group member or group. This type of evaluation requires that the group function as a whole as well as that individual group members engage in self-evaluation for personal improvement in the classwork.

McMaster and Fuchs (2002) reviewed cooperative learning research from 1990 to 2000. They concluded that the effectiveness of the approach continues to need further research but that strategies that incorporate individual accountability and group rewards are particularly promising. They noted that

> in light of inconclusive findings in the literature regarding the efficacy of using CL with students with LD, teachers may wish to use caution in deciding whether to use CL to improve these students' academic performance. Research that reveals which features are most essential to CL's effectiveness, when and where it is most successful, and whether it results in sufficient academic gains for students with LD should help to better inform teachers of its utility in the classroom. Teachers who choose to implement CL might also systematically evaluate whether it is indeed benefiting their students, and explore the use of other empirically validated teaching methods when CL does not elicit desired academic gains. (p. 116)

Universal Design for Learning

The concept of universal design emerged out of the field of architecture and then was applied to education. The general meaning of *universal design*, from an architectural perspective, is "the design of products and environments to be usable by all people, to the greatest extent possible, without the need for adaptation or specialized design" (Mace, 1997, p. 2).

Applying this concept to education, Pisha and Coyne (2001) described universal design as "the development of educational curricula and materials that include potent supports for access and learning from the start, rendering them effective for a far wider range of students than traditional materials" (p. 197). The term that has emerged to describe the application of these principles to educational situations is **universal design for learning** (UDL).

Universal design as applied to education suggests that various aspects of the classroom and the instructional dynamics can be adjusted in such a way that certain students who need these adjustments can benefit within a system that offers the adjustments to all students. As Thoma, Bartholomew, and Scott (2009) note, "UDL is not a set method for instruction, but rather a framework for instructional design that is built on the principle that all students can learn; multiple means of content delivery and student assessment should be part of daily lessons and planning to enhance this learning process" (p. 9).

In practical terms, UDL provides learners with various ways to acquire information/knowledge, alternative ways of demonstrating what they know, and various features that support their participation in ongoing instructional activities. Examples of UDL at the secondary level might include such options as note-taking supports, alternative formats for taking tests, and extended time for taking tests that is made available to all students.

The main attractions of UDL include the following:

- It attends to individual needs in a general fashion that does not draw attention to any one individual.
- This approach is *proactive* rather than reactive—that is, it avoids "retrofitted changes and accommodations to classroom instruction" (Scott, McGuire, & Shaw, 2003).
- Developing curricula and materials that attend to the needs of students with special needs increases their utility for all students (Meyer & Rose, 2000).
- UDL capitalizes on accessible technologies and electronic resources.

Technology Applications

The use of technology in classrooms is very common in schools throughout the country. The revolution in technology for persons with disabilities received significant support with the Technology-Related Assistance for Individuals with Disabilities Act of 1988. Although subsequent legislation has reinforced educational programs, this act provided a foundation for assisting persons with disabilities to exercise greater control over their own personal lives, increase participation and contribution to activities in their communities (including home, school, and workplace), increase interaction with individuals who are non-disabled, and take advantage of opportunities that exist and that are taken for granted by individuals who are not disabled.

The proliferation of technology in classrooms in today's schools is astounding. The introduction of tablets and other mobile devices as part of ongoing instruction is changing the way many teachers design and implement lessons, manage their classrooms, and communicate with others. Certain kinds of technology are particularly useful for certain students such as those with autism and other communication-related disabilities. IDEA requires that assistive technology be considered for students who might need various devices or services. A significant number of students who qualify under IDEA will benefit from technology that assists them in their routine classroom activities. All students, however, are likely to benefit from the use of instructional technology that enhances the way instruction is provided.

Instructional Technology. Instructional technology refers to the use of hardware and software that assists teachers in the planning, delivery, and evaluation of instruction. This type of technology is not restricted to use with students with disabilities; it is useful and applicable for instructional purposes with all students in a classroom. Examples of instructional technology would include software that allows teachers to generate instructional materials, techniques for polling students during instruction, and systems for collecting, charting, and interpreting data on the progress of students. A vast array of instructional technology is now available to teachers. A growing amount of this technology is being developed and shared by teachers themselves.

Assistive Technology. Assistive technology (AT) provides an important vehicle for instruction and a complementary source of learning adaptations for learners. "Assistive technology devices include any item, piece of equipment or product system, whether acquired commercially, modified, or customized, that is used to increase, maintain, or improve the functional capabilities of individuals with disabilities" (Beirne-Smith, Patton, & Kim, 2006, p. 436).

The potential outcomes of the use of AT devices include the following:

- Helping students meet the challenges of daily life
- Providing vehicles to help overcome barriers to inclusion and independence
- Compensating for an individual's functional limitations
- Fostering social interactions with peers (Beirne-Smith et al., 2006)

AT options vary from low-tech applications (e.g., pencil grips, currency recognition apps on a smartphone) to high-tech ones (e.g., voice synthesizers, print reading software). The advent of the iPad opened up a range of relatively inexpensive AT options for many students. Without question, the use of AT with students with special learning needs may make a substantial difference in their academic progress or ability to communicate with others. In addition, there are numerous devices to enable people with challenges to access computers (e.g., voice recognition software, word prediction software, switches, eye gaze, screen readers, refreshable Braille screen, Touch Windows). Teachers should become familiar with a range of devices that are often used in educational settings, how the AT needs of students can be evaluated, and, if AT devices are used, how they work.

 Check Your Understanding 2.4 Click here to gauge your understanding of the concepts in this section.

CHAPTER 3

Teaching and Differentiating Instruction in a Multi-Tiered System of Education

LEARNING OUTCOMES

Upon completion of this chapter, the reader should be able to:

3.1 Identify and describe the major components of multi-tiered systems of education operating in schools today.

3.2 Recognize the key roles and skill sets that special education teachers need to possess in the contemporary context of schools.

3.3 Articulate a comprehensive model for differentiating instruction within both general education and special education settings.

3.4 Describe the major collaborative arrangements that special education teachers will encounter in their roles within schools.

Schools continue to experience significant changes in recent times. One of the most notable changes is the implementation of new models for addressing students who are struggling in school. The most prominent model that has evolved in recent years involves a multi-tier system that is predicated on how well students who have been identified as having some problems respond to the interventions that are provided. This system that is being used in many schools throughout the country places a heavy emphasis on the involvement of general education teachers in the initial efforts to address student needs and implies that the roles of special education teachers continue to change.

This chapter covers four major topics. First of all, a thorough description of what a multi-tiered system of education looks like is provided. Second, the changing rules that both general education and special education teachers are experiencing are explored, with an emphasis on the role of special education teachers. Third, an overview of how to differentiate instruction for students who might be in a variety of educational environments, particularly general education, is presented. Finally, different collaborative arrangements, now more important than ever, are reviewed.

MULTI-TIERED SYSTEM TO EDUCATION AND RESPONSE TO INTERVENTION

Multi-tiered instructional models have emerged for at-risk and special learners in a majority of schools throughout the country. Balu et al. (2015), in their study of response to intervention (RtI) practices (reading) at the elementary level, found that schools that had been implementing these practices for three or more years reported an 86% full implementation rate. It should be noted that a range of terms, such as *multilevel*, *tri-level*, *three-tiered*, and *four-tiered*, may be used to describe this multi-tiered system, and, as a result, the way a system is implemented varies from school to school.

In general, tiered instruction provides layers or levels of intervention to meet student needs, increasing in intensity as a student progresses through different tiers over time (see Figure 3-1), and predicated on how the student responds to evidence-based practices at the various levels of intervention.

Hoover and Patton (2007) defined the three tiers in the following way:

Tier 1: High-quality core instruction: "High-quality, research-based, and systematic instruction in a challenging curriculum in general education" (p. 9). The anticipated outcome is that all students initially receive quality instruction and achieve expected academic and behavioral goals in the general education setting. Approximately 80% to 85% of all students would be anticipated to receive tier 1 instruction—that is, universal supports (McLeskey & Waldron, 2011).

Tier 2: High-quality targeted supplemental instruction: "Targeted and focused interventions to supplement core instruction" (Hoover & Patton, 2007, p. 9). The anticipated outcome is that students who do not meet general class expectations and exhibit need for supplemental support will receive more targeted instruction. Learners may receive targeted, tier 2–type instruction within the general education classroom (e.g., separate grouping) or in some other setting (e.g., different location within the school). Regardless of location, students need to receive various types of assistance in terms of differentiations, instructional and curricular adaptations, more specialized equipment, and technology in order to target

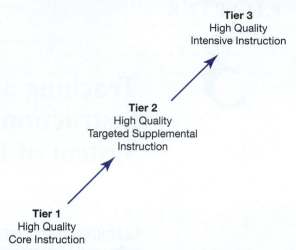

Instructional Levels in a Multi-Tiered System

Tier 3
High Quality
Intensive Instruction

Tier 2
High Quality
Targeted Supplemental
Instruction

Tier 1
High Quality
Core Instruction

FIGURE 3–1 Three-Tier Instruction for At-Risk and Special Learners

instructional-related needs. Critical within tier 2 is the documentation of students' responses to the interventions used, which serves as important pre-referral data should more formal special education assessment be determined necessary. Approximately 10% to 15% of students would be anticipated to receive tier 2 instruction or targeted supports (McLeskey & Waldron, 2011). Students who make insufficient progress in tier 2 are likely to be considered for more formal special education consideration.

Tier 3: High-quality intensive intervention: "Specialized interventions to meet significant disabilities" (Hoover & Patton, 2007, p. 9). If individuals are found eligible for special education services, tier 3 provides students with more intensive, evidence-based interventions within a range of possible special education settings. Approximately 1% to 5% of students may require intensive or special services through high-quality intensive intervention or specialized supports (McLeskey & Waldron, 2011).

This process can be conceptualized as one of successive levels where students who are identified as struggling are provided high-quality core instruction within the general education classroom. This instruction is associated with "reasonable and targeted" differentiated instruction that teachers provide to identified students (Hoover & Patton, 2007, p. 9). Those students who do not respond to this initial level of intervention over a reasonable amount of time will require additional high-quality targeted supplemental instruction. Some students who receive tier 2 instruction will benefit in ways that allow them to return to tier 1 status. However, some students will not respond favorably to supplemental instruction and will need more intensive instruction. Often, this next level implies consideration for special education services.

▶ **LEARNING MODULE 3.1** Click here to learn more about multi-tier systems of support.

As noted in the above description, an important element within a multi-tiered model is how a student "responds" to the evidenced-based practices that should be implemented at the various tiers in a well-designed and implemented system. Typically referred to as RtI, this key component of multi-tiered systems is predicated on the following notions:

- Teachers—specifically, general education teachers, are prepared properly to function within a multi-tiered system of instruction.
- Students who are truly struggling are identified appropriately.
- Teachers are using evidence-based practices.
- Student progress as a result of the prescribed intervention is monitored regularly and systematically.
- Decisions about how well a student is responding are based on data and not conjecture.

Response to intervention is considered so noteworthy that RtI is recommended under IDEA, although not required, as the method to be used for identifying students with learning disabilities. However, RtI is most relevant to this discussion because of the process by which students receive high-quality instruction, and their progress as a function of this intervention is monitored with quantifiable data to determine if they are making appropriate progress toward the successful achievement of specific benchmarks within the academic curriculum (Hoover & Love, 2011).

Special education teachers must understand the RtI process that is being implemented at the schools where they work. Most important, special education teachers need to understand what roles they need to fulfill at the various tiers within this process. Clearly, if and when a student moves to tier 3, the role of special education teachers becomes more evident. However, it is crucial to note that special education personnel can and should play important roles in tiers 1 and 2 as well. The next section of this chapter elaborates on this point.

 Check Your Understanding 3.1 Click here to gauge your understanding of the concepts in this section.

THE CHANGING ROLE OF SPECIAL EDUCATION TEACHERS

The sophistication of what it takes to be an effective special education teacher is reflected in the ongoing documentation of professional standards and competencies that are needed. One of the best sources that chronicles the evolving demands of being a special education teacher is the set of professional competencies that the Council for Exceptional Children (CEC) publishes on a regular basis. The most recent version (CEC, 2015) highlights the range of knowledge and skills that teachers need to have. New areas, such as transition, have been added to this resource since its beginning in the 1960s.

Over the years, various emphases can be noted in regard to how special education was delivered and accordingly to the knowledge and skills that teachers needed. As Hoover and Patton (2008) have noted, the early days of special education were often characterized as focusing on self-contained classroom settings. Following the focus on self-contained settings, the era of the "resource room" became a dominant theme. Over the years, as "mainstreaming"—now more properly referred to as inclusion—became more of the norm, the need for special education teachers to be proficient in working with general education teachers became a necessity. Today, given more recent changes to the way services are provided to struggling students, the role of special educators has morphed somewhat from earlier times.

Special education teachers have always had to be good at managing behavior and accommodating the needs of students—whether that was in special education settings or in general education settings. Competence in these areas remains; however, subtle changes have occurred. Moreover, other areas, which arguably have always been important, have emerged as being critical to the overall effectiveness of the special education teacher in today's schools, especially within multi-tier systems, in addressing the needs the students who are struggling in school.

Hoover and Patton (2008) identified five critical areas in which special educators must become highly proficient within the context of the demands of teaching in schools today: data-driven decision maker, implementer of evidence-based intervention, implementer of socioemotional/behavioral supports (i.e., manager of behavior), differentiator of instruction, and collaborator. Table 3-1, based in part on this model of Hoover and Patton (2008), provides a sample of some of the subskills that are associated with these various roles. It should be noted that the degree of "need" of these various skills will be a function of the type of students and the settings in which they are placed.

The point to be made is that, for those teachers who will be working in a multi-tier system that in large part involves students in general education settings, these roles/skills are unquestionably important. Put another way, preservice teacher training programs must ensure that these skills are covered in coursework, and in-service programs provided by schools must ensure that teachers are provided opportunities to enhance their current knowledge and skill levels in these areas. All five of these key roles, along with their associated subskills, are addressed in this book. The topics of evidence-based intervention and data-driven decision making are woven throughout Part 2 of this book. The topic of behavioral supports is covered in depth in the next chapter. The topics of differentiating instruction and collaboration are addressed in more detail in the next two sections of this chapter.

 Check Your Understanding 3.2 Click here to gauge your understanding of the concepts in this section.

TABLE 3–1 Special educator roles and selected subskills

1. **Evidence-based intervention**
   - Subject knowledge
   - Instructional strategies across subjects
   - Direct instruction
   - Proficiency and mastery
2. **Differentiation**
   - Adaptations (accommodations, modifications)
   - Differentiation strategies
   - Cultural relevance
   - Learning strategies instruction
   - Peer-tutoring models
   - Academic engaged time
3. **Behavioral supports**
   - Behavior and classroom management
   - Positive behavioral supports
   - Self-management instruction
   - Cultural considerations
   - Functional behavioral assessment
   - Behavior intervention planning (BIP)
4. **Data-based decisions**
   - Effective decision-making
   - Data analysis
   - Skills assessment
   - Curriculum based assessment
   - Eligibility for special education
5. **Collaboration**
   - Professional communication
   - Collaborative teaching
   - Parent–school partnerships
   - Cultural and linguistic considerations
   - IDEA tenets and regulations
   - State and district referral and assessment processes

DIFFERENTIATING INSTRUCTION

The concept of **differentiated instruction**, as advocated by Tomlinson (2014) and others (Patton, 2016; Smith, Polloway, Patton, & Dowdy, 2012), has become an important dimension of classroom instruction. To a certain extent, the term is a reformulation of the basic idea of "individualizing instruction" that has been espoused for many years within special education; however, the current term borrows from gifted education and has been applied consistently to general education settings.

The essence of this concept is that a wide range of student needs can and must be accommodated within general education classrooms. This results from the reality that most public school classrooms have students displaying a wide variety of academic, social, behavioral, and personal needs. Both general education and special education teachers have to have the skill sets to deal with the challenges that confront them regardless of educational placement.

Tomlinson (2001) is often credited with the introduction of the term *differentiating instruction* as it applies to general education classrooms, although at its very essence, many of the ideas associated with differentiating instruction have been part of the special education experience for many years. The important change in recent years is the widespread consideration of this idea in general education settings. Tomlinson (2014) defines differentiating instruction as follows:

> A teacher proactively plans various approaches to what students need to learn, how they will learn it, and/or how they can express what they've learned in order to increase the likelihood that each to learn as much as he or she can as efficiently as possible. (p. 170)

It is important to point out that various models of differentiation have emerged over the years. However, as Tomlinson (2015) notes, "There is no formula for differentiation—no single way to respond to student variance" (p. 179). The important point is that teachers can and should develop their own models as long as, whatever model is used, it is comprehensive in nature so that the needs of students who display a vast array of challenges are considered and addressed.

The integration of the principles of universal design for learning (UDL) and differentiated instruction provide a potentially powerful way to address the individual needs of a range of students within the general education classroom. This point is particularly noteworthy because more students who are at risk, who have special needs, or who have debilitating learning-related disabilities are in these settings.

Teachers seeking to educate all of their students are faced with the challenge of meeting the instructional needs of these students to prepare them for a competitive world. Much of the information instructors must teach is complex and abstract. New vocabulary is necessary, and the applicability of new information to everyday life must be understood. As a result, being able to differentiate instruction requires skill sets that can be complex, with significant variance from the mindset that all students are alike (Tomlinson, 2014).

Unfortunately, many students have limited interest in learning things that they do not understand or that seem irrelevant to their immediate future. This lack of motivation among students is a formidable barrier. If teachers are unable to introduce new information in an understandable manner, students will become frustrated and will not persist on their own to learn the material. If teachers are unable to teach students how to acquire new concepts and to have them relate these concepts in a meaningful way, the students will not pursue the new content areas presented to them in their classes.

Teachers must focus on techniques and strategies that enable students to succeed in school while gaining access to the general education curriculum. Central to this success are classroom **adjustments**. Such efforts are critical to the success of students with disabilities in terms of their access to the general curriculum (Hedeen & Ayers, 2002). Further, "the need to adapt curricula increases as the variability of student abilities and learner characteristics increases" (Hoover & Patton, 2005, p. 43).

 LEARNING MODULE 3.2 Click here to learn more about differentiated instruction.

In this chapter, we use *adjustments* as a generic term to include both accommodations and modifications. **Accommodations** typically refer to changes in input and output processes in teaching and learning; they do not minimize course or task content itself. Some examples include extended testing time or a distraction-reduced testing setting. **Modifications** refer to changes in content or standards; they change the task or course content itself (Polloway, Epstein, & Bursuck, 2003). Examples in a college-level course in foreign language might include the substitution of the study of culture for the language instruction requirement.

Key Elements of Differentiating Instruction

Differentiating instruction can be conceptualized on two different levels. On a more global level, various adjustments can be made within a curriculum or in a classroom that are designed so that all students can benefit from the features. To a great extent, this macro level of differentiation is akin to the idea of universal design for learning noted previously.

When adjustments are made on a more individual level, differentiating instruction reflects a micro level of attending to individual student needs. At this level, attention is given to the unique challenges that a specific student presents in the classroom. In this case, the changes made for a certain student may not need to be made for other students in the class. In some instances, the adjustment cannot be made for logistical reasons. For instance, only a limited number of students can actually be given preferential seating.

The model of differentiating instruction described below is based on a model that covers a range of areas for which either macro-level or micro-level adjustments can be implemented. This model, depicted in Figure 3-2, is composed of six major areas (Smith et al., 2012): setting, content, materials, instruction/intervention, management/behavior, and personal-emotional. All of these areas with the exception of the last two are discussed below. The others are covered in detail in the next chapter. It should be noted that in the following discussion, the area of instruction is broken down into more specific topics.

Setting Differentiation

The setting dimension refers to the way a classroom is set up, organized, and utilized. This dimension includes considerations such as the way desks are arranged in the class, where students are seated, specialized equipment that might be needed (e.g., adaptive equipment, chairs, desks), and accessibility

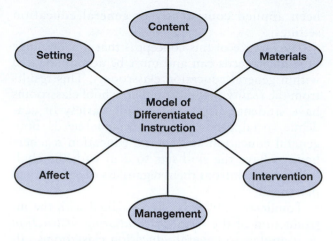

FIGURE 3–2   Model of Differentiated Instruction

issues. Perhaps the most common adjustment that is made in this area is preferential seating.

Content Differentiation

Adjustments made in this area involve reducing the amount of content that is covered, altering the content that is covered, or adding additional content that needs to be covered. In some cases, it may be necessary to make the decision not to cover some material. This decision may be made based on any number of factors—most often related to a student's inability to understand various topics. Teachers need to be cautious about modifying content because students with special needs, according to IDEA, must have access to the general education curriculum.

For many students with special needs, it may be very important to teach certain skills that are not part of the explicit curriculum. For example, it is quite likely that students may need additional time acquiring, developing, or refining skills, such as study skills and social skills. These two topics are so important that individual chapters have been devoted to covering them.

Materials Differentiation

A wide variety of materials are used in school settings, including print materials as well as non-print materials, such as maps, globes, models, photographs, and videos. More and more schools are also moving to the use of digital-only materials.

The key concerns that precipitate the need to make adjustments to instructional materials for the most part cut across the different types of materials. These concerns include the following:

- The student does not display the skills necessary to handle the material.
- The conceptual complexity of the material exceeds the level at which the student understands (i.e., insufficient background knowledge or experience).
- The linguistic complexity of the material is such that the student is unable to extract meaning from it. Primary sources of problems are vocabulary and syntactic factors.
- The amount of information presented to students is overwhelming. Typically, emphasis has been placed on breadth of rather than depth of coverage.
- The design or format features of materials (e.g., advanced organizers, layout, organization, graphics, cuing, clarity, use of examples, practice opportunities) are lacking or insufficient, thus making them difficult to use.

Textual materials refer to any type of material that requires reading as the primary means of obtaining information. Text-based materials typically used in classrooms include textbooks, workbooks, worksheets, literature, weekly periodicals, handouts, and increasingly more digital text.

Three general approaches can be implemented to address problems that arise with text-based materials: (a) substitution of an alternative material in place of the existing textual material, (b) content enhancement techniques that include strategies to increase comprehension and tactics for retaining information over time, and (c) use of supplemental materials to assist in the use of text material. The first technique aims to avoid the problems associated with existing textual material. The second and third options support the student primarily in using existing material, particularly when the student is in a general education setting.

One type of material adjustment warrants particular attention. *Graphic organizers*—graphically based materials that provide visual models for presenting curricular content—have been widely promoted as a particularly efficacious approach to content learning by students with special needs (Wehmeyer, 2002). As such, the widespread use of graphic organizers has become an important aspect of the application of universal design for learning. While these materials can be extremely important for use with students who are struggling, they actually have value for all students in the classroom.

Graphic organizers can be developed for content in any instructional area. For example, graphic organizers can provide outlines for note taking from lectures, a template for organizing reports and speeches for oral presentation in class, a format for deriving key content information from reading assigned as homework, and a prompt to assist students in monitoring their own errors in writing as part of a proofreading strategy. The chapters in Part 2 of this text provide a wealth of examples of graphic organizers. Semantic maps in reading (Chapter 7) and paragraph development models for writing (Chapter 8) are particularly good examples.

The following discussion of various other techniques for adapting instructional materials with textual material is based in part on the recommendations of Schumm and Strickler (1991):

- **Use an audio version of textual material**— Although this technique can be viable and attractive at face value, its use is dependent on the availability of material in digital format, the amount of time it takes to listen to the material, and the interest of the student in using this alternative format. Ideally, the material being used is already available in an audio format. Otherwise, unless volunteers or other students are available to do the taping, taping may be difficult to do. It is also important to realize that this technique assumes that the student has good listening skills. Furthermore, it requires a significant amount of time to listen to the audio material.
- **Read the material aloud**—This suggestion has the same advantages and limitations as taping.
- **Pair students**—This technique has short-term and targeted usefulness and requires the availability of such supports whenever the textual material is being used.
- **Use other ways to deliver the material**—Other vehicles (direct experience and media) for delivering information are useful for presenting content-laden topics.
- **Work with students individually or in small groups**—This works when students can understand the textual material to some extent and time is available on a regular basis for this activity.

- **Simplify existing material**—The teacher can simplify vocabulary, terminology, and expressions that are difficult for students to understand. In place of rewriting complete textual passages, the teacher can place a transparency over a page of written material and, with a marker, cross out the more difficult words and write a more understandable equivalent in the margin (Hoover & Patton, 2005).

A variety of ways exist for enhancing content so that students are better able to understand what they read. The following recommendations focus on tactics for improving comprehension of textual, particularly grade-level, material:

- Preview the reading assignment to prepare the students for the specifics they will encounter. This pre-reading activity should introduce the students to new vocabulary and concepts that may pose problems. The use of a diagram or story frame may be helpful (see Chapter 7).
- Teach students how to use format features, including the ability to use headings, boldface type, visual aids, opening sections, and summaries of textual material, to gain additional meaning from the textual material.
- Use a study guide to support the students through the reading material by having them respond to questions or statements related to the passages they are reading or have read.
- Adjust the reading assignment to reduce the length of the assigned reading or to slow the pace at which content is being covered.
- Adapt text-based activities, such as reorganizing and rewriting the "end-of-chapter" questions that are often included with textbooks. For students experiencing reading problems, these types of questions can be frustrating.

Attention also needs to be given to any type of learning aid (e.g., outside readings, games, in-class projects) that might be part of the ongoing instructional program. Caution must be exercised to ensure that students know how to use these materials. If textual material (e.g., lab manuals) is part of the learning aid, the preceding specific suggestions may need to be implemented. In regard to the use of instructional games, students need to possess appropriate game-playing skills and behaviors—this is crucial if students play games in cooperative situations without teacher involvement or supervision.

ENHANCEDetext
video example 3.2
Watch this video to learn more about differentiating instruction.

Instructional Differentiation

This particular dimension focuses on the basic elements of how a teacher provides instruction and what students have to do as a result of that instruction. An elaborate discussion of this particular dimension is provided elsewhere (Smith et al., 2012); however, five areas of adjustment are covered in the section of the chapter: instructional delivery, products/assignments, homework, testing, and grading. All of these topics have relevance for both general education and special education settings.

Instructional Delivery Adjustments. The way a teacher delivers instruction is critically important. The following adjustments may be helpful to students in classroom situations:

- **Location**—Proximity to students who are experiencing learning-related problems can help students attend to the important dimensions of what is occurring in the classroom, give them easier access to support, and minimize behavioral problems that might arise.
- **Multisensory experiences**—Multisensory activities can have a positive impact and thus can be instructionally useful.
- **Lecture-related tactics**—Teacher-controlled adaptations include scheduling the session so that more breaks are possible, organizing the lecture so that a variety of instructional methods (e.g., discussion, media) are utilized, moving around the room, being responsive to the audience and to specific students, highlighting important points, and providing advanced organizers. In addition, note-taking skills and listening strategies may need to be taught. If the lecture format allows for discussion, then the students may also need to develop question-asking skills.
- **Instructional variation**—Consideration of how a teacher can present information and how a student responds to that information can lead to a more expansive way of looking at instruction. Based on earlier work of Cawley, Fitzmaurice-Hayes, and Shaw (1988) instructional variation

can be accomplished by altering input and output options, as noted below:

Student input (instructional delivery) options: Read, listen, watch.

Student response options: Write, speak, identify (i.e., point to or choose from options), do something.

Based on these options, a teacher theoretically would have 12 ways to design a lesson or activity. It should be noted that the combination of read (input) and write (output) is often the most used option.

Product and Assignment Adjustments. A key consideration is using a variety of *work product options*. To provide some choice about options is desirable and is supported by the emerging emphasis on self-determination (see Chapter 13). Too often, teachers tend to make the same assignments, as noted above. For students with special needs who have strengths in areas in which they are seldom allowed to show their ability, having alternative products might be just what they need (Smith et al., 2012).

Another key area relates to the need to adapt in-class and out-of-class (see the homework discussion that follows) assignments given to learners with special needs. Teachers can alter assignments in the following ways: shorten assignments (i.e., break them into smaller versions), change the criterion that has been established that designates successful completion of the assignment, allow more time to complete the assignment, reduce the difficulty of the content, and change the output mode.

Homework Adjustments. A staple of the education diet is homework. The research literature generally supports the value of homework in achievement and learning good work habits. When this conclusion is combined with the reform literature supporting increased use to enhance quality, it is apparent that students with special needs must be able to respond effectively, especially as they spend more time in inclusive settings. Prior to the early 1990s, fewer than a dozen articles and only a handful of papers were published on the topic; since that time, increased interest in this topic has emerged, and a much larger research base now exists on this topic.

Although homework presents special problems for students with disabilities and their families, intervention efforts can result in beneficial outcomes.

The following suggestions (adapted from Patton, 1994) provide direction for developing and implementing homework practices, including making adaptations for learners with special needs:

- **Assign homework from the beginning of the year**—Getting students accustomed to the routine of having homework is best accomplished by assigning it early and continuing with it on a regular basis.
- **Establish a class routine for homework**—If the homework process is to run efficiently, adequate time must be allocated to assign, collect, and evaluate homework. Teachers need to have a reasonable amount of time to inform students of their assignments.
- **Communicate consequences**—Students need to know the procedures that are expected of them as well as the consequences of violating these procedures. Logical consequences for non-completion of assignments should be determined beforehand.
- **Minimize demands on teacher time**—Homework is only one of many duties that teachers must manage. Therefore, any mechanism created to handle homework must demonstrate efficiency. If individualized assignments are indicated, they can be provided by adapting the general assignment rather than developing completely different activities.
- **Present instructions clearly**—A thorough explanation of a homework assignment should include (a) the purpose, (b) directions for completing the assignment, (c) an estimate of how long the assignment should take, (d) a note when due, (e) the format to be used, (f) the materials needed to complete the assignment, and (g) how it will be evaluated. Teachers also should query students to determine whether they understand what is assigned or let them begin working on it in class.
- **Use assignment books**—Homework assignment books can help compensate for organizational difficulties. Typically, the students will write their assignments in these books, and the teachers can initial the books before the students leave the class, confirming that the correct assignment has been recorded. Folders also can be used to provide a quick and simple way for the teacher to evaluate completion of the assignment, thus underscoring the importance of turning in assignments on time.

- **Evaluate assignments**—Homework that is collected, evaluated, and used to determine a grade is more meaningful to students and has a positive effect on achievement. The challenge is to find ways to manage this aspect of the homework process efficiently, such as through the use of assignments that can be evaluated through peer grading or self-correction techniques or by paraeducators.

- **Help students recognize the purpose and relevance of the assignment**—The major reasons for homework are practice opportunities, completion of unfinished work, preparation for future course activities or upcoming tests, and extension. Homework is best used for proficiency, generalization, or maintenance types of learning activities. Guided by a clear purpose for giving homework, teachers should also identify specific objectives for each assignment and inform students of these objectives when an assignment is introduced. Further, teachers should show students how a particular assignment relates to their scholastic or non-academic lives.

- **Adapt assignments**—As more students face the challenges of completing homework assignments in general education, practical ways to adapt assignments must be identified. Options to be considered include shorter assignments, extended timelines, alternative evaluation techniques (i.e., based on effort, not accuracy), fewer assignments, extra-credit opportunities, alternative response formats, and group assignments.

ENHANCEDetext
video example 3.3
Watch this video to learn more about developing classroom adaptations.

- **Develop self-regulation skills**—A significant outcome of a successful homework system is the students' taking responsibility for outside class aspects of their own learning. Teachers should help students understand that the effort they put forth can lead to academic success.

- **Consider student preferences**—It is beneficial to consider students' views on homework practices. A number of studies address the issue of student preferences (e.g., Nelson, Epstein, Bursuck, Jayanthi, & Sawyer, 1998).

- **Communicate with parents**—If a smooth school–home communication system is operating, this suggestion is moot because many ongoing opportunities to share views on homework exist. Nevertheless, parents should be contacted regarding homework to request their views and to be informed of their child's school-based performance.

Testing Adjustments. Another area of critical importance is classroom testing. Adaptation options include the following:

- Test preparation (study guides)
- Test construction (space, number of questions)
- Test administration time
- Form of response (oral, written)
- Site of testing (distraction-free)
- Forms of feedback
- Curriculum modification
- Use of portfolios
- Use of checklists
- Development of shared grading approaches between general and special educators

Polloway, Bursuck, Jayanthi, Epstein, and Nelson (1996) identified the testing adaptations that teachers indicated were most helpful to students. They provided a list of the most helpful adaptations. The top five are as follows:

- Give extra help preparing for tests.
- Give individual help with directions during tests.
- Read test questions to students.
- Simplify wording of the test questions.
- Give practice questions as a study guide. (p. 140)

Grading Adjustments. Along with testing and homework, grading is one of the most discussed topics related to students with special needs. Grading is a required form of student evaluation and record keeping and an integral part of our educational system. This topic is particularly noteworthy when students with special needs are in general education classes.

Grading issues have become more significant for students with disabilities given increased school inclusion. Salend (2005) stressed the role of communication in the grading process, particularly as related to the usage of differentiated instructional strategies in inclusive settings. The special education teacher generally needs to provide a clear description of an individual student's strengths, weaknesses, capabilities, and needs, thus giving the classroom teacher additional data on which to base a letter grade evaluation. The solution that emphasizes cooperative efforts is the one most likely to succeed.

To facilitate this process, teachers should jointly consider possible adaptations that will be effective and also be deemed acceptable by general education teachers (Polloway, Bursuck, et al., 1996). Grading adaptations may include the following:

- Altering grading criteria (e.g., variant weights for assignments, individualized contracts)
- Supplementing letter and number grades with additional information (e.g., comments, portfolio)
- Providing alternatives to number or letter grades (e.g., checklists) (Munk & Bursuck, 2001)

More comprehensive lists of grading adaptations is provided by Munk and Bursuck (2004). An interesting perspective was provided in research by Nelson, Jayanthi, Epstein, and Bursuck (2000). They noted that middle school students preferred these adaptations:

- Open notes
- Multiple choice over short answer/essay
- Simplified words in questions
- Open-book tests
- Practice questions

On the other hand, middle school students least preferred the following practices:

- Teacher reading questions aloud
- Tests with fewer items than others
- Tests covering less material for some students
- Teaching of test-taking strategies

To implement an effective grading intervention, teachers may wish to use the concept of personalized grading plans (PGPs) (Munk & Bursuck, 2001, 2004). Munk and Bursuck (2001) described the implementation of the PGP model as follows:

> During Stage 1, the student, parents, and teachers identify . . . what purpose they believe the grade should meet. During the second stage, the student, parents, and teachers review their school's grading policy and a menu of possible grading adaptations.

During the third stage . . . the student, parents, and the teachers meet together to review their perceived purposes for a report card grade, and identify one or more mutually agreed upon purposes that will be used to steer selection of a specific adaptation. In Stage 4, the team collaborates to implement the PGP. Stage 5 involves evaluating the effects of the PGP on the student's grade(s), the student's and parent's satisfaction with the accuracy and meaning of the grade, and the teachers' perceptions of the accuracy and usefulness of the PGP. (p. 212)

The following summative recommendations on grading are adapted from Smith, Polloway, Doughty, Patton, and Dowdy (2016) and Polloway, Bursuck, and Epstein (2001):

- Plan for general and special education teachers to meet regularly to discuss individual student progress.
- Use cooperative grading agreements (e.g., grades for language arts might reflect performance in both the general education classroom and the resource room).
- Emphasize the acquisition of new skills as a basis for grades assigned to provide a perspective on the student's relative academic gains.
- Investigate alternatives for assessing what has been learned (e.g., oral examinations for poor readers in a science class).
- Use narrative reports as a portion of or adjunct to report card grades. Such reports can include comments on specific objectives within the student's IEP.

 Check Your Understanding 3.3 Click here to gauge your understanding of the concepts in this section.

COLLABORATIVE ARRANGEMENTS WITHIN AND OUTSIDE OF SCHOOL

As noted earlier, the emphasis in education on providing the vast majority of students with access to the general education curriculum and doing so within the general education classroom whenever possible. As a consequence, special educators must operate as part of a team in many aspects of his or her role, including screening, making assessments, planning individual programs, developing placement options, providing direct or indirect support, and monitoring success. Teachers must work with many others to operationalize the required aspects of all initiatives or changes in effect within the instructional program. Through collaboration, the learning needs of students are assessed and then subsequently addressed. Educators work collaboratively using their unique resources and special expertise (Hoover & Patton, in press).

Working with General Education Teachers

General education personnel at all K–12 levels are important partners in many different types of collaboration. The particular configuration of the special and general education interaction may vary, depending on which student or program situations exist. A key form of collaboration is *cooperative teaching*, or co-teaching, in which special education teachers work alongside general education teachers and provide effective instruction in inclusive classroom environments. As Murawski and Lochner (2011) noted, "If educators with varying areas of expertise and frames of reference are able to come together and collaborate on a daily basis in the same classroom, all students will benefit more: socially, behaviorally, perhaps most importantly, academically" (pp. 174).

Several different variations of the co-teaching model exist. At the core, general education and special education teachers are working together; however, the way they function within the classroom differs according to the structure of the co-teaching arrangement. Four co-teaching options (Thousand, Villa, & Nevin, 2007) include the following:

- **Supportive teaching**—One teacher is the primary instructor—the other teacher moves around the classroom and provides support to students.
- **Parallel teaching**—Teachers work with separate groups of students within the same classroom space.
- **Complementary teaching**—The teacher with expertise takes the lead, and the other teacher provides ancillary instructional functions, such paraphrasing, modeling, or emphasizing key points.
- **Team teaching**—Teachers simultaneously deliver a lesson or activity.

Several barriers or challenges may interfere with establishing effective collaborative relationships between special and general education teachers (see Table 3-2). These challenges can be addressed by effective cooperative work and advocacy to enhance the educational programs of all students.

Consulting with Other School Professionals

As noted in the section of this chapter dealing with the changing role of special education teachers, the need to be a good collaborator was emphasized. In addition to working with general education teachers, special education teachers need to be

---

TABLE 3–2   Challenges in school collaboration

- Lack of administrative support and encouragement of collaborative activities
- Attitudinal issues
- Teacher's focus on the class as a whole rather than on individual learning needs
- Required coverage of content standards overlaid with needs for curricular accommodations
- Insufficient preparation or confidence to differentiate instruction for diverse learners, especially those with extreme behavioral events
- Lack of funds needed to directly support all students needing individualized help
- Insufficient time allocated for real collaborative efforts to work
- Intensification of teachers' daily challenges when students with exceptionalities are included within a full class load
- Lack of real assistance due to the caseloads among special educators and delays with referrals
- Absence of an efficient and effective pre-referral system that would assist general education teachers with students prior to an official referral and eligibility determination
- Students' lack of self-determination/self-advocacy and other collaborative skills

prepared to work with a host of other professionals at their schools. Some of the other professionals with whom special education teachers are likely to work include speech and language pathologists, occupational therapists, physical therapists, school psychologists, diagnosticians, school counselors, school nurses, and a range of other outside-of-school professionals.

One of the key reasons why it is important to know how to work with other professionals results from the fact that many students with special needs require related services to allow them to benefit from their educational experience. The expertise that these other professionals provide can be extremely important to ensuring that a student receives an appropriate education. As a result, special education teachers should be familiar with the backgrounds, skill sets, and rules that these professionals play in the school system. Moreover, special education teachers must develop collaborative skill sets that maximize the interaction among these various professionals.

Working with Paraeducators

Paraeducators are school employees who contribute to providing appropriate services to students with special needs. These individuals may also be referred to as educational assistants, teacher aides, or instructional assistants. As Gerlach (2015) points out, these individuals "work under the direction of certified licensed staff members to help provide instructional and other services to students and their families" (p. 9).

Special education teachers who work with students with more significant support needs are likely to have the additional responsibilities of "planning, scheduling and directing the work of paraeducators" (Gerlach, 2015, p. 45). Some of the major responsibilities that a teacher will have in working with paraeducators include the following:

- Establishing and clarifying roles
- Planning the tasks that paraeducators will perform
- Developing schedules for paraeducators
- Delegating responsibilities
- Monitoring the day-to-day performance and providing feedback
- Coaching and mentoring
- Maintaining effective communication (Gerlach, 2015, p. 46)

Partnerships with Families

Collaboration is not just a priority consideration within schools. It is also important in terms of working with the parents and families of students with special needs. Since the advent of P.L. 94-142 in 1975, parents have always been encouraged to participate in the special education process and are equal members of the IEP team. However, the amount and quality of this participation have varied greatly. Parents must consent to the evaluation of a student's educational abilities and needs, the determination of necessary services, and the actual placement of their child in any type of special program. Parents have the right to obtain an independent educational evaluation of their child. Some parents engage the process fully, whereas others participate minimally for a variety of reasons.

As noted, parents are key contributors to the development of their child's IEP. In addition, they have the right to challenge or appeal any decision related to any aspect of the special education process. IDEA also encourages efforts to increase student involvement in the decision-making processes related to their education, especially as related to transition planning. Further, parents have the right to educational records, the right to obtain an independent educational evaluation, the right to request a due process hearing, the right to appeal decisions, and the right to initiate civil action when appealing a final hearing decision.

Successful home–school collaborative partnerships are characterized by the following attributes (Wehmeyer, Morningstar, & Husted, 1999):

- Prompt honest, open sharing of information, impressions, and judgments
- Two-way sharing of information without fear of being negatively judged
- Mutual respect for each other's expertise and sensitivity to new areas of learning
- Shared goals, planning, and decision making

A key element of home–school communication is the meeting or conference, whether formal or informal. Some specific suggestions for teachers are identified in Table 3-3. Effective collaborative programs with parents and families represent yet another key aspect of the professional role of special educators.

TABLE 3–3 Principles of effective meetings with families

- Prepare for the meeting by discussing the meeting with parents well in advance, agreeing mutually on a time and location for the meeting, organizing your notes, reviewing pertinent information, and planning an agenda—with input from the family and student when possible.

- Create a positive atmosphere, agree on the purpose of the meeting, employ good communication skills, take notes of what is being discussed, and end the meeting with a positive statement and appreciation to the family members for coming.

- Be honest and direct.

- Avoid technical terms.

- Be clear and concise.

- Do not speculate about issues for which you have no information. Discuss only what you know and about which you have data (i.e., what you can document).

- After the meeting, organize your notes for future reference, initiate action on any items requiring attention, determine when a follow-up meeting is needed, and send out a summary of the meeting.

 Check Your Understanding 3.4 Click here to gauge your understanding of the concepts in this section.

4

Strategies for Classroom Management and Positive Behavior Support

LEARNING OUTCOMES

Upon completion of this chapter, the reader should be able to:

4.1 Identify the essential factors and programs that establish a positive and successful school climate.

4.2 Identify the key factors related to a well-organized and well-managed classroom, including research-based behavioral interventions that enhance appropriate classroom behavior.

4.3 Discuss the student diversity considerations that relate to classroom management and supports.

One of the most important issues for teachers is managing their classroom and providing interventions for students who need particular support for appropriate behavior. These issues have been compounded by years of public concern as teachers and school administrators have had to confront the threats regarding school safety and effectiveness. Coupled with the growing diversity of learners and the complexity of working toward meeting the demands of federal legislation, teachers and educational leaders are challenged with the task of thinking about school behavior and classroom management in different ways (Lewis, Mitchell, Trussell, & Newcomer, 2015).

Since the 1980s prominent researchers have recognized the need to focus on a non-aversive school environment to support the quality of every student's life as well as their academic and social experiences. This focus has been termed positive behavior support (PBS) (e.g., Dunlap, Kincaid, Horner, Knoster, & Bradshaw, 2014). Historically, PBS is "characterized as a multicomponent process that is guided by the values of the individual, his or her family, and the organizational and community context in which support is provided" (Dunlap et al., 2014, p. 134). The positive approach was implemented to reduce target behaviors that interrupted the learning environment of the student(s). It includes assessing and redesigning the school and classroom environment, teaching social skills, and reinforcing desirable behaviors while intervening on disruptive behaviors.

Over the years, PBS has become a strong evidence-based practice and is recognized as a preferred intervention approach for early childhood, elementary, and secondary schools. This recognition has become evident because of the systematic approach to positive behavior rather than emphasizing punitive methods of discipline. Dunlap et al. (2014) further characterized PBS as

1. an emphasis on instructional procedures and an avoidance of interventions that involved pain and stigmatization,
2. a continued emphasis on supporting observable and measurable behavior, and
3. an insistence that all interventions be based on an understanding of and respect for a person's life, circumstances, preferences, and goals. (p. 134)

As the popularity of PBS grew, researchers began to expand on this philosophical and applied approach. For example, Lewis and Sugai (1999) coined the term *effective behavior support* (EBS) to describe the collection of efforts of several researchers who were addressing severe behavioral needs of students in the classroom (e.g., Sugai & Horner, 1999). Eventually, with the 1997 and 2004 reauthorizations of IDEA, the combination of functional behavior assessment, PBS, and EBS approaches were incorporated, and the term *positive behavioral interventions and supports* (PBIS) emerged (Sugai & Simonsen, 2012). The PBS approach and the PBIS applications have merged with school efforts and is commonly known as schoolwide positive behavior support (SWPBS). We refer to the SWPBS framework in the first section of the chapter when looking at a schoolwide, universal approach to keeping schools and classrooms well managed and safe.

Using each tier of the SWPBS framework, as it relates to school and classroom management behavior support systems, is the basis for the organization of this chapter. Specifically, within the first universal level/tier of SWPBS, the implementation of schoolwide approaches that include teachers and administrators address school safety, an orderly environment, and the culture or climate of the school before teachers can address classroom issues. Therefore, the first section of this chapter includes schoolwide PBS as the preferred evidence-based initiative that will address school safety.

Addressing the intersection of classroom management with specific interventions (all three tiers; Lane & Menzies, 2015), the next section of the chapter involves how teachers implement, organize, and manage their classrooms as well as classroom interventions that address the second and third tiers of the PBIS framework. This section contains (a) prerequisite strategies for setting up and organizing the classroom, (b) behavioral principles to produce a positive climate, and (c) research-based interventions. The final section of the chapter considers the students and discusses benefits for considering cultural background and classroom diversity that may interact with school, classroom, interventions, and teacher factors related to PBIS.

SCHOOL FACTORS: POSITIVE AND SUCCESSFUL SCHOOLS AND CLASSROOMS

For the past 30 years, research has supported the notion that school and other child-oriented environments must establish positive communities (sometimes called cultures or climates) for children to learn and flourish. Sprague and Walker (2005) supported the concept that school climate is a powerful variable when considering the safety and well-being of students. They continued by advocating that "whole-school interventions . . . clearly communicate and enforce consistent behavioral expectations for all students and . . . create a climate of competence and mutual respect within the school setting" (p. 8). Furthermore, a climate of competence and mutual respect fosters a sense of community or belonging to something that is worth the effort of participation. This established attitude begins at the school level with teachers and administrators and then translates into the classroom with teacher–student and peer relationships.

ENHANCEDetext
video example 4.1
Watch this video to learn more about positive environments in the classroom.

This section emphasizes Schoolwide Positive Behavior Support (SWPBS) systems as well as focusing on the cornerstones of positive behavior support mechanisms: (a) functional behavioral assessments

(FBAs) and (b) positive behavioral intervention plans (BIPs). We highlight an evidence-based SWPBS that is a stellar example of how to implement a schoolwide program (a universal or primary intervention): the Best Behavior program (Sprague & Golly, 2004).

Schoolwide Positive Behavioral Interventions and Supports

In general, PBS is the "integration of valued outcomes, behavioral and biomedical science, empirically validated procedures, and systems change to enhance quality of life and minimize/prevent problem behaviors" (Horner, Sugai, Todd, & Lewis-Palmer, 2005, p. 360). Positive behavior support focuses on the prevention of academic and school failure and the enhancement of positive behavior interventions through a three-tiered system (see Chapter 2 for a full explanation of the three-tiered system). This three-tiered system begins with the initial tier, primary/universal interventions, that enhances protective factors within the environment and can occur at the school level or the classroom level. At the classroom level, approximately 90% of the student population responds to the intervention. This student response-to-intervention data make a universal intervention most cost effective (Lewis et al., 2015).

At the school level, researchers have investigated SWPBS systems extensively for several years (e.g., Lane & Menzies, 2015; Sabornie & Pennington, 2015; Simonsen & Sugai, 2009). The goal for the support system is to improve discipline at the school level so that each student feels respected as an individual in the community. Sprague and Walker (2005) outlined the key practices of SWPBS as follows:

1. Clear definitions of expected behaviors (i.e., appropriate, positive) are provided to students and staff members.
2. Clear definitions of problem behaviors and their consequences are defined for students and staff members.
3. Regularly scheduled instruction and assistance regarding desired positive social behaviors is provided to enable students to acquire the necessary skills to effect the needed behavior change.
4. Effective incentives and motivational systems are provided that encourage students to behave differently.
5. Staff commit to implementing the intervention over the long term and to monitoring, supporting, coaching, debriefing, and providing booster lessons for students, as necessary, to maintain the achieved gains.
6. Staff receive training, feedback, and coaching in the effective implementation of the system.
7. Systems for measuring and monitoring the intervention's effectiveness are established. (p. 63)

Best Behavior Program. Although several approaches to SWPBS have been documented over the years (e.g., Embry & Flannery, 1994; Knoff & Batsche, 1995; Taylor-Green et al., 1997), this chapter features one program. The Best Behavior program highlights general school behaviors that indicate positive outcomes with regard to discipline referrals and staff satisfaction with their work (Sprague & Golly, 2004). Additionally, the program is based on 30 years of experience and research in education and related fields. The importance of this program is that the authors have provided a standardized staff development process for improving school and classroom discipline. The primary goal of the program is to facilitate the academic achievement and healthy social development of children and youth.

The Best Behavior program follows the previously listed key elements of SWPBS and packages the information so that it is user-friendly. The program begins by having school and staff delegate a group of individuals to be a representative school team to be trained to develop and implement the school rules (e.g., be respectful, be responsible, be safe). The team is involved in teaching the rules and establishes positive reinforcement systems for the rule-governed behavior. Specific and effective classroom management methods and curriculum adaptations (some covered in the second section of this chapter) are outlined. Finally, the cornerstones of SWPBS, functional behavioral assessment, and behavioral intervention plans are outlined in the Best Behavior program.

Functional Behavior Assessment

Because universal interventions within the SWPBS framework may not be effective for all students, secondary and tertiary prevention interventions (see the three-tiered system discussion in

Chapter 2) must be considered. As part of a behavior interventions and supports system, a functional-based approach to determine environmental events that trigger and maintain problem behavior is appropriate.

Functional behavior assessment (FBA) provides a contextual view of specific behaviors and behavioral patterns (McConnell, Patton, & Polloway, 2006). In doing so, teachers can determine the cause(s) of a given behavior and thus provide a basis for intervention (Gresham, 2004). Using an FBA approach requires professionals to understand and evaluate a behavior within the broad context of the student's home and school environment. A typical FBA format provides a structured way to analyze the contextual aspects of a behavior by asking for an exact description of the specific behavior in question along with information regarding precipitating conditions, consequences that follow the behavior (an A-B-C analysis), and hypotheses about the purpose the behavior serves. A manipulation of hypothesized antecedent (A), behavior (B), and consequence (C) is conducted to verify the hypothesis. Once the hypothesis is confirmed, an intervention can be implemented. A completed sample of the descriptive portion of an FBA is shown in Figure 4-1. It provides a link to specific assessment techniques that can be used to analyze behaviors. This form also allows professionals to add other qualitative information (e.g., academic, social/peer, family) or quantitative data collection that might play a factor in the demonstration of a behavior.

A functional behavior assessment provides a valuable approach to more fully understanding a behavioral pattern as a basis for selecting intervention strategies. Further, it provides a basis for developing a behavioral intervention plan. The information obtained from the FBA can then be used as a critical aspect of the steps of successful behavioral change programs (i.e., definition and measurement of a target behavior, identification of behavioral occurrences, identification of factors causing or maintaining the behavior, and determination of appropriate procedures for intervention; Simonsen & Sugai, 2009). It also is an essential element in developing or guiding positive behavioral supports in which interventions are focused on (a) modifying antecedent events, (b) teaching alternative behaviors, (c) reinforcing alternative behaviors, (d) reinforcing the approximations of desired behavioral goals, and (e) extinguishing undesirable

behaviors by withholding reinforcement (Simonsen & Sugai, 2009).

Functional Behavior Assessment Technology. A very useful technological tool in behavioral assessment is an interactive training module developed by Liaupsin, Scott, and Nelson (2004, 2006). This self-paced interactive CD-ROM is used to instruct teachers in observing behavior, plotting events, conducting FBA interviews, and reviewing archival records of students. It comprises over 70 PowerPoint slides that help a facilitator (or an individual) guide participants toward conducting accurate assessments and thus creating effective behavioral intervention plans.

 LEARNING MODULE 4.1 Click here to learn more about Functional Behavioral Assessment: http://iris .peabody.vanderbilt.edu/module/fba

BIPs. Under IDEA, students with disabilities are protected from arbitrary suspension or expulsion from school in instances in which their behavioral difficulty was determined to be related to their disability. This provision clearly has decreased the likelihood that such students could be denied a free, appropriate public education. The unforeseen result was that the protection of the rights of an individual became perceived as a potential threat to school discipline in general and to the safety and security of other students, teachers, and staff (McConnell et al., 2006). Teachers—both general and special education—are concerned with the problem of balancing individual rights (including teachers and students) with equitable school discipline policies (Yell, Rozalski, & Miller, 2015).

The extent of serious behavioral problems associated with students with disabilities has been controversial. Nevertheless, clearly a distinct minority of such students does present troublesome behaviors that challenge a school's ability to educate all students effectively. As a result, when regulations for the amendments to IDEA were developed in 1999, a key issue was determining the appropriate balance between the rights of students with disabilities and the need for an orderly learning environment (McConnell et al., 2006).

The legal resolution of this debate was the incorporation of a requirement for specific practices in the 1997 amendments to IDEA. Foremost among

Student's Name: **Mike Harris**

Background Information

The following sources of background information were considered for this FBA.

☑ Parent information/interview (see Parent Contact form)　　　Attached? ☑Yes ☐No
Summary of parent information: **Mike's parents have had problems with him at home. They think positive approaches work best.**

☐ Behavior checklist or rating scale　　　Attached? ☐Yes ☐No
Summary of checklist or rating scale:

☑ Recent observation data (see data collection forms)　　　Attached? ☑Yes ☐No
Summary of observations: **Frequency data from math observation indicated that Mike follows only about half of teacher directions.**

☑ Discipline records　　　Attached? ☑Yes ☐No
Summary of discipline records: **Five referrals this semester.**

☑ Assessment information　　　Attached? ☑Yes ☐No
Summary of assessment information. **Mike is learning disabled (LD) in math and emotionally disturbed (ED).**

☐ Information from other agencies or service providers　　　Attached? ☐Yes ☐No
Summary of other information.

☑ Review of prior BIP (see Reasons and Review form, Section Three)　　　Attached? ☑Yes ☐No
Summary: **Music is a motivator. Detention not working.**

☐ Student interview/conference　　　Attached? ☐Yes ☐No
Summary:

☐ Video- or audiotape　　　Attached? ☐Yes ☐No
Summary:

☐ Teacher/administrator interview(s)　　　Attached? ☐Yes ☐No
Summary:

SECTION ONE

FIGURE 4–1 Sample Functional Behavioral Assessment

Source: From *BIP 3 Behavioral Intervention Planning: A Comprehensive Guide for Completing a Functional Behavioral Assessment and Developing a Behavioral Intervention Plan*, 3rd Ed. (p. 32-34), by Kathleen McConnell, James R. Patton, Edward A. Polloway 2006, Austin, TX: PRO-ED. Copyright 2006 by PRO-ED, Inc. Reprinted with permission.

(continued)

Student's Name: **Mike Harris**

Analysis of Behavior

Prioritized Behavior #   1   Following directions

Antecedents (Events or conditions occurring before or triggering the behavior)	**Behavior** (Exactly what the student does or does not do)	**Consequences** (Actions or events occurring after the behavior)	**Function of Behavior** (Hypothesized purpose of the behavior)

Antecedents
(Events or conditions occurring before or triggering the behavior)

☐ Setting, subject, or class:

☐ Time of day:

☐ Person(s):

☐ Interruption in routine:

☑ Directive or request to:
begin an assignment

☐ Consequences imposed:

☐ Lack of social attention

☑ Difficulty or frustration:
with assignments

☐ Other(s):

Behavior
(Exactly what the student does or does not do)

Behavior in observable, measurable terms:

Refuses to follow directions, Ignores, says "no," argues

Baseline measures of behavior

Frequency of behavior:
50% of requests

per

Duration of behavior:

per incident

Intensity of behavior:

Consequences
(Actions or events occurring after the behavior)

☐ Behavior is ignored
    ☐ Planned
    ☐ Unplanned

☑ Peer attention

☑ Adult attention
    ☑ Reminder(s)
    ☑ Repeated directive or request
    ☑ Private meeting or conference
    ☑ Reprimand or warning

☐ Change in directive or request

☐ Loss of privilege:

☐ Time out in classroom

☑ Administrative consequence:

☐ Parent contact

☐ Other(s):

Function of Behavior
(Hypothesized purpose of the behavior)

☑ Avoidanc or escape
    ☑ Avoid a directive or request
    ☑ Avoid an assignment
    ☐ Escape a situation or a person

☐ Attention
    ☐ Gain peer attention
    ☐ Gain adult attention

☐ Self-control issue
    ☐ Express frustration
    ☐ Express anger
    ☐ Vengeance
    ☐ Power of control
    ☐ Intimidation

☐ Sensory or emotional reaction
    ☐ Fear or anxiety
    ☐ Sensory relief or stimulation

☐ Other(s):

FIGURE 4–1   (continued)

Student's Name: __Mike Harris__

Analysis of Behavior

Prioritized Behavior #   2   Verbal aggression

Antecedents (Events or conditions occurring before or triggering the behavior)	**Behavior** (Exactly what the student does or does not do)	**Consequences** (Actions or events occurring after the behavior)	**Function of Behavior** (Hypothesized purpose of the behavior)
☑ Setting, subject, or class: **math class**	Behavior in observable, measurable terms: **Threatens, yells, and curses at teacher**	☐ Behavior is ignored ☐ Planned ☐ Unplanned	☑ Avoidance or escape ☑ Avoid a directive or request ☑ Avoid an assignment ☐ Escape a situation or a person
☐ Time of day:		☐ Peer attention	
☐ Person(s):		☑ Adult attention ☐ Reminder(s) ☐ Repeated directive or request ☑ Private meeting or conference	☐ Attention ☐ Gain peer attention ☐ Gain adult attention
	Baseline measures of behavior Frequency of behavior:		
☐ Interruption in routine:	**2 times per class**	☑ Reprimand or warning	☑ Self-control issue ☐ Express frustration ☑ Express anger ☐ Vengeance ☑ Power of control ☑ Intimidation
☐ Directive or request to:		☑ Change in directive or request	
☐ Consequences imposed:	Duration of behavior: per incident Intensity of behavior:	☐ Loss of privilege:	☑ Sensory or emotional reaction ☑ Fear or anxiety ☐ Sensory relief or stimulation
☐ Lack of social attention	**Escalates to loud yelling, moves too close to teacher**	☑ Time out in classroom	
☑ Difficulty or frustration: **math assignments**		☑ Administrative consequences: **Removal from class Detention**	☐ Other(s):
☐ Other(s):		☑ Parent contact	
		☐ Other(s):	

FIGURE 4–1   (*continued*)

these were the establishment of clearer guidelines for the removal of students with disabilities from the regular school setting, the need for functional behavioral assessments, and the establishment of a requirement for the development of a **behavioral intervention plan** (BIP) for individual students who present challenging behaviors within the school setting (McConnell et al., 2006).

Given the latitude in IDEA, appropriate practice suggests that BIPs include the following components:

Student's Name: <u>**Mike Harris**</u>

Behavior #   1   Behavior to Be Decreased: **Refuse to follow directions**

Replacement Behavior: **Say "okay" and begin**

Specific Behavioral Objective	Interventions*	Person(s) Responsible	Evaluation Method(s)/Timeline
Mike	Positive environmental supports:	**Teachers**	Method(s):
will:	**Contract**	will:	**Check grades for zeroes**
Say "okay" and begin assignment within 2 minutes	**Visual cues** **Partner for assignments**	**Use contract, provide visual cues, assign partners**	**Review contract with Mike** **Contact parents**
Under these conditions:	Instructional strategies:	**Principal**	Timeline:
When given a verbal direction	**Repeat directions** **Provide an extra example**	will: **Administer detention**	**2 weeks, 4 weeks, 6 weeks**
To meet these criteria:	Positive reinforcement:		
Improve from 50% to 80% of time	**Points for music time or early lunch, home reward—car races**	**Mr. Harris**	
		will:	
	Reductive consequences:** **Make up work before school** **Lunch detention**	**Reward Mike with a trip to the car races**	

Additional Information: **Mike has a secondary diagnosis of emotional disturbance.**

FIGURE 4–2   Sample Behavior Intervention Plan

Source: From *BIP 3 Behavioral Intervention Planning: A Comprehensive Guide for Completing a Functional Behavioral Assessment and Developing a Behavioral Intervention Plan*, 3rd Ed. (p. 35-36), by Kathleen McConnell, James R. Patton, Edward A. Polloway 2006, Austin, TX: PRO-ED. Copyright 2006 by PRO-ED, Inc. Reprinted with permission.

Student's Name: __Mike Harris__

Behavior # 2 Behavior to Be Decreased: **Verbal aggression**

Replacement Behavior: **Express feelings without threatening**

Specific Behavioral Objective	Interventions*	Person(s) Responsible	Evaluation Method(s)/Timeline
Mike will: **Express a complaint or frustration without verbal threats**	Positive environmental supports: **Visual cue to calm down** **Bonus points on contract**	**Math Teacher** will: **Cue Mike** **Use contract** **Call parents**	Method(s): **Check discipline referrals** **Review contract** **Conference with Mike**
Under these conditions: **In math class**	Instructional strategies: **Anger management class**	**Counselor** will: **Provide anger management class**	Timeline: **2 weeks, 4 weeks, 6 weeks**
To meet these criteria: **100% of time**	Positive reinforcement: **Music time** **Early lunch** **Call parents**	**Mike** will: **Attend anger management class, practice new ways to express feelings**	
	Reductive consequences:** **Lunch detention** **In-school suspension**		

Additional Information:

*Interventions must include positive behavior supports (positive environmental supports and positive reinforcement). The BIP may not contain only reductive consequences.

**All students are subject to the student code of conduct (SCC). Short-term disciplinary consequences that do not involve a change of placement may be imposed for any SCC violation.

FIGURE 4–2 (*continued*)

the overall goals to be achieved, attention to planned activities, the persons responsible for implementing the proposed activities, timelines to be followed, and plans for intervention. Figure 4-2 illustrates a sample BIP completed in case study format. Additionally, Figure 4-3 illustrates a flow chart that depicts the FBA to BIP process that can be followed by educators.

 Check Your Understanding 4.1 Click here to gauge your understanding of the concepts in this section.

Addressing Student Behavior Through an FBA and a BIP

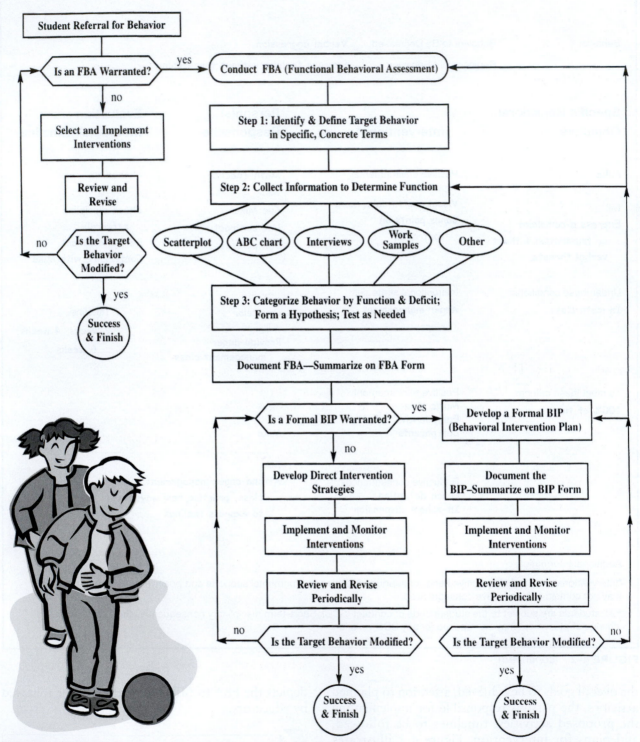

FIGURE 4–3 Addressing Student Behavior through an FBA and a BIP

Source: Some information in this document was adapted from *Addressing Student Behavior*, which is a copyright-free technical assistance guide prepared by the New Mexico Public Education Department, 2010 (p. 10). http://www.ped.state.nm.us.

FACTORS RELATED TO CLASSROOM ORGANIZATION AND MANAGEMENT

Lane et al. (2015) discuss the importance of a safe, positive and orderly classroom and how teachers and students will encounter difficulties in the areas of teaching and learning if certain factors are not in place. Specifically, they identify how teachers manage the classroom as well as initiate the intervention strategies (i.e., low-intensity strategies) used to ensure that behavior is supported. This section of the chapter is divided into three areas. The first two areas are universal interventions that occur in the classroom: (a) classroom organization and prerequisite elements of classroom management that must be present for effective classroom behavior and academic instruction to occur and (b) behavioral principles and behavioral support strategies to increase successful behavior in the classroom. The third area consists of high-intensity strategies to decrease behaviors and still be supportive of the PBS framework.

The first area begins with the prerequisite elements of physical and instructional dimensions of management that are intrinsically associated with effective teaching. Three topics are included as considerations and activities that teachers need to perform so that their classrooms function efficiently: (a) functions of the physical arrangement of the classroom, (b) successful classroom management, and (c) organizing and planning for instruction.

As this area begins, we recognize that a strong case can be made for the value of flexibility in instruction and thus in classroom organization. At the same time, however, students with special needs profit from classrooms and instructional programs that are well organized, orderly, and predictable. The discussions that follow in this chapter should provide a basis for developing classrooms and programs that promote learning through structure, organization, and behavioral support and yet promote interest and involvement through flexibility, variety, and responsiveness.

Managing the Physical Environment

The classroom environment is a crucial determinant of successful teaching and learning, yet discussions of teacher competencies frequently overlook it. In two comprehensive reviews of critical instructional factors, Simonsen, Fairbanks, Briesch, Myers, and Sugai (2008) and Evertson and Weinstein (2006) noted the importance of a positive climate in the classroom, partly related to an orderly school environment. The issue of environmental planning takes on a new meaning with the inclusive education movement. Needed accommodations might include (a) seating arrangements that stimulate responding and discourage distractibility, (b) technology that assists in highlighting important points, (c) charts that provide reminders of specific rules, and (d) classroom areas that encourage cooperative interaction and sharing. Although a prosthetic environment—that is, a classroom designated to facilitate learning (Doyle, 2006)—is physically separate from the teacher–student dyad, conceptually it is an extension of the teaching–learning paradigm. Antecedents and consequences emerge from any environment. The effectiveness and efficiency with which they are managed are enhanced in a well-planned environment. The discussion of various environmental aspects in this chapter should assist teachers in planning an effective environment and should provoke further thinking about environmental options.

Environmental Design. Historically, U.S. education has recorded dramatic changes with regard to what the school environment should be and how it should appear. The one-room school of the turn of the 20th century eventually led to graded, self-contained classes. Later, the emphasis shifted to open classrooms, which were aesthetically pleasing with carpeted floors, non-distracting illumination, brightly colored walls and furnishings, and ample space in which to create. However, many schools became disenchanted with this concept and returned to more traditional, structured situations. Later, emphasis is being given to the advantages of cooperative learning situations and more cooperative teaching arrangements between special and general education (Bauwens & Hourcade, 1995).

Though some students with special needs still receive special education in resource or self-contained settings, the primary setting for these students is in more inclusive settings. Within these settings, students with special needs will need supports to ensure that their experiences are successful. Also, it needs to be noted that not all students benefit from the same type of educational setting. For these reasons, educators must remain vigilant about how students with special needs are progressing regardless of setting.

Students who are disabled may initially require more structure and guidance than their peers. However, one of a teacher's major goals must be to help students learn how to handle and control their own behavior in less structured situations. This fact is particularly significant in light of school inclusion. Therefore, classroom arrangements should provide structure, organization, and regimentation when needed as well as freedom, exploration, and choice. To achieve these seemingly conflicting goals, teachers should conceptualize the degree of structure along a continuum from highly structured to less structured arrangements and determine which best suits the needs of particular learning tasks. Educational environments must be flexible and adaptable to individual needs, must allow for differing levels of need within a given group of students, and must change as students grow.

Several noteworthy considerations related to designing and organizing an educational environment (adapted in part from Doyle, 2006; Reeves, 1989) include the following:

- **Sense of community**—Students need to feel welcome in a classroom as an important member of this community—this is especially important in inclusive settings. The teacher plays a crucial role in creating an accepting and nurturing classroom environment.
- **Personal territory**—Students and teachers alike need a sense of their own turf. This may include a place to keep personal possessions as well as a place to be alone to think and to be separate from the group.
- **Authentic motivation**—A classroom setting in which students are motivated to participate in the learning process has three fundamental factors: collaboration (learning together in teams), content (relevant and meaningful), and choice (opportunities to make a decision about what is learned) (Kohn, 1993).
- **Classroom flexibility**—Patterns of use within a classroom need not be fixed or predetermined. The environment must allow itself to be manipulated by its users so that spaces can be changed.
- **Environmental acknowledgment**—A school facility must allow its occupants to stamp their presence on it. It must be ready to accept the graphic presentation of student activities and interests so that the building reflects who the students are and how they are doing.

- **Flexible seating and work areas**—Classrooms should acknowledge that people work in a variety of natural postures (e.g., sitting up straight, lounging, leaning, and standing). It should offer a variety of seating and work-surface heights to accommodate individual styles.
- **Barrier-free**—The environment must be able to accommodate students whose disabilities demand special attention (e.g., physical or vision needs).

**ENHANCEDetext
video example 4.2**
Watch this video to learn more about classroom environment considerations.

Classroom Arrangement. Each classroom teacher must operate within certain administrative guidelines and physical limitations. Whether the room is a small resource room or a large general education setting, these dimensions are essential for developing a prosthetic, effective environment.

The starting point for classroom arrangement is the same as that for all other instructional strategies: the assessment of students' strengths and needs in core curricular areas and in their response to various environmental demands. After this initial assessment, teachers may begin to develop a prosthetic environment. As the teacher and students become a community, the classroom should be adaptable and flexible.

When students are in inclusive settings, their needs will be addressed as a result of the collaborative efforts of the general and special educators. Even though special educators do not have sole responsibility for the inclusive classroom design, they can make reasonable suggestions for accommodating specific students. In general, recommendations for special settings are frequently applicable for the general education classroom as well.

There are multiple strategies available for desk arrangements in the classroom. Weinstein (2007) described the advantages and disadvantages of three approaches: vertical rows, group circles, and small clusters. Advantages of vertical rows are that they create an orderly environment and create opportunities for students to physically interact with each other. A disadvantage is that vertical rows make it difficult for students in the back to see or hear the teacher. A large-group circle allows the teacher and students to see each other easily, facilitates discussion, and provides an alternative to traditional row-by-row seating, but it also limits opportunities for physical interaction among students. Small clusters facilitate student interactions and provide an alternative to traditional row-by-row seating, but they require teachers to move about the room, make it difficult for teachers to see all of the students at all times, and can restrict total group discussion.

Study Carrels   Classrooms can benefit from having at least one study carrel for use with students who have learning-related difficulties. Carrels or cubicles have the two main purposes of limiting outside stimuli and providing a specific place for concentrated study.

A study carrel should be designed to minimize the distraction of various other classroom activities, and thus it should be placed in a quiet area. Cubicles come in many shapes and forms. Some are commercially produced, while others are little more than a small table and chair placed in the back corner of the classroom. The carrel becomes a work area for the student who uses it as a special place for concentrated study. Use of carrels should emphasize the positive features they afford (i.e., a quiet place to work) rather than association as a location to be placed for inappropriate behavior.

Interest Centers   Especially at the elementary level, interest centers can add variety to classroom instruction and enrich the curriculum. Interest centers can be used for instruction in which a student works at the center to review something previously learned or apply something learned in a new way, the promotion of social interaction for two or more students who are working together, and the development of independent work skills and self-direction.

Teachers should consider several key components of interest centers: (a) characteristics of the user, (b) objectives that the activities are designed to meet, (c) interest value to students, (d) procedures and directions, and (e) materials or equipment needed. Because centers are intended for students, the user is the most important element. In developing ideas for effective interest centers, teachers should keep in mind the user's characteristics (e.g., behavior, language). In effect, an interest

center becomes a well-planned lesson presented primarily without the teacher's direct assistance with a particular learning objective.

For centers to be effective, they must be engaging. Students must find the activities as well as the materials used in the centers stimulating. Additionally, procedures and directions go hand in hand in promoting effective use. Procedures are general guidelines telling students how to use the center; directions tell them how to perform the specific activities.

Prerequisites to Successful Management

Classroom Procedures.   In keeping with the initiative of positive behavioral support systems, the classroom culture or climate has a tremendous impact on a positive learning environment. It is an effective preventive method that will help teachers and students be successful (see Table 4-1). Classroom procedures are the key to this success. Antecedents to learning can be traced back to teachers' initial planning in setting up their instructional days. As Simonson et al. (2008) concluded in their review of critical instructional factors, proactive management—structuring the classroom as a basis for management—is the key element in avoiding disruptions and increasing instructional time. In addition to concern for the physical and temporal environment, a number of procedural aspects of teaching are important. Marzano, Marzano, and Pickering (2003) focused on the six specific elements involved in planning classroom procedures that contribute to the success of students in secondary environments. These elements include (a) group work, (b) seatwork and teacher-led instruction, (c) general behavior, (d) beginning and ending class, (e) transition in and out of the classroom, and (f) use of materials and equipment (see Table 4-2 for a secondary school example of a breakdown of subjects under each of the five elements).

Classroom Rules.   Most children and adolescents function best when they know what is expected of them. Students need to be aware of what a teacher expects and will accept. Explaining classroom rules and then posting them are sound practices to aid in preventing problem behaviors; students should not have to test the limits if the teacher has clearly explained the distinction between acceptable and unacceptable behaviors. Classroom rules should be

TABLE 4–1 Aspects of building positive climate

Factor to Consider	Topic Elements	Detailed Elements
Classroom ecology	• Well-organized environment • Predictable • Seating arrangement	• Books, materials, etc. have a place • Posted routines, schedules, etc. • Differentiating seating for different activities (e.g., carrels)
Teacher	• Order, structure, and consistency • Clear, realistic expectations • Choices for students • Able to interpret communicative intent of students	• Use routines, rules, and consequences • Use of goals, rubrics, and modeling • Differentiate materials and content • Be culturally and behaviorally responsive
Classroom community	• Classroom problem solving • Students have input into classroom decisions	• Classroom meetings to generate options • Students vote on class decisions; negotiation
Curriculum	• Develop lessons for student success • Curriculum stresses student interests and talents	• Differentiate lessons for academic and social success • Give options for students to meet same standard/objective
Social emotional learning (SEL)	• Students encouraged to express feelings • Students encouraged to socially interact with others • Students' psychological needs met (belonging, safety, competency, and self-esteem) • Positive teacher–student relationships	• Teach appropriate social skills (e.g., giving and accepting negative feedback) • Use peer-assisted learning/group projects • Use cognitive behavioral interventions and student success • Use communication skills and humor

TABLE 4–2 Secondary school classroom

Subject	Procedures or Expectations
1. Group work	Expectations for student movement in and out of groups Assignment of leadership and roles in each group Delineation of the relationship of each group to the class activity Establishment of group communication with the teacher
2. Seatwork and teacher-led activities	Establish expectations for student attention during presentation. Determine acceptable student participation procedures. Create class rules concerning "talking" among students. Establish procedures on obtaining help. Create rules for behavior when work has been completed.
3. Beginning and ending of class procedures	Taking attendance Addressing student absences and makeup work Setting tardiness procedures Ending the period with clear expectations for homework
4. General behavior	Setting rules for bringing materials to class Being in assigned seat at beginning of class Being respectful to others and respecting others' property
5. Transitions and interruptions	Procedures for leaving and returning to the room Routines and rules for fire and disaster drills Split lunch periods
6. Use of materials and equipment	Distributing materials Collecting materials Storing common materials Creating procedures for using electronic equipment

few in number, clearly defined, and linked to specific consequences when violated. Teachers should encourage students to discuss the rules and assist in their formulation and development. Students benefit from learning the give-and-take process of developing and modifying classroom rules.

Group Management. A classic contribution to classroom management is Kounin's (1970) research on which teacher variables predict compliance and appropriate behavior in students. Berliner (1988) noted that Kounin's work is "enormously influential . . . and has given us a set of concepts that help us understand the process of monitoring a workplace free from deviance and in which students attend to their assignments" (p. 32). The following variables are among those related to successful classroom management:

1. "*With-it-ness*," essentially awareness, refers to the teacher's ability to follow classroom action, be aware of possible deviance, communicate awareness to the class, and intervene at the initiation of the problem. Doyle (2006) referred to a similar concept of "the content of monitoring—what teachers watch when scanning the room" (p. 109).
2. *Overlapping* indicates an ability to deal with two events simultaneously and thus to respond to target behaviors promptly.
3. *Movement management* refers to smooth transition between activities. When the teacher can maintain momentum between instructional periods, the degree of behavioral compliance is likely to increase.
4. *Group alerting* consists of specific skills for maintaining attention throughout various teaching lessons, as with a specific signal or procedure that involves all students.
5. *Accountability and format* include the methods that teachers develop to ensure a group focus by actively involving all students in appropriate activities.
6. *Avoiding satiation* on instructional activities refers to the ability to vary activities to prevent inappropriate behaviors.

These principles will minimize the time needed for problem management, thus leading to an increase in the time available for individualized instruction. They provide for classroom management that is based on prevention.

Grouping for Instruction. A major organizational concern is instructional grouping. A discussion of how best to group for instruction must first address a concern for individualization. Among the foremost principles on which special education was founded is the importance of individualization in instruction. In many cases, the primary justification for the provision of special services has been the assumption that instruction must be geared to the individual's specific needs.

Nonetheless, a distinction should be made between individualization and one-to-one instruction. Individualization refers to instruction appropriate to the individual, whether or not it is accomplished on a one-to-one basis. By this definition, individualization can be accomplished through one-to-one or one-to-two ratios, in small groups, or even occasionally in large groups. Even though individualization presumes that instruction is geared to the needs of the individual student, it does not mean that it is provided on a one-to-one basis. The following discussion focuses on one-to-one versus group instruction.

Instructional Concerns Three predominant concerns—instructional effectiveness, efficiency, and social benefits—are important in the context of inclusive education.

Effectiveness is a measure of whether the skills taught have been learned by students. Research on the effectiveness of grouping alternatives has been equivocal, with advantages cited for one-to-one instruction. More commonly, comparable results have been reported.

In particular, direct instruction programs, characterized by small-group work, have demonstrated effectiveness for students identified as learning disabled, intellectually disabled, disadvantaged, and slow learners (e.g., Smith, Polloway, Doughty, Patton, & Dowdy, 2016).

Efficiency refers to the amount of time required for something to be learned. Most research in this area has favored the use of group instruction because an undeniable benefit of group instruction is an increase in the number of students who can be served. Even more urgent is the reality that more students receive their education in general education settings where group instruction is very much the core of the instructional routine.

A third consideration relative to the efficacy of group or one-to-one instruction is that of *social outcomes*—whether there are benefits or detriments. A key social benefit of group instruction is simply the opportunity for learning to participate with others. On the other hand, a predominant focus on one-to-one instruction can result in greater difficulty for students who are included in general education classrooms where the student–teacher ratio is much higher than in special education.

A potential solution to the problem of isolation or rejection and one that further enhances learning is peer instruction as it relates to socialization and learning. A variety of peer instructional strategies can be used. Smith et al. (2016) summarized them as follows:

- Peer tutoring—An opportunity for peer instruction that benefits both the tutor and the student being tutored. Examples include reviewing directions, drill and practice activities, recording material dictated by a peer, and providing pretest practice (e.g., spelling).
- Classwide peer tutoring—This approach divides classes into two teams for competition of several weeks' duration. Students work in pairs and are tutored and provide tutoring on the same material. Students accumulate points for their team by giving correct answers and using correct procedures, and individual scores on master tests are then added to the team's total.
- Group projects—This cooperative learning alternative allows students to pool their skills and knowledge in order to complete a specific assignment. Group projects are uniquely appropriate for inclusive settings where the talents of high, average, and low achievers can be blended together into specific aspects of the task.

Implications Research on grouping arrangements encourages the consideration of group experiences for students who are disabled. A variety of positive benefits can accrue from the use of group methodology, including the promotion of observational learning, facilitation of overlearning and generalization, the teaching of turn-taking, increased and better use of instructional time, more efficient student management, and increased peer interaction. What seems to be the most critical variable favoring group instruction is increased contact with the teacher. In Stevens and Rosenshine's (1981) classic review of best practices, the importance of "academic engaged time" and its relationship to higher achievement levels was clearly demonstrated. The opportunities for teacher demonstration and corrective feedback are strong arguments in favor of group instruction.

Grouping for Acquisition Meeting students' diverse needs across different stages of learning requires organization. The teacher's goal is to maximize teaching to ensure optimal **acquisition** of skills and abilities. For the teacher to work daily with each child, the problem becomes one of ensuring the highest degree of learning efficiency.

An initial option is to work with each student on a one-to-one basis. This approach has the advantage of providing the learners with instruction specifically tailored to their needs and abilities. Individual teaching appears to be ideal for the acquisition stage of learning. However, as noted earlier, a one-to-one arrangement has a number of drawbacks (e.g., inefficiency).

Teaching lessons to the entire class provides another alternative, which can increase instructional time for each child. Teachers can thus supervise each student throughout entire periods and can provide constant instruction of a large-group nature. However, because large groups may not properly accommodate individual needs, such instruction may drastically reduce the acquisition of skills, knowledge, and concepts.

The clear alternative to one-to-one and large-group models is to provide instruction in small groups. The use of grouping should not dictate rigid adherence to a standardized grouping arrangement across all subjects. To assist students in acquisition learning, the group can organize around a specific skill the members need to acquire. Groups should be flexible and fluid; they should neither restrict a student's improvement beyond the group mean nor force the child to work too fast.

Bickel and Bickel (1986) noted that grouping for instructional purposes has positive benefits under the following conditions:

1. Number and size of groups are dependent on student characteristics and content taught.
2. Different groupings are used for different subjects.
3. Frequent shifts among groups occur during the school year as well as between years.
4. Groups are based on current levels of skills.
5. Groups are established as a result of instruction.

6. There is a combination of small-group and whole-class instruction.
7. Groupings are responsive to instruction. (p. 494)

How do large-group and one-to-one models fit into this grouping picture? Large-group instruction never quite accommodates the acquisition stage of learning, but it can provide the class with general introductions, serve as a forum for classwide discussions, and allow more advanced students a chance to review what other students are seeing for the first time. On the other hand, individual attention will continue to demand some class time. It may be essential for students who are unable to learn in the small-group setting, who are working on a skill different from the focus of the rest of the class, or who are receiving assistance with specific aspects of work assignments. One-to-one instruction suggests the need for supports such as a paraeducator, cooperative teaching, or resource services.

Ideally, grouping can afford the teacher some organizational flexibility while providing a vehicle to give individuals what they need. For example, a class divided into three groups during a one-hour academic period could provide several advantages: each child would receive 15 or 20 minutes of teacher-directed, small-group instruction; the teacher would need to plan for only a limited number of children outside the group at any one time; and the teacher could still supervise individual students occasionally and briefly. Thus, this flexible system would allow maximum efficiency at each learning stage.

If acquisition of a skill or concept is important, then its learning cannot be left to chance. Instruction through flexible grouping arrangements is essential to sound teaching that maximizes the probability of learning.

Grouping for Proficiency and Maintenance
A system for ensuring **proficiency** and **maintenance** must accompany acquisition learning strategies. Small-group instruction provides a regular opportunity for students who are not working directly with the teacher to pursue educational activities that further develop and maintain what was acquired through teacher-directed instruction. Some simple techniques and activities to assist in fluency building and overlearning of skills previously taught include the following:

- Being tutored by a peer
- Participating in group projects

- Preparing individual seatwork folders
- Using instructional games
- Using software programs
- Working cooperatively with partners
- Writing a short composition
- Reading assignments silently
- Tutoring other students

In addition, several guidelines may help teachers keep these activities going smoothly:

1. Ensure that students display acceptable independent working and interpersonal relationship skills.
2. Choose assignments that can be accomplished independently to avoid constant interruptions by students.
3. Be sure directions for completing each task are clear.
4. Build in self-correction methods so that students will receive immediate feedback.
5. Vary the activities, allowing each student to experience several different activities during a period.
6. Allow students some freedom to choose their activities.
7. Allow time to provide feedback or reinforcement for independent work.

Finally, after acquisition, proficiency, and maintenance, the fourth component of learning that should be planned for is generalization. Instruction should provide the basis, for example, for generalizing from the resource room to the inclusive setting, from learning in the school to learning in the community, and from learning new content by building on previously learned material and through working with different instructors.

Lesson Planning. Lesson plans should focus directly on the teaching objectives for each student. Thus, plans should be consistent with prior assessment of students' specific learning needs.

Lesson plans force teachers to identify what they will teach and how. The important aspect for the teacher is not the format of the lesson plan but rather the careful consideration of what will be taught and how. The essential concern is whether the system used by the teacher results in sufficient preparation for teaching.

Figure 4-4 illustrates a typical lesson plan format. Because teachers present varied types of material to many students, experienced teachers may

Sample Lesson Plan
Instructional Objective:
Materials-equipment-supplies:
Teacher-directed activities:
• Anticipatory set:
• Input and modeling:
Guided Practice:
Independent Practice:
Evaluation:
Special Considerations:
• Early finishers:
• Anticipated problems:
• Special adaptations:

FIGURE 4–4 Sample Lesson Plan

not regularly write such detailed lesson plans; however, many do, and they are particularly valuable to beginning teachers (Maroney & Searcy, 1996) because constructing detailed plans assists in focusing precisely on the instructional process.

Regardless of format and specificity, all plans should attend to the questions of why, what, and how. An assessment of needs determines *why*. The *what* is expressed as objectives stated in terms of observable student performance, which can be evaluated to determine whether the student has attained the objective.

The *how* of the lesson plan is the method of presentation; it describes the teaching process and any materials or programs to be used. All plans should also provide for evaluation of teaching efficiency and effectiveness.

Some specific suggestions on developing lesson plans include the following:

1. Create interest in and clarify the purpose of lessons. This is particularly important for students with special needs.
2. Provide direct instruction on key topics to help students acquire an initial grasp of new material.
3. Assign independent practice, some of which can be accomplished in class and some of which should be done as homework.
4. Plan activities for students who finish early.
5. Anticipate problems that might arise during the course of the lesson and identify techniques for dealing with them. (Smith et al., 2008)

Positive Behavior Support Strategies

A major factor in successful teaching is the ability to implement educational strategies that increase a student's motivation to perform while assisting in the development of appropriate classroom behavior. The teacher's role is as a change agent whose primary goal is designing and implementing effective interventions, which should be key components of a teacher's repertoire. Therefore, this section focuses on strategies for changing behavior with an emphasis on those approaches that have been found particularly effective with students who have special needs.

In considering the various techniques to assist in behavior change, the primary focus is on effectiveness. To facilitate effectiveness, the teacher should reflect on two key concerns. The first is the need to be systematic. Haphazard modification is misleading in the interpretation of results. It can also be confusing and possibly detrimental to the student who needs structure and predictability. The need for a systematic policy of record keeping to accompany teaching techniques cannot be overstated, particularly for children with more serious learning difficulties.

The majority of intervention efforts undertaken to produce behavior change are oriented toward increasing appropriate, desirable behaviors. For students with special needs, this orientation includes a variety of adaptive behaviors, most notably academic, social, and daily living skills. The most pedagogically sound method of providing consequences to increase appropriate behavior is through positive reinforcement.

Principles of Positive Reinforcement. Reduced to its simplest terms, positive reinforcement refers to the supplying of a desirable consequence after appropriate behavior. In more precise terms, it refers to those consequent environmental events that increase a specific desired behavior by presenting a positive reinforcer. Positive reinforcement can be simply a smile or a wave extended to a courteous driver, a weekly paycheck, or a thank-you from someone receiving a gift. The classroom presents constant opportunities for the use of positive reinforcers. The key is to select the "least intrusive" reinforcer that will produce the desired results.

Positive tools can be used in three basic ways. First and most common, reinforcement can be made contingent on appropriate target responses selected to be increased. This approach provides motivation for building new skills. Second, positive events can be used to reinforce a behavior incompatible with one to be decreased. An example might be reinforcing on-task time to decrease out-of-seat behavior. Third, teachers can positively reinforce peers to demonstrate to a given student that certain actions will receive reinforcement.

Successful use of positive reinforcement initially involves determining reinforcer preferences. With a wide variety of alternatives available, a teacher can establish a menu of reinforcers most effective for an individual student. A menu could include a list inclusive of free time, use of a software game, or some tangible prize.

The following techniques can be used to develop a menu:

- Direct questioning of the student
- Indirect questioning of parents, friends, or past teachers
- Observation of the student within the natural environment
- Structured observation (i.e., arranging specific reinforcement alternatives for selection)
- Trial and error of a variety of reinforcers (i.e., reinforcer sampling)

Generally, teachers can construct a reinforcement menu by selecting from a pool of three types of reinforcers: social (most commonly, praise), tangible, or activity reinforcers. The latter two are discussed below.

The addition of *tangible reinforcement* to an instructional program may enhance the value of the social reinforcers with which they should be paired. Tangible reinforcers can be a powerful component of the reinforcer hierarchy for many students.

The tangible item with primary reinforcing value is food because it is desired instinctively. However, because highly desirable edible items, such as sweets, are often nutritionally unsound, the volume of food intake should be considered. One method for young children of using food is to break it down into small pieces that can be earned for specific steps in an instructional task. For adolescents, obtaining a beverage at the end of the day may become the focus of points earned through earlier instructional periods.

Other paired reinforcers might be considered to promote delaying gratification. Pairing allows

certain items to serve as symbols of reinforcers and to be exchanged later for other reinforcers. In our society, money serves this purpose; in the classroom, this same principle can be applied through the use of points or tokens. Both represent items that learners desire; they will work to earn those tokens because they have learned that they are paired with the actual reinforcers. On a basic level, tokens can be used in an individual instructional session to reinforce appropriate behavior and then can be exchanged immediately upon task completion. On a grander scale, tokens can become the exchange medium for a classroom-based economy, which is discussed later.

Activities can also be highly reinforcing positive consequences. As an incentive, an activity should be an event in which a child earns the right to participate because of appropriate behavior. The teacher must distinguish between positive activities that the child normally has been accustomed to, such as lunch and recess, and those that are contingent on certain behavior. This concept requires that the activity be desirable for the student as well as extra.

In addition to activities like recess, many other alternatives are available to the teacher. Depending on the student, free time, being first in line, taking the lunch money to the office, or assisting with school maintenance can become positive consequences. Table 4-3 contains other activities that might be reinforcing to individual students.

Reinforcement Schedules   An important consideration after the selection of a particular consequence is the schedule according to which it is presented

TABLE 4–3   Activity reinforcers

Selecting topic for group discussion
Selecting a game or activity for recess
Reading to a friend
Using the tablet computer
Listening to music
Having extra time in a favorite subject
Taking attendance
Handing out papers
Helping correct papers
Being team captain
Helping put up a bulletin board
Reading comics, magazines
Playing games
Doing arts and crafts
Keeping behavioral point records

to the learner. In general, schedules can be defined as either continuous or intermittent. A **continuous schedule** indicates that reinforcement is given with each occurrence of a given behavior; it is most useful for teaching and learning at the acquisition stage.

Intermittent schedules provide reinforcement less frequently and are more advantageous for maintenance/proficiency and generalization learning. Six intermittent schedules are fixed ratio, fixed interval, fixed response duration, variable ratio, variable interval, and variable response duration. A fixed ratio schedule specifies a particular relationship between occurrences and reinforcement (e.g., 5:1) and can be illustrated by piecework (e.g., stacking bricks) or rewards given according to the number of worksheets completed (e.g., a token given for every worksheet completed with 90% accuracy). Fixed interval reinforcement specifies the amount of time that will elapse before reinforcement—for example, using classroom timers and awarding points to all students working when the buzzer sounds at regular five-minute intervals. A fixed duration schedule differs from a fixed interval schedule in that the target behavior must have occurred for the duration of the entire interval in order for the individual to earn the reinforcement. Variable ratio, variable interval, and variable duration schedules allow planned alterations in the frequency, elapsed time, or duration of time, respectively, between reinforcers.

Reinforcement schedules should be selected according to specific instructional objectives. For certain goals, such as completing worksheets or establishing quiet time during reading, fixed schedules may be most appropriate. In many situations, however, variable schedules are more effective because students are unable to predict receipt of reinforcement as precisely; thus, programming tends to produce behaviors most resistant to extinction. The variable ratio schedules inherent in slot machines illustrate how effective these contingencies can be in maintaining desired responses. Variable interval or duration schedules are most appropriate for non-discrete behaviors, such as on-task or in-seat behaviors.

Gradual Change Processes The basic principles of positive reinforcement can create a false picture that learning, as defined by behavior change, is simply a matter of selecting the correct reinforcer and scheduling it effectively. For most educational objectives, learning is best characterized as a gradual process of behavior change. The purpose of **shaping** is to reach an academic or behavioral goal through the gradual achievement and mastery of subgoals. The process involves establishing a shifting performance criterion to reinforce gradual increments in performance. As it is most precisely defined, it refers to the gradual change in performance that is tied to a single behavior, to distinguish it from **chaining**, which generally refers to multiple, related behaviors, such as those involved in getting dressed.

A shaping program includes four steps (Martin & Pear, 2015): specification of a final desired behavior, selection of the starting behavior, choosing of the specific shaping steps, and movement through the steps at an appropriate pace, with reinforcement provided accordingly. Because shaping is based on a series of small, more easily achieved subgoals, it provides the teacher with a valuable strategy for building responses that are well beyond a child's present functioning.

Shaping behavior through successive approximations to the desired goal is one of the basic uses of reinforcement. When combined with both task analysis and prompting, it can be the basis for teaching precise, manageable skills to students. Such an approach provides the foundation for chaining, or the linking of skills to complete a complex behavioral task. Forward chaining can be used to teach sequential steps in consecutive order, as with self-help skills such as shaving; backward chaining can effectively teach skills such as dressing by beginning just short of the completed task and gradually requiring the student to complete more steps within the task hierarchy.

Positive Reinforcement Programs. Effective teaching often requires the use of systems for implementing reinforcement strategies. This section describes several reinforcement programs that have been successfully used in classroom situations.

Premack Principle The most basic concept for dealing with consequences is the classic *Premack principle* (Premack, 1959). It is often called "Grandma's law" because it is reminiscent of the traditional dinner table remark, "If you eat your vegetables, then you can have your dessert." The principle asserts that a low-probability activity can be increased in frequency when paired with a high-probability activity. For example, a student who finishes a spelling lesson (a low-probability behavior) will be allowed to go out and play volleyball for 10 minutes (a high-probability behavior). Because volleyball is a desirable activity, the student has increased incentive to finish the lesson.

Contingency Contracting   Contracting represents a potentially effective, versatile management system. Contracts can be oral or written; they state the work assignment that the learner has contracted to complete and the consequences that the instructor will provide upon completion. Contracts should be perceived as binding agreements between student and teacher; signatures on written contracts emphasize this perception. In his classic work, Homme (1969) identified 10 fundamental rules of contracting:

1. The contract reward should be immediate.
2. Initial contracts should call for and reward small approximations.
3. Small rewards should be given frequently.
4. The contract should call for and reward accomplishment rather than obedience.
5. The performance should be rewarded after it occurs.
6. The contract must be fair.
7. The terms of the contract must be clear.
8. The contract must be honest.
9. The contract must be positive.
10. Contracting must be used systematically.

Although contracts are usually associated with individuals, contingency contracting can also be handled efficiently and effectively within a large-class setting. For example, a teacher responsible for a one-hour arithmetic period can make assignments that a student will need approximately 50 minutes to complete.

The remaining 10 minutes can then be given to students to play games, explore the Internet, or work at an interest center, contingent on the completion of specific academic tasks. Although the instructional time has been decreased by one-sixth, the students' motivation to complete their work and gain their free-choice time will probably compensate for the reduced time.

Figure 4-5 illustrates a simple form for an individual contract. Changes and elaborations depend on the instructional goals of the specific situation. Contracts can be an extremely useful technique in a classroom situation. They can be age appropriate, can provide initial training in understanding formal contracts, can facilitate home–school coordination, and can serve as an appropriate step toward self-management.

Group Contingencies   Group contingencies are another possible source of effective intervention strategies. They represent peer-mediated interventions and can include independent contingencies (i.e., all members of the group work individually toward reinforcement provided on an individual basis), dependent

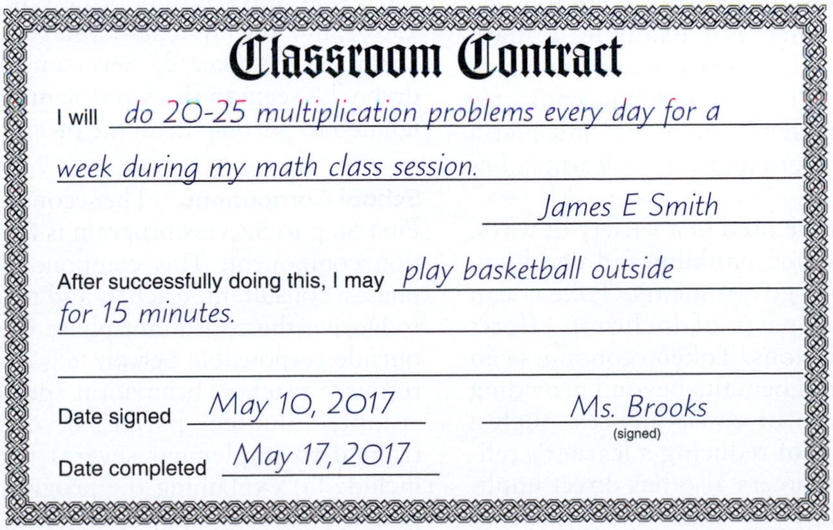

Classroom Contract

I will _do 20-25 multiplication problems every day for a week during my math class session._

James E Smith

After successfully doing this, I may _play basketball outside for 15 minutes._

Date signed _May 10, 2017_   _Ms. Brooks_
                                        (signed)
Date completed _May 17, 2017_

FIGURE 4–5   Sample Contingency Contract

contingencies (i.e., reinforcement is contingent on performance of a designated student), and interdependent contingencies (i.e., reinforcement is contingent on the performance of a group of students).

Token Economies Another systematic method for programming reinforcement is through the establishment of a **token economy**. In general, a token system is based on items symbolizing actual reinforcers, much like the use of monetary rewards. Just as adults receive money for their performance, students can earn tokens for appropriate behavior and completion of tasks. Just as adults can exchange their money for food, clothes, shelter, and entertainment, students can redeem their tokens for items they desire.

Token systems afford the teacher a number of distinct advantages over other forms of contingency management. Tokens can help bridge the gap between a specific behavior and the actual reinforcer with a minimal disruption in instruction. In addition, the interest generated by obtaining tokens may actually increase the value of the reinforcer for which they are exchanged. Tokens can be constructed to ensure portability and availability and can allow for a flexible reinforcement menu without incorporating a variety of reinforcers into the instructional class activities. Finally, token economies can have positive effects on teachers by emphasizing the need to reinforce students frequently and consistently.

Tokens can also be beneficial in enhancing skill training and academic learning. Amounts to be paid when work is completed can be established for specific assignments. For example, a math sheet might be worth 10 tokens when completed with 90% accuracy. With this added incentive for work completion, teachers frequently find that a student's quantity of work and rate of learning improve dramatically.

Token systems can be used in a variety of ways. Outgrowths may include banking and checking, stores, and classroom governments. Tokens can also become integral parts of inclusion efforts and home–school relations. Token economies can have direct educational benefits beyond providing an organized program of consequences. Such a system's ultimate goal of reducing a learner's reliance on external reinforcers also has direct implications for the possible success of self-regulatory forms of behavioral intervention (discussed later).

First Step to Success Program

This chapter covers a variety of interventions based on reinforcement principles to increase appropriate behavior. What is of particular interest is the ability of teachers to take these interventions and integrate them into their classroom as an early, universal, or secondary intervention. By doing this, teachers are able to address unwanted behaviors from occurring or give support to children who need additional interventions for difficult behaviors.

The First Step to Success program, developed by Walker et al. (1997), is one of the most comprehensive behavior-change programs that can be found for young children (pre-K to grade 3) today. The program targets the behavior of young children who exhibit emerging antisocial behavior patterns (e.g., oppositional behaviors, aggression toward others, tantrums, conflicts and confrontations with peers and teachers, and rule infractions). The program consists of three components that exemplify the use of behavioral assessment, consultant- and teacher-based intervention, and parent involvement/ reinforcement. The following summary presents these three components (Walker et al., 1997).

Screening Component. The first component of the program was developed to evaluate each child with regard to behavioral indicators that would help teachers identify children most appropriate for the program. For young children, the Early Screening Project (Feil, Severson, & Walker, 1998) may be used. Older children might be assessed through the Social Skills Rating Scale (Gresham & Elliott, 1990) and the Systematic Screening for Behavior Disorders (Walker & Severson, 1992). The children who seem to show problem areas are then designated to participate in the program.

School Component. The second component of the First Step to Success program is the school intervention component. This component comprises three phases: consultant, teacher, and maintenance phase.

During the consultant phase of the program, an outside responsible person (e.g., school counselor, resource teacher, behavioral specialist, teacher assistant, volunteer parent, or college student) is trained to implement several tasks. These tasks include (a) explaining the program to the teacher, parents, child, and peers; (b) ascertaining a consent to participate from all participants; (c) initiating the program in the classroom for the first five program days (20 to 30 minutes per day); (d) developing a negotiated list (among the teacher, child, and parent) of school rewards and home privileges to be earned by the child; (e) implementing the first five days of the program and training the teacher in the application of all aspects of the program; and (f) turning the program over to the teacher, supervising its operation, and beginning the HomeBase program with the parents.

As soon as the teacher is trained, the teacher phase of the component begins. Annemieke Golly, the First Step to Success trainer (personal communication), describes the mechanics of the actual component:

> The First Step program is based on five research-based principles: (1) develop clear expectations, (2) directly teach expectations through examples and nonexamples, (3) provide lots of feedback when students are doing well, (4) minimize a lot of attention for minor misbehavior, and (5) have very clear consequences for unacceptable behavior. These principles are effective strategies when working with all students, including students with special needs and/or students with a diverse cultural background. Students are taught school skills through one-on-one role-play situations to (a) follow directions, (b) get along with others, and (c) stay on task.
>
> During the first few days of the program, the coach provides feedback to the child in the classroom using a card that is green on one side and red on the other side. The child earns points on the green side of the card. When enough points have been earned during a small period of time, the child gets to pick a fun activity for the entire class. The strategy works extremely effective to elicit positive interaction from peers who might have rejected the child before. In fact, teachers report that the First Step to Success program significantly increased positive peer interactions as well as their own teaching behavior and classroom atmosphere.

The maintenance phase of the school component extends the program for up to 10 days. During this time, the students' dependence on the program is slowly reduced. The feedback and points are substituted by giving occasional rewards contingent on exemplary performances. Additionally, the teacher at school and the parents at home verbally reinforce the students' behavior, primarily with praise and expressions of approval.

After the maintenance phase is completed, the HomeBase component is the final piece of this program. It is designed to teach the parents/caregivers six lessons to build child competencies and skills in school adjustment and performance. These lessons consist of (a) communication and sharing, (b) cooperation, (c) limits setting, (d) problem solving, (e) friendship making, and (f) development of confidence. The goal of this component is to build a strong, positive relationship between the home and the school. Parents and caregivers are recruited to be partners with the school to work cooperatively to help the student be successful in school. Once in place, data are collected to determine effectiveness. Seeley et al. (2009) reported that the First Step to Success intervention yielded "significant and moderate-to-large post intervention effects on school-based measures of ADHD and disruptive behavior symptoms, social functioning, and academic functioning" (p. 37).

Behavior Reduction Techniques

Successful teaching requires the ability to resolve problem behaviors successfully. The use of reductive strategies requires an initial consideration of the techniques most natural to the classroom and school environment. The following list provides a sequence of selected strategies from least to most restrictive alternatives:

1. Natural and logical consequences
2. Differential reinforcement
3. Extinction
4. Time out from positive reinforcement
5. Response cost

Natural and Logical Consequences. Before teachers consider high-powered consequences for inappropriate behavior, attention should be given to consequences that are natural and/or logical relative to a given behavior. Although in some instances these may be behaviorally defined as punishment, their cognitive relationship to the behavior itself makes them more attractive alternatives. As Elias and Schwab (2006) noted, the use of natural and logical consequences can result in children and adolescents learning responsibility.

Natural consequences occur when a parent or a teacher "does not intervene in a situation but allows the situation to teach the child. The technique is based on the old adage: 'Every generation must learn that the stove is hot'" (West, 1986, p. 121). Two examples illustrate how this process can operate in a classroom setting. A student may refuse to do classwork or homework. The natural consequence is that he receives no credit for the work. The teacher need not say or do anything. In another situation, a child may habitually forget her permission slip to attend a class function away from school. The natural consequence is that she has to stay behind when the class goes on a trip. Natural consequences are an effective means to teach common sense and responsibility and important social emotional skills of "understanding and anticipating the consequences of one's actions, self-regulating, and learning to problem solve more effectively for the future" (Elias & Schwab, 2006, p. 331).

With certain behaviors, natural consequences could result in severe eventualities, such as injury. For example, having a person depend on the natural consequence of walking into the street without looking (i.e., struck by a car) would clearly be inappropriate. In these instances, consideration should be given to alternatives that are **logical consequences** of the behavior. Logical consequences attempt to tie the disciplinary response directly to the inappropriate behavior (West, 1994). For example, when a student pushes another child in the hall, the teacher may give the child the choice of not pushing or of going back to the classroom, waiting until the group has reached its destination, and then starting out alone. In considering the use of behavior reduction strategies, the teacher is encouraged to continuously evaluate how natural and logical consequences can enhance a management program.

Differential Reinforcement Strategies. A number of strategies are available to reduce inappropriate behaviors through positive reinforcement strategies. As outlined by Martin and Paer (2015), these include **differential reinforcement** of a low rate of responding (DRL), differential reinforcement of the omission of behavior (or of other behavior) (DRO), and differential reinforcement of incompatible (DRI) or alternative behaviors (DRA).

A DRL strategy employs reinforcement based on the successive reduction of behavioral occurrences; it can thus be used, for example, to gradually decrease talking out of turn during an instructional period. DRL is an underused yet effective tool for changing behavior.

As a classroom example, consider a program for students in sixth grade. An initial average problem level of 10 examples of profanity per day is determined. An initial criterion standard of 5 is set.

Reinforcement (e.g., an agreed-upon group activity) is then based on staying below this level in a given period. Subsequently, the standard can be lowered to 3, to 1, and to 0, thus essentially shaping down the behavior as the rate of behavior is successively reduced.

DRO procedures call for reinforcement based on the omission of a given behavior or the occurrence of other behavior. Martin and Pear (2015) described two types of DRO schedules. With momentary DRO, reinforcement is delivered if the target behavior is not occurring at the end of an interval (e.g., when the bell rings). It is best used to "catch" students who are or are not behaving appropriately. For example, it could be used to decrease the occurrence of out-of-seat behavior. With whole-interval DRO, students are reinforced if the target behavior does not occur for the entire time period. To return to the previous example, reinforcement in this case could be tied to a student's remaining seated for a period of 10 minutes. Subsequently, with a DRO schedule sequence, the time could be increased to the entire instructional period; the inappropriate behavior is effectively omitted during these successively longer periods.

DRI and DRA approaches can be used to strengthen behaviors that are not compatible with or that represent an alternative to the targeted inappropriate behavior. Thus, the reinforcement of hand raising could be used to decrease the occurrence of calling out in class. When using a DRI approach, teachers should select an incompatible behavior that requires "doing something" so that the student is not reinforced for simply "sitting quietly" (Kerr & Nelson, 2009). A traditional measure of whether the behavior selected is appropriate is to ask, "Can a dead person do it?" The following example underscores the importance of this consideration.

Positive methods, via differential reinforcement, represent a valuable option and should be considered before more restrictive means are selected. Thus, they offer an attractive alternative to reliance on aversive techniques.

Good-Behavior Game One example of the use of differential reinforcement (especially DRL) is the good-behavior game. Originally reported by Barrish, Saunders, and Wolf (1969), it divides a class into teams or groups. Each person within the group has specific standards for meriting free time. Teams that remain below the maximum number of occurrences of inappropriate behavior receive the designated reinforcement (i.e., interdependent group contingency). The technique is easy to implement and has been used successfully in general education as well as in special education settings (Bradshaw, Zmuda, Kellam, & Ialango, 2009; Lannie & McCurdy, 2007; Leflot, van Lier, Onglena, & Colpin, 2010; McCurdy, Lonnie, & Barnabas, 2009; Tanol, Johnson, McComas, & Cote, 2010).

Although group contingencies such as those in the good-behavior game may seem unfair to individual students who are penalized for the actions of others, any technique that effectively enhances classroom management ultimately serves their best interests. Naturally, the teacher must modify the structure of the game if one student consistently misbehaves for attention-seeking purposes and thus penalizes the team.

Extinction Procedures.

As behaviorally defined, **extinction** refers to the withholding of reinforcement that previously maintained a specific behavior or behaviors. Analysis of antecedents, behaviors, and consequences relative to a particular situation may indicate that change can be effected by removing the reinforcer maintaining the behavior, thus extinguishing the response. The most typical use of extinction in the classroom occurs when teacher attention has inadvertently been tied to students' inappropriate behavior. For example, the teacher may originally have spoken to students only when they were disruptive. An extinction procedure would then involve withholding attention at these times so that only appropriate behavior elicits reinforcement. For other behaviors, peers may need to be involved in the intervention plan if their attention has been maintaining the inappropriate behavior. For example, if a child is using infantile language to receive others' attention (e.g., laughter), then peers will need to be trained to withhold their laughter in response to this behavior.

Several cautions are needed concerning the use of extinction. First, extinction should be used only for a behavior for which it is apt to be effective. Thus, for example, its utility is likely to be greater for talking out in class than for self-stimulatory behavior (e.g., twirling a pencil). Second, the initial withholding of attention or other forms of reinforcement may prompt a dramatic rise in the target behavior as students increase their efforts to receive attention. The efficacy of the procedure thus cannot be truly evaluated until several hours or perhaps days have passed. Third, extinction occasionally produces an initial aggressive response. A fourth concern is consistency of application. Without a commitment to consistency, the teacher may accidentally reinforce the undesirable behavior on an irregular basis and thus inadvertently maintain it at a higher rate of occurrence. Finally, other students may begin to imitate the behavior being ignored, thus exacerbating the situation. Alberto and Troutman (2006) aptly commented on the use of extinction:

> "Just ignore it and it will go away. He's only doing it for attention." This statement is one of the most common suggestions given to teachers. In truth, extinction is much easier to discuss than to implement. It will go away, all right, but not necessarily rapidly or smoothly. (p. 308)

Time Out.

Punishment through withdrawal of positive reinforcement is best typified by **time out**, which generally entails preventing a student from receiving the positive reinforcement that otherwise would be available (hence its full name, "time out from positive reinforcement"). Time out can include planned ignoring, contingent observation (i.e., the student is removed from but can still observe the group), exclusion from the time-in environment, and seclusion in an isolated room or cubicle (Kerr & Nelson, 2009). The discussion here focuses primarily on the last of these forms.

Teachers should observe several cautions in using time out. First, the effectiveness of time out depends on the presence of positive reinforcement in the classroom and its absence in the time-out area. Without both of these elements, the procedure can be of only limited assistance to the teacher. For example, if Susan dislikes the classroom situation (e.g., there is a substantial amount of yelling by the teacher and difficult work assignments) and she is sent to the hall for time out, where friends wander by and chat, she has been rewarded for her behavior, not punished. This approach in the long run could increase her misbehavior.

A second caution about time out pertains to the other end of the spectrum. The time-out area should be bland and unstimulating but not a dungeon. Time out may occur in a corner of the room or in a small room adjacent to the classroom. It should be used sparingly for short periods (i.e., 5 to 10 minutes). If it needs to be used frequently for a particular child, the teacher should consider alternatives.

Use of time out naturally varies according to the space available, the type of students, and the teacher. Regardless of the circumstances, however, time out should be (Gast & Nelson, 1977)

- selected only after trying alternative solutions,
- preceded by an explicit statement about when it will be used,
- accompanied by a brief explanation of why it is being used,
- kept brief,
- documented through record-keeping procedures,
- terminated contingent on appropriate behavior, and
- combined with reinforcement for incompatible behavior.

Time out must be used carefully. The student must know in advance that the teacher will not accept a particular behavior. Classroom rules must clearly indicate which specific behaviors merit time out, and the teacher must enforce the rules consistently. The teacher should also consider any legal aspects that may apply in a given school district.

Response Cost. A second example of punishment based on withdrawing positive reinforcement is the use of **response cost (RC)**. Such procedures include, in particular, subtracting points or tokens within established reinforcement systems. RC procedures can be used concurrently with positive reinforcement in the classroom, producing a reasonably rapid decrease in behavior, and they can be combined with other procedures to yield a comprehensive behavior program (Martella, Nelson, & Marchand-Martella, 2003).

Walker, Ramsey, and Gresham (2004) noted that RC is likely to have maximum effect when the teacher has clearly explained the system to the students, has closely tied it to a reinforcement system, and has developed an appropriate feedback and delivery system. In addition, they suggest seven rules for implementation:

1. RC should be implemented immediately after the target response or behavior occurs.
2. RC should be applied each time a target behavior occurs.
3. The student should never be allowed to accumulate negative points.
4. The ratio of points earned to those lost should be controlled.
5. Subtraction of points should never be punitive or personalized.

6. A student's positive, appropriate behavior should be praised as frequently as opportunities permit.

 LEARNING MODULE 4.2 Click here to learn more about addressing disruptive behaviors: http://iris.peabody .vanderbilt.edu/module/bi1 (Part 1) http://iris.peabody .vanderbilt.edu/module/bi2 (Part 2)

Considerations: Strategies for Adolescents

Although many of the tools previously discussed in this chapter have been used effectively with older students, special circumstances should be considered in selecting a strategy to implement with adolescents. An overriding principle is to avoid behavioral issues, if at all possible. The nearby Teacher Tips provide ideas for preventing issues. In light of the inherent difficulties in motivating students with long histories of school failure and chronic patterns of inappropriate behavior, intervention programs must be carefully evaluated to determine their likely outcome. First, natural and logical consequences relative to the outcome of the behavior should be emphasized (e.g., being late results in detention). Second, careful attention should be given to the reinforcers controlled by a student's peer group. The use of peer-mediated strategies should be carefully considered as possible interventions. As noted earlier, these strategies can be dependent (e.g., students are reinforced based on the behavior of the child), interdependent (e.g., reinforcement is given to a group working together), and independent (e.g., all students work on similar tasks for similar reinforcement, but the reinforcement is contingent only on the individual's performance).

For use with adolescents, reinforcers that require a minimum of teacher intervention should be sought; this concern is particularly important with response cost procedures that can be associated with confrontational outcomes. A point system, for example, would be easier to use than a token system if something must be removed from a student's total.

Most important, teachers must carefully choose strategies based on their anticipated reception by adolescents. In the case of positive reinforcement programs, the system must be designed in an age-appropriate fashion; for example, token programs using Daffy Dollars or the like are obviously high-risk approaches at the secondary level. Furthermore, backup reinforcers for any systematic positive reinforcement program must reflect students' interests and must be varied. For behavior reduction strategies, teachers should obviously avoid interventions with potential for exacerbating current situations.

Self-Management

Student-regulated strategies, including self-management, can be defined as interventions that, though initially taught by the teacher, are intended to be implemented independently by the student. Specifically, self-management requires "students to systematically monitor their own behavior in order to assess whether or not a targeted behavior has occurred and then record the results in some manner" (Holifield, Goodman, Hazelkorn, & Heflin, 2010, p. 230). To date, self-management interventions have been implemented with both high- and low-incidence disabilities.

The goal of self-management programs for students with disabilities is to "increase independence and inclusion within schools and society" (Southall & Gast, 2011, p. 155). The emphasis on self-management of one's own behavior represents a shift from extrinsic to intrinsic control. This transition can be facilitated by considering these procedures: (a) gradually reducing the frequency and amount of extrinsic reinforcement provided, (b) gradually delaying access to extrinsic reinforcement through the use of feedback to students, (c) gradually fading from the application of artificial reinforcers to reliance on naturally occurring reinforcing events, and (d) teaching self-control through an emphasis on the cognitive aspects of behavior change (Wallace & Kauffman, 1986).

ENHANCEDetext
video example 4.3
Watch this video to learn more about self-management.

A number of specific aspects of self-management can be utilized. Self-instruction includes a cognitive approach to management, using self-cuing to inhibit certain inappropriate behaviors and to direct appropriate ones. It typically involves instruction in a specific verbal strategy that students perform to complete a task or control a behavior.

The self-determination of reinforcement places on the student the primary responsibility for selecting reinforcers so that they can be self-administered, contingent on performance of the specified appropriate behavior. Self-evaluation or self-assessment involves the learner in determining the need for change in behavior and then measuring (in some form) the change. Young, West, Li, and Peterson (1997) highlighted components of self-evaluation, done in consultation with the teacher:

- Determining the expectations or standards for acceptable behavior for each of the settings in which behavior is monitored
- Comparing the counts or ratings of behavior (based on self-monitoring) to the standards
- Determining whether the behavior is acceptable or should be changed in either quantity or quality

The most researched self-management strategy is the technique of self-monitoring, or recording, of behavior. Self-monitoring, particularly of on-task behavior, is a relatively simple technique that has been validated with children of diverse abilities.

One classic common approach to self-monitoring involves an easily implemented series of techniques that can be used in both general and special education classrooms (Hallahan, Lloyd, & Stoller, 1982). It consists of the use of a tape-recorded tone that sounds at random intervals, averaging every 45 seconds, and a self-recording sheet. Children are instructed to ask themselves, each time the tone sounds, whether they were paying attention and then to mark the yes or no box on the self-recording sheet. Although this strategy has been used with accompanying reinforcement for correct use of the self-recording sheet, in most instances it has been successful simply with appropriate training in the techniques.

Self-monitoring procedures have been used with varied groups of students and settings (e.g., Bialas & Boon, 2010; Crabtree, Alber-Morgan, & Konrad, 2010; Harris, Friedlander, Saddler, Frizzelle, & Graham, 2005; McDougall, 1998; Rafferty & Rimondi, 2009). Soares, Vannest, and Harrison (2009) introduced the use of computer aided self-monitoring to increase academic performance among students with more severe behavioral problems.

 Check Your Understanding 4.2 Click here to gauge your understanding of the concepts in this section.

In his book *Your First Year of Teaching: Guidelines for Success*, Richard Kellough (2005) outlined 50 errors that new teachers should avoid. Kellough contended that it is easier to avoid these errors than try to remediate the behaviors that are caused by the teacher's inexperience. Although all 50 errors cannot be outlined here, following are five of the errors Kellough described. These errors were selected because they are some of the errors that new teachers (and old) fall into quite easily.

1. **Inadequately attending to long-range and daily planning.** Because teachers are so busy, they may fall into the trap of working from a day-to-day philosophy.
2. **Emphasizing the negative.** Teachers can easily fall into a negative mode by emphasizing what students are doing wrong. Remind students of the correct procedures with rationales why these procedures benefit them.
3. **Not requiring students to raise their hands or allowing students' hands to be raised too long.** Allowing students to communicate their need by raising their hands gives them assurance that they will have the teacher's attention. Once raised, however, the teacher must recognize the student in a timely fashion.
4. **Being too serious and no fun.** Students (especially adolescents) enjoy teachers who are willing to work with them and help make learning fun. Although teaching is a serious business, young people love to use humor to communicate.
5. **Relying too much on teacher talk.** Teachers may continue to lecture or talk to students when they want to give them a lot of information. Too much talking, however, can create confusion and boredom. If students are not able to detect what is the information that is most important, they will tune the teacher out.

Source: Kellough, R. D. *Your First Year of Teaching: Guidelines for Success* (3rd ed.) © 2005, pp. 18–21. Reprinted by permission of Pearson Education, Inc., Upper Saddle River, NJ.

STUDENT DIVERSITY CONSIDERATIONS

During the past 15 years, SWPBS researchers have devoted considerable time investigating the diversity among students as a possible factor related to classroom management (e.g., Cartledge, Lo, Vincent, & Robinson-Ervin, 2015; Fallon, O'Keefe, Gage, & Sugai, 2015; Fallon, O'Keeffe, & Sugai, 2012). These researchers recognize that schools and classrooms of today are experiencing more diversity in the student population than ever before and may not reflect the cultural sensitivity that is needed for many students (Cartledge et al., 2015). The diversity we speak of includes both cultural diversity as well as diverse learners in the classroom. The final section of this chapter discusses the topic of the individual child and the sensitivity that teachers and administrators need to exhibit when working with each child (as well as his or her family).

Considering Diversity in Classroom Management

As we discuss diversity in the classroom, many definitions of diversity and culture are to be considered. In doing so, we selected the following key terms to be defined. According to Barrera, Corso, and Macpherson (2003), *cultural diversity* may be defined as "behavioral, value, linguistic and other differences ascribed to peoples' cultural backgrounds." *Cultural competence*, however, may be considered as "the ability to skillfully address communication and learning across diverse cultural parameters. It is more specifically defined . . . as the ability to craft respectful, reciprocal, and responsive interactions across diverse cultural and linguistic parameters" (p. 6). It is precisely these definitions that outline the acknowledgment of students as being considered unique and contributing members in any school.

By attending to cultural diversity and how it relates to classroom management, classroom climate, and classroom instruction, teachers become culturally competent to address the needs of each individual child in their classrooms. Barrera et al. (2003) outlined three benefits of recognizing and attending to the challenges of the culturally diverse student. First, teachers have a *professional responsibility to address the needs of shifting demographics* in the schools of today. Children from diverse backgrounds are becoming a significant population in schools in the United States. Many teachers will

For Native American children the transition from home and tribal community learning environments to formal school can often present challenges when academic or social issues arise in these settings. School staff can make assumptions about students and their families when they have little knowledge about the critical nature of children's cultural upbringing or linguistic background. They may also rely on standard school-based procedures and policies that may not consider the ways that parents and families may traditionally socialize their children or communicate with them when important issues arise concerning their behavior or actions.

In many Native American societies, family structures and the role of both the immediate and extended adult members can be important aspects of a young child's upbringing. Among some Pueblo Indian tribes, for example, it may be that male relatives from the child's maternal side play a key role in the teaching, discipline and guidance of young children in addition to parents. Adults of the community may also play a critical role in the socialization of children into more traditional cultural aspects that take place in both family and community contexts and through varied learning experiences (Romero-Little, 2010). For Pueblo Indian children, the formation of cultural values, social behaviors and identity are embedded in the traditional practices that may be acquired through a number of different ways such as quiet listening and observation, imitation, peripheral and active participation alongside adult role models (Romero-Little, 2008). Thus, young children not only learn how to communicate verbally and non-verbally, but also how to interact with family members as well as other adults in the extended family and community.

Dealing with Native American children's social, emotional, and academic issues in school, therefore, can pose a challenge for personnel who may be unfamiliar with the sociocultural and home environment of these children. Family structures may be different from one Native American culture to another which school staff may not be able to differentiate. When personnel insist on communicating only in modalities that they have been trained to use, these may in fact, be perceived as indifferent, overbearing or intimidating to Native parents and this can result in ineffective interaction and poor communication. When a child needs guidance in how to change certain behaviors, standard school procedures and processes may not always work, hence educators and practitioners bear the responsibility to respectfully explore the ways that will work best to communicate and interact with Native children and their families. Sensitivity to communication styles, both verbal and non-verbal, can provide important clues in developing more appropriate strategies when speaking to children and their parents. Inclusion of key extended family members may be another important aspect of working with families. Finding ways that will work best while validating and honoring Native American cultural values and perspectives should be at the heart of on-going, informed, and respectful practice by professional and caring educators.

Christine Sims is an enrolled tribal member of Acoma Pueblo in New Mexico. She is an associate professor in the College of Education and director of the American Indian Language Policy Research and Teacher Training Center at the University of New Mexico.

come into contact with at least one child from a diverse background. Attending to the individuality of that child may make the difference in his or her becoming a successful student.

A second benefit for addressing the challenge of culturally diverse students in the classroom is the *professional responsibility of supporting a student's developmental, social, and academic growth*. Barrera et al. (2003) stated that "one of the core needs of all children is to have their behaviors and beliefs mirrored and valued by adults around them" (p. 18). Learning the values, beliefs, and customs of an individual can greatly contribute to understanding the student's classroom behavior. This knowledge can greatly influence how a teacher interacts with students as well as how behavioral assessments are conducted and interpreted.

Finally, the *professional responsibility of developing appropriate and responsive curriculum* can be a benefit for every student, including the culturally diverse student. Understanding the expectations and experiences of individual children (including children with disabilities) and how they are associated with specific cultures can influence how teachers determine a student's status in relation to goals of the classroom management procedures and interventions that are implemented.

Sims (see the prior Diversity in the Classroom box) talked about the communication of a child's behavior with family members. If we apply the previous three benefits with Sims's advice, we can further see how students of different backgrounds may behave differently depending on the family's expectations of that behavior. Understanding these differences and responding to them accordingly can enhance any classroom management system.

Vaughn, Bos, and Schumm (2006) offered five suggestions to enhance classroom management when responding to diversity in the classroom. First, teachers must remember that students are children/adolescents first. That is, teachers should respond first to accepting, recognizing, and valuing students as members of the community—respecting their common needs and goals. Second, teachers should focus on abilities and expertise of all members of the classroom. Third, teachers should celebrate diversity in student learning and behavior as well as cultural backgrounds and languages. Fourth, teachers should demonstrate a high regard for all students. Finally, teachers should provide opportunities for students to work in mixed-ability groups. In keeping with the child as an individual with specific needs, we conclude this chapter with the need for developing individual programs for students with disabilities.

Mihalas, Morse, Allsopp, and McHatton (2009) introduced the importance of cultivating caring relationships between students and teachers. Although Mihalas and her colleagues suggested relationship building between students with emotional and behavioral disorders and their teachers, the concept applies to all classrooms, including classrooms with diverse populations. Possible practices used when advocating for caring teacher–student relationships include the following teacher behaviors: (a) advocating for students, (b) getting to know students regarding their lives and how their background would influence their behavior and learning, (c) inviting students to be active participants in their education, (d) listening to their students and understanding what is being communicated as well as checking for the students' understanding, (e) asking for student feedback regarding teacher performance, (f) journaling with students as a way to establish effective communication between teachers and students, (g) dedicating time to solve problems as a class and with individual students, (h) celebrating student successes, and (i) teaming with other teachers or professionals to implement these practices.

Finally, Cartledge et al. (2015) recommended two effective strategies that are considered culturally responsive interventions. These strategies are "(1) using culturally responsive procedures to conduct functional behavioral assessments of student behaviors to determine behavior strengths and (2) implement culturally responsive social skill instructions to promote desired social behaviors" (p. 419). With regard to functional behavioral assessments, Cartledge believes that the use of direct observations within the classroom (if that is where the problem is occurring) may be particularly appropriate for students of diverse backgrounds. If the function of the behavior can be targeted, the student might readily respond to the prescribed intervention. Additionally, Cartledge et al. recommend the use of culturally responsive social skills instructions where peer-mediated instruction is used to enhance cooperation and appropriate peer interactions as well as student engagement. Finally, the use of peers from the same diverse backgrounds can enhance the generalization of social skills within the school environment. More information regarding social skills instruction can be found in a later chapter in this book.

 Check Your Understanding 4.3 Click here to gauge your understanding of the concepts in this section.

ACTIVITIES

1. Provide supports to promote on-task behavior by pairing the special needs student with a study buddy or learning partner who is an exemplary student.
2. Students choose a picture of a large reward they would like to earn (e.g., ice cream). The teacher cuts the picture into puzzle pieces. When the class or student meets the criteria, they earn a piece of the puzzle. When the puzzle is complete, they earn the reward.
3. Students are placed in teams where they will monitor each other. Students are directly

taught the target behavior, monitoring techniques and procedures for the game. The teacher makes goals individually or for the class as a whole. For example, the teacher can set the criteria that each group that earns 80% of the points over the course of the day will earn the reward, or the teacher may require the class to earn 80% of the points collectively. Teacher determines the interval at which the group monitors and evaluates the behavior of the group.

4. The teacher has a surprise box filled with positive reinforcers. At the end of every class, students who behaved well get an item from the surprise box. Teachers should set the criteria for good behavior.

5. To encourage students to work toward appropriate behavior, the teacher tells the students to follow certain rules when they are in class and further that they can earn points that can be used to obtain reinforcement for doing so.

6. To help prevent challenging behavior, the teacher creates a daily schedule and ensures that students are aware of it. The teacher may find a student version of a weekly planner. The teacher places class schedules prominently in the classroom. Students will be prompted to refer to their schedules, and the teacher will preview what is about to happen at various times throughout the day. The teacher will use the previews to clearly specify criteria and outcomes for activities.

Spoken Language

Lynda Miller

LEARNING OUTCOMES

Upon completion of this chapter, the reader should be able to:

5.1 Discuss the nature of language including the evolution of language, the function of language, and the relationship between communication, language, and speech.

5.2 Identify and discuss the primary components of our system of language.

5.3 Identify the types of language disabilities and disorders that may be present in students.

5.4 Discuss formal and informal language assessment strategies.

5.5 Understand and identify effective instructional strategies for teaching spoken language.

Educators working with students with special needs need to develop and support the language development of these students. In order to do so, it is important that they have a thorough understanding of communication, language, and speech; are familiar with the components of language; are sensitive to the potential language difficulties they may experience; and can collaborate in implementing assessment and instructional strategies in spoken language. This chapter addresses all of these important concerns.

NATURE OF LANGUAGE

Humans have been using language to communicate in one form or another for millennia. Early primitive language-like systems were most likely used by *Homo habilis* approximately 2.3 million years ago (Fitch, 2010), while most modern languages emerged less than 100,000 years ago (Newmeyer, 2005). Every culture has some kind of spoken language, and most have a corresponding written language system. In the United States, the most spoken language is English; the second most is Spanish. In the world, it is Chinese, followed by Hindi, English, and Spanish.

In the United States, there are over 300 living languages still spoken by at least some native speakers (U.S. Census Bureau, 2013). Of those whose native language is not English, nearly 60% of people sampled in the 2010 census claimed to speak English very well, while another 20% claimed to speak English well.

EVOLUTION OF THE ENGLISH LANGUAGE

Circa	Status
55 BC	Obscure Germanic dialect, first becoming primarily Celt speaking, then Latin speaking following Roman invasion of British Isles
AD 410	Romans abandon Britain, various Germanic tribes invade, Anglos and Saxons prevail, and language they spoke became known as *Englisc*, Old English, or Anglo-Saxon.
8th to 11th centuries	Most famous epic poem in Old English from era was *Beowulf*.
1066	Normans conquered Britain, bringing rural dialect of French, influenced by German.
11th to 13th centuries	English had no status (French and Latin dominate) and was largely spoken rather than written.
14th century	English regains dominance. Chaucer writes *The Canterbury Tales* in English.
Late 16th to early 17th centuries	Shakespeare writing in English, as changed considerably and as understandable to people reading his work today.
19th century	American English heavily influenced by British English, Spanish (with settlement of the West), and Black English when Africans were brought to the South.
19th to 20th centuries	Many enslaved persons from West Africa, where hundreds of languages were spoken, which led to English-based creoles, as "forms of simplified English combined with many words from a variety of African languages" (Maslin, 2011a, para. 28).

Sixty-two percent of those who spoke a language other than English at home spoke Spanish or Spanish creole (U.S. Census Bureau, 2013).

Languages evolve over time. The box provides an illustration of the development of the English language based in part on Maslin (2011a).

Many people use language without thinking about what it is, how it works, or how it influences their thinking, relationships, and values, among other things. For most, language is like water to a fish—essential but not anything to think about. It's just there, part of the fabric of life. Unlike fish, though, people can survive without language—but at great cost.

One way to think about language is that it is a system for organizing and expressing what we know (McLuhan, 1964). Language has evolved considerably since humans first began using actual speech rather than prearranged signals to communicate with each other. It has become more complex and varied and now functions as a powerful, complex system by which we categorize what we know and think, communicate with others, and even develop the values we do.

Language in our modern world is a social tool, a shared code that allows people to communicate with each other. Owens (2013) suggested that language represents the collective thinking of a culture and that every culture is, in turn, influenced by its language. Facility with the language of one's culture serves as a primary means by which we participate in the relationships, experiences, events, rituals, politics, and learning that make up everyday life.

People use language to communicate thoughts, ideas, desires, and needs to others. As with any system, language operates through several sets of rules that govern the arrangement of arbitrary symbols in relation to one another. The rules of any given language determine how sounds, words and word parts, and phrases can be combined to make meaning. Because these rules, too, are arbitrary, they can be used to describe almost anything. A person can use any allowable combination of these language parts to describe virtually a thing, an idea, an experience, or a feeling. Because there is no inherent reason why a horse, for example, is called a horse or why compassion is called compassion, the rules of language remain independent of the way the world works.

Further, because the forms and content of language are arbitrary, language can never be a complete description or explanation for anything. In other words, language *mediates* between the thing, experience, process, or feeling and the saying of it. The act of saying something is one step (at least) removed from the actuality of what it represents. This arbitrariness and the mediational quality of language can be difficult for children to grasp and often pose special difficulties for students, as will be shown in the chapter.

Besides being rule governed, language is unique because it is a generative system, meaning it is creative. Using the finite rules of language and a finite set of words (e.g., nouns, pronouns, verbs), a person can generate an infinite number of meaningful utterances. First, words can be used to refer to more than one thing, as in "That is some *sweet* sounding music," "I'd like *sweet* iced tea," and "She has a *sweet* nature." Second, things can be called more than one name, as in *davenport* and *couch* or *curtains* and *drapes*. Third, words can be combined in varied ways to mean the same thing, as in "May I have more gravy, please?" or "Is there more gravy?," both of which mean "I want gravy!"

Typically developing children do not learn all the possible word combinations. Rather, they learn the rules underlying their spoken language, which means that they can understand and create an infinite variety of word combinations, sentences, and phrases in order to communicate.

Spoken language underlies most school-based learning in the early grades and predicts children's success with reading, spelling, writing, and literacy in general (Polloway, Miller, & Smith, 2012). Many children diagnosed with learning disabilities have spoken language difficulties that interfere with their ability to succeed in reading, writing, and spelling, without which they cannot make the transition from learning language to using language to learn.

Relationship of Communication, Language, and Speech

Language is only one of the forms of communication people use. Communication can occur through various means, both verbal and nonverbal, including the following: speaking, signing, alternative and augmentative communication systems, reading, writing, music, dance, mathematics, codes, games, and glyphs (symbols that convey information nonverbally, such as road signs). This list demonstrates that communication need not be solely linguistic (e.g., words, word parts, phrases, sentences). Much of communication occurs either through other codification systems (music, dance, mathematics, or codes) or through nonverbal, paralinguistic, or metalinguistic signals, discussed below.

A large portion of communication occurs via nonverbal cues, including head, hand, and general body posture; gestures; facial expressions; head, body, and hand movements; eye contact; and physical distance. Most people are identifiable by the way they utilize nonverbal cues, such as arm waving, winking, standing too close, showing no facial expression, frowning, and crossing their arms. For some students with difficulties, learning appropriate nonverbal cues is challenging and may result in social rejection or ostracism.

Paralinguistic signals—intonation, emphasis (stress), speed/rate of delivery, and pause/hesitation—are superimposed on speaking, writing, and/or signing to convey attitude or emotion. Consider, for example, how using either a rising or a falling intonation alters the meaning of this sentence: *Are you serious!* (falling intonation) compared with *Are you serious?* (rising intonation). Spoken with a rising intonation, the sentence becomes a sincere (or not-so-sincere) question, while using a falling intonation signals not a question for the listener but rather a comment on the speaker's perception. Besides indicating emotion, asides, and/or emphasis, paralinguistic markers convey information about the speaker's relationship to the listener(s), the importance of the information being communicated, and the status and role of the participants.

Metalinguistic skills include being able to reflect on and talk about language and all its aspects, being able to separate it from its content enough to manipulate and play with it. For children learning language, developing metalinguistic abilities allows them to define words; identify homonyms, antonyms, and synonyms; recognize homophones; identify syntactic and morphological elements; and match sounds to letters (Polloway et al., 2012). An inability to see language in this way poses a serious difficulty for students learning to read, write, and use language to learn.

Culture and Language

According to the National Center for Education Statistics (2015), approximately 4.4 million students (9.2%) spoke a native language other than

English. Each language represents a separate culture, which means that teachers must be aware of and responsive to a variety of cultural differences. The most successful teachers are those who appreciate cultural diversity and take steps to ensure that cultural differences are seen not as problems to be overcome but rather as opportunities to assist all students in learning to the best of their ability (Polloway et al., 2012).

Cultural differences in language present several challenges for educators. One is that many educators have limited opportunities to learn the skills that prepare them to teach students from cultures other than their own. The following box provides further information.

CULTURALLY RESPONSIVE CLASSROOMS

Classrooms that are culturally responsive share some basic characteristics:

- The teacher and school communicate their expectation that all students will succeed.
- The teacher acts as a guide and knowledge consultant as well as an instructor.
- The teachers in these classrooms inform themselves about the cultures represented in their classrooms.
- The teacher uses social situations that are culturally appropriate as part of instruction.
- Students are given opportunities to participate in how curriculum can be enhanced through incorporating the various cultural backgrounds in their classroom.
- The teacher designs activities that help students learn academic language.
- The teacher engages in ongoing dialogue with students and their family members and includes issues that are important to them in the curriculum and classroom activities.

A second challenge is that the curriculum in most schools in the United States rests on the assumption that children will enter school with some metalinguistic abilities already developed (e.g., knowledge of the alphabet, how print works on the page, that print represents spoken language). However, this assumption is usually true only of typically developing children from homes in which

- the native language is the language of school,
- print is visible and valued,
- adults talk about language and provide opportunities for children to demonstrate their own linguistic knowledge,
- adults tell stories and encourage children to tell stories,
- children are read to, and
- children have had multiple opportunities to interact with print and print artifacts (e.g., books, magazines, menus, signs).

Children from these homes usually arrive at school able to understand and tell stories, respond to adult questions in a way that demonstrates what they know, and, at least in basic ways, talk about language and its parts. For children from some cultural backgrounds, such activities may be unfamiliar and result in their feeling overwhelmed or confused.

A third challenge is providing fair and accurate assessments of the language abilities of children whose dominant language is not English (see below). One of the primary problems is that educators may not differentiate between language differences related to cultural factors and language differences that stem from a language disorder. In addition, tests may be biased against students from minority cultures because they contain items that represent values and/or knowledge different from those held by these students, don't really test what they purport to test, or are unavailable in any language other than English (Polloway et al., 2012).

A fourth challenge is that parents often face significant obstacles. For example, the lack of access to adequate health care for their children can result in their missing school or having difficulty focusing when in school. Nutrition may be enough of a problem that a child's brain development is slowed, with potentially devastating effects on cognitive growth. They may not be able to provide access to books and writing materials, and funds may not be available to provide the child with the cultural activities and experiences that other children are exposed to. Parents may not fully appreciate that the early years are a critical predictor of children's academic success and may not realize the importance of engaging them in conversation.

However, many children who enter school from diverse backgrounds, including impoverished circumstances, learn and adapt quickly to the school environment and go on to perform as well as or better than their peers. Some who display differences in their language abilities may require individualized modifications in the classroom, whereas others may need intervention aimed specifically at a language disorder.

DECONSTRUCTING LANGUAGE

School-age children with language disorders often experience later difficulties in learning to read, write, and learn. Thus, understanding how language works is fundamental to understanding how to provide instruction to these students. In school-age children, an estimated 7% have an identifiable language disorder that is often associated with later difficulties in learning to read, write, and learn; 61% of speech and language clinicians in schools reported that they provided services to children with language disorders (American Speech-Language-Hearing Association, 2012). Teachers are highly likely to have one or more students with a language disorder in their classes.

To offer the most effective instruction, teachers benefit from becoming proficient with the components of language and the terminology used to describe them. The most prevalent model used by language professionals comprises five parts: use, content, form, narrative, and nonverbal. In addition, any discussion of language must include a description of the literal and figurative levels of language use.

How People Use Language: Pragmatics

Most people don't think about how they change their language patterns depending on the various settings in which they communicate with others. To negotiate different communicative contexts, we use a set of implicit rules that govern how we change how we talk depending on to whom we are talking and what the circumstances are. Pragmatics describes the functions of language, or what we are trying to make happen through our language patterns, particularly in social situations.

This set of implicit rules is a kind of "code of conduct," first described by Bates (1976), that includes these components:

- We tell the truth when we're communicating.
- We cooperate with our conversational partners.

- We offer only information we believe to be new and relevant to each conversational partner.
- We ask only for information from our conversational partners that we truly want to have (i.e., we don't ask obvious, "dumb" questions).
- We give our conversational partners just the right amount of information to make our point (not too much and not too little).
- We are unambiguous in our conversations.
- We alter our language to fit each social setting.

Of course, no one actually strictly adheres to these rules. In fact, violations of the rules are themselves conventionalized and carry separate meanings. For example, the use of satire or irony in storytelling or journalism is, strictly speaking, a violation of the truth principle. So are "little white lies." Similarly, idioms violate the truth principle because, though they say one thing, they actually mean something different. For example, when someone asks how we are and we reply "fine" even if we don't feel fine, that reply violates the truth principle in favor of the politeness required. Overall, polite forms offer people a way to navigate through a wide range of the social situations in which they find themselves. Using polite forms—all the tacit rules—allows people to get their message across without insulting others or treating them as subordinates.

Learning the conventions for violating the rules makes up an important aspect of language acquisition and frequently appears as one aspect of some language disorders. In addition, because cultural and dialectal variations of these rules exist, students communicating across dialects or from culturally different communities can suffer communication breakdowns or misunderstandings. They can sometimes be diagnosed as having a language disorder when none exists.

Another aspect of language use is **discourse**, which is defined as a linguistic unit (e.g., a conversation, a story, a speech) larger than a sentence. In almost all cultures, children are first exposed to **conversational discourse**, which, though it varies in form and content across cultures, functions primarily as a way to communicate within social-interactive contexts. As children's language develops, they become more proficient with the nuances of both conversational partners and conversational contexts. In the early stages of language development, children generally adhere to the code of conduct of language use and take the rules at face value. Only gradually do they learn that there are sanctioned ways to violate those rules, including the notion of polite forms and how they are used within their culture.

Almost all cultures use **narrative discourse**, which involves characters, plot, setting, and resolution of the conflict. In stories, the characters are usually fictional, and their motivations are driven by a problem that the character then goes about trying to resolve. The character's efforts toward resolution constitute the plot, which may involve various episodes that alternately increase and release tension typically until the problem is resolved in some sort of final way.

In most cultures, children learn to relate experiences using narrative discourse. They themselves are the main character, and what they do and what happens along the way become the plot, usually resulting in a happy ending. As children become more adept with stories, their ideas, vocabulary, and grammar become more complex; they include dialogue, and they exhibit an increasing amount of creativity. Children who are read to and become readers themselves are able to incorporate into their stories more complexity and ingenuity as well as showing increasing mastery of the mechanics characteristic of the narrative form.

In many cultures, children are routinely included in oral storytelling activities and are expected to become proficient storytellers as soon as their language skills allow. In other cultures, only specific elders are allowed to tell the stories, and children are expected to remain silent. In cultures with a strong tradition of oral storytelling, narrative discourse often includes poetic and dramatic discourse.

Dramatic discourse is used whenever a scene, story, or play is conveyed to an audience either live or through radio, film, television, or via the Internet. Children acting out scenarios or playacting stories may use dramatic discourse by describing or showing the set, utilizing lighting effects, demonstrating what the characters look like and what they're wearing, and how the actors talk to each other and use interruptions, silence, ignoring someone, and speaking simultaneously. Often, young children playing together will construct make-believe scenarios in which they first negotiate who is going to be which character

(e.g., "I'll be Batman, and you be the Joker"), how to portray the setting (e.g., throwing a blanket over two chairs to simulate a cave), and what sort of costumes to wear. In addition, they will negotiate what the characters should say.

Poetic discourse utilizes language "which focuses on the expression of feelings, ideas, imaginations, events and places through specific rhymes and rhythms" (Literary Devices, 2015). Children are exposed to poetic discourse when they hear song lyrics or play rhyming games or when adults read (or sing) poetry or songs to them. Nursery rhymes expose children at an early age to the most basic form of poetic discourse. Films for children often contain music with lyrics that also exhibit some of the characteristics of poetic discourse.

When children enter school, they are immersed in **classroom discourse** (i.e., the language used in teaching and learning). The primary characteristics of classroom discourse are that the teacher does most of the talking, takes most of the turns, determines the topic, decides which students will talk, evaluates students' responses in order to correct or redirect them, uses decontextualized language (i.e., the context is not immediately apparent), and sometimes requires students to talk about language or the components of language.

Adults in **language-literate households** frequently converse with their children using classroom discourse, particularly in their efforts to teach their children about the world and how to display their knowledge about it to adults. However, children from homes that are less language literate may not be exposed to classroom discourse until they enter school and, therefore, have little experience demonstrating their knowledge in ways that are expected in the classroom.

Expository discourse includes the non-narrative discourses common to textbooks, articles, essays, editorials, and some online blogs. Usually, the expository discourse forms are seen in print; however, depending on the circumstances, speakers may use them in presentations, speeches, or lectures. The most common types of expository discourse are

- descriptive (describes a thing, process, event, experience, or idea),
- explanatory (explains how something works or how to do something), and
- argumentative/persuasive (attempts to convince or persuade the audience/reader of something).

Although some children are exposed to expository text (orally or in print) before they enter school, they are usually not expected to understand the structure or function of print-based expository discourses until they have learned to read.

Forms of Language

The structures of language are grouped into three categories: phonology, morphology, and syntax. Sign language, because it combines visual, gestural, and postural components, also includes a fourth category, cherology, which is a way to describe the basic units of any given sign language.

Phonology comprises the set of rules governing which sounds in a language are pronounceable and used to make meaning as well as how they can be combined to make meaning. Different languages have varying rules for how this works. For example, although in English /t/ and /l/ cannot be combined at the beginning of a word to make meaning, in Tlinglt (a native Alaskan language), /t/ and /l/ at the beginning of a word are pronounced "kl." Another example is from languages that use few vowels but include combinations of dental, lateral, alveolar, or palatal *clicks* as phonemes (e.g., Nelson Mandela, Xhosa language). The first time many people outside Africa heard a language using clicks was in 1966 when Miriam Makeba sang "The Click Song."

ENHANCEDetext
video example 5.1
Watch this video to learn more about language clicks.
http://www.youtube.com/watch?v=M3lfENV_U6M&feature=related

The smallest linguistic units to carry meaning are *phonemes*, which are the pronounceable sounds in a language. Thus, in each language, some sounds carry meaning, and some do not. In English, how one pronounces /t/ or /p/ makes no difference in meaning, though in other languages (e.g., Bengali, Hindi), adding a puff of air to /p/, for example, indicates a shift in meaning and is considered a separate phoneme. English consists of a set of 44 phonemes that are further categorized into vowels and consonants, the latter including voiced, voiceless, oral, nasal, and place and manner

English Spelling	IPA Notation
alter	/ɑltɚ/
church	/tʃɝtʃ/
remember	/rimɛmbɚ/
clinging	/klɪŋɪŋ/
opportunity	/ɑpɚtunɪti/

FIGURE 5–1 Five English Words Represented in Phonetic Notation (IPA)

of articulation. Phonemes are typically represented by a notational system, the International Phonetic Alphabet (IPA). Figure 5-1 shows phonemes associated with five common English words.

Morphology is the set of rules governing how phonemes can be combined into larger units (syllables and words) in order to convey meaning. Morphemes are the smallest grammatical units that carry meaning. Morphological rules govern the specific phonemic combinations that can be used by any given language to indicate, for example, past tense (e.g., "The three girls *swam* across the pond"), plural number (e.g., "The *dogs* were barking at the intruder"), pronoun differentiation (e.g., "*My* brother's sons gave *him* a puppy for *his* birthday"), or possession ("The truck *driver's* brakes failed, but he managed to get *his* rig stopped without incident").

Syntax is the set of rules governing how phrases and sentences must be constructed in order to convey meaning. For example, syntactic rules include those governing word order ("The dog ate the bone" and not "The bone the dog ate" or "The bone ate the dog") and those governing active or passive voice ("The chairperson counted the votes" [active], "The votes were counted by the chairperson" [passive]). Syntactic rules allow people to construct unique utterances in order to perform these common functions to greet, comment, seek attention, request information, acknowledge others, and respond to others; negate, refuse, reject, protest, indicate absence, and assert falsity; direct others to carry out instructions; tell stories; teach, describe, or explain things; bargain and negotiate; repair conversations; and persuade others.

Content of Language

Language content is usually discussed in terms of **semantics**, or the meaning(s) behind words, how humans map words to their experience of reality. In children, semantics is described through analysis of their oral vocabulary development (preschool and early elementary) and then their reading and written vocabulary. Learning the semantic aspects of language involves learning

- how words relate to their referents (the actual thing, idea, concept, feeling, event, or process a particular word stands for) and
- that the relationships between words and referents are **arbitrary** and **symbolic** (i.e., words are symbols that represent some thing, idea, concept, event, or process).

Children learn these two aspects of semantics gradually. Their earliest words are more **iconic**, with meaning closely tied to the word (e.g., "moo," "choo-choo," "bowwow").

Literal and Figurative Language. Language users employ language on different levels of abstraction, ranging from the literal and concrete to the abstract and figurative. At the literal level, language functions to convey the concrete, primary meaning of a word or phrase, as in "The man slept deeply." In the earliest stages of language development, children use concrete, literal language to get things done in a direct and efficient way.

At the figurative level, language conveys a more abstract and secondary meaning through expressing one thing but being understood as meaning something different, as in "The man was sawing logs all night." In the figurative meaning, the man slept deeply, even though the sentence says otherwise on the literal level. Children see that they can use language in a less direct way to alter how—and how efficiently—they can get things to happen. Table 5-1 lists examples of figurative language forms.

Many types of humor rely on figurative expressions or words or phrases with double meanings. Puns use double meanings to convey humor:

- "We saw an old beater," which could mean an eggbeater or a car.
- "When we took 12 rabbits and put 6 in one pen and 6 in another, we were splitting hares," which plays on the pronunciation of "hare" to evoke its homonym in the expression "splitting hairs."

Riddles also use double meanings as a way to express humor, as in the following:

- "Why didn't the skeleton cross the road? Because it didn't have the guts," which refers both to "courage" and "innards."

TABLE 5–1   Figurative language forms

- Polite forms (e.g., "Might you have a table for two next Wednesday at 7:00" or "Would you mind helping me with this puzzle?")
- Idioms (as in the "sawing logs" example above)
- Simile (e.g., "She sings like a bird" or "He's as fast as a cheetah")
- Metaphor (e.g., "This car is a racehorse")
- Satire (e.g., an essay, a story, a play, or a novel that ridicules or scorns human vices)
- Irony (e.g., the expression of something other than the literal meaning, as in "You look fantastic," meaning the opposite)
- Adage (a metaphorical saying embodying a common observation, e.g., "The early bird gets the worm")
- Proverb (a short maxim, e.g., "You can't teach an old dog new tricks")
- Allegory (fiction using symbolic characters and actions to express a truth regarding human existence, e.g., "Spiderman" or "Avatar"),
- Alliteration (e.g., "She sold seashells on the seashore")
- Personification (e.g., "The sun smiled down on us that day")

- "What is the smartest insect? A spelling bee," which refers to the insect and the spelling game.

To be able to understand and use figurative language, children must develop the ability to reflect on language, talk about it, and manipulate it. This is called **metalinguistic ability** and begins to emerge when children first grasp the idea that different people can have the same name. As children become more proficient with language, they learn how to use it to better get what they want (e.g., through using indirect language to request a wanted object or food, "I *need* to have this popsicle" vs. "Give me a popsicle!"). Gradually, most children discover that idioms say one thing but mean another, that polite forms are required in certain social situations, and that language parts can be rearranged. At higher levels of language development, people use metalinguistic abilities to understand and express ideas in graceful and artistic ways.

For schoolchildren, one of the most important aspects of metalinguistic ability is **phonological (and phonemic) awareness,** the understanding that speech consists of sounds and syllables. Phonological awareness is a basic prerequisite for learning to correlate speech sounds with printed letters in order to decode the written word and evolves out of the child's awareness that language has parts that can be talked about and analyzed.

How Children Acquire and Develop Language

Language is typically described as a stage-by-stage process as follows:

1. Early communication and emerging language—typically from just after birth through 12 months of age
2. Toddler language—between 12 and 24 months
3. Preschool language—between ages two and five
4. School-age language—ages five through the elementary school years
5. Adolescent/advanced language—through the adolescent years

We focus our attention below on stages 4 and 5.

School-Age Language. Typically developing children entering elementary school exhibit several language characteristics:

- They know most of the basic words in their native language and dialect.
- They know how to use almost all of the phonological sounds in their native language/dialect.
- Their syntactic skills are well enough developed that they use declarative sentences with ease (e.g., "My sister came to visit last week and brought her new puppy"), know how to ask questions of different sorts (e.g., "Do you want to play this game?") and form negatives (e.g., "I don't want to go outside right now"), and use imperatives (e.g., "Put that down!)." They may still have difficulty understanding complicated passive sentences (e.g., "The criminal was arrested by the police").
- They are able to use polite forms with relative ease, can make indirect requests ("More juice would be really good"), can take turns, and know when their conversational partners do not understand what they have said and provide relevant information to clarify.

Children from literate families arrive at school with several advantages over children from families that may be semi-literate in that they are more likely to know how stories and books work, how to talk about language, and how to demonstrate to adults, through specific conversational routines, what they know and have experienced. That is, they know how to demonstrate their knowledge in the ways in which teachers expect their students to show what they know. They are familiar with various "artifacts" associated with print (e.g., pencils, pens, computers, smartphones, paper, magazines, books, and e-readers), and they know that language is a powerful tool for producing results—for getting what they want in a given conversational exchange.

Perhaps the most important developmental shift to occur during this stage is what is called the oral-to-literate shift, which means the ability to communicate not only in the immediate context of the here and now but also across time and place, a process that includes reading, writing, and other more formal oral and electronic language genres. The children who are most successful in making this shift are those who have intact and well-developed oral language abilities in all areas (Paul & Norbury, 2012).

In the early school years, children continue to add new words to their vocabularies, but they also learn to refine how they use words, a large part of which is influenced by their developing ability to read. They learn how to

- choose among words for the most precise meaning to fit what they are trying to express,
- use the same words to mean different things (e.g., *sweet cookie*, *sweet girl*),
- distinguish among words with similar meanings (e.g., *knife*, *dagger*), and
- classify words into categories and hierarchical subcategories (e.g., animal>mammal>clawed>omnivore>bear).

It is during these early school years that children complete their elaboration of the English pronoun system (see Table 5-2).

In addition, children figure out that pronouns have antecedents that can appear in previous sentences or, more complicated, previous conversations. For example, children become able to decode sentences such as these: "Monica's mother told her to come home. She [Monica's mother] had something she [Monica's mother] wanted her [Monica] to do."

Syntactic development in this stage is both an expansion of forms that children have already acquired and the acquisition of some of the more difficult semantic forms. Examples are shown in Table 5-3.

When they enter school, most children have acquired most of the phonemes in the adult system.

TABLE 5–2   English pronouns

	Singular			Plural		
	1st	*2nd*	*3rd*	*1st*	*2nd*	*3rd*
Subjective						
Female	she	you			you	
Male	he	you			you	
Neutral	I*		it, one	we*		they
Possessive						
Female	her, hers	your, yours			your	
Male	his	your, yours			your	
Neutral	my, mine*		its, one's	our*		their, theirs
Objective						
Female	her	you			you	
Male	him	you			you	
Neutral	me*		it, one	us*		them
Reflexives						
Female	herself	yourself			yourselves	
Male	himself	yourself			yourselves	
Neutral	myself*		itself, oneself	themselves*		themselves

*Self-referring pronouns are assumed to carry the gender of the person using them.

TABLE 5–3   Adult syntactic forms children learn in the early school years

- Expand noun and verb phrases (e.g., putting adjectives in the correct order, as in *big black dog* and not *black big dog*).
- Use some (not all) passive sentences (e.g., *The bone was eaten by the dog* and not *The dog was eaten by the bone*).
- Use exceptions to the regularization rules for plural and tense markers (e.g., *ate, swam, drove, children, mice, deer, sheep*).
- Embed more complicated structures (e.g., *My friend has a song I know you'll think is crazy*).
- Conjoin sentences with conjunctions other than *and* and *but* (e.g., *You can have either this truck or that one; We can't go because it's raining*).

TABLE 5–4   Phonemes acquired last by most children

ʃ	as in *she*
θ	as in *thimble*
s	as in *see*
z	as in *zip*
ð	as in *there*
l	as in *lake*
r	as in *read*
ʒ	as in *measure*

However, some children are age eight or older before they finish acquiring all the phonemes, and some may exhibit inconsistency in their use throughout this stage of language development. Among the last phonemes children acquire are shown in Table 5-4.

Most children entering school are decent conversationalists, though they will continue to develop proficiency with conversational discourse throughout their years in elementary school and sometimes even beyond. They are much more adept at maintaining topics during a conversation, they can clarify something they have said that resulted in a conversational breakdown (called a *conversational repair*), and they are now using indirect requests (i.e., polite forms) to get what they want. Throughout their years in school, these conversational skills become increasingly important in peer interactions.

Moving from Oral to Literate Language. As mentioned earlier, one aspect of school-age language development has particular importance for school success: making the transition from being primarily oral to being increasingly literate, which requires proficiency with narrative, classroom, and expository discourses.

Types of Discourse. The **narrative** abilities of children vary with the circumstances in which they are telling a story, particularly who their listeners are, how much time they have to tell the story, and whether there are other people vying for a turn to talk. Their abilities will also reflect the culture(s) in which they have spent their years prior to entering school. Some cultural groups tell stories in a linear, chronological sequence (European American cultures), while others may tell stories in a series of tales with multiple events and episodes (African American cultures).

Before age seven, most typically developing English-speaking children tell stories that are somewhat incomplete, but beginning around age seven, children begin to be able to tell stories that have a plot driven by resolving some sort of problem or conflict. When this happens, children also begin using stylized beginnings and endings, such as *once upon a time* and *they lived happily ever after* (Owens, 2013).

By around age eight, the stories told by most typically developing, English-speaking children sound more like adult stories because they have a clear plot that is developed around a problem or conflict that is resolved by the end of the story. These stories include important details that are not irrelevant, such as when and where the story takes place, and their characters' feelings, thoughts, and motives are developed throughout the story (Hulit & Howard, 2011).

In addition, children across cultures introduce dialogue for the characters in their stories, and they develop an increasing ability to switch between their characters and the narrator as their story unfolds (Owens, 2013).

School success depends on children understanding how classroom discourse works. As noted earlier, with classroom discourse, the teacher chooses almost all the topics to be talked about; takes most of the turns; determines whether, when, and how long students talk; when students should relinquish turns; and whether their responses are correct or acceptable. Children making the shift from being primarily oral communicators to acquiring the skills necessary to develop proficiency as literate language users are expected to learn to understand and use various expository discourse styles.

The most prevalent types of **expository discourse** children encounter in the early school years are description and explanation. Both forms of discourse differ from conversational and narrative discourse in that they are more decontextualized. That is, rather than referring to shared experiences, events, or settings, they function to state facts or hypotheses, to ask questions and draw conclusions, and to interpret, classify, synthesize, and summarize. The format of expository discourse depends on the paragraph (oral at first, then written) with a topic sentence that states the main idea, the body of the paragraph elaborating on the main idea, and a summary sentence or sentences.

Later during the school years, children encounter a more abstract and complicated argumentative or persuasive discourse. Most school-age children develop some proficiency with the oral forms of argument or persuasion, which do not always contain all the components characteristic of this type of discourse. However, when they enter middle school, children begin learning about the formal characteristics of argumentative/persuasive discourse and are soon expected to be able to present written examples of successful arguments.

Figurative Language and the "Metas." During the school-age years, children's abilities to understand and use figurative language expand considerably. They become able to understand and use various forms of humor, including riddles, puns, and witticisms and metaphors, similes, idioms, proverbs, adages, and maxims. This expanding ability with figurative language is described as *metalinguistic*, *metapragmatic*, and *metacognitive*.

In this stage of language development, children develop substantial **metalinguistic ability**, especially as they meet the challenges of learning about defining words; identifying homonyms, synonyms, and antonyms; resolving semantic ambiguities (e.g., *Visiting relatives can be a nuisance*); identifying sounds in words and learning their corresponding letters in print; and identifying the various syntactic and morphological characteristics of both oral and printed language (Polloway et al., 2012).

One of the most critical metalinguistic abilities for children is phonological awareness, which has been identified as the best predictor for spelling ability in elementary school (Nation & Hulme, 1997) and as a predictor of reading skills (Hogan & Catts, 2004). **Phonological (or phonemic) awareness** is the ability to recognize individual phonemes in spoken language, that is, to identify the sounds, syllables, and sound structure of words (Owens, 2013). This also includes the ability to manipulate sounds either through segmenting words or syllables into their individual phonemes or through blending phonemes together to form syllables or words.

To make the correspondence between sounds and letters and decode words, children rely on this awareness to identify the sounds in the first place. Developmentally, most children leaving second grade decode well enough to comprehend what they are reading, and by the end of fourth grade, most will be able to decode fluently enough to use reading as a vehicle for learning. However, some children do not develop these abilities until they are older, which makes learning to read and write more difficult and requires skilled intervention from teachers knowledgeable about these processes (Polloway et al., 2012).

Children in this stage of development also acquire a more elaborate understanding and ability with the **meta-pragmatic** aspects of manipulating conversation, narrative, classroom, and expository discourse and become able to evaluate the specific requirements of each type of setting (i.e., conversation with a peer, demonstrating their knowledge to a teacher, disagreeing with a classmate) and how to manage the pragmatic aspects of each. The specific pragmatic aspects children learn include the following:

- identify who has more or less authority and how to change one's speaking and/or writing accordingly;
- the degree of formality required in this situation, either with a particular conversational partner or in the classroom (oral) or for a specific audience of readers (written);

- the role of cultural differences among participants in conversations or classroom discussions or among potential readers of something written;
- how to manage conversational breakdowns with peers or with teachers or other adults;
- how to interrupt appropriately; and
- how to manage other people's interruptions.

Children in the school-age years also develop **metacognitive ability**, which allows them to reflect on and manage their own thinking and learning processes. The two metacognitive processes that have been described most thoroughly are **comprehension monitoring** and **organizational and learning strategies** (Paul & Norbury, 2012). Comprehension monitoring involves recognizing when one does or does not understand something (such as a teacher's instruction or something the student is reading), an ability most children acquire between the ages of five and eight. After age eight, most children also begin to exhibit compensatory strategies, including recognizing they need help and asking for it, analyzing context for clues, reasoning through, and checking to see if there is additional information somewhere (e.g., chalkboard, book, computer).

A related development occurs when children begin to exhibit the ability to process new information through such means as analyzing what they already know or inferring from what they already know (Wallach, 2007). For example, the child may ask herself a question such as "What do I already know about this?" or "What do I need so I can understand this?" Or she may infer from what she already knows: "This is about whales. Whales are mammals. I know mammals are warm-blooded. Does that mean whales are warm-blooded, too?"

Adolescent/Advanced Language. By the time children have reached adolescence, most have become familiar with and able to engage in the language required for the intense social interactions they engage in with peers, for manipulating the literate language forms of academics, and for engaging in critical thinking through reading and writing (Paul & Norbury, 2012).

Vocabulary, Syntax, Conversation. Adolescents continue to add to their vocabularies, but they also further refine the meanings and usages of the words they already know, such as discovering how words are related through language family (i.e., Greek and Latin), derivation (e.g., poor, impoverish), meaning (e.g., antonyms, synonyms), and sound (e.g., homonyms). By late adolescence, most have learned how to define words using more sophisticated structures than they used in earlier stages of development. For example, where previously they might define a word using simple, one-word descriptions, now, during adolescence, they are able to provide definitions, such as "An edict is a proclamation" [superordinate term] "carrying the force of law" [description of characteristics].

Most syntactic growth during adolescence occurs across sentences rather than within sentences. Adolescents begin using more coordinate and subordinate clauses as well as sentence structures more typical of literate (i.e., printed) language, including low-frequency types that don't work well in oral language, such as passive constructions. Their sentences are usually longer and tailored for specific discourse types, and their sentences usually contain more morphosyntactic markers to mark interrogatives, negatives, and verb tenses than do those of younger children (Polloway et al., 2012).

Most adolescents can be skilled conversationalists, especially with peers. They understand that different listeners require different amounts and types of background information, and they know how to efficiently and effectively repair conversational breakdowns and how to request and provide clarification when needed. They maintain topics appropriately; take, maintain, and yield turns; and interrupt according to the politeness rules of their culture. Owens (2008) reported that when conversing with peers, teens in the United States use specific strategies to make sure their listeners know what they are talking about, give both verbal and nonverbal positive feedback, and respond directly to what their conversational partners have just said.

Discourse. By adolescence, most students will have mastered the art of negotiating classroom discourse regardless of individual variations in teachers and teaching styles. They will have read and written numerous narrative pieces, giving them additional experience and practice with narrative discourse, and they will have been exposed to a wider variety of expository discourse. Nonetheless, during adolescence, they continue to develop their skill within discourse types, and they begin developing proficiency with an argumentative/persuasive discourse.

As described above, argumentative/persuasive discourse differs from the other discourse types in that it puts forward a fact or proposition as a thesis, then uses a set of logically ordered statements to support the thesis. Although argumentative and persuasive discourse use the same formal structure, they differ slightly in their basis. Argumentative discourse expresses a statement or proposition, along with a set of supports for the proposition. A typical example of argumentative discourse is an essay in which the speaker or writer proposes an idea (the proposition) and provides several supporting statements for the idea (the arguments) and a summary iteration of why the arguments support the proposition.

Persuasive discourse offers a statement of belief, along with a set of reasons describing how the belief is "true." Advertisements commonly use persuasive discourse in an attempt to convince the listener or reader of the validity, superiority, or truthfulness of a particular product. Both argumentative and persuasive discourse can express disagreement with facts, beliefs, or interpretation of events.

Argumentative (or persuasive) discourse is the most abstract and decontextualized discourse students experience and, with appropriate instruction, learn to understand and use. The nested organizational scheme of this type of discourse presents another level of difficulty for students, especially those with language/learning disorders (Polloway et al., 2012). However, typically developing children usually acquire some facility with this discourse type by the end of secondary school.

Figurative Language. One of the most striking developments in adolescents' language is their increased ease with figurative language. One of the most obvious examples is slang, which changes generationally and is influenced by movies, television, music groups, music videos, and the various forms of electronic communications used by adolescents. Because conversation with peers is vitally important, a proficiency with slang is a prerequisite for belonging to a peer group. Just as important is that adolescents must master the abbreviations and emoji used in virtually every text message.

Reading is one of the primary ways adolescents acquire experience with various types of figurative language. If they attend schools in which writing is stressed, they may also have experienced opportunities to practice using these figurative forms in

TABLE 5–5 Types and examples of figurative language

Metaphor: "He's *a machine*," meaning rugged, strong, invulnerable.
Simile "She's *like a computer* in math," meaning highly skilled.
Allegory: Extended narratives (poems, parables) conveying hidden meaning.
Irony: Expressing meaning that usually means the opposite, such as "He's so *bad*," meaning good, cute, smart, or funny.
Idiom: "It's raining *cats and dogs*," meaning it's raining hard.
Satire: Using language to make fun to improve behavior, policy, or procedure.

their own writing. Table 5-5 shows some of the more common types of figurative language and examples for each.

By adolescence, much of the school process rests solidly on the metas described earlier. Adolescents must use their metalinguistic abilities to analyze, manipulate, and synthesize both oral and printed language. Writing is particularly demanding because it requires students to focus or reflect on and manipulate language forms, content, and usages. Students with more experience in writing tend to develop more skill with the metalinguistic processes necessary to succeed in the secondary curriculum, particularly note taking, paraphrasing, summarizing, recognizing and using figurative language forms, and understanding and using diverse literate styles in their own oral and written language.

An advantage gained from developing skill with figurative language is that, at the same time, these students are developing strong metapragmatic abilities. For example, deciding ahead of time what to say (either orally or in print), how to say it, and the discourse type to use and using humor appropriately in discourse all demand metapragmatic proficiency.

The secondary curriculum requires students to be able to reflect on their understanding of what's happening in the classroom and how they can most effectively and efficiently learn what is expected of them (i.e., metacognitive ability). They are expected to devise learning strategies that work best for them and to modify them when they encounter new, more demanding learning tasks. To do this, they use their metacognitive skills to, first, analyze what they know, what they're expected to learn and how, and how best to accomplish that learning and, second, to apply the results of their analysis. The development of strong metacognitive

skills allows adolescents to become less dependent on specific support from teachers and more independent in figuring out their own unique learning strengths and needs and how to use those strengths in order to meet their learning needs.

The secondary curriculum carries special metalinguistic, metapragmatic, and metacognitive demands. Students must negotiate multiple teaching styles and communication rules, a wide assortment of decontextualized language forms, increasing amounts of work requiring increased length of time focusing (including increased demand that students be self-organizing), working independently, and using logical and critical thinking (Paul & Norbury, 2012).

 Check Your Understanding 5.2 Click here to gauge your understanding of the concepts in this section.

LANGUAGE DISORDERS

The National Institute on Deafness and Other Communication Disorders (2015) reported that between 6 million and 8 million people in the United States have some form of language impairment, which exists whenever a person has difficulty understanding and/or using any of the aspects of language—content (semantics/vocabulary), form (phonology, morphology, syntax), or use (pragmatics)—be that spoken, written, or both. Specific language impairment (SLI) can occur after a period of normal development. SLI has been reported by Ziegler et al. (2005) to affect 7% of all schoolchildren.

Some language disorders may be the result of infection, tumor, stroke, epilepsy, brain injury, hearing loss, chromosomal anomalies, or motor functioning disorders. Frequently, however, the cause is unknown.

Language Difference versus Disorder

The U.S. Census Bureau (2013) reported that more than 55 million people—20% of the population over age five—speak a language other than English at home. It is estimated that by 2025, one in four students in schools will be an English Language Learner (ELL). Therefore, it is imperative that teachers not confuse language disorders with language differences arising from differences in dialect, culture, ethnicity, or influence of a foreign language. Children from culturally and linguistically diverse (CLD) backgrounds can exhibit characteristics that, without careful analysis, may be confused with a language disorder.

The primary factor that differentiates a language disorder from a language difference is that the way children from CLD circumstances learn language (both primary and secondary languages) is significantly different from the way children with language disorders learn language. Although children with language disorders often have difficulty acquiring new language content, forms, or usages, children from CLD families usually show no such difficulty when given appropriate instruction, a topic addressed below in the assessment and teaching sections.

Even within one culture, the way children develop language is not consistent, nor is the way families regard verbal communication consistent across different cultures. In some middle-class American families, children learn language through the use of what is called *parentese*, a drawn-out, exaggerated way of speaking that highlights particular sounds, phrases, or words, and/or by one or more parent acting as a language coach for their child, pointing out particular sounds, words, or sentences and relating their meaning. In contrast, in many other cultures, children learn language primarily through observing the adults around them and, as they grow older, through socializing with peers. Language development looks different from culture to culture.

Determining whether a child has a language disorder or is simply a "late bloomer" can be difficult, particularly in young children. The American Speech-Language-Hearing Association (2015d) reports four factors that differentiate slow language development from a true language disorder, shown in Table 5-6.

Compared with their peers, the language abilities of children from CLD backgrounds can be mistakenly thought to represent language disorders. Some children learning a second language learn the two languages at the same time from birth and are called simultaneous bilinguals; others, who learn one language first (L1, their primary language) and another one second (L2), are called sequential bilinguals. Whereas children who learn two languages from birth (simultaneous bilinguals)

TABLE 5–6 Factors that differentiate slow development from disorder

- Age-appropriate receptive language abilities are typical of late bloomers, while the receptive language abilities of children who have language disorders are usually significantly delayed.
- Children who use a large number of gestures associated with different communicative intentions are more likely to catch up to their peers in language development (i.e., they are likely to be late bloomers).
- The older the child is who is still behind his or her peers in language development, the more likely that child will have a language disorder and will not catch up, especially if he or she exhibits slow growth when peers are in a period of rapid progress.
- Children showing little progress in language development are more likely to develop language disorders than slow talkers who continue to make noticeable changes in their language.

often enter school with abilities in both languages equal to those of their peers, when children who are sequential bilinguals enter school, their abilities in the second language are often less developed than those of their peers and may be mistaken for a disorder.

Children learning a second language (L2) often learn enough to be able to converse informally with peers and adults. However, their L2 abilities may not yet have developed sufficiently for them to be able to engage easily in the formal academic language required for success as they proceed through the elementary school years (Roseberry-McKibbin, 2014). As a consequence, these children may have a difficult time reaching the common core standards for their grade.

 ENHANCEDetext
video example 5.2
Watch this video to learn more about the stages involved in learning a language.

An important consideration in differentiating between a disorder and a difference is that children with a true language disorder will experience difficulties in both languages. That is, the characteristics of the language disorder will appear in both their first (native) language (L1) and their second language (L2); their primary language abilities will display markers characteristic of a language disorder. On the other hand, if there are no concerns regarding a child's first language acquisition, any delays or deviations from normal use in the second language should not be attributed to a language disorder. Instead, such delays or deviations should be considered a language difference. Later sections on assessing and teaching spoken language will describe some methods to distinguish between language difference and language disorders and instructional techniques that work well with CLD children.

Language-Based Learning Disabilities

Polloway et al. (2012) reported that language-based learning disabilities (LLD) are the most common type of learning disability, primarily because most learning disabilities involve deficits in reading, writing, or spelling, which are based on oral language abilities. LLD include difficulties with any or all of the child's phonological, semantic, syntax, pragmatic, and discourse systems.

School-age children diagnosed with LLD often have a history of delayed speech and language development during preschool. The American Speech-Language-Hearing Association (2015c) described the risk factors associated with LLD as well as some of the problems typically exhibited by children with LLD as follows:

- learning the alphabet,
- retrieving specific words,
- learning new vocabulary,
- understanding questions and directions,
- recalling spoken or printed letters and numbers,
- understanding and recalling stories or classroom lectures,
- learning sound–letter correspondences,
- mixing up letters in words when writing, and
- spelling.

 Check Your Understanding 5.3 Click here to gauge your understanding of the concepts in this section.

ASSESSING LANGUAGE

In young children, the primary goal of language assessment is to determine their level of development in order to assist them in moving to the next developmental level. However, for school-age children, the primary goal of assessing language skills is driven primarily by the purpose and goals for instruction and, if need be, intervention. The overall goal of assessing language skills is to ascertain the student's needs in order to design appropriate teaching strategies, classroom modifications, and accommodations to help the student succeed. More specifically, assessing a student's language abilities is done to determine whether they are developed well enough for the student to make the shift from orality to literacy, which is required to succeed in school. For elementary students, language assessment focuses on discovering how (and how well) they use language to participate successfully in the classroom; talk about language and its parts; understand and tell stories; learn to read, write, and spell; and comprehend the various types of expository text.

For adolescents, language assessment is aimed at discovering how adept they are with the social discourse used by their peers; how they interact with literate language forms, including the various discourse genres characteristic of the secondary grades; and the extent of their metalinguistic, metacognitive, and metapragmatic abilities and how successful they are in exercising them appropriately for learning.

Types of Assessment

Two types of assessment are typically used to evaluate students' language: standardized and non-standardized. Standardized assessments compare students' language development with other children of the same chronological age. Table 5-7 shows some of the more commonly used standardized instruments used for assessing language.

Standardized tests are designed to be administered and scored the same way each time, usually in a quiet room with no one present except the student and the examiner. As a result, they do not reflect a student's ability to use language in contexts other than the testing situation. In addition, they tend to underestimate the language abilities of children for whom English is not their native language.

Non-standardized assessment procedures include criterion-referenced procedures, curriculum-based language assessment, developmental scales, interviews, questionnaires, observational checklists, language sampling, and dynamic assessment.

Criterion-referenced procedures assess the child's ability to attain a certain level of performance. They are used to establish what the child knows about a specific language function, form, or content and

TABLE 5–7 Common standardized language assessment instruments

Clinical Evaluation of Language Fundamentals—Fifth Edition (Wiig & Secord, 2014)

Comprehensive Receptive and Expressive Vocabulary Test—Third Edition (Wallace & Hammill, 2013)

Expressive One-Word Picture Vocabulary Test—Fourth Edition (Martin & Brownell, 2011)

Oral-Written Language Scale—Second Edition (Carrow-Woolfolk, 2011)

Pragmatic Language Skills Inventory (Gilliam & Miller, 2006)

Receptive One-Word Picture Vocabulary Test—Fourth Edition (Martin & Brownell, 2010)

Structured Photographic Expressive Language Test—Third Edition (Dawson & Stoute, 2013)

Test for Examining Expressive Morphology (Shipley, Stone, & Sue, 1983)

Test of Adolescent and Adult Language—Third Edition (Hammill, Brown, Larsen, & Wiederholt, 2007)

Test of Adolescent/Adult Word Finding—Second Edition (German, 2014)

Test of Language Development—Intermediate—Third Edition (Newcomer & Hammill, 1997)

Test of Language Development—Primary—Fourth Edition (Newcomer & Hammill, 2008)

Test of Pragmatic Language—Second Edition (Phelps-Terasaki & Phelps-Gunn, 2007)

Test of Preschool Vocabulary—Second Edition (Mathews & Miller, 2014)

Test of Word Finding—Third Edition (German, 2014)

The WORD Test 2: Adolescent (Bowers, Huisingh, LoGuidi, & Orman, 2005)

to design instructional targets based on the results. Criterion-referenced approaches are usually used with school-age children and adolescents.

Curriculum-based language assessment is the process of evaluating the student's use of language as he or she interacts with the curriculum in the classroom. One of the easiest ways to assess these abilities is to develop a checklist similar to the one designed by Allison (2015) that lists the core curriculum language skills associated with the student's grade and then to observe whether the student demonstrates the ability to use each skill.

Developmental scales are used more often with children in the emerging and developing stages of language development. These scales provide developmental milestones against which the child is compared in order to determine where along the scale a particular aspect of language development lies. Interviews, observational checklists,

and questionnaires are used to collect information about a child's use of language in specific situations. Evaluators use interviews, observational checklists, and/or questionnaires with parents, caregivers, teachers, and students of all ages.

Language sampling aims to discover detailed information about the child's use of the structural aspects of language (i.e., syntactic and morphological forms). Examples include the number of morphemes per sentence, number and type of embedded clauses, number and type of conjunction, complex sentence usage, proportion of simple to complex sentences, type of complex sentences used, and number of disruptions.

Dynamic assessment is a method used to observe how a child changes a language behavior when given structured help. First, the evaluator determines what the child knows about a specific language behavior (e.g., including setting in a story). Then, in a series of sessions (i.e., mediated teaching), the evaluator provides information and supports the child uses to begin incorporating the language behavior (see American Speech-Language-Hearing Association, 2015b).

Assessing Students from CLD Backgrounds

Students from CLD backgrounds sometimes exhibit language characteristics similar to those shown by students with language disorders. Because these characteristics sometimes represent an actual language disorder or delay, an assessment may be recommended.

Peña and Bedore (2008) reported that identifying language disorders in bilingual children and designing appropriate language instruction is challenging for two reasons. First, the tests available for assessing children's language do not accurately discriminate between bilingual children with and without a language impairment. Second, although there are many models for planning language intervention and instruction for CLD children, there is little evidence-based research that describes what actually works. Further, determining the most effective language of instruction for bilingual children is fraught with political and cultural differences of viewpoint and power.

A comprehensive model for assessing CLD students was developed by Damico, Smith, and Augustine. (1996). Their approach is based on these principles:

- Build a collaborative team that includes the student and parents. Team members combine knowledge of language, assessments, and the student's culture, strengths, and needs in the classroom and knowledge of bilingualism.

- Before referring the student for special education testing, use the team to design modifications that support his or her particular needs. Assess how the student is doing after the modifications have been in place for long enough to see any differences.
- Design assessment around the student's particular cultural characteristics, determining which of the student's difficulties that may be attributable to cultural background will guide the choice of assessment instruments and procedures used. Assess both conversational abilities and formal academic language abilities.
- Give greater emphasis on how well the student functions than on test scores through the use of specifically designed rating scales, protocols, or checklists; role-playing; and/or interactive computer probes.
- The team uses all the collected data to determine the student's linguistic and academic competence.

Peña, Summers, and Resendiz (2007) advocated using a greater number of informal measures than standardized tests in assessing the needs of CLD children, primarily because most standardized instruments have been designed for and normed using children for whom English is the primary language. Table 5-8 (adapted from Peña et al., 2007) shows some of their procedures that lead to designing appropriate instruction.

Table 5-9 illustrates the process used to assess the language abilities of a young African American girl and to use mediated instruction for discovering the student's responsivity to learning how to include character descriptions in stories.

ENHANCEDetext
video example 5.3
Watch this video to learn more about the challenges associated with learning a second language.

Assessing Students Who Need Alternative and Augmentative Communication Systems

Students with certain disabilities often need to use augmentative or alternate communication (AAC) systems in order to communicate. AAC refers to methods people use to communicate when speech may be difficult. The most common of these methods involve facial expressions, gestures, and writing. AAC "includes all forms of communication (other than oral speech) that are used to express thoughts, needs, wants, and ideas" (American Speech-Language-Hearing Association, 2015d, para. 1).

AAC systems, both unaided and aided, are used by people with significant speech and/or language problems to either supplement or replace nonfunctional speech. Unaided communication systems are those that utilize the speaker's body to communicate by using gestures, body language, facial expressions, and/or sign language. Aided communication systems require tools or equipment and may include paper and pencil; codes; communication boards or books; communication charts; speech-generating devices, such as computers or voice generators; smartphones with AAC apps; and/or written output.

Communication aids and electronic devices can include representations of objects, events, and people using pictures, photographs, drawings, letters, words, sentences, special symbols, or any combination. Assessment for students using AAC systems or devices should focus on whether the student would benefit from a low-tech device, such as pointing with a head stick or laser light, or from a high-tech device, such as a computer that produces synthesized speech. In addition, assessment should include attention to the suitability of the symbol system used (iconic symbols are easier for younger children, while more abstract symbols may work for older students); whether the system or device is easy for the child, family, and teachers to use; the social effectiveness of the system; and its suitability for promoting language development (Polloway et al., 2012).

Polloway et al. (2012) recommended that adolescents using an AAC system or device receive an assessment addressing several issues, including determining whether the current AAC system/device

- is adequate for the communication demands of the curriculum,
- is equal to the student's cognitive abilities,
- can expand to meet students' developing communication and cognitive growth,
- is appropriate for non-academic communication needs, and
- can be maintained independently by the student in vocational, recreational, domestic, and academic settings and, if not, how will maintenance be provided.

TABLE 5-8 Questions to guide assessment of CLD children

1. "Which language or dialect should be used to assess and ultimately intervene with the student?"
   - Ask parents and teachers to record, hour by hour, the language(s) the child uses and hears.
   - Which language(s) is used by the child's primary conversational partners?
   - What is the percentage of time the child is exposed to each language?
   - What is the percentage of time each language is used at home?
   - What is the percentage of time each language is used at school?
   - Determine which language is the child's stronger language.

2. How can the child's language performance needs at home and in the classroom be determined—a checklist for parents and teachers.
   - Do you and others understand the child when he or she speaks English a second language (e.g., Spanish)?
   - Is the child able to follow directions at home in his or her first language?
   - Where do you see the child communicate and perform the best?
   - Which contexts are hardest for the child? What language is used in these contexts?
   - What strategies help the child succeed in communicating? Do they result in the child's communication improving?
   - Which language suffers the most communicative breakdowns?

3. Is it appropriate to translate tests from English to second language (e.g., Spanish) to assess the child?
   - Translating tests can render individual items more or less difficult in the second language, thus invalidating the normative process.
   - What is considered an impairment in one language may not be in the second, so the test may not target appropriate language targets.

4. If the child speaks a dialect:
   - Is the child familiar with taking tests? If not, standardized testing may result in artificially lowered scores.
   - Use a standardized test that has been designed for the child's dialect. Options for children who speak dialects or are Spanish-English bilingual:
     - *Diagnostic Evaluation of Language Variance*—designed for children who speak African American English (Seymour, Roper, & de Villiers, 2003).
     - *Expressive One-Word Picture Vocabulary Test—Fourth Edition* (Gardner & Brownell, 2011).
     - *Preschool Language Scales—Fourth Edition, Spanish* (Zimmerman, Steiner, & Pond, 2002).
     - *Test of Narrative Language*—bias analysis shows limited item bias for targeted groups of English-speaking children (Gillam & Pearson, 2004).
     - Use informal assessments such as dynamic assessment or providing contextual support during the testing.

5. What other measures can help determine if there is an impairment?
   - Non-word repetition tasks differentiate between children with and without language impairment. Non-word repetition tasks are included in:
   - *Diagnostic Evaluation of Language Variance* (Seymour et al., 2003).
   - *Comprehensive Test of Phonological Processing—Second Edition* (Wagner, Torgeson, Rashotte, & Pearson, 2013).
   - Language sampling can be done in conversation, dialogue, and answering questions in varying contexts, including on the playground, in the lunchroom, and before/after school. Children with language impairments show shorter, less complex utterances; fewer vocabulary words; simpler syntactic structures; and less pragmatic complexity and success.
   - Analysis of the child's narrative abilities. The stories of children with language impairments are less developed and shorter, use less sophisticated language and truncated episode structure, and usually fail to take the listener's perspective into account.
   - Analysis of the child's ability to learn new skills when instruction includes dynamic assessment. Children with language impairments typically have significant problems understanding and generalizing the strategies they learned during the mediated teaching sessions and are less responsive during the teaching sessions (i.e., they exhibit problems attending to the task, lack persistence and motivation, have difficulties with solving problems, and are relatively inflexible).

TABLE 5–9 Assessment and mediated instruction: Child speaking African American English

Amarisa is an eight-year-old African American second grader. Her teacher has been concerned about her ability to understand classroom instructions and answer questions. She also indicated that she uses African American English (AAE) dialect, and she wanted to make certain her language development was progressing appropriately. The clinician recommended the following assessment procedures:

1. Administer the Comprehension Subtest of *Stanford-Binet Test of Intelligence Scale—Fourth Edition* (Thorndike, Hagen, & Sattler, 1986).
2. Observe her in the classroom and interview a family member to determine how well she communicates in the classroom and outside it.
3. Analyze a language sample to determine whether she produces complex sentences and uses various conjunctions, articles, and modal auxiliaries.
4. Administer the *Diagnostic Evaluation of Language Variation Screening Test* (a non-word repetition task).

	Results of Assessment Procedures	
Test/Procedure	**Score/Result**	**Significance**
Comprehension Subtest of the *Stanford-Binet Test of Intelligence Scale*	Standard score = 99	Mean score = 50
Diagnostic Evaluation of Language Variation Screening Test	**Language Variation Status** Strong variation from mainstream American English	No further testing
	Diagnostic Risk Status Developing language normally. Amarisa converses easily with family and friends and interacts easily with peers outside the classroom. Her mother reports that she is shy about talking in the classroom.	
Language sample	Use of AAE indicates that her language development is typical for children her age speaking AAE.	

Given these results, the team designed the below mediated instructional lesson to see how she responded to this type of instruction. Because she enjoys books and stories, the lesson centers on including appropriate episode structures.

Objective: Teach Amarisa (A) stories should contain information about characters.

Teaching Sequence:

1. Show A *The Ugly Duckling* and have her retell the story. Remind her before she begins to describe the characters.
2. Tell A what you're going to do in this lesson and why it is important.
3. Using the story, help A describe the main characters.
4. If A describes the characters without much help from you, help her extend the concept to another story. If she has difficulty, help her evaluate why it is important to describe the characters in a story.
5. Help A plan how to describe the characters when she tells another story.
6. Help A respond to the questions throughout. Use prompts, cues, and models as needed to support her.
7. Help A figure out how she can remember to describe the characters next time she tells a story.

Strategy	Examples of Instruction	What You Did to Support Amarisa	How Amarisa Responded
What you're going to do.	"Today we're going to talk about telling stories. When we tell stories, we usually describe the characters."	Pointed to each character as I talked.	Looked carefully at the characters.
Why that's important.	"Telling about the characters is important because it tells your listener who they are and what they are like."	Asked Amarisa how she would describe who she is and what she's like.	"I'm tall and my eyes are brown. I'm like an ice cream cone."
Help Amarisa describe the main characters.	"Let's look at *The Ugly Duckling* again. Let's see if we can describe the mother duck, the duckling, and the old woman." Help Amarisa describe who they are and what they look like. "What does the mother duck look like?" "What does the baby duck look like?" "What can you tell me about the baby duck?" Help Amarisa use descriptive words and phrases.	Asked Amarisa what made the mother duck look different from the others. Ditto re: the baby.	"She pretty! She green and shiny. . . . The baby bigger than the others, and kinda brown. He feel bad because the others tease him."

(continued)

TABLE 5–9   *(continued)*

Strategy	Examples of Instruction	What You Did to Support Amarisa	How Amarisa Responded
Help Amarisa extend the concept to another story.	"How would you change the story if there were a dog and a cat instead of ducks and a swan? What would you say about the dog and the cat?" "Would the dog and cat do the same things as the duck and the swan?" "Have you ever read or heard another story that described things about the characters?" If not, present a familiar story and help her discover the character information.		"I'd say the dog was big and fluffy and the cat was orange and round."
Help Amarisa plan.	"The next time you tell a story, what are you going to remember to put in it?"		"What the characters look like and feel."
Help Amarisa generalize her learning.	"We've been talking about describing the characters in your stories. How are you going to remember to describe characters when you make up your own stories?"		"How the baby duck look when he see his self in the water! He beautiful!"

 Check Your Understanding 5.4 Click here to gauge your understanding of the concepts in this section.

TEACHING SPOKEN LANGUAGE

One of the most effective ways to teach spoken language is within the context of academic learning standards. Individualized education programs (IEPs) should be linked with their state learning standards so that their IEP goals, objectives, and benchmarks reflect the learning standards deemed most appropriate for them by the school team. The linking process involves identifying the state standards applicable to the student's age or grade level and then generating goals geared to help the student achieve the applicable standards.

Every state publishes a list of standards (in many states, the common core standards) to specify what are the critical aspects of learning for students to achieve. The academic standards most likely to be addressed on IEPs for students with language disorders include communication, listening, receptive and expressive language, speaking, reading, writing, and spelling. Often these categories are subsumed into English Language Arts Standards (see, e.g., the Common Core State Standards Initiative, 2010). Table 5-10 shows an example using Indiana's Speaking and Listening Standards subset of the English Language Academic Arts standards for grade 3.

Literate Language Forms

Children entering elementary school face formidable challenges if they have language disorders, particularly when they are expected to make the transition from the world of oral language into the literate world of print. These children have particular difficulties when the curriculum shifts from teaching them to read to using reading as a way to learn. Perhaps the most important aspect of language instruction for elementary-age children with language disorders is literate language forms (i.e., narrative, classroom, and expository discourse) and metalinguistic, metapragmatic, and metacognitive abilities. The discussion below focuses on skill development for both oral and written expression.

Teaching Discourse Types. One of the most powerful approaches to teaching discourse types to students with language difficulties is dynamic assessment/mediated teaching. In this approach, assessment is an integral part of the teaching process (Miller, Gillam, & Peña, 2001). The approach begins with asking the student to look through a wordless picture book and then tell the story the pictures tell. (Although the description here describes using the approach with one student, it can be used in a group setting, and students can analyze each other's stories.)

Using the story features shown in Figure 5-2, the teacher than analyzes the student's retelling of the story as a baseline measure for comparison with a second story the child tells following two mediated teaching sessions.

TABLE 5–10   Designing instruction for grade 3 student based on Indiana's Common Core Standards for Language Arts

One of the standards focuses on the student's ability to engage in collaborative conversation with peers about grade-appropriate topics and texts. One of the abilities is for the student to be able to determine the purpose of listening through either describing or paraphrasing key ideas or specific details from a text read aloud, information presented orally, or information presented through other media.

Step 1: Standard becomes the annual goal for the student: *To determine the purpose for listening through describing or paraphrasing key ideas or specific details from a text read aloud, information presented orally, and information presented through other media.*

Objective 1: To determine purpose for listening through describing or paraphrasing key ideas or specific details from text read aloud.

Objective 2: To determine purpose for listening through describing or paraphrasing key ideas or specific details from information presented orally.

Objective 3: To determine purpose for listening through describing or paraphrasing key ideas or specific details from information presented through other media.

Step 2:   Whether or not the student is receiving special education services, use the IEP format to describe the following:

* present levels of performance, the student's learning strengths, and how the student's disability affects his progress in the general curriculum;
* which people and/or programs are going to be involved in assisting this student meet these objectives (including personnel, frequency, location, and duration of services); and
* goals and objectives (from step 1), including how they will be evaluated and by what objective criteria, and expected date of accomplishment.

Step 3:   Develop specific instructional strategies for the following:

1. *Have student listen to a recording of short descriptive text that she can follow by reading. Ask her to:*
   * *describe the main idea of the text.*
   * *describe three important details from the text.*
   * *state a conclusion from the textual description.*
   * *summarize the text by first stating the main idea, then listing three important ideas/details, then stating a conclusion.*
2. *Follow the same step-by-step procedure using a recording of a different short text but without support of her being able to follow by reading along.*
3. *Follow the same procedure using other media (e.g., video).*

---

* Story components
  ○ Setting: time and place
  ○ Character information
  ○ Temporal order of events
  ○ Causal relationships
* Story ideas and language
  ○ Complexity of ideas
  ○ Complexity of vocabulary
  ○ Grammatical complexity
  ○ Knowledge of dialogue
  ○ Creativity

FIGURE 5–2   Story Features Used in Dynamic Assessment/Mediated Teaching

After the first story has been analyzed, the teacher conducts two teaching sessions utilizing this set of mediation strategies to support the student's learning about stories:

1. Intention to teach: explain what the goal is for the session.

2. Meaning—explain why the goal is important in telling good stories.
3. Example—show specific examples of targeted story structure or element.
4. Planning—help the student think about what new skill(s) he or she has learned and how he or she will use it the next time he or she tells a story.
5. Transfer—summarize the session to help the student think about using his or her new narration skill in related situations (story time, show-and-tell).
6. Hypothesizing—by asking a series of "what if" questions, help the student develop metacognitive awareness of alternative strategies or responses in telling the story.
7. Self-evaluation—help the student become aware of his or her own learning.

The sessions are designed to be fluid and dynamic rather than static, and the idea is to provide the student with support, explanation, examples, and opportunities to try things out while focusing on what it is that makes a story good, that is, worth listening to.

Following the sessions, the teacher has the student tell a second story, using a different wordless picture book, which they together analyze using the same criteria used to analyze the first story. By comparing the student's performance on each aspect of narration, the teacher and student can determine which areas need to be targeted for instruction and which are likely to develop on their own given adequate opportunities to interact with stories.

Polloway et al. (2012) described an approach for teaching narrative discourse to use with students whose language skills are developed well enough that they can use worksheets as a guide (see Figure 5-3). Students can use the worksheets as they analyze a story heard or read to determine its ideas and language, components, and episode structure.

Adolescents are expected to understand and manipulate more complex aspects of stories, which include

- understanding what motivates characters,
- identifying how characters feel and plan in response to the main problem or conflict,
- drawing inferences based on what the author presents in the story,
- summarizing episodes and the story as a whole, and
- providing listeners (or readers) with enough cohesive markers (e.g., pronouns, conjunctions, ellipses, definite articles) that they know how things in the story hang together (Scott, 2012).

In the secondary grades, students encounter a variety of forms of narrative discourse, each of which, while obviously exhibiting the primary aspects of narrative discourse, exhibits a unique set of characteristics. Some of the most common are novel, comic book, folktale, myth, tall tale, personal essay, autobiographical narrative, oral history, and creative nonfiction.

Table 5-11 shows a set of questions to guide students' learning about the more abstract aspects of narrative discourse; the questions can be modified for students to use in writing their own narratives.

For students who struggle with narrative, comic books and graphic novels offer two advantages:

TABLE 5–11 Questions to guide students' narrative discourse learning

- Who is communicating with the reader in the story?
- Which voice did the author use to communicate: a character's voice, the author's "own" voice, or a relatively "objective" voice?
- From what position or angle regarding the story did he or she tell it? Where was the "camera" (above, periphery, center, front, or shifting)?
- What channels of information did the narrator use to convey the story to the reader (author's words, thoughts, perceptions, and feelings; character's words and actions; or character's thoughts, perceptions, and feelings)?
- How much of the story was "telling" (describing action) and how much "showing" (i.e., having the characters engage in a scenario that "shows" an idea)?

they exhibit a less complex narrative structure than novels, and they use visual images to convey a significant portion of the meaning. Specifically, the visual images convey setting and character information that, because it is present visually, does not need to be described linguistically.

Using comic books is a good way to introduce students to the idea that printed forms of narration encompass various components. You can target setting, character information, temporal order, and causal relationships. Students can identify and orally describe the settings, which are usually provided visually in the comic. Next, students can write their descriptions of the setting as a way of practicing the inclusion of setting in their written narratives. They can experiment with different ways to describe the same setting.

The same approach can be used to help students learn to include information about the characters. At first, the students can identify and orally describe the specific characteristics of each character, focusing on aspects such as clothing, physical features, and body type. Then students can develop descriptions of the characters, again experimenting with the effects produced by using different adjectives or shifting focus from describing physical appearance to state of mind or mood and the language required to successfully describe these character attributes.

The comics can be cut into individual panels so that students can see how temporal order works, and, by rearranging the panels, students can play with how meaning is altered when temporal

Story Components

This story takes place _____ and _____.
                              (where)   **(when)**

The main character: _____.
                    (describe what s/he did, looked like, said, thought, felt)

Events in this story happened in this order: _____.
                                      (first, next, then, and then, last)

Events in this story happened because: _____.
                              (describe why things happened as they did)

Story Ideas and Language

The literal events that occurred in this story were: _____.

Some things that happened that weren't described in words were: _____.

Some things this story could mean that weren't described in words were: _____.

Some words that were used that mean more than one thing were: _____.

Some examples of figurative words used in this story are: _____.
                                              (simile, metaphor, irony, satire)

Some examples of grammatically complex sentences used in this story are: _____.
                                              (compound, complex, compound/complex)

An example of dialect I particularly liked and why: _____.

Here's what made this story interesting: _____.

Episode Structure

Here's what happened to start the story: _____.
                                              (the problem or conflict)

Here's what the main character(s) did in response to the problem or conflict: _.

Here's how the main character(s) felt about the problem: _____.

Here's what the main character(s) intended to do about the problem or conflict: _.

Here's how the problem was solved: _____.

Here's how the main character(s) reacted to the solution: _____.

If there was another episode in this story, what happened to start it? _____.

How did the main character(s) in this episode react to the problem or conflict? _.

How did the main character(s) feel about this problem or conflict? _____.

How was this problem or conflict resolved? _____.

If there was more than one episode, how were the episodes related to each other? _.

How did the overall story end? _____.

How did the main character(s) feel about how the overall problem was resolved? _.

Source: Polloway, E.A., Miller, L., & Smith, T.E.C. (2012). *Language instruction for students with disabilities* (4e). Denver: Love Publishing, pp. 224 & 225.

FIGURE 5–3 Worksheets for Narrative Discourse

sequence is changed. At first, they can orally describe what is happening and use appropriate linguistic markers, such as "first," "then," "and then," and "finally." After they've had some practice with orally describing temporal order, they can begin writing a description of the unfolding of events, again practicing the use of appropriate linguistic markers.

Causal relationships can be targeted by having the students focus on which events seem to result in which consequences. With the comics cut into individual panels, students can experiment with rearranging the causes and the effects to see if events still make sense. All the while, they can be orally describing their perceptions of why things in the panels are happening the way they are. After experimenting with rearranging the panels and orally describing the resulting causal relationships, the students can write out two or three scenarios depicting the different causal relationships emanating from their experiments. Emphasis in each scenario should be on describing which event(s) resulted in which consequences.

Purdue University's Online Writing Lab (2015b) offers resources on a wide range of aspects for teachers and students. These include incorporating writing across the curriculum, information and links to resources for both teachers and students, and extensive resources on the ESL Teacher Resources page (Purdue Online Writing Lab, 2015a) (e.g., materials, lesson plans, quizzes, online conversational partners, audio and video, forums, analysis tools).

For some students, the various types of discourse they encounter in school are familiar from their experiences at home. For others, however, classroom discourse may pose particular difficulties, primarily because some of its rules are never verbalized by teachers, and thus constitutes a hidden curriculum—an unwritten, informal, and often unacknowledged code of conduct to which students are expected to adhere in the classroom. In education, the hidden curriculum conveys information to students regarding how they should interact with peers and their teachers, how they should perceive people who are different from themselves (e.g., different race, group, or class of people), and which ideas and behaviors are acceptable.

A typical example of classroom discourse is what happens when the teacher initiates a topic, a student responds, and the teacher evaluates the response:

> T. *Who knows the origin of Memorial Day?* Pauses. *Remember, you need to raise your hand.* Waits for students to raise hands. *Tony?*
>
> S. *World War I?*
>
> T. *No, that's what most people think, though, isn't it?* Points to another student. *Jessica?*
>
> S. *The Civil War?*
>
> T. *Yes, that's right. And who knows when it was first celebrated?*

Notice in the above interaction that the teacher emphasizes that students need to raise their hands, which is one example of the types of behaviors teachers find most desirable in students. Others include working well in teams or groups, participating in class discussions, following directions, being respectful to others, and appearing interested.

Many students, particularly those with disabilities, struggle with these teacher expectations and will need direct instruction regarding how to recognize the various aspects of classroom discourse and how to respond appropriately. For example, these behaviors can be used as standards, with students progressing toward them at varying rates, depending on their language abilities. They can be fine-tuned into a set of steps progressing from the least linguistically demanding through increasing levels of linguistic load. In addition, teachers can add redundancy to instructions, slow speaking rate, and help students develop skill with the metas, a topic addressed below.

By the time students reach third or fourth grade, they are expected to begin using their reading skills to read texts that teach them new information. Those texts typically use one or more forms of expository discourse, which, as discussed above, differ significantly from the narrative discourse of stories. In the middle elementary grades and later, the most common types of expository discourse that students encounter are descriptive and explanatory.

Most typically developing children begin producing oral descriptions before they begin school, and, once they enter school, their verbal descriptions become tied to academic content. In addition, much of classroom discourse contains elements of description and explanation. By third or fourth grade, students are expected to read, understand, and write descriptive and explanatory discourse, and by the time they enter the secondary grades, they are expected to read and understand argumentative/persuasive texts. By the time they leave secondary school, most students will also be expected to produce their own written argumentative/persuasive discourse.

Students usually encounter expository discourse first in oral forms, such as lecture, oral reports, laboratory reports, and research reports. Later, they interact with printed forms of expository discourse, such as essays, descriptions, letters, explanations, and argument/persuasion. To begin teaching students about expository discourse, one approach is to show them how to differentiate narrative from non-narrative genres, which requires that they first understand what constitutes a good narrative, or story, a topic discussed earlier in this chapter. Once students can discriminate the narrative from non-narrative, they can begin to learn

the characteristics of the non-narrative discourse genres. Figure 5-4 is a schematic showing four types of non-narrative discourse genres.

The schematic can serve as a model for designing worksheets that students can fill in with specific details. Once they become familiar with each type, they can begin developing oral and/or written work, first by looking at the schematic for whichever particular discourse genre they're working on and then, as they become more proficient, without looking at the schematic. Table 5-12 shows a format for expository communication (see also Chapter 8).

Students can use this format to create a checklist to follow as they begin learning how to comprehend and orally describe the organizational characteristics of the expository text. A rubric system can be used to help students increase their skill with expository text (see Figure 5-5).

Because each discourse type is typically associated with specific words, once they can recognize the various types of expository text, you can

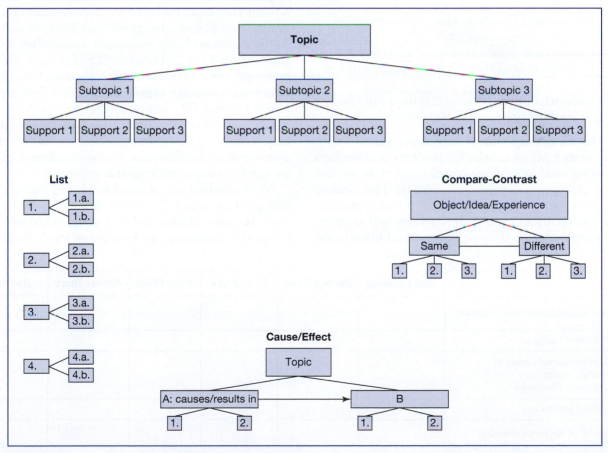

FIGURE 5–4 Types of Non-Narrative Discourse Genres

TABLE 5–12 Basic outline format for expository communication

Title (the subject of the report or essay)
Topic sentence (statement of the overall idea of the report or essay)

  I. First main idea
    A. Fact 1
    B. Fact 2
    C. Fact 3, etc.
  II. Second main idea
    A. Fact 1
    B. Fact 2
    C. Fact 3
 III. Conclusion (re-statement of the topic sentence, the conclusion)

provide students with a list of which words they can use for each genre, such as these:

- **Cause and Effect:** *because, therefore, thus, is seen to be.*
- **Compare and Contrast:** *same, different, alike, although, however, yet, still, but.*
- **Descriptive:** *is called, is defined as, refers to.*
- **Explanation:** *is explained as, since, then, therefore, is a function of.*
- **Problem/Solution:** *therefore, thus, a possibility is, is probably the case.*

The Secondary School Educators (2015) website offers a set of rubrics for students and teachers showing how to evaluate compare/contrast, expository, debate, and persuasive essays. Their rubric for expository essay emphasizes focus, organization, conventions, and understanding and support, each rated along a six-point scale. In addition to the rubrics, the site also provides a tutorial on rubrics for any assignment.

Thirteen Ed Online (2015) offers a lesson plan for 10th, 11th, and 12th graders on how media shapes perception of events through analyzing the subtexts present in the audio, language, and visual aspects of media coverage of tragic events. Students have opportunities to explore how the media shape their opinions and emotional reactions to tragic events. After looking at various news organizations' home pages, students convey their own opinions and emotions by creating their own home page designs.

Figurative Language

For some children, learning that language exists on more than one level is a delight, while for others, it's a mysterious and troubling task that seems to make little sense. However, the ability to use non-literal forms of language is necessary in order to participate fully in social interactions, which often rely on idioms, slang, and shortcuts, and to access written language, particularly poetry, music lyrics, drama, and fiction. An inability in this area can result in a student being ostracized or belittled. Websites oriented toward teaching English as a second language are a rich source of ideas about teaching figurative language types. Table 5-13 provides a number of helpful examples.

The earliest types of figurative language elementary students learn about are usually homonyms, synonyms, and antonyms. Numerous lesson plans for teaching them are available online.

Most children are exposed to idioms and idiomatic phrases well before they enter school. However, because idioms vary by geographic region, cultural influences, and education level, children

	Just Learning	Getting There	Sometimes	More Often	Almost There	Got It!
Text Organization and Structure						
Cohesive Features						
Developmental Levels of Syntax, Vocabulary, and Cohesion Strategies						
Writing Mechanics						
Sense of Audience (Reader)						

FIGURE 5–5 Rubric for Expository Discourse

TABLE 5–13 Resources for teaching figurative language

Type	Source	Resources Available
Homonyms	YourDictionary.com (2015)	706 sets of homonyms, 56 online homonym quizzes, lesson plans
Homophones	K12 Reader (2015)	Homophone worksheets for grades 4+
Homonyms	Internet TESL Project (2015)	Self-study homonym quizzes about common English homonyms
Synonyms	Readwritethink (2016)	Lesson plans using word webs to teach synonyms, varied resources
Synonyms, antonyms.	TeachNet.com (2015)	Provides a lesson plan for middle school students using sports headlines
Homonyms, synonyms, antonyms	Sass (2015)	List of online lesson plans, elementary through secondary levels
Idioms	Miller (2015)	Lesson plan for third- through fifth-grade students that includes a list of common idioms.
Idioms	ESL Gold Net (2015)	Section to teaching idioms along with attention to slang, proverbs, and clichés
Idioms	Rizzo (2015)	Using *Amelia Bedilia* (Parish, 2012) to devise lesson plan for fourth through sixth grade; model for teaching other idioms through other books
Idioms	Idiom Connection (2015)	Collection of English idioms with quizzes in categories: animal, heart, food, fish, clothes, business, body, money, number
Idioms, slang	Internet TESL Journal (2015)	Idiom quizzes, organized into categories (idioms, phrasal verbs, and slang) by level of difficulty; allows student to select idiom in a sentence and then click to see what it means in literal English
Varied simile and metaphor	A to Z Teacher Stuff (2015)	Links to lesson plans and rubrics for teaching alliteration, simile, metaphor, poetry, imagery, onomatopoeia, personification, proverbs, puns
	Teacher Vision (2015)	Lesson plans for grades 3 through 12 addressing both simile and metaphor
Analogy, symbolism, personification, metaphor, etc.	Rekate (2015)	Lesson plan using Martin Luther King Jr.'s "I Have a Dream" speech to teach fifth- through ninth-grade students
Allegory	National Endowment for Humanities (2015)	Lesson plan for teaching allegory and the art of persuasion using Orwell's *Animal Farm*; introduction, guiding questions, objectives, activities, lesson assessment
Slang	Many Things (2015)	Aimed at ESL students, offers comprehensive list of common American slang
Slang	ESLprintables.com (2016)	Links to lesson plans centered on teaching various elements of slang
Metaphors	English Linx (2015)	Worksheets for grades K through 5, 6 through 8, and 9 through 12

entering school do not necessarily know the exact idioms commonly used by their schoolmates. Also, children from families that are less oriented toward literate uses of language may not recognize that idioms are figurative expressions.

Merriam-Webster Dictionary (2015) defines slang as "an informal nonstandard vocabulary composed typically of coinages, arbitrarily changed words, and extravagant, forced, or facetious figures of speech." In other words, slang is a set of specialized idioms and idiomatic expressions that change frequently. Because slang is a variant of idioms, teaching students about slang is virtually the same process as teaching them about idioms.

Learning to reflect on and talk about communication, language, speech, and one's own learning are among the most critical skills students learn in school. Teaching students **metapragmatic** skills focuses on helping them recognize that the "rules" governing how language is used in different situations can be talked about, analyzed, and broken. According to Polloway et al. (2012), metapragmatic instruction for elementary students emphasizes showing students how to

- decide when to violate the "tell the truth" principle,
- identify the unspoken rules governing classroom discourse,
- participate in classroom discourse,
- demonstrate knowledge appropriately in the classroom,

For secondary students, Polloway et al. (2012) emphasized how important it is to understand and be able to participate successfully in the unspoken classroom rules (the hidden curriculum, discussed earlier), which requires significant metapragmatic ability. They recommend utilizing a set of questions to assess students' awareness of the different sets of classroom rules required by their individual teachers.

If one of your teachers doesn't tell you specifically, how do you know the following?

- When it's okay to talk during class
- How you're supposed to ask him or her for help
- How you're supposed to respond to his or her questions to the entire class
- When it's okay to talk to other students during class
- Whether you're supposed to give short or long answers when asked to respond to the teacher's question(s)
- How to disagree with another student or with the teacher

- talk about different types of discourse (e.g., slang, school talk, home talk, church talk),
- participate successfully in different types of discourse,
- talk about discourse rules, and
- use different discourse genres in their writing.

The Teacher Tips box provides guidance for enhancing student language as related to class engagement and participation

For elementary students, one of the most important **metalinguistic abilities** they must acquire is **phonological and phonemic awareness**, which plays a major role in learning to read and write. This will be discussed further in Chapter 6. The discussion below highlights approaches to assist children in developing an awareness of the phonetic and phonemic aspects of spoken language.

A rich resource for teachers is the University of Missouri's (2015) set of teaching tips for phonemic awareness. The site includes links for phonemic awareness assessment, worksheets and activities, and specific techniques, including rhyming, songs, tongue twisters, games, and decoding strategies.

The University of Oregon Center on Teaching and Learning (2015) hosts a website with a wide variety of resources for teaching phonemic awareness. The site describes the critical features of phonemic awareness instruction, how phonemic awareness develops, examples of phonemic awareness skills, and curriculum maps for each grade. The site offers teaching strategies and examples for sound isolation, blending, and segmenting; student benchmarks for first and second grades; and a guide to evaluating phonemic awareness programs and materials.

The **metacognitive strategies** students need in order to succeed in school involve learning how they learn, how to manage their learning, and how to manage learning problems or breakdowns. In essence, metacognition is the ability to discover how one naturally attends and learns. Table 5-14 shows the developmental sequence that most students go through without assistance. Table 5-15 then provides a list of sample strategies you can use for teaching metacognition.

Teaching Spoken Language to CLD Students

Because the school population in the United States is increasingly culturally and linguistically diverse, teachers are more aware of and respectful to a

TABLE 5–14   How metacognitive awareness develops

1. First, students become aware that they think. As a consequence, they begin to understand
   - which factors affect their own thinking,
   - different strategies they can use to learn something, and
   - which strategy to use for a specific learning situation,
2. Later, students become able to regulate their thinking and learning by
   - planning ahead and setting goals,
   - monitoring their progress and their learning, and
   - evaluating how they did; that is, did their strategy(ies) work, and might a different strategy(ies) have worked better?

TABLE 5–15 Sample strategies for teaching metacognition

1. Encourage students to think aloud so they begin to notice their thoughts.

2. Ask students direct questions about how they're learning a particular concept or skill. Ask them to reflect on how they might have made some assumptions prior to learning the concept or skill and whether those assumptions influenced them in any way.

3. Show students how to ask their own questions in order to increase their comprehension of a particular concept or skill. For example, you might describe the process you use when learning a new skill, such as using a new tool or a new app.

4. Provide opportunities for students to feel safe making mistakes while they're learning something new. Then encourage them to reflect on the possible causes of what went wrong and how they might change their strategy to increase their chance of learning the concept or skill.

5. Provide opportunities for students to engage in some challenging learning situations. Encourage them to describe how they plan to engage in learning in this situation.

6. Provide time for your students to solve some learning problems in teams. Encourage each team member to discuss possible approaches to their specific learning situation. After the team has engaged in learning the new concept or skill, encourage each member to describe specific metacognitive he or she learned from the others.

wide variety of cultural groups. One of the ways this is happening is through teachers developing cultural competence, which includes knowing that culture affects child-rearing practices, everyday life activities, how disabilities are viewed, and communication (e.g., eye contact, gestures, taking turns, interrupting, humor, asking and responding to questions). Teachers know that students with a foreign accent or limited English skill are not intellectually inferior, slow, or incapable learners. Teachers who are successful with CLD students share a number of characteristics in that they

- use ongoing and varied assessment as an integral part of instruction (the teacher knows exactly what each student is learning on any given day);
- ensure respectful activities for all the students in their classroom;
- frequently change how students are grouped so that all students work with a variety of peers, which ensures that every student has the opportunity to work sometimes with peers who are at the same level of readiness or who are at different levels of readiness and/or interests;
- use student differences as a basis for instructional planning;
- measure student growth based on each student's baseline skills;
- provide a wide variety of materials and activities; and
- understand that a student's literacy in his or her first language (L1) can be used to help the student develop literacy in English (L2) (they use the skills in L1 as a bridge to those the student is learning in L2).

The Brown University Education Alliance (2015) website Teaching Diverse Learners is a resource for teachers with CLD students providing in-depth descriptions of literacy for elementary students and the challenges faced by CLD students, extensive discussion of instruction for CLD students, a list of 10 strategies successful teachers employ, literature review of current research and teacher resources, and teaching and learning strategies based on culturally responsive teaching and language support for students. There are sections on assessment that explore initial assessment, ongoing assessment, and high-stakes testing; language educational policies with suggestions for best practices for implementing equal access plans; and information and suggestions for school–family relationships, family involvement, and cultural awareness.

Peña et al. (2007) proposed designing instruction for CLD children based on two fundamental principles. First, mediated instruction that focuses on their underlying skills that can be used to support language learning, regardless of the language or dialect the children speak, has been shown to increase children's ability to learn specific language structures. The authors conclude that an important aspect of mediated instruction aimed at underlying cognitive skills helps children develop behaviors for learning in general. Second, mediated instruction that focuses on skills that are specific to the language, dialect, and circumstances in which the children need language in order to communicate effectively and interact successfully has been shown to help them understand their language goals, why they are important, and how they can use their new skills to enhance their own learning.

The following Teacher Tips box shows a sample mediated instruction lesson for the same second-grade

Mediated Instruction Focused on Setting Information in a Story

Lesson Objective: Teach that stories contain information about time and place.

Teaching Sequence: 1. Show Amarisa (A) *Two Friends* (a wordless picture book that shows a dog looking for a friend, a cat, and finally finding the cat) and have her retell the story. Remind her before she begins to include information about when and where the events take place. **2.** Tell A what you're going to do in this lesson and why it is important. **3.** Using the story, help A describe time and place. **4.** If A describes the setting without much help, help her extend the concept to another story. If she has difficulty, help her evaluate why it is important to describe time and place in a story. **5.** Help A plan how to describe the setting when she tells another story. **6.** Help A respond to the questions throughout. Use prompts, cues, and models as needed to support her. **7.** Help A figure out how she can remember to describe the setting as she tells a story.

Strategy	Examples of Instruction	What You Did to Support Amarisa	How Amarisa Responded
What you're going to do	"Today we're going to talk about telling stories. When we tell stories, we tell when and where the events happen."	Reminded her what she learned about including character information.	"Oh, yeah. The baby was big and kinda brown."
Why that's important	"Telling about when and where things happen is important because it tells your listener about the world the characters live in."	Asked Amarisa to describe her seventh birthday and how it was different from her 8th.	"My mom have a party this year. Last year we go to my granmommy's."
Help Amarisa describe the setting	"Let's look at *Two Friends* again. Let's see if we can see where and when things are happening." Help Amarisa describe where the dog and cat are at the beginning of the story. "When do you think this story happened? Was it yesterday? Ten years ago? A hundred?" Help Amarisa use time/place words and phrases.	Pointed out the pictures in the story that showed where and when.	"Oh, he sleeping. It night there." "He swimming in a river."
Help Amarisa extend the concept to another story.	"How would you change the story if the dog and cat lived on a different planet? How would you change the story if it happened in the year 3000?" And "Can you think of another story that tells where the characters are and when things are happening?" If not, present a familiar story and help Amarisa discover the setting.		"It cold on the moon. And dark on one side." "In 3000 they ride in a space ship." "In the Ugly Duckling, they in a lake."
Help Amarisa plan	"We've been talking about telling about time and place. The next time you tell a story, what are you going to remember to put in it?"		"Tell the place and the time, like now or the future."
Help Amarisa generalize her learning	"We've been talking about putting time and place in your stories. How are you going to remember to include time and place when you make up your own stories?"		"I think about the dog swimming in the river. Or him sleeping at home at the end."

student previously described in Table 5-9. This lesson was built from information gleaned during the prior session on setting information in her stories. During that session, the student responded well as the lesson guided her understanding of how to include setting information in a story. She was able to recognize where and when the story took place, generalize her learning to another story (*The Ugly Duckling*), and tell her teacher how she planned to remember to include setting information the next time she told a story. The teacher designed the mediated lesson below for the student's group, who were each telling the group their favorite story in preparation for completing a story guide that would act as a template to use in writing a story over a five-day period. Although the teacher addressed each of the five students and elicited their responses, she recorded only the questions, supports, and responses related to the one student.

LEARNING MODULE 5.1
Click here to learn more about effective instructional practices for teaching English Language Learners:
http://iris.peabody.vanderbilt.edu/module/ell>

Teaching with Technology

Today's children are surrounded by digital technology from infancy and use a variety of devices on a daily basis. An estimated 94% of teenagers in the United States use the Internet daily (Infoplease.com, 2015). According to Business Insider (2015), teens sent almost 10 times as many texts as Americans over age 55, more than an estimated 2,000 per month. The most popular app for teenagers (and all ages) is Facebook (International Business Times, 2014). However, those in the business world are discovering that many students do not know how to communicate effectively in various media, are unable to analyze and interpret data available in electronic formats, are unable to differentiate between fact and opinion delivered in electronic formats, and have difficulty managing and prioritizing tasks while using various technology applications.

With rapidly evolving communication technologies more readily available in an increasing number of classrooms, students with special needs now have more opportunities to use technology in a number of ways. These efforts are consistent with the emphasis on universal design for learning (UDL), which was discussed in Chapter 2. As the National Center on Universal Design for Learning (2016) noted, the three basic principles of UDL are

- multiple means of representation (the "what" of learning), to give learners various ways of acquiring information and knowledge;
- multiple means of expression (the "how" of learning), to provide learners alternatives for demonstrating what they know; and
- multiple means of engagement (the "why" of learning), to tap into learners' interests, offer appropriate challenges, and increase motivation.

The center's Web pages offer a variety of resources for integrating UDL with the Common Core State Standards (2015b). Two key technology resources, Internet usage and AAC, are discussed below.

Internet Resources. One of the richest technology resources available is the Internet, which is invaluable because it is so vast. That same vastness, however, can be intimidating and confusing without forethought and planning. As a means of teaching students with special needs, the Internet offers a wide range of resources related to specific aspects of language instruction. Many resources related to teaching language arts can be used and/or modified for students needing specific language instruction. Table 5-16 lists additional online resources for using technology in developing language instruction.

Augmentative and Alternative Communication

Some students with special needs communicate partially or exclusively by using one or more augmentative and/or alternative communication (AAC) devices as discussed previously in this chapter. Examples of AAC systems and devices and assessment strategies were noted. The most common AAC system used with individuals who have very limited or nonexistent verbal ability is the Picture Exchange Communication System (PECS). Using a changeable picture format, this system is used to build vocabulary and to consistently express basic functional desires, feelings, and observations (Silverman & Miller, 2017).

TABLE 5–16 Technology resources for language arts

Web2-4LanguageTeachers.com iPad apps for teaching oral skills http://web2-4languageteachers.wikispaces.com/iPad+apps+-+oral+skills	iPad in the Classroom iPad apps for students to use in the classroom http://ipadintheeslclassroom.weebly.com/esl-apps.html
Web2-4LanguageTeachers.com iPad apps for teaching listening skills http://web2-4languageteachers.wikispaces.com/iPad+apps+-+listening+skills	My English Teacher iPhone and Android apps for students to use http://www.myenglishteacher.eu/blog/9-most-popular-ios-and-android-apps-to-learn-english-language/
Web2-4LanguageTeachers.com iPad apps for teaching writing skills http://web2-4languageteachers.wikispaces.com/Web2+tools+-+writing+skills	English with Jennifer a compendium of videos for almost every aspect of language arts learning http://englishwithjennifer.com/youtube_videos.html
Web2-4LanguageTeachers.com iPad apps for teaching vocabulary http://web2-4languageteachers.wikispaces.com/iPad+apps+-+vocab+skills	

Mobile devices with touch screens are used more frequently than most other devices for varied reasons including that they

- are multi-functional,
- support a wide variety of apps,
- offer easy accessibility to an extensive range of technology sources through the Internet and through mobile apps,
- are easier to navigate than a computer mouse,
- provide tactile input,
- are easy to use,
- are multi-sensory,
- are less expensive than other AAC devices,
- offer instant gratification,
- do not require special training, and
- allow for innovative uses.

Students who are unable to use mobile devices are often able to use AAC devices that produce synthesized voice. These devices provide students with help matching words and sentences to their intended meanings, thus improving phonological awareness. In addition, children using voice output devices show greater speech and language growth than children using different sorts of systems, and AAC devices have been shown to increase children's language literacy development.

Speech recognition software has progressed so that it can be used to help students who have difficulty with reading and writing. It allows the student's voice to interface with a computer through turning spoken language into digitized text or turning commands into actions. Both Microsoft and Apple operating systems have speech recognition built in, which makes it easy for teachers and students to try them out to see whether speech recognition is a good fit for a particular student's needs.

For using AAC in the classroom, an informative resource is a guide from the Georgia Department of Education (2015), developed by Jennifer Thomas, that emphasizes how to use AAC to help a student develop functional language skills. After listing the specific steps necessary for selecting the appropriate AAC tool, Thomas gives a detailed example of a rubric to identify the communication skill to focus on with the student, its message/purpose, the student's current communication, and the desired communication. She details how to help the student use the device to communicate specific intentions (e.g., gaining attention, requesting assistance) in an appropriate manner. The guide also shows examples of various communication systems, such as the PECS, and communication boards, ranging from simple to complex.

 Check Your Understanding 5.5 Click here to gauge your understanding of the concepts in this section.

ACTIVITIES

Elementary Level

Using the list of games below, construct your own specialized versions to reflect whichever language concepts you're focusing on. Have your students pair off and play the following.

1. Hangman, using familiar words.
2. Crossword puzzles, using familiar words and concepts, perhaps from a story or science project.
3. Word search—find words embedded in seemingly random arrays of letters that you construct.
4. "Begins with . . ."—Select a picture that shows numerous animals, actions, or things and construct a game sheet that shows the first letter of three or four words shown in the picture, followed by the appropriate number of blank boxes that corresponds to the number of letters in each word. For example, if there's a goat in the picture, the sheet would have "g ☐☐☐" and so on for the other words.
5. Construct a set of anagrams using words the students are practicing for spelling.
6. Construct a set of misspelled words and ask students to first identify which are misspelled and then to spell them correctly.
7. Recruit a parent or volunteer to teach some American Sign Language (ASL) to the students. Have them describe how ASL is different from English.
8. Have the students work in teams to develop a communication board for a hypothetical student who is temporarily unable to talk and needs a way to communicate. You can make it more realistic by having the students take turns role-playing the student who is unable to speak whose job is to try out the boards designed by each team and tell the teams how well each worked and how their board could be made better.
9. Have students work in teams to make up three riddles. Each team presents them to the other teams and gets feedback on what makes them funny and how they could be made even funnier.
10. Read a poem to the students and have them write their own, using the same number of words and the same style. Change the type of poem each time so that the students gain experience writing in different styles.

Secondary Level

These activities give students experience learning about different types of discourse and corresponding styles of writing:

1. Divide students into teams of three or four each. Select a different short piece of fiction (three to five pages) for each team to read. Select pieces with considerable dialogue. Then have each team create an adaptation of their story that they then perform for their classmates. Emphasize the importance of dialogue and the presence of a narrator to speak the lines of the story that are not in dialogue. Provide time for them to create some basic scenery and costumes. Have the students create a critique sheet each team can use to critique the other teams' *adaptations* (not their performances).
2. Screen four or five songs that are popular with your students, making sure they contain appropriate content and words. Have the students read them aloud. Have each student then select one and write his or her own song using the same number of words, verses, and style. Have the students read or sing their songs aloud and tell how their song is like the song they chose to emulate.
3. Divide students into teams. Have each team find one example of each of the following types of cell phone advertising:

   - A geographically relevant ad that uses GPS to push ads for businesses that are close by
   - Two examples of ads on Facebook from Facebook persuading the user to add friends, use more services, or receive news targeted to each user

   After the teams have collected their examples, have each team select two ads they found and describe the persuasive techniques of each

4. Divide students into teams and have them design a video (on either a computer a cell phone) that presents their case for modifying a school or community policy with which they disagree. When each team presents their video, the rest of the class offers a critique, using what they've learned about the characteristics of persuasive discourse. Have the class decide which video (or videos) are successful enough that they should be presented to the school administration (or to the people responsible for formulating school policy) or to community leaders.

Reading: Word Recognition

Ed Polloway and Jacqueline Lubin

LEARNING OUTCOMES

Upon completion of this chapter, the reader should be able to:

6.1 Discuss the nature of reading and reading difficulties, identifying reading problems and challenges experienced by students with special needs.

6.2 Identify general reading considerations, discuss the central role of reading instruction within the school curriculum, and identify key distinctions between decoding and holistic instruction.

6.3 Identify appropriate assessment strategies for determining instructional needs and evaluating student progress.

6.4 Identify key areas of word-recognition instruction and describe effective strategies within these areas.

6.5 Define fluency, identify reasons for its importance, and discuss strategies to promote fluent reading.

The ability to read is essential for living in today's world; personal independence requires at least functional literacy. Failure to read restricts academic progress because proficiency in math, English, science, or social studies depends in part on an ability to read. Most careers require at least minimal reading skills. Reading is also a key to personal and social adjustment and to successful involvement in community activities. As a consequence, this text includes two chapters on reading, with an introduction and a focus on word recognition and fluency in this chapter and on reading comprehension in the next. Reading, reading failure, and ways to teach reading should be dominant concerns for teachers working with students with special needs.

READING AND READING DIFFICULTY

The five key components of reading include phonemic awareness, phonetic analysis, fluency, vocabulary development, and comprehension (National Reading Panel [NRP], 2000). Building on this foundation, Figure 6-1 outlines these five areas as well as several related word analysis strategies (e.g., structural analysis and contextual analysis) that are addressed within this text.

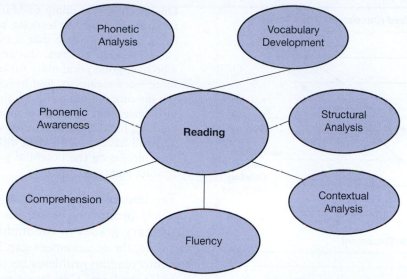

FIGURE 6–1   Key Reading Components

Source: Graphic Models and Instructional Tools for Students with Special Needs (p. 5), by E. A. Polloway & J. Lubin, 2016, *Lynchburg College Journal of Special Education*, Lynchburg College, Lynchburg, VA. Used with permission.

The acquisition of reading skills is a challenging task for many children. As opposed to oral language acquisition, reading acquisition has been characterized as an "unnatural" process (Shaywitz, 2003) that creates difficulties for students at the emergent literacy, beginning reading, and fluent reading levels. Thus, before considering the problems that children may experience, it is helpful to first conceptualize what children achieve at these three levels.

Tompkins (2006) explained that literacy develops in three stages: emergent, beginning, and fluent. At the emergent level, children show interest in books, pretend to read, and use pictures and patterns to retell a story. They are able to recognize environmental print and some letter names. Their high-frequency word vocabulary ranges from 5 to 20 words. At the second level, children's high-frequency vocabulary increases to 20 to 100 words. They are able to match phonemes with graphemes and spoken words to written words. They are able to read slowly, decode some sounds, and point to words when reading. They can monitor their reading and make reasonable predictions. At the third level, fluent, children can read most words automatically and with expression. Their high-frequency vocabulary has increased to 100 to 300 (or more) words. They are independent readers who like silent reading, as they are able to use various strategies effectively to decode unfamiliar words and garner comprehension.

Media reports underscore the problems that students experience in reading. Common estimates of the scope of reading problems include the following:

- Up to 20% of the total school population
- Up to 50% of the students in some inner-city schools
- 75% of individuals identified as juvenile delinquents
- 85% of students with disabilities

Students who progress at a slower rate in spite of reading interventions have been referred to by a variety of terms. These include, for example, reading disabled, dyslexic, treatment resisters, or nonresponders. The key question, though, is not how they are labeled but rather how we understand their challenges as a basis for effective education.

A critical focus for problem readers is the gap between their age and grade placement and their reading achievement level and, consequently, the gap between students with reading difficulties and those who are progressing in a typical fashion.

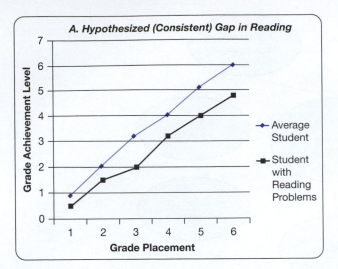

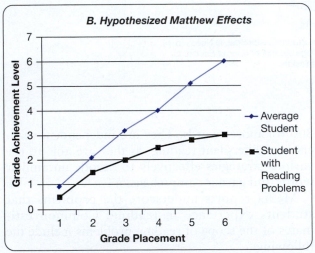

FIGURE 6–2 A Model for Matthew Effects in Reading

Source: Graphic Models and Instructional Tools for Students with Special Needs (pp. 6–7), by E. A. Polloway & J. Lubin, 2016, *Lynchburg College Journal of Special Education*, Lynchburg College, Lynchburg, VA. Used with permission.

Figure 6-2 illustrates two models of underachievement. The first reflects a static gap that may typify some students who fall behind and stay behind (in parallel sense) their peers.

The second model in Figure 6-2, however, shows an increasing gap developing as students proceed through school. This gap is unfortunately common to many students with reading disabilities. It has been referred to as a reflection of *Matthew effects*, based on the biblical verse from Matthew 25:29: "For everyone who has will be given more and he will have an abundance. Whoever does not have, even what he has will be taken from him." As Stanovich (1986) explained,

One mechanism leading to Matthew effects is the facilitation of further learning by a previously existing knowledge base that is rich and elaborated . . . . The very children who are reading well and who have good vocabulary for reading more, learn more word meanings, and hence read even better. On the other hand, those who experience reading difficulties will often develop a failure set about reading, have diminished motivation for success, and will have compounding difficulties over time, thus increasing the potential gap related to their reading ability. (p. 381)

The impact of the Matthew effects become particularly prominent as students progress to later elementary grades to the middle school level. By this time, the achievement gap has often increased, and thus reading problems become most noticeable in older students. Consistent with this perspective, Hock et al. (2009) concluded that "in all component areas of reading, struggling *adolescent* readers were found to score statistically lower than their proficient reader counterparts. . . . While the areas of greatest deficit were fluency and comprehension, many poor readers also demonstrated significant deficits at the word level (order to act, decoding, word recognition, and rate) (p. 34).

A number of hypotheses have been offered as to the source of reading problems. One common problem cited often, though not consistently confirmed by research, is the complexity of the English language (e.g., 1,120 ways to spell 44 phonemes). (See Table 6-1 for a listing of English language phonemes.)

A broader view was espoused by Mathes and Torgesen (1998), who identified three stumbling blocks to successful reading:

- Understanding and using the **alphabetic principle** that written spellings represent spoken words, that words are made up letters, that the letter system has a purpose and letters correspond to specific sounds, and ultimately that 26 letters (graphemes) are used to map the 44 sounds (phonemes) (see also Figure 6-3)
- Transferring spoken language comprehension skills to reading and learning new strategies
- Lacking the motivation to read or failing to develop an appreciation of its rewards

Regardless of the inherent reasons for reading problems, the critical element is our educational response. A key need is for an increased intensity of

TABLE 6–1 English language phonemes

Consonant Phonemes		Vowel Phonemes	
Phonetic Symbol	**Spelling Example (Common Graphemes)**	**Phonetic Symbol**	**Spelling Example (Common Graphemes)**
/b/	ball	/a/	bar
/d/	dig, down	/æ/	sat, after
/f/	fish, photograph	/ai/	by, pie, dry
/g/	mug, goal	/aʊ/	now, south
/h/	home, hot	/ɔ/	claw, thought
/j/	yet	/ɔi/	choice
/k/	cup, luck, kale	/e/	pet
/l/	lazy, call, lap	/ei/	reign, play
/m/	more, hammer	/i/	tea, flee
/n/	name, knife	/o/	fox
/p/	pig	/ou/	grow, boat
/r/	run, wrap	/u/	blue, influence
/s/	cite, same	/ʊ/	boot, food
/t/	time, trap	/ʊə/	poor, manure
/v/	vote	/^/	cut
/w/	what	/ɜ/	purse, prefer
/z/	zip, zebra		
/dʒ/	judge, ridge		
/l ʒ /	treasure		
/ʃ/	nation, ship		
/tʃ/ /	perch, church		
/ŋ/	sing		
/θ/	thing		
/ö /	mother, them		

Source: Graphic Models and Instructional Tools for Students with Special Needs (p. 11), by E. A. Polloway & J. Lubin, 2016, *Lynchburg College Journal of Special Education,* Lynchburg College, Lynchburg, VA. Used with permission.

instruction. A second variable is academic engaged time, which is critical to success in learning to read. Given the fact that not all of the time available in the school day actually involves engagement, the key is to maximize the amount of time available and therefore ensure that students have the opportunity to be highly engaged in the process of reading.

Swanson (2008) reported on 21 observation studies of students with learning disabilities and classrooms. Four key areas of concern were noted. First, the students spent limited time engaged in instruction in key areas of reading (e.g., phonics, fluency, comprehension). Second, the grouping structures that were used were often inappropriate and did not frequently include small-group instruction. Third, comprehension instruction was not only limited but also primarily focused on literal-type questions. Fourth, students were not engaged in actual reading of textual material for a sufficient enough time frame to make a difference in terms of, for example, fluency.

The majority of contemporary special education research on reading problems has focused on students with learning disabilities. Attention to the reading achievement and instruction of students

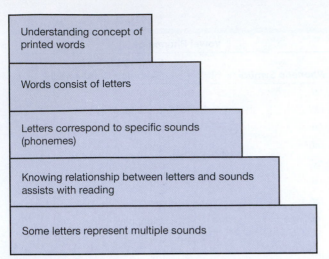

| Understanding concept of printed words |
| Words consist of letters |
| Letters correspond to specific sounds (phonemes) |
| Knowing relationship between letters and sounds assists with reading |
| Some letters represent multiple sounds |

FIGURE 6–3 Elements of the Alphabetic Principle

Source: Graphic Models and Instructional Tools for Students with Special Needs (p. 9), by E. A. Polloway & J. Lubin, 2016, *Lynchburg College Journal of Special Education,* Lynchburg College, Lynchburg, VA. Used with permission.

with intellectual disabilities (ID) has not been as extensive (e.g. Joseph & Seery, 2004). Because reading challenges are significant for these students, their need to reach a level of minimum literacy is consistent with many capabilities.

Research on reading instruction for individuals with ID and in particular for those with more significant disabilities has been relatively limited for many years. However, a number of recent papers have provided research-based perspectives on effective instruction for these students. While a full discussion of these considerations is beyond the scope of this chapter, the reader is referred to the excellent discussions on research-to-practice provided by Allor, Mathes, Jones, Champlin, and Cheatham (2010); Allor, Mathes, Roberts, Jones, and Champlin (2010); Cooper-Duffy, Szedia, and Hyer (2010); and Knight, Browder, Agnello, and Lee (2010).

Students with emotional and behavioral disorders (E/BD) also typically experience significant problems in reading even if these problems may not have been the primary basis for their referral. With regard to students with E/BD, Nelson, Benner, and Gonzalez (2005) noted,

> Unfortunately children with or at risk of emotional disturbance (ED) face enormous challenges learning to read. Many of these children have reading problems. . . . Further compounding the reading problems of children with or at risk of ED is a growing body of evidence that suggests that they are likely to respond poorly to generally effective pre-reading and reading intervention. (p. 3)

 Check Your Understanding 6.1 Click here to gauge your understanding of the concepts in this section.

GENERAL READING CONSIDERATIONS

The importance of reading for all students is universally accepted. Reading must be a significant part of the school day, and teachers should seek ways to integrate reading instruction into other areas of the curriculum. Given the frequency of difficulties among students with disabilities, additional practice to maintain and refine skills is essential. In addition, such opportunities provide a place for students to generalize their reading ability. Thus, adolescents can improve their comprehension skills while acquiring basic vocational competencies from trade books; younger students can benefit from vocabulary development while learning basic science concepts.

Agreement on how best to teach reading (particularly beginning reading) has been debated at least for the last 80 years. The key emphases in the reading debate have been decoding-based emphases (e.g., phonetic analysis approaches that teach sound–symbol correspondences) and holistic approaches (e.g., placing primacy on meaning). The following discussion briefly highlights these concerns.

Decoding-based programs typically emphasize a skills-based, "bottom-up" approach to reading. Usually focused initially on teaching sound–symbol correspondences in language (e.g., c-a-t→cat), they are characterized by the direct teaching of a sequence of skills that begins with an emphasis on the phonological basis of language and thus provide a foundation for the subsequent transfer of skills to reading comprehension. This general approach is consistent with research on phonological difficulties in students with special needs.

Holistic approaches, often seen as a **whole-language** emphasis, focus on the meaningfulness of language, stress the importance of the child's language as a bridge to literacy, and include speaking, listening, and expressive writing as integral parts of literacy development. This approach builds on the diversity of literary experiences that children are exposed to prior to entering school. For example, as a result of having been read to by parents, young children often develop an awareness of the structure of texts and understand the implicit relationship between speech and print.

Pressley and Fingeret (2005), in their review, noted that those young students who have difficulties and are struggling are the ones who benefit most significantly from decoding skills instruction at the primary grades. Students with disabilities require intensive, direct instruction on basic skills that may not be available in classrooms that have adopted a purely whole-language focus. At the same time, they also indicated that those who are of high ability may benefit more from emphases that are inclusive to a greater extent of holistic instruction and tied more directly to, for example, language experiences.

Students require comprehensive instructional programs (e.g., decoding and comprehension emphases, teacher- and student-directed instructional experiences) derived from evidence-based approaches to instruction. Thus, teachers of students with special needs must be prepared to focus on teaching word-recognition and analysis skills as well as on the promotion of meaning through well-designed reading comprehension programs. Students with reading difficulties need intensive intervention over a period of time in order to be equipped with skills to access the general curriculum (Vaughn & Wanzek, 2014). Reading instruction needs to be provided in a conducive environment (i.e., small-group or one-on-one settings) that targets specific elements of reading. Effective interventions require an intensity associated with daily, direct instruction for 45 minutes or more (Vaughn & Wanzek, 2014). Educators must be cognizant that in order for students with disabilities to make meaningful improvements, intensive reading instruction using scientifically based interventions is required.

Validated approaches to reading instruction include the following:

- Phonemic awareness instruction
- Systematic, explicit instruction in decoding skills
- Exposure to varied texts
- Vocabulary instruction on word meanings, structure, and origins

- Direct teaching of comprehension strategies for prediction, summarizing, clarification, questioning, and visualization (Moats, 2003)

This chapter next examines assessment in reading in general and instruction of skills related to word recognition in particular as well as fluency. The next chapter focuses on assessment and instruction in reading comprehension. The approaches discussed here provide a foundation for the development and implementation of comprehensive reading programs.

 Check Your Understanding 6.2 Click here to gauge your understanding of the concepts in this section.

ASSESSMENT

Reading presents the reader with many challenges and consists of many essential components. The teacher must understand the many facets of the reading task and know how to determine which skills each student does or does not possess. The teacher also needs to determine each student's reading level before implementing any program. The central purpose of reading assessment is instructional planning.

The National Joint Committee on Learning Disabilities (NJCLD, 2008) noted that assessment should be "designed to gather multiple sources of qualitative and quantitative information, including measures that reflect student background knowledge, readability of textbooks used in different subject areas, classroom expectations, information about the use of literacy skills outside the school setting, and the need for in the level of ability to use assistive technology. . . . [Further, the information should be] integrated so that data interpretation results in a clear profile of the student's strengths and weaknesses, describes the literacy needs of the student, and provide specific recommendations that are tied to instruction, learning/behavioral supports, and transition planning" (p. 214).

Informal and formal assessment instruments can assist the teacher in determining an individual's level of reading competency. Instruments of both types can help determine an approximate reading level for determining where to begin instruction and how to begin to analyze specific strengths and weaknesses.

Classroom-Based Assessment

A key concern in assessment is the ongoing use of performance data as teachers monitor the progress of students and make determinations concerning their specific instructional needs. Complementing these data with information about strengths and interests will provide a strong foundation for instructional planning (NJCLD, 2008).

Informal reading inventories (IRIs) typically contain a word-recognition inventory, oral reading passages, silent reading passages, and comprehension questions to accompany the passages. Three classifications of reading ability can be determined from these inventories. The *independent reading level* refers to vocabulary that a student can read without teacher assistance and content that can be comprehended at a high level while still identifying approximately 95% of the words correctly. Library books and seatwork instructions should be at the student's independent level. The *instructional level* refers to vocabulary and content that the student can read with some outside assistance. Students should be 85% to 95% accurate at this level. The *frustration level* is that at which the student cannot read with any degree of independence, accurately identifying fewer than 80% of the words. These ranges are included for illustration purposes; views vary on precisely what percentage of accuracy is associated with any given level.

An IRI can also provide for an analysis of errors, which can give added information on specific word analysis difficulties; for this reason, mispronounced words should be recorded phonetically. The errors can be classified in common areas, such as incorrect sounds, full reversals, partial reversals, or incorrect beginning, medial, or final consonants. A sample scoring sheet is shown in Figure 6-4.

An oral reading inventory samples a student's oral reading and comprehension capabilities at various levels. The format, administrative procedures, and scoring practices may vary. However, it is advantageous to record the student's reading so that the

---

1. <u>Mispronunciations</u>: Incorrect pronunciations are written above the word.

   alligator
   (E.g., The elevator stopped working this morning.)

2. <u>Assistance</u>: The letter <u>A</u> is written above each word pronounced for the child after allowing five seconds to elapse.

   A
   (E.g., Peter's mom can play the piano, guitar and saxophone.)

3. <u>Omissions</u>: A circle is placed around each word or portion of word that the student omits.

   (E.g., The teacher described the vagrant as unambitious, (lackadaisical) and sloppy.)

4. <u>Letter or Word Inversions</u>: The traditional typographical mark is used to indicate this type of error.

   (E.g., My brother walked bare/foot on the white, sandy beach.)

5. <u>Self-correction</u>: The letter C is written above the word of the independently corrected error.

   C
   reward
   (E.g., He was given an award of excellence by the mayor.)

6. <u>Insertions</u>: A caret is used to indicate additions inserted by the reader.

   of art
   (E.g., They visited the museums∧ in Washington, D.C.)

7. <u>Hesitations and Repetitions</u>: Although not errors, are identified using check mark and wavy line, respectively.

   ✓
   (E.g., Every holiday, we have family dinners after which a family photograph is taken.)

FIGURE 6–4 Assessment of Oral Reading

Source: Graphic Models and Instructional Tools for Students with Special Needs (p. 13), by E. A. Polloway & J. Lubin, 2016, *Lynchburg College Journal of Special Education*, Lynchburg College, Lynchburg, VA. Used with permission.

TABLE 6–2 Step-by-step: Curriculum-Based Measurement (CBM)

Step 1: Select a passage with approximately 600 words from . . . text designed for students in or about to enter the grade level. Ensure the passage has a reasonable starting point, which includes appropriate content and limited number of specialized words. . . .

Step 2: Produce two copies of the reading material: a student's copy—type the text in approximately the same font and size as the original; and a teacher's copy.

Step 3: For the teacher's copy, include similar text as the student's copy; however, on the right hand side of the page, make a column for line-by-line cumulative word counts. . . . On the bottom of the page, create a rate box with space for the following information: Words Read in Two Minutes, Total Number of Scored Miscues, Total Number of Words Correctly Read in Two Minutes, and Average Number of Words Correctly Read in One Minute (or Correctly Read Words/2).

Step 4: The student reads aloud for two minutes using the student's copy. At the end of two minutes, the teacher puts a slash mark after the last word read.

Step 5: As the student reads, the teacher marks miscues on the teacher's copy by putting a line through miscued words or writing in an inserted word. Miscues are responses to texts that differ from expected responses. . . . Miscues include use of nonsense words, substitutions (e.g., ran for rain), omissions, reversals (words not read in the correct order . . .), inserted words, and no attempt to say a word. However, self-corrected words, repeated words, hesitations, words read with an accent or dialect, and improper intonation resulting from ignored punctuation marks are all scored as correct. . . .

Step 6: Teachers should observe carefully what readers do when they encounter a difficult word. They should try to note answers to the following questions: Do students try to sound it out, use context cues, ask for help, give up? Do some of the mistakes make sense? . . . How are errors corrected? . . .

Step 7: After a student reads the text for two minutes, the teacher calculates the student's oral fluency rate or number of words correctly read in one minute. This is done by dividing the total number of words read correctly in two minutes by 2. . . .

Step 8: Oral fluency rates should be kept for each . . . student. The same text can be used at three points over the traditional academic year to measure oral fluency development: September, January, and May.

Source: Information from Unrau, Norman, *Content Area Reading and Writing: Fostering Literacies in Middle and High School Cultures*, 1st Edition, © 2004, pp. 102–103. Reprinted by permission of Pearson Education Inc., Upper Saddle River, NJ.

teacher can listen critically and analyze errors as a basis for instruction. IRIs can also assess silent reading. Achievement and skill difficulties can be determined by students' responses to comprehension questions.

Curriculum-based measurement (CBM) assesses a student's academic progress by sampling his or her mastery of the actual curriculum. For example, to assess reading progress, one- to three-minute oral reading samples can be taken under the assumption that as the decoding process becomes more automatic, more attention can be allocated to comprehension. CBM also can help teachers monitor fluency, track oral reading miscues, and support student self-monitoring of skills. CBM

procedures do not emphasize assessing a student's performance in relation to a standardized sample but rather focus on the ability to perform the specific skill stated in the accompanying behavioral objective. An example of the use of the CBM process in reading is provided in Table 6-2.

Checklists developed from a summary of competencies are also an effective informal procedure. The teacher selects a particular area to assess and, during a classroom lesson, observes and records a student's skills on the checklist. For example, in observing comprehension skills during small-group reading lesson, the teacher might focus on the specific skills reflected in Figure 6-5.

Student Names	Main Idea	Sequence	Cause and Effect	Details	Fact vs. Opinion
James	X	X	X	X	X
Aretha		X	X	X	
Lincoln	X	X	X		
Patrice		X	X		

FIGURE 6–5 Checklist of Comprehension Skills

Student's name:_____   Age: _____
Class placement: _____   Teacher: _____

Key: N = Not acquired   P = Needs practice   M = Mastered

Reading levels: Independent _____   Tests used: IRI _____
                Instructional _____   Survey _____
                Frustration _____   Diagnostic _____
                                                      Other _____

Sight word vocabulary: SORT _____   Dolch list_____   Other _____

Phonics:
    Consonants

b	c	d	f	g	h	j	k	l	m	n	p	q	r	s	t	v	w	x	y	z

Vowels

	a	e	i	o	u	y
Long sound						
Short sound						

Digraphs

ch	sh	th	wh

Variant vowels

ar	er	ir	or	ur	au	al	on	ow	oi	oy

Blends

bl	cl	fl	gl	pl	sl	br	cr	dr	fr	gr	pr	tr	wn	ap	st

Comprehension: Factual questions _____   Main idea _____
               Inferential questions _____   Sequence of events _____
               Application questions _____   Cause and effect _____

Reading interests: _____
Comments:_____

_____

FIGURE 6–6   Reading Assessment Summary

Tailoring reading lessons to meet each student's needs can be facilitated by efficient, simple record-keeping procedures. Figure 6-6 provides a form to use to analyze a student's strengths and weaknesses in various reading areas. To use this form, teachers should establish criteria for the evaluation of which skills require practice or have been mastered. Figure 6-7 is a sample class profile of word analysis skills in a format that is appropriate for other reading skill areas as well. Figure 6-8 presents some specific questions that teachers can then use to translate assessment information into individualized teaching plans. Once information about each student is organized and easily accessible, a teacher can individualize group instruction.

Formal Instruments

Formal tests provide specific guidelines or tools for screening and other administrative purposes (e.g., eligibility). The instruments typically provide teachers with standard score and grade-level information and may provide data on specific skills.

Some formal instruments can be used to analyze skills in the same way as informal inventories are used. If word lists or paragraphs are read orally by a student, the teacher phonetically records the errors at the time of the reading or later from a tape recording. Once categorized, the errors provide a picture of the student's needs.

The purposes of formal instruments are on a continuum ranging from surveying global reading

Skills		Students							
		Jon	Mary	Paul	Bob	Beth	Andy	Sam	Roy
Reading levels	Independent								
	Instructional								
Consonants	Initial								
	Final								
	Blends								
Vowels	Long sound								
	Short sound								
	Variant								
	Prefixes								
	Suffixes								
Comments									

Key: N = Not acquired P = Needs practice M = Mastered

FIGURE 6–7 Class Profile of Selected Word Analysis Skills

performances to pinpointing specific strengths and weaknesses. Diagnostic tests are used primarily to identify specific problems and to highlight skills needing remediation. Table 6-3 summarizes information on selected formal reading assessment instruments.

Check Your Understanding 6.3 Click here to gauge your understanding of the concepts in this section.

WORD-RECOGNITION INSTRUCTION

The remainder of this chapter is devoted to instructional strategies for enhanced word-recognition skills. The majority of students with special needs will experience problems in decoding because of difficulties related to phonemic awareness and to using sound–symbol correspondences to phonetically analyze words and thus will profit from direct instruction in those areas as well as from instruction in other word-recognition strategies (see Figure 6-9).

1. What are the student's specific strengths?
   a. What specific phonetic knowledge is mastered: letter names? letter sounds? blending?
   b. What specific knowledge of structural analysis is mastered: plural endings? prefixes? suffixes? compound words?
   c. What sight-word categories are mastered: Dolch list? content-area words?
   d. What specific comprehension skills are mastered: vocabulary? getting the main idea? summarizing? making inferences? recognizing cause and effect?
   e. Does the student comprehend best when reading orally or silently?
   f. What is the student's reading level?
2. What skills are priority concerns (based on the state standards)?
3. What is the next needed skill in each area that can be taught to the student at this time?
4. What is the student's attitude toward reading and reading instruction?
5. What reading program is most appropriate for the student?
6. What independent practice and reinforcement activities can the student engage in successfully?
7. What serves as a reinforcer for the student?

FIGURE 6–8 Assessment Considerations to Assist in Instructional Planning

TABLE 6–3 Formal reading assessment instruments

Test Name	Areas of Focus	Ages/Grades
Gray Oral Reading Tests—Fifth Edition (GORT-5) (Wiederholt & Bryant, 2012)	Measures oral reading fluency and comprehension. Includes two equivalent forms, each containing 16 developmentally sequenced reading passages with five comprehension questions each. It has an optional miscue analysis system that allows analysis of reading errors.	6–0 to 23–11
Gray Diagnostic Reading Tests—Second Edition (GDRT-2) (Bryant, Wiederholt, & Bryant, 2004)	Includes four reading subtests: letter and word identification, phonetic analysis, reading vocabulary, and meaningful reading.	6–0 to 18
Woodcock Reading Mastery Tests—Third Edition (WRMT-III) (Woodcock, 2011)	Includes nine tests, with increasing level of difficulty. It assesses reading *acquisition skills* using tests such as Phonological Awareness and Rapid Automatic Naming and *reading achievement* with tests such as Listening Comprehension, Oral Reading Fluency, and Passage Comprehension.	4–6 to 79–11
Wide Range Achievement Test—Fourth Edition (WRAT-4) (Wilkinson & Robertson, 2006)	The subtest can be administered in approximately 10 minutes. It is composed of a group of words that the student reads orally. Words pronounced incorrectly are marked phonetically to aid in determining the need for remedial instruction.	5 to 94
Test of Phonological Awareness—Second Edition: PLUS (TOPA-2t) (Torgesen & Bryant, 2004)	Measures young children's awareness of beginning and ending sounds. Intended for K-level students who can benefit from phonological awareness instruction. An early-elementary version of the test is intended to assess difficulties present in first and second graders.	Grades K–2
Lindamood Auditory Conceptualization Test—Third Edition (LAC-3) (Lindamood & Lindamood, 2004).	Criterion-referenced instrument focused on the discrimination of one speech sound or phoneme from another and the segmentation of the spoken word into component phonemic units. Intended to identify students at risk for reading and spelling problems because of poor phoneme–grapheme correspondence ability and ability to distinguish and manipulate sounds.	5–0 through 18–11
Slosson Oral Reading Test—Revised—Third Edition (SORT-R3) (Slosson, Nicholson, & Hippsman, 2002)	Individualized test using lists of 200 sight words. Word lists progress in difficulty from primer to high school.	Preschool through Adult

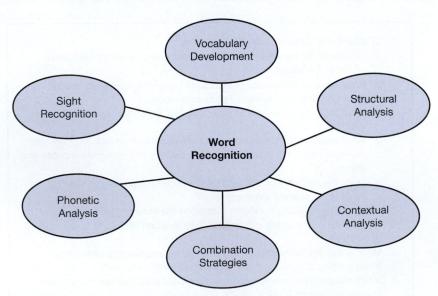

FIGURE 6–9 Word-Recognition Emphases

Source: Graphic Models and Instructional Tools for Students with Special Needs (p. 14), by E. A. Polloway & J. Lubin, 2016, *Lynchburg College Journal of Special Education*, Lynchburg College, Lynchburg, VA. Used with permission.

Phonemic Awareness

A crucial foundation to reading is the ability of young students to learn and use the productive relationships between the sounds and symbols of their language system. Teachers must attend to this area if problems are to be prevented in children who are at risk for reading failure and if remediation is to be achieved for these young readers who fail to make satisfactory progress.

The importance of facility with phonology is best understood by first considering the importance of phonemic awareness. Troia (2004) described it as "the deepest level of phonological awareness, which is most crucial to success in reading (and spelling). It facilitates the process by which many beginning readers identify printed words, converting single letters and letter strings into their corresponding phonemes and then re-assembling the sounds to pronounce the written word" (p. 1).

Key concerns within phonemic awareness include syllable awareness, segmentation related to the first sound in a word, onset-rhyme awareness, onset-rhyme blending, onset-rhyme segmentation, the blending of individual sounds, and the segmentation of individual sounds (Bursuck & Damer, 2007). Thus students must learn to *discriminate* between words and between sounds, *identify* certain sounds within words, *manipulate* the sounds in words, *identify* phonemes (e.g., ax = a/k/s, bake = b/a/k, thing = th/i/ng), and *isolate* sounds in words, such as in the initial, medial, and final positions.

Because the phonological system is the primary problem area for students with reading disabilities, it requires explicit instruction for those who do not learn

---

CULTURALLY RESPONSIVE CLASSROOMS

The field of reading instruction has begun assembling a synthesized understanding of English language learners (ELLs) and instruction in phonemic awareness and word recognition. The same principles of instruction for English speakers can be applied to ELLs, with certain adaptations; however, ELLs can be very different from one another in terms of their literacy backgrounds. Children who begin learning English after they are already literate in their first language have already developed certain word-level skills and may not need the same types of instruction as a native English speaker first learning to read.

One important finding is that teachers do not have to wait for English learners to acquire English proficiency before beginning phonemic awareness instruction. However, teachers need to keep in mind certain differences between their native English speakers and their English learners as well as certain instructional caveats.

- The sounds of English are likely different in some way from the sounds of the student's first language. This means that children may have difficulty hearing and/or producing certain English sounds.
- After learning about sound differences between the child's first language and English, teachers will need to help children both hear these differences and account for these differences in writing. Teachers should not overemphasize standard English pronunciations. Students who have repeated exposures to the sounds and pronunciations of English through planned oral activities and wide reading will steadily improve in their pronunciations.

- If English language learners have developed high levels of phonological awareness in their first language, it is likely that they will also have high levels in English, particularly if their first language used an alphabetic writing system as opposed to a logographic system such as Chinese.

One challenge in word-recognition instruction with ELLs is that these children are much more frequently attempting to decode or recognize words for which they have no spoken counterpart. When an English-speaking student tries to decode the word *moon*, successful decoding efforts lead to a known word and its accompanying denotations and connotations. For the English language learner, decoding the word *moon* may be the same as decoding the nonsense word *poom*: the end goal of attaching decoded word to meaning is not achieved. Teachers can address meaning through approaches such as picture support and simple explanations and/or definitions.

Teachers should keep in mind that studies have shown that effective instructional practices have enabled English language learners who have initially lagged behind their English-speaking peers to perform as well as, and sometimes even better than, those same peers in a full range of literacy tasks. The key to these improvements is systematic instruction.

Laura Smolkin is a professor of elementary education at the University of Virginia's Curry School of Education.

to read independently. Instruction based on these considerations promotes the ability to be aware of phonemes in words and serves as a foundation for the use and application of sound–symbol correspondences in reading as a component of phonetic analysis.

Torgesen and Mathes (2000) identified these instructional principles for phonemic awareness:

1. Instruction should begin with easier and move toward more difficult tasks. . . . Many programs begin with general listening activities designed to help children attend to sequences of individual sounds, and then move to activities that help children become aware of individual words in sentences, and then syllables in words. . . . Once children have some beginning proficiency with sound comparison tasks, they can be moved to training activities that involve segmenting beginning sounds and blending of onset-rhyme patterns (i.e., c-at, d-og). The final series of tasks should be those that involve completely segmenting the sounds in simple words, or blending all the sounds, or manipulating the sounds in words (e.g., "What word do we have if we say *cat*, but don't say the /k/ sound?").

2. Instruction . . . should take place for 15 to 20 minutes every day throughout the kindergarten year. . . . For children who require more intensive instruction, small group or individual tutoring should be provided daily. . . .

3. Instruction should involve both *analytic* and *synthetic* activities. Analytic activities require children to identify individual sounds within whole words (e.g., "Tell me some words that begin with the same sound as *dog*,"). . . . Synthetic activities involve blending together separately presented phonemes (e.g., "What word do these sounds make: /f/a/t/?"). (pp. 45–48)

In its review of studies on phonemic awareness, the NRP (2000) concluded the following:

- Instruction in (phonemic) awareness is effective in enhancing the ability of children to attend to and manipulate speech sounds in words.
- Instruction in the manipulation of phonemes—the sounds of language—subsequently assists students in learning how to read.
- Instruction is most effective when the focus of instruction is on the manipulation of phonemes with letters and when children are taught within small instructional groups.

- Phonemic awareness is always a means and not an end, and consequently the inclusion of letters is important so that the phonemic skills can be transferred to reading and writing tasks.
- The provision of early instruction of phonemic awareness is not a guarantee of later success in literacy.

Phonetic Analysis

Teaching **phonetic analysis** (e.g., phonics) builds on phonemic awareness as students learn how to apply their knowledge of the phonology to the written word. While phonemic awareness provides an explicit awareness of a word's sound structure, such as through phoneme blending (e.g., /c/ /a/ /t/ = cat) and through phoneme segmentation (e.g., bat = /b/ /a/ /t/), phonics provides instruction in critical sound–letter (phoneme–grapheme) correspondences (Gillon, 2004).

Phonetic analysis provides a strategy to attack unknown words by applying a learned rule. Bursuck and Damer (2007) noted that systematic phonetic analysis programs are ones in which teachers explicitly teach students to relate sounds and letters, to blend sounds into words, and to break words into sounds. In so doing, they also help the students understand the relationships between sounds and letters, promote the application of phonics skills as they are reading words and sentences, and stress alphabetic knowledge, phonemic awareness, vocabulary development, and text reading along with systematic phonetic analysis instruction.

Phonetic analysis can be used as an initial step in a developmental program with young students just beginning to learn to read, or it can be used as a remedial technique with students who have developed a strong sight vocabulary but lack the skills needed to analyze unfamiliar words. The teacher's goal is to produce fluent readers with the necessary skills to decode unknown words. Once decoded, the words should become part of the students' sight-word vocabularies so that they can be read without analysis when next encountered.

The two most common forms of phonetic analysis are analytic phonics and synthetic phonics. Pullen and Lloyd (2008) defined the former as "teaching students to analyze letter-sound relations in previously learned words to avoid pronouncing sounds in isolation" (p. 2). They described synthetic phonics as "teaching students explicitly to convert letters into sounds (phonemes) and then blended sounds to form words" (p. 2).

Phonics Instructional Sequence The sequence presented below for learning phonetic skills is adapted from the classic work of Orton (1964):

1. /b/, /s/, /f/, /m/, /t/ in initial and final positions
2. Short /a/
3. All consonants except the five already learned
4. Short vowels (/o/, /i/, /u/, /e/)
5. Consonant digraphs (/sh/, /ch/, /th/, /wh/)
6. Initial consonant blends (/bl/, /br/, /st/)
7. Final consonant blends (/nd/, /nk/)
8. Long vowels (final /e/, double vowels)
9. r-influenced vowels (/er/, /ir/, /ur/, /ar/)
10. Suffixes (-s, -ing, -ed)
11. Vowel teams (/ai/, /ea/, /ow/, /ea/)
12. Vowel diphthongs (/oy/, /au/)
13. Prefixes (e-, pre-, un-)

This sequence introduces five consonants, then short /a/. It allows the formation of short words quickly (e.g., *bat, fat, tab*) to provide immediate decoding experience.

Typically, consonant sounds are taught initially because they are easier than vowels to learn, are most consistently associated with only one sound, and are the first sound in most words. Teachers first must ensure that students can discriminate between the sound being taught and different consonant sounds at the beginning of a word. Consonant sounds can be taught with keywords and pictures. Individual consonants and digraphs should be introduced one at a time and then reviewed along with the sounds previously taught. Before moving to vowel sounds, students should have mastered common consonant sounds in the initial and final positions and should be able to blend teacher-pronounced sounds into words. Once vowel sound instruction is initiated, this sequence is effective to integrate vowel and consonant instruction:

1. Provide the child with auditory experiences to discriminate between similar vowel sounds. A student must be able to hear how a sound is different and unique before he or she can reproduce it in a new word or identify it in a word to be spelled.
2. Teach students to blend a vowel sound to final consonants and blends, and to spell these stems (e.g., p-*ack*).
3. Teach students to use onset-rhyme to blend initial consonant sounds to these stems (*b* + *ack* = *back*).

4. Present words containing the vowel sound being taught and have the student rehearse: Find the vowel, cover all the letters that come before it, pronounce the vowel stem, add the initial consonant or blend, and pronounce the whole word.
5. When the child can analyze words (which in isolation contain the sound in question), provide guided opportunities that allow the child to use the new sound to decode unknown words in context.

Direct Instruction A key instructional strategy for teaching reading skills, and particularly for teaching decoding skills, is direct instruction. The attributes of direct instruction include the fact that it is an explicit and systematic approach to teaching that is focused on clear outcomes. The teacher is directly responsible for the instructional activities, but high student engagement is a key aspect. Instruction begins with ensuring student attention and then a precise sequencing of content is essential. Teachers monitor student responses and provide corrective feedback. Most important, direct instruction is intensive and explicit. By actively engaging students in requiring higher rates of appropriate responses and by carefully matching instruction to student ability and skill level, teachers are able to ensure that the instruction provided is consistent with student needs. The use of instructional prompts to support learning, the systematic fading of the prompts, and the provision of feedback also are critical (Rock, Thead, Gable, Hardman, & Acker 2006).

ENHANCEDetext
video example 6.1
Watch this video to learn more about direct instruction and the teaching of reading.

NRP The NRP (2000) evaluated research on phonetic analysis instruction and reported the following:

- Programs that involve the use of systematic phonics instruction make larger contributions to achievement than do programs that provide no such instruction or unsystematic phonics instruction.

- Systematic phonics instruction can be effective through a variety of delivery modes including tutorial approaches, small-group instruction, and class instruction.
- Instruction is most effective when taught to younger children (i.e., Grades K–1). It should begin with basic foundational knowledge, which includes instruction on letters and phonemic awareness.
- Systematic phonics instruction results in significant improvement in the reading performance of young children at risk for developing further problems and also for readers with disabilities. However, in general, low-achieving readers nevertheless make less progress.
- Rather than interfering with students' ability to read and comprehend textual material, systematic phonics instruction has a positive effect on their growth in this area as well.

The NRP (2000) concluded with this caution: "phonics teaching is a means to an end. . . . Students need to be able to blend sounds together to decode words, and they need to break spoken words into the constituent sounds to write words. Programs that focus too much on the teaching of letter-sound relationships and not enough on putting them to use are unlikely to be very effective" (section 2, p. 96).

Sight-Word Vocabulary

For learners with a disability, a key component is learning **sight words**. Through a whole-word approach, students learn to recognize important high-frequency words without analysis. Students must achieve **automaticity** with the sight words they have learned—they must recognize them immediately and automatically—to be able to move continuously through a written passage. Fluent readers use their sight vocabulary consistently, applying phonetic analysis only to new words. Sight-word development often focuses on the recognition and rapid recall of words in text. However, another critical aspect is the development of word knowledge or vocabulary. Because of its clear ties to comprehension, we consider *vocabulary development* in the next chapter.

To be remembered, sight words must already be in the learner's speaking and comprehension vocabulary. The most common source of sight words is from high-frequency word lists (see Table 6-4).

TABLE 6–4 50 high-frequency words

after	did	his	school	through
always	done	inside	semester	two
any	each	just	subject	what
because	first	morning	teacher	where
become	friend	need	teenager	which
black	give	open	tell	while
book	great	people	the	white
choice	help	please	their	why
class	her	remember	there	yes
could	here	run	they	your

Source: Graphic Models and Instructional Tools for Students with Special Needs (p. 16), by E. A. Polloway & J. Lubin, 2016, *Lynchburg College Journal of Special Education*, Lynchburg College, Lynchburg, VA. Used with permission.

As can be noted in the list, a substantial number of these words are phonetically irregular, do not lend themselves to decoding, and thus are best learned as sight, or whole, words. If a basal series is used, words from the particular program can become a focus of sight-word instruction.

With all students, but especially with those experiencing reading difficulty, a variety of strategies should be used to teach sight words, and success is often a function of multiple exposures to achieve automaticity. Thus, the challenge of sight-word instruction is to provide students with multiple exposures to words through varied means.

The **Fernald method** (Fernald, 1943) is a classic multisensory approach combining language experience with visual, kinesthetic, and tactile (VAKT) instructional techniques. The program consists of four steps: eliciting a word from the student, writing it large enough for the student to trace, saying the word as the student traces the word, and having the student write the word from memory. These steps are intended to provide ways to develop a sight vocabulary by offering the students multiple ways of experiencing the word. Words can then be alphabetically filed in a word bank. When several words have been learned, the student uses them to dictate a story to the teacher. As the student progresses, the procedure can be modified in various ways. For example, tracing can be done with letters made of sandpaper, smooth paper laid on sandpaper, or sand sprinkled on glue. Teachers should focus on the potential benefits of teaching new words through multiple means. Rather than rigid adherence to the sequence outlined by Fernald, teachers are encouraged to investigate multisensory strategies that are effective for individual students and enhance their recognition of sight words.

Another approach to teaching sight words is using pictures together with sight words. Picture–word combination can be used in two ways (Blackwell & Laman, 2013). First, the teacher uses a direct representation of the word where the child is shown a pictorial illustration and the written word. Second, the word is morphed into a picture where the letters of the word are manipulated to create a graphical image which represents the meaning of the word (Blackwell & Laman, 2013). Sheehy (2005) explained that "the graphic form of the word itself is altered, the new shape being an intermediate form between picture and word" (p. 295). In this transformative instructional style, the child is shown three representations of the word: the written word, a picture, and a morphed illustration. The morphed approach has proven to be more effective than teaching sight words in isolation (Sheehy, 2005). Several strategies that can be used to enhance fluency also have merit for strengthening sight vocabulary. In a subsequent section, repeated readings, unison reading, and paired reading are discussed in detail.

Another strategy for sight word instruction is using games. Blackwell and Laman (2013) defined "game-based teaching . . . as the use of a game to deliver lesson material either during regular instruction or in between lessons when games are defined as an enjoyable activity by the participant(s)" (p. 44). Several games can be used to teach sight words, including a modified version of bingo. (See also Activities 2, 4, and 5 under "Sight Vocabulary.") Games can be commercially generated or teacher-made.

Functional Reading and Sight Words. Sight word instruction is consistent with the concept of **functional reading**, which refers to a level of literacy necessary for information and protection. An understanding of this concept is particularly important for teachers of secondary students who must decide how to teach reading. Instruction at this level raises a number of difficult questions: Which reading program should the current teacher select? Is it best in the limited time remaining to teach functional reading so that students will know some words for their own protection and safety? Or is there still time to teach students decoding strategies, aiming toward an acceptable level of literacy?

After weighing these factors, the teacher can decide to concentrate efforts on functional reading, exert a final effort toward teaching remedial skills, or focus primarily on one option but include the other in a less intensive form. Students need to understand clearly what the goal is and how it will be measured at specific intervals. When goals are organized into small steps, adolescent students are motivated by their progress, which suggests that the problems they have faced unsuccessfully throughout their school careers may have solutions.

Reading for protection requires minimal but practical competence. Generally, this is the level of reading achievement that enables minimal survival in today's word-dependent world. Survival words should be taught as sight words, consistent with the strategies described earlier in the chapter. The teacher should provide actual experiences that demonstrate the word's meaning, produce a concrete object, or identify a special characteristic of the concept. A list of 25 survival words and survival phrases is presented in Table 6-5.

Fortunately, most students with disabilities learn to read well beyond the level of survival words. The next stage of functional reading addresses what the world of work requires and thus focuses on sufficient skills to fill out applications and related forms, pass a driver's test, follow simple factor check-in directions, order from a restaurant menu, and handle similar life tasks.

Teachers can use a combination of strategies to teach this level of functional reading. Using a sight-word approach, the specific vocabulary of applications and forms can be taught. The most important step is teaching students to generalize this knowledge by providing practice with the variety of formats and situations that they are likely to encounter. Many workbooks contain samples of forms and applications.

Structural Analysis

Structural analysis skills enable students to use larger segments of words for decoding cues. Recognition of root words, compound words, prefixes, suffixes, contractions, and plurals allows students to use clusters of letters to assist in reading a new word. Structural analysis is an essential

TABLE 6–5 Survival words and phrases

Beware of dog	Exit	Keep away	No turns	Restrooms
Boys	Exit only	Keep closed	On	Slippery when wet
Bus stop	Flammable	Keep off	One way	Slow down
Closed	Girls	Keep out	Off	Smoking prohibited
Danger	Go	Ladies	Open	Step down
Do not cross	Help	Men	Out of order	Stop
Do not enter	Help wanted	No parking	Poison	Walk
Do not touch	Hospital zone	No right turn	Private	Warning
Don't walk	Hot	No smoking	Pull	Watch your step
Down	In	No swimming	Push	Women
Entrance	Information	No trespassing	Quiet	Wrong way

Source: Graphic Models and Instructional Tools for Students with Special Needs (p. 17), by E. A. Polloway & J. Lubin, 2016, *Lynchburg College Journal of Special Education,* Lynchburg College, Lynchburg, VA. Used with permission.

word-recognition strategy that directly influences fluency; continued letter-by-letter phonetic analysis slows the reading process and will inhibit comprehension. The strategies suggested for teaching phonics also apply to teaching the structural elements related to meaning units, that is, morphemes in words (e.g., prefixes, suffixes).

Morphemic Analysis. This form of word analysis focuses on morphemes, which are the smallest units of meaning found within words. For example, the word *really* consists of two morphemes: *real* and *ly*. Root words that can stand alone are referred to as the *free morphemes*, while affixes (suffixes and prefixes) are classified as *bound morphemes* because they must be attached to a free morpheme.

Instructional programs for students should help them discern the meaning units that are within words. Consequently, the focus of instruction should be on identifying common prefixes as well as common suffixes so that students will attend to their presence, realize they constitute a separate syllable with distinct meaning, identify the root word to which they are bound, and consequently be able to break down the word according to its structure (hence structural or morphemic analysis). Table 6-6 provides a summary of common prefixes, suffixes, and roots; these can be used to frame specific instructional units that will enhance the ability of students to take advantage of meaning units within words.

Morphological instruction is important in helping students learn unknown words. Teachers must plan instruction carefully to ensure effectiveness.

In a study conducted by Pacheco and Goodwin (2013) to find out the different strategies middle school students used to decipher unknown words, they discovered that when students started their analysis of words using root words, they were more effective than when starting with prefixes or suffixes. The researchers recommended that effective morphological instruction should begin with teachers guiding students to focus on root words, followed by affixes.

TABLE 6–6 Morpheme meanings: Examples and non-examples

Morpheme: Prefix/Suffix/Root	Meaning	Example	Non-Example
bi-	two	bicycle	binder
un-	not	unlikely	unite
pan-	all	pandemic	panther
-ject	to throw	interject	subject
-hood	body of people	priesthood	likelihood
port	to carry	teleport	report
post	after	postdate	poster
-able	capable of being	suitable	table
-pel-	to drive	compel	spelling

Source: Graphic Models and Instructional Tools for Students with Special Needs (p. 18), by E. A. Polloway & J. Lubin, 2016, *Lynchburg College Journal of Special Education,* Lynchburg College, Lynchburg, VA. Used with permission.

Other components of morphemic analysis include the identification of compound words as well as contractions. Typically, these represent more limited challenges for readers but nevertheless are important areas of focus within instruction as students understand these other ways of viewing meaning units in the process of word recognition.

Syllabication. Another key area of structural analysis is syllabication. The core of instruction in syllabication is to learn two rules central to success. The first rule, dividing syllables between two consonants, can be illustrated by the word *rabbit*. Instruction can emphasize that *rabbit* should have two syllables (that is, two sounded vowels), should be divided between *b* and *b* (two consonants together), and then should be read as two small words (*rab-bit*) and blended in to one word.

The second core rule is dividing syllables between a vowel and a consonant. It can be illustrated by the word *favor*. Division between syllables would fall between *a* and *v* (because of the vowel–consonant–vowel combination), and the word would be read and blended (*fa-vor*). These two basic rules can extend to words with more syllables (e.g., *discussion* and *tomato*, respectively) and with both combinations present (e.g., *envelope*, *remainder*). The nearby Teacher Tip provides detailed steps for teaching syllabication skills that is particularly apt for older students.

TEACHER *Tips*   **Secondary Level**

Syllabication Strategy

The syllabication method is used to teach students to recognize and count syllables, to apply two rules to words with two or more syllables, and to rely on vocabulary to correct any distortions in pronunciations. Without a multitude of rules to memorize, students can read longer words using the phonetic generalizations learned previously. The steps for the syllabication strategy (as adapted from Polloway et al., 2012) are as follows:

1. Student identifies how many syllables are heard in known words. Student will divide a known word orally.
   a. Teacher orally explains concept and demonstrates on known words.
   b. Student is given words to divide orally.
   c. Sample word list: *tomato, sunshine, toe, cucumber.*
2. Student recognizes that a word has as many syllables as vowels heard.
   a. Teacher writes known words, and student tells how many syllables are heard and how many vowels are seen and heard.
   b. Process continues until student learns that the number of vowels heard equals the number of syllables.
   c. Sample word list: *tomato, sunshine, toe, cucumber.*
3. Student determines how many syllables an unknown word will have.
   a. Review the two rules of the silent *e* and that when two vowels come together, one sound results.

   b. Teacher writes unknown word; student determines which vowels will be silent and predicts number of syllables.
   c. Sample word list: *domino, barbecue, stagnate, mouse.*
4. Student syllabicates words that follow the vc/cv (vowel consonant/consonant vowel) pattern.
   a. Teacher writes and student divides two-syllable words.
   b. Student practices dividing and pronouncing two-syllable vc/cv words.
   c. Teacher demonstrates process of dividing longer known words:
      i. Determine number of syllables.
      ii. Establish first division by starting with first vowel and look for vc/cv pattern, then divide.
      iii. Establish second division by starting with second vowel and look for vc/cv pattern, then divide.
      iv. Continue procedure until all syllables are determined.
      v. Pronounce word.
   d. Student practices dividing and pronouncing unknown words that contain vc/cv pattern.
   e. Sample word list: *rabbit, bitter, pepper, mixture.*
5. Student syllabicates words that contain the v/cv (vowel/consonant vowel) pattern.
   a. Follow instructions for step 4, substituting the v/cv pattern.
   b. Sample word list: *labor, favor, basic, demand.*

(continued)

6. Student syllabicates words that contain both vc/cv and v/cv patterns.
   a. Teacher writes and student divides known words that contain both patterns.
   b. Student practices dividing and pronouncing unknown words with both patterns.
   c. Sample word list: *envelope, cucumber, remainder, resulting.*
7. Student syllabicates words that have a vcccv (vowel consonant consonant consonant vowel) or vccccv pattern.
   a. Teacher writes and student divides known words containing vcccv or vccccv patterns until student recognizes that the division is based on consonant blends and digraphs.
   b. Student practices dividing and pronouncing unknown words containing both patterns.
   c. Sample word list: *concrete, pitcher, contract, merchant.*
8. Student syllabicates words ending with *cle* (i.e., consonant *le*).

   a. Teacher writes and student divides known words ending with *cle* until student generalizes that when preceded by *cl*, the final *e* is not silent but produces a syllable that contains *cle* and the preceding consonant.
   b. Student practices dividing and pronouncing unknown words containing the *cle* ending.
   c. Sample word list: *candle, rattle, dribble, staple.*
9. Student recognizes the *y* in the medial or final position as a vowel.
   a. Teacher tells student that *y* will be a vowel in the medial or final position.
   b. Teacher writes and student divides known words containing *y* in both positions.
   c. Student practices dividing and pronouncing unknown words that contain *y* in the medial or final position.
   d. Sample word list: *funny, my, cranky, style.*
10. Student divides and pronounces unknown words containing mixed patterns.
11. Student syllabicates and pronounces unknown words in context.

Teaching syllabication skills builds on the student's existing sound–symbol skills to analyze longer words beyond the student's current reading vocabulary. With success to the degree that such a task can be done automatically, students can then incorporate it within the process of reading a passage without significant interference with comprehension.

Contextual Analysis

Contextual analysis involves the identification of an unknown word based on its use in a sentence or passage. It functions as a system of syntactic and semantic cuing. Context clues potentially may help readers identify words and derive word meanings.

At the early elementary level, students' listening vocabulary and comprehension may supersede their decoding skills, and thus their ability to use context may be relatively effective. They can use structural and meaning cues to follow the sentences to anticipate forthcoming words and make a guess about one that they might not be able to recognize on sight. Context clues may be a useful strategy for young children, particularly for its impact on

comprehension. Its use with older students, however, is more problematic; it is discussed below.

Contextual Analysis for Older Students. Difficulty in the use of context becomes evident as students move to middle school. The challenge for teachers is to find a way to encourage the use of context primarily when it assists in enhancing comprehension of text (e.g., through vocabulary development) and figuring out the occasional word but not to overemphasize it to the point where it becomes a primary strategy used by students.

Stanovich and Stanovich (1995) spoke directly to this issue in noting that "research has consistently indicated that the word recognition of better readers is *not* characterized by more reliance on contextual information. . . . There *is* considerable evidence that better readers are better able to use contextual information to facilitate their *comprehension* processes. . . . However, research . . . has shown that hypotheses about context use in comprehension were inappropriately generalized to the *word recognition* level. . . . In summary, contextual information is simply no substitute for the ability to decode the words on the page" (pp. 90, 92).

Applying Multiple Word Strategies

CRUSCH is a word-recognition strategy for identifying unknown, polysyllabic words encountered in text. CRUSCH refers to the following:

- Consonant—Focus on the initial consonant sound.
- Rapid—Rapidly focus on initial consonant, vowel sounds, and prefixes and suffixes while reviewing whole words.
- Unimportant—Skip over unimportant words that do not require precise pronunciation (e.g., names).
- Syllabicate—Apply syllabication strategies if word pronunciation is essential.
- Context—Use contextual analysis for periodic (i.e., infrequent) determination of meaning for new vocabulary words.
- Help—Seek help (e.g., from teacher, peer, dictionary).

CRUSCH can assist students in thinking about how they will respond when confronted with unknown words. Although research indicates that mature readers are most successful when they respond to the inherent sound–symbol correspondences in their reading, the steps as outlined will give those who experience difficulty ways to generate meaning for new vocabulary words, focus on the most efficient sound–symbol correspondences that provide key graphophonemic cues, ignore the need for pronunciation of words that do not affect meaning, and utilize more complex syllabication strategies when they are necessary to determine the pronunciation of a particular word and/or an understanding of its meaning.

Phonemic Awareness and Word-Recognition Curricular Programs

Several instruments have been designed to help learners develop reading skills. These instructional programs may assist with phonological awareness, phonemic awareness, word recognition, decoding, and fluency (and, in some cases, comprehension skills). Several reading intervention programs are noted below.

The **Lindamood Program for Reading, Spelling, and Speech** (Lindamood & Lindamood, 1998) focuses on the development of phonemic awareness by enabling learners to identify and sequence individual sounds in their order within words to promote competence in reading, spelling, and speech. The key element is learning consonant and vowel sounds through feedback from articulating the sounds. It includes a training manual, a research booklet, videotapes, photos of correct formation for phoneme pronunciation, and a variety of instructional materials. A comprehensive review of related research by Truch (1998) focused on the effectiveness of the Lindamood program within the context of an analysis of the role of phonological processing in reading and spelling.

Phonological Awareness Training for Reading was developed by Torgesen and Bryant (1994) and is designed to increase phonological awareness in young children with particular emphasis on kindergarten children at risk for failure and first- and second-grade children who have already begun to experience difficulty in learning to read. It is an approximately 12-week-long program that teaches sensitivity to phonological structures. The program includes a training manual, picture word cards, rhyming picture cards, and a variety of other instructional materials. It is based on validation studies conducted by the senior author under the auspices of the National Institute of Mental Health. Wanzek, Dickson, Bursuck, and White (2000) reported that the program includes a number of key features: It is consistent with preferred curriculum design principles, requires limited adaptations for at-risk learners, is user-friendly, and provides teachers with an explicit script to follow for instructions.

The **Reading Mastery Program** (Engelmann, 2003) relies on auditory and sound-blending skills. The program presents a phonetic alphabet of 40 symbols taught in a highly sequential manner before introducing letter names. In each lesson, the teacher reads the material to a small group of students and asks individuals to respond orally when given certain designated symbols. Student behavior and responses are monitored during exercises. The program contains reading materials using specialized symbols and seatwork activities focused on both word analysis and comprehension. Other materials in this series are teacher's guides, lesson plans, reading books, workbooks, spelling books, and take-home readers. The program is highly structured, sequences each step of learning, and contains criterion objectives for each learning task as a developmental program in beginning reading instruction for any student, but these programs are more commonly used for remedial purposes.

The **Corrective Reading Program (CRP)** (Engelmann, 1999) is a direct instruction program for upper elementary, middle, and high school students who have not mastered decoding and/or comprehension skills. The program is divided into two strands, decoding and comprehension, each with three levels of skill development. The comprehension strand presents a variety of formats involving real-life survival situations that are excellent for the adolescent learner. CRP promotes academic engaged time by providing group lesson plans using teaching strategies that require students to answer aloud and in unison. Each lesson is fast paced, keeping students thinking and providing less opportunity for students to become distracted. Because CRP uses the direct instruction approach, it provides a script for teachers to follow. Special motivation for adolescent students is provided in a group reinforcement component, with each student receiving additional points based on the group's performance. Some research (e.g., Polloway, Epstein, Polloway, Patton, & Ball, 1986) has indicated that students with learning disabilities as well as those who were mildly intellectually disabled increased decoding and comprehension skills after participating in the CRP for an academic year. Further, when implemented with 11th- and 12th-grade peer instructors, CRP was effective in increasing achievement test scores and oral fluency (Harris, Marchand-Martella, & Martella, 2000).

The **Spalding Method** (Spalding Education International, 2000; Spalding Method Catalog, 2002) for literacy instruction is a total language approach that involves explicit, multisensory instruction in spelling, writing, and listening/reading comprehension. Specifically, the essential components for this method include phonics instruction, writing, comprehension instruction, literacy appreciation, and a philosophy centered on the development of critical thinking skills for children. The program is commonly used with both general and special education students in grades K through 12. The Spalding program utilizes a variety of techniques in the course of literacy instruction. For example, during phonemic awareness training, students are taught explicitly to segment spoken words and syllables as well as blend sounds into spoken words. Students also learn to speak and write 70 common sound–symbol relationships. Both of these techniques are reinforced through daily phonogram and spelling reviews. In addition, the program incorporates extensive fluency training, vocabulary instruction, and comprehension strategies through which teachers may provide modeling and immediate feedback. Another essential component of the Spalding program is providing students with quality literature and then encouraging independent reading to complement the other elements of the program.

The **Wilson Reading System** (Wilson Language Training Corporation, 2015) is a well-regarded reading program that provides an important focus on decoding skills. The program is based on the Orton-Gillingham approach to instruction in reading and consequently has a strong emphasis on phonetic analysis skills. The program uses a "sound tapping" system to highlight letter–sound correspondences. It includes an extensive set of word lists, sentences, and stories that can be decoded. It also includes two levels of vocabulary in order to make the program applicable to students from primary grades through secondary school. Malmgren and Trezek (2009) reported on the research of the Florida Center for Reading Research regarding the degree to which various reading curricula address the key components of reading: phonemic awareness, phonics, fluency, vocabulary, and comprehension. The Wilson Reading System received four ratings of three (highest rating) (with a two rating on vocabulary development). Wilson and O'Connor (1995) also provided data on the effectiveness of students with learning disabilities across grades 3 to 12 in terms of skills, comprehension, total reading scores, and spelling.

The **Edmark Reading Program** (Edmark Associates, 2002) consists of two levels designed to teach basic sight vocabulary. The program was originally designed to instruct students with intellectual disabilities through a systematic approach that would encourage motivation and cooperative behaviors, but it has been used successfully with other students, primarily to help them acquire a basic sight vocabulary. For each lesson, students are asked to follow a systematic method of learning, with emphasis on errorless discrimination. Following each lesson, the student participates in a set of various activities, including stories, direction cards, and picture/phrase cards. Both levels introduce words in groups of 10. There are posttests given at the end of each group for review. The stories and activities that follow each lesson have story ideas that relate to real-life situations to capture student interest. Level 1 includes lessons for 150 basic sight vocabulary words. This level also introduces simple endings (-*ed*, -*ing*, -*s*); its goal is to have the nonreader at a first-grade level. Level 2 introduces 200 new words. This level includes more complex words, including compound words; its goal is to have the student reading at a third-grade level.

Peer-Mediated Strategies

With reading instruction being critical to student success, students must be provided the maximum amount of instruction time within the school day. However, meeting students' needs when their ability levels are significantly at variance is difficult. One approach is to use peer-mediated strategies.

In the area of reading, the best-researched intervention using peers at the elementary level is the Peer-Assisted Learning Strategies (PALS) approach (Fuchs & Fuchs, 2005; What Works Clearinghouse, 2012). The PALS program matches a student with a peer and includes a higher and lower performer within the class. Although the roles of tutors are reciprocal, the program has the student who is higher performing reading first for each of the activities as a way to model the goal performance.

PALS is an effective instructional tool across educational levels (Fuchs & Fuchs, 2005; Rafdal, McMaster, McConnell, Fuchs, & Fuchs, 2011; Spörer & Brunstein, 2009). For example, Kindergarten Peer-Assisted Learning Strategies (K-PALS) has proven effective for improving reading skills of kindergarten students with and without disabilities. In fact, when used in the inclusive classroom, K-PALS has shown gains for students with disabilities in the areas of initial alphabetic principle and decoding skills, including word attack, spelling, and oral reading (Rafdal et al., 2011).

LEARNING MODULE 6.1
Click here to learn more about PALS: A reading strategy for grades K–1: http://iris.peabody.vanderbilt.edu/module/palsk1

In addition, PALS can enhance reading comprehension of secondary students (Spörer & Brunstein, 2009). The use of PALS by older students has shown improvement in self-regulated behaviors as well as summarization skills (Spörer & Brunstein, 2009).

LEARNING MODULE 6.2
Click here to learn more about PALS: A reading strategy for high school students: http://iris.peabody.vanderbilt.edu/module/palshs

Fuchs and Fuchs (2005) summarized PALS findings across multiple studies as follows:

- Some instructional content reserved for older and more sophisticated learners can and should be directed to younger children. This content includes decoding and word recognition in kindergarten and fluency building in first grade.
- PALS is a means of transforming knowledge about reading instruction, developed and highly controlled in artificial context, into routines and programs that real teachers in the real schools can implement.
- In spite of our treatments' general effectiveness and robustness, they did not help all individual children. There was always 10% to 20% who did not respond to either of our most successful treatments.
- Teaching of some higher order reading skills, including those that may appear developmentally appropriate, may be unproductive: First graders who received instruction in word-reading skills outperformed those participating in both word-reading and comprehension activities because, we believe, the activities designed to strengthen comprehension inadvertently interrupted reading practice. (p. 42)

Check Your Understanding 6.4 Click here to gauge your understanding of the concepts in this section.

FLUENCY

A key concern is to develop fluency in reading. It serves as an appropriate bridge between word recognition and comprehension because as students are able to more fluently read sentences and passages, they are subsequently better able to follow the text meaning. *Fluency* is defined as "the ability to read text accurately, quickly, and with expression. All three of its elements—accuracy, speed, and expression—are essential if students are to understand what they read" (Bursuck & Damer, 2007, p. 169). More specifically, these three components are *speed* (i.e., rate with a goal of 100 words per minute [wpm] by grade 3 and 300 wpm for adults), *accurate word recognition* (i.e., automatic recognition of most words read), and *expressive reading* in terms of phrasing, intonation, and rhythm (Tompkins, 2006). The development of fluency is a complement to comprehension; the process of reading through passages continuously and smoothly can enhance comprehension.

Kubina and Hughes (2007) noted that "many students, even when they become accurate decoders, do not automatically become fluent readers and must be taught to do so by providing meaningful practice through repeated exposure to text" (p. 1). Effective strategies for promoting fluency can include the use of repeated readings, unison reading (in which the teacher and student read a text together), paired reading that includes a more mature reading with a less skilled reader, and of course regular opportunities to engage in the reading process both orally and silently.

It is also important to consider fluency for students with intellectual disabilities. Allor, Mathes, Roberts, Cheatham, and Otaiba (2014) reported that interventions for students with lower IQ should include validated reading instruction in which delivery is explicit and systematic. They reported that

> a student with an IQ of 75 would require 52 weeks of intervention to move from 20 words per minute (wpm) to 60 wpm on first grade reading passages. Students with IQs between 70 and 80 require approximately one and a half school years to move from 20 wpm to 60 wpm. . . . A student in the *mild* range . . . would require approximately three academic years to move from 10 wpm to 60 wpm. (p. 302)

Repeated Readings

With **repeated readings** or *multiple oral readings (MOR)*, students receive a selection approximately 200 words in length with instructions to practice reading it orally while listening to a tape of the same material. When students decide that they are ready, their time and errors are recorded. After further oral practice, another time/error check is made. This procedure continues until the student

reads 85 words per minute, at which time the process begins again with new material.

Moyer (1982) outlined the following steps for MOR:

1. Choose materials at a level that results in limited difficulty in word recognition.
2. Read initially at a comfortable pace.
3. Reread three to four times, increasing the speed with each reading.
4. Use passages of approximately three to four paragraphs on the average; vary according to the student's needs.

A derivative of multiple oral readings is timed-repeated readings (Sample, 2005). With this approach, teachers can (a) select a passage of approximately 100 words, (b) have students reread the passage until they reach a predetermined rate of fluency with regard to words per minute and also word-recognition accuracy, (c) engage in self-assessment by graphing the results to show continued improvement, and (d) use self- or peer-mediated strategies to enhance further performance.

The NRP (2000) concluded that repeated reading can positively affect students' reading:

> In the early stage of reading instruction, the beginning reader may be accurate in word recognition but the process is likely to be slow and effortful. With increased practice and repeated exposure to the words in a text that the student reads, word recognition continues to be accurate [and improvements are] evident in the speed and ease of word recognition as well. Continued reading practice helps make the word-recognition process increasingly automatic. (pp. 3–8)

Based on its review of research since the publication of the NRP's report, Pressley and Fingeret (2005) concluded that multiple readings is an effective approach to enhance fluency. Further, they indicated that teacher guidance was the critical component and resulted in more significant gains in both fluency and reading comprehension than occurred when the student was assigned to reread passages on his or her own.

Although repeated readings have been recognized for decades as an approach to promote reading achievement, there is need for caution in its usage. The What Works Clearinghouse (2014) reported that "repeated reading was found to have potentially positive effects on reading comprehension [but] no discernible effects on alphabetic, reading fluency, and general reading achievement for students with learning disabilities" (p. 1). It therefore serves as a complementary strategy rather than a major instructional reading approach.

Unison Reading

Several approaches represent forms of *unison reading*, in which the teacher and the students read aloud in unison or echo fashion. The instructor sits behind the student and reads slightly faster and louder, pointing to the words as they are read. This method can be used for 5 to 10 minutes daily. Progress usually occurs quickly, so this strategy should be terminated if no improvement is noted in a reasonable period of time. Because research on this technique has been mixed, teachers should evaluate its effectiveness when using it.

Teachers may also want to use *imitative reading*, which is a similar procedure for improving the fluency of students with reading difficulties. The teacher reads very simple, short segments aloud as the student follows silently. The student then tries to read the same phrase or sentence aloud. The procedure is repeated until the student reads the material with fluency.

Paired Reading

With this approach, two students who have similar instructional reading levels read aloud in unison (Henk, Helfeldt, & Platt, 1986). Material familiar to both students is used in the initial stages of paired reading. After the two develop a sense of trust and cooperation, less familiar text can be introduced. As they work together, one student can assist when the other hesitates or makes an error. Recording of these oral reading sessions can help both students evaluate their reading fluency.

Oral Reading

Oral reading is an important component of a total program. It is particularly necessary in the early stages of instruction because it gives the teacher insight into the beginning reader's knowledge of sight words and decoding skills. Oral reading has three core purposes: diagnosis, conveying of directions or instruction, and personal pleasure. For learners with special needs, oral reading has four additional purposes: articulation and vocabulary

practice, memory reinforcement, rereading for better comprehension, and group participation.

Oral reading can assist the development of correct word pronunciation by providing the reader with disabilities who seldom verbalizes with a structured opportunity to speak. When reading aloud, the student takes in information both auditorily and visually, adding an additional pathway to learning that is often necessary for memory. Rereading a passage orally after it has been read silently assists comprehension, particularly when the teacher designates a purpose for each reading.

Continuing oral reading for students with special needs longer than for children without disabilities is often beneficial. However, the students also clearly need practice and guidance in the transition from oral to silent reading (directed and encouraged by the teacher) because silent reading is the critical skill to develop. This fact will be discussed further in the next chapter with regard to how silent reading promotes comprehension.

 Check Your Understanding 6.5 Click here to gauge your understanding of the concepts in this section.

ACTIVITIES

Elementary Level

The activities listed serve as a basis for reinforcing skills in word recognition. The activities are grouped according to activities for word analysis and sight vocabulary.

Word Analysis

1. Initial consonant sounds can be practiced by gluing pictures of simple objects on small cards. Have students place the cards on a grid on which each square has a consonant letter corresponding to the beginning sound of an object on the cards. Consonant blends and final consonant sounds can be drilled in the same manner.

2. Make word wheels of word families, changing only the initial consonants. These devices not only give practice in consonant sounds but also are excellent for sound blending. Word wheels are two circles made of oaktag, one smaller than the other and fastened together

in the center with a brass fastener so that they can rotate. The different word bases (e.g., *ag*, *ad*, *at*) are written on the exposed edge of the larger circle, and the different initial consonants are written on the edge of the smaller circle. As students rotate the top circle, different words are formed, which students can read aloud to a friend.

3. Make two-part puzzles with an initial sound on one part and a word family on the other. Have students put the puzzles together and pronounce the words. Animal shapes are popular and can be cut between the head and body or body and tail. Use the same idea for contractions, compound words, and root words with endings. Character combinations are popular also: Snoopy and his doghouse, Woodstock and his nest, and Batman and his cape. Three-part puzzles can be made to accommodate adding prefixes and suffixes to root words (e.g., *unfolded*).

4. Have students make notebooks for sounds. As sounds are presented, students can cut out pictures of objects that begin with each specific sound and glue them into the book. Later, students can write words that they have learned to recognize or spell that begin with each specific sound.

5. List on the board the letters for the vowels, blends, or consonants that have been studied. Have students stand in a large circle with one student in the center. The student in the center tosses a ball to a student in the circle and calls out one of the letters from the board. The student who catches the ball has to say a word that contains the sound that was called. That student then goes to the center and throws the ball.

6. Create a "Word Forest" in the reading corner. Decorate the corner with several tree and leaves cutouts. Write the name of different word families on the stem of trees. Below the trees, place cutouts of leaves with various consonants and consonant blends. Have students create different words by sticking leaves on the tree to create a word. During reading, ask students to identify and write words pertaining to a word family in the forest. They should then stick it on the appropriate tree. Students can be ask to identify the onset and rime of words.

Sight Vocabulary

1. List words on the board. Have two students stand with their backs to the lists. As you call out a word, the students turn; the first to find the word receives a point.

2. Make a game board of oaktag with a path of squares. Mark "start" and "finish" squares and various outer squares with directions like "move ahead three squares," "move back three squares," or "shortcut" with a path to another square. Write words that are to become sight vocabulary words in the open squares with a grease pencil. Students then throw dice to determine how far they are to move. They must pronounce the word they land on to remain in the game. The game can be varied by changing the words, and several boards can be made to fit the season of the year.

3. Put pictures of words like *ball* or *car* on one side of a card and write the word on the other side. Make a game board similar to a bingo card, with each sight word written on it for each child. Place cards with the word-side up in a pile. Students take turns drawing cards. They must be able to say the word correctly before placing it on their boards. The picture on the back makes the game self-correcting. If the student cannot recognize the word, the card is placed at the bottom of the pile. The first student to get four words in a row in any direction wins the game.

4. A form of Concentration can be played by making two sets of identical cards with sight words. Begin with five pairs of cards. Place the cards spread out in two areas, face down on a flat surface. The child turns up a card in one set and then tries to find the card that matches in the other set. When a match is made, the student pronounces the word and gets to keep the cards.

5. Use a chart-sized pegboard and attach hooks on which index cards can be hung. Write vocabulary words on index cards, punch a hole in each card, and hang the cards from the hooks on the pegboard. Give students a rubber jar ring to toss at a hook on the board. When a ring lands on a hook, that card is removed from the hook, and the student pronounces the word to earn a point. The one with the most points wins. The game can be varied by using beanbags to throw at a card on a board or at cards hung from a miniature clothesline with pins.

6. Divide class into two groups. Explain to students that they are going to play a game in which they will be given five minutes to identify specific words in songs. Have students listen to a few of their favorite songs while reading the lyrics on the computer. Stop songs at strategic points and ask students to identify specific sight words and frequency seen. For example, the teacher can ask, "How many times did the word *the* appear?" Give students a few seconds to write a number. Then, together with the students, go through the lyrics again and count the number of times the word appears. All those who wrote the correct number gain a point for the group.

ENHANCEDetext
video example 6.2
For many students who experienced difficulty in reading, motivation is a key concern. Watch this video to learn more about motivational considerations.

Middle and Secondary Levels

1. Recognition of prefixes and suffixes can be practiced by listing words on the board or on a worksheet and having students underline the prefix, suffix, or both. You may also call out words while students write the prefix or suffix they hear in the word, or they may find and write different words containing the same prefix or suffix.

2. Write multisyllabic words on small cards, one word per card. Place the cards in an envelope and clip it to a manila folder. Inside the folder, draw several columns, numbered 2, 3, 4, and so on, as room permits. The student counts the number of syllables in the word on the card and writes in the proper column. The cards have the correct number of syllables written on the back, or an answer sheet can be provided for immediate feedback.

3. For compound words, develop exercises such as the following:
   • Matching drills using two lists of words with pairs that can be combined

   • Adapting the cloze procedures in which one half of each compound word is left blank (e.g., *When the winter blows, we huddle around the _____ place*)
   • Giving students ridiculous pictures to label (e.g., a stick of flying butter for butterfly)
   • Providing a list of invented words or colloquialisms to be defined (e.g., *slamdunk, skyhook*)

4. To enhance an ability to use prefixes and suffixes, consider activities such as the following:
   • Color coding of the designated affix being taught
   • Providing word wheels with root words in the center surrounded by prefixes or a suffix in the center surrounded by root words
   • Doing a speed listing of all the words that begin with a prefix (e.g., *un-: undress, untie, uncover, undo*)

5. To enhance fluency and aid in vocabulary development in subject areas (e.g., social studies, science), select a short passage, three to four sentences long, on the topic to be discussed. In groups of three or four, ask students to take turns reading one sentence each. Students will do this until each person has read each sentence once. Then the group must come up with one word that comes to mind after reading and share it with the class. The sharing can include writing on the board, typing it on the computer that can be projected for all to see, or writing on paper to be posted on the classroom wall. During classroom discussion, students' attention will be continuously reverted to words so that connections can be made.

6. Have students create a vocabulary booklet that is divided per subject. Under each subject, have the students divide paper into three columns: words of interest, words unknown, and words liked. At the end of each week, the students must share one of the words with the class.

ENHANCEDetext
video example 6.3
Watch this video to learn more about reading instruction in small groups.

Reading: Comprehension

LEARNING OUTCOMES

Upon completion of this chapter, the reader should be able to:

7.1 Identify the nature of reading comprehension, the principal components of comprehension, the levels of comprehension, the nature of text structures, phases in which the reader engages in order to comprehend text, and the types of challenges faced by students with reading disabilities.

7.2 Identify formal and informal measures for assessing reading comprehension.

7.3 Describe specific strategies that can be used to build vocabulary to strengthen students' reading skills.

7.4 Identify the importance of reading text comprehension strategies, the process of teaching such strategies, and specific examples of comprehension strategies.

Although word analysis and word recognition are clearly important basic skills, they are not the primary goal of an instructional reading program. The goal of reading is comprehension—obtaining meaning from printed material. Reading comprehension is the most critical skill students need to be successful in school. This chapter addresses both word knowledge and reading comprehension in general.

NATURE OF READING COMPREHENSION

Reading comprehension can be defined as "the process that excerpts and, at the same time, creates meaning having the student interact and be involved with written language. . . . Reading comprehension requires the reader to make connections with the text and, in addition, to the reader's prior knowledge. . . . It is a complex task that involves a range of language and cognitive processes and skills that students must master in order to make sense of written text" (Watson, Gable, Gear, & Hughes, 2012, p. 79). The definition conveys the complexity of this skill and also suggests the complexities that are associated with effective instruction.

A strong argument can be made that comprehension is the most important academic skill that is taught in school. It is required throughout the school experience, and it must be applied to a variety of types of textual material. Further, reading continues to be an important focus regarding the demands of adult living (i.e., lifelong learning).

Comprehension involves far more than being able to answer questions after one has read some type of printed material. Its importance is evident not only in most school contexts but also in most life contexts, as the demand of being able to comprehend oral and written information on a daily basis is apparent.

A number of key concepts associated with comprehension are addressed prior to the subsequent discussions of assessment and intervention. These topics include the principal components and levels of comprehension, types of text structures, and phases of the reading process.

Components of Comprehension

The two main components of comprehension are word knowledge (vocabulary) and text comprehension. Word knowledge simply means that students understand the meaning of words and word variations (such as with figurative language). Clearly, a difference exists between word identification and recognition and word knowledge. Text comprehension means that students are able to make sense out of passages of varying lengths and to use this information in a variety of specific ways.

Reading comprehension skills can be conceptualized as including three semi-distinct levels: literal, inferential, and critical. Students need to develop proficiency in each of these areas:

- **Literal comprehension**—refers to information as printed in text. Attention to literal recall includes comprehension for details, sequence of events, and major characters in the story. Most reading programs have traditionally addressed literal comprehension as their primary concern.
- **Inferential comprehension**—requires the reader to move beyond the literal information to infer the meaning of text. Although it is often mistakenly referred to as a lower-level skill, deriving the main idea from text is a good example of inferential comprehension as is summarization. In this case, students are required to consider what they have read and infer the primary focus of the author.

- **Critical comprehension**—requires the reader to analyze and evaluate the information that has been read, typically to develop new perspectives relative to the content. It may include separating fact from fiction, analyzing for the presence of bias, and interpreting events and situations. All comprehension draws on prior knowledge, but critical comprehension in particular asks the reader to use new information, for example, to compare and contrast it with other information learned at a prior time or to make judgments related to what was read.

Types of Text Structure

To fully recognize the complexities of reading comprehension, it is necessary to recognize that different types of textual material exist and that they present different demands to the reader. As a result, students need to recognize differences in text structure and use appropriate strategies for the type of material they are reading. Two major forms of text structure are narrative and expository.

Narrative text is related to storytelling. It is manifest in material such as short stories, legends, science fiction, and other types of fiction. Narrative structure often includes clear story elements, or *story grammar*, including characters, setting, themes, a central problem or conflict, a sequence of events that forms the story line, and a resolution to the conflict.

Expository text relates to material that is factual. Examples of expository text include textbooks, biographies, newspapers, magazines, catalogs, and other nonfiction materials. Expository text will not have the story grammar elements associated with narrative text but is likely to have other types of structures that students must be able to master (e.g., cause-and-effect or compare/contrast features). In addition, expository text (such as illustrated with this text) typically will incorporate headings and graphics into the textual material.

Phases of the Reading Process

Reading comprehension requirements also can be examined across the three phases of before, during, and after reading. Table 7-1 outlines the three phases and highlights specific reading actions associated with each respective phase.

TABLE 7–1 Reading phases

Phase	Reading Actions
Before reading	• Purpose and motivation for reading established
	• Adequate reading vocabulary (in place or activated)
	• Awareness of text structure
During reading	• Awareness of one's reading by monitoring comprehension
	• Words, phrases, and sentences read accurately and quickly
	• Connections made between/among sentences/statements
	• Questions generated and answered about what is being read
	• Background experiences called upon to make predictions and establish relevance to content encountered
	• Content that is of central importance, that is supportive or supplemental, and that is not important identified
	• Inferences made in regard to topics presented
After reading	• Reflections made on what has been read
	• Main idea and key points identified
	• Summarization of what was read
	• Connections made from what was read to new situations

Comprehension Difficulties

Reading comprehension is problematic for many students. Spencer, Quinn, and Wagner (2014) analyzed extensive data on over 400,000 elementary students. They concluded that there were two primary groups of students experiencing difficulty in comprehension. The first are individuals who also have difficulty with adequate decoding skills. The second, smaller group includes individuals who do not experience decoding difficulties but reflect deficits in oral language, such as in terms of vocabulary knowledge.

A combination of key factors associated with the student, the textual material, and the comprehension process contribute to the difficulties that students may have. Key areas of possible difficulties include problems in decoding, limited working memory, prior knowledge deficiencies, failing to use background knowledge, inability to develop or use strategies to monitor reading, syntactical difficulties, vocabulary deficits, and unfamiliarity with text structures, such as expository or narrative text (see Chapter 6) (Berkeley, Scruggs, & Mastropieri, 2010; Wagner & Meros, 2010; Watson et al., 2012).

An important area of concern regarding the development of comprehension skills in students, particularly those students with reading difficulties, is determining what instruction students are receiving. It is informative to consider research on comprehension instruction. As reported by Klingner, Urbach, Golos, Brownell, and Menon (2010) in their observational study of special education teachers working at the elementary school level, during their 124 observations, no comprehension instruction occurred in 42 of the lessons, while in 30 of them, the only comprehension activity was to ask students primarily literal questions about their reading. Otherwise, when additional comprehension instruction was provided to the remaining lessons, it was typically through prompting students to use a strategy rather than via the provision of explicit and systematic instruction. They concluded that "teachers continued the practice of mentioning skills and provided opportunities to practice but neglected to offer explicit instruction in the skill" (p. 73).

Secondary Level Students. The most significant problem faced by adolescent learners is their ability to read effectively. Ample evidence exists within the literature to confirm the fact that a significant number of students at the secondary school level experience serious problems with reading comprehension (Solís, Vaughn, & Scammacca, 2015). A challenge for teachers is that students' specific problems vary greatly and may likely reflect years of failure experiences in schools. Hock et al. (2009) noted that "many students will need instruction in all reading components (word identification, fluency, comprehension, vocabulary), but at different levels of intensity" and that "secondary schools must develop ways to provide an array of instructional alternatives that address students' reading needs, especially for students with learning disabilities" (p. 35).

The problems that adolescent learners face were summarized by the National Joint Committee on Learning Disabilities (NJCLD, 2008), which noted that the academic demands on students in secondary school included more complex reading tasks; a greater volume of information; exposure to more complex linguistic forms; the consequences of universal reliance on high-stakes tests and the implications of such tests for graduation; a greater reliance on print as the medium of learning; the challenges of vocabulary, particularly within expository text structures in the content areas; and higher demands for students to achieve more within time limitations.

Because the adolescent who struggles with reading is likely to have experienced considerable frustration and failure in past efforts to learn or improve reading skills, the teacher must overcome not only skill deficits but also problems in attitude, motivation, and fear related to failure expectancy.

 Check Your Understanding 7.1 Click here to gauge your understanding of the concepts in this section.

ASSESSING READING COMPREHENSION

This section focuses on other procedures specifically assessing comprehension. The assessment of reading in general was covered in the previous chapter, where many of the techniques discussed included subtests or methods for obtaining information about proficiency in certain aspects of reading comprehension.

The assessment of reading comprehension must go beyond merely asking questions to determine whether the examinee was able to obtain literal meaning from what he or she has read. Assessment should look at vocabulary (word knowledge) as well as some of the more complex areas of comprehension (e.g., inferential and critical aspects). Further, assessment must include analysis of the strategic behaviors that are required during the reading process as well.

Formal Instruments

Formal measures provide results that allow for comparisons with other students of similar age or grade level. Typically, the results are reported as percentiles, grade or age equivalents, or standard scores. The diagnostic value of the results from formal tests varies depending on the test and how responses are analyzed. Examples of formal instruments are highlighted in Table 7-2.

TABLE 7-2 Formal assessment instruments

Test Name (Reference)	Areas of Focus	Applicable Ages
Gray Oral Reading Tests—Fifth Edition (GORT-5) (Wiederholt & Bryant, 2012)	Taps comprehension by asking examinee to answer five questions after reading short passages orally.	6–0 to 23–11
Gray Diagnostic Reading Tests—Second Edition (GDRT-2) (Bryant, Wiederholt, & Bryant, 2004)	Includes two subtests that provide information related to comprehension: Reading Vocabulary and Meaningful Reading.	6–0 to 13–11
Gray Silent Reading Tests (GSRT) (Bryant & Blalock, 2000)	Examinees read sequenced reading passages silently and five comprehension questions follow each passage in a multiple-choice format.	7–0 to 25–0
Woodcock Reading Mastery Tests—Third Edition (WRMT-III) (Woodcock, 2011)	Includes nine tests, with increasing level of difficulty. It assesses reading acquisition skills using tests such as Phonological Awareness and Rapid Automatic Naming and reading achievement with tests such as Listening Comprehension, Oral Reading Fluency, and Passage Comprehension.	4–6 to 79–11
Test of Reading Comprehension—Fourth Edition (TORC-4) (Brown, Wiederholt, & Hammill, 2009)	Includes five subtests: Relational Vocabulary, Paragraph Construction, Sentence Completion, Text Comprehension, and Contextual Fluency.	

Informal Measures

A wide range of informal techniques can be used to obtain information on how well a student comprehends words and text. Assessment techniques can be incorporated in ongoing reading materials or can be accomplished through the use of related but different materials. The majority of these measures would be classified as curriculum-based measures (CBMs).

Table 7-3 describes informal techniques for assessing reading comprehension, developed by Watts (2015) and adapted in part from information provided by Blachowicz and Ogle (2001).

TABLE 7–3   Reading comprehension: informal assessment strategies

Strategy	Description and Implementation
Change Questioning	• Vary type of questions asked • If student is not responding correctly to literal questions; change to interpretive or vice versa. • Note this and watch for improvement • Model *how* to respond to various types of questions
Cloze Passages	• Include a paragraph (or set of paragraphs) with missing words at strategic points • Student read the passage and use context clues to determine the missing word • A scoring rubric is used to determine comprehension level
Direct Observation	• Observe student in different texts—informational text is more difficult • Take notes and keep in student file • Form and test hypothesis for instruction
Informal Reading Inventories	• Helps determine independent, instructional, and frustrational reading levels • Student reads a set of graded word lists and reading passages (orally and silently) • Student is asked comprehension questions at varying levels • Score determines reading level
Oral Reading Speed	• Choppy reading—analyze for decoding issue of word or whole phrase • Helps develop fluency
Pocket Vocabulary	• Student has to "pocket" word for vocabulary that has been introduced • Known vocabulary should kept in "pocket" at all times • At any time, student can be asked to hand any adult in school the pocket words to read and tell definition.
Retelling	• Requires student to recall parts of a story, for example, "tell me about you just read" • Ask for more details if student do not say much, by rephrasing the question or making it more specific, for example, "what happened after . . ." • Works for entire passage, and specific word issues • Helps with recalling of facts, sequencing, and developing vocabulary
Running Record	• Students read from textual material with identified level of readability • Teacher listens to student read roughly 100 words in book used for reading instruction • Mark check for each word read correctly • Write in word said (and write underneath word that should have been said) • Helps determine student's reading instructional level
Think Alouds	• Students openly share thoughts about reading material before, during or after reading. • Activates prior knowledge, and so leads to more inferential thinking • Helps teacher know how student is processing text as it provides information on student understanding of the reading material

Source: Watts, J. (2016). Assessment strategies. In Graphic Models and Instructional Tools for Students with Special Needs (p. 22), by E. A. Polloway & J. Lubin, 2016, *Lynchburg College Journal of Special Education*, Lynchburg College, Lynchburg, VA. Used with permission.

For many struggling readers, the techniques highlighted in Table 7-3 may be used to determine the nature of their reading difficulties and thus lead to effective instruction.

One final consideration related to assessment is student *self-monitoring* in reading comprehension, which involves self-recording students and accepting responsibility for assessment of their learning progress. Examples of aspects of comprehension for which self-recording of comprehension behaviors can be effective include accurate responding to comprehension questions, accurate identification of the main idea for an individual paragraph for a short passage, generation of summarization statements, and on-task behavior (Joseph & Eveleigh, 2011).

 Check Your Understanding 7.2 Click here to gauge your understanding of the concepts in this section.

WORD COMPREHENSION: BUILDING VOCABULARY

Vocabulary knowledge includes both oral and reading vocabulary. Our focus in this chapter is on the latter. However, struggling readers experience difficulty when attempting to read words that may not be part of their working vocabulary (Watson et al. 2012). Much of what happens in classrooms on a daily basis is associated with vocabulary acquisition. Harris, Schumaker, and Deshler (2011) noted the importance of vocabulary development given the fact that students need to learn a substantial number of words every year in order to be successful in academic programs across subjects and also the importance for students in terms of the impact on reading comprehension in general and performance on high-stakes assessments as well.

The report of the National Reading Panel (NRP, 2000) contained the following findings related to vocabulary instruction, noting, not surprisingly, that vocabulary instruction leads to gains in comprehension. Their analysis of research on word comprehension highlighted the following:

- The need for direct instruction of vocabulary words
- The importance of repetition and multiple exposures to vocabulary

- The value of teaching vocabulary words that will be useful in many contexts and the value of vocabulary derived from content materials
- The use of computer-assisted instruction to teach and practice vocabulary
- The importance of varied strategies for success in vocabulary development

Pressley and Fingeret (2005) noted that "students acquire vocabulary from exposure to vocabulary, for example, in texts that they read, with repeated encounters with vocabulary increasing learning. Even so, learning vocabulary words from text context is never certain, nor is it certain that vocabulary will be learned well even if students are provided the definitions for newly encountered vocabulary words" (p. 20). They recommended that teachers "flood" students with vocabulary exposure by making sure that new lessons are replete with opportunities for students to be immersed in an environment with new words.

Key considerations to help plan vocabulary instruction are presented in Table 7-4. These serve as guidelines for instructional strategies to build stronger word meaning and understanding among students. Several of these areas are discussed further below.

A number of specific strategies are discussed further below. All these represent ways in which instruction can be designed to enhance vocabulary development.

One way to organize for instruction on vocabulary words is to work with students to classify new words to which they will be introduced, such as in their reading. Following a model presented by Higgins, McConnell, Patton, and Ryser (2003), students can be presented with a list of new vocabulary to be learned and then asked to classify the words based on how well they know it. For example, students can indicate they have never heard of the word, may have heard of it but do not know what it means, may have a limited understanding of what it is, or that they know the word and are able to use it appropriately.

A critical part of vocabulary development is repeated exposures to the word in print. Repeated reading, an approach that is associated with reading fluency, also coincidentally has merit for developing word comprehension. Repeated or multiple oral readings is a strategy in which students read the same passage a series of times. By providing for

TABLE 7–4 Strategies to enhance vocabulary instruction

Strategy	Process
Clustering words	Grouping words for instruction based on meaning units in order to facilitate conceptual knowledge and link learning opportunities.
	Emphasize similarity of meaning to other known words.
	Illustrate opposites in meaning to other known words.
Exposures	Provide repeated exposures to specific words to promote fluency.
	Note the frequency of word appearances within text and ensure multiple exposures.
Linkages	Emphasize linkages to prior reading and other experiential opportunities.
Text relevance	Stress the importance of new words being taught in terms of their impact on text understanding.
	Pre-teach words that will appear in daily reading passages to introduce new vocabulary.
Multiple meanings	Provide instruction on vocabulary multiple meanings depending on context. Provide illustrations of multiple contexts.
Mnemonics	Use mnemonics (such as keyword mnemonics) to teach students associations between vocabulary words and meanings.
Technology	Use computer-assisted instruction to enhance vocabulary development by providing students with words to respond to for both recognition and meaning.

total vocabulary control through the redundancy of reading passages, students are presented with the same words multiple times, accuracy can improve, and words can become part of a student's reading lexicon. (See also Chapter 6.)

A useful way to build word meanings is through the application of graphic organizers. A sample graphic organizer focused on enhancing the meaning of individual words as part of an overall is presented in Figure 7-1.

One area of importance related to vocabulary development and word comprehension relates to morphological analysis. The importance of learning about morphemes within the context of word structures was discussed at length in the previous chapter with a particular focus on word recognition to enhance reading skills; it is certainly also important from a comprehension perspective.

Harris et al. (2011) identified an approach to morphological analysis (meaning cues) that directly relate to enhancing vocabulary. A *generative* approach has as its purpose the teaching of the meanings of words while promoting the ability of students to determine the meaning of other new words (hence generating new vocabulary). Such an approach involves teaching students how to segment words into their morphological parts while connecting each of these parts with meaning. Harris et al.

use as an example the word *dictate*, teaching students that *dict-* refers to saying or talking and consequently that this route can assist students in learning words, including *prediction*, *dictating*, *dictator*, and so forth. Then ultimately, that meaning connection provides an understanding of the words' likely definitions. A large number of polysyllabic words can be analyzed in this fashion in order to help students generate meaning and attack new words.

Another important strategy to promote vocabulary development is the use of mnemonics. Mnemonics provide "structured ways to help remember and recall information. Mnemonics instruction combines presentation of important information with explicit strategies for recall" (Brigham & Brigham, 2001, p. 1). They are particularly helpful in the area of vocabulary development.

Lubin and Polloway (2016, p.222) summarized the confirmed impact of mnemonics:

Research over almost three decades has demonstrated that mnemonic instruction is effective with students with learning problems. It has helped students retain, maintain and generalize concepts which they would have otherwise forgotten. They have improved the academic achievement of typically developing students and students with learning disabilities, intellectual disabilities and emotional and behavioral disorders.

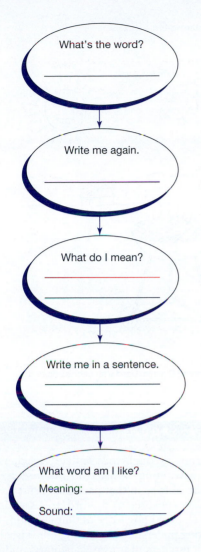

FIGURE 7–1 Vocabulary Graphic Organizer

Source: Graphic Models and Instructional Tools for Students with Special Needs (p. 15), by E. A. Polloway & J. Lubin, 2016, *Lynchburg College Journal of Special Education*, Lynchburg College, Lynchburg, VA. Used with permission.

As specifically related to word comprehension and vocabulary development, mnemonics can provide significant assistance to students in learning the meaning of the words. Using the same example as above, Harris et al. (2011) provided the example of *dictate* being paired with a keyword or rhyming word (in the example provided, the rhyming word of *-tate* was used with the mnemonic related to it that the principal tells the school secretary, Judy Tate, what to write).

One particularly valuable type of mnemonic for vocabulary development is the use of keywords.

Keywords provide the learner with a way to change the vocabulary word into a similar word that is easy to picture, relating the picture to the vocabulary word's meaning, and then ultimately retrieving the word by thinking of the keyword in the visual image and thus being able to define the meaning of the word. In Figure 7-2, a keyword strategy is used in order to remember the meaning of the word *meteorologist* (with the acoustical link to the keyword of *meat-eater*).

LEARNING MODULE 7.1 Click here to learn more about secondary reading instruction focused on teaching vocabulary and comprehension in the content areas: http://iris.peabody.vanderbilt.edu/module/sec-rdng

Further discussion on word comprehension and vocabulary is presented in the nearby Culturally Responsive Classroom Tip.

If students are being taught through the use of basal reading programs, opportunities are provided for multiple exposures and reinforcement of vocabulary words as they progress through a particular level of the book. They provide students with a consistent exposure to a basic vocabulary that provides for repetition.

ENHANCEDetext
video example 7.1
Watch this video to learn more about direct and indirect strategies for teaching vocabulary.

The nearby Elementary Teacher Tip discusses a unique type of book, predictable or pattern books, that provides another way to present students with multiple exposures to the same word as well as help to build fluency.

We conclude this section with mention of the Language Experience Approach (LEA) often used in elementary and middle school classrooms in particular. Although such programs may endeavor to be more comprehensive in their approach to reading and reading comprehension, it is included here because of the opportunities for the use of a language experience strategy to promote vocabulary development. With LEA, students are encouraged

METEOROLOGIST = A person who studies the weather.
(Meat-Eater)

Windy   Rainy   Clear   Sunny

While I wait for
my meat to cook,
I'll study the weather.

FIGURE 7–2 Keyword Mnemonic for Vocabulary

Source: Nolan, K. (n.d.). Reconstructive elaborations. Lynchburg, VA: Lynchburg College. Used with permission.

CULTURALLY RESPONSIVE CLASSROOMS

Proficiency in English makes a large difference in students' reading comprehension abilities. . . . Children's English vocabulary knowledge and English oral language proficiency are directly related to their success in English reading comprehension.

Research has shown that vocabulary knowledge is highly correlated with reading comprehension. Given that an average English-speaking kindergarten child comes to school knowing between 5,000 and 7,000 words, the challenge for English language learners (ELLs) is great indeed. Therefore, intensive efforts at enhancing children's vocabulary knowledge must begin as soon as the ELL arrives at school.

In the primary grades, teachers can use various approaches to pre-teach vocabulary prior to working with students' own reading materials or in preparation for read alouds. Teachers can take sentences from the text that contain new vocabulary and paraphrase those sentences with simpler vocabulary. They can also provide quick demonstrations of a word's meaning.

Effective support of students' comprehension does not end with an introduction to new words prior to the reading event. Teachers' questioning during the reading event must reflect an awareness of words that have multiple meanings. If a geographic text says,

"A river runs through that valley," teachers must, through questioning, assist students in determining the meaning of *runs* in that particular sentence.

Multiple exposures to a word are essential for a child's developing knowledge of that word. In addition to supporting understanding through the visual modes mentioned, teachers of upper elementary, middle, and high school students can encourage ELLs to supply definitions in their own words. Teachers can additionally make use of peer teaching for new vocabulary.

One area of particular importance is the vocabulary that provides cohesion to a text. Words such as *whereas* or *while* are difficult to present through pictures or demonstrations, but they are critical in determining the meaning of a sentence and can impact understanding of text.

Teachers should create opportunities for students to talk as well as to listen. Opportunities for discussion and use of new vocabulary can be found in small-group work in content studies such as math, science, and social studies, where new vocabulary is linked and reinforced thematically.

In the area of comprehension, there are two issues critical to work with ELLs. First is the nature of the material; the second concerns how students are taught to approach a text. Background knowledge is critical to text comprehension; therefore, it makes sense that there can be cultural influences on comprehension.

Finally, teachers of ELLs can make use of comprehension strategy instruction typically recommended as part of a balanced literacy program. When using cognitive strategies such as predicting or summarizing, teachers should keep in mind that continuing work on English language learners' oral English abilities cannot be neglected.

Laura Smolkin is a professor of elementary education at the University of Virginia.

Predictable Books

An interesting way to promote vocabulary development along with fluency in reading can come through the use of predictable books. *Predictable books*, children's books or stories that use repetition, provide, as the name suggests, consistent re-use of repetition that can give students opportunities for multiple exposures to individual vocabulary words. In turn, the multiple exposures enhance the likelihood of the development of proficiency in word knowledge.

A good example of a book using a high level of reputation is *Brown Bear, Brown Bear, What Do You See?* (Martin, 1983). Another example that reflects a cumulative pattern within the story can be seen in the familiar story of the gingerbread man. Another example that reflects familiar day, month, or time sequences is found in Maurice Sendak's (1962) *Chicken Soup with Rice*. These three types of predictable stories—through the use of rhythm, rhyme, and redundancy—give semantic and syntactic language cues that stimulate fluent reading for children with disabilities and that can enhance vocabulary development and sight-word recognition.

To use predictable books as a strategy for promoting reading, the teacher can initially read the story aloud to children, possibly using an enlarged version or distributing multiple copies of the material so that children can read along for most of the story. Subsequently, instructional activities can be designed for students to practice reading the stories to the teacher or to peers and consequently having multiple exposures to the individual vocabulary words that may be presented within the book.

---

to verbalize their thoughts and experiences, which are then written down by the teacher or the student and can be read. These stories are re-read by the student and by other students as the program progresses. Word lists are made from the words used in the stories to develop word-recognition skills and a working vocabulary. Because the words are from the students' own language, there is an inherent benefit in terms of word comprehension and thus vocabulary development.

To briefly summarize, the language experience approach would typically include the following stages (Tompkins, 2005): providing an experience for a student or group of students that will help to stimulate writing, having classroom discussion about the experience prior to actually writing out the story, having students dictate the story while the teacher records it, providing text of the recorded dictation (e.g., electronically, in small books, in notebooks), and then having students read and reread the stories for the continual opportunity to practice the words and promote fluency.

 Check Your Understanding 7.3 Click here to gauge your understanding of the concepts in this section.

TEXT COMPREHENSION STRATEGIES

The key focus of instruction for students with special needs is the provision of systematic and explicit instruction on skills and strategies in order to allow students to better engage textual material. As students are taught strategies to facilitate comprehension, teachers should monitor the effectiveness of these strategies in enabling the students to achieve success on identified comprehension skills.

The teacher's task is also to ensure that appropriate attention is given to different levels of comprehension based on the learning needs of individual students. Through effective teaching, instructors can work with groups of students and incorporate a concurrent focus on literal, inferential, and critical comprehension questions within the same lesson. Such an approach enhances inclusion efforts for students with special needs when they are participating in larger group instruction with other students.

The NRP (2000), after reviewing 203 text comprehension studies, identified eight successful evidence-supported instructional techniques:

- Question answering
- Comprehension monitoring
- Question generation
- Graphic and semantic organizers
- Story structure
- Cooperative learning (peer-mediated)
- Summarization
- Multiple-strategy teaching

This section of the chapter generally follows these successful evidence-supported instructional techniques. The discussion within each of the subsections highlights key information about the implementation of the relevant teaching and learning strategies. It should be noted that several of these areas have some inherent overlap, which will be noted within the subsequent discussions.

Question Answering: Teacher-Directed Strategies

Questioning by teachers is the instructional strategy used most often in teaching comprehension. As a general approach, this has frequently been found to be effective, particularly when students are taught to ask themselves questions before, during, and after the reading process. Questioning permeates the reading process. Factual, inferential, and analytical questions are all essential for comprehension development.

Frequently, the majority of questions that teachers ask are factual, and the answers are directly stated in the text, requiring no higher-level thinking by students. Teachers can stimulate students to begin inferential and critical thinking through higher-level questioning. Students who can decode the material adequately can, with guidance and practice, become critical readers. If properly

guided and questioned, slow learners as well as gifted students can learn to make inferences from the material they have read. Questions that stimulate thought and motivate students to higher levels of comprehension can be asked on material at any readability level. Evaluative and interpretive questions also apply to every level of readability.

Comprehension requires connecting what is read with prior knowledge of the topic. The printed material provides new information; to understand it, readers use various information sources within their own memories. Thus, each reader's background of concepts directly influences the comprehension of passages read. Most instruction therefore should be initiated prior to reading the material. The teacher must stimulate students' thinking about the topic before oral or silent reading begins. Strategies include setting the purpose for reading to arouse students' prior knowledge and the use of the directed reading/thinking activity.

Setting the purpose in advance of reading is one way to stimulate students' prior knowledge. A teacher can introduce a selection by saying, "As you read, think about what you would do if you were caught in a flood as Van is in this story." Immediately, students' prior knowledge (or lack of it) concerning floods comes to mind and thus helps prepare them for the passage to be read.

One of the most useful questioning techniques to teach comprehension of content or expository material is the *directed reading/thinking activity* (DRTA). Students are taught to make predictions about what they are going to read before they begin reading the text. While reading, the students test and refine the predictions they made in advance. These predictions generate divergent questions and stimulate expanded thinking. DRTA teaches students to verify and defend their predictions and gives them guidelines for reading to learn. The following procedures make up the DRTA technique:

1. Students examine the story title, pictures, and subheadings.
2. Individually or in a group, students list information they anticipate finding in the selection.
3. Students read the selection.
4. Students then look at each prediction on their list and decide whether it was correct or incorrect.
5. When uncertainty or disagreement occurs, students defend their positions by locating validating information in the text.

DRTA stimulates students to generate their own questions. Their predictions become questions when they search the text for supportive information.

Traditionally, many teachers have taught comprehension solely by asking students questions after they have read a specific passage. Thus, instructional lessons might typically include questions such as the following after a reading sample:

- What is the main idea?
- What are the sequential events that took place in the story?
- Who are the main characters?
- What do you conclude about the story?

General questions such as these provide a basis for evaluating whether students have understood the passage they have completed.

Teacher-directed, overt, explicit teaching of comprehension is effective in all grades. However, comprehension instruction is not just asking questions at the end of story or having students do workbooks. Effective instruction includes students asking questions throughout the text and modeling think-alouds and so forth. Teacher questioning strategies may test students' comprehension without necessarily directing or instructing them in comprehension strategies, and thus they may fail to directly and explicitly teach students strategies they can use. So the discussion that follows focuses on student-directed instruction to enhance comprehension of content and comprehension skills.

Question Generation and Comprehension Monitoring

Teacher questioning is a staple of reading comprehension instruction. However, as noted, it also is essential that students learn to ask themselves questions in order to become more effective and independent readers and develop self-efficacy as readers. The considerations of question generation by students and comprehension monitoring are closely related, and both are discussed in this section.

The central consideration related to these two related areas is the effective use of comprehension strategies by students. Berkeley et al. (2010) noted that "systematically employing strategies is very likely to improve students' ability to construct meaning from text" (p. 433). Reading comprehension strategies have been referred to as being

"among the most thoroughly researched interventions in special education" (Brigham, Berkeley, Simpkins, & Brigham, 2007, p. 3). As Brigham et al. (2007) noted, comprehension strategies require students to ask themselves questions and answer those questions about textual material prior to, during, and following the reading process. Strategies that can help students be more effective in reading text fall under the general focus of directly teaching students strategies for monitoring their own reading (referred to as comprehension monitoring, self-monitoring of reading, or metacomprehension).

In emphasizing the use of comprehension monitoring approaches, Mastropieri and Scruggs (1997) reported that several common features of strategies and strategy instruction help promote enhanced reading comprehension:

- [giving] clear, explicit instruction in a strategy associated with enhancing reading comprehension
- [using] detailed self-monitoring procedures containing cards that require students to mark off steps as they proceed
- informing students about the purpose of the strategy instruction
- attributing success to controllable factors (e.g., reminding students that the use of a strategy would be beneficial to them and would influence success) (p. 205)

As noted above, comprehension monitoring is directly related to the development of *self-generated questions*. Wong's (1982) classic work in this area showed that the lack of metacognitive skills or, in other words, the inability to monitor their comprehension (e.g., self-monitoring, predicting, and controlling one's own attempts to study and learn) limits students' success in learning to read. Self-questioning is one way to stimulate development of the poor reader's metacognitive skills and to improve comprehension monitoring. Bryant (2001) noted that a key goal is to "teach them when and how to use effective comprehension monitoring strategies before, during, and after reading so they can 'repair' comprehension problems and understand text" (p. 1).

To facilitate a strategy of using self-generated questions, students can first be trained in question phrasing or writing. This orientation includes identification of good and poor questions, discrimination between questions and statements, and awareness of question words. Students are then instructed to read the story, describe what it is about, and generate two questions. Finally, students answer their own questions or exchange questions with peers. Teachers can further enhance students' metacognitive skills by directly teaching and modeling comprehension processing.

Main Idea.   One of the most critical skills in the area of text comprehension is finding the main idea from a reading passage. Depending upon the reading level, this may be finding the main idea in a paragraph or in a longer reading passage. Determining the main idea is important both in narrative text (in which the reader has to determine story themes) and in expository text (in which the reader must determine the key thesis based on the relationship of ideas in text) (Jitendra & Gajiria, 2011).

Main idea instruction illustrates the role of self-questioning and comprehension monitoring. Watson et al. (2012) stressed that identifying the main idea within a passage is an essential component of reading comprehension.

For an example, consider that students can be instructed to perform the following self-questioning tasks (Schewel & Waddell, 1986):

1. Identify the main idea of a paragraph and underline it.
2. Develop questions related to the main idea and write them where they can be referred to easily.
3. Check those questions with the teacher's models to be certain that they are correctly stated.
4. Read the passage, answer the questions, and learn the answers.
5. Continually look back over the questions and answers to note the accumulation of information.

Several learning (or study) strategies can also be used to help with thinking while reading. A key one to use for paraphrasing and summarizing is RAP (Hagaman & Reid, 2008; Schumaker, Deshler, & Denton, 1984, cited in Ellis & Sabornie, 1986). With the RAP strategy, students are instructed to do the following:

- Read a paragraph or passage.
- Ask yourself: Who/what it is about? What is happening?
- Put the main idea in your own words.

The series of steps that facilitate student use of a variety of comprehension strategies, including RAP, are as follows: describe the strategy to the student, model or demonstrate it, provide verbal rehearsal opportunities as guided practice, provide independent practice, review for mastery and recall, and plan for collaboration.

Successful use of RAP can facilitate students' paragraph-by-paragraph reading of text by using a self-monitoring strategy to continue to think about what is being read. Hagaman, Luschen, and Reid (2010) provided a detailed discussion of the use of RAP with third-grade students. These students learned the strategy in approximately four or five lessons consisting of 20 to 30 minutes of direct instruction, using a self-regulated strategy development (SRSD) model (see also Chapter 8). Instruction in the use of the strategy was systematic and explicit, and the results were positive in terms of enhanced comprehension skills. They concluded, "The RAP strategy . . . can be extremely effective for improving reading comprehension. The strategy is flexible and can be used for elementary, middle, and high school students across many different content areas" (pp. 27–28).

Jitendra, Hoppes, and Xin (2000) recommended the use of a *main idea prompt card* to help students find the central theme of the paragraph or passage. This strategy formalizes self-questioning by cuing students as to the key questions they can pose to themselves while reading. Students can be given a series of printed prompts to consider to help them determine the main idea based on these questions:

- Who (or what) is the subject?
- What is the action?
- Why (or where, when) did something occur?
- How was something done (or how did it look)?
- Thus: what is the main idea?

Student-questioning strategies are important for other comprehension skills as well. Most significantly, they provide a way for students to continue to think well they are reading, hence the concept of mid-comprehension. Pressley and Fingeret (2005) provided the following recommendations, which are particularly apt when considering student-directed strategies that promote comprehension monitoring:

- Teach a small battery of strategies: prediction, summary, questioning, imagery

- Explain and model these strategies
- Encourage students to use them until they begin to self-regulate (p. 50)

To this list of recommendations can be added importance of generalization of skills and strategies. The NJCLD (2008) noted "for struggling learners, particularly those with learning disabilities, it is not sufficient to simply teach and learn strategies; continued support for the use and generalization of strategies is required for real change to occur" (p. 215).

ENHANCEDetext
video example 7.2
Watch this video to learn more about comprehension strategies.

Graphic and Semantic Organizers

Graphic organizers focus attention on important information, provide students with visual formats to assist them in organizing information for better comprehension, and can facilitate peer learning through group instructional formats. Several graphic aids apply well to teaching students who struggle with reading comprehension. The use of such graphic aids provides a way to enhance the teacher-directed and student-directed questioning strategies that are being used to build comprehension skills. Graphic aids provide systems where students can organize their thoughts and make notes on what they are going to read or have read; they also recall and provide a basis for further study. They also frequently serve as advanced organizers that provide an introduction to or an overview of the passage to be read.

Kim, Vaughn, Wanzek, and Wei (2004) summarized research on the effects of graphic organizers on the reading comprehension of students with learning disabilities. They concluded, "Our findings support the use of semantic organizers, cognitive maps with and without mnemonics, and framed outlines to promote [comprehension]. . . . When students were taught to use graphic organizers, large effect sizes were demonstrated on reading comprehension. . . . Visual displays of information enhance reading comprehension by helping them organize the verbal information and thereby improve their recall" (p. 116). Examples of graphic strategies are presented and discussed below. Graphic organizers have been associated with increases in learning in the areas of vocabulary knowledge and text literal and inferential comprehension (Dexter & Hughes, 2011).

Semantic mapping is based on the assumption that new information is learned and understood when it is integrated with prior knowledge. The teacher's role is twofold: to continually work on building students' knowledge background through experiences, discussion, and literature and to teach students to stimulate their own schemata about a topic before beginning to read a passage. The teacher might instruct students in the use of self-questioning (e.g., "What do I already know about the Civil War?") or prediction strategies. Students with disabilities often have limited experiential backgrounds and need additional guidance in gaining knowledge from the experiences they encounter.

Brainstorming is an essential element in the mapping process. The student's active participation in this activity stimulates prior knowledge and encourages students to associate new information with what is already part of their schemata (Schewel, 1989).

Semantic mapping is a method of promoting comprehension that stimulates prior knowledge of the topic. Semantic maps are diagrams developed by students and teacher before students read an assigned selection. The maps can be re-used after reading to further stimulate comprehension. The procedure is as follows:

1. The teacher presents a stimulus word or a core question related to the story to be read.
2. Students generate words related to the stimulus word or predict answers to the question, all of which the teacher lists on the board.
3. With the teacher's help, students then put related words or answers in groups, drawing connecting lines between the topics to form a semantic map.
4. After reading the selection, students and the teacher discuss the categories and re-arrange or add to the map.

Semantic mapping can appear in various forms. Figure 7-3 presents an example of a semantic map related to content on reading comprehension.

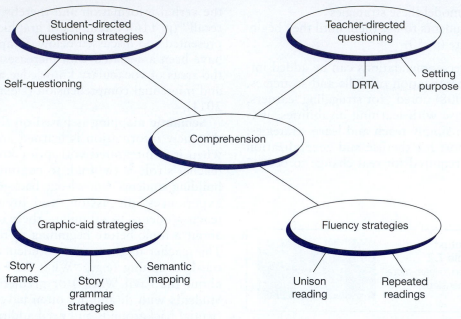

FIGURE 7–3 Semantic Map

Earlier, the importance of students being able to identify the main idea in text was noted. Figure 7-4 provides a graphic organizer that can afford students a strategy for looking at a paragraph, page of text, or short passage, identifying key details and then using that information to conclude what the main idea was for the individual reading assignment.

Story Structure

An additional strategy validated by the NRP (2000) is the use of story structures. Frequently, such structures take the form of graphic organizers as discussed above. They also may be referred to a story grammar strategies or story maps.

Story structures or story grammar strategies can enhance the reading and writing skills of students with special needs; the concept builds on many of the previously mentioned strategies. Malmgren and Trezek (2009) noted that "text structures vary dramatically between narrative (fiction) and expository (nonfiction) texts and should be taught as distinct skills. Familiarizing students with story grammar elements directing them to identify elements such as character, setting, conflict, resolution, have been shown to increase their comprehension of narrative texts. Although story

grammar elements are typically part of the elementary curriculum, struggling adolescent readers still benefit from instruction in this area" (p. 7). Extending this generalization further, Garwood, Brunsting, and Fox (2014) further reported in their review of the literature that story mapping was among the most significant techniques in terms of positive effects for reading comprehension for students with emotional and behavioral disorders.

Story grammar strategies are included in this section, although they can complement a variety of graphic and nongraphic approaches to promoting comprehension as discussed in prior sections of the chapter. The following list outlines a series of strategies that provide ways to enhance learning for students in the context of story structures (Hagood, 1997):

- Teach students to use self-questioning techniques to increase their comprehension of a narrative text.
- Teach students to use story maps to organize a story's components (i.e., use visual organizers to enable students to enhance their understanding; see Figure 7-5).
- Develop group narrative dramatizations through the use of visual, auditory, and kinesthetic learning channels.

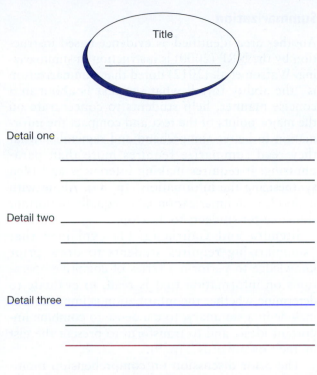

FIGURE 7–4 Main Idea Map

Source: Graphic Tools and Instructional Models in Reading, Writing and Math for Students with Special Needs (p. 27), by E. A. Polloway & J. Lubin, 2016, *Lynchburg College Journal of Special Education*, Lynchburg College, Lynchburg, VA. Used with permission.

- Teach students to analyze and critically compare the elements of two similar stories (e.g., use graphic organizers to discuss similarities and differences between stories).
- Teach students to manipulate and analyze the components of story grammar (e.g., re-write stories by changing the setting of a story and modifying other elements that change when the setting does).

Peer-Mediated Strategies

A variety of peer-mediated strategies can enhance the development of text comprehension skills. While a full discussion of cooperative learning is beyond the scope of this chapter, the discussion below highlights several examples of strategies that

can enhance comprehension through techniques that involve peers.

A strategy that involves questioning and additional activities to activate comprehension and that commonly includes both student-generated questions and peer mediation is *reciprocal teaching* (RT), developed originally by Palincsar and Brown (1984). This approach is based on the assumption that comprehension is enhanced when students read a text and then take turns leading small-group discussions with their peers. RT includes four specific strategies:

- *Questioning* about the content read
- *Summarizing* the most important information
- *Clarifying* concepts that are unclear
- *Predicting* what is occurring

The key to the effectiveness of RT is that the approach enables students to learn specific strategies

Questions	Answers (to be developed by students)
Who are the characters?	• Snow White • Seven Dwarfs • Wicked Queen • Prince Charming • Magic Mirror
Where does it take place?	A faraway land
When does it begin?	Once Upon a Time
What is the problem?	Snow White is in an enchanted sleep due to a poison apple.
What is the goal?	To awaken Snow White with true love's kiss.
What are the events?	• Magic Mirror reveals Snow White is the fairest in the land. • Wicked Queen tries to have Snow White killed. • Snow White escapes and meets Dwarfs. • Snow White eats poison apple. • Prince Charming kisses Snow White.
What is the result?	The Prince and Snow White live happily ever after.

FIGURE 7–5 Story Map: Snow White

Source: Meade, A. In Graphic Models and Instructional Tools for Students with Special Needs (p. 29), by E. A. Polloway & J. Lubin, 2016, *Lynchburg College Journal of Special Education*, Lynchburg College, Lynchburg, VA. Used with permission.

that foster their comprehension rather than simply asking them questions about what they have read. By using this approach, a variety of questions can be modeled, practiced, and used in an active fashion. The planned outcome is that students can then generate appropriate questions themselves while reading.

Another example of a successful peer-mediated technique is the Collaborative Strategic Reading (CSR) (Klingner, Vaughn, Arguellas, Hughes, & Leftwich, 2004). This technique includes four specific strategies: Preview, Click and Clunk, Get the Gist, and Wrap-Up. These are defined as follows (Klingner et al., 2004):

- Preview—brainstorming about the topic and predicting what will occur in the story.
- Click and Clunk—clicking along through words read smoothly. When clunking on difficult words, use fix-up strategies, such as analyzing clues within the sentence, prefixes and suffixes, word parts, and/or use of a picture.
- Get the Gist—deciding who or what the topic of the paragraph is about and identifying the main idea.
- Wrap-Up—asking questions about what was read and reviewing what was most important from the assignment.

These strategies are taught to the whole class using expository texts, and then cooperative groups implement their roles (i.e., Leader, Clunk Expert, Gist Expert, Announcer) and the specific techniques as noted above.

Another popular strategy that involves peers is typically referred to as *think-pair-share*. This straightforward strategy would include the following steps:

- *Think* on your own, individually about the reading passage.
- *Pair* up with a peer (or group of peers) to talk about the passage.
- *Share* your own responses with your pair (or group).

One final peer-mediated strategy was discussed at length in the prior chapter. *Peer-Assisted Learning Strategies* (PALS; Fuchs & Fuchs, 2005) provides a way in which students may take turns as a reading coach and a reader, respectively. (See Chapter 6 for more detailed information on implementation.)

Summarization

Another area identified as evidence-based instruction by the NRP (2000) is instruction in summarizing. Watson et al. (2012) noted that summarization is "the ability to tell what the text is about in a concise manner, help students to concentrate on the major points of the text and compact the information to better comprehend and remember what they read summarize requires more than paraphrasing; it requires making inferences and then synthesizing the information" (p. 85). Along with main idea, summarization is an equally important skill area for students to develop.

Jitendra and Gajiria (2011) explained that "summarizing requires students to draw prior knowledge to perform a series of cognitive operations on information that is read, to evaluate to determine whether the information is important to include in a summary, to condense to combine important ideas, and to transform to present the gist in 'their own words'" (p. 9).

The prior discussion on comprehension monitoring relates as well to the development of summarization. Students are challenged to read and synthesize the important ideas from text, building on their ability to remain. A strategy that can be used to promote summarization is ICER:

- Identify main ideas within the paragraphs (or pages) of the text.
- Connect the main ideas.
- Eliminate information that is not relevant or redundant.
- Restate what is most important about what was read.

Another approach that can be used to promote summarization is the 3-2-1 strategy (Cash, 2011). Using this strategy, students are asked to identify the *three* most important details or actions from what they have read, identify *two* interesting things from the reading passage, and list *one* question still remaining after the reading has been completed.

Figure 7-6 illustrates a strategy for summarization (which also reflects two other evidence-based practices: working with peers and using a graphic organizer). This graphic organizer is intended to provide students with a strategy for working with their peers in summarizing the information they learned from their reading assignment. It builds on the concept of thinking and sharing with peers discussed earlier.

Summarizing
What do I know after reading?
• _____
• _____
• _____
What questions do I have for my partner?
• _____
• _____
• _____
What answers do I have for my partner?
• _____
• _____
• _____
How can I summarize what I read in one paragraph?
_____
_____
_____
_____
_____

FIGURE 7–6   Summarizing: Graphic Organizer Strategy

Source: Graphic Models and Instructional Tools for Students with Special Needs (p. 24), by E. A. Polloway & J. Lubin, 2016, *Lynchburg College Journal of Special Education*, Lynchburg College, Lynchburg, VA. Used with permission.

**ENHANCEDetext
video example 7.3**
Watch this video to learn more about moving from during reading to after strategies in reading.

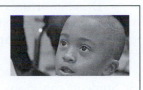

In concluding the discussion of summarization strategies, we present an overall strategy developed by Mason, Meadan-Kaplansky, Hedin, and Taft (2013). They presented the concept of TWA to help students focus on what is important across the three phases of reading identified earlier: Thinking before reading, thinking **W**hile reading, and thinking **A**fter reading. Instruction can focus on these three phases as follows:

• Think before reading—to include attention to the purpose of the author, what you already know about the topic, what you would like to learn about the topic.

• While reading—including thinking about the speed and pace of your reading, the linkage between what you know and what you are reading, and the re-reading of parts to enhance understanding.

• After reading—including thinking about the main ideas across the reading passage, summarizing the information from the passage, and identifying what you have learned overall.

LEARNING MODULE 7.2   Click here to learn more about secondary reading instruction and content-area learning with vocabulary and comprehension strategies: http://iris.peabody.vanderbilt.edu/module/sec-rdng2

Multiple-Strategy Teaching.   The eighth strategy identified by the NRP (2000) is listed as multiple-strategy teaching. As noted in the report, this refers to "teaching in which the reader uses several of the procedures and interaction with the teacher

Explicit and Systematic Instruction

As noted throughout this chapter, many strategies are available to enhance the comprehension of students who experience difficulty reading. These include graphic organizers, learning strategies, question generation strategies, and strategies focused, for example, on the main idea in summarization. In each case, however, it is essential to not lose sight of the fact that the effective use of such strategies will likely occur only when they are directly taught, systematically and explicitly, in order to ensure their accurate and continued usage. For older students who have experienced past difficulty in reading, it should be a core assumption that without such a focus, achievement gains will be unlikely to be realized.

Systematic instruction requires a focus on instruction of carefully selected and useful set of skills and strategies and that those skills and strategies are organized in a logical sequence for instruction. Students must know what is expected and why it is important. *Explicit instruction* provides a clear purpose for learning accompanied by clear and understandable directions. It focuses on the skills and strategies that are needed by students and includes a process that addresses the importance of modeling and demonstration, guided practice, independent practice, maintenance, and generalization.

---

over the text. [It] is effective when the procedures are used flexibly and appropriately by the reader or the teacher in naturalistic context" (pp. 4–6).

 Check Your Understanding 7.4 Click here to gauge your understanding of the concepts in this section.

ACTIVITIES

The following activities relate to specific aspects of enhanced reading comprehension.

Elementary Level

1. Have students read to remember something they can share with their peers. When they finish, have them volunteer information to the class and write their statements on the board. At first, begin with three pieces of information from each student. Write these statements on the board and have students place them in the sequence in which they occurred in the story.

2. Have students complete these reading follow-up activities:
   - Write a letter to a main character in the book suggesting other ways the character might have solved the problem or acted in the situation.
   - Write sentences from the story that show that someone was excited, sad, happy, or ashamed.
   - Draw a picture of something in the story that indicates that the setting is past, present, or future.
   - Find three pictures in magazines that are reminiscent of the main characters in the story. Under each picture, write your reasons for selection.
   - Draw a picture of one memorable scene from the story, showing as many details as possible. Accompany it by a map reflecting these details.
   - Make a poster advertising the book.

3. Students can motivate others to read by sharing a book they have enjoyed. Some ways for them to share are listed here:
   - Publish a book review column for the school paper with short reviews and reactions to books read.
   - After reading a biography or book of fiction, describe the main characters and their common problems. Tell how these problems were or were not solved.
   - Prepare a collection of something (e.g., rocks, animals, plants) the class has read about, with appropriate information for an exhibit.
   - Make a poster (either flat or three-dimensional) showing a scene or stimulating interest in a book.

- Make and decorate a book jacket; write an advertisement to accompany the book.
- Write a letter to a friend or a librarian recommending a book you especially liked.
- Dress as one of the characters in a book and tell about yourself.

4. In designing reading instructional lessons, consider the following:
   - Use active reading strategies so that students will comprehend and retain information better.
   - Always give students a purpose for reading and gradually train them to set their own purposes.
   - Teach them to make predictions about content before beginning to read.
   - After reading, have students defend or reject their predictions.
   - Encourage students to ask themselves after each paragraph, "What is the main idea?"

5. Exaggerate events, characters, and behaviors in stories. A big, old, nearsighted owl that lost its spectacles in the stream is certainly more interesting than just a wise, old owl. Likewise, a little girl who makes many friends because she is kind and generous (something she learned from her grandmother, who lives in a one-room apartment) is more interesting than a little girl who makes a lot of friends because she is nice (Buck, 2008).

6. Have students work in small groups to shape and highlight the sounds of interesting poems with vocal inflection, coloring, and orchestration. Have them generalize these behaviors to their own spontaneous storytelling (Buck, 2008).

Middle and Secondary Level

1. Journal writing can be used to enhance comprehension. In character journals, students can comment on a story they have read in the voice of one of the characters. In this way, they may think more about what they are reading.

2. In groups, have students write and produce a videotaped commercial advertising a novel they have read. Each student will serve on his or her group's "ad committee," which will determine the type of commercial to be produced (e.g., public service announcement, testimonials) and how the information will be presented. The goal of each group should be to create an informative, entertaining commercial about their book that will convince "viewers" to read that book. Commercials may also be shared with other classes and teachers.

3. Reading instruction often must occur in the context of content areas.

ENHANCEDetext
video example 7.4
Watch this video to learn more about guided reading in the content areas.

4. After reading a selected story or novel, ask the students to paraphrase the story and develop a script for a class play. The students make props, costumes, and puppets if desired. For a shorter version, students role-play parts of the story without verbalizing the information. The remainder of the class guesses the part of the story that is being dramatized. This activity reinforces the events of the story and improves comprehension.

5. Students can use K-W-L charts as a technique to focus attention, with K representing what is known, W what the student wants to know, and L what has been learned.

6. An activity that includes reading for information, survival, and amusement uses menus from the community's restaurants, fast-food chains, or food counters. Give students specific assignments to compare prices, develop lists of meals, or identify the top 10 places to go on a special date. Students might also construct a composite menu to be printed in the graphics department and used for personal review. This menu can provide a basis for a variety of exercises to develop vocabulary, attack skills, and word recognition.

7. Art and reading can be combined in book review collages. Students should select a book that they have completed and then cut out words and pictures from magazines and newspapers to illustrate the idea of the book (Buck, 2008).

CHAPTER

8

Written Language

LEARNING OUTCOMES

Upon completion of this chapter, the reader should be able to:

8.1 Discuss the special problems and challenges of written language as experienced by students with disabilities.

8.2 Identify the importance of writing within the curriculum.

8.3 Identify specific assessment strategies that can be used across the three domains of written language.

8.4 Discuss the appropriate role of and effective strategies for handwriting instruction.

8.5 Identify effective strategies for spelling instruction.

8.6 Identify and discuss approaches to instruction in written language that are effective for students with special needs.

Written language subsumes the three areas of handwriting, spelling, and written expression and demands that the individual draw from an array of mechanical, memory, conceptual, and organizational skills in order to communicate successfully. Therefore, it is not surprising that writing can present significant challenges to students with special needs, who may have deficits in oral language, reading problems, low societal expectations for success, inconsistent encouragement and reinforcement for appropriate usage, and limited motivation or expectation for success.

PROBLEMS AND CHALLENGES IN WRITTEN LANGUAGE

Writing opens a critical avenue for communication. At initial levels, students develop the capability to write their names and other personally identifying information and write short stories. At advanced levels, they need to take notes, respond to test questions, develop elaborate compositions and essays, and write letters of inquiry and complete job applications as they transition into adult life. Further, they need to develop the ability to communicate through both expository and narrative writing, such as in compositions, stories, reports, and research papers.

Written language warrants increased attention in educational programs for students with special needs, particularly as students are challenged to be successful in inclusive classrooms. An increased attention to writing instruction corresponds with the increased focus on standards-based education with the related federal requirements that all students be included in schoolwide assessments (Gregg, Coleman, Davis, & Chalk, 2007). It is, however, important to place in accurate context the writing difficulties of children and adolescents who have disabilities by noting that such problems are also experienced by large numbers of students who are not identified as being disabled.

Lienemann, Graham, Leader-Janssen, and Reid (2006) reviewed research on achievement data and noted that approximately 75% of students at the 4th-, 8th-, and 12th-grade levels achieved only partial mastery of grade-level skills and knowledge. Further, MacArthur and Phillippakos (2010) cited the National Assessment of Educational Progress (NAEP) in noting that only 6% of students with disabilities were proficient in writing skills. The writing of students with disabilities reflected fewer ideas, typically were more poorly organized, and generally were of lower overall quality.

Baker, Chard, Ketterlin-Geller, Apichatabutra, and Doabler (2009) stressed the implications of writing skills or problems beyond the school setting. They noted, "The majority of public and private employers state that writing proficiency is critical in the workplace and directly influences their hiring and promotion decisions. Writing is no longer a requirement limited to the daily tasks of professionals, but it is a workplace demand that extends to nearly all living-wage jobs" (p. 304).

This chapter initially provides an orientation to the importance of written language in the school curriculum. Subsequent major sections then focus on assessment in writing and the three instructional areas of handwriting, spelling, and written expression.

 Check Your Understanding 8.1 Click here to gauge your understanding of the concepts in this section.

WRITTEN LANGUAGE IN THE CURRICULUM

The writing process requires the translation of thoughts into the written word. It involves two distinct processes. **Text generation** involves the transfer of ideas into representations in language; this is commonly referred to as written expression. **Transcription** involves the translation of such language representations into the format of written language, most commonly through handwriting (or keyboarding) and spelling.

The model presented in Figure 8-1 provides an overview of written language and illustrates the role of handwriting and spelling as supportive skills to written expression. The model has been adapted from a prior model provided by Polloway, Miller, and Smith (2012).

Writing remains important throughout school, although, as Penner-Williams, Smith, and Gartin (2009) noted, "the goal changes as the student matures. In writing at the primary grades, the focus is on the mechanics of the process so that the students can learn how to write-letter formation, punctuation [while] at the upper elementary levels and beyond, the goal is for the student to be able to communicate what they have learned, seen, experienced, or felt" (p. 163).

A number of specific facets of writing serve as general programming considerations. First, writers must draw on *previous linguistic experiences*. Thus, prior problems in listening, speaking, or reading may be reflected and perhaps magnified in the area of writing. To write in a coherent, understandable manner, one must be able to think, read, and comprehend in a logical way.

Second, special considerations apply to handwriting and spelling, including that any difficulties experienced in the process of "text transcription can negatively affect the message writers are endeavoring to share and therefore create interference with other writing processes. As a result, poor performance in spelling and handwriting can have a negative impact on students' perception about their academic competence" (Graham & Harris, 2006, p. 64).

Third, writing involves a complex blend of *ideation reflected in content and technical skills reflected in craft*. Particularly when teaching the mechanical aspects of writing (e.g., handwriting, spelling, grammar), the goal is to use craft

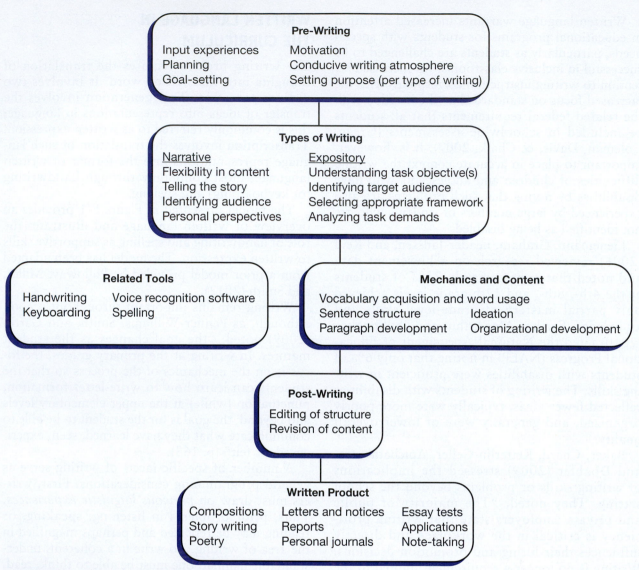

FIGURE 8–1 Written Language Model

Source: Graphic Models and Instructional Tools for Students with Special Needs (p. 28), by E. A. Polloway & J. Lubin, 2016, *Lynchburg College Journal of Special Education*, Lynchburg College, Lynchburg, VA. Used with permission.

to enhance ultimately the expression of content. Thus, work on technical skills is more effective if the skills taught are of a high degree of importance in terms of subsequent usage in actual writing.

Fourth, writing must be viewed as both *process* and *product*. Products frequently have served as the primary educational goal, and educators need to ensure that students learn how to reach that goal. However, they need to understand the process behind the product, which provides an opportunity

to emphasize the concept of the working draft. An emphasis on process is central to effective writing.

Fifth, writing also provides a communication link for *personal expression*. In this sense, writing is not simply a goal but also a vehicle. Writing provides opportunities for the expression of feelings and attitudes.

Sixth, a comprehensive program develops skills in narrative and expository forms of written language. Narrative writing may include a creative emphasis that stresses individual expression. Expository writing is more functional, serving a utilitarian purpose and stressing skills that are directly applicable to school achievement, postsecondary success, and independent living. Teachers, particularly at the secondary school level, should carefully evaluate standards for learning along with both current writing ability and expected future needs to determine which skills will benefit each student most.

 Check Your Understanding 8.2 Click here to gauge your understanding of the concepts in this section.

WRITTEN LANGUAGE ASSESSMENT

For students experiencing difficulty in acquiring writing skills, the teacher must be able to assess his or her potential to develop this skill. Several formal tests provide guidance in the process. A selection of appropriate assessment instruments is presented in Table 8-1.

Handwriting Assessment

There are limited diagnostic options available on handwriting, and therefore the most common assessment tools for that area are teacher observations and related informal techniques. Thus, once screening has been accomplished, a close visual

TABLE 8–1 Formal writing assessment instruments

Test Name (Reference)	Areas of Focus	Ages
Test of Early Written Language—Third Edition (TEWL-3) (Hresko, Herron, Peak, & Hicks 2012)	Measures early writing ability. Consists of two subtests: Basic Writing and Contextual Writing Subtest. The basic writing subtest focuses on the practical, tool, or perfunctory mechanism of writing. The Contextual Writing Subtest measures a child's skill in constructing a writing sample. To attain a overall writing score, both subtests must be administered.	4.0–11.11 years
Test of Written Expression (TOWE) (McGhee, Bryant, Larsen, & Rivera, 1995)	Measures ideation, vocabulary, spelling, and mechanics within the broader area of written expression. Includes actual writing sample from a story prompt. Two assessments are used to evaluate students' writing skills. In method 1, 76 items that touch on various skills related to writing are administered. In method 2, the student is required to read or listen to a prepared story starter that must be used as a stimulus for writing an essay.	6.6–14.11 years
Test of Written Language—Fourth Edition (TOWL-4) (Hammill & Larsen, 2009)	TOWL-4 is a comprehensive norm-referenced test that uses pretests and posttests to evaluate student growth in writing. The test consists of forms A and B to avoid contamination by memory. The test consists of eight subtests: Contextual Conventions, Contextual Language, Story Construction, Vocabulary, Spelling, Style, Logical Sentences, and Sentence Combining.	9.0–17.11 years
Test of Written Spelling—Fifth Edition (TWS-5) (Larsen, Hammill, & Moats, 2013)	The TWS-5 is a norm-referenced test of spelling administered using a dictated word format. It facilitates teach–test–teach situations. This test is used to identify students with scores significantly below those of their peers who might need interventions to improve spelling proficiency and to document the progress of spelling intervention programs.	6–18 years
Oral and Written Language Scales—Second Edition (OWLS- II) (Carrow-Woolfolk, 2011)	The OWLS-II evaluates the receptive and expressive (oral and written) language of children and young adults. There are four scales: Listening Comprehension, Oral Expression, Reading Comprehension, and Written Expression. Students' broad level of language ability and specific performance in listening, speaking, reading, and writing may be determined from the results.	3.0–21.11 years (for listening comprehension and oral expression scales) and 5.0–21.11 years (for reading comprehension and written expression scales)

examination should give the teacher information on which to build a program to help a student develop or improve specific handwriting skills.

Spelling Assessment

For spelling, many achievement tests contain sections devoted to this area. These tools generally provide a global estimate (e.g., grade-level scores) of a student's achievement. The teacher must then analyze and evaluate the responses to determine exactly what the problem is. One available instrument with further diagnostic attention in writing is the *Test of Written Spelling—Fifth Edition* (TWS-5) (Larsen, Hammill, & Moats, 2013), which measures a student's ability to spell both phonetically regular and phonetically irregular words (see also Table 8-1).

Informal approaches to assessment are of particular value to the teacher in planning spelling instructional programs. Calhoon, Greenberg, and Hunter (2010) identified three ways in which spelling can be assessed: by responding to the dictation of words said out loud, by assessing student writing samples including spelling words, and by asking students to recognize words that are correctly spelled within the context of multiple choices. These three approaches collectively can provide varying opportunities to observe student performance as the basis for instruction.

A way to conceptualize spelling assessment is to consider the learner's progression through stages of spelling proficiency with attention to identifying developmental errors. Beirne-Smith (2012, summarizing Gentry, 2000) outlined a five-stage system:

1. **Precommunicative spelling.** Spellers randomly string together letters of the alphabet without regard to letter–sound correspondence (examples: *opsop* = eagle; *rtat* = eighty).
2. **Semiphonetic spelling.** Letters represent sound, but only some of the letters are represented (examples: *e* = eagle; *a* = eighty).
3. **Phonetic spelling.** Words are spelled as they sound as the speller represents all of the phonemes in a word, though the spelling may be unconventional (examples: *egl* = eagle; *ate* = eighty).
4. **Transitional spelling.** A visual memory of spelling patterns is apparent as spellings exhibit conventions of English orthography such as vowels in every syllable, vowel digraph patterns, correctly spelled inflectional endings,

and frequent letter sequences (examples: *egul* = eagle; *eightee* = eighty).
5. Words are spelled correctly. (p. 399)

Error analysis also can provide specific information to develop a spelling instructional program; it should be based on careful scrutiny of patterns in a student's misspellings. Areas of specific attention (*with sample words*) include the following:

- Additions of unneeded letters (*necessary*)
- Omissions of needed letters (*togehr*)
- Reversals of letters (*bog* for *dog*)
- Reversals of whole words (*was* for *saw*)
- Letter-order confusion (*recieve*)
- Final consonant changes (*trys* for *tries*)

Another approach is to develop a simple diagnostic spelling survey of words containing some of the most common spelling errors and administer it to students as an informal test. For example, an assessment could emphasize letter changes at the end of words:

- Change *y* to *i* when a suffix is added (*happiness*)
- Change *y* to *i* in plurals and tense (*flies*)
- Final *e* makes preceding vowel long (*rate*, *cane*)
- Drop final *e* when suffix is added (*liking*, *using*)
- Final consonant is doubled when suffix is added (*stopped*)

Written Expression Assessment

Polloway (2009) noted that initial and ongoing analyses of writing are necessary components to guide instructional practices for all students. Further, he stated that "a key aspect of such a commitment (to writing success) must include a careful assessment of students within this domain. With so much of school success and postsecondary success contingent on the acquisition and use of effective writing skills, it is critical that teachers take advantage of relevant assessment data to provide a basis for designing effective instructional programs" (p. 132).

A contemporary concern is the increased emphasis on school standards in the assessment of writing. The challenges experienced by students with disabilities in writing have been highlighted by the increased use by states of high-stakes tests aligned with standards of learning. Such testing puts "increased pressure on students who have difficulty writing, and that difficulty can, in turn, affect their ability to graduate, attend college, and seek postsecondary employment outside of entry-level positions" (Jacobson & Reid, 2010, p. 158).

TABLE 8–2 Informal written language assessment procedures

Technique	Description	Methodology	Example	Comment
Type-token ratio	Variety of words ratio used (types) in relation to overall number of words (tokens)	$\dfrac{\text{Different words used}}{\text{Total words used}}$	Type = 36 Token = 100 Ratio = 36/100 = .36	Greater diversity of usage implies more mature writing.
Index of diversification	Measure of diversity of word usage	$\dfrac{\text{Total number of words used}}{\text{Number of occurrences of most frequently used word}}$	Total words = 64 Number of times word *the* appeared = 8 Index = 8	Increase in index reflects broader vocabulary.
Average sentence length	Words per sentence (WPS)	$\dfrac{\text{Total number of words used}}{\text{Total number of sentences}}$	TW = 64 TS = 8 WPS = 8	Longer length reflects more mature writing ability.
Error analysis	Measure of word and sentence usage	Compare errors found in sample with list of common errors.	—	Determine patterns, prioritize instruction.

Thought-unit length	Measure of writing maturity	1. Determine number of discrete thought units (T-units)
		2. Determine average length of T-unit: $\dfrac{\text{Total words}}{\text{Total number of T-units}}$
		3. Analyze quantitative variables:
		  a. Number of sentences used
		  b. Number of T-units
		  c. Number of words per T-unit
		4. Analyze qualitative nature of sentences
			"The summer was almost over and the children were ready to go back to school."
			Quantitative: (1; 2; 5–10) *Qualitative:*
			1. Compound sentence
			2. Adverbs: of degree —*almost;* of place —*back*
			3. Adjective—*ready*
			4. Infinitive—*to go*
			5. Prepositional phrase of place—*to school*
				Provides information on productivity and maturity.

A number of norm-referenced assessment instruments are available for written language. Table 8-1 provided an analysis of selected formal instruments that can assist teachers and diagnosticians in selecting appropriate instruments for particular purposes (e.g., screening, determining current level of performance, or evaluating educational programs). One diagnostic tool that can provide a more comprehensive analysis of written language abilities is the *Test of Written Language—Fourth Edition* (TOWL-4) (Hammill & Larsen, 2009), which was developed to assess the adequacy of abilities in handwriting, spelling, and the various other components of written expression. The test includes scales for vocabulary, thematic maturity, word usage, and style.

Because formal tools cannot fully evaluate the total scope of written expression, informal assessment approaches should receive primary attention. Effective assessment strategies in writing are comprehensive in scope, derived from the curriculum, and reliant on data from a variety of sources.

Writing assessment can be based on a variety of approaches that typically may include holistic scoring, in which global judgments are made about individual writing samples; analytic scoring, which focuses on specific dimensions of writing; and *curriculum-based measurement* (CBM). The latter may include a prompt for writing a brief passage with assessment that may be focused on measures such as "number of words written, number of correctly spelled words, and number of correct word sequences (defined as two adjacent words that are correct)" (Coker & Ritchey, 2010, p. 177).

The techniques described in Table 8-2 facilitate an informal analysis of a number of aspects of writing. The key to using any of these procedures is to analyze students' writing samples. Frequent opportunities to communicate must be part of the weekly experiences of all students possessing basic skills in the area. Teachers should plan a sequence of skills that will be evaluated on an ongoing basis and should resist the temptation to provide corrective feedback for all types of errors simultaneously. Error analysis should thus focus on an individual skill deficit as a basis for remediation. Although this set of assessment procedures focuses on a variety of specific writing skills that emphasize craft in particular, most important is the successful communication of ideas (i.e., the content). Content is often best assessed via holistic writing measures.

Penner-Williams et al. (2009) highlighted the strengths of informal assessment as including their coordination potentially with the daily classroom activities without the interruption of classroom routines and the fact that they are typically completed by the teacher who is naturally more familiar with students in terms of his or her strengths and weaknesses. Possible weaknesses include the fact that informal assessment typically does not include comparison with a normative sample and consequently that teachers cannot make comparisons to age peers. In addition, the unstructured nature of some informal assessment procedures can fail to provide consistent, useful information on instructional effectiveness.

 Check Your Understanding 8.3 Click here to gauge your understanding of the concepts in this section.

HANDWRITING INSTRUCTION

Historically, the importance of handwriting was perhaps related to the traditional observation that attractive handwriting once meant that a person was well educated and wealthy and was a status symbol that separated socioeconomic classes before education was compulsory in America. While such an observation sees no such attention in contemporary society, handwriting instruction certainly has remained a core focus of the curriculum for students at the elementary level.

Graham and Harris (2005) surveyed teachers to determine handwriting practices in the schools at that time. Primary-grade teachers reported that they spent an average of 72 minutes a week on instruction (Graham & Harris, 2005). They further indicated that 12% of those students experienced difficulties.

Cahill (2009, pp. 223–224) posited that "handwriting is closely linked to academic achievement, especially composition and literacy skills. . . . Even if students do not intend to use handwriting as their primary mode of communication, instruction and practice with handwriting may support their academic achievement." Failure to master skills can have a negative impact on how much students write, their writing quality and grades, and the time taken to complete assignments.

Even though handwriting has been a staple of the school curriculum for years, technological advances have caused some educators to question its relevance as an important skill to be taught. Nevertheless, as Polloway et al. (2012) noted,

> Although the advances made in technology have clearly impacted on the everyday use of handwriting for some people, competencies in this skill remain important. . . . Without the ability to communicate with handwriting, individuals will be [less] able to make notes, take down information quickly, and communicate with others. (p. 336)

Many children are delayed or disabled for reasons that also may impact their handwriting skills. For example, they may have deficits in attention or visual memory, or they may have physiological problems that inhibit the development of fine motor skills. In addition, they may be more susceptible to the effects of poor teaching in the primary grades. Because writing combines fine motor skills, sequencing, language, memory, attention, thinking skills, and visual-spatial abilities, it may be quite difficult. Difficulties with handwriting at an automatic level may result in students being frustrated with written assignments, failing to complete such assignments, and experiencing lower self-efficacy (Cahill, 2009).

All students, but especially those with disabilities, are disadvantaged when handwriting is not taught correctly and frequently. Bertin and Perlman (2000) noted that "handwriting is a basic skill that needs to be systematically taught so that children can learn to use written language to communicate their knowledge and express their ideas" (p. 1). Research has shown a relationship between handwriting skills and the overall writing process (Graham, Harris, & Fink, 2000).

In instructing learners with special needs, teachers should remember that the ultimate goal is legibility. Efforts to achieve perfect reproduction are doomed to failure; even when reasonably successful, they may be short-lived triumphs because most students eventually develop their own personal style. Therefore, instructional programs should avoid stressing the perfection associated with some recognized standards and instead encourage a legible yet unique style.

Instructional Considerations

Prerequisites. The development of pre-writing skills builds on visual acuity and its coordination with motor movements. Therefore, when students who are disabled enter formal schooling, they must engage in the same type of visual and motor activities that typically developing children may have mastered by that time. Developing visual-motor integration and establishing handedness (i.e., preferred hand for writing) are central concerns at this stage. To achieve these two goals, numerous activities have typically been suggested: manipulation of objects, tracing of objects in sand, manipulation of scissors for cutting paper, and crayon and finger painting.

There are however, several important considerations about such training. While some activities (e.g., cutting with scissors) are clearly important for their own worth, regardless of their relationship to writing, there is no empirical support confirming that the above types of prerequisite exercises directly assist in refining existing writing skills. Instead, the focus on non-writing fine motor activities may simply take time away from direct instruction in writing. Rather, the handwriting process itself provides fine motor practice and thus can accomplish both linguistically relevant goals (i.e., objectives that promote language development) and motoric goals. As a result, prerequisite skills often are best developed by directing students to write letters and words rather than via readiness instruction. For students with significant motoric difficulties, occupational therapists can provide assistance to both teachers and students.

Stages in Writing Development. To provide an overview, it is beneficial to consider specific stages associated with the development of handwriting skills. For students through first grade, key considerations include the following:

- Learning how to hold pencil
- Recognizing upper- and lowercase
- Writing names and common words

As students progress through primary education, considerations include the following:

- Forming upper- and lowercase manuscript
- Using wide-lined paper and "beginner" utensils
- Learning to read cursive
- Joining letters
- Continue manuscript while learning cursive
- Mastering both forms
- Developing personal style

The discussion below focuses on manuscript writing and then progresses to cursive writing.

Manuscript Writing. Because manuscript writing is the initial instructional focus for most students, the teacher's first tasks are to determine an instructional sequence of letters and to select instructional methodology; this decision is most often governed by the curriculum followed in the general education classroom. There is no correct letter to start with in teaching manuscript writing; however, certain letters lend themselves to that function. For example, the letters of a child's first name have high utility value and thus have a positive effect on motivation.

To ensure an appropriate instructional sequence, the teacher can group different letters by their shapes (see Figures 8-2 and 8-3) or can follow the letter sequence in one of the commercial manuscript workbooks available. Another alternative is to follow the order in which letters are introduced for reading. Attention also should be given to the relative similarity of strokes required for the letters.

For students who experience difficulty in beginning writing, modifications of the writing implement can be considered; the greatest problem often encountered is the child's use of the correct grip on the utensil. A variety of aids have been used to facilitate appropriate grip, including the larger primary-sized pencils, tape wrapped around the

o a d g q / b p / c e /
t l i k / r n m h / v w
x y / f j / u / z / s

FIGURE 8–2 A Sequential Grouping of Lowercase Manuscript Letters According to Common Features

FIGURE 8–3 A Sequential Grouping of Uppercase Manuscript Letters According to Common Features

pencil, use of a multisided large pencil, and the adaptation of a standard pencil with a *Hoyle gripper* (a three-sided plastic device that requires the child to place two fingers and the thumb in the proper position). Although there is not definitive research on handwriting instruction on the benefits of modifying writing utensils, it is prudent to assess the grip of individual students in order to determine whether an adaptation is warranted.

The most effective approach to teaching specific letters and words is one in which teacher presentation is consistent. Most programs assume that these forms are best taught in isolation but that opportunities must be provided for their use in actual writing exercises. In their classic paper on handwriting, Graham and Miller (1980) provided an excellent review of effective instructional techniques and sequences to facilitate letter formation. The procedures that follow are based in part on the specific steps they outlined for instruction.

First, the teacher demonstrates the formation of individual letters while students observe the specific strokes involved. Students' attention should be directed to the distinctive features of these letters and their comparison with letters previously learned. As the children begin to transcribe letters, the teacher should use prompting (e.g., manual guidance during writing, directional arrows) and tracing to facilitate the task. When there is no longer a need for this more intrusive type of prompt, instruction becomes a function of copying—typically, from near-point (i.e., from a paper on the student's desk) and then from far-point (e.g., the board). While students are copying and then writing from memory, they should be encouraged to engage in self-instruction by verbalizing to themselves the writing procedures being followed. After

a letter can be written from memory, repetition of the form is needed to ensure learning and enhance proficiency. Finally, corrective feedback from the teacher, extrinsic reinforcement, or self-correction can be used so that the letter will be retained and increased legibility will be achieved.

Once the student has made appropriate progress acquiring competence in the formation of manuscript letters, the transition to cursive should begin, often in third grade. Criteria for the transition include manuscript proficiency, ability to write all letters from memory, and self-initiated imitation of cursive forms.

Cursive Writing. The set of skills acquired while learning manuscript writing is helpful to students when they begin to learn how to write in cursive form. The movement to cursive should stress the key features of that style: paper positioning, the pencil remaining on the paper throughout the writing of individual words, all letters starting at the baseline, a left-to-right rhythm, an appropriate slant to the right, connection of letters, and the spacing between words. Students can begin with manuscript letters that directly evolve into cursive forms.

Instruction in cursive writing can follow the same format used with manuscript form: (a) start with letters that students are presently working with while following a predetermined sequence (see Figures 8-4 and 8-5) based on common features or follow the sequence found in commercial cursive writing workbook, (b) consistently use the terms *uppercase* and *lowercase* to describe a letter, and (c) work with previously written words to promote transfer and overlearning. In addition, teachers need to prompt students as to whether they should be writing in cursive or manuscript. When students begin to use cursive writing, they will also be using more complex language forms and will be able to record them in sentence and paragraph form.

FIGURE 8–4 A Sequential Grouping of Lowercase Cursive Letters According to Common Features

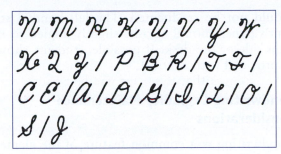

FIGURE 8–5 A Sequential Grouping of Uppercase Cursive Letters According to Common Features

Perspective: Manuscript and Cursive Writing. The question of teaching manuscript versus cursive handwriting has been debated for many years. Rationales for teaching only manuscript traditionally include its similarity to book print, the relative ease of letter formation, and its benefit in not confusing students with a second writing form. Rationales for cursive have included its natural rhythm, amelioration of problems with spacing and reversals, social status, and speed.

Despite the various claims and disclaimers about the merits of these forms, the question is often moot because most students will already been taught according to the traditional sequence in the general education classroom (i.e., manuscript followed by cursive in the second or third grade). Students with more significant disabilities, however, are typically best taught first in manuscript because it makes fewer motoric demands and is consistent with (and thus reinforces) the printed words in reading. Because most students ultimately will learn both forms, they subsequently will use the form of handwriting with which they feel most comfortable and at which they are most proficient. No clear empirical data establish that one form of handwriting is clearly and inherently better than the other for a given population of students.

Handwriting Program Alternatives

The traditional approach to instructional sequences is still commonly followed by the majority of general education classrooms and schools. Thus, a common program used is the classic Zaner-Bloser approach, which identifies both manuscript and cursive handwriting forms. There are however, several options worth noting:

- **D'Nealian handwriting program**—The purpose of the D'Nealian program (Thurber, 2008) is to reduce teaching or learning time by initially establishing the letter formations, rhythm, size, slant, and spacing that will be used for cursive writing. The program stresses continuous skill progression with transition from manuscript to cursive. Materials are available for readiness through eighth grade. The teacher's edition suggests ways to modify instruction for those experiencing motor coordination and other handwriting problems. The instructional sequence provides an alternative to traditional instruction.

- **Handwriting without Tears (HWT)**—HWT (Olsen, 2015), while not designed specifically for students with special needs, has a number of elements that make it appropriate. The program pays specific attention to the developmental progression of fine motor skills, and provides teacher guidance in facilitating posture and pencil grasp. Letters are introduced according to the developmental difficulty of the pencil strokes involved in their creation. HWT uses a multisensory approach and begins by introducing capital letters and numbers that are written in gray blocks with prompts to eliminate and correct letter reversals. It simplifies the structure of letters by reducing writing strokes to long lines, short lines, large curves, and short curves. All letters, both capital and lowercase, can be created using these four shapes, which are introduced based on the directionality and difficulty of the line–curve combinations. This reduction in the complexity of manuscript writing allows students to more easily visualize letters and identify similarities between letters. Students using HWT demonstrate significant improvement in letter size and spacing (Owens, 2004). HWT provides an alternative to traditional instruction when teaching children who have been unsuccessful in the acquisition of handwriting skills. (*Note:* The authors thank Crystal Wimmer for assistance with HWT.)

- **Mixed script**—Mixed script programs use a simplified script that combines elements of both manuscript and cursive writing, thus simplifying the task of learning letter forms and eliminating the need for transition from manuscript to cursive. Whether such a mixed script is formally taught or not may be moot; many writers naturally gravitate to it. Graham and Harris (2005) reported some limited data that suggest such writers may be faster and also may have higher levels of legibility.

- **Keyboarding**—Instruction in keyboarding is an alternative to handwriting instruction that may be particularly beneficial for students who have significant problems with fine motor coordination. Given the dominance of technology in communication, all students who have not already demonstrated proficiency should receive instruction so that they can learn to look at the screen rather than their fingers in the process. In addition to teaching typing and computer skills, the advantages of keyboarding include faster speed, higher degree of legibility, and inherent motivational advantages.

- **Voice-recognition software**—Another key alternative approach is through *voice-recognition software*. The promise of this technology is particularly significant for students who have motoric difficulties with handwriting and keyboarding (e.g., some students with cerebral palsy). Programs such as *Naturally Speaking* from Nuance are reasonable in cost and can achieve in excess of 95% accuracy in recognition after appropriate training.

Left-Handedness

Left-handed students (approximately 10% of the U.S. population, or two or three students in each general education classroom) often encounter problems in writing that may accentuate the other problems already present in students with learning difficulties. They cannot see letters adequately as they form them because the left hand blocks out a letter shortly after it is written. The primary difference between right- and left-handed writers is in their physical orientation. That is, "right-handed students pull their arms toward their bodies as they write, whereas left-handed students push away. As left-handed students write, they move their left hand across what they have just written, often covering it" (Tompkins, 2005, p. 615).

One simple strategy is for left-handed students to grasp the writing utensil farther away from the tip while maintaining the same grip on the pencil or pen. They should not be encouraged to hook their hands to see better; this practice is tiring and may cause more problems. However, students who are already successfully writing in a hooked fashion

should not be reeducated. The left-handed student's paper should also be slightly angled to the right side of the desk. If possible, students should be provided with a model.

Handwriting Legibility Maintenance Considerations

Handwriting is a common feature of the elementary classroom and is very seldom part of an instructional program at the middle or secondary school level. Nevertheless, there are advantages in instructional activities that promote the continued legible transcription of writing. For example, a key consideration would include preparing adolescents for the world of work and for the forms and applications that so frequently specify "please print." Teachers can continue to provide practical opportunities for using manuscript writing beyond the elementary school level.

Direct instruction of new skills rarely occurs for older students; therefore, key goals for upper elementary and middle school students are in the areas of proficiency and maintenance. Teachers may assume that handwriting was taught in elementary grades and that the students will independently maintain good handwriting skills just by doing the writing required for daily assignments. However, the value of guided practice should not be overlooked.

The goal of proficiency and maintenance learning activities is to enhance and retain both accuracy and fluency. Consequently, the teacher must periodically evaluate retention and use direct instruction to maintain both accuracy and speed. Penmanship tends to deteriorate with time, and the importance of repetition to enhance retention is relatively infrequently stated in reference to handwriting.

The first concern in developing a maintenance program is to evaluate the handwriting of each student. To facilitate this process, teachers can maintain checklists of specific letters and skills for individual students with the student's involvement. A second concern is for student self-evaluation and correction. The greatest improvement occurs when students are taught to evaluate their own handwriting and are encouraged to improve, such as by self-monitoring letter forms and by self-grading, finding their own mistakes, and making corrections.

A classic technique to promote proficiency is *selective checking* (Lovitt, 1975). A teacher using this technique selects a specific letter to be evaluated at the end of a given daily assignment. A model is provided for the student, with an established criterion for acceptable legibility. After reviewing the specific examples of the letter-of-the-day within the particular task, the teacher uses illegibility as the basis for assigning additional practice exercises and correct letter formation as the basis for reinforcement.

Cahill (2009) provided a list of practices that can enable students to enhance their handwriting skill and maintain legibility. Her examples included writing subjects in a notebook of assignments on a daily basis, signing in or out of the classroom, writing words from spelling lists multiple times, copying vocabulary word definitions, writing letters and numbers in sequence, and copying assignments from the board.

Because most adults write in a form of cursive, some support can be generated for having persons with special needs write in this way to foster inclusion. However, only in personal signatures does cursive writing take clear precedence over manuscript. An analysis of the writing of many adolescents and adults typically will reveal reliance on a mixed script with elements of manuscripts and cursive merged (see the previous text).

 Check Your Understanding 8.4 Click here to gauge your understanding of the concepts in this section.

SPELLING INSTRUCTION

Although limited efforts have been made to ascertain the prevalence of spelling disorders, it is generally assumed that such problems are widespread, with primary teachers indicating that 26% of their students experienced difficulty (Graham & Harris, 2005). The challenge is exacerbated because the English language has 26 letters, 300 different letter combinations, and 17 vowel and 27 consonant phonemes and thus over 500 spellings to represent phonemes. Calhoon, Greenberg, et al. (2010) noted that the processes involved in spelling require the individual to use "orthographic memory" that includes an ability to focus on sounds associated with letters, morphemes within words, syllables, and also odd or unusual word forms.

Individuals experiencing difficulty in spelling are typically classified as demonstrating isolated deficits in specific spelling skills or as exhibiting a general pattern of academic and language-learning disabilities, of which spelling is just one symptom (Beirne-Smith, 2012). Given the fact that reading and spelling are correlated, it is not surprising that many students who have difficulties with reading also experience problems with spelling. Further, given the fact that both reading and spelling draw on an understanding—or lack of understanding—of the alphabetic system, it is likely that students with reading disabilities will also experience problems in spelling (Calhoon, Al Otaiba, & Greenberg, 2010).

Beirne-Smith (2012) provided this analysis of spellers of variant ability:

> Proficient spellers . . . typically depend on sensitivity of patterns of letters, have visual ability to distinguish when words look correct, and have strong phonemic awareness and knowledge of spelling patterns. . . . When faced with unfamiliar words, proficient spellers access, devise, or apply strategies to determine the correct spelling of the word. They use their knowledge of phonemic and morphemic rules to spell the word phonetically, generate several alternative spellings of the word, and then use revisualization to determine the correct spelling, or they consult an outside source such as the teacher, a peer, or the dictionary. . . . Less fluent spellers, in contrast, seem to lack skills essential to producing correctly spelled words. [They] experience word confusions, recall failures, and have unexpected problems remembering certain words. (p. 375)

Troia (2005) noted the following in his review of research concerning the importance of spelling (which included attention to handwriting as well):

- Instruction has a demonstrable impact on measures associated with those skills as well as writing fluency.
- Students with and without problems benefit from basic skills instruction.
- Spelling instruction improves decoding performance.
- Composing strategies should be taught alongside these basic skills to influence their parallel development.

Although the emphasis on spelling has waned somewhat in light of, for example, spell-checkers on computers, it remains an important skill. Because writing is communication, spelling must be accurate enough for the reader to understand.

Instructional Considerations

Spelling instruction should begin soon after young students have started to learn to read because they will be attempting to write certain words that they can read. The close ties among spelling, reading, and writing should lead to integrated language instruction. Santoro, Coyne, and Simmons (2006) noted that "spelling instruction can strategically integrate two critical aspects of beginning reading for kindergartners at risk of reading difficulties: phonemic awareness and alphabetic understanding. . . . Spelling does appear to intensify beginning reading instruction and help improve (reading and spelling) skills" (p. 131).

General Considerations.

A number of specific considerations can assist in designing an effective spelling program regardless of classroom settings. These considerations, based broadly on a review of the relevant literature, include the following:

- Stress initial instruction on spelling high-frequency words.
- Include a focus on misspelled words from student's writing.
- Link instruction in spelling and reading, having students learn to spell words that they are in the process of learning to read.
- Present words in units of about 6 to 12 words, emphasizing common structural elements.
- Teach word patterns by focusing on meaning units (morphemes: prefixes, suffixes, root words).
- Teach students error-correction procedures for individual words.
- Teach strategies that are based on a systematic word study procedure (see examples below).
- Promote accuracy and maintenance through periodic spelling review.
- Link instruction in spelling and actual writing to promote generalization.
- Use reinforcement to ensure motivation.

Regardless of the word list selected or the approach utilized, spelling instruction will be effective only if students have opportunities to use the target words in written assignments and to proofread their work for possible errors. Although learning words in isolation is recommended to facilitate acquisition, maintenance and generalization are achieved only when students are encouraged to make regular use of the words they have learned.

However, because students risk interruption in the conceptual task of writing when they ponder the correct form of a difficult word, they can be encouraged to write an approximation of the word initially and then review it and correct it as necessary during the post-writing phase.

Word Selection.

The first words that students write are often meaningful to them, not just because they are new but because they are usually the names of people, places, and things with which they are familiar. Teachers should also make other new words as meaningful as possible, such as by using new words to make up stories about students' immediate environment, thus facilitating a transition from the old to the new, or by placing new words in colorful sequence on a bulletin board, thereby causing students to be interested in finding out what the words are and how to spell them.

Word selections can be made from a variety of sources. Based on a student's ability and interest level, a teacher can select from frequency-of-use-in-writing lists (see also Chapter 6), linguistic word families (e.g., *fan/tan/pan*), words used regularly within a student's oral expressive vocabulary, lists from specific basal or remedial programs, commonly misspelled words, and words taken from the student's list of mastered reading words.

An initial list of high-utility words for spelling instruction adapted from reading (Tompkins, 2006) is presented in Table 8-3. These words were selected because of their common occurrence in reading at the elementary level as well as for their utility in initial writing compositions. It provides an illustration of a beginning point for the spelling curriculum.

General Teaching Strategies.

A variety of instructional strategies can assist students who are having difficulty with spelling. Teachers should plan a program allowing for regular, systematic instruction while drawing from a variety of word-study techniques that are effective for particular students. The most successful word-study techniques can draw on multisensory approaches, promote revisualization of words, build on phonetic analysis skills, assist students in formulating specific rules for accurate spelling, and promote self-correction.

A classic example of a word-study technique is the **Fernald multisensory approach** (Fernald, 1943). The following specific procedures are based on her directions for children learning new words

TABLE 8–3 High-utility spelling word list

a	about	After	again	all	always
am	and	another	any	are	around
as	at	away	back	bad	ball
be	because	been	before	began	behind
best	better	big	blue	book	box
boy	but	by	call	come	can
children	could	day	did	do	does
down	each	eat	even	ever	every
far	fast	find	first	fly	for
found	friend	from	fun	get	girl
give	go	good	got	grow	had
hand	happy	has	have	he	help
her	here	him	his	home	house
how	i	if	in	into	is
it	it's	jump	keep	know	last
left	let	like	little	live	long
look	made	make	man	many	may
me	my	name	need	never	new
next	night	no	not	now	of
off	on	once	one	only	or
other	our	out	over	play	put
ran	red	ride	right	room	run
said	sat	saw	say	school	see
she	show	small	so	some	something
stop	story	take	tell	than	that
the	them	then	these	they	thing
think	this	thought	through	time	to
together	too	try	two	under	until
up	us	very	walk	want	way
was	water	we	went	were	what
when	where	who	why	will	with
woman	work	yes	you	your	zoo

Source: Graphic Models and Instructional Tools for Students with Special Needs (p. 35), by E. A. Polloway & J. Lubin, 2016, *Lynchburg College Journal of Special Education*, Lynchburg College, Lynchburg, VA. Used with permission.

and provide an example of the multisensory nature of the approach:

1. Look at the word very carefully and say it over to yourself.
2. See if the word can be written just the way you say it.
3. Shut your eyes and see if you can get a picture of the word in your mind. If you cannot, remember the parts that are written the way you say them. Pronounce the word to yourself or feel your hand make the movements of writing the word.
4. When you are sure of every part of the word, shut your book or cover the word and write it, saying each syllable as you write.
5. If you cannot write the word correctly after you have looked at it and said it, ask the

teacher to write it for you. Trace the word with your fingers. Say each part as you trace it. Trace the word carefully until you can write it correctly. Say each part of the word as you write it.

6. If the word is difficult, turn the paper over and write it again.
7. Later in the day, try writing it from memory.
8. Make your own dictionary.

Approaches based on Fernald (or having similar features to that program) are focused on varied strategies for promoting revisualization of words. Such instructional strategies can be used for any words regardless of whether or not they are linguistically regular (and follow certain sound–symbol correspondences). Such approaches essentially require attention to looking at the word, saying it to yourself, closing your eyes and revisualizing it, covering the word, spelling it, and checking for accuracy.

For words that are linguistically regular, spellers have the additional advantage of relying on sound–symbol correspondences to assist in the learning process. Because within English there is a productive (if imperfect) relationship between sounds and symbols, such an emphasis can be important as a mediating influence. The foundation in phonetic analysis therefore shows the relationship between reading and spelling again in this instance. Specific strategies that take advantage of such approaches include selecting words that follow certain word families and are linguistically regular, repeating the word after listening to the teacher pronounce it, saying each sound within the word while looking at the letters, and then writing the word while naming the letters.

An emphasis on *spelling rules* can also be beneficial. An instructional sequence that can be followed may include select the rule, develop a related word list, promote understanding of the rule through word study, teach the rule generalization by focusing on the word characteristics within the list, use and apply the rule, and identify exceptions.

Mnemonic Strategies. Accurate spelling of difficult words can be facilitated through the use of *mnemonic strategies*. Because the task of learning a series of mnemonic devices can challenge a student's memory, their use in spelling should be limited to examples that students can retain and use

regularly. The following limited list of examples provide a start in such efforts: *a principal is your pal*; *there are three e's buried in cemetery*; *stationery is paper*; *meant is the past tense of mean*; and *a secretary can keep a secret*.

Invented Spellings

A component of some language instructional programs has been *invented spellings*. Typically, students' creations of spellings reflect a direct application of phonology to words (e.g., *mi* [my], *lade* [lady], *nit* [night]) (Tompkins, 2005). The concept of invented spelling is based on the assumption that students should be able to express themselves initially in writing without having to be concerned with spelling accuracy. When students invent their own spellings, teachers are naturally provided with helpful assessment data. Further, it is logical to assume that the temporary use of invented spellings, such as within a given writing assignment, may have a positive effect on writing fluency and creativity by not interfering with the writing (i.e., conceptual) process.

The efficacy of invented spellings used with students with special needs, however, is largely unexplored territory (Graham, 2000) and has not been validated empirically. There remains disagreement as to whether acceptance or encouragement to create new spellings ultimately will have a positive effect on the writing of students or whether it may reinforce incorrect revisualization and hence lead to misspellings in the future. Teachers are advised to consider its use only on an experimental basis and to research it for effectiveness.

Spelling for Middle and Secondary School

Spelling is less often a primary instructional focus beyond the elementary level. Nevertheless, one important consideration, also relevant at the elementary level, is to assist students in the development of word-study strategies that can be used on an independent basis after instruction and support by the teacher. A simple strategy—the 5C's (derived in part from McLaughlin & Skinner, 1996)—for use in studying words is outlined below:

- *Copy* each spelling word while saying each letter.
- *Cover* each word and then write the word from memory.
- *Compare* each word as written to its actual spelling.

- *Correct* any misspellings for each word that is not spelled correctly.
- *Continue* the process until all words are spelled correctly.

Another consideration is to make spelling functional. Thus, students should have as many functional words in their spelling vocabularies as possible. Functional words help young students communicate more effectively and help older individuals gain and maintain employment, adjust to environmental and social demands, and thus achieve social independence. Teachers can draw up a list of community-relevant, functional words for students to learn. Functional word lists can be integrated into the reading program and can help students develop skills not only for spelling but for life in general.

 Check Your Understanding 8.5 Click here to gauge your understanding of the concepts in this section.

WRITTEN EXPRESSION INSTRUCTION

Written expression builds on all other language domains. Therefore, effective writing derives from knowledge and skills in listening, speaking, reading, handwriting, and spelling. It is multifaceted in terms of challenges and required skills and strategies. It also is associated with multiple purposes including *narrative* (writing stories and personal essays), *informative* (sharing knowledge and communicating instructions, ideas, and messages), and *persuasive* (influencing the reader's action and bringing about change).

Based on their review of research, Butler, Elaschuk, and Poole (2000) noted that effective writers analyze the requirements of the task and plan accordingly, identify goals, use strategies to achieve their goals, adjust goals as needed, and monitor the success of their endeavors. On the other hand, Troia (2002) characterized the writing of ineffective students—such as those with special needs—as producing writing that is "shorter, less linguistically sophisticated, more poorly organized, more mechanical errors, poorer in overall quality . . . [and reflective of] difficulties in executing and regulating the cognitive and meta-cognitive processes underlying proficient writing" (p. 251).

Special concern relates to students at the secondary level. Chalk, Hagan-Burke, and Burke (2005)

aptly summarized the importance of writing instruction for older students:

> Written expression is a fundamental skill for today's high school students. Those who lack the ability to adequately demonstrate conceptual knowledge and communicate their thoughts and beliefs in writing are at grave disadvantage. Being facile with written language and writing is required to pass state and district exams, advance from grade to grade, and to graduate from high school. An alarming number of students with learning disabilities struggle to develop writing skills sufficient to satisfy these crucial benchmarks. (p. 85)

Because writing instruction occurs as a significant curricular concern across levels of schooling, the following discussion integrates further consideration for teaching adolescents rather than including a separate section at the end.

Writing Stages

The process of writing can best be conceptualized by a multicomponent model—a series of sequential stages that not only define the process but also guide the necessary instruction (see Figure 8-1 for a model that illustrates the stages). Writing models typically divide the process into the three stages: pre-writing, inclusive of planning and organizing; writing, or the drafting of ideas into sentences and paragraphs; and post-writing, or revision and editing.

Viewing these three stages of writing as distinct and significant enables instruction to focus on the specific tasks facing the would-be writer. In practice, though, these phases are not perfectly discrete and linear (e.g., planning and rethinking continues to take place during the post-writing stage, and revising may take place during the drafting stage). Nevertheless, an initial focus on distinct stages of writing can promote a process orientation that will assist students in thinking about what they are writing.

To discuss the broad array of writing instructional strategies, this section focuses on general principles of instruction across the three stages of writing. Although the lines between these stages can blur and writing is a recursive process, they are presented here separately.

Pre-Writing Stage

Pre-writing consists of what the writer considers prior to the act itself. Input includes the various forms of stimulation that assist in forming a basic intent to write, such as environmental experience, reading, listening, and media exposure. Motivation includes the effects of various stimulating activities, as well as the external factors that reinforce writing. In addition, the purpose for writing must be established to assist in organization.

Instruction taking place during this stage should reflect the reality of the way students present themselves for instruction. In particular, assumptions should not be made that students have had the necessary experiential prerequisites to develop ideation, that they have a desire to communicate via written means, or that they understand their purpose in writing and their intended audience. As a consequence, teachers need to focus on devoting sufficient time to writing, providing rich experiences and assisting students in getting ideas, structuring content, setting purpose, determining audience, and building vocabulary (Scott & Vitale, 2003).

Given the challenges that students with special needs often have with writing, the first important consideration in instruction is sufficient opportunity for students to develop their writing ability. Thus, they need a *substantial amount of time to write*.

The second concern is the *classroom environment*. Santagelo and Olinghouse (2009) stressed the importance of the physical environment enhancing motivation for writing and ultimately writing skills. Key features that they identify included expansive classroom libraries, an environment that is print rich with access to varied writing materials and active usage of these materials, showcasing examples of students writing, and providing alternative spaces to enable students to work in a comfortable fashion within the classroom.

Related is the third concern of *motivation*, which is particularly important for adolescents with disabilities. A substantial amount of research focused on the writing of students without disabilities argues that motivation must come from within; teachers can stimulate students, but, by this theory, they cannot actually motivate them. According to this logic, if students have something meaningful or interesting to think about, their writing will reflect it. This premise, however, presents difficulty because writing does not just happen much of the time for many students. Teachers of students with special needs should consider ways to promote motivation, such as using external reward systems to complement the internal motivation of reluctant writers.

A fourth consideration is *stimulation*. Teachers should strive to provide opportunities to expose students to varied experiences through listening and reading; provide them with a chance to discuss and clarify ideas on a given topic, thus encouraging active thinking about the task at hand; promote brainstorming with peers; develop story pictures, outlines, and webs with students to organize ideas; and establish a conducive, supportive classroom atmosphere. Effective teachers provide stimulation before students write. Though stimulation is clearly insufficient for the achievement of competence in writing, it helps start writers thinking clearly.

Students can be stimulated initially by topics of personal interest. Teachers should generate a collection of possible themes to use as general assignments. Some examples include the following:

- I knew something was wrong when I heard that sound . . .
- When I was a baby . . .
- The day I became a . . . (pick an animal)
- When I become 18 . . .
- The greatest YouTube video . . .
- The challenges of high school . . .
- If I could change Instagram, I would improve it by . . .
- My favorite movie . . .
- My preferred type of music . . .
- My favorite sports figure . . .
- If I could be someone else, in the world for one day, I would most like to be . . .

A fifth and critical aspect of pre-writing is *planning*. Graham and Harris (2009), in assessing the planning process in writing, concluded that the behaviors students engaged in planning were predictive of performance in writing. Students had particular difficulty with the self-regulation of the processes involved in the planning stage. The key is successful instruction on how to effectively plan, which can result in a strong and positive impact on writing performance.

A component of planning is *setting the purpose*. The writer must have a clear understanding of who the audience is and thus what the purpose is. Expressive and functional writing have different intents and thus require different formats. For students with special needs—and for many other students in inclusive settings as well—planning is an area given insufficient attention.

Writing Stage

The *writing* or *drafting* stage incorporates the craft and content aspects (see below) of written language. Considerations include vocabulary usage, sentence form, paragraph sense, the overall sequence of ideas, consistency, clarity, and relevance. The important challenges that all students face include developing applicable content, organization, goal setting, and using appropriate mechanical skills (Harris, 2010).

It is of little surprise that problems and deficits in this phase are common in many students. The educator's key concern is to determine how skills are most effectively taught and learned.

An overview of writing characteristics is presented in Table 8-4. Specific considerations related to the work of good and poor writers are noted below.

Elaborating on the summative information in Table 8-4, skilled writers use cognitive processes to plan, produce, and revise; use knowledge of writing genres; reflect sensitivity to writing functions and to audience; and self-regulate through the writing process (Harris, 2010). On the other hand, unskilled writers produce shorter and less sophisticated work, tend to be more poorly organized, exhibit more mechanical errors, produce less relevant content, and engage in limited or no revision (Harris, 2010; Troia, 2002, 2005).

General Instructional Considerations. It is useful to consider the distinctions between the two roles inherent in the writing process: the author and the secretary (Isaacson, 1989). Whereas the *author* role is concerned with *content* (the formulation and organization of ideas and the selection of words and phrases to express those ideas), the *secretarial* role emphasizes *craft* (the physical and mechanical concerns of writing, such as legibility, spelling, punctuation, and grammatical rules). Both roles are critical to a writer's success.

There is an important interplay between the craft and content of writing and therefore between the author and secretarial roles. Graham and Harris (2009) identified three central considerations: the challenge of shifting attention from content to mechanical aspects without losing basic ideas for the composition or straying from the plan, the loss of ideas because of the problems due to slow speed in writing or keyboarding the text, and an overall possible loss in thinking about core ideas in the composition when the students focus must be on mechanical considerations.

The roles of author and secretary can be applied in the two instructional emphases of *teach–write* and *write–teach*. The former emphasizes formal grammar instruction, structure, skills exercises, and often a reliance on worksheets. Another traditional emphasis was diagramming sentences (for a historical review of this non-validated practice, see Schuster, 2005). Even though the teach–write approach may be common, it lacks validation for learners without disabilities as well as those with special needs. A major concern is that these instructional activities can be completed without opportunity for actual writing. At the same time, such activities can damage motivation to write and may usurp a major block of time, something that writing programs often have in limited supply. Thus, although skills are important, they may not be truly learned—that is, applied—in this fashion.

The alternative is more a write–teach focus, with initial stress on the primacy of the author role, on ideation over form, with structure emphasized later. The write–teach approach is process oriented and capitalizes on the desire to write without stifling that effort. Structure is then taught within the context of actual writing opportunities.

TABLE 8–4 Writing characteristics

Stages of Writing	Unskilled Writer	Skilled Writer
Planning	Minimally engaged in planning processes	Extensive planning to set goals and direction
Transcribing	Inconsistent message in writing, mechanical difficulties, abrupt conclusion	Clear sequence, consistent message, relative absence of mechanical problems, logical conclusion
Revising/Editing	Absence of revision of content and editing of specific mechanical concerns	Revision to focus on clarity of ideation and editing to identify and correct mechanical difficulties

Source: Graphic Models and Instructional Tools for Students with Special Needs (p. 30), by E. A. Polloway & J. Lubin, 2016, *Lynchburg College Journal of Special Education*, Lynchburg College, Lynchburg, VA. Used with permission.

The process approach to writing typically includes these emphases (Troia & Graham, 2002):

1. Frequent opportunities for writing using a predictable routine
2. Mini-lessons in which instruction in critical writing skills and strategies takes place when the need for such instruction becomes evident
3. The formation of a community of writers writing for authentic purposes and audiences
4. Teacher and peer conferencing activities during which students receive individualized feedback about the substance and form of their compositions
5. Regular occasions for sharing and publishing written work (p. 292)

The process writing approach has been associated with effectiveness in the improvement of the writing of students with learning disabilities. A focus on process enables the students to understand and follow the sequential stages involved in the writing process (Gillespie & Graham, 2014).

A writing process approach leads to a number of clear implications for instruction. Most significant is that for writing to improve, students need to write regularly. Rankin-Erickson and Pressley (2000) reported that effective teachers had students write from four days per week to several times per day.

However, once the opportunity to write is confirmed, the development of structural or mechanical skills still needs direct instruction because writing opportunities alone will not yield competence. A process approach may overrely on informal or incidental methods of instruction when explicit instruction in skills and strategies is still needed for learners with special needs (Troia & Graham, 2002). Troia (2005), for example, found that exemplary writing teachers use a balanced approach to instruction, emphasizing the explicit teaching of skills and strategies. A process approach combined with explicit instruction remains most fruitful.

Thus, the challenge is to enhance the acquisition of skills without interfering with the writing process. Graham (1992) offered three well-reasoned tenets to assist with instructional decision making: (a) maintain a balanced perspective between the extremes of decontextualized teaching of mechanics and complete de-emphasis on skills information to the extent to which acquisition becomes incidental, (b) focus on teaching skills that are likely to benefit the student rather than unlikely to produce benefits that generalize (e.g., learning to spell high-frequency words versus learning to diagram sentences), and (c) tie instruction on skills to the context of real writing opportunities. Students should be shown that these skills reflect conventions followed to enhance communication.

Effective strategies can be based on the implementation of a supports model for students with special needs. Particular strategies that appropriately fit under the concept of a supports model include selective checking and feedback, focused skills for teacher editing, peer writing groups and writing communities, sufficient time to develop skills, and teaching self-monitoring of skills.

In terms of supports for students in writing, the critical area for consideration is technology. The benefits of technology, in the forms of keyboarding and voice-recognition software, as an alternative to handwriting have been discussed earlier in the chapter. In addition to those considerations, an effective writing program should include instruction and use of technologies that directly support written expression. Obviously, word processing programs are universally used for writing and should be a core component of the program for students. The opportunity to take advantage of assistance in areas diverse as spelling and grammar have tremendous benefit for all students and certainly for students with special needs. In addition, voice-recognition programs offer students with limited keyboarding/typing skills, including those with motoric challenges, the opportunity to significantly enhance their writing output and quality.

A key way to provide such support is through *teacher conferencing*. The teacher reads written assignments and provides feedback directly to students, most often in an oral conference. Such an approach provides an opportunity to introduce and reinforce specific skills and writing conventions. As students enhance their skills, teachers must ensure that they have many chances to develop and use these skills. Vaughn, Gersten, and Chard (2000) noted that such *guided feedback* includes "providing frequent feedback to students on the quality of their work, elements missing from their work, and the strengths of their work" (p. 103).

Positive Writing Environment. As described by Graham, Harris, and Larsen (2001), overall classroom practices that are exemplary in promoting an appropriate writing environment include the following:

- A literate classroom environment where students' written work is prominently displayed, the room is packed with writing and reading material, and word lists adorn the walls.
- Daily writing with students working on a wide range of writing tasks for multiple audiences, including writing at home.
- Extensive efforts to make writing motivating by setting an exciting mood, creating a risk-free environment and promoting an "I can" attitude.
- Regular teacher–student conferences concerning the writing topic the student is currently working on, including the establishment of goals or criteria to guide the child's writing and revising efforts.
- A predictable writing routine where students are encouraged to think, reflect, and revise.
- Overt teacher modeling of the process of writing as well as positive attitudes toward writing.
- Cooperative arrangements where students help each other plan, draft, revise, edit, or publish their written work.
- Group or individual sharing where students present work in progress or completed papers to their peers for feedback.
- Follow-up instruction to ensure mastery of targeted writing skills, knowledge, and strategies.
- Integration of writing activities across the curriculum and the use of reading to support writing development.
- Frequent opportunities for students to self-regulate their behavior during writing, including working independently, arranging their own space, and seeking help from others. (p. 77)

Vocabulary Development. A key focus of the writing stage is building vocabulary. Because students' oral vocabulary typically is much larger than their written vocabulary, teachers should look for ways to facilitate transition from oral vocabulary to writing. This can be accomplished by introducing them to objects and experiences outside their daily lives and assisting them in writing about these events.

Within the context of specific writing tasks, several strategies may promote vocabulary development. Students can generate specific words that might be needed in a writing assignment, and the teacher can write them on the board for illustration and later reference. A list of words can also be kept on a bulletin board for students to copy and place in a notebook for later use. This is especially helpful with high-frequency words (e.g., Dolch words) that may also be spelling demons in order to minimize interruptions in the conceptualization process (see also the list of high-utility words presented in Table 8-3).

Instructional activities should also focus on the development of descriptive language. Students can brainstorm alternative words to use in a specific instance and then systematically substitute them in their own written compositions. This exercise can target synonyms as well as adjectives and adverbs to increase the descriptiveness of writing. However, for older students who may still have very limited writing abilities, the most appropriate goal is the acquisition and correct use of a limited number of functional words.

Vocabulary building can also be facilitated by reinforcement strategies. A variety of contingency arrangements can be used; collectively, reinforcement strategies for specific targets, such as use of unusual words, produces not only gains in that area but often also generalization to related skills (Polloway et al., 2012).

ENHANCEDetext
video example 8.1
Watch this video to learn more about the use of word walls as related to vocabulary development.

Sentence Development. Another significant aspect of writing instruction is sentence development. The sentence is the nucleus of structural work with students and the basis for teaching about appropriate syntax. Often, struggling writer's efforts are characterized by sentence fragments, safe and repetitive short sentences, or rambling prose without any structure.

It is important to balance an emphasis on "real writing" with focused instruction on patterned sentence guides and structures (Isaacson, 1989). With such guides, students can enhance their efforts to communicate effectively. The simplest form of patterned guide presents a picture for which students must write a sentence, following a set pattern (e.g., "The [dog] is [running]").

Datchuk, Kubina, and Mason (2015) illustrated the benefits of such beginning simple sentence construction skills built on providing the students with a picture of an object, animal, or person and accompanying that picture with a one- to three-word prompt that described the particular activity. Students can then be taught how to develop sentences relevant to each of the pictures. They reported success with such a strategy with a group of fourth and fifth graders with emotional/behavioral disorders or learning disabilities. Datchuk et al. (2015) noted that the "construction of simple sentences represents a core skill for more advanced writing tasks such as complex sentences, paragraphs, and multi-paragraph compositions" (p. 48).

Within the context of sentence instruction, students can also be taught appropriate grammatical structure. Strategies should reflect ways in which these mechanical skills can be incorporated directly into the writing act. A simple sequence of activities for students who are learning to apply grammatical rules includes the following steps:

- Selecting the correct sentence from group of sentences presented
- Correcting sentences in other students'(or models from the instructor) work including identifying and changing the sentences
- Editing one's own work
- Developing self-monitoring strategies (see the discussion on post-writing to follow later in the chapter).

One example of a strategic approach for teaching grammar is illustrated by Figure 8-6, which focuses on noun–verb agreement, a common area of difficulty for many students. The strategy involves providing students with a sheet that enables them to determine appropriate word usage. Figure 8-7, which follows, uses a similar strategy in terms of pronoun choice. (*Note:* The authors acknowledge the assistance of Larry Mays and Jessica Scott in the development of these two respective models.)

Several alternative pattern guides are available. Using a **sentence extension** approach, Phelps-Terasaki and Phelps-Gunn (2000) developed a program to analyze sentences into a series of *wh*-questions (who, what, when, and where) instead of initially labeling nouns, verbs, adjectives, adverbs, and prepositions. This technique is beneficial because it avoids the density of instruction in parts of speech and keeps instruction meaningful and

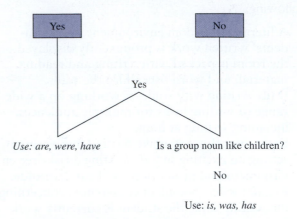

FIGURE 8–6 Noun–Verb Agreement

Source: Graphic Models and Instructional Tools for Students with Special Needs (p. 38), by E. A. Polloway & J. Lubin, 2016, adapted from L. Mays, *Lynchburg College Journal of Special Education*, Lynchburg College, Lynchburg, VA. Used with permission.

relevant. The program contains four units focused on beginning sentence writing, expanding sentence writing to paragraph development, paragraph writing for a purpose, and theme writing.

A sentence extension model can be used in two ways. One approach is to take a sentence and *analyze* it according to specific word categories, thus outlining the specific parts of a sentence. The second option is to have students generate a series of words or phrases to fit in each of these columns; at that point, a sentence or series of sentences can be *synthesized*. Both exercises emphasize a direct relationship between words and sentences and facilitate sentence sense.

Another option is **sentence combining**. Sentence combining provides a way for writers to increase syntactic maturity, develop more interesting sentences in order to express their ideas in varied ways (Saddler & Preschern, 2007), and improve the overall quality of writing. A sample set of clusters to be combined is shown here:

Most of us remember Groper. We remember him from our high school days.

He was angular. He was muscled. He had huge hands.

The quarterback would send him down. The quarterback would send him out into the flat.

And then the football would come. It looped in an arc. The arc spiraled.

Groper would go up. He would scramble with the defense. The defense clawed at his jersey.

He was always in the right place. He was always there at the right time. (Strong, 1983, p. 38).

Pronouns	Question	Applicability	Example
it's (or) its ?	Can you replace the word with: <u>it is</u> or <u>it has</u> ?	Yes→	it's
		No→	its
who's (or) whose ?	Can you replace the word with <u>who is</u> or <u>who has</u> ?	Yes→	who's
		No→	whose
I (or) me ?	Is I/me the SAME person as the subject of the sentence?	Yes→	use I ("The winner was I." Winner and I <u>are</u> the same person)
		No→	use me (1. "Sally called me." Sally and me are <u>not</u> the same person. 2. "The ball hit me." Ball and me are <u>not</u> the same person.)
Stan and me (or) Stan and I ?	If you take "Stan" away, is it still right?	Yes→	Keep what you have* *remember "be polite," and put yourself last.
		No→	Switch to the other one* *remember to "be polite," put yourself last

FIGURE 8–7 Use of Correct Pronouns

Source: Graphic Models and Instructional Tools for Students with Special Needs (p. 31), by E. A. Polloway & J. Lubin, 2016, *Lynchburg College Journal of Special Education*, adapted from J. Scott, Lynchburg College, Lynchburg, VA. Used with permission.

In Figure 8-8, a series of cluster sentences (based on this concept as discussed above) are presented to further illustrate how sentence combining can be set up in order to assist students in learning how to build more elaborate sentences, including compound and complex sentences.

Sentence combining is a promising intervention to enhance writing skills. By providing systematic instruction, the approach can directly impact the quality of the writing of students generate. In particular, the process of manipulating kernel sentences within the clusters and then rewriting them helps students understand sentences to a higher degree and thus be able to revise them and enhance them. As sentence combining skills advance, the consequence can be a positive impact on the quality of the compositions that students write (Graham & Harris, 2009; Saddler & Preschern, 2007).

Paragraph Development. Just as sentences are the transition from words to organized thoughts, paragraphs represent the transition from sentences to a unified composition. Instruction in paragraphing thus provides training in organization. Students learn that paragraphs are a matter of making assertions and elaborating on those assertions.

To begin, teachers can identify a topic sentence and request THAT students then provide elaboration ON THAT SENTENCE AS THEY build their paragraph. Subsequently, students can generate the first sentence while the teacher monitors their efforts. Later, teachers can have students support their topic sentences with two or three follow-up sentences and, as appropriate, one clincher (or transition) sentence (see Figure 8-9 for an example).

A helpful technique to assist in building paragraphs as well as a useful skill for writing in general is paraphrasing. An example of a paraphrasing strategy is **RAP** (see the full discussion and reference to research in Chapter 7). The acronym comes from **R**ead a paragraph, **A**sk yourself what the main ideas and details in the paragraph were, and **P**ut the main idea and details into your own words.

Because paragraphs also can function as short compositions, they lend themselves well to the use of specific strategies that are applicable to developing compositions in general (see below). It is helpful for students to see the transition from five-sentence paragraphs that might include an introductory sentence, three sentences with details, and a concluding sentence to more extensive compositions that include five paragraphs, respectively, with an introduction, three details, and a conclusion.

```
1. It was her birthday.

2. She was very happy.

Cluster: _____, and she _____.

3. She had planned all year for her party.

4. She had reserved the location with a swimming pool.

Cluster: As a result of _____ , she was able to _____.

5. Her father had assisted her.

6. He was very helpful too.

Cluster: Her father, _____, had _____.

7. Her father had ordered all the decorations.

8. She was very surprised when it came a month before her birthday.

Cluster: Prior_____, and she _____.

9. She was bubbling with joy.

10. "I love you daddy," she whispered in his ear while she hugged him.

Cluster: Feeling _____, she said "_____."
```

FIGURE 8–8 Story Cluster Sentences for Sentence Combining

Source: Graphic Models and Instructional Tools for Students with Special Needs (p. 32), by E. A. Polloway & J. Lubin, 2016, *Lynchburg College Journal of Special Education*, Lynchburg College, Lynchburg, VA. Used with permission.

Composition Strategies. Composition writing is the key goal in written language. The central concern in instruction is teaching students effective strategies for independent writing. Writing strategies provide vehicles to enable students to enhance their writing across all stages of the writing process. Students benefit from writing instruction that helped them develop specific strategies for brainstorming, semantic mapping or webbing, goal setting, and composition revision (Chalk et al., 2005).

The key element is to encourage students to think about—and talk to themselves, their teachers, and their peers about—the writing process. As MacArthur and Phillippakos (2010) noted, "Self-regulation is an important component of strategy instruction; students need to learn not only how to use specific writing strategies but also when and where they are appropriate and how to manage strategies independently" (p. 439). Self-regulation requires the use of a writer's inner voice to assist them, for example, in following the general structure and intent of composition while remaining cognizant of the preceding phrase, sentence, and thought.

Troia (2002) provided the following recommendations to promote writing strategy use, maintenance, and generalization:

1. Model strategy use and provide opportunities for student practice.
2. Teach students both self-regulatory behaviors as well as the strategies that are task specific.
3. Communicate to students expectations for use and transfer and then reinforce these applications.
4. Promote "mindfulness" and help students think about generalization of strategies on similar as well as dissimilar tasks.

Another key concern is to have students engage in meaningful writing experiences.

ENHANCEDetext
video example 8.2
Watch this video to learn more about such experiences.

Within the area of composition writing are several key concerns, including especially narrative or story writing and expository writing. Vaughn et al. (2000) noted the importance of "teaching of the conventions of a writing genre. These 'text structures' provide a guide for undertaking the writing task at hand,

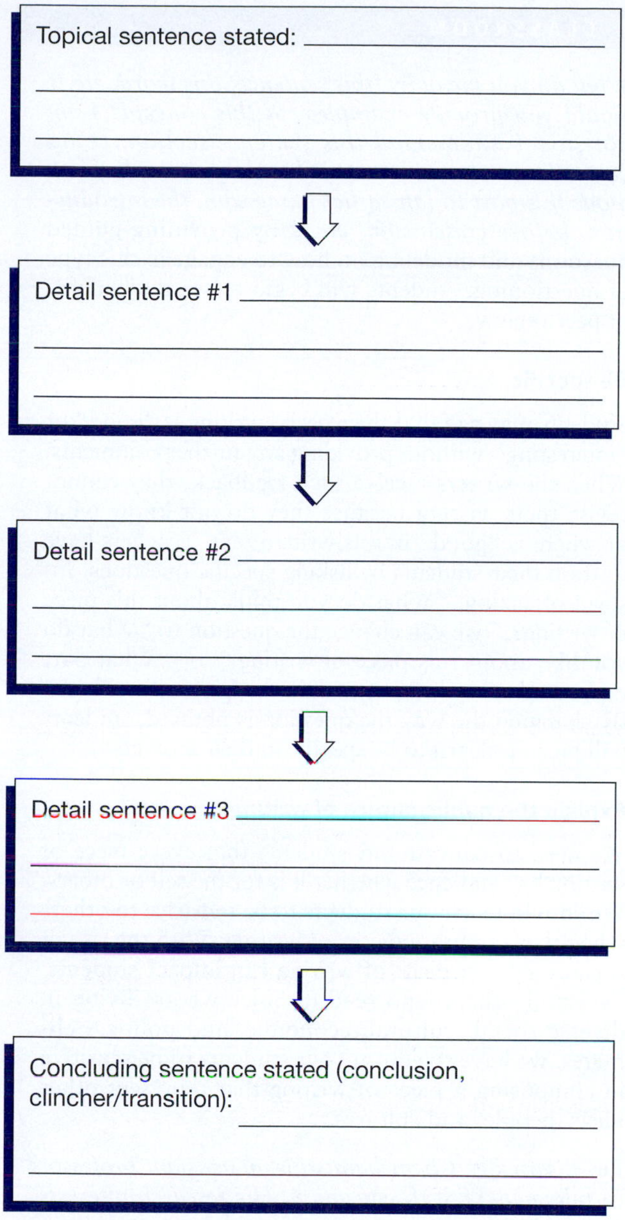

FIGURE 8–9   Graphic Organizer: Paragraph Writing

Source: Graphic Models and Instructional Tools for Students with Special Needs (p. 33), by E. A. Polloway & J. Lubin, 2016, *Lynchburg College Journal of Special Education*, Lynchburg College, Lynchburg, VA. Used with permission.

whether it is a persuasive essay, a personal narrative, or an essay comparing and contrasting two concepts" (p. 103). Narrative and expository writing are discussed next along with relevant strategies.

One alternative that can be considered for students who are struggling with writing compositions is dictation. Gillespie and Graham (2014) noted that having students dictate their compositions to be recorded or transcribed by a scribe was associated with increased improvements in writing when compared to students who actually wrote the compositions by hand. This observation reinforces previous discussion concerning challenges related to transcription, including handwriting. It also is suggestive of the possible benefits of the use of voice-recognition software for students.

There are numerous aspects of writing and types of writing (e.g., narrative, expository, persuasive, descriptive, argumentative). The discussions below focus on two key areas of narrative writing and expository writing as a way to illustrate strategies for enhancing writing.

Narrative Writing. Writing interesting stories and personal narratives is an important focus of writing instructional programs. Beginning in the elementary grades and continuing through secondary school, students are expected to develop compositions that effectively relate stories they have encountered in their readings, personal perspectives on individual experiences, and other such manuscripts. To be effective, students need to be taught appropriate strategies for such work.

Among the strategies that have proven to be evidence-based practices, an important approach is the self-regulated strategy development (SRSD) program developed by Karen Harris and Steve Graham. SRSD has been researched on numerous occasions with students across a wide range of ages and grade levels and has been used effectively for both narrative writing and expository writing.

According to Baker et al. (2009), the SRSD focus

is on providing teachers with a comprehensive approach to writing instruction that can help students write more effectively and coherently across writing genres. . . . It seems very reasonable to expect that the majority of students in elementary and middle school settings could benefit from this approach. . . . Because SRSD does have strong evidence of effectiveness for students at risk for learning disabilities or with learning disabilities, the approach could serve as the basis for writing instruction with increased intensity . . . for students who continue to struggle. (p. 315)

Asaro and Saddler (2009) summarized the goals of the SRSD strategy as "helping writers master the higher-level cognitive processes involved in writing, developing the ability to monitor their use of effective writing strategies, and form positive attitudes about writing and themselves as writers" (p. 269).

All students struggle with their writing from time to time. Students who are English Language Learners (ELL) or have written language deficits seem to hesitate and are not confident in their writing. One way to address these writing issues is through the use of the peer review process. Peer review is a messy yet an important process for our students, regardless of their language background, because the process promotes student–student interactions in which they will have a chance to practice and use their language skills in meaningful ways. In a peer review activity, students need to negotiate and discuss meanings they want to convey in their writing through speaking, listening, reading, and writing. By clarifying their written intent to other students, the peer review process can help students learn that every piece of writing needs to be revised in order to convey your intent clearly.

Many ELL students do not like the peer review activity because they think that their peers are not "experts" or "teachers." Teachers have to introduce and train students about the process of doing peer review and allow students to interact with their written drafts. When teachers introduce the peer review activity to students, we have to teach students to make a decision whether the comments will focus on the content or the grammatical errors. If it is an earlier draft of student writing, content feedback may be more important than grammatical feedback. The following peer review activities are listed as suggestions for teachers to implement peer review activities in their classes:

Teach students how to give feedback during peer reviews.

Teachers cannot assume that students are prepared to conduct a successful peer review session without training. Teachers must prepare and teach students how to ask questions and provide feedback to each other. A list of questions can be provided to students during the peer review process. For example,

What do you mean by (this sentence, this word, etc.)? Could you provide examples for this concept? I am not sure I understand this sentence/section; could you tell me more about it? What do you think if you move this part to (an earlier paragraph, the introduction, before conclusion, etc.)? By providing guided questions and modeling on how to engage in this type of questioning, students will begin to see the benefits of peer review.

Be specific.

Students may say that their peers' writing is "good" or "interesting" without providing any further comments. When the writers receive such feedback, they cannot revise their writing because they do not know what or where is "good" in this written text. Teachers have to train their students by asking specific questions. Instead of asking, "What do you think about this piece of writing?," we can change the question to "What do you like about this piece of writing?" or "What part do you agree or disagree with in this piece of writing?" By changing the way the question is phrased, students will begin to learn to be specific in their answers.

Explain the public nature of writing.

We need to educate our students that every piece of writing has audience whether it is for the self or others. We should teach our students to be sensitive to others when they compose pieces of writing. With the rise of social media, a piece of writing can impact students' lives and others who read it. Since we are living in diverse social, cultural, economic, and political climates, we have to educate our students to be sensitive in composing a piece of writing that represent other ideas, people, and cultures.

Dr. Pisarn Bee Chamcharatsri is an assistant professor of bilingual/TESOL education. His research interests are writing, teacher preparation, and language policy.

Sandmel et al. (2009) identified two key SRSD mnemonics used in story writing. The first is *POW*—"pick my idea, organize my notes, write and say more" (p. 25); this mnemonic is intended to lead students through the process of writing (across genres). The second SRSD mnemonic is *W-W-W What-2 How-2*—"Who is the main character? When does the story take place? Where does the story take place? What does the main character do or want to do; what do other characters do? What happens then? What happens with other characters? How does the story end? How does the main character feel; how do other characters feel?" (p. 26). This mnemonic (see the following text for further information) provides a sequence for learners to consider each of the key elements of a story and ensures that they pose these questions for themselves in order to frame the composition.

Instruction provided to students with learning disabilities related to planning, writing, and revision through the use of instruction in writing strategies has proven effectiveness. Such instruction (and the benefits to students) is clearly exemplified by the SRSD approach (Gillespie & Graham, 2014), which is evidence-based practice.

LEARNING MODULE 8.1 Click here to learn more about the SRSD writing strategy: http://iris.peabody. vanderbilt.edu/module/srs

Another related approach for teaching narrative writing is **story grammar**. With such a cuing system, students learn to focus on the setting of the story to be written, the main and supporting characters, the problem in the story and the plan to solve it, and the ending or resolution. With such a cuing system, students can check off each of these five elements as they plan and write their narrative. Figure 7-7 presented a story map that can be adapted for writing a story summary as well as for organizing notes for reading comprehension.

Graphic organizers can facilitate the teaching of narrative text for planning and writing. Figure 8-10 presents a framework that highlights specific questions associated with narrative writing, adapted from a prior model developed by Englert and Mariage (1991).

Narrative Story Frame

Characters
- _____
- _____
- _____

Setting
- _____
- _____
- _____

Plot
- _____
- _____
- _____

Story Problem or Conflict
- _____
- _____
- _____

Problem Resolution
- _____
- _____
- _____
- _____
- _____

FIGURE 8–10 Narrative Story Frame Graphic Organizer

Source: Graphic Models and Instructional Tools for Students with Special Needs (p. 27), by E. A. Polloway & J. Lubin, 2016, *Lynchburg College Journal of Special Education*, Lynchburg College, Lynchburg, VA. Used with permission.

Explanation Writing
Provide setting background (for task to be explained)
First, (initial step)
Second, (second step)
Third, (third step)
Finally, (last step)

FIGURE 8–11 Explanation Organization Form

Source: Graphic Models and Instructional Tools for Students with Special Needs (p. 36), by E. A. Polloway & J. Lubin, 2016, *Lynchburg College Journal of Special Education*, Lynchburg College, Lynchburg, VA. Used with permission.

Expository Writing.   In addition to story writing, students also need to be taught *expository writing* skills. For many students with disabilities, this is a daunting challenge. Assisting these students to understand the various structures inherent in such writing requires a significant commitment.

One helpful way to teach expository text structures is to teach students to use advanced organizers as vehicles for enhancing their planning and writing. Figure 8-11 presents a framework that highlights specific questions associated with the task of explanation (also adapted from a prior model of Englert, 1989).

Another useful strategy that can be used in expository writing (and story writing) is Rooney's (1988) *wheels for writing*. This approach includes a focus on the use of circles or wheels to provide a graphic organizer for planning and writing. With this approach, the student is taught to begin with five wheels: the first for the "start" of the paper, the next three for the three main ideas within the composition, and the fifth a "therefore" or conclusion. These five wheels then become circles around which specific ideas in the form of details can subsequently be developed. For example, if the focus of an essay was on writing instruction, the first wheel might provide an introduction and summary of writing considerations and problems, the second wheel on pre-writing, the third wheel on the writing or drafting stage, and the fourth wheel on post-writing, with the final wheel serving as a conclusion related to, for example, a summary of the evidence-based practice in this area.

SRSD, as noted earlier, can also be used in an adapted form for expository writing assignments. In this case, the focus of students' work is, for example, on persuasive writing themes in which the goal is communicating perspectives on a particular topic or issue.

Similar to the narrative writing approach noted previously, Sandmel et al. (2009) identified the first mnemonic to be used in SRSD again as POW to lead the student through the process of writing. While POW is also used in expository writing, the difference comes with the second mnemonic, TREE, which was designed specifically for expository writing purposes. For *persuasive writing*, this mnemonic enables students to organize their notes and then write: "TREE: Topic sentence—tell what I believe; Reasons (three or more)—why do I believe this? will my Readers believe this? Ending—wrap it up right; and Examine—do I have all my parts?" (Sandmel et al., 2009, p. 25). The mnemonic corresponds well with the model of developing a five-paragraph essay, with the first paragraph discussing the topic, the next three paragraphs discussing the reasons, and the final paragraph serving as a conclusion (Harris, 2010).

Baker et al. (2009) summarized research on SRSD in noting that it is "a comprehensive approach that can help students write more effectively & coherently across genres. . . . Because SRSD does have strong evidence for effectiveness for students at risk for LD or w/ LD, the approach could serve as basis for writing instruction with increased intensity . . . for students who struggle" (p. 315). In a related vein, Taft and Mason (2011) noted that the approach has been found effective for use with students identified as learning disabled or emotionally and behaviorally disordered or with attention deficit disorder, mild intellectual disabilities, or speech and language impairment. In addition, Mastropieri et al. (2015) also reported positive effects with adolescent students with emotional and behavioral disorders.

As a concluding note, it is important to note that the growing research on writing interventions for students with learning disabilities in particular has consistently shown that such interventions have demonstrated effectiveness when sufficient time is given to directly instructing students regarding the teaching skill and process. The simple provision of a procedure or of a graphic organizer, such as the examples provided above, in the absence of systematic and explicit instruction, was not effective (Gillespie & Graham, 2014). The nearby Teacher Tip highlights information related to note taking, an important consideration related to writing for students particularly at the middle and secondary school level.

Note Taking

Note taking is an important skill for students to acquire. While also often considered a study skill (and thus discussed also in Chapter 11), the core element of note taking is, of course, writing.

Boyle and Rivera (2012) conducted a synthesis of the literature on note taking for students with disabilities and reported that students who were taught specific techniques consistently performed at a higher level on quizzes and tests. The key implication is that to be effective, such strategies need to be taught through the use of explicit instruction, including a reliance on modeling and guided and independent practice.

Specific strategies that are associated with demonstrated effectiveness include the use of guided notes ("teacher-prepared outlines of the lecture that are meant to guide students through the lecture. Guided notes provide students with an outline of the content from the lecture and contain designated spaces for students to record more detailed information about specific lecture points" (Boyle & Rivera, 2012, p. 137).

A second alternative is strategic note taking, which provides students with cognitive prompts, such as recording a series of main lecture points, recording vocabulary that is new to a given lesson, and summarizing key points in the lecture, as a way to enhance their note-taking activities. The process is facilitated with specialized paper cuing students to indicate the information using the strategy of cluster-prompting the recording of three to six ideas, using prompting for listening to cues and recording key points associated with these cues, prompting the noting of key vocabulary words, and prompting the writing of words that can be used to categorize key lecture points (Boyle & Rivera, 2012).

Other strategies that can be used include providing students with a split-page paper format in order to assist them in recording lecture notes and using self-questioning strategies before, throughout, and following class lectures. In each case, explicit and systematic instruction will be necessary to facilitate proficiency.

Post-Writing Stage

The post-writing stage includes the *editing* of the craft aspects of writing and the *revising* of content, with both emphases having the goal of improving the written product. The term *proofreading* also has been used to refer to post-writing concerns.

The general goal of writing instruction is to enable students to communicate effectively with others while achieving personal satisfaction in the process. To achieve this goal, the post-writing stage must become a routine and integral part of the writing process. Students must be sold on the concept of the "working draft" as the initial effort to get the information to be shared on paper. Post-writing must acquire a positive association, removed from any connection with punitive action. Students should be assisted in deriving personal satisfaction from writing that comes from looking at it as a process rather than as a one-draft polished product.

Successful post-writing requires active involvement of the writer in the careful editing and revision of what has been previously written. Initially, students must have the opportunity to establish the concept of editing and revision. Training can begin with anonymous papers and direct instruction to, for example, identify correct and incorrect sentences,

find three spelling errors, or correct all punctuation errors on a given page. After reaching an acceptable criterion, students can shift to their own work.

Focusing on the full spectrum of editing and revision is an overwhelming task for any student who has difficulties with writing. Therefore, only one or two skills should be stressed at any time. A helpful approach for the initiation of editing activities is the error-monitoring strategy indicated by the acronym COPS (Schumaker et al., 1981):

- **Capitalization**—Have I capitalized first word and proper nouns?
- **Overall appearance**—Have I made handwriting, margin, messy, or spacing errors?
- **Punctuation**—Have I used end punctuation, commas, and semicolons correctly?
- **Spelling**—Do the words appear to be spelled correctly?

The COPS process is intended to be introduced one step at a time. Students should first learn a particular skill and then learn to edit for that skill. After they have been trained to proofread for each of the four components separately, they can be directed to use all four at the same time. The procedure has been validated for use with students who are at or above the middle school level (Shannon & Polloway, 1993), though it may be successfully used at the upper elementary level as well. One simple change that can be made to the COPS strategy is to substitute "U" (CUPS) to focus more specifically on *word usage* as a way to edit written work.

There is, of course, far more to the post-writing stage than the editing areas of capitalization, overall appearance, punctuation, and spelling. If students acquire these skills, instruction should then focus on the higher levels of editing, with special attention to content and organization. One strategy for use in the revision process is *REVISE* (Polloway & Lubin, 2016, p. 37):

- Reread your paper to confirm overall purpose achieved.
- Edit using COPS.
- Vocabulary selected to be appropriate for purposes.
- Interesting and lively topic developed.
- Sentence written to be complete and varied.
- Evidence provided to support your points.

One effective way to enhance writing at the post-writing stage is to engage peers in the process. This approach is typically referred to as writer's workshop.

ENHANCEDetext
video example 8.3
Watch this video to learn more about writer's workshop.

Another approach to editing is the use of the EDIT strategy. Woods-Groves et al. (2015) followed the steps of EDIT (based on Hughes et al., 2010) as follows:

- Enter your first draft;
- Do a spellcheck;
- Interrogate yourself using the . . . COPS questions [see above]
- Type in corrections and run the spellchecker. (p. 97)

They used the strategy with young adults with developmental disabilities and reported that these students demonstrated learning and application of the strategy in the identification and correction of errors within word documents.

Improving and maintaining skills in writing in general and in expository writing in particular requires practice. Because writing skills are especially difficult for many students to master, they should be provided with frequent opportunities to practice. Teachers can provide them with a wide variety of writing opportunities, such as job or college applications, letters requesting freebies, written math problems, thank-you letters, want ads, imaginary obituaries, advice columns, descriptions of items for magazine advertisements, critiques of TV shows or films, book reviews, travel brochures, and business letters.

The Teacher Tips for elementary level students provides a list of validated practices for writing instruction. These practices subsume aspects of all three key curricular areas within writing.

TEACHER *Tips*   Elementary Level

Validated Instructional Practices

- Establish environment where students understand that there is an audience: teachers, other students, and individuals beyond class.
- Encourage legible styles as alternatives to formal styles that may be taught but abandoned.
- After legibility is achieved, focus on maintenance.
- Relate spelling instruction to emphases within reading to take advantage of words that have significant personal interest, are from linguistic families, and are important for all writing efforts (i.e., high frequency).
- Beyond initial instruction, emphasize handwriting and spelling as tools to be improved with writing skills.

- Teach writing through process approach in which students learn the importance of and strategies related to the three stages.
- Use strategies to promote error monitoring and sentence, paragraph, and composition generation.
- Provide text structures/graphic organizers as models.
- Emphasize the importance of expression of ideas, with error monitoring to follow during post-writing.
- Use student–teacher conferences to review and make recommendations for changes in craft and content.
- Have students write often to develop skills and reinforce interest.

Check Your Understanding 8.6 Click here to gauge your understanding of the concepts in this section.

ACTIVITIES

Elementary Level

Manuscript Writing

1. Make name tags for all students, and have them copy their names.
2. Write students' names at the top of a sheet of primary writing paper and have them copy their names.
3. Make dot letters and have students form the letters by connecting the dots.
4. Write students' names or other letters of the alphabet in very large letters (36 inches tall) on large paper (can be obtained from newspaper printers). Have students fill in the letters with tempera paints (Buck, 2008).
5. After a series or group of letters has been learned, have the children write the letters on primary writing paper.
6. Have the class dictate several sentences about some event that has previously occurred and then have students copy the sentences that you have written on the board or chart paper.

Cursive Writing

1. Make dot cursive letters and have students form the letters by connecting the dots.
2. Play Concentration using cards with manuscript or cursive letters copied on them. Ask students to match the cursive and manuscript forms of a letter.
3. Let students collect samples of cursive writing to share and compare. Signatures from staff members, parents, or other community members can be interesting.
4. A classroom mailbox encourages students to write notes to their friends during specified times of the day or at home. Notes must be legible in order to be read and answered. The students especially want to use their best handwriting when they are writing to someone special outside the classroom (e.g., principal, last year's teacher).

5. As students get older, a handwriting goal is to increase speed without loss of legibility. The students write an assignment for a certain amount of time. When time is up, each letter is evaluated against pre-set criteria. One point is given for each correctly formed letter. The writing assignment can be content material, classmates' names, ABCs, or sentences that contain all the letters of the alphabet (Alston & Taylor, 1987).

Spelling

1. Have students keep words that they can spell in a box to be reviewed periodically. They can also be used for spelling games, alphabetizing, homework assignments, or creative writing.
2. The Dolch and other word lists can be grouped into different sets of words (e.g., nouns, adjectives). Have students pick out words that they do not know how to spell.
3. Show the children that there is some linguistic regularity to English by giving them a word or stem and having them form and spell other words (e.g., *ad*: had, dad, mad; *amp*: damp, lamp, stamp; *oe*: hoe, foe, toe).
4. Divide the class into two teams and list spelling words on the board in short columns. While students from each team stand with their backs to the board, pronounce a word. The students then turn and find the word on the board; the first person to find the word gets a point for the team.
5. Play bingo. Give each student a playing card. Instruct students to write a word from a current spelling list on each square of their cards. Collect and redistribute the cards. The game proceeds until the first student to cover the appropriate squares says "bingo!"
6. Students may enjoy opportunities to make, as well as solve, spelling puzzles. Students can make word searches by placing spelling words in different spaces on graph paper (diagonally, horizontally, vertically) and then filling in the other blocks with random letters. The puzzles can be exchanged and solved by classmates.

Written Expression

1. At the beginning of the day, set aside a silent writing time to write in journals. The aim of this activity is to foster enjoyment; therefore, entries should not be evaluated.

2. Develop visual imagery as a prerequisite to writing. Students can imagine making an angel in the snow, flying a kite in March winds, eating ice cream on a hot summer day, or burying a friend in a pile of leaves. Initially, have students relax and think at their desks. Later, have students list adjectives associated with their images. Finally, direct students to write sentences or paragraphs.

3. Use progressive writing exercises. The object is to pick up where a classmate has left off and write for two or three minutes. The final writer should write a conclusion. One student can read the finished product.

4. A class newspaper can help students improve written expression. Assignments can be made according to ability and interest. Class, school, community, national, or international topics can be reported.

5. Use photos to teach students topic sentence development. Start by describing the photograph and then write sentences and paragraphs.

6. Direct students to write responsible letters to elected officials. Help students express their opinions on various political or social issues.

7. A motivating activity is Contest Week. Many contests merely require students to place their name and address on a postcard and mail it to a company or radio station. Others require them to express ideas or opinions.

8. Cut pictures out of the newspaper and remove the captions. Students write a title and caption based on what is happening in the picture, read their ideas to the class, and then write a short article about what they believe is going on.

9. Have students obtain a copy of or transcribe the lyrics of a favorite song. Then have them rewrite the words in standard English.

10. To help students expand their sentences while reinforcing the concepts of subject and predicate, have them write a simple sentence on the board, dividing it into subject and predicate (e.g., *The dog barks*). Working in pairs, have students add details to both parts. Then have them share their expanded sentences. Discuss the differences between the simpler and expanded versions.

11. Technological support can be used on a regular basis to enhance writing and support the skills associated with post-writing. Word processing opportunities have been validated for two decades on their positive effect on the length and quality of writing efforts and, importantly, on the way that the revision and editing process is viewed.

12. For essay writing on examinations, Hughes, Schumaker, and Deshler, (2005) developed the ANSWER strategy, which is based on the following steps: "Analyze the action words in an essay question, Notice the requirements of the question, Set up an outline, Work in the details of the outline, Engineer an answer, and Review the answer" (Woods-Groves et al., 2012, p. 213).

Mathematics Instruction

Ed Polloway and Andrew Bruce

LEARNING OUTCOMES

Upon completion of this chapter, the reader should be able to:

9.1 Identify national initiatives in mathematics and recognize their impact on the teaching of mathematics to students with mathematics difficulties.

9.2 Understand mathematics assessment procedures that measure student progress.

9.3 Identify general and evidence-based mathematics instructional strategies for students with special needs.

9.4 Identify effective procedures and strategies for teaching mathematics computation.

9.5 Identify effective instructional procedures and strategies for mathematics problem solving.

Mathematics is an important part of everyday life. It pervades much of what we do at home, in the workplace, and in our communities. Mathematics is an integral part of the business, manufacturing, science, technology, and, of course, all educational sectors. Effective instruction is necessary to help students attain life goals such as high school graduation, post-secondary success, and securing employment. Because of the integral nature of mathematics in today's society, instruction in mathematics has joined reading at the forefront of educational community considerations.

This chapter first provides an overview of national initiatives to enhance mathematics education, followed by a brief discussion of mathematics difficulties and assessment of mathematics difficulties. General instructional considerations are then highlighted, which then lead into subsequent discussions about the key areas of computation and problem solving. The chapter concludes with a discussion of specialized mathematics curricula and activities for use across educational levels.

MATHEMATICS INITIATIVES AND DIFFICULTIES

America has been concerned with the mathematical competence of its youth for decades. Numerous reports have been issued concerning the importance and focus of mathematics instruction (Bryant et al., 2008; Coyne, Kame'enui,

& Carnine, 2007; Klein, 2003; Rosenfield & Beringer, 2009). Over the past couple of decades, different education organization have proposed recommended standards and practices in an attempt to improve mathematics instruction in the classroom.

National Initiatives

In 2000, the National Council of Teachers of Mathematics (NCTM) produced comprehensive standards divided into two main categories: Content Standards (Number and Operations, Algebra, Geometry, Measurement, and Data Analysis) and Process Standards (Problem Solving, Reasoning and Proof, Communication, Connections, and Representation). The Content Standards describe what knowledge and skills the students should learn, and the Process Standards highlight the ways of acquiring and using content knowledge. Table 9-1 represents examples of the Content Standards for children in Grades 3 to 5, with descriptions of what instruction should enable students to know and do.

Underscoring the consensus concerning the broad scope of U.S. mathematics curricula, the NCTM (2006) later acknowledged that the country's curricula had resulted in a lack of clear, consistent priorities and focus. NCTM acknowledged that teachers are stretched "to find the time to present important mathematical topics effectively in depth" (p. vii). This document was written as an initial step toward providing a more coherent and focused curriculum (pre-K–8). NCTM (2006) regarded curricular focal points as mathematics topics for every grade level, designed to organize or structure the curriculum and instruction of mathematics for children. The NCTM stated,

> The decision to organize instruction around focal points assumes that the learning of mathematics is cumulative, with work in the later grades building on and deepening what students have learned in the earlier grades, without repetitious and inefficient re-teaching. A curriculum built on focal points also

TABLE 9–1 Example of standards 2000, grades 3–5

Example Content Knowledge	Standard	Example of Required Expectation
Number and Operations	Understand numbers, ways of representing numbers, relationships among numbers, and number systems	• Understand place-value structure of base-10 numbers and be able to compare whole numbers with decimals
	Understand meaning of operations and how they relate to one another	• Recognize and generate equivalent forms of commonly used fractions, decimals, and percentages
	Compute fluently and make reasonable estimates	• Understand effects of multiplying and dividing whole numbers
Algebra	Understand patterns, relations, and functions	• Develop fluency with basic number combinations for multiplication and division and use the combinations to mentally compute related problems
	Represent and analyze mathematical situations and structures using algebraic symbols	• Describe, extend, and make generalizations about geometric and numeric patterns
	Use math models to represent and understand quantitative relationships	• Represent and analyze patterns and functions, using words, tables, and graphs
		• Identify properties as commutativity, associativity, and distributivity and use them to compute with whole numbers
		• Represent idea of a variable as an unknown quantity using a letter or symbol
		• Express mathematical relationships using equations
		• Model problem situations with objects and use representations such as graphs, tables, and equations to draw conclusions
		• Identify and describe situations with constant or varying rates of change and compare them

has the potential to offer opportunities for the diagnosis of difficulties and immediate intervention, thus helping students who are struggling with important mathematics content. (p. 5)

More recently, the Common Core (see also Chapter 1) advanced a new set of mathematics standards. Getting bogged down reviewing every mathematics standard in the Common Core would be counterproductive. Instead, it is beneficial to understand the general intent of the new standards. Common Core mathematics standards were created to shift mathematics instruction in three ways. First, a common complaint about mathematics instruction in the past has been that the curriculum was far too broad for students to master essential concepts. The Common Core standards seek to narrow and deepen the focus of mathematics instruction in the classroom (Common Core State Standards Initiative [CCSS], 2010).

Second, mathematical concepts build on each other, yet mathematics is often presented as a series of incoherent skills and concepts. The reality is that what is learned in one year will be essential for student understanding in the future. For example, a student learning how to solve algebraic equations involving fractions will have difficulty if they never mastered adding, subtracting, multiplying, and dividing with fractions in previous grades. The Common Core has standards linked from year to year so that mathematical concepts are not just learned once and discarded. For example, students in fourth grade must "apply and extend previous understandings of multiplication to multiply a fraction by a whole number" (Standard 4.NF.4). This standard is revisited in fifth grade, when students are to "apply and extend previous understandings of multiplication to multiply a fraction or whole number by a fraction" (Standard 5.NF.4). In addition to standard coherence between grades, the Common Core standards seek to create coherence within grades. For example, instead of having a separate unit on data displays, data displays are integrated into other lessons throughout the year (CCSS, 2010).

Third, the new Common Core standards seek to increase the rigor of mathematics instruction. Rigor can often be misinterpreted to mean introducing mathematical concepts earlier or having students complete more work. The standards address rigor by calling for a deeper level of mathematics mastery. The Common Core standards

do not abandon a traditional focus on procedural skills and fluency but rather call for mathematics educators to also focus on real-life application and conceptual understanding as well (CCSS, 2010).

In 2008, the National Mathematics Advisory Panel (NMAP; U.S. Department of Education [USDOE], 2008), a presidential commission tasked with reviewing mathematics research, presented a comprehensive report based on extensive research in mathematics instruction. This report did not present a set of standards for students to learn; rather, the report highlighted effective instructional approaches for mathematics teachers. Although findings are highlighted throughout this chapter, we note here an overview of their recommendations. The NMAP stressed the mutually reinforcing benefits of conceptual understanding, procedural fluency, the automatic recall of facts, and problem-solving skills as core considerations within a comprehensive curriculum. Miller, Stringfellow, Kaffar, Ferreira, and Mancl. (2011) further elaborated in stressing the need to address conceptual, procedural, and declarative knowledge as follows:

- **Conceptual knowledge:** deep understanding of the meaning of mathematical operations as well as an understanding of the relationships and connections among the operations that results in the ability to generalize and apply mathematics understanding to various situations and settings.
- **Procedural knowledge:** the ability to solve problems using a step-by-step process that ultimately results in an accurate solution.
- **Declarative knowledge:** ability to memorize information is factual in nature. Proficiency in all three knowledge types enhances students computation competence and increases the likelihood of success in other areas of mathematics. (p. 38)

When considering Common Core standards, NCTM standards, and NMAP recommendations, teachers should carefully reflect on the purpose of mathematics instruction. Assuming that the ultimate goal in mathematics instruction of learners with special needs is to help them prepare for using mathematics at a later point in their lives, programs must include content that is based on the type of mathematics that will be needed. For example, math programs appropriate for students going on to higher education would vary from programs designed for students who will be entering the workforce immediately after leaving school. In either case, students must receive effective instruction so that they will acquire a range of skills extending beyond computational competence. Implicit within the goals of mathematics education for students with learning problems is the idea that these students must receive opportunities, encouragement, and intensive instruction on using fundamental math skills to solve everyday problems.

Mathematics Difficulties

The difficulties faced by students who experience mathematics disabilities add to the challenges of providing effective mathematics instruction. Students with mathematics disabilities are typically identified between third and fifth grade, which is somewhat later than those identified for reading. Data reports indicate that as many as two-thirds of eighth graders with disabilities score below the basic level on math assessments. Satsangi and Bouck (2015) noted that about 5% to 8% of students are identified as having a disability in mathematics, while Dennis, Bryant, and Drogan (2015) similarly estimated that around 5% to 10% of all students exhibit persistently low math achievement.

Although many students are not officially identified with a mathematics disability until later in elementary school, mathematical problems usually begin early. Students who have math disabilities typically experience problems in a variety of areas across multiple aspects of mathematics instruction. Some of the most common early difficulties experienced by students include recognizing and writing numbers as well as mathematical symbols, counting without the use of their fingers, and understanding the language of math. As mathematics instruction gets more complex in elementary school, new deficits emerge: failing to verify answers and settling for the first answer, recalling number facts automatically, experiencing a long time to complete calculations, having difficulty with subtraction with regrouping, ordering numbers, performing arithmetical operations, accomplishing multidigit calculations, switching from one operation to another, and problem solving (Bryant & Bryant, 2008; Salend, 2011). As mathematics instruction becomes more complex, students with disabilities often struggle and fall even further behind their peers. Unfortunately, these early mathematics difficulties often signal later trouble in more advanced mathematics. Siegler et al. (2012) examined thousands of students from the United States and the United Kingdom and found that the greatest predictor of success in high school mathematics was students' mastery of fractions and division in late elementary school. These skills were more influential on high school mathematics performance than other factors, such as socioeconomic status, gender, ethnicity, and general intelligence. It is essential that students falling behind in mathematics receive timely and intensive instruction.

 Check Your Understanding 9.1 Click here to gauge your understanding of the concepts in this section.

ASSESSMENT

Educational assessment is the systematic process whereby information about students is collected and used to make decisions about them. A basic question is, What are the student's strengths and weaknesses? In other words, a major instructional reason for assessing students is to obtain diagnostic information. Other motivations for assessing students may stem from a need to determine eligibility for services, to choose the most suitable program within the three-tiered model (see Chapter 2), and to evaluate student progress and program effectiveness. All these reasons for assessing students occur regularly in educational settings and are inexorably entwined with providing appropriate education.

Assessment is often equated with testing. Although testing is one way to answer some educationally relevant questions, it is not the only way. Information about students can and should be obtained through other techniques as well: direct observation of students' behaviors; interviews, checklists, and rating scales; and examination of students' work. Assessment in mathematics should utilize all of these techniques in analyzing students' skills. Further, affective dimensions (e.g., how students feel about math) as well as communication and process evaluation (e.g., how students are able to communicate their math knowledge as well as their critical thinking skills) are worth investigating, too.

It is important, when assessing, to focus on what you hope to get from the assessment. Assume that Lyndsay responds to the following algorithm as indicated: $3/10 + 1/5 = 5/10$. Is the response right or wrong? Technically, the student did not simplify her answer, so the answer given did not match the correct answer of $1/2$. Realistically, she demonstrated that she understood how to find a common denominator and how to add fractions. As the teacher, it is important to decide what skill or knowledge is most important and to dig deeper to fully understand how a student is performing. Teachers must always be careful that the assessments they give provide the type of information they desire.

Standardized Measures of General Achievement

General achievement instruments are formal devices that usually assess a range of skill domains (e.g., reading, mathematics, written language) and result in a variety of derived scores (e.g., percentiles, standard scores, grade equivalents). Achievement tests focus on assessing skills or knowledge that have been taught, as opposed to ability tests that attempt to assess a capacity to learn instead of what has already been learned. These norm-referenced achievement tests are designed to show how a student's score compares with the scores of other students on whom the test was standardized. From an instructional perspective, such tests provide some general indication of the skill or subject areas in which students are strong or are having difficulty. However, these instruments are not intended to be diagnostic and therefore offer limited information and guidance about student needs or where to start teaching.

There are two major types of achievement tests: individual and group. Individual tests have enjoyed a great deal of popularity in special education. Some of the more commonly used include tests such as the *Wide Range Achievement Test, Fourth Edition* (WRAT–4; Wilkinson & Robertson, 2006) and the *Diagnostic Achievement Battery, Fourth Edition* (Newcomer, 2014). Most individual achievement tests are developed for school-age populations and administered in a one-on-one basis, although the calculation portion of the WRAT–4 can be administered in a small group. If one requires standardized data related to

math performance for adult populations, then one is referred to tests that extend coverage to this age range (e.g., WRAT–4) or to tests that are developed specifically for adult groups (e.g., Scholastic Abilities Test for Adults).

Both types of achievement tests are limited from an instructional perspective, as they give only one or two different samples of any major skill area. As a result, they may not tap certain skills at all and do not provide enough examples to establish error patterns. That being said, they do provide a snapshot of general student levels of performance.

Standardized Diagnostic Measures

Instruments that assess specific academic areas in more detail than the general achievement measures help teachers determine particular problems and strengths of students. For the most part, instruments in this category are attractive because of their potential diagnostic usefulness; they usually contain a number of mathematically related subtests. Some of the more commonly used instruments are featured in Table 9-2.

These tests can be broken up into different subtests, and within each subtest are a group of subskills. Evaluating deficits in specific subskills can be instructionally useful, but educators should be wary of using subskill deficits for diagnostic purposes, as these scores are derived from a small number of questions. Thus, to obtain the information necessary to plan instructional interventions, teachers must augment these tests with informal, teacher-constructed measures. For example, if a student has difficulty with two items on an addition subtest ($66 + 4$ and $86 + 29$), then it is advisable to explore this skill with additional problems ($16 + 8 + 15$; $37 + 20$; $66 + 44$; $145 + 159$; $390 + 148$; $524 + 386$). Such an analysis provides a more detailed assessment of the student's ability to do two- and three-digit addition problems that require regrouping and handling a zero.

KeyMath3 Diagnostic Assessment. An example of a diagnostic assessment is the *KeyMath3 Diagnostic Assessment* (Connolly, 2007). The *KeyMath3* is an individually administered diagnostic instrument designed to address the development of math concepts from ages 4.2 (e.g., number sense and rote recall) to 21 (e.g., solving linear equations) and to facilitate the communication

TABLE 9–2 Formal, standardized diagnostic mathematics tests

Test	Grade	Subtests	Results	Remarks
KeyMath3 Diagnostic Assessment (Connolly, 2007)	K–8	Three areas/10 subtests Basic Concepts: Numeration, Algebra, Geometry, Measurement, Data Analysis, Probability Operations: Mental Computation and Estimation, Written Computation: Addition and Subtraction, Written Computation: Multiplication and Division Applications: Foundations of Problem Solving, Applied Problem Solving	Derived scores for total test. Three areas, 10 subtests: Standard scores Grade equivalents Age equivalents Percentile ranks Derived scores for individual subtests: scaled scores (mean = 10, SD = 3), percentile ranks	Individually administered Two Forms—A, B Written responses required on subtests in operations Software available for converting scores and developing profiles
Stanford Diagnostic Mathematics Test—Fourth Edition (SDMT-4) (Beatty, Gardner, Madden, & Karlsen, 2002)	1.5–13	Three subtests: Number system and numeration Computation Applications (Shortened version of SDMT, 4th edition, for quick identification of students needing more assistance in math)	Criterion-referenced scores performance levels Norm-referenced scores Percentile Stanines Scaled scores	Group administered Four overlapping levels: Red: Grades 1.5–2 Orange: Grades 3–4 Green: Grades 4 Purple: Grades 5–6 Brown: Grades 7–8 Blue: Grades 9–13
Test of Mathematical Abilities—Third Edition (TOMA-3) (Brown, Cronin, & Bryant, 2012)	3–12	Five subtests: Math Symbols and Concepts Computation Math Everyday Life Word Problems Attitude toward Math	Mathematical Ability Index Subtest Scaled Scores Percentiles Age equivalents Grade equivalents	All subtests except general information can be group administered

and interpretation of results of the assessment so that educators can assemble an intervention plan that is appropriate for students with disabilities. The *KeyMath3* was revised to address the current progress monitoring demands placed on educators. When administered every three months, the assessment will generate growth scale values (e.g., a developmental scale) that will chart the progress and skill level of a student. Thus, the test may tell the teacher how much progress a student has made and where growth needs to occur and, based on the results, what intervention might be helpful.

Curriculum-Based Measures

The most instructionally useful methods of assessing mathematical performance and diagnosing mathematics difficulties are measures based on the curriculum being used. This approach allows an in-depth probe of specific skills based on the types of problems encountered in everyday instructional situations and instructional goals set for students.

A procedure that can be followed in collecting curriculum-based data is to ask students to complete a sheet containing multiple samples of math skills that are being taught (see Figure 9-1). Students are given two minutes to solve as many of these items as they can. This sheet and alternative forms of it are administered on a regular basis. The results of each data collection can be graphed;

12 + 23	22 + 53	73 + 43
16 + 23	71 + 43	14 + 23
51 + 32	61 + 62	14 + 42

FIGURE 9–1 Sample Curriculum-Based Assessment Sheet

decisions can be made as to whether students are progressing toward the intended goal. Curriculum-Based Measures are a good tool for focusing on increasing student procedural fluency.

Advantages of curriculum-based measurement approaches are many: (a) items or problems assess a specific skill; (b) tests include enough problems to ensure knowledge or lack of knowledge regarding a specific skill; (c) if the teacher has concerns about the validity of assessment results, similar problems can be constructed and given to the student, and those results can be checked against previous results; and (d) student-specific data can guide instructionally meaningful decisions.

Informal Assessment

By subdividing and expanding the concepts and skills assessed by informal tests, teachers can pinpoint the difficulties students have in acquiring specific mathematics understanding, comprehension, and skills. Some effort is required here, as most standardized instruments do not provide guidance or assistance in analyzing individual responses. The following diagnostic techniques may be used to analyze individual student responses.

Error Patterns. Carefully examining the work samples of students often provides clues to patterns in the types of arithmetic errors they are making. One system for doing so is as follows:

- **Random responding (RR)**—Student errors are without any recognizable reason.
- **Basic fact error (BF)**—Student performs the operation correctly but makes a simple error (addition etc.).
- **Wrong operation (WO)**—Student performs the wrong operation (e.g., adds instead of subtracts).
- **Defective algorithm (DA)**—Student does not perform the operation appropriately; the steps involved are out of sequence or are performed improperly.
- **Place value problems (PV)**—To some extent, this category is a subset of the previous category. The student knows the facts and the beginning stages of an operation but is deficient in some aspect of place value.

Whether teachers use this or another system, recognizing students' systematic errors is a diagnostic skill that has great bearing on instruction.

Task Analysis. The process of task analysis can be utilized to determine an ordered set of steps needed to solve a problem. As with the analysis of error patterns, task analysis can help a teacher pinpoint where student error is coming from. Diagnostic information may be obtained from checklists corresponding to thorough task analyses of specific computational operations. These lists can be found in commercial instruments, or they can be developed by teachers based on their understanding of different mathematics procedures. Table 9-3 is an example of one such task analysis. Knowledge of the steps involved in solving this subtraction problem can be used to help isolate specific problems. Prerequisite skills for the task are listed first.

Student Verbalizations. A useful practice for determining the nature of the problems that students are experiencing in math is to have them verbalize

TABLE 9–3 Task analysis of a subtraction problem

Computational Task: 400–175

Prerequisite Skills Required

1. Visually discriminate numbers.
2. Write numerals.
3. Name and match numerals.
4. Match numerals.
5. Identify the minus sign and state the concept of takeaway.
6. Compare basic subtraction facts.
7. State the concept of regrouping for computing problems.

Math Procedures Required

1. Identify the problem as subtraction.
2. Identify the starting point.
3. Recognize cannot compute 0 minus 5.
4. Move to the tens column to regroup.
5. Recognize, state, refuse to group 0 tens.
6. Move to the hundreds column.
7. Identify 4 hundreds as a number that can be regrouped.
8. Regroup the hundreds: cross out 4; write 3 above 4; place 1 on tens column.
9. Regroup tens: cross out 10; write 9 above 10 in tens column; place 1 on ones column.
10. Subtract 10 minus 5. Write 5.
11. Subtract 9 minus 7. Write 2.
12. Subtract 3 minus 1. Write 2.
13. Read the answer correctly (225).

the procedure they are employing in solving a given task. After such an analysis, teaching strategies can address the specific problems. This is not a difficult procedure to use, but it does require teachers to structure their class periods such that they have an opportunity to work individually with students. The benefits of scheduling time for this activity outweigh the hassles of scheduling the time.

Evaluating students' communication and learning of mathematics can be done through interviewing techniques. The hypothesis that students can learn through guided self-questioning and suggested self-management of learning (e.g., Andrade & Valtcheva, 2009) is tested by asking questions that reflect the students' ability to communicate their mathematics knowledge as well as give the instructors insight into their problem-solving ability. Generic questions such as (a) What was the best thing to happen in mathematics?, (b) What is the biggest worry affecting your work in mathematics?, (c) How do you feel in mathematics class?, and (d) How could we improve mathematics classes? are found to show students' conceptions of mathematics as well as their increased use of technical mathematical terms (Shapiro, 2010a, 2010b). Other, more specific questions or directives, such as having the students ask themselves questions regarding a math rubric, can be helpful (Andrade & Valtcheva, 2009). In this self-evaluation format, the students and the teacher co-construct a rubric that meets the criteria of performing, for example, a word problem. The students then monitor themselves according to each step of the rubric. This criterion-referenced self-assessment uses a rubric to scaffold self-assessment of each problem.

Journal Writing. Journal writing is an opportunity to introduce self-evaluation skills with mathematics learning. As with having students verbalize their mathematical thinking, journal writing also attempts to understand student mathematical thinking. Although teachers won't have the same ability to understand student thinking in depth, journal writing has the benefit of assessing the mathematical thinking of an entire class at once. Through journal writing, teachers may be able to identify whether students are choosing to use mathematical procedures, principles, and facts without being cued or questioned on tests. Journal writing may be able to identify when students are distinguishing strategies within the problem-solving process.

Spinelli (2012) provided the following suggestions:

1. Discuss a math problem completed in class successfully.
   - What did you do to solve the problem?
   - What was easy?
   - What challenges did you encounter?
   - What did you learn?

2. Discuss a problem you completed in class unsuccessfully.
   - Where did you get stuck?
   - How were you able to complete the problem?
   - How might you be able to solve this problem?

3. Think about and describe how you might solve a problem in a totally different way. Write about:
   - Important issues in mathematics
   - The most interesting thing I learned in class today
   - What I understand best about the math lesson today
   - What I need more help with
   - Two examples of problems I solved
   - Ways to use math skills in real life
     (p. 334)

 Check Your Understanding 9.2 Click here to gauge your understanding of the concepts in this section.

MATHEMATICS INSTRUCTIONAL CONSIDERATIONS

The NMAP (USDOE, 2008) emphasized that mathematical instruction should focus on conceptual understanding, procedural fluency, and the automatic recall of facts. These three components of mathematics instruction are mutually reinforcing to the overall mathematical capabilities of students. As those are the three types of mathematics skills required for mastery, how then should a teacher go about helping their students develop these skills?

The NMAP (USDOE, 2008) report called for the use of rigorously researched instructional techniques. Fortunately, the field of special education has had a number of researchers examining what instructional methods work best with students with disabilities. One review by Riccomini (2011) stressed that students who are struggling need systematic and explicit instruction, clear problem solving methods, carefully sequenced examples, and increased opportunities to think aloud. Further, Miller et al. (2011) summarized mathematics research by noting "the need to implement explicit mathematics instruction, use concrete and representational models, teach cognitive strategies, and administer mathematics timings (to help students become more fluent in computation abilities)" (p. 45). Similarly, Doabler, Fien, Nelson-Walker, and Baker (2012) identified core research-based principles of instruction in mathematics, including pre-teaching prerequisites, teaching math vocabulary, explicit instruction, concrete math models, practice and review, and academic feedback mechanisms. Based on the above studies and a number of other special education mathematics reviews (e.g., Butler, 2005; Jitendra, 2013; Maccini & Gagnon, 2000; Miller et al., 2011; Riccomini, 2011), the following discussions will highlight many of the shared components of effective mathematics instruction:

- Explicit instruction
- Progress monitoring
- Cognitive and mnemonic strategies for problem solving
- Concrete—semi-concrete—abstract model
- Automaticity and fluency in computation
- Building concepts and embedding math in real situations

In this section, we examine research-based general teaching methods, mathematics-specific teaching methods, and, finally, how to intensify mathematics instruction within the current school reality of multilevel models of instruction (e.g., response to intervention [RtI]).

Teaching Techniques Effective across Subjects

This section highlights strategies found to be effective across subject areas and then discusses their specific applications in a mathematics instructional setting. A subsequent section then discusses teaching methods specific to mathematics.

Explicit Instruction. A core consideration in mathematics, as with other subjects (e.g., see Chapter 1), is explicit instruction. Students with challenges in mathematics learning need instruction that is delivered in explicit fashion. Manel, Miller, and Kennedy (2012) cited the USDOE (2008), which defined explicit instruction "as an approach in which teachers provide clear demonstrations and models for solving problems, multiple examples for solving the problems, and extensive practice opportunities of the newly learned skills and strategies" (p. 153). Further elaborating, explicit and systematic instruction includes the use of clear teacher directions, sequenced instruction, consistent instructional routines that include appropriate feedback to students, modeling and demonstration of skills and processes, guided practice by students with multiple practice opportunities (Dennis et al., 2015; Doabler et al., 2012). Explicit instruction relies on carefully planned teacher-led lessons intended to build student fluency, recall of facts, and/or conceptual understanding.

The USDOE (2008) noted that "explicit, systematic instruction was found to improve performance of students with learning disabilities in computation and solving word problems. . . . Significant positive effects were also found for direct instruction and other forms of explicit instruction to enhance automaticity and enhanced problem representation." Doabler et al. (2012) posited that "there is converging evidence that explicit and systematic instruction is the most effective method for teaching students with or at risk for math disabilities" (p. 205).

A primary example of explicit instruction is direct instruction, with evidence-based research spanning over 50 years. A direct instruction approach to teaching mathematics is teacher directed, structured, and demonstrative of the components of effective instruction presented introduced and discussed earlier. Historically, researchers have found that "direct instruction provides a comprehensive set of prescriptions for organizing instruction so that students acquire, retain, and generalize new learning in as humane, efficient, and effective a manner as possible" (Silbert, Carnine, & Stein, 1990, p. 1). The attitude that virtually all students can learn mathematics is inherent in direct instruction.

Silbert et al. (1990) provided techniques for constructing effective lessons and developing specific instructional procedures. They suggested an eight-step sequence:

1. Specify objectives that are observable and measurable.
2. Devise problem-solving strategies that can be useful across situations.
3. Determine necessary pre-skills and teach those first.
4. Sequence skills in an appropriate order.
5. Select a teaching procedure related to the three types of tasks required of students
6. Design instructional formats, including the specifics of what the teacher does and says, correction procedures, and anticipated student responses.
7. Select examples based on what students are learning and what they have been taught previously.
8. Provide practice and review, including guided and independent practice.

Cognitive and Mnemonic Strategies. Another teaching strategy that is effective across subject matter and that has also been found effective for mathematics instruction is the use of cognitive and mnemonic strategies. Cognitive and mnemonic strategies facilitate student understanding and performance both in mathematics computation and ultimately in problem solving. For purposes of discussion here, mnemonics provide memory tools that enable students to remember the specific steps involved in, for example, an arithmetical algorithm, a process, or a problem-solving strategy. A simple mnemonic in mathematics computation would be *MOMA*, which provides the list of specific steps in completing two-digit multiplication problems as follows:

Multiply
Put "**O**" to hold place (a zero)
Multiply
Add

Cognitive or learning strategies provide more than just the memory; they also outline the cognitive steps involved in a particular mathematics task. For example, a learning strategy for problem solving, using a mnemonic to summarize the cognitive steps involved in the process, would be *SOLVE* (Freeman-Green, O'Brien, Wood, & Hitt, 2015):

Study the problem
Organize the facts
Line up a plan
Verify your plan with action
Evaluate your answer

Mancl, Miller, and Kennedy (2012) noted that "strategy instructional models focus on the processes involved in solving problems. This type of instruction involves systematic explanations, modeling, questioning, demonstrations, reminders to use certain strategies or procedures that have been taught, step-by-step prompts or multi-process instructions, and teacher-student dialogue and feedback" (p. 153). Further, Swanson, Orosco, and Lussier (2014) reported that "the majority of studies validating the use of cognitive strategies suggested such training facilitates problem-solving accuracy because it reduces or compensates for the demands placed on the limited cognitive processes of children with math abilities" (p. 150). When students are given a series of questions or steps to follow, they don't have to give any of their focus or thought to what to do next. They can instead focus on other aspects of the problem. Several more examples of mnemonic devices are given through this chapter as the discussion turns toward effective instructional techniques for specific mathematics concepts.

Continuous Monitoring of Progress. The importance of continuous progress monitoring was underscored by the prior discussion in the assessment section and in other chapters in this book. It is sufficient to note at this point that effective instruction in mathematics requires teachers to be constantly vigilant in terms of the response of students to the specific skills and processes being taught. Because mathematics presents "permanent products," it can be a straightforward process to monitor achievements and difficulties across mathematics subdomains. The assumption of ongoing progress monitoring is that modifications of instruction will follow based on student performance. Doabler et al. (2012) noted that "review and practice opportunities should provide teachers with accurate snapshots of student performance and understanding" (p. 205).

Progress monitoring in mathematics is practically important because students may develop incorrect algorithms in response to specific problems, such as in computation. Consequently, failure to provide feedback on a regular basis to students results in the risk of the students developing perseverating on such error patterns. Also, simply marking problems completed by students as correct or incorrect fails to provide the necessary feedback for correction and future performance. Doabler et al. (2012) noted further that "although mistakes are expected to occur and learning, unattended errors are likely to lead to later misconceptions in math. As a result, teachers require procedures for correcting errors, eliciting correct responses, and modeling correct responses" (p. 205). These responses should be provided in a clear and timely manner.

Mathematics-Specific Effective Teaching Techniques

Concrete–Semi-Concrete/Representational–Abstract Model.

An important consideration related to effective mathematics instruction is teaching students to master concepts through reliance on the concrete, semi-concrete (or representational), and abstract (CSA/CRA) model. This model first involves the use of tangible, three-dimensional objects or manipulatives that facilitate the learning of the mathematic concept by creating a mental image of the particular concept being taught. Once the students are able to grasp the concrete example of the concept, the semi-concrete level is introduced, which is a representation of the concrete example (e.g., drawing on paper). This begins the process of translating concepts students know about the mathematical relationships between physical objects to a mere representation of those relationships. The semi-concrete stage can include, for example, the use of tally marks in arithmetic computation, drawings of geometric shapes, or pictorial representations. The semi-concrete stage of instruction begins to help the student relate real-world mathematics concepts to images seen on a page.

The term *abstract* in this model of instruction refers to the numbers and symbols we use to represent mathematical problems (e.g., $6 + 5 =$, $20 \div 4 =$). There is nothing inherently meaningful about how we write the number six or the addition sign; therefore, symbols like 6, 9, +, and = are considered abstract. While introducing the concrete and the semi-concrete level, teachers can begin to introduce abstract representations of those concepts so that students will begin to pair concept with symbol. Mastery of mathematical concepts in the CSA model may take longer than simply teaching students how to solve an algorithm, but the conceptual understanding developed will help students generalize their mathematical knowledge to new and unique problem types.

Figure 9-2 provides a schematic for illustrating the CSA (CRA) model. It reflects the three stages of the model in attacking this simple addition task (and is adapted from the student work product). At the concrete stage, students are understanding the meaning of numerals and the concept of addition, while at the abstract stage, they are completing tasks using symbols and moving toward automaticity.

Numerous research studies have supported the efficacy of applying the concrete–semi-concrete–abstract model to mathematics instruction. For example, Strickland and Maccini (2012) noted that the integration of concrete manipulatives, sketches of manipulatives, and abstract notation with a graphic organizer was an effective strategy to improve student conceptual understanding and procedural fluency for multiplying two linear expressions. Scheuermann, Deshler, and Schumaker (2009) reported that use of the CSA model resulted in significant increases in procedural performance on basic facts, fractions, perimeter, simple equations, addition, and subtraction. Further, they found that the emphasis on teacher-directed instruction using the sequence produced positive effects that had long-term maintenance associated with them. Flores (2010) presented research on the use of the CRA model in teaching

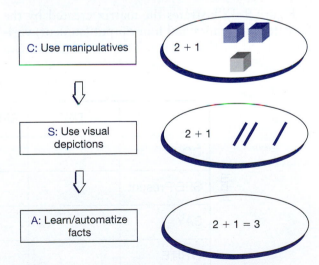

FIGURE 9–2 Concrete–Semi-Concrete–Abstract Model

subtraction with regrouping. For students at the level, benefits were noted in terms of fluency in subtraction problems with clear evidence of positive gains for students in acquiring skills and maintaining them. Flores, Hinton, and Strozier (2014) used the CRA model to effectively teach computation skills (learning digits in particular) to students with autism spectrum disorders and developmental disabilities. They noted that "the students made progress at or above the expected rate of progress for students without disabilities, increasing the number of digits written at a rate of one or more digits per week" (p. 552).

An outgrowth of the CSA/CRA model is the **interactive unit**. Originally presented and developed by John Cawley, the interactive unit increases to four the considerations by further dividing the abstract or symbolic stage in order to include both verbal and written components. The interactive unit therefore presents the 16 cells that illustrate ways in which to both provide instruction (input, as the teacher) and respond (output, as the student). Consequently, there would be 16 ways to teach a particular skill from early computation through algebra. The four input and output variables are based on the following:

> **Do:** use of manipulative (concrete stage)
> **See:** display (input); identify (output) (semi-concrete stage)
> **Say:** verbal (abstract)
> **Write: graphically** symbolize with numerals (abstract)

Figure 9-3 illustrates the matrix created by the four (teacher) input and four output (student) variables as identified above. The model illustrates potential combinations of 16 ways in which teachers can present and students can respond to mathematic instruction.

Concrete-Manipulative Instruction. The above discussion of the concrete–representational–abstract model for math instruction illustrates the importance of mathematical concepts being developed based on concrete learning experiences provided to students. For math curricula, this most often refers to the use of manipulatives in order to provide such experiences. As Satsangi and Bouck (2015) noted, manipulatives provide objects that assist students in learning more abstract or symbolic mathematical processes and concepts. Table 9-4 provides a list of potential manipulatives that can be used as tools for promoting concrete learning opportunities (derived in part from Satsangi & Bouck, 2015; West, n.d.).

The following guidelines are helpful in ensuring appropriate usage of manipulatives to provide a concrete experience for students learning mathematics concepts and processes:

- Select manipulatives relevant to the concept being taught.
- Choose manipulatives that are appropriate for the academic/developmental level of students.
- Avoid manipulatives that are inappropriate for the particular skills or processes being taught (e.g., use of popsicle sticks for two-digit multiplication problems)
- Provide opportunities for student interaction with the manipulative devices.
- Explicitly teach the use of the manipulative devices using appropriate teacher-directed verbal explanations while encouraging student self-questions.

Output

	DO	SEE/Identify	SAY	WRITE
DO				
SEE/Present				
SAY				
WRITE				

Input

FIGURE 9–3   Interactive Unit: 16 Cells

TABLE 9–4 Possible manipulatives

Manipulatives	Uses and Applications
Base-10 blocks	Place value, addition, subtraction, decimals, square roots
Fraction towers, fraction strips	Equivalent fractions, adding and subtracting fractions, multiplying and dividing fractions, percent and decimal equivalents
Hands-on equations	Solving linear equations, solving word problems
Measurement tools	Balance, graduated cylinder, thermometer, clocks, money
Geo-strips, angle fixers, geo-boards	Geometry
Algebra tiles	Algebraic problem solving

- Use the manipulatives across situations and settings as appropriate.
- Monitor student use of manipulatives.
- Find efficient ways to store and distribute and collect manipulatives as needed.
- Provide for transition of the concrete manipulatives to representational and then symbolic application.

ENHANCEDetext
video example 9.1
Watch this video to learn more about the use of manipulatives in problem solving.

An important alternative to the traditional use of manipulatives is the advent of the use of virtual manipulatives. Virtual manipulatives are provided to students through technology including software programs or Web-based sources. Satsangi and Bouck (2015) noted that "virtual manipulatives offer users greater organization on-screen in the manner in which each manipulative is presented in the procedural steps incorporated within each. . . . [They] provide built-in constraints that lessened much of the cognitive load experienced by students when solving mathematical problems" (p. 175).

By definition, virtual manipulatives would not truly be considered to be concrete because they cannot be physically manipulated. Satsangi and Bouck (2015) opined that they would likely be characterized essentially as between the concrete and semi-concrete stages given that they are neither completely concrete nor visual drawings or representations that might be created by students to illustrate specific math processes.

Automaticity in Computation. Another important consideration in mathematics instruction is the achievement of automaticity—and thus fluency—in mathematical facts and processes. By simple definition, automaticity combines accuracy with speed. Therefore, for example, students become automatic with addition facts; they are functioning at the level of "see it and say it" or "see it and write it." In this sense, it reflects the fact that students have reached a level where calculations of, for example, $5 + 6 = 11$ would no longer have to be considered; rather, automatic responding would yield the correct answer. With automaticity for basic skills achieved, students are far better equipped for advance computational work and certainly for successful problem solving. Automaticity in mathematics is achieved much the same way as automaticity in reading. Initial skills are taught by a teacher, students practice those skills with close teacher guidance, students practice independently, and students move into a maintenance phase. As the US Department of Education [USDOE] (2008) noted, "Computational proficiency is dependent on sufficient and appropriate practice to develop automatic recall of facts. It also requires fluency with standard algorithms for four operations." Doabler et al. (2012) stressed the importance of "purposely designed review and practice to facilitate student automaticity of math skills and maintenance of previously learned material" (p. 205). The USDOE (2008) spoke to this issue in recommending "that high-quality computer-assisted instruction drill and practice be considered a useful tool in developing automaticity, freeing working memory so that attention can be directed to more complicated aspects of complex tasks."

For some math facts and calculations, the alternative to automaticity through mental computations comes from the use of calculators, assuming that students understand the concepts that they are working on and understand the use of the technology. For example, Yakubova and Bouck (2014) focused on calculator use by students with mild intellectual disability. They stressed the importance of technology in supporting students working in math, using both scientific and graphing calculators. They concluded that "calculators as assistive technology support not only students' correct performance in mathematics, but also efficiency of solving mathematical problems. . . . Calculators resulted in a degree decreased amount of time spent on answering subtraction competition in word problem-solving questions. Thus, calculators can serve as a cognitive prosthesis and augment mathematical performance of students" (pp. 123–124).

Building Concepts and Embedding Math in Real Situations.

Much of the prior discussion deals with the importance of students conceptual understanding of mathematics prior to engaging in, for example, computational tasks, which may be completed by rote but for which students may have limited understanding of meaning. The CSA, for example, places primary emphasis on conceptual learning as a basis for further mathematical work.

Burns et al. (2015) stressed the importance of conceptual understanding, which

> recogniz[es] and understand[s] the core underlying ideas of a subject such as the relationships and reasons that underlie the math problems in a certain area. . . . It is knowledge that is generalized to a specific area and underlying core principles, and does not necessarily refer to a specific set of problems. . . . Conceptual understanding may provide the basis for procedural fluency. For example, students with conceptual understanding should be able to apply the certain concepts of understanding to solving familiar problems, even if they do not have procedural fluency regarding a certain topic" (pp. 52–53).

Cawley and his colleagues (Cawley, 2002; Cawley, Fitzmaurice-Hayes, & Shaw, 1988) stressed the importance of teaching students to understand mathematical concepts rather than just having them memorize rote responses to basic facts or algorithms. Teaching students to learn mathematical concepts through everyday situations can promote learning and motivate students to want to learn the

concepts. Using a real-life situation as an anchoring technique or a connective strategy to the mathematical concept can help students see the relevance of the concept and how to employ it on a daily basis (Van de Walle, Karp, & Bay-Williams, 2010).

Such applications of mathematical skills to strengthen conceptual understanding necessarily relate to the question of generalization. Opportunities for applying basic skills to new situations should be programmed systematically with teachers giving students many chances to apply their acquired skills in new contexts and settings. Another way to do this is to integrate math into other subject areas; this can be done easily in a subject like science but also in other subjects.

Mathematics Instruction within a Multi-Tiered System

Many schools across the country are implementing multi-tiered systems of instructional support (e.g., RtI) for struggling learners (Balu et al., 2015). Multi-tiered systems were developed in part to reduce the number of students who fall behind in school due to poor instruction and to reduce student delays in receiving extra support. When implemented correctly, multi-tiered systems have been shown to increase the mathematics performance of students with math disabilities and/or difficulties (Bryant, Bryant, Gersten, Scammacca, & Chavez, 2008). That being said, there is some evidence that multi-tiered systems are not being implemented properly in all schools, which may reduce the program's overall effectiveness (Balu et al., 2015). As teachers, it is important to understand how such systems are should work and, specifically, what mathematics instruction for students should look like within these systems.

Tier I.

Tier 1 instruction is a push to have classroom teachers use a combination of evidence-based instructional methods, systematic screening, and continuing assessment of student progress. All of the instructional techniques discussed in this chapter would be ideal candidates for evidence-based practice at the tier 1 level (e.g., explicit instruction, cognitive and mnemonic strategies, monitoring of progress, CRA).

The role of screening and assessment at the tier 1 level is important for a couple of reasons.

First, frequent assessment can help identify students who are struggling earlier than waiting for a series of failures to accumulate. This puts teachers in a proactive stance, looking for ways to catch problems early. Evidence has repeatedly demonstrated that mathematics interventions are effective when introduced early in a child's education (Mononen, Aunio, & Koponen, 2014). Second, frequent screening can provide a method for classroom teachers to reflect on their effectiveness. If one student is falling behind the rest of the class, then he or she might need extra support and help. If, however, half of a teacher's class is performing poorly, the teacher needs to reexamine his or her teaching practices. This is a key element of effective tier 1 instruction because teachers often want to blame poor results on their students instead of considering that the problem might lie within their own teaching practices. Tier 1 serves to provide quality instruction to every student, give feedback on teacher effectiveness, and identify students who need extra support in addition to quality instruction.

Tier 2. Students who fall behind their classmates in spite of quality tier 1 instruction move to supplemental tier 2 instruction. Tier 2 mathematics instruction is effective for a few reasons. First, tier 2 mathematics instruction targets a specific set of skills or concepts instead of tackling the whole curriculum (Powell & Fuchs, 2015). This allows students to focus more on essential mathematical concepts. Second, tier 2 interventions take place in small groups, allowing the teacher to give more immediate corrective feedback and to monitor student engagement more closely than in a whole-class environment. Third, tier 2 interventions are designed to be done in addition to tier 1 instruction, thereby increasing the total amount of time students spend learning about mathematics. Unfortunately, Balu et al. (2015) found that many schools implementing multi-tiered systems pull students out of tier 1 instruction to administer a tier 2 intervention, thereby nullifying one of the key benefits of tier 2 instruction.

Tier 2 mathematics interventions often involve a standard (i.e., non-individualized) intervention program. These programs are developed, tested, and validated for different mathematical concepts, skills, and grade levels. When implementing a tier 2 intervention program, teachers should use the program as it was originally designed; that way, every student in tier 2 receives the same quality instruction. A list of researched tier 2 mathematics interventions can be found in the Academic Intervention Tools Chart from the National Center on Intensive Intervention.

Tier 3. Even with effective tier 1 instruction and the use of a researched tier 2 program, some students will continue to fall behind. Students identified for tier 3 mathematics instruction need not only more of the same but also their instruction intensified in some manner. To intensify instruction, teachers can either change what students are learning (i.e., curriculum, program) or change how teachers present the material. Powell and Fuchs (2015) recommended using the same curriculum from tier 2 as a foundation for tier 3 instruction and finding ways to intensify that instruction. Unlike in tier 2, where teachers are supposed to implement the program as designed, teachers in tier 3 have several options for altering or changing how the program is presented. Powell and Fuchs (2015) created a list of effective means of intensifying instruction for students most at risk of mathematics failure (discussed below).

Smaller Steps   Instead of presenting problems and concepts as a whole, they can be broken down into smaller chunks. For example, if a tier 2 intervention focused on teaching students how to add fractions with unlike denominators in one lesson, a teacher could break that lesson into several parts. One day could focus on finding least common denominators, another on the mechanics of adding fractions with common denominators, and a third on changing improper fractions to mixed numbers and simplifying. Breaking problems and concepts into smaller steps is an effective method for students with disabilities.

Precise Language/Repeat Language   Teachers should use the correct mathematical terms in class and should be consistent in using those terms. Switching the vocabulary used to describe the same concept can adds unnecessary confusion to a struggling learner.

Have Students Explain   An effective teaching method mentioned earlier in the chapter is having the teacher model thinking out loud as they work through a problem. Tier 3 instruction allows a personalized enough instructional flexibility where teachers can have students explain their thinking, allowing teachers to target the underlying causes of student error.

Modeling/Manipulatives Modeling and manipulatives should be used in every level of mathematics instruction, but tier 3 allows more modeling and the use of a variety of manipulatives to represent a mathematical concept. For example, when first introducing multiplication to a class, a teacher might have students sort objects into four piles of three to represent 4×3. After working on a couple of examples, the class moved on to more abstract representations of multiplication. During tier 3 instruction, the student could work on more examples than the whole class had time for. In addition to the one model, other methods of representing multiplication (e.g., skip counting on a number line) could be used to reinforce the same concept.

Worked Examples Worked examples are problems that have already been solved. Some of them are correct, and some are incorrect. Teachers then ask the student guiding questions about what the person solving the problem did and if he or she was correct. These worked examples can lead to the student later doing the problems on his or her own.

Repeated Practice As with any skill, repeated practice provides more opportunity for growth. Unfortunately, students with learning difficulties often don't benefit from practice as quickly as their peers. Often, more exposure to the same concepts is needed for students to master a concept or skill.

Error Correction Teachers should be providing specific feedback to students at every level of mathematics instruction, but tier 3 allows that feedback to be immediate and very specific. Problems should not just be marked wrong; teachers should ask the student guiding questions to help them identify and correct their own error immediately.

This list of methods for intensifying instruction for individual students who are struggling is not exhaustive, but it does give a picture of the way in which a teacher can alter instruction to help those who are struggling.

 Check Your Understanding 9.3 Click here to gauge your understanding of the concepts in this section.

TEACHING MATH COMPUTATION

As discussed earlier, the NMAP (USDOE, 2008) called for mathematics instruction to focus on conceptual understanding, procedural fluency, and automatic recall of basic math facts. This section discusses specific strategies for building computational fluency. Computational competence remains important for two valid reasons: it is valuable for determining correct answers in problem-solving tasks, and it helps a person determine the reasonableness of responses in everyday situations (Cawley, Miller, & Carr, 1989). In arithmetic computation, students must possess certain skills to learn new facts and operations or must develop them quickly to progress in mathematical learning. Each competency must be understood before the larger computational skill can be mastered. Effective teachers must incorporate methods of checking for student understanding in these competency areas and be prepared to provide instruction to students when needed. A list of computational competencies is provided in Table 9-5.

An integrated approach to computational instruction includes attention to specific, logical steps in introducing new skills and processes to students, ensuring acquisition, promoting proficiency, and maintaining such skills. The following steps are recommended within such an approach. The first consideration is to explain and demonstrate the specific math skill and concept. Teachers take responsibility for ensuring that students understand what is to be taught and learned. Context is provided by associating the particular skill or process with prior size processes learned by the students. The relevance of this particular mathematical skill is emphasized so that students are motivated to learn how to do this.

Second, the specific skills need to be taught explicitly. Teacher demonstration, as noted above, followed by opportunities for student responding (such as with guided practice) and followed by extended, independent practice, all follow the sequence associated with explicit instruction. The NMAP (USDOE, 2008) concluded that students with learning problems need to receive explicit and

TABLE 9–5 Computational competencies

Pre-Computational Skills

1. Can discriminate among quantities, shapes, and sizes
2. Understands one-to-one correspondence
3. Can name symbols for numbers
4. Can name symbols in order from 1 to 10
5. Can recognize numerals from 0 through 9
6. Can write numerals from 0 through 9

Addition

1. Can make combinations using at least two numbers from 1 to 10
2. Can add at least two numbers less than 10 to yield a sum greater than 10
3. Can count sequentially past 30
4. Understands place value and understands concept of zero
5. Can add two-place numbers to two-place numbers without carrying
6. Can count sequentially to 100
7. Can add sets of numbers using the process of carrying
8. Can count sequentially past 200
9. Can add sets of numbers yielding a sum greater than 100
10. Can count sequentially past 1,000
11. Can add sets of numbers yielding a sum greater than 1,000
12. Can add numbers with decimals
13. Can add fractional numbers

Subtraction

1. Can subtract a one-place number from another one-place number to yield values between 0 and 9
2. Can subtract a one-place number from a two-place number less than 10
3. Can subtract a set of numbers from another set of numbers without borrowing
4. Can subtract a set of numbers from another set of numbers using borrowing
5. Can subtract numbers with decimals from each other
6. Can subtract fractions from each other

Multiplication

1. Can multiply a one-place number by a one-place number
2. Can multiply a two-place number by a one-place number
3. Can multiply a three- (or more) place number by a one-place number
4. Can multiply a two-place number by a two-place number
5. Can multiply a three- (or more) place number by a two- (or more) place number
6. Can multiply a decimal by a whole number
7. Can multiply a fraction by a fraction

Division

1. Can divide a one-place number by a one-place number
2. Can divide a two-place number by a one-place number
3. Can divide a three- (or more) place number by a one-place number
4. Can divide with numbers containing decimals
5. Can divide with numbers containing fractions

systematic instruction. It should include opportunities to think aloud and ask and answer questions while they are engaged in solving problems.

The third consideration is to seek ways in which students can develop the ability to self-instruct as they work on, for example, skills acquisition. Such efforts can include, for example, mathematics attack strategies as illustrated above in the discussion on mnemonic and cognitive strategies. Students are thus given the opportunity to develop independence as they practice and maintain skills and the use of arithmetic and other mathematical processes. A simple and straightforward strategy for self-instruction would include the following steps:

1. Teacher models task, saying steps aloud.
2. Students complete task, teacher verbalizes.
3. Students complete task, verbalizing aloud.
4. Students complete task while whispering.
5. Students complete task with lip movements.
6. Students complete task, thinking to self.

Fifth, consistent again with the discussion above, it is important for students to develop automaticity with regard to specific skills and processes. As noted, automaticity frees students from routine calculations in order to facilitate more advanced mathematical tasks that build on these automatized skills.

Finally, it is important to conclude with confirmation of the fact that computation skills do not stand alone. Their value and utility come only through their use and application in problem solving and ultimately in real-life usage of mathematics. Think of mathematics computational fluency as a parallel to reading fluency. As readers get more and more fluent, they devote more of their attention to understanding and making connections with complex content. Similarly, as students no longer have to devote their focus to solving simple computations, they can focus on the conceptual understanding and real-world connections that permeate all of mathematics. Consequently, instruction in computation should be coordinated with application in these areas.

Pre-Computational Skills

A student must demonstrate certain pre-computational skills in order to be able to handle arithmetic processes successfully. Initially, students may learn to count without meaning (by rote); next, they learn to count with meaning, that is, with numerals associated with sets of objects; and, finally, students learn to recognize different numerals and to write them.

During the same period, students must learn to distinguish among quantities, shapes, and sizes of different common objects. Also, students learn to differentiate among numbers as well as letters. Other concepts that teachers need to foster at the pre-computational level include big/little, long/short, few/many, more/less, and round/square.

One of the most important pre-computational skills that students need to acquire is a knowledge of one-to-one correspondence, the idea that every one thing seen can be matched to one other thing that may or may not be seen. Teaching one-to-one correspondence begins by having a student match similar objects; later, this task can be made more difficult by shifting the dimensions of the objects the student is to match. For example, a student may first be required to match a red token with a red token; later, the teacher requires the student to match a token with a token, ignoring color or size.

Learning to write numerals from 1 through 9 is the activity that bridges the gap between pre-computation and computation. The writing of numerals should be coordinated with the learning of manuscript handwriting, but it is not totally dependent on mastery of handwriting.

Time

A procedure to begin teaching about time is an opening activity of the school day that requires a child to affix some symbol on a calendar showing the days of the week. Concepts of the days of the week and the months of the year are often presented when describing certain events during a particular time period, such as Monday being the first school day of the week or Christmas coming in the last month of the year.

As an option, if math is taught every day using small groups, it may be advantageous to begin each session with a quick, clear, precise presentation of the days of the week, months, and year. This is an example of a concept that is easy to present but may be exceedingly difficult for students to understand.

Learning to tell time on a clock is a difficult task for many children, and this difficulty may be compounded for students with learning problems. A

Peer-Mediated Strategies

Cooperative learning approaches involve the grouping of students so that the group members accomplish a particular goal. In the past, researchers (e.g., Johnson & Johnson, 2009; Sapon-Shevin, 2008) applied the cooperative learning method to mathematics instruction and reported effective instructional results in primary grades.

Implementing a cooperative learning program in mathematics requires that teachers structure the group work to promote a group effort toward meeting the academic goal. Esmode (2009) noted that cooperative learning fosters positive social skills, positive interdependence (group goals), and individual accountability (responsibility). Thus, it is important to incorporate group goals and individual accountability into the cooperative learning lesson.

One cooperative learning model is the think-pair-share model (McTighe & Lyman, 1988). Using this model, students are required to follow three steps: (a) think, (b) pair, and (c) share. During the "think" step, students listen to a question or presentation about a mathematic situation and then think about how they might solve the problem.

After the children are able to think about a solution, they are grouped together to undertake the "pair" step of this model. Within their groups of pairs, students must share their ideas and solutions with their partners; this allows the students to communicate in mathematical language with one another and to practice their skills in a safe, manageable, small-group atmosphere.

The final step, the "share" step of the model, requires the teacher to place the students in larger groups. The students are then encouraged to share their paired discussions within a larger-group framework. In this way, different ideas are shared and students realize that there is more than one way to solve a problem.

Another peer-mediated strategy for math learning is peer tutoring. The use of peer tutors to enhance instruction has been well documented. Okilwa and Shelby (2010) emphasized this enhancement when they reviewed research that look at the use of tutors for math instruction. The use of tutors proved to be beneficial in enhancing the learning of math as well as other subject areas. Additionally, the use of corrective feedback by the tutors seemed to be an important component in the tutoring of students with learning disabilities.

---

prerequisite to telling time is an understanding of time itself. Concepts of today, tomorrow, yesterday, next week, and soon are basic to understanding time. Next, students need to understand that certain things happen at certain times, like lunch, recess, cleanup, and dismissal. The schedule of events aids in teaching time. An extension of posting a daily schedule is to write in the approximate (if possible, exact) times that specific activities occur. Later, the teacher can use a clock face to show the different times that these familiar activities happen. Teachers should keep in mind that the entire process of teaching temporal measurement must be evaluated in light of digital watches and clocks, which clearly alter the skills students need to be taught.

Money

Monetary skills are among the most important life skills that students will need later in their careers. Most of the critically important math skills that we use as adults involve monetary concepts and

activity. As a result, effective instruction in this area provides a good preparation for the demands of adulthood.

Children usually enter school with some knowledge about money. A real-life interest in this concept develops over time. Students use money to buy lunch and go to school-sponsored activities. Teachers can easily take advantage of these activities to help students gain a more precise knowledge of money. A unit on different coins up to a dollar can be coordinated with instruction in addition and subtraction skills during the primary years.

One of the best ways to teach coin recognition and change making is to use real coins to make simulated purchases of various items; for example, a student may use two quarters to purchase a 30-cent candy bar and must then determine how much change should be received. With this approach, the teacher does not have to worry about transfer of learning from play money to real money. Using real coins has the further advantage of providing concrete items for students to manipulate.

Addition

In most mathematics programs, the skill area of addition forms the base of the arithmetic operational ladder. Many specific addition-related skills are used in other operations, such as multiplication and arithmetic reasoning. Students who manifest deficits in basic addition skills are likely to have trouble in all other areas of computation as well.

Initial instruction in addition focuses on the concrete representations of the arithmetic reality being taught. Traditional techniques have included varied objects, popsicle sticks, counters, and Cuisenaire roads, which can be used directly for counting. The abacus—the ancient Egyptian counter containing different-colored beads—is also a useful device for teaching addition skills.

Throughout arithmetic instruction, teachers should be careful to emphasize only one new concept at a time and should continue to teach this concept until students reach a predetermined mastery level. Continued instruction does not mean that students must learn arithmetic facts through boring repetition; short, intensive practice using a variety of ways to teach the same concept should be used to promote overlearning.

As students have demonstrated an understanding of one-to-one correspondence and the ability to recognize numbers from 1 to 9, they should be given opportunities to make additive combinations using at least two numbers. While students master initial combinations, they may rely on the concrete, but a gradual transition should be made to visual representations (pictures, tally marks) of the process. The last step in this sequence is for students to be able to understand the process of addition and to represent this process exclusively with symbols and signs. Encouraging students to verbalize what they are doing rather than just having them respond to worksheets enhances the achievement of this last stage.

Having students take responsibility for learning is an important component of achievement throughout mathematics instruction. As an example, Figure 9-4 illustrates a self-recording card that can be given to students in order for them to track their progress in addition as well as throughout other mathematical tasks.

Subtraction

Most of the methods and procedures used for teaching addition can be used for subtraction instruction. Again, initial instruction starts in a concrete manner, then paired with visual representations, and then associated with the introduction of number symbols. For example, Flores et al. (2014) reported successful intervention on the teaching of subtraction (and multiplication) with regrouping using the concrete representational abstract sequence. As noted previously, the CRA/CSA model "involves an instructional sequence in which the operation is taught using manipulative objects; once mastery is demonstrated using objects, instruction involves the use of drawings and pictures. Once students demonstrate mastery the representational level they learn a strategy for solving problems that involve numbers only" (Flores et al., 2014, p. 548).

The act of borrowing from one place to the next may be one of the most difficult parts of the

	# problems completed	# problems correct	Overall self-rating (1-5)
Monday			
Tuesday			
Wednesday			
Thursday			
Friday			

FIGURE 9–4 Self-Recording

subtraction process to grasp. Many students fail to understand why one cannot switch the 1 and 3 around when subtracting 23 from 41. It makes sense because we teach students that they can add in either direction (commutative property). Behind this confusion is a fundamental lack of understanding of place value. Getting students to perceive that the position a number occupies indicates something more about a number than just its name can be accomplished in several different ways. Initially, students need to see that regrouping numbers permits the lesser number to be subtracted from the greater number. For example, in subtracting 4 from 23, regrouping 23 into 2 tens (20) and 3 ones (3) and then changing this arrangement to 1 ten and 13 ones makes it easy to subtract 4 from 13 and then add that number to the 10 not used to get an answer of 19. Cawley et al. (1989) recommended the use of expanded notation to help students understand this process (e.g., 23 = 20 + 3). Students must understand that the 2 in 20 really stands for 2 tens. Another way to help students understand borrowing is to show the relationship of carrying in addition to borrowing in subtraction, using examples similar to the following:

22	13	33	26	60	44
−9	−9	+7	−7	−16	+16
13	22	26	33	44	60

The first problem in each set shows the operation of borrowing, whereas the second problem shows the opposite operation of carrying. Once students understand the relationship, they can check their work by reversing the original operation. Concrete and representational depictions of subtraction problems are another good method to help students understand the relative values of different place values.

Mnemonic strategies can also be very helpful in assisting students in understanding and following the subtraction algorithm (as well as for other arithmetical processes). An example from Miller (1997) illustrated such a strategy for subtraction, *SCATES*:

Say the problem (become aware of the sign)
Circle the smallest number (if on top, continue with SCATES; if not, just subtract)
Ask and then borrow
Take one away

Exchange and give one to "neighbor"
Subtract

ENHANCEDetext
video example 9.2
Watch this video to learn more about strategies for teaching addition and subtraction.

Multiplication and Division

As typically taught in schools, both multiplication and division demand a great deal of rote memory, and some persons with disabilities may frequently use neither process after they leave the formal learning environment.

Multiplication can be thought of as a faster, more efficient way to add, and most students prefer a more facile method once they learn it; this is also an argument for the use of calculators. There are other similarities between multiplication and addition; carrying from one place to another in multiplication is much the same as in addition. Also, the principle of reversibility (commutative property) applies to both; that is, the same answer results, regardless of the positions of particular numbers in the original combination.

Instruction in multiplication must also focus initially on concrete examples involving sets. Later, the concrete examples can lead to practical examples that may vary in level of abstraction. When students come to multiplication, they should have a good grasp of addition and subtraction facts. If so, they should be encouraged to begin checking answers to multiplication problems. This self-checking can be done in the same way that other arithmetic work is done, or students can be shown how to use a calculator for checking.

Division requires many of the skills and manipulations learned in multiplication. Teachers must provide clear and systematic instruction in this area. When beginning instruction in division, it is a good idea to require students to check all answers by multiplying the divisor by the quotient. For example, if the student divides 21 by 7 and gets the answer 3, the 7 should then be multiplied by the 3 to determine whether the product is actually 21. This process helps students develop a greater understanding of the relationship between multiplication and division.

Every attempt should be made to use practical examples to make multiplication and division relevant. In addition, having the student to verbalize various problem-solving operations enhances generalization and transfer of skills.

The importance of teaching students how to reason and problem solve cannot be overemphasized, yet traditional teaching of multiplication and division relies heavily on memorizing multiplication tables. Students may be taught to learn computational skills in such a rote fashion that this process itself interferes with understanding and learning problem-solving skills, or these students may learn rote computational skills but fail to learn how these skills are applied in practical situations, making the instructional time and effort expended impossible to justify.

Attack strategies using mnemonics facilitate students having an increased understanding of procedures to follow in both multiplication and division. Previously, one such a strategy using an acronym for multiplication, MOMA, was presented. Another strategy is this acrostic for long division:

Dear (divide)
Mother (multiply)
Shall (subtract)
Cook (compare)
Brownies (bring down)
Again (continue the process as needed to complete the problem)

A strategy to promote procedural fluency and work toward enhance automaticity is to use *count-bys* in multiplication and division. With this strategy in multiplication, students can be taught to take the smallest number being multiplied and count by that number, making/marks or tally marks to indicate reaching the larger number. An example is as follows:

3 × 6
111111
Count by 3s

Similarly, the strategy can be applied also for division. In this instance, students identify the divisor and count by that number until reaching the dividend. Tally marks again are kept in order to determine what the quotient for the problem would be:

45/5
Point to divisor
Count by 5 until reach 45

Because teaching children how to use a calculator may circumvent rote learning, this will be the option of choice for many students. Teachers should use teaching time to explain and clarify what multiplication and division processes are and to give examples of how the processes may be applied to their everyday lives. Calculator usage for all multiplication problems beyond one-digit multiplication or division problems with one-digit divisors becomes an obvious choice as long as students understand the concepts that underlie what they are doing by the machine.

Fractions

For many students, fractions present significant difficulties. Unfortunately, the mastery of fractions, both conceptual and computational, offers unique challenges. For students who have incorrectly overgeneralized their whole-number mathematics experiences, fractions represent a radical new way to view and understand numbers (Bruce, 2015).

Part of the reason fractions are so difficult for students to understand is that they can represent many different mathematical constructs. Mathematics educators have identified five different constructs that can be represented by fractions (Van de Walle et al., 2010). Fractions can represent a part–whole relationship (slices of pizza), a measurement of length (5/8 of an inch), division (10/4 = 10 ÷ 4), an operator (2/3 of 30 people), and, finally, a ratio (probability of flipping a coin and getting heads: 1/2). Students with disabilities need clear, carefully designed instruction to help them understand each of the above five fraction constructs.

Fractions can also be difficult because they seem to contradict mathematical concepts that served students well when working with whole numbers. For example, students often believe that when multiplying, the product is always greater than the multiplicand. As long as students multiply whole numbers, their assumptions about multiplication work. As soon as a number between 0 and 1 is multiplied, student assumptions no longer work. Another misconception that often causes difficulty with fractions is when students assume that larger numbers in fractions mean that the value of the fraction is greater. For example, a student might think that 10/30 > 1/2 because 10 and 30 are larger than 1 and 2. Yet another difficulty many students have is seeing both the numerator and the denominator as representing one number instead of two distinct numbers. Teachers need to be aware of these misconceptions and take appropriate steps to correct them.

In addition to the conceptual difficulties students have with fractions, understanding the computational procedures for solving fraction problems can be difficult as well. The process for addition, subtraction, multiplication, and division of fractions each has its own set of rules that seem arbitrary when separated from a real conceptual understanding of fractions. For example, many students were taught to solve division problems with fractions by the saying, "Ours is not to question why, just invert and multiply." Yet many teachers, let alone students, cannot explain what the division of fractions means or come up with a real-world application (Lamberg & Wiest, 2015).

Developing computational fluency with fractions can be done with many of the same approaches already discussed through this chapter. Repeated examples, modeling, opportunities to practice, and clear and corrective feedback are all effective methods to help students gain computational fluency with fractions. Computational fluency with fractions can also be facilitated by the use of mnemonic strategies. For example, the MAD strategy provides information on the steps involved in changing a mixed number into an improper fraction (that may be used for further computation). The steps are as follows:

Multiply the denominator by the whole number
Add answer to numerator, which becomes new numerator
Denominator stays the same

Example:

6 2/3 (6 × 3 = 18)
18 + 2 = 20
20/3

Although this chapter does not fully discuss developing the conceptual understanding of fractions, there are a few key considerations teachers should keep in mind. The following suggestions from Van de Walle et al. (2010) are some practical activities that will build key conceptual understanding of fractions that students desperately need:

- Present fractions using an area model. This can be done using the traditional "pieces of pie"

representation, rectangular shapes, folded paper, pattern blocks, or drawings on graph paper.
- Present fractions using a length model. This helps students understand fractions as a unit of distance. Length models can be explored through the use of Cuisenaire rods, fraction strips, rulers, or number lines. Length models can be used to help students conceptualize the addition, subtraction, multiplication, and division of fractions.
- Present fractions using a set model. Set models can be used with groups of objects like coins or tokens. The set model is particularly good at helping students conceptualize simplifying fractions. Students might be given nine checkers and asked how many checkers are red. If three checkers are red, then they might form two groups of three black checkers to find that 1/3 are red. Conversely, they might form three groups of one red and two black checkers, each group being 1/3 red.
- Offer many opportunities for students to partition shapes and number lines. Too often, students are never presented the opportunity to divide the whole up for themselves. On a simple level, this might look like asking a student to divide a circle into fourths or to draw partitions on a number line. On a more complex level, this sort of thinking can help solve complex problems like figuring out 3/7 of 35. Students could partition 35 into seven parts to figure out how many in each part and then know that they have three of those parts.
- Ask students sharing questions and provide sharing activities. These questions might ask how to share three cookies between two friends or four pizzas among six students.
- Provide opportunities for students to count fraction parts. This process is called iterating and helps build an understanding of the relationship between the part and the whole. An easier example would be to give students a piece of string 3−1/2 feet long and ask how many thirds are in it. Students would then measure out how many 1/3 lengths of string fit together to make 3−1/2 feet. A more difficult version of this type of activity would be to provide the student with a piece of string and say that the string is only 3/4 of the whole. Then ask them to find 1/2, 1−1/2, or 3 times the whole. To do this, the student needs to be able to break the originally given piece down into three parts

and realize that each of those parts represents 1/4 of the whole.
- Make sure to use accurate vocabulary and ask frequent questions, like "What does the denominator of the fraction tell me?"
- Provide opportunities for students to practice estimating the values of fractions.

Algebra

Although algebra is generally thought of as a specific course taken generally in eighth or ninth grade, algebraic thinking is actually introduced and reinforced throughout elementary school. Algebra is mathematics focused on patterns, functions, and the use of symbols to represent mathematical problems.

ENHANCEDetext
video example 9.3
Watch this video to learn more about pre-algebra instructional activities.

Below are some skills and concepts that will be of particular importance for students with disabilities to understand:

- Present equations in nonstandard formats. Most school textbook mathematics problems are written in the traditional $4 + 3 =$ _____ format (Powell, Driver, & Julian, 2013). The problem with this is that students who are presented with only the standard format begin to conceptualize the symbol = as meaning "put the answer here." Unfortunately, the = sign should be understood more as a balance between two equal parts of an equation. Not understanding symbols correctly is often a roadblock to successful completion of more advanced mathematics. Make sure to present problems in both nonstandard (e.g., _____ $= 4 - 2$) and standard formats.
- Students with disabilities have difficulty understanding that variables can represent more than one value. In an equation like $y = 3x - 5$, any number could be substituted for x. The key is to help students understand that they should be really interested in understanding how y

changes in response to changes in the value of x. A good way to help students with disabilities understand this concept is through the creation of tables. Have students make a table with three columns. On the left, they choose a value for x; in the center, they plug that value into the equation; and on the right, they write down their answer. Then they choose a new value for x and repeat the process in the next row.
- Another key issue that students with mathematics disabilities struggle with is remembering the properties of the number system (e.g., the associative, distributive, and commutative properties of addition and multiplication). Students often do not see the value in memorizing and understanding these properties, but they help immensely when students have to simplify and solve complex equations.
- Finally, one issue that students with disabilities often struggle with is completing a set of complex steps. Algebra is full of problems requiring complex steps to complete. Similar to other sections of this chapter, mnemonic devices can help guide students through complex processes. For example, when working with polynomial equations, students are often taught the technique FOIL. Let's say the students were presented with $(x + 2)(x - 3)$. They could factor the problem through the following steps:

  First (multiply $x \times x$)
  Outer (multiply $x \times -3$)
  Inner (multiply $2 \times x$)
  Last (multiply 2×-3)
  Finally, students can then add the answers from each of these four steps to find $x^2 - x - 6$.

- Other mnemonic devices besides FOIL should be used as needed. For example, PEMDAS (Parenthesis, Exponents, Multiplication and Division, Addition and Subtraction) is useful for helping students remember the order of operations when solving complex problems. Another mnemonic that might be useful is DiRT to help students remember the formula that Distance = Rate $\times$ Time.

Functional Mathematics

This section highlights some considerations related to functional mathematics for adolescent learners with disabilities. Further information about this consideration is provided later.

Many learners with special needs require that their programs reflect a realistic examination of their subsequent environments. If postsecondary education is not likely, then the curriculum should reflect an orientation toward the life skills and knowledge needed to survive in the community and on the job, that is, an adult outcomes-oriented mathematics curriculum (Cronin & Patton, 2007).

While post-secondary-bound students can benefit from life skills instruction if they are to successfully adjust as adults, those students in particular who continue to struggle in their secondary mathematics courses are in great need of mathematics skills related to real life. If they have been unsuccessful in their academic mathematics courses, curriculum decisions must be made to provide them with life skills needed to be productive citizens (see Chapter 14). These students must acquire mathematics skills that will have practical value in their post-secondary lives. For most of these students, their secondary mathematics courses will be the last opportunity in their secondary education to learn these skills.

Topics covering financial matters such as paychecks, checking and savings accounts, and home budgets are important items to cover, as will be discussed later in the chapter. One of the easiest and most effective ways to deal with these topics on the high school level is to print paychecks and issue these checks to students at the end of the week. By explaining various types of withholding, students are forewarned that deductions are made from paychecks and that they will actually receive less money than expected (i.e., take-home pay). Students can use numerous commercial materials in the exercise, but classroom instruction based on students' actual experiences with paychecks and yearly taxes is the most effective teaching technique. Students need to become familiar with various time schedules, reimbursements, deductions, taxes, and the corresponding calculations involved with each.

Home budgeting can be taught with reproductions of bills and statements for utilities, rent, food, and clothes. Basic bookkeeping skills can also be taught at this time. During the process, students should be maintaining home records and filing receipts. Banking skills should also be taught directly. Students should learn how to deposit and withdraw money, write checks, and maintain a savings account using both traditional methods and modern, electronic methods. It may be advisable to expose students to the variety of financial software now available as well.

Check Your Understanding 9.4 Click here to gauge your understanding of the concepts in this section.

TEACHING PROBLEM SOLVING

The mastery of computation skills or the compensatory use of calculators provides students with the tools to solve problems but does not teach them the process of how to solve daily mathematics problems. Problem solving, therefore, has been targeted as one of the major areas of professional focus.

One reason why problem solving is so important yet so difficult to teach is that it requires many complex skills. Krawec, Huang, Montague, Kressler, & de Alba (2013) noted the fact that "similar to reading comprehension, math problem solving is a complex skill that requires students not only to calculate an answer but also to comprehend and integrate the problem information, generate and maintain mental images of the problem, and develop a viable solution path" (p. 80). Fuchs et al. (2011) indicated that students who are unable to employ a variety of arithmetic competencies also have difficulties in solving mathematical word problems. Furthermore, the fluency of these represent essential skills to gaining skills in the area of problem solving. All of these factors can be significant obstacles for students with special learning needs and must be taken into account when assessing and planning instruction. Additionally, students with learning problems, as well as students from bilingual or different cultural backgrounds, may experience language and vocabulary problems that compound their inability to understand a word problem.

The problem-solving process includes necessary attention to (a) translating the problem in order to determine what it is saying, (b) integrating the problem information to create a structural representation, (c) planning the operations to use in solving the problem, and (d) carrying out the solution by completing the planned computations (Mayer, 1985, as cited by Kingsdorf & Krawec,

2014). Each of these four stages requires a certain type of knowledge or skill (e.g., identifying the type of problem, identifying relevant information, carrying out computations). This process can create challenges for students with disabilities. For example, Kingsdorf and Krawec (2014) found that use of this four-phase model clarified the types of errors that students make in problem solving; the model was successful in identifying four of the most common six error types. These included number selection, operation selection, inclusion of all relevant information, and computation (with the latter being least likely to differentiate students with learning disabilities from students who are not disabled). The other two were random error and omission errors that are not directly related to the Mayer model but rather, the authors concluded, reflect self-monitoring and motivation, necessary for persistence during the problem-solving process. Figure 9-5 provides a graphic model for considering necessary components of the problem-solving process.

To teach problem solving, teachers must help students make appropriate decisions, understand the vocabulary being used, use the available information, identify sequences or patterns in the problem, and develop strategies that allow them to work through a solution (Bley & Thornton, 2001).

Problem-Solving Strategies

Students need effective problem-solving tools. By teaching these tools, students begin to think in mathematical terms, and they will begin to organize their thoughts into logical steps or strategies (Harris, Carnine, Silbert, & Dixon, 2007). These strategies are designed so that the students can acquire a meaningful application of the information. To accomplish this outcome, the teacher must explicitly teach the strategy so that the students can apply it to a variety of mathematical situations. Several strategies have been developed to help students experience more success when learning to solve problems.

An effective strategy uses a sequence of tasks to be performed when a word problem is encountered, such as the following:

1. Read (or listen) carefully.
2. Write a few words about the kind of answer needed (e.g., kilometers per hour).
3. Look for significant words and eliminate irrelevant information.
4. Highlight the numbers that are important.
5. Draw a diagram or sketch when appropriate. This graphic does not have to be a work of art but should depict what the problem is describing.
6. Decide on the necessary calculations and identify a math sentence for this situation.
7. Perform the calculations.
8. Evaluate the answer to determine its reasonableness.
9. Write the answer with the appropriate units.

Table 9-6 illustrates another option for a formal strategy for the respective steps necessary for problem solving.

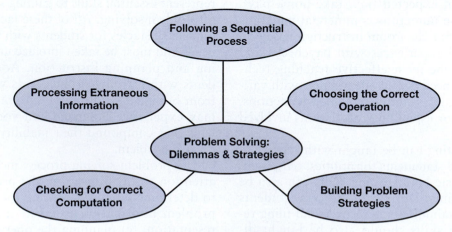

FIGURE 9–5 Problem Solving: Dilemmas and Strategies

Source: Graphic Models and Instructional Tools for Students with Special Needs (p. 40), by E. A. Polloway & J. Lubin, 2016, *Lynchburg College Journal of Special Education*, Lynchburg College, Lynchburg, VA. Used with permission.

A mathematics class should be about learning and not performing (Boaler, 2016). This statement became evident when I visited an 11th-grade mathematics classroom where students with learning disabilities (SLD) were reluctantly reviewing single-digit addition facts without regrouping because they were yet to achieve mastery. Some students may never master basic facts, so it is possible that they may or may not ever experience problem solving in later grades (Fuchs & Fuchs, 2005). As the class progressed, however, the same students were presented with a multiple-step word problem about a koala climbing a tree that included similar addition and subtraction facts. The students eagerly and successfully represented, reasoned about, and solved the problem. Their emotional and cognitive investment became evident in this task. This situation corroborates that problem solving is a distributed product of a collective intelligence activity. This manifested as participants drew from and applied their own resources while their distributed intelligence served as a learning tool for development (Pea, 1993). Similarly, we have learned that while the type of tasks is important, the surrounding context, social interactions, and purpose are crucial to spark either learners' genuine and purposeful mathematical reasoning or their simple recall of procedures (Nunes-Carraher, Carraher, & Dias Schliemann, 2004). Additionally, one must consider the children's existing knowledge as well as the idea that inquiry approaches foster their autonomy (Isenbarger & Baroody, 2001).

Another aspect of learning mathematics is the environment of the lesson. At school, students with LD, culturally and linguistically diverse students, and English learners face situations where they feel and act differently from their peers. When teachers and peers view their behaviors and learning processes to be "disrespectful" or slow, it can result in peers' and teachers' misunderstanding the behaviors and not relating the behaviors to their race, culture, or language (Skiba et al., 2006). Thus, teachers should monitor their interactions with students so that mathematics education includes tasks that support students' reasoning and are linked to students' knowledge and interests (Torres-Velasquez & Lobo, 2005). Moreover, these suggestions became evident when the students in the above example were engaged in a task that was both challenging and meaningful to them and allowed them to think. The use of representations and their investment in an engaging task generated productive learning attitudes. Although some procedures were wrong, they collaboratively revised them with peers and teacher. This interaction kept them learning and interested. Mistakes are sources of learning, so when teachers or parents change "the message they give about mistakes and wrong answers in mathematics . . . it has an incredibly liberating effect on [students]" (Boaler, 2016, p. 15). This practice promotes a "growth mindset" that encourages students to view mistakes as a challenge and motivation to work hard. In contrast, a "fixed mindset" reinforces ability as a rigid trait, which limits one's willingness to make and learn from mistakes (Boaler, 2016).

While the mastery of basic facts is useful, problem solving promotes the application of knowledge to real or fictional situations and enables the assessment of students' comprehension and reasoning strategies for future instruction (Zhang & Xin, 2012). Problem solving does not necessarily mean a word problem (e.g., equally sharing a bagel could be a problem-solving task). Fortunately, the teaching of mathematics in special education supports that students "can successfully learn problem-solving skills when instruction is designed to promote understanding" (Jitendra & Star, 2011, p. 18) and that teachers should "nurture the mathematic intelligence and curiosity" so they achieve their potential (Baroody, 1987, p. 268). Finally, students learn algebra and arithmetic when solving simple-structured or real-world problems along with effective instruction (Zhang & Xin, 2012). Mathematics think-aloud, Solve It!, and Dynamic Strategic Math are some promising strategies for teaching problem solving.

Carlos A. López Leiva is an assistant professor in bilingual/mathematics education at the University of New Mexico. His research interests include social processes of learning and mathematical and linguistic identity development of diverse learners.

Table 9-7 provides an additional alternative strategy for problem solving.

A key challenge in solving word problems relates to the step of knowing which operation to use in the solution. A model that can be used to determine the correct operation is based on two considerations. These two rules assist in thinking about the correct operations in problems that involve whole numbers. They are useful when the question is non-cued (if there are clear cues, there

TABLE 9–6   Problem-solving strategy: SOLVE-IT

Say the problem to yourself (repeat)

Omit information that is not needed

Listen for clue words within the problem

V Change *vocabulary* to numbers and symbols

E Write the math *equation*

Indicate the answer

Transfer your answer back to problem's original context

TABLE 9–7   Look & create, select usefully, review and re-strategize (if necessary)

Look for operational terms in word problems

Create a concrete or mental picture of word problem

Select a strategy to be used

Use that strategy

Review strategy and solution

Re-strategize if answer is incorrect

Source: Graphic Models and Instructional Tools for Students with Special Needs (p. 43), by E. A. Polloway & J. Lubin, 2016, *Lynchburg College Journal of Special Education*, Lynchburg College, Lynchburg, VA. Used with permission.

is no need for a model) and when problem does not include multiplying or dividing fractions.

The first step is determining the following:

- Do you have the big number, or do you have to get the big number?

- If you have the big number, use subtraction or division.
- If you need to get the big number, use addition or multiplication.

The second step is determining the following:

- Do the items represent same-size or different-size groups or individual numbers?
- If they are same-size groups, then you will divide or multiply.
- If they are different-size groups or just individuals, then you will add or subtract.

In Figure 9-6, the problem relates to, first, needing to get the big number and, second, having same-size groups. Hence, the operation as noted is multiplication. The box reflected in the figure can be used to assist students in working through problems.

There a number of additional effective strategies that can be used to encourage thinking as students develop the ability to solve problems. They also provide a real-life perspective in the sense that problems are not always clear when confronted with a problem to solve. Three examples are provided below.

The first example is having students determine the correct verb or action word within a word problem in order to demonstrate an understanding of the problem. Essentially, this works like the cloze procedure (see Chapter 6). A typical problem

Which Operation?

❹ The boy scouts were going to go caving. Each of the scouts had flashlights and had to carry extra batteries. The scout leader gave them 40 batteries and wanted each scout to carry an equal amount. How many batteries does each boy scout have to carry?

	Have the Larger Number	Need the Larger Number
Same Size or Equal Groups	÷	×
Different Size or Unequal Groups	−	+

Explanation

Rule 1: We have the larger number, in this case it is 40 batteries. These need to be distributed to each scout. Rule 1 tells us that we must subtract or divide.

Rule 2: We have one group of the same size, 5 scouts. Rule 2 tells us we must divide.

FIGURE 9–6   Problem-Solving Strategy: Determining Correct Computation

Source: Ryser, G., Patton, J. R., Polloway, E. A., & McConnell, K. (2006). *Practical ideas that really work for teaching math problem solving.* Austin, TX: PRO-ED (p. 182). Used with permission.

Can't Tell

Read the problem found on the page number provided. Read each statement and check the box that shows whether the statement is true, false, or if you can't tell. Prove the true and false statements in the space provided.

❶ Page _____   Problem _____

	TRUE	FALSE	CAN'T TELL
• _____	☐	☐	☐
_____			
_____			
• _____	☐	☐	☐
_____			
_____			
• _____	☐	☐	☐
_____			
_____			

❷ Page _____   Problem _____

	TRUE	FALSE	CAN'T TELL
• _____	☐	☐	☐
_____			
_____			
• _____	☐	☐	☐
_____			
_____			
• _____	☐	☐	☐
_____			
_____			

FIGURE 9–7   Can't Tell

Source: Ryser, G., Patton, J. R., Polloway, E. A., & McConnell, K. (2006). *Practical ideas that really work for teaching math problem solving*. Austin, TX: PRO-ED (p. 92). Used with permission.

might read as follows, with the student either filling in the missing word or choosing the correct word:

- Juan had three pieces of candy. He ____ two pieces. He now has one piece. (ate, bought, gave away)
- Saranda had a mathematics assignment to work on 20 multiplication problems. She ____ 15 problems. She must work on five more problems. (completed, skipped, added)

In Figure 9-7, an example is given of the concept of "can't tell." Students must determine that there is insufficient information for certain problems; in those case where they cannot tell, they learn to say that, and no problem solution is required.

Figure 9-8 provides a strategy for having students follow up on the previous example of cannot tell by learning to read carefully to determine what is missing before they can solve a problem.

Another way to consider learning about problems is having students write their own problems. Figure 9-9 provides such an example.

As students are working on word problems, the curriculum can be developed to challenge students with problems of increasing difficulty. In the same way that students move through computational mathematics by learning, for example, addition, subtraction, multiplication, and division, problem solving can be considered as teaching students through a graduated problem sequence moving from problems that are easier to problems that are more difficult. Table 9-8 illustrates a graduated problem sequence.

This section concludes with a summary of recommended and non-recommended practices for teaching problem solving. Table 9-9 is based in part on the work of Cawley, Miller, and School (1987, pp. 91–92).

**ENHANCEDetext
video example 9.4**
Watch this video to learn more about further considerations related to strategies to solve problems.

What's Missing?

Read each problem and decide what additional information you need to solve the problem. Below each problem are four statements. Circle the letter of the statement that describes the missing information. Next, provide the missing information (you will have to make it up), and use it to solve each problem. Choose one problem to present to the rest of the class.

❶ A gardener is planting a garden with green peppers, broccoli, sweet potatoes, and tomatoes.
She has 15 tomato plants, 6 broccoli plants, and 12 sweet potato plants.
How many plants did she have altogether?

A The time of year the gardener is planting her garden

B The number of plants the gardener has already planted

C The size of the garden

D The number of green pepper plants the gardener has

❷ A bowl of punch is made of pineapple, strawberry, and cranberry juices.
The punch contains 1.5 quarts of fruit juice in all.
If 0.62 quart of it is pineapple juice, how much cranberry juice is in the punch?

A The number of people who will drink the punch

B The amount of strawberry juice in the punch

C The number of cups in the punch

D The size of the punch bowl

❸ Twenty-four students are to go on a field trip.
How many cars are needed to take the children?

A The number of children that can go in each car

B The number of adults going on the field trip

C The distance to the field trip

D The day of the week the children are going on the field trip

❹ David is saving to buy a new shirt. He has saved for 2 months. Last month he saved $25.00. How much did he save this month?

A The price of the shirt

B The color of the shirt

C The total amount saved

D The jobs David did to earn money

FIGURE 9–8   Missing Elements in a Problem

Source: Ryser, G., Patton, J. R., Polloway, E. A., & McConnell, K. (2006). *Practical ideas that really work for teaching math problem solving.* Austin, TX: PRO-ED (p. 84). Used with permission.

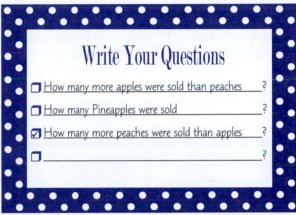

FIGURE 9–9 Students' Writing Problems

Source: Ryser, G., Patton, J. R., Polloway, E. A., & McConnell, K. (2006). *Practical ideas that really work for teaching math problem solving*. Austin, TX: PRO-ED (p. 88). Used with permission.

Basal math programs and several specialized programs are highlighted in this section.

Basal Textbook Programs

The most frequently employed approach to teaching math is the use of basal textbooks, which all major publishers produce. These textbooks are written primarily for students in general education math classes; however, most teacher's editions included in these series offer suggestions for addressing the needs of students with learning-related problems. Nevertheless, teachers of students who are experiencing difficulties in math must be prepared to augment or adapt these texts as necessary.

TABLE 9–8 Simple math computation matrix

	Add, No Distractor	*Add, with Distractor*	*Subtract, No Distractor*	*Subtract, with Distractor*
1 digit, 2 items	Mary had two apples. Her brother gave her two bananas. How many fruits does she have?	Mary had two apples. Her brother gave her two bananas and a lollipop. How many fruits does she have?	Mary had nine apples and five bananas. Her brother ate two apples and one banana for lunch. How many fruits does she have left?	Mary had nine apples and five bananas. Her brother ate one banana, one carrot and two apples for lunch. How many fruits does she have left?
2 digit, 2 items	Jon bought 22 pencils and 17 pens. How many items did he buy?	At the bookstore, Jon bought 13 pencils, 12 pens and 10 magazines. How many pens and pencils did he buy?	Jon bought 22 pencils and 17 pens. He gave 10 pens and 13 pencils to his best friend. How many pens and pencils does he have left?	Jon bought 22 pencils and 17 pens. He gave 10 pens, 12 magazines and 13 pencils to his best friend. How many pens and pencils does he have left?

Source: Graphic Models and Instructional Tools for Students with Special Needs (p. 44), by E. A. Polloway & J. Lubin, 2016, *Lynchburg College Journal of Special Education*, Lynchburg College, Lynchburg, VA. Used with permission.

TABLE 9–9 Problem-solving practices

Recommended Practices	Non-Recommended Practices
Making the solving of problems why students acquire and apply computational skills.	Stressing the use of cue words in order to directly indicate the operation.
Reading problems to students or re-writing them as needed rather than ignoring problem solving.	Marking problems completely wrong if students make an error in computation if they followed the correct problem-solving process.
Developing long-term instructional sequences for teaching problem solving.	
If the computational skills are too complex for word problems, simplifying the computational skills needed	Assuming students can solve problems automatically if they can do the computation.
	Not realizing problem solving is the basis for applying mathematics to daily living.
Using problems that include real-life applications.	
Monitor progress and modify instruction.	

Although there are many commonalities across basal series, there are notable differences as well. The more attractive series include specific suggestions for dealing with diverse needs and offer ways to augment lessons. A key variable to consider is the amount of practice included to achieve mastery of the skill(s) being taught. Many commercially available textbooks now come with sets of supplementary hands-on materials as well, and these must be evaluated in terms of students' needs.

Textbook usage with students who have learning problems has distinct advantages as well as some disadvantages that may be characteristic of some books. Some of the advantages are the following:

1. Skill development is laid out in a comprehensive and sequential fashion.
2. A number of primary and supplemental materials are provided: text, teacher's edition, student workbook, ditto masters, quizzes and placement tests, and record-keeping procedures.
3. Some series are oriented to real-life situations and use student-relevant examples.
4. Some series provide a hands-on, activity-oriented approach.

Some of the disadvantages are the following:

1. Teacher's editions do not provide specific teaching strategies for acquisition-stage learning (e.g., scripted instructions for teachers).
2. Enough practice may not be provided (proficiency stage).

3. Movement from one skill or topic to another may be too rapid.
4. Sometimes there is not enough review of previously acquired skills and knowledge (maintenance stage).
5. Linguistic and conceptual complexity may inhibit student understanding.
6. Types of activities may have limited variety.
7. The activities may lack relevance to students.
8. Problem-solving applications are often too contrived.

Corrective Mathematics

Corrective Mathematics (Engelmann & Carnine, 1981) is a remedial program developed for use with students in grade 3 through a post-secondary level. Its primary focus is on four basic operations, referred to as *modules*. Each module contains certain strands: facts, computation operations, and story problems. The addition module also has a strand on reading and writing numbers. The program was developed for students who have not mastered addition. Students do need certain pre-skills to use this program, although advanced reading skills are not required; poor readers can be placed in this program.

Corrective Mathematics is a systematic sequence of skill development following the direct instruction paradigm. Each module contains a presentation book, answer keys, and a student book. Each module also includes a placement test, a pre-skill test, and a series of mastery tests. Using a teacher-directed approach, each presentation book provides specific instructional information for each of the many lessons. Each task within the lesson has a script telling exactly what the teacher should say and do as well as what the students should say and do. Each daily lesson involves some type of teacher-directed activity; most lessons also require some independent student work.

One feature of the program is the built-in point system by which students can accumulate points for successful performance with workbooks in groups, in game situations, or on the mastery tests. Systems for awarding and monitoring points are programmed into the materials. A common theme in the Corrective Mathematics program is the concept of teaching to criterion. The idea is that at the completion of any exercise, each student should be able to perform a given task without error.

In their literature review concerning the direct or explicit instruction of mathematics programs, Przychodzin, Marchand-Martella, and Azim, (2004) outlined the supportive research that has accumulated over a period of 40 years. Their review concluded that direct instruction mathematics programs are effective and viable programs for students with significant mathematics difficulties.

TouchMath

This program has been used extensively in the schools and in particular with students with learning difficulties, including students with intellectual disabilities. Developed by Bullock, Pierce, and McClellan (1989), the program is a multisensory dot-notation system. "The dot-notations are touch points using one dot for the numbers 1–5 or a dot-notation with a circle around the dot/s to indicate to double touch points to assist students with and without disabilities with basic counting and computational skills" (p. 545).

Figure 9-10 and Figure 9-11 present two examples of the TouchMath system. The first illustrates the cuing system for the touch points for the nine numerals that provides an overview to the process of using the program. The second illustrates the use of the program in order to teach addition.

Waters and Boon (2011) focused on the use of the TouchMath program for high school students with mild intellectual disabilities. "The findings indicated that the use of the touch point strategy was effective for all three students in acquiring three-digit money computational problems with regrouping. Findings from this study not only add to the previous literature based on the touch math program but also provide new insights and

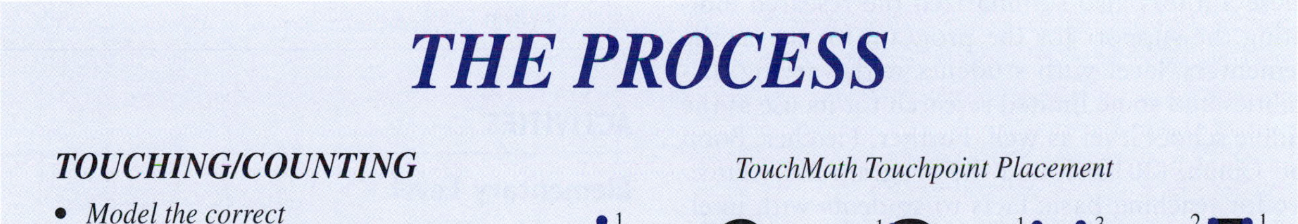

THE PROCESS

TOUCHING/COUNTING

- Model the correct touching/counting process

- Single dots are touched and counted once

- A dot with a circle is touched and counted twice

- Touch the points on the numbers and count aloud

TouchMath Touchpoint Placement

FIGURE 9–10 TouchMath Process

Source: Bullock, J., Pierce, S., & McClellan, L. (1989). *TouchMath.* Colorado Springs, CO: Innovative Learning Systems.

ADDITION

PREREQUISITES

- *Counting/writing numbers 1-50*
- *Using correct process for touching and counting*
- *Continuous counting*

PROCESS

- *Begin at the top of the column*
- *Go straight down the column, continuously counting*
- *After writing the answer, repeat the problem aloud for reinforcement*
- *Move toward the addition of several numbers*
- *Model the addition statement*
- *Adding two digit numbers utilizes an arrow over the right column which indicates where the student should begin*
- *Addition with regrouping adds a box over the ten's, hundred's, etc. column for carrying numbers forward*

FIGURE 9–11   TouchMath for Addition

Source: Bullock, J., Pierce, S., & McClellan, L. (1989). *TouchMath.* Colorado Springs, CO: Innovative Learning Systems.

applications to teach money computational skills to students at the high school level." (p. 553). These authors also summarized the research indicating the support for the program for use at the elementary level with students with varying disabilities and some limited research for its use at the middle school level as well. Further, Fletcher, Boon and Cihak. (2010) found the program more effective for teaching basic facts to students with intellectual disabilities when compared to just using a number line strategy within the context of teaching single-digit addition problems.

Browder, Trela, Gibbs, Wakeman, and Harris (2007) highlighted the following advantages of the use of this program for students with developmental disabilities: reinforces math skills using visual, auditory, and kinesthetic modalities; assists students' retention of math facts; provides them with a strategy to generate quicker and more accurate responses; and helps students solve problems without counting on fingers in front of peers (e.g., for older students who may no longer commonly be using manipulatives).

 Check Your Understanding 9.5 Click here to gauge your understanding of the concepts in this section.

ACTIVITIES

Elementary Level

Pre-Computational

1. To develop the ability to count from 1 to 10, have students play rhyming games, such as Buckle My Shoe.
2. Make different cutouts of three basic shapes (circles, triangles, rectangles); have students identify each shape. After students can identify each different shape, have them compare the sizes of the different shapes to determine which is larger, smaller, and so on.
3. Students can learn the concepts of "more" and "less" by comparing groups of objects. Start with one object in one group and two

or more objects in another group. Have the student identify which group has more and which has less. This activity could also be used to teach sameness.

4. Draw a line of objects, such as apples; have a pupil put an *X* on the number of objects designated by the numeral at the beginning of the line.

5. Have students match strings to kites, sails to boats, or stems to flowers to help develop an understanding of one-to-one correspondence.

6. Make up ditto sheets with similar but different-size figures (e.g., animals, toys, buildings) in each of several boxes. Have students cross out the largest and/or smallest figure in each box.

7. Using a felt board or pocket chart, have students match a set of objects with a numeral. For example, they might match two apples with the numeral 2.

8. Using a felt board or pocket chart, have students match a number word with a set of objects. Next, have students match a numeral and a number word with a set of objects.

9. Group objects in sets from 1 to 10; place several numerals next to each set and instruct students to circle the correct numeral.

10. Instruction in writing numerals from 1 through 9 should be started when a student is learning to write in manuscript. Have students trace the numerals to be learned, make the numerals by connecting dots, and finally write the numerals independently.

11. Have students complete dot-to-dot puzzles of simple designs (e.g., circle, square, triangle) and then of more complicated pictures (e.g., boats, animals, cars).

12. Cut numerals from old calendars and paste each on cardboard. Ask students to arrange the numbers in proper sequence without using the calendar page (Crescimbeni, 1965).

13. Request students to count silently the number of times you bounce a ball or buzz a buzzer. Challenge a student to state the correct number; if correct, ask that student to take your role.

14. Make seasonal puzzles with number as cues (e.g., jack-o-lanterns with different numbers of teeth, turkeys with different number of tail feathers, Christmas trees with different numbers of decorations). The student must count the items, find the puzzle piece with the corresponding numeral, and fit the pieces together.

15. Bender (2005) discussed the concept of **number sense**. He described number sense as "a student's conceptual understanding of basic number and numeration concepts such as counting, or recognizing how many objects are present in a set, and how a number may be used to represent that set of objects" (p. 7). In this regard, a child must figure out what a number means and how to relate that number to the real world. By doing so, the child develops meaning with regard to figures as symbols and what they mean in relation to counting or a set of objects. A student with number sense can take a quantity and develop a one-to-one relationship to objects. For example, a child would be able to pick out five pieces of candy to give to his or her four friends and keep one piece of candy for him- or herself. A child who does not have number sense would not be able to make that relationship. Teachers need to work on number sense for all children in the elementary grades, as number sense changes as a child matures.

16. As teachers move from the concrete, students may still need some visual help with computations. This help can be secured through the use of number lines. A short number line with numbers stopping at 10 should be used first. Later, as students progress to numbers past 10, a longer number line can be used.

Beginning Number Line

0—1—2—3—4—5—6—7—8—9—10

Advanced Number Line

0—1—2—3—4—5—6—7—8
—9—10—11—12—13—14—15

These number lines can be taped to students' desks or made of heavy cardboard and kept inside the desks. For younger children, number lines on the floor can be used to illustrate counting through movement. Familiarity with number lines will be useful later as students move into subtraction.

Computational

1. Have students make combinations of less than 10 by first counting real or pictured objects and then writing the correct number.

2. To ensure understanding of addition (or any other operation), introduce the concept of the missing element. This can be done in a way that is similar to the following example:

$$1 + 4 = \underline{\hspace{1cm}} \quad 1 + \underline{\hspace{1cm}} = 5 \quad \underline{\hspace{1cm}} - 4 = 5$$

3. An abacus is a good, concrete way to introduce students to the idea of place value. Show students when they get to 10 beads in the same row on the combinations and then write the number indicated on the abacus.

4. Have students play counting games in which the counting changes direction every time a bell rings.

5. Strengthen concepts of "before" and "after" by having students find the missing number in a series.

6. Help students learn to carry by covering all but the number column they are working with in a given problem.

7. Start work with fractional numbers by having students actually manipulate the fractional part to see that all parts are equal.

8. As students manipulate equal fractional parts, give them a chance to label them; for example, if there are four parts, then each part should be labeled one-fourth, or 1/4.

9. As students learn to count and write numerals, encourage them to make their own number line using tape or some other material.

10. Beginning instruction in subtraction should focus on actually taking away concrete objects, then crossing out pictures of objects, and finally working with pure abstraction.

11. Help students perceive the relationship of addition and subtraction by having them first add two sets of numbers and then subtract the two numbers from the derived sum.

12. Make a handout sheet with objects in sets like those in activity 12. Have students write how many objects are in each set. Then instruct students to write the same statements, using only numbers.

13. To show the relationship between addition and multiplication, have students first add the same number several times and then multiply that number by the number of times it was added.

$$\begin{array}{ll} 3 + 3 + 3 + 3 + 3 = 15 & 3 \times 5 = 15 \\ 6 + 6 + 6 = 18 & 6 \times 18 = 18 \end{array}$$

14. Concepts of "more" and "less" can be further developed by using multiplication facts. Require students to underline which is more or less.

More	Less
2 threes or 5	3 fives or 18
3 twos or 7	4 twos or 10

15. A student with a short attention span can sometimes do as much work as another student if arithmetic work is broken into smaller segments. To achieve this goal, cut a worksheet into small parts (e.g., rows of problems) or make up arithmetic problems on three-by-five cards that the pupil picks up each time a problem is completed.

16. After students learn basic division facts, have them show how a given number is divided into several equal parts.

$$6 = \underline{\hspace{1cm}} \text{ twos} \quad 6 = \underline{\hspace{1cm}} \text{ threes}$$

$$12 = \underline{\hspace{1cm}} \text{ sixes} \quad 12 = \underline{\hspace{1cm}} \text{ threes}$$

$$12 = \underline{\hspace{1cm}} \text{ twos} \quad 12 = \underline{\hspace{1cm}} \text{ fours}$$

Middle and Secondary Levels

1. Make a math center using index cards with basic computational skills of addition, subtraction, multiplication, or division on each card. Arrange the cards according to sequential skills (i.e., basic addition facts, carrying, and so on). Students can check their own recording sheets to show individual growth. Commercially prepared activity cards, such as Contemporary Math Facts Activity Cards (Prentice Hall Learning Systems), cover all math areas.

2. Many recently developed electronic games can be used to teach or reinforce math skills. Pupils also can check their work with them.

3. Simple calculators can be used to check work. In addition, these devices can be used for motivation; a student who finishes work on time or ahead of time can check it with the calculator.

4. More metric-related activities are needed to help students with disabilities understand the different systems of measurement. To show the difference in liquid measurement, empty a liquid from a container with a known measure to a container showing the metric equivalent.

5. Using pictures of various items that can be bought in restaurants, direct students to make up menus and choose what they will eat. Have them write the name of the food and its price and then add the prices to determine the total bill. As a bonus, figure out what the tip would be.

6. Give students practice reducing fractions to the lowest terms by making fraction cookies. Reduce all the fractions in the recipe and follow the directions as given.

Ingredients

a. $^4/_2$ cup of sugar
b. $^2/_4$ cup of milk
c. $^3/_3$ stick of margarine
d. $^4/_8$ cup cocoa
e. Bring ingredients to a boil in a saucepan. Cool slightly.
f. Add $^2/_2$ cup peanut butter and $2^2/_4$ cup oatmeal.
g. Drop on waxed paper.
h. Makes $1^4/_4$ dozen cookies.

7. Let two students roll dice to practice addition facts. The object of the game is to be the first player to score 100 points from the totals on the dice rolled. The players take turns rolling the dice; each may continue to roll as long as neither die shows a 1 but may stop voluntarily at any point. When either die does show a 1, the player gives up the turn and loses all points earned during that turn. If a 1 is rolled on both dice, the player gives up the turn, loses all points, and starts again at zero (Mercer, 1979).

8. Have each student draw a place-value chart. Draw a card from a deck of 10 with a digit (0 to 9) written on each. Direct students to record that digit in any column they wish. Continue drawing until five cards have been drawn. The student with the largest number wins. Require the winner to read the winning number correctly. Modify as appropriate.

9. Cut a piece of tagboard into a circle as large as the center of a car tire. Tape the tagboard into the center of a tire. Write these directions on the circle: (a) measure the radius of the circle, (b) tell the diameter of the circle, and (c) find the circumference of the circle. Use different types of tires and other circular items to vary this activity.

10. Real Life Math, Living on a Paycheck, is a math-based consumer education simulation program. Students move out of their parents' homes to Willow, U.S.A., the city where they get their first jobs and their first apartments. Students hunt for and choose apartments. They sign leases, pay security deposits, start paying rent, and move in. They buy starter furniture and basic household needs. Students who think they will have trouble affording an apartment on their own choose roommates and begin making joint decisions.

11. After filling out applications and being interviewed, students get a job. They receive paychecks based on actual school attendance. For 70 simulated days, they budget their money to do the following:

- Rent and furnish their apartments
- Buy cars and gas fill-ups
- Pay bills
- Buy groceries
- Pay for leisure activities
- Buy clothes
- Pay for medical care

The 70 simulated days can translate to a one- or two-semester course activity. Choosing possible shortcuts, limiting elaboration, keeping all students working together, and doing activities in groups as needed to stay on track allow the program to be completed in one semester.

LEARNING OUTCOMES

Upon completion of this chapter, the reader should be able to:

10.1 Understand the content of the social studies curriculum and the academic challenges students with special needs may encounter in social studies.

10.2 Discuss and implement assessment strategies in the area of social studies.

10.3 Identify instructional techniques and strategies that may be used to teach social studies to students with special needs.

Although the instruction of social studies has traditionally been one of the least emphasized content curricular areas, it is the subject matter that is of the utmost importance when teaching students to become productive citizens of our country. It is a subject that can develop the problem-solving and analytic skills students need to navigate through life and exercise their civic duty as citizens of this country and the world. Additionally, learning about the human condition and why societies function the way they do provides a framework for students to understand and empathize with other people in their own country and around the world. It helps students make sense of their nation's past and why the present circumstances are taking place. It encourages students to become actively involved in their communities in order to learn about themselves and others. Additionally, social studies instruction challenges students and teachers to think critically so that effective decisions may be made toward establishing a better future for themselves and others.

Increased attention is being paid to the adult outcomes of learners with special needs. As a result, preparing them to be contributing, competent citizens and active participants in their communities has become a major goal of education. Perhaps as much as any other subject area, the functional aspects of the subject area of social studies become obvious. At its very core is citizenship education. Moreover, this content area promotes informational skills and value development that contribute substantially to an understanding of human diversity, societal complexity, and general world knowledge.

The idea that social studies is considered a critical or core subject area for all students has often been overlooked (Bailey, Shaw, & Hollifield, 2006). Researchers in the area of social studies have found that 72% of surveyed teachers indicate that this subject receives a low priority when considering curricular importance in general education (Farkas & Duffett, 2010). These teachers state that the emphasis on mathematics and language arts (i.e., reading, writing) has taken center stage due to the pressure for students to compete in the world market. The Center on Education Policy (2006) reported that its 2005–2006 study of 229 school districts (representing 15,000) elementary schools in all 50 states indicated that 71% of all the surveyed districts had reduced instructional time in at least one other subject to make time for reading/language arts and math. As a result, a National Assessment of Educational Progress (NAEP, 2010) study indicated that social studies is not included in every state's standards and testing and that in those states that do include social skills testing, 75% of the fourth-grade students and 88% of the eighth-grade students scored below the desired Basic Skills Proficiency level. Historically, these results and sentiments are also reflected for students with special needs. Patton, Polloway, and Cronin (1994) concluded that the teaching of social studies to students with mild learning difficulties often mirrored social studies as a low priority.

SOCIAL STUDIES CURRICULUM AND LEARNERS WITH SPECIAL NEEDS

Curriculum

The specific curricular goals of social studies can be extracted from professional organizations and councils, state standards, competency requirements, and professional literature. Goals have also been predicated on the pervading contemporary philosophy (Zevin, 2010). For example, prior to the late 1970s, the "new social studies" movement was prevalent, espousing inquiry-oriented techniques and including disciplines beyond history, geography, and civics (Birchell & Taylor, 1986). This orientation was replaced in the late 1970s and early 1980s by a "back-to-basics" movement that emphasized five primary areas: reading skill development, American history and heritage, geography (including map and globe skills), American government, and tradition, values, attitudes, and beliefs (Birchell & Taylor, 1986).

A new orientation arose in response to the criticism of social studies programs that emerged during the 1980s. McGowan and Guzzetti (1991) summarized the spirit of these reforms:

> Reformers advanced "kinder, gentler" social studies, founded on a content framework largely drawn from history and geography, but enhanced with teaching strategies encouraging student engagement, subject matter integration, global awareness, social participation, and the formation/application of significant ideas. (p. 16)

The Board of Directors of the National Council for the Social Studies (NCSS, 1994) then adopted the following definition of social studies:

> Social studies is the integrated study of the social sciences and humanities to promote civic competence. Within the school program, social studies provides coordinated, systematic study drawing upon such disciplines as anthropology, archaeology, economics, geography, history, law, philosophy, political science, psychology, religion, and sociology, as well as appropriate content from the humanities, mathematics, and natural sciences. The primary purpose of social studies is to help young people develop the ability to make informed and reasoned decisions for the public good as citizens of a culturally diverse, democratic society in an interdependent world.

Most recently, the Common Core State Standards Initiative (2010), adopted by most states, have impacted the social studies curriculum. Bulgren, Samson Graner, and Deshler (2013) noted that the Common Core Standards challenge students to "engage more in higher-order thinking and reasoning than just on the acquisition of factual information." (p. 17). Further, "content literacy standards are now included in . . . graduation requirements, making informational-text' importance grow in social studies classes" (Ciullo, Falcomata, & Vaughn, 2015, p. 15).

The scope and sequence of any social studies program for special education students will depend on where the student receives such instruction. Given widespread inclusion, most students with learning problems are taught in general education classes, where they have the best access to the general curriculum, while a much smaller number may be in a secondary school program that covers the key elements of the general education curriculum but emphasizes a more functional orientation that will be useful to them in adjusting to adulthood (see Chapter 14).

TABLE 10–1 Typical social studies themes by grade level

Grade Level	Theme
K	Self, school, community, home
1	Families
2	Neighborhoods
3	Communities
4	State history, geographic regions
5	U.S. history
6	World cultures, Western Hemisphere
7	World geography or history
8	American history
9	Civics or world cultures
10	World history
11	American history
12	American government

The K–12 curricular sequence in social studies has been fairly standard in classrooms across the nation. The common grade-level themes reveal two major patterns: a focus in grades K–6 on expanding environments (movement from family/neighborhood to world perspective), followed by recurrent attention (grades 7–9 and 10–12) on contracting environments. Other subjects, such as economics, may be options that are available to students (see Table 10-1).

This sequence represents social studies curricula in general. However not all states, and not all commercially available textbook series adhere to this sequence. The themes designed to guide social studies curriculum are woven into the general sequence depicted in Table 10-1. The scope of the social studies curriculum at the high school level may vary considerably from one state to another; however, courses such as American history and world history are typically required for graduation. In addition, particular states commonly require that students take units pertaining to their own state histories and cultures.

Considerations for Students with Special Needs

In past decades, issues concerning social studies instruction for students with special needs were often downplayed simply because a significant number of learners with disabilities were not receiving social studies instruction while they were often in special education settings for most of their instructional day. In a classic study of special education for students with "mild" learning problems, Patton, Polloway, and Cronin (1987) found that no social studies instruction was occurring in almost one-third of the classes where it should be taught. Further, of all the subject areas to which students with special needs are exposed, social studies has been studied and written about the least. For example, more attention has been paid to science than to its companion subject area, social studies.

Regardless of the past perception of social studies as a low-priority subject, more students with special needs are experiencing the social studies coursework at higher rates than ever before for two reasons. First, IDEA (2004) mandated that students with disabilities be provided with access to the general education curriculum. Second, each year, more students with disabilities are spending more time in inclusive settings. As students are required by IDEA to participate in the general education curriculum, consideration of this academic area becomes critically important in order to provide appropriate instruction (Scruggs, Mastropieri, & Okolo, 2008).

Thus, as this situation concerning access to social studies instruction has changed and far more students are in general education social studies classes, there has been an increased focus on how to teach them (e.g., De la Paz, Morelles, & Winston, 2007). Given changes in placement and hence curricular access, it is important to consider why such students may face challenges in such classes. The discussion below briefly addresses some key student characteristics as well as common problems faced by students with special needs related to curricular and skill demands. In addition, a brief discussion on preparation of teachers concludes this section.

Learner Characteristics. Common problems that may be experienced in social studies instruction may relate to student learning problems. Perhaps foremost are possible difficulties in reading and, particularly, comprehension. Ciullo et al. (2015) noted that components of reading comprehension that often prove difficult for students with learning disabilities include recall of facts, summarizing key points in main ideas, locating details that are supportive of the main ideas of text material, following the sequence of events, and making inferences from available text data.

In addition, common challenges students may face relate to difficulties with written expression, strength of vocabulary to understand and retain, note-taking difficulties in lecture-based classes, and conceptually being able to find the *big ideas* in the social studies curriculum within myriad factual details.

Collectively, these types of difficulties can negatively impact students as they attempt to learn new information and also as they seek to apply what they have learned in social studies. Therefore, such classes present particular difficulties for students at risk for failure to succeed in content classes. Problems are often most significant for students at the secondary school level, where their reading skills are significantly below students who are not disabled (Ciullo et al., 2015).

Challenges with Curricular Materials. Few materials are designed with the idea of accommodating students' learning differences right from the start (Scruggs et al., 2008), which would be reflective of universal design for learning (see below and also Chapter 3). Given the heavy reliance on the use of textbooks (Jarrett, 1999a) and the demanding features of these books, it is no surprise that many students have difficulties with these materials. Moreover, much of the accompanying tasks that students are required to use as in-class activities or as homework (e.g., worksheets to complete) present a similar set of challenges for students.

Lenz and Schumaker (1999) identified some design characteristics that are major determinants of how useful materials are for students with diverse learning needs. Some of these design qualities are as follows:

- **Abstractness**—Much of social studies involve the understanding of concepts. For many students with diverse learning needs, being able to grasp complex concepts is not easy. This is particularly the case for students with mild intellectual disabilities.
- **Skills**—A range of skills is expected from students in the social studies area. The ability to skim or scan textual passages is essential to complete assignments and to study for tests. The ability to organize information gleaned from reading textual material is essential.
- **Strategies**—To effectively master the content of this subject area, the appropriate and efficient use of various strategies is required. For example, in classes where the memorization of facts

that are embedded in the textual material is demanded for success on quizzes or tests, certain strategic behaviors are needed. Many students do not possess these strategies.

- **Background**—Without question, those students who come to social studies with rich experiential backgrounds are at greater advantage in mastering what is presented, read, discussed, and tested. One of the most challenging aspects of teaching social studies is the overwhelming amount of new vocabulary that is introduced. Mastropieri and Scruggs (1992), in an early evaluation of textbooks, identified an amazing number of new vocabulary words introduced (750 in one series and 1,831 in another). This aspect of the learning process can be daunting to the student with learning needs.
- **Quantity**—The volume of information that is presented in a any secondary level social studies textbook chapter is massive. The amount of detail that must be assimilated and related to more general themes borders on overwhelming. The fact that many students with diverse learning needs become frustrated easily when trying to operate in this type of inclusive setting is not hard to understand.

Challenges with Skill Demands. Social studies contains many complex topics, issues, and concepts. For example, the concept of "community" is abstract, requiring certain cognitive and conceptual skills. The subject also favors students with rich experiential backgrounds who find many topics more meaningful as a result of their varied experiences. In addition, most social studies classes demand proficiency in a variety of areas, particularly reading, writing, oral expression, interactive/group skills, study skills, and research-related skills (e.g., Internet and library skills). Smith and Smith (1990) suggested that students need a significant set of "social studies skills," including the following:

- **Acquiring information**—reading, study skills, information search, technical skills (e.g., Internet skills)
- **Organizing and using information**—classifying, interpreting, analyzing, summarizing, synthesizing, evaluating, decision making
- **Participating socially**—personal skills, group interaction, social and political skills (i.e., related to group dynamics) (p. 5)

Providing a summative perspective, Bouck, Courtad, Heutsche, Okolo, and Englert (2009) noted that social studies instruction is particularly challenging for students who have disabilities given the abstract nature of the curriculum, the reading levels of the textbooks, the demands of lectures on oral comprehension and processing skills, and the challenges of independent seatwork.

Teacher Preparation. Another concern related to social studies instruction is the training background of special education teachers, many of whom report being unprepared to teach social studies. Brophy, Alleman, and Knighton (2009) underscored the lack of training for teachers in the area of social studies instruction. Many secondary level special education teachers, in particular, are unfamiliar with curriculum, instructional practices, and appropriate materials in this area. This has become a particularly problematic issue with the provision that all teachers must be "highly qualified."

Although more students with special needs are included in social studies courses, the low priority for teaching social studies is nevertheless often reflected in special education teacher preparation programs. Few special education training programs require or even offer coursework in which topics were dedicated to how to teach social studies to students with special learning needs. Patton et al. (1994) in the past found that a significant number of special education teachers reported that they had received no training of any type (i.e., preservice or in-service) in this area. Not surprisingly, many special educators feel unprepared and uncomfortable teaching social studies. However, many of them are assigned to teach in this area, especially at the secondary level, and may find themselves teaching or co-teaching social studies courses to students in diploma programs. The requirement of students being taught by "highly qualified" teachers has addressed this issue, especially for special education teachers at the secondary level.

Regardless of these concerns, the reality is that an increasing number of students with special needs is being taught in inclusive settings. Even though, as McCoy (2005) noted, "the role of the special education teacher is to be the instructional strategist, not the content specialist" (p. 3), teachers will need to be able to accommodate their needs in the context of the demands of the general social studies classes. As a result, special education teachers need to possess at least a working knowledge of content and clearly will need to possess skills in being able to provide assistance in modifying curricular materials and designing effective cognition strategies that will work within the instructional practices used in these classes (De la Paz et al., 2007).

 Check Your Understanding 10.1 Click here to gauge your understanding of the concepts in this section.

DIVERSITY IN THE CLASSROOM

Social studies has the potential through content and skills to empower students to think critically about their present and future roles as members of a diverse society. Regardless of the nature of a student's place in the world, the power of learning history, geography, political science, sociology, anthropology, and economics provides a foundation for developing a critical consciousness. As an instructor of Native American studies, my goal is to introduce the youth to issues and concepts in this field of study with three major objectives: (1) to engage in intellectual activity within a community of learners; (b) to examine issues of race, ethnicity, social class, culture, gender, and language in relation to Native peoples now and in the past; and (c) to reflect on ways that my course can relate to youth now and in the future. Embedded in all of the lessons are pedagogical activities that encourage youth to reflect on cultural identity. For example, one lesson focuses on the question, What is an Indian? Prior to viewing the documentary *Half of Anything* (a 2006 documentary by Jonathan Tomhave, Hidatsa/Prairie Band of Potawatomi/Hocak, produced by Native Voices, University of Washington), which addresses Native identity, blood quantum, assimilation, skin color, and hairstyles, I ask the youth, "What are you? Why do you identify yourself in this way?" The documentary provides perspectives including Sherman Alexie (writer, poet, filmmaker) and John Trudell (Santee Sioux and Mexican activist, poet, and musician).

In the post-viewing debrief, I ask the students to identify responses that are new, challenging, or similar to their own constructions of cultural identity.

Their responses cover a broad range from youth who recently learned about their affiliation with a Native Nation to youth who have a strong foundation of cultural identity as a tribal specific Native person. Wexler (2009) noted that "if young people can make sense of their experiences by locating themselves and their situation within historical understanding and community meaning, they are better able to overcome hardship and sustain psychological health" (p. 271). The implications for curriculum and instruction of Native American studies in this instance and in the field of social studies in the larger context of this discussion are enormous. By embedding a connection among critical consciousness, knowledge, and identity, there is a natural merger of the cognitive and affective domains. For example, Native youth can gain an appreciation for and knowledge about activism, decolonization, sovereignty, and rights as they relate directly to Indigenous peoples. Through this process of reflection in becoming critical readers of the world, they can rearticulate their roles as members of society upon release. They can ask questions that interrogate taken-for-granted assumptions about the representation of Indigenous peoples, for example, in popular culture or the continued use of Indigenous peoples as sports mascots. They can think critically about the meaning of cultural sovereignty within the context of their own Native Nations and engage in movements to revitalize and preserve Native languages. They can guide the next generation of youth about the value of learning to critically read the world as a means of sustaining Indigenous cultures, languages, traditions, and histories. Through the liberating potential of social studies, students develop a strong foundation of identity for exercising agency that sustains a healthy outlook on life.

Glenabah Martinez, Ph.D. is an associate professor and associate dean for educator preparation at the University of New Mexico. His research focuses on Indigeneity, youth, and education with a particular emphasis on Indigenous youth, critical pedagogy, and the politics of social studies curriculum.

ASSESSMENT IN SOCIAL STUDIES

Four key reasons exist for collecting information on students in most academic areas: monitor progress, make instructional decisions, evaluate student achievement, and evaluate program effectiveness (National Council of Teachers of Mathematics, 1995). We focus mainly on the first two reasons in discussing social studies assessment below.

A number of techniques are available for collecting information on students' knowledge and skills in social studies. Spinelli (2012) noted that student assessment must be an indication of the quality and depth of the students' knowledge of social studies as well as evaluating whether the knowledge gained is accurate. In doing so, teachers must use evaluations that are appropriate according to the different instructional approaches used (e.g., textbook-oriented instruction, inquiry-oriented instruction). For example, a teacher might assess student knowledge of his textbook instruction by evaluating vocabulary development, reading comprehension, or ability to interpret graphs and charts. In contrast, if the teacher was using an inquiry approach to instruction, student assessment might entail the evaluation of planning, researching and problem-solving abilities (to name a few). Aligning the instruction to the evaluation is of the utmost importance when assessing student achievement.

Although there are several assessment tools, the major ways of measuring performance include standardized testing, curriculum-based measurement (CBM), performance measures, rubrics, and various student-centered assessment techniques. Before these assessment tools are discussed, one might note that the traditional use of weekly quizzes and regularly scheduled tests is still prevalent in many secondary level social studies classes. This long-standing process is organized in the following way: students read the textbook, listen to in-class presentations, participate in discussions, and then are evaluated via a closed-book quiz or test. Though this scenario might be common, other ways of assessing students exist and should be considered. These assessments are as follows.

Due to the emphasis on standards and accountability, standardized, norm-referenced group achievement tests are given to students throughout the United States as part of the system to determine annual yearly progress. Students are usually assessed via high-stakes tests in social studies at specific grade levels, depending upon the state in which a student resides.

Curriculum-based measures are generally teacher-made, non-standardized tests that relate closely to the actual curriculum to which students are being exposed. This type of assessment is extremely useful, as it allows for a monitoring of student progress in the specific lessons being presented. Additionally, it allows teachers to use decision-making instruction based on the data gleaned from these measures.

In subjects like social studies, where projects and other types of hands-on activities are used, this type of assessment is a good fit for evaluating student performance. According to Stepanek and Jarrett (1997), performance assessments "typically focus on the process of solving problems or completing complex tasks. The emphasis is on what students can do, not just what they know" (p. 11).

Similar to behavioral checklists is the rubric assessment (Finson & Ormsbee, 1998). A rubric assessment refers to the use of specific guidelines to help navigate the grading of the student's work. A teacher may use **analytic rubrics** that outline specific criteria to determine the level of a student's performance. This type of rubric is objective in nature. A more subjective assessment is the **holistic rubric**, which implies that a teacher assesses and rates the overall quality of the student's work (e.g., as superior, acceptable, inadequate, or unacceptable). Either rubric system can be used for the assessment of a social studies project/performance.

Spinelli (2012) identified some additional ways in which students can be involved in the assessment process. Each of those assessment strategies are discussed here:

- **Portfolios**—Portfolio assessment is one of the most popular techniques used in schools. Portfolio assessment implies the accumulation of student products to reflect their performance. This increasingly implemented method is attractive for use with students with special needs because it deemphasizes the need for optimal demonstration of competence in a standardized format. Instead, it allows students to show their best work that has been generated over time. This list has been adapted and modified from Spinelli (2012) to highlight a number of examples that may be part of a social studies portfolio (see Table 10-2).

TABLE 10–2 Suggested entries for social studies portfolios

- Map of gerrymandered congressional or state election districts
- Data tracking on election trends for particular offices
- Travel brochure
- Historical character biographical blurb
- Historical event report
- Concept map
- Geographic topographical map
- Video of famous battle
- Timelines for historic events
- Transcript of an historic speech
- Letter to the local paper editor on a community issue
- Interview with a political candidate
- Photographs
- Oral history with witnesses to historic events

- **Journals and learning logs**—Journals are resources for students to use their written languages skills. In journals, students are able to write in depth about a particular concept or era that they have been studying. Journal writing allows students to write about their impressions of an injustice or analyze the facts in the case of a particular outcome (e.g., the Civil War). Because journal writing does involve writing skills that students with special needs may not have, teachers might structure the journal entries or explicitly teach students how to write in their journals.

Learning logs might entail fewer higher-order thinking skills as well as written language skills. Students write what they have learned that day or week as a way of summarizing and synthesizing information. This will necessitate explicit teacher instruction and structured guidance in teaching students how to paraphrase their knowledge (a paraphrasing strategy would be useful).

- **Think-alouds**—According to Spinelli (2005), the think-aloud technique asks the student to verbally explain the processes he or she used in solving a problem or performing an activity. The teacher may have to spend some time showing students how this technique works.
- **Self-evaluation questionnaires**—This type of questionnaire allows students to evaluate their own performance as well as other aspects of the social studies activities in which they have participated.

- **Interviews**—Interviews are useful not only to determine what a student has learned but also to determine interest and attitudes. If there is sufficient time to do this, teachers are encouraged to gather information through conversations with students as an adjunct to other techniques. This evaluation is of particular importance for those students who have difficulty with writing but are able to verbally express themselves.

 Check Your Understanding 10.2 Click here to gauge your understanding of the concepts in this section.

SOCIAL STUDIES INSTRUCTION

General Approaches to Teaching Social Studies

Two major instructional approaches for this age-group may be considered to be the textbook/lecture/discussion approach and the inquiry approach. These are discussed below and summarized in Table 10-3. Another important option is based on the teaching of big ideas, which is also discussed below.

Textbook and Lecture Approach. Of the various ways to cover social studies content, the most historical and frequently used techniques in general education setting have been the textbook, lecture, and discussion format. For example, this was the case in the 1970s (Turner, 1976), remained so during the 1980s and into the 1990s (Hayes, 1988; Steinbrink & Jones, 1991; Woodward, Elliott, & Nagel, 1986), and remains so today.

This approach is characterized by an emphasis on textbooks, lectures, and discussion as the primary mechanisms for organizing the course and disseminating information. Teachers familiar with textbook series in social studies know that the most significant problem is readability or, more specifically, students' inability to manage the textual material and ultimately to comprehend the material. Scruggs et al. (2008) noted that social studies textbooks require that students learn vocabulary and are able to comprehend the factual nature of the subject. These are difficult skills for most students with special needs who lack the literacy skills necessary to navigate through the social studies textbook. If the goal of social studies is to teach problem-solving skills, decision-making skills, and moral and ethical thinking, how can a student do so if a textbook is limiting his or her access to a broader network of information?

TABLE 10–3 Two instructional approaches in social studies

Approach	Positive Features	Negative Features	Components
Textbook/lecture/discussion	Has been simplified in series Includes good aesthetic features (e.g., illustrations) Includes good resource/reference materials Introduces content-related terms Lessens teacher's workload (i.e., preparation time)	Presents readability problems Introduces language complexity Develops too many concepts too quickly May lack sufficient organizational aids (e.g., headings and subheadings) Makes understanding difficult because of superficial and disconnected coverage of topics Does not adequately accommodate special learners in teacher's guides Is typically used only in combination with discussion	Teacher's guide Student text Student workbook Supplemental materials (e.g., filmstrips)
Inquiry	Emphasizes organizational problem-solving skills Is student centered Capitalizes on student curiosity and interest	Requires organizational and problem-solving skills Demands self-directed behavior (i.e., independent learning) Requires the use of outside materials that may not be readable and/or available (e.g., in Braille or on tape) Requires special skills of the teacher	Trade books Reference materials Library work Fieldwork Media Student reports (oral or written) Microcomputers

Kinder, Bursuck, and Epstein (1992) underscored the problems with the textbooks used in social studies in their evaluation of 10 eighth-grade history textbooks. They found that the readability of all the textbooks was one or more years above the grade level. They also found important differences in certain organizational dimensions of the textbooks that have an effect on a student's ability to use them successfully.

Most major publishers have developed a social studies series, and some of the series accommodate individual differences better than others. Teachers should examine these series closely, looking for certain features in the student materials (e.g., controlled reading levels, organizational elements, language demands, conceptual levels) and in the teacher materials (e.g., guidelines for adapting instruction, additional activity-oriented ideas for covering the topic, supplemental materials). These factors can make a big difference in increasing the ability of reading-challenged students to use these materials. Further, teachers shall consider texts that emphasize, for example, in history, the relationship between events and activities and how they are made explicit (Harniss, Caros, & Gersten, 2007).

ENHANCEDetext
video example 10.1
Watch this video to learn more about considerations related to reading in the content area of social studies.

Inquiry Approach. Inquiry, also referred to as a process approach, puts a premium on skills used in solving problems or addressing issues. Although attractive in many ways, this approach requires that students possess certain abilities and prerequisite skills, such as the social studies skills previously noted. Many general education social studies teachers find that they must explicitly teach some of these "social studies skills" and provide organizational supports for many students in their classes. As more and more states are including "inquiry" as a component of their content standards, teachers are required to include inquiry approaches in the social studies classrooms (Newby & Higgs, 2005). In fact, the inquiry approach has been a key factor of education reform in social studies (Morocco, Hindin, & Mata-Aguilar, 2001).

A completely inquiry-oriented approach for teaching social studies to learners with special needs must be used with caution. As with process approaches in other academic areas (e.g., science), structured instruction helps students make connections across topics and concepts and is therefore recommended and often necessary. Thus, it is important first to assess whether students can effectively use inquiry skills and then to present a schema of substantive information via a systematic teaching paradigm. Scruggs et al. (2008) outlined a number of positive features (e.g., engagement and hands-on activities, positive impact on motivation, potential for increased learning) and negative features (e.g., difficulty some students have from learning from "discovery" approaches, still need instruction on vocabulary and knowledge, independent use of discovery strategies difficult to promote) of constructed (i.e., inquiry) approaches to social studies (and science).

Rieth et al. (2003) and Gersten, Baker, Smith-Johnson, Dimino, and Peterson (2006) developed inquiry-oriented social studies programs that focus primarily on the study of detailed analysis of videos (e.g., *To Kill a Mockingbird*) to develop investigative skills as well as integration of information across social studies areas. Such a program can be very interesting and meaningful to students because it deals with local community issues as well as national issues and helps develop decision-making skills using topics to which students can relate. These authors also suggested that high expectations should be maintained, as these special students showed increases in higher-order thinking (e.g., reasoning) as well as motivation in their learning. Scruggs et al. (2008) underscored that learners with special needs are too infrequently afforded opportunities to experience innovative, dynamic programs. Such programs should be considered and their effectiveness should be evaluated.

ENHANCEDetext
video example 10.2
Watch this video to learn more about the inquiry method.

While the above discussion presented a dichotomous analysis, many teachers have developed social studies programs that combine features of the textbook/lecture/discussion approach with inquiry- or issue-oriented elements. For example, a program might use a textbook but also regularly include video-based, inquiry-oriented activities.

Many efforts are developed at a local level. They can be engaging, relevant, and appropriate for special learners. However, it remains important that the customized curriculum not deviate too much from the general education curriculum and the state standards in terms of content even though methodology and selected topics may be very different.

Big Ideas. A third general method is the big idea approach (Brophy et al., 2009; Coyne et al., 2007). Teaching a large amount of information, as in the area of social studies, can be a difficult and daunting task. Thus, one instructional adaptation for organizing the breadth and depth of social studies information is through the use of big ideas. Coyne et al. (2007) noted that "big ideas are important concepts and principles that are more specific than thematic strands . . . and fundamentally different from transitional social studies concepts such as democracy and community" (p. 207).

Brophy et al. (2009) noted that big ideas have been recognized for a century (Dewey 1902, 1938) as an instructional approach to convey information. They stated,

> Powerful ideas have several distinctive characteristics. First, they are fundamental to the subject area in general and the major instructional goals in particular. They tend to cluster in the midrange between broad topics such as transportation and particular items of information such as the fact that the fuel used in airplanes is not the same as the fuel used in cars. Most are concepts, generalizations, principles, or causal explanations. Examples within transportation include the categories of land, sea, and air transportation; the progression from human-powered to animal-powered to engine-powered transportation; role of transportation in fostering economic and cultural exchange; and the development of infrastructure to support a given form of transportation once it gets established (e.g., roads, service stations, traffic control mechanisms). (p. 59)

Teaching with the big idea approach helps children make more connections with other powerful ideas. Brophy et al. (2009) posited that the big idea approach goes beyond teaching "propositional knowledge (what it is, why and how it was developed)" as well as the "procedural knowledge (how to use it)" and the "conditional knowledge (when and why to use it)" (p. 59).

When selecting big ideas, teachers should choose those concepts that exemplify an efficient and broad acquisition of knowledge. Above all, the choice of one or two yearly big ideas should function as a mechanism to organize and connect information so that students can identify and associate the social studies content with their own lives. For example, Coyne et al. (2007) employed one type of big idea called the *problem–solution–effect* model (*ProSE* strategy model). The "problem" (e.g., economic, human rights) is usually present in every social studies concept. Once the problem is identified, possible solutions can be considered (e.g., using the ADMIT model developed by Carnine (1995): accommodation, domination, movement, invention, tolerance) to overcome the problem. Finally, the solution will result in an "effect" or the outcome or consequence that might end, continue, or solve the problem. It then may be cyclical, as new problems may arise. The lead-up to the U.S. Civil War creates a readily apparent example of the ProSE model and its recycling as problems are identified, solved, and reconsidered.

Winchester et al. (2009) focused on teaching American Civil War history to two groups of students with learning disabilities. One group was taught using a traditional textbook-based approach with related activities, including textbook reading, teacher-led discussion, lectures, written assignments, and recitation of facts. The other used the big idea, problem–solution–effect model and text from Carnine, Crawford, Harniss, and Hollenbeck, K. (1995) that dealt with historical concepts in order to provide a framework for enabling students to make meaningful connections among facts and relied on graphic organizers to assist students in organizing themselves in terms of focusing on the critical information within a given chapter. There were significant advantages for students using the strategy-based approach and conceptually organized text versus the traditional text the implication. Students benefited more from strategy-based instructional sequences than simply from textbooks that rely on memorization but do not include explicit instruction on how to organize facts to understand and recall them.

Applying a problem–solution–effect big idea to each studied concept can be repeated throughout the year to help students see connections throughout history and within other subject areas of social studies (e.g., civics, law, economics, political science). Coyne et al. (2007) suggested (a) multiple perspectives and (b) factors of group success (i.e., motivation, leadership, resources, and capability) as other big ideas that can be employed to adapt social studies curricula to diverse learners. The discussion below on content enhancement routines reinforces the value of a big ideas approach to social studies curricula.

Instructional Strategies for Students with Special Needs

Social studies, as all subject areas, requires sound instructional practices that maximize the probability that learning will occur. Although the components of effective instruction are introduced in other chapters of this text, they also apply to the area of social studies. In addition, certain instructional-related topics that are unique to this subject area are noteworthy. Strategies that have received research support in terms of learning include advanced organizers, graphic organizers, concept maps, small-group instruction, extended practice, peer tutoring, teaching note-taking skills, using guided notes, study guides, reciprocal teaching (i.e., question, summarize, clarify information while reading text passages; see Chapter 7), content enhancement routines, technology-based instruction, and mnemonics (e.g., Ciullo et al., 2015; Fontana, Scruggs, & Mastropieri, 2007; Scruggs, Mastropieri, & Marshak, 2011). A number of these strategies are discussed below following a further consideration of universal design.

Universal Design for Learning. As discussed earlier, the philosophy of designing curriculum, materials and equipment, and instruction in such a way that all students with diverse needs can be included appropriately is strongly recommended. The Virginia Department of Education (2016) defines universal design for learning (UDL) as "a concept or philosophy for designing & delivering products & services usable by people with a wide range of functional capabilities, which include products & services directly usable with or without assistive technologies." Bouck et al. (2009) noted that "universal design for learning focuses on creating curricular content accessible to all students. . . . Consequently, it does not imply one way of

teaching are ones-size-fits-all model but rather offers a range of options . . . it is intended to remove [learning] barriers and make learning accessible" (p. 14). Relevant to the social studies, UDL can attend to individual needs in a general fashion, stress a proactive approach to students' learning needs, capitalize on technology, and emphasize a continuum of students with learning needs.

A number of simple strategies can be used in social studies programs that evoke UDL principles. These include lecture notes placed on website and/or handouts; the use of advanced and graphic organizers; content enhancement strategies; study guides; the use of assistive technology; assessment variance that may use, for example, more frequent tests on more limited material or alternative response formats; class presentations characterized by clarifying, repeating, and encouraging question asking; and adapted reading level options.

The use of "choice" is one method of working with students with disabilities (e.g., Kerr & Nelson, 2010) as well as all students. For students who do well with teacher–student decision-making tasks, the use of choice as a UDL can be considered when trying to meet the needs of diverse students in a general education classroom. Employing choice, teachers might consider the use of "menus" to structure activities and evaluations of their students. Menus come in a variety of forms. For example, the use of a "tic-tac-toe menu" is a common option for teachers. This menu "is a basic menu with a total of eight predetermined choices and one free choice for students" (Westphal, 2009, p. 6). Westphal (2009) recommended that teachers who use a tic-tac-toe menu create each choice box with the same (a) level of difficulty, (b) weight for grading, and (c) expectation for completion time and effort. She continued by stating that this menu is flexible (can cover one topic in depth or several lesson objectives) as well as easy for students to understand and efficient for teachers to use.

Graphic Organizers. An important strategy to consider in social studies instruction is the use of graphic organizers (GOs). Ciullo et al. (2015) noted that "graphic organizers are visual displays that arrange words using boxes, cells, arrows, or other visual cues picked key concepts in a comprehensible format" (p. 16). GOs can help to inform the learner regarding purpose and topics to learn, provide organization to instructional lessons,

Main Ideas	Germany	United States	Similarities	Differences
Targets	Jews, Roma, persons with disabilities	African Americans		
Strategies	Property theft, concentration camps, Holocaust, extermination	Voting denial, housing and transportation access, human rights denied, lynching		
Organized groups	Nazi Party Related national groups	State and local governments, Ku Klux Klan		

Big Idea: Racism was widely practiced in both countries with dehumanizing strategies.

FIGURE 10–1 Racism in 1930s

support curriculum adaptation and augmentation, and facilitate student participation through group formats. A simple graphic organizer to promote knowledge acquisition in the context of a comparison and contrast task is presented (partially completed) in Figure 10-1.

Graphic organizers can help focus on big ideas (as discussed above) for social studies instruction Consistent with elements in Figure 10-2, the graphic organizer can provide for an overriding statement of the big idea question, opportunity for individuals to identify the people or groups involved, a way to identify key vocabulary, a framework to identify the events that relate to the big idea, and then a conclusion that enables a summary to be provided in terms of the impact of this particular idea/initiative (Ciullo et al., 2015).

In research on GOs and students with learning disabilities, Dexter and Hughes (2011) reported increases in vocabulary knowledge, comprehension, and inferential knowledge. Consistent with research on effective instruction, it should also be noted that students must be explicitly taught how to use GOs (e.g., how concepts are related, how to combine information to frame the picture of the content being learned). The benefits of graphic organizers and other content enhancement strategies have also been demonstrated in the teaching of history (e.g., Bulgren, Deshler, & Lenz, 2007; Williams et al., 2007).

Depending upon the use and student responsiveness, Ciullo et al. (2015) highlighted that graphic organizers can be used collaboratively where students work with teachers and filling in the components or can be used as a way for students to

research information and complete graphical boxes. Much of the research on social studies comprehension through the use of graphic organizers has occurred at the secondary level. Nevertheless, the challenges for success with informational text and social studies are often significant as well at the upper elementary school level, and hence GOs should be considered across grade levels. Graphic organizers are also a key component of content enhancement strategies discussed below.

Content Enhancement. The prior discussion of big ideas provides a context for the use of content enhancement and content enhancement routines. Content enhancement has been advocated especially for learners with special needs because of their apparent lack of prior knowledge, possible attention and memory problems, confusion with concepts, and challenges related to the lack of clarity concerning curricular relevance. A number of content enhancement techniques is available to teachers to use in social studies.

Bulgren and colleagues (Bulgren, 2004; Bulgren et al., 2013) discussed the value of formal content enhancement routines that provide an organizational structure for students in understanding information to be learned. Content enhancement routines include advance organizers, graphic organizers, embedded strategy steps, interactive learning, study guides, charts, outlines, visual-spatial displays, and mnemonics, which have been found to improve student performance and are supported by analyses from the What Works Clearinghouse.

One example of a content enhancement routine is the question exploration routine (Bulgren et al., 2013).

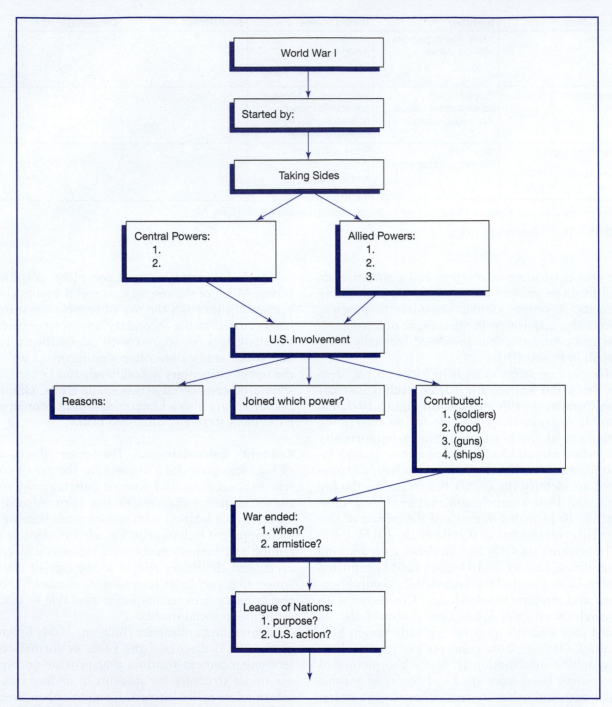

FIGURE 10–2 Graphic Organizer for World War I

It "supports the comprehension of key ideas and details, and analysis of sources, summarization of central ideas and how they develop, determination of causes and effects, an explanation of understandings" (p. 22). Using this routine, the teacher works with students to answer the following within the construct of a graphic organizer (adapted from Bulgren et al., 2013):

- What is the critical question?
- What are key terms and explanations? (comprehending key ideas, details)

- What are supporting questions and answers? (analyzing sources, evaluating effects)
- What is the main idea answer? (summarizing central ideas)
- How can we use the main idea? (analyzing, comparing sources)
- Is there an overall [big] idea? Is there a real-world use? (evaluating claims and reasoning)

ENHANCEDetext
video example 10.3
Watch this video to learn more about varied strategies for promoting learning in social studies.

Mnemonic Strategies. Mnemonic strategies are useful for helping students deal with vocabulary, terminology, and other label tasks that are associated with social studies instruction. Such instruction utilizes memory devices to increase knowledge and retention. Mnemonic strategies have been used in special and general education for decades as a way to convert difficult-to-remember concepts into more memorable ones (Lubin & Polloway, 2016). Lubin and Polloway further noted that "mnemonic strategies can be used across subject areas in lessons where new vocabulary, technical terms, the names of people places or things, number patterns and formulae need to be learned. . . . [It] has utility for any academic task that requires factual recall . . . and has been found to be effective in enhancing performance across subject areas (Therrein, Taylor, Hosp, Kaldenberg, & Gorsh, 2011)" (p. 6).

Lubin and Polloway (2016) noted in their review that "acquiring and retaining social studies concepts tend to be a great challenge for students with disabilities. Many students with LD lack the skills needed to extract information from expository text (Hall, Kent, McCulley, Davis, & Wanzek, 2013) and lack a retrieval strategy. . . . Mnemonic instruction has proven not only to promote the acquisition of social studies content but make abstract information more concrete . . . . [It] goes beyond teaching the concepts; it provides students with specific strategies to retrieve information at a later date. Therefore, mnemonic instruction is an appropriate tool to use in the social studies classrooms as it gives students with disabilities the opportunity to acquire content knowledge, make causal connections and learn a retrieval strategy that can be used beyond the classroom" (p. 12).

Scruggs et al. (2011) recommended the use of a variety of mnemonic strategies with the most commonly used ones in social studies instruction being linguistic (e.g., keywords), first letter, and visual (or pictographic) mnemonics. Lubin and Polloway (2016) reported that students tend to be most familiar with the use of acronyms and acrostics and found them to be most helpful (McCabe, Osha, & Roche, 2013), while keywords are the most frequently cited strategy used in educational research with students with disabilities. Common and effective mnemonic strategies are discussed below.

First-Letter Mnemonics First-letter mnemonics include acronyms and acrostics. As Mastropeiri and Scruggs (2010) stated, first-letter "strategies can be used for remembering lists of things. For example, the HOMES strategy prompts recall of the names of the Great Lakes . . . if students are familiar enough with the names of the Great Lakes that thinking of a single letter will prompt the entire name" (p. 243). Table 10-4 and Table 10-5 present sample social studies acrostics and acronyms, respectively.

Linguistic Linguistic mnemonics include keywords, which help associate the new concept with familiar words and/or phrases to help remember the item. Mastropieri and Scruggs (2010) noted that the **keyword method** "is used to strengthen the connection between a new word and its association information. For example, the Italian word *strada* means road. To strengthen this association, the learner is first provided with a 'keyword' for the new word, *strada*. The keyword is a word that is familiar to the learner, but that sounds like the new word and is easily pictured. In this case of *strada*, a good keyword is straw. . . . Next, a picture is created of the associates interacting together" (p. 237). A picture of a road with a straw scarecrow beside it might be used. Possible keyword uses in social studies include vocabulary words and definitions, technical terms and definitions, famous people and contributions, states and nations and their capitals, and wars with causes and effects. Uberti, Scruggs, and Mastropieri (2003) noted that students with learning disabilities benefited from

TABLE 10–4   Social studies acrostics

Category	Data to Be Learned	Sample Acrostic(s)
Assassinated American Presidents	Lincoln, Garfield, McKinley, Kennedy	Lunatic gunmen maliciously killed.
Cabinet offices (in order of creation, 1–25)	State, Treasury, Defense, Justice, Interior, Agriculture, Commerce, Labor, Health/Human Services, Housing and Urban Development, Transportation, Energy, Education, Veterans' Affairs, Homeland Security	See The Dog Jump In A Circle and Leave Her House To Entertain at Virginia Homes in the Suburbs
Central America nations	Mexico, Belize, Guatemala, El Salvador, Honduras, Nicaragua, Costa Rica, Panama	My best girl, Elizabeth, has no Cocoa Puffs!
Confederate States (seceding from Union)	Virginia, North Carolina, Florida, Georgia, Texas, Mississippi, Alabama, Louisiana, Arkansas, Tennessee	Virgil needs fundamentally good teaching methods about learning ability techniques
Continents	Africa, Asia, Antarctica, Australia, South America, Europe, North America	4As simply exhibit necessity
First 16 American Presidents (in order) (Lubin & Polloway, 2016)	George Washington John Adams Thomas Jefferson James Madison James Monroe John Quincy Adams	**W**ashington **A**dams **J**ust **M**ade **M**any **A**dmirers, ====
	Andrew Jackson Martin Van Buren William Henry Harrison John Tyler	**J**uggling **V**arious **H**eavy **T**rumpets. ====
	James Polk Zachary Taylor Millard Fillmore Franklin Pierce James Buchannan Abraham Lincoln	**P**lease **T**ry **F**ollowing **P**retty **B**oy's **L**egacy.
Oceans of the World	Southern, Arctic, Pacific, Indian, Atlantic	Silly Ants Play In Attics
Virginia Geographical Regions	Tidewater, Piedmont, Blue Ridge, Shenandoah Valley, Appalachians	Tim Picks Blue Stars Again

Source: Graphic Models and Instructional Tools for Students with Special Needs (p. 46), by E. A. Polloway & J. Lubin, 2016, *Lynchburg College Journal of Special Education*, Lynchburg College, Lynchburg, VA. Used with permission.

TABLE 10–5   Social studies acronyms

Category	Data to Be Learned	Sample Acronym
Continents	Africa, Asia, Antarctica, Australia, North America, South America, Europe	4ANSE
Great Lakes	Huron, Ontario, Michigan, Erie, Superior	HOMES
Virginia Rivers of Chesapeake Bay Watershed	James, Potomac, Rappahannock, York	J-PRY
WWI Powers Allied Powers Central Powers	France, Italy, Russia, England Turkey, Austria-Hungary, Germany	FIRE TAG

Source: Graphic Models and Instructional Tools for Students with Special Needs (p. 48), by E. A. Polloway & J. Lubin, 2016, *Lynchburg College Journal of Special Education*, Lynchburg College, Lynchburg, VA. Used with permission.

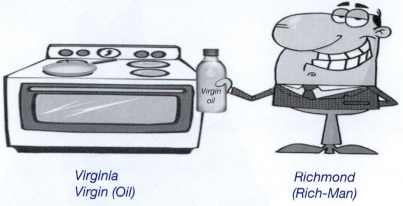

Virginia
Virgin (Oil)

Richmond
(Rich-Man)

FIGURE 10–3   Keywords for Virginia State Capital

Source: Lubin, J., & Polloway, E.A. (2016). Mnemonic instruction in science and social studies for students with learning disabilities: A review. *Learning Disabilities: A Contemporary Journal, 14 (2)*, p. 212.

keyword method more than other students so that their achievement matched that of the students who were non-disabled. Figure 10-3 and Figure 10-4 illustrate the use of keywords in learning state capitals of two selected states.

Visual Mnemonics Visual mnemonics, including pictographics, use pictures or visualizations to create an association to the target concept. Mastropeiri and Scruggs (2010) noted that teachers can create a picture that helps the student remember the concept or words that are being learned. "Mnemonic pictures are not difficult to create and, once created, can be used again and again to improve students' memory of important content. In some cases, materials have already been created" (p. 244). Figure 10-5 provides a sample visual (pictographic) mnemonic.

There is consistent evidence that mnemonic instruction is helpful for students with disabilities to learn and recall social studies facts and concepts. Further, students not only learn content but also appear to be more motivated to do so. However, it needs to be emphasized that mnemonic instruction is effective only if used for the intended purpose of helping students remember (Lubin & Polloway, 2016).

Study Skills.   Study skills in various forms make up an essential component of effective instruction in social studies. Its importance is evidenced by the fact that we have devoted an entire chapter to the topic (see Chapter 12). When it is determined that a student has problems with certain study skills, those skills need to be taught explicitly. Instruction should be based on present levels of educational performance that are established through valid assessment and related to goals that should be included in the student's IEP.

Classroom Adaptations.   A number of techniques can be implemented that will enhance the probability that students with special needs will learn social studies content. Table 10-6 provides recommendations for accommodating student needs as a function of the

Connect

Connecticut
(Connect)

Hartford
(Heart)

FIGURE 10–4   Keywords for Connecticut State Capital

Source: Lubin, J., & Polloway, E.A. (2016). Mnemonic instruction in science and social studies for students with learning disabilities: A review. *Learning Disabilities: A Contemporary Journal, 14 (2)*, p. 212.

▶ **ENHANCEDetext**
video example 10.4
Watch this video to learn more about enhancing recall in social studies via flash cards.

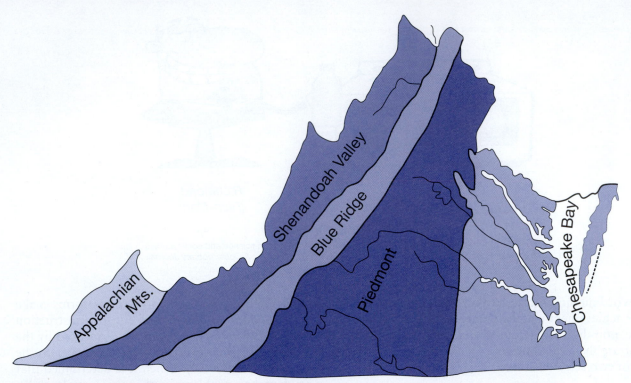

FIGURE 10–5 Virginia Geographical Regions (left to right) Always Search Before Pitching a Tantrum

Source: Hall, E. (n.d.). *Geographical regions of Virginia.* Unpublished manuscript, Lynchburg College, VA. Used with permission.

typical types of demands and activities encountered in the social studies classroom across grade levels.

Strategies for enhancing textbook use were outlined by Munk, Bruckert, Call, Stoehrmann, and Radant (1998), who suggested that teachers (a) prioritize materials to reduce the amount and complexity of the text, (b) pre-teach vocabulary words prior to reading the assignments so that decoding and comprehension may be enhanced, and (c) paraphrase passages or have students retell

---

TEACHER *Tips*   **Secondary Level**

The Institute of Education Sciences (2013) (based on Vaughn, Swanson, Roberts, Wanzek, Stillman-Spisak, Solis, & Simmons, 2013) favorably reviewed and evaluated the program of *Promoting Acceleration of Comprehension and Content through Text* (PACT). PACT is an instructional practice that includes five interrelated components the teachers use over the course of a 10-day unit:

- *Comprehension canopy:* an overarching question is introduced on day one and reviewed each day is new knowledge is gained.
- *Essential words:* 4 to 5 key terms are introduced and then reviewed throughout the unit.
- *Knowledge acquisition:* each day, students read in various settings (whole class, small group, paired,

and individually) and record notes from their readings and teacher presentations in a log.

- *Team-based learning comprehension check:* students complete regular multiple-choice and open-ended knowledge checks. Students complete the questions on their own and then verify their answers and groups, using resource materials to answer questions, when necessary.
- *Team-based learning knowledge acquisition:* at the end of the unit, students engage in debate, requiring students to use textual evidence, think critically, evaluate team members contributions, synthesize perspectives, present a final written product to the entire class, and respond to feedback. (p. 1)

TABLE 10–6 Adaptation techniques

Instructional Practice	Area of Concern	Suggestion
Textual materials	Readability	• Use other content-area books that cover the same material—lower readability. • Have the text put on tape (e.g., Recordings for Blind). • Use supplemental reading materials that can be read for access to content. • Use peer-directed grouping.
	Vocabulary	• Introduce new words and terminology prior to students encountering this material. • Use teacher-generated glossaries. • Incorporate various word acquisition practices (e.g., card games).
	Comprehension	• Preview textual material with students (e.g., identify key terms, concepts). • Discuss all pictures, figures, tables, and graphs. • Use advanced organizers. • Use reading guides. • Use semantic maps and other graphic organizers. • Ensure that students have competencies in skimming and scanning. • Help students learn how to go through the text more than once for different purposes. • Discuss what was read.
Class lectures	Attention	• Teach self-monitoring techniques. • Use self-monitoring aids (e.g., checklists). • Make sure that lectures are not too long or complex (i.e., break up into briefer segments). • Infuse lectures with discussion and other engaging activities.
	Comprehension	• Provide students with advanced notes, PowerPoint slides, various types of graphic organizers, or general outlines of what is to be covered. • Introduce new terminology before lecturing. • Discuss all graphics that are presented in class.
	Note taking	• Teach note-taking skills. • Provide teacher-prepared notes/outlines that contain missing information that must be filled in during the lecture.
Instructional materials	Procedural issues	• Ensure that students know how to use the materials and equipment. • Develop criteria or qualifications for using certain equipment (e.g., utility knives).
	Conceptual difficulties	• Teach map and globe skills. • Preview and discuss all vocabulary and concepts that might be problematic.
Projects	Following directions	• Clearly presented instructions and verify understanding—always provide directions in written format.
	Self-direction	• Monitor progress. • Set up intermediate deadlines. • Use cooperative group projects if individual work is not possible.
	Content development	• Require outlines from students soon after giving the assignment. • Allow variant formats for a final product—capitalizing on student strengths and interests. • Have students submit drafts of their work prior to the final product.
Media	Vocabulary	• Introduce and discuss new vocabulary and terminology prior to viewing.

(continued)

TABLE 10–6 *(continued)*

Instructional Practice	Area of Concern	Suggestion
	Comprehension	• Allocate time to discuss background information and context prior to viewing.
		• Use various graphic aids when viewing.
		• Discuss key points after viewing.
Web-based activities	Procedural issues	• Make sure that students know how to access the sites and information you prescribe.
		• Choose websites that are well designed and easy to navigate.
		• Teach students to use bookmarks and ways to organize their bookmarks so that they can retrieve important information.
	Comprehension	• Provide graphic aids to assist students in acquiring the appropriate information.

what they have read after each paragraph or page. Teachers may want to supplement the reading of content with taped texts.

Because textbooks are used so widely in social studies education, certain techniques may be needed to help students with special needs deal with these materials. Lovitt and Horton (1991) recommended a number of techniques for adapting textbook material, including the following:

- **Advanced organizers**—written material or oral discussion related to textual material to be read
- **Study guides**—selected important information from the textual material, usually in the form of questions or statements that help guide students' understanding of the material
- **Vocabulary drills**—timed activities in which students relate terms to their appropriate definitions
- **Graphic organizers**—graphic representations of key information (e.g., vocabulary or content), including visual-spatial illustrations

Peer-Mediated Learning. Cooperative learning arrangements have been found useful for increasing achievement, student involvement, and motivation (Manning & Lucking, 1991) and recommended for students with special needs (Carin, Bass, & Contant, 2005). Social studies can utilize activities that are ideal for creating opportunities for students to work together cooperatively. Most of the various cooperative learning methods (e.g., jigsaw, teams-games-tournaments) can be used to develop effective instruction. Peer tutoring, including class-wide peer tutoring, also represents an important peer-mediated strategy in social studies.

Technology-Based Instruction. Technology is used extensively in education. The growing amount of innovative media and online resources offers intriguing interactive possibilities for engaging social studies topics. The possibilities of using the Internet for instructional purposes are almost endless. It is possible to find websites that address virtually any topic, thus providing a way to enrich instruction. Computers, tablets, and smartphones are well suited for use in social studies. One of the most exciting uses of these devices relates to its interactive capability.

With digital technology readily available, more options are now available in terms of innovative, alternative products that students can pursue to demonstrate skill and knowledge acquisition. Westphal (2009, p. 25) suggested a number of products because of their flexibility in meeting the needs of diverse children. She categorized these products as being visual (e.g., crossword puzzles, advertisement, book cover), kinesthetic (e.g., play, model, bulletin board display), or auditory (e.g., speech, interview) in nature.

One social studies–relevant product is the Web-Quest, which provides online learning activities whereby teachers and students engage in inquiry-based learning to develop links that take students on a "quest" for information. In their book *Using WebQuests in the Social Studies Classroom*, Thombs, Gillis, and Canestrari (2009) instructed teachers on the mechanics of creating this product. Careful use of QuestGarden (an online tool that guides teachers and students through the construction of a WebQuest) is a helpful tool to integrate technology in the classroom (Dodge, 2005). Thombs and her colleagues emphasized that

WebQuest is a flexible, problem-solving strategy that can "transport students from the present to the past and back or in and out of personal and cultural connections to the social sciences" (p. 20).

Another example of a technology option is the Virtual History Museum (VHM), which provides a series of short Internet readings that are presented by computer, an opportunity to observe historical documents, and promotion of discussion (Okolo, Englert, Bouck, Heutsche, & Wang, 2011). Bouck et al. (2009) noted that VHM provides a universally designed approach to social studies instruction. It provides support to students with disabilities and scaffolding so that they can increase both their participation as well as ultimately their achievement within social studies. As Bouck et al. (2009) noted, the teacher acts as a curator for the students as they explore the virtual museum. Among the areas available for study are American history, world history, geography, aspects of culture, history of individual states, and other areas related to social studies.

Additional computers can be used in social studies to promote content enrichment. A substantial amount of media exists that can be used to supplement what is being taught in social studies classes. Some software that has been designed to show simulations and creating maps/timelines are particularly useful (some examples can be found in Table 10-7).

Media. Teaching social studies can involve many different instructional practices. Within the classroom setting, teachers can employ discussions, demonstrations, and learning centers. The efficient use of media is another way of making content

TABLE 10–7 Sample computer applications

- Word processing/desktop publishing: school newspapers, reports
- Databases: data on community demographics, information on legislators, CD-ROM encyclopedias
- Spreadsheets on economic trends, census data
- Graphs/charts on demographic information
- Electronic field trips
- Online databases

interesting and instructionally relevant. A substantial number of videotapes, films, and digitized media are also available for instructional use. Russell (2007) indicated that 100% of social studies teachers reported using films at least once a month to help teach content. Other studies indicate that the use of film in the social studies classroom is even more frequent—once a week (e.g., Stoddard & Marcus, 2006). Given that the use of film is a common practice in the general education classroom, some attention is given to this aspect of teaching social studies. Teachers may wish to consider using an entire film or clips from a film to enhance the knowledge and understanding of a concept. In doing so, careful consideration should be given to the Motion Picture Association of America (MMPA) rating given to the film or documentary as well as the age appropriateness of the film. Table 10-8 illustrates some films that might be used in a social studies classroom.

To maximize the use of this film in the classroom, Russell (2009) suggested that teachers should employ a four-stage model when utilizing film as part of their instructional technology. This model requires that teachers consider (a) preparing

TEACHER *Tips*   Elementary Level

Cultural immersion is an approach to immerse students in a culture. For example, if the topic under consideration is a particular foreign country and its culture, then students might be introduced to its food, dress, music, and any other identifiable characteristics.

Sensoy (2010) provided an example of how to combine culture and with a first day of school activity. The example is based on Michel's (1998) article titled "What's in a Name?" in *American Indian*:

"Michel described the Ho-Chunk naming ceremony, and her own Ho-Chunk name, *Wakanchunk mahnee* (Holy Walker) given by her grandfather" (p. 155).

An activity called "What's in a Name?" can be introduced to the elementary or secondary students. The lesson may focus on history as well as culture and how it relates to surnames as well as nicknames. Students might research their own surnames and determine their origin and what they meant to their ancestors.

TABLE 10–8 Films to enhance secondary social studies instruction

Subject Being Taught	MPAA Rating	Example of Film
Poverty and homelessness	Not Rated	*From Homeless to Harvard: The Liz Murray Story*
	PG	*August Rush*
	PG-13	*The Pursuit of Happyness*
Women's rights/suffrage	Not Rated	*Iron Jawed Angels*
Nonviolence/religion	PG	*Gandhi*
Animal rights	PG-13	*Gorillas in the Mist: The Story of Dian Fossey*
Consumerism	Not Rated	*Walmart: The High Cost of Low Prices*
	PG	*Confessions of a Shopaholic*
Integration	Not Rated	*I Sit Where I Wanta: The Legacy of Brown v. Board of Education*

the lesson plan as well as adhering to the legal requirements for showing a film in the classroom, (b) previewing the film prior to presenting it to a class of students, (c) watching the film with the students, and (d) presenting a culminating activity after the film is watched. This model should be studied if students with special needs are to reap the benefits of this technology. Ensuring that the film is presented for a purpose and that the instruction is taking place is of the utmost importance.

Field Experiences. Field experiences (i.e., field trips) for many teachers may conjure up unpleasant memories (e.g., kids too hyped up, gift shops). However, appropriate use of this type of learning activity can enrich the world knowledge of many students with limited experiential backgrounds. Field experiences involve planning and preparation: instructional objectives should be identified, students should be told what to look for, and follow-up discussions should be scheduled. For example, a trip to a local cemetery can lead to a fascinating discussion of history and local culture.

Service Learning. Service learning is fast becoming a practice with promising evidence to support its use. Kaye (2010) stated that "*service learning can be defined as a research-based method where guided or classroom learning is applied through action that addresses an authentic community need in a process that allows for youth initiative and provides structured time for reflection on the service experience and demonstration of acquired skill and knowledge*" (p. 9). By engaging classrooms and

schools in community involvement projects, students learn civic responsibility as well experiencing the social studies curriculum authentically through social action. Kaye outlined several kinds of service learning initiatives that can be implemented. They include the following:

- **Direct Service**—Direct service projects have students engaged in activities that directly affect and involve other adults or children. An example might be the tutoring of young children or helping military families package care boxes for deployed family members.
- **Indirect Service**—Indirect service projects benefit communities or environmental efforts but do not involve direct contact with recipients (e.g., donating clothing or food for individuals who are homeless). Usually, these projects require team efforts so a whole class can participate by taking leadership roles, exhibiting planning and organizational skills, and working collaboratively with others.
- **Advocacy**—This category requires that students have a certain amount of knowledge regarding issues in their community or government. Teaching students to meet and talk to their state senators with regard to particular issues is one form of advocacy. Students can write letters, sponsor a town meeting, and speak publically about issues they wish to promote.
- **Research**—Research-based service learning projects provide ways to combine Social Studies with other subject areas such as science. For example, students might team up with scientists to test local water reservoirs for safe drinking

water. Based on information collected, these projects require students to develop the science experiment, create a hypothesis, test the hypothesis, and write a report on the findings. The findings might be beneficial to the whole community. (p. 11)

 Check Your Understanding 10.3 Click here to gauge your understanding of the concepts in this section.

ACTIVITIES

1. Obtain pictures of different people in the community, show one picture, and have students discuss what that person does, how the person is important to the community, and what would happen if this person did not do the job. Students need to be aware of sources of help in the community. Examples can include police officers, postal workers, doctors, and rescue squads.

2. To develop awareness of societal values, discuss the Declaration of Independence and the Bill of Rights of the Constitution. List specific values, rights, and responsibilities on the board. Discuss applications to the school setting.

3. Grandparents are an often-overlooked treasure of information. A great way to investigate history is to ask them about past events. Students might also request autobiographical information from them.

4. For additional work on map skills, have students make maps of their neighborhoods. If cameras are available, have students take pictures of various significant sites.

5. Develop a unit on tools. Other subject-area content can be easily incorporated into it (e.g., science, career education). Have students study the tools used by workers in different vocations today and in times past.

6. Another neighborhood-based activity to assist students in refining their map and directional skills is a walk rally—similar in format to a road rally. Give students directions (e.g., written prompts, pictures) that they must

use to follow a pre-planned course. They are to answer questions along the way and ultimately reach a designated destination.

7. To assist students with map work and learning the location and capitals of the 50 states, enlarge a map to fit on a bulletin board. Then make cards that have a state's name on one side and the capital on the other, within an outline of the shape of the state. Have students match the outline of the state on the map with the name on the card and then identify the capital. They can check themselves.

8. To help students remember the great amount of information found in a social studies curriculum, mnemonic strategies are great aids. For example, if memorizing the capitals of the 50 states, sayings like the following can help: Charles Ton lives west of his friend, the Rich Man (Charleston, West Virginia, and Richmond, Virginia).

9. Study cards can help special needs learners prepare for exams. On one side of an index card, print the important event, name, or place covered in the chapter. On the back, make a mark of any sort to use as a key. On another card, print information that explains, defines, or identifies the word printed on the first card. Place the same symbol on the back of this second card. Students can then study at school or at home by reading the study cards and matching them. The cards are self-checking, provide instant reinforcement, and let students work on information in small, manageable pieces.

10. Combine practice of written expression and reference skills by having your class make a travel brochure for a state or region of study. Have students use library sources to gather interesting information about a specific area, tourist attraction, or culture found within this region. Then have them prepare a paragraph that highlights the facts and sparks interest in visiting that spot. They can also find pictures that add meaning to their writing. Both pictures and paragraphs can be cut, pasted, and copied to make a brochure for all to read.

11. Have students conduct opinion polls on several topics. This exercise requires students to use various data-gathering and interpretive skills.

LEARNING OUTCOMES

Upon completion of this chapter, the reader should be able to:

11.1 Discuss the nature of the science curriculum and identify the major challenges that science may pose to students with learning challenges.

11.2 Identify ways to assess science performance.

11.3 Discuss effective instructional practices related to science education for students with special needs.

Science is a major subject area along with language arts, math, and social studies. It is knowledge, facts, concepts, principles, theories, and laws; it also is process and methodology. During the elementary grades, science introduces students to critical content and concepts on which more advanced courses in this area are based. Furthermore, science develops skill sets that will be tapped in later coursework as well as in life outside of school.

Science is very much a part of everyone's daily life. It includes topics that can have a major impact on our personal, family, workplace, and community needs, and, as Sunal and Sunal (2003) stressed, "it is the right of all citizens to be scientifically literate, since literacy affects the quality of life of every person" (p. 262). Science should be made meaningful to students in a long-term sense as well as relevant to their current needs.

Students are typically curious about their surroundings and about the people and things inhabiting them. As a result, they have a natural interest in seeking information about their environment and the events occurring within it. Teachers should take advantage of this curiosity by exposing students to science topics that capitalize on their interests and backgrounds. This subject area is rich with topics and issues that provide wonderful opportunities for active student involvement and ways to relate knowledge and skills to students' everyday lives.

Teaching science can be exciting and rewarding. Few subject areas are as inherently interesting to teach, actively involve students as much, and can be made as relevant to students of diverse backgrounds. However, not every student will share this enthusiasm. Even though many students are stimulated when presented with an engaging science program, others are not and may require other engagement strategies.

While science may be one of the most fascinating subjects to teach, it is also one with unique challenges for teachers. The following example, although it involves a student with advanced language skills, illustrates both points:

> I was invited to go on a "reef walk" with a class of gifted third and fourth graders. While we were wading in some shallow water, we came upon a familiar marine organism called a "feather duster." Being cognizant of being with a group of young students but forgetting that they were students with vocabularies which were well advanced of their non-gifted peers, I was about ready to say something like "Look how that thing hangs on the rock." Before I could get my highly descriptive statement out, one of the students offered the following: "Notice how securely anchored the organism is to the stationary coral." All I could say was "Yes, I do." (Blackbourn, Patton, & Trainor, 2004, p. 213)

How exciting to be out on a reef actually seeing, touching, and experiencing nature, but how threatening to realize that a student may know more about something than you do or that someone may ask you a question for which you do not have an immediate answer. Many teachers who do not have extensive science training express reservations about teaching science. Nevertheless, by using effective instructional techniques, by refusing to feel intimidated by the subject itself, and by recognizing the intriguing aspects of this subject area, teachers can provide dynamic and socially valid science programs.

SCIENCE CURRICULUM AND STUDENTS WITH SPECIAL NEEDS

Content of Science Instruction

Different sources yield different goals for science education. Consider the following four goal clusters for science education:

- Science for meeting personal needs
- Science for resolving societal problems
- Science for career awareness
- Science for preparation for further study (Yager, 1989, p. 151)

Though all of these goal clusters may be appropriate for students with special needs, some are likely to be more important than others for certain students.

On an instructional level, three major objectives are woven throughout science education: the acquisition of relevant content and knowledge, the development of inquiry-related skills, and the nurturing of a scientific attitude. Many of us have experienced science instruction that focused largely on content acquisition with little opportunity for hands-on activities. However, currently more emphasis is given to the importance of skill acquisition and activity-oriented instruction. These objectives are all important, and none should be emphasized to the detriment of the others.

Although one might suggest that science is every place we cast our attention, science can be organized into three general areas:

- Life science (the study of living things, including biology, zoology, botany, and ecology)
- Physical science (the study of non-living things, including chemistry and physics)
- Earth/environmental science (the study of topics, including astronomy, meteorology, oceanography, and geology)

In extracting the key initiatives set forth in a series of national standards documents, Sandall (2003) identified the following common recommendations:

- Scientific literacy is for all students.
- Science is active, hands-on learning and in-depth study of fewer topics.
- Science should emphasize critical thinking, problem solving, and developing mathematics and science as a way of thinking and reasoning.
- Science should emphasize integration and interdisciplinary activities.
- Science should emphasize application of science, mathematics, and technology to real-life situations. (p. 18)

Gurganus, Janas, and Schmitt (1995) suggested that a set of common themes or concepts exists that can serve as a guide for what should be covered in science education. These concepts include systems (life in an aquarium), models (model of the heart), scale (amount of moisture in air), change (seasons), stability (phases of the moon), diversity (fingerprints), structure/function (types of teeth), matter (dissolving solids into liquids), and energy (heat produced through friction).

Recently, the Next Generation Science Standards (NGSS, 2016) were announced, based on the National Research Council's framework for K–12 science education. NGSS addresses the STEM disciplines (science, technology, engineering, mathematics). The focus of the standards is on core concepts and major ideas related to scientific inquiry and on students thinking critically and solving problems as related to an understanding of concepts within science. Visit the NGSS website for more details.

A vast number of topics could be incorporated into a science curriculum, but given the trend to cover fewer topics while spending more time on individual topics, one must select topics to the exclusion of others. It is possible to address major concepts by selecting appropriate related units of study.

During the elementary years, the topics (as derived from Delta Science Modules II) represented in Table 11-1 are typically incorporated in varying degrees into the classes.

The importance of quality science programs at the elementary level is generally recognized because this level of science instruction provides the foundation in skills, knowledge, and attitudes for further science study that supports a sound science education program. Cawley, Foley, and Miller (2003) identified four curricular models that can be found at the elementary level:

- **Spiral curriculum**—textbook-driven approach where topics are repeated each year—common model of science instruction at the elementary level.
- **Intensified curriculum**—more in-depth coverage of fewer topics—more hands-on, activity oriented.
- **Integrated curriculum**—combines two or more areas that are used as the basis of the curriculum.
- **Theme-based curriculum**—approach is organized according to broad-based themes.

Most elementary programs follow a spiral curriculum orientation. In this curricular structure, the curriculum is driven by the textbook series that has been adopted. For example, a topic like plants will be introduced at an early grade level and covered a number of times in subsequent grades in more conceptually complex ways. Table 11-1 illustrated how topics are repeated across grade levels.

The nature of science programs for students at the secondary level will depend on the program

TABLE 11-1 Modules for elementary students

Grades	Life	Earth	Physical
K–1	From seed to plant Observing an aquarium	Finding the moon Sunshine and shadows	Investigating water properties
2–3	Using your senses Butterflies and moths Classroom plants Plants and animals	Amazing air Weather watching Soil science	Force and motion Length Sink or float? States of matter
3–5	Animal behavior Dinosaur classification Food chains and webs Insect life Plant/animal life cycle Small things and microscopes	Earth movements Solar system Water cycle Weather instruments	Electrical circuits Looking at liquids Magnets Measuring Powders and odors Sound
5–6	Fungi—small wonders Pollution Pond life You and your body	Erosion Oceans Rocks and minerals Solar energy Weather forecasting	Color and light Electromagnetic lenses and mirrors Simple machines
6–8	DNA: from genes to protein Plants in our world	Astronomy Earth moon and sun Earth processes	Chemical interaction Electrical conduction Newton's toy

orientation these students are following. If students are in the general education curriculum, they will take courses such as life science/biology, physical science, chemistry, physics, and earth science. If students are in a curriculum that affords access to the general education curriculum but is not provided in an inclusive setting, materials and procedures may not differ significantly from those used in the general education setting; however, different textbooks might be used and different activities conducted.

If students with special needs are in an alternative curriculum, they may be exposed to functional science content that is completely related to life skills or technical/vocational applications. Science provides a great opportunity to link classroom instruction to real-life topics. It has functional importance in the lives of students; that is, it includes many topics that are functional in nature.

Science Instructional Considerations for Students with Special Needs

Students with special needs are being exposed to science more so than in the past for a number of reasons. First and foremost, IDEA mandates that students with disabilities must be provided with access to a general education curriculum that includes science. Second, each year, more students with disabilities are spending increased amounts of time in inclusive settings where they will likely have instruction in the area of science.

Science instruction must be designed for and accessible by all students, not just those who will be future scientists and certainly including students with disabilities. For decades, this was not the case. For example, Patton, Polloway, and Cronin (1994) found in their classic study of special education teachers that substantial numbers of students were not receiving any science instruction and that those who were did not have much time allocated to this subject area each week. This trend of neglect has changed dramatically for two primary reasons: a greater number of students with learning-related problems are in inclusive settings for a greater part of their instructional day (including science classes) and the mandate in IDEA that students with disabilities must have access to the general curriculum that is provided to all students.

In recent years, there has been some increased attention to science education for students with disabilities. For example, information is now presented at the What Works Clearinghouse, the Access Center presents information through the Office of Special Education Programs, and the *Journal of Science Education for Students with Disabilities* provides a forum for practice in the field of science education as related to the teaching of students who have special needs. The National Science Teachers Association (NSTA, 2004) has established a position statement and policies related to science education and students with disabilities that focuses on recommendations for overcoming educational and physical barriers, the development and use of assessment tools, and the education of science teachers about teaching students with disabilities, as well as the selection of science curriculum and the encouragement of students with disabilities to seek careers in science and science-related fields.

Science instruction can however pose some significant challenges for teachers and students with disabilities. Factors that must be recognized and addressed represent an interaction of student features and the nature of science instruction. Therrien, Taylor, Hosp, Kaldenberg, and Gorsh (2011) noted that students with disabilities may find it challenging to learn science concepts and may perform at a significantly lower level in science exams than their peers. Two noteworthy considerations include learner characteristics and instructional demands. A third consideration has to do with the preparation of teachers for science education for students with special needs. These three considerations are discussed below.

Learner Characteristics. A detailed list of some of the student characteristics that can increase the difficulty in learning science is provided in Table 11-2. The first column is a brief description of select student characteristics. The second column describes how the particular student feature can become a barrier during science instruction.

Instructional Demands. The demands of science learning for students with special needs begins with the ability to respond to the common presentation modes of text reading and class presentations given that "the main instructional strategies used in traditional general education classrooms typically include textbooks and/or lectures. Students with disabilities typically struggle to grasp concepts when these are the sole techniques used in classrooms"

TABLE 11–2 Learning characteristics and impact on science performance

Characteristic	Implications
Cognitive abilities	• Difficulties in thinking, problem solving, or reasoning • Difficulties understanding conceptually complex science content, instructions, or activities • Limited ability to acquire and use learning strategies • Problem with both working memory and long-term retrieval of information • Limited ability to analyze and evaluate one's learning-related behavior
Reading	• Limited ability to use science textbook at levels that other students are able to do • Struggle to read science lab manuals and materials • Difficulties in comprehending textual material • Limited ability to take notes on science reading material • Trouble in using other types of reading skills, such as skimming and scanning
Writing	• Limited ability in generating science lab notes • Limited ability in writing an extensive report or paper
Math	• Difficulties in understanding various math concepts used in science • Problems in performing calculations • Problems in measurement
Study skills	• Ineffective note-taking skills in science lectures • Limited ability to use science online resources • Problems in analyzing and making sense of graphs, tables, figures, and other graphically presented materials • Poor strategies for preparing for tests • Problems in organizational skills
Language	• Difficulty following and understanding material presented in science lectures • Limited ability to develop and present an oral report
Attention	• Difficulty focusing and sustaining attention to lectures • Problems following directions • Struggle with finishing work

(Therrien, Taylor, Watt, & Kaldenberg, 2014, p. 8). Therrien et al. further noted that, given that instruction often includes textbook or lecture presentations in general education classrooms as a primary method of instruction, the approach can be problematic for students who have content knowledge limitations, problems linking prior knowledge with newly presented information, and limited in motivation.

Carnine, Silbert, Kame'enui, and Tarver (2004) highlighted some characteristics of content-area textual materials that can be challenging particularly for students with reading difficulties:

- **Vocabulary**—It is usually more difficult than that used in narrative text.
- **Content**—Often the information presented is not familiar to students and can cause conceptual problems.

- **Style and organization**—There may be extensive use of headings or subheadings. Writing is very succinct and matter-of-fact.
- **Special features**—Graphics and illustrations play an important part in presentation of information.

Given the heavy reliance on the use of textbooks and the demanding features of these books, it is not a surprise that many students have difficulties with these materials. Consider as an example Table 11-3, which summarizes the vocabulary list from the more than 75 terms presented in just one seventh-grade science textbook chapter.

In addition to challenges with textual material, another instructional demand that may prove problematic for students with special needs is the ability to engage effectively in class discussions that

TABLE 11–3 Sample science textbook vocabulary

- Electrical energy
- Electrical power
- Electrical circuits
- Positive and negative charge
- Transferring charge
- Static electricity
- Conservation of charge
- Electrical fields
- Electrons
- Electric and gravitational forces
- Conductors and insulators
- Insulator materials
- Static discharge
- Atomic collisions
- Calculating electric force
- Voltage
- Amperes
- Closed loop
- and 75 other terms

Source: Buck, G. (2015). *Science vocabulary*. Unpublished manuscript, Lynchburg College, VA. Used with permission.

are frequently part of the text/lecture approach to science teaching. Further, for classes that have an activity-based focus, participation in laboratory activities may be difficult for students to learn procedures and participate in a meaningful fashion. These may present in terms of difficulties with core science-related skills. Most of these skills relate closely with the inquiry

Teacher Preparation. In the past, science was a low priority in the educational curriculum for students with special needs. However, as students with learning problems spend more of their instructional day in the general education classroom, consideration of challenges associated with science instruction becomes critically important. Science is a subject area for which states have developed content and performance standards and on which many students with special needs will be tested.

The typical general education classroom contains students with a range of diverse needs. General educators who teach science often feel unprepared to work with special learners. Many general education teachers are faced with significant challenges

in meeting the needs of students with learning and behavior problems, given the nature of the presenting problems that this group of students brings to the classroom. As Scruggs, Mastropieri, and Okolo (2008) noted in regard to students with learning disabilities, these students will need active support in order to learn.

General education teachers can be overwhelmed by the enormity of the task to provide appropriate education to students who present an array of diverse needs. Having the knowledge and skills in how to adapt or differentiate instruction for students with special learning needs is essential (Smith, Polloway, Doughty, Patton, & Dowdy, 2015). Of particular importance is the ability to make adjustments in how students are presented information (i.e., typically by the teacher) and how they respond to various instructional demands (e.g., assignments, homework).

While general education teachers may be challenged by the need to provide effective instruction to students with learning difficulties, special education teachers may more likely be challenged by the content to be taught. They need to acquire a comfort level with the subject of science. Not only will special education teachers have to teach this subject, but they will also be working with their general education colleagues in teaching this subject. Getting to a comfort level with science instruction includes a recognition that no one will ever know every science fact or even be able to recall instantaneously information that was formerly in one's memory.

Certain competencies are desirable in special education teachers who work with students with special needs in the area of science. The following list is intended as an illustrative compendium of such competencies:

- Knowledge of basic content in the area of science
- Awareness of state content and performance standards for particular grade levels
- Knowledge of various approaches to and materials for teaching science to students with special learning needs
- Ability to adapt materials and techniques to accommodate the needs of learners
- Knowledge of skills needed to plan and carry out science investigations
- Understanding of laboratory skills
- Ability to apply relevant science education research to the educational programs of special populations
- Ability to work cooperatively with other teachers in delivery of science to students with special needs

 Check Your Understanding 11.1 Click here to gauge your understanding of the concepts in this section.

ASSESSMENT IN SCIENCE

The assessment of content, process, and performance in science may pose significant difficulty for teachers of students with special needs. This difficulty surrounds the questions of what assessments are most suitable and appropriate for students with special needs.

There are multiple purposes of assessment in science, including to monitor educational progress or improvement (summative assessment), formative assessment to provide feedback to teachers and students, and accountability assessment to serve as the driving force for changes in practice. While all three purposes of assessment are important for the total

learning process (Stull, Varnum, Ducette, & Schiller, 2011), we focus here on formative assessment. Tweed (2005) noted that formative assessment provides ways in which teachers can have data that enables them to focus instruction directly on student learning. It can enable learning targets or goals to be seen as a progression within the content area.

Athanases and Achinstein (2003) observed more notable gains for lower-achieving students when formative assessment was incorporated into their regular assessment. This observation may be because in formative assessment, "students become active participants with their instructors, sharing learning goals and understanding how their learning is progressing, what steps they need to take and how to take them" (Stull et al., 2011, p. 30).

A number of formative assessment techniques exist. They may be presented in the form of curriculum-based measures, performance measures, portfolios, journals and learning logs, and other student-centered techniques. These techniques may be used to supplement or vary the traditional assessment (i.e., regular tests and quizzes that take place in many science classrooms).

Curriculum-based measurement (CBM) is used by teachers to find out how students are progressing materials learned. It generally consists of teacher-made tests that are in line with the curriculum being taught. Through CBM, a teacher observes students' performance to see whether there is need for a different instructional strategy, reteaching, individual support, and so on.

Performance-based assessment is particularly effective at evaluating student performance in an activity-based subject such as science. In performance-based assessment, the teacher employs the use of student activities, as opposed to formal tests, to assess how well students have mastered what is taught and what is expected of them. Stepanek and Jarrett (1997) suggested that in performance-based assessment, the focus is on what students can *do*, as it underscores the process of problem solving or completing complex tasks.

Portfolios represent another type of performance-based assessments. Portfolios usually involve the compilation of students' work to show their progress. Mueller (2011) described a portfolio as a "collection of a student's work specifically selected to tell a particular story about the student." This method, when used in combination with tests, provides a more complete picture of students' skills

TABLE 11–4 Suggested entries for science portfolios

- Evaluation of group presentations on given topics
- Entries on periodic student self-assessment
- Goal settings sheet at the beginning of the term
- Report on science experiments and observations
- Graphic organizer, timelines, flowcharts, and Venn diagrams as representations of science concepts
- Concept map showing the interconnectedness of various concepts
- Pretest and posttest assessing knowledge concepts such as formulas and gases (student keeping track of his or her own progress)
- Experiment log
- Reflective essay at the end of a science unit
- Teacher evaluation of student's oral science report
- Go green (sustainability) development posters
- Scientific time series investigations
- Student-selected science homework assignments
- Videotapes of student completing laboratory experiments or projects
- Parent/teacher/student science conference reports

and abilities. Special educators find this strategy particularly helpful, as it removes the weight of examinations on students with disabilities. It also allows students to showcase their best efforts without the time constraints. Table 11-4 provides examples of the types of entries that could be included in science portfolios.

Science, in particular when hands-on activities are implemented, provides a great opportunity for students to maintain records of activities in which they have been involved. This is often accomplished through the use of **journals and learning logs**. For some students with special needs, some structure and explicit instruction may be needed at first so that they get the idea of what is expected.

Rubrics are a type of performance assessment that delineates a "set of clear expectations or criteria used to help teachers and students focus on what is valued in a subject, topic, or activity" (Airasian & Russell, 2008, p. 223). A rubric may be analytic or holistic in nature; that is, it may be general or task specific. Both the analytic and holistic type of rubric can be used in the assessment of science.

 ENHANCEDetext
video example 11.1
Watch this video to learn more about assessment strategies in science.

In **self- and peer evaluations**, students engage in reflecting, making judgments, and then reporting on their peers or their own behavior, process, or work. Instruments such as checklists, Likert scales, or holistic scales, among others, may be used in self- and peer evaluations. The results of such evaluations are generally used to assess attitude and performance.

Think-alouds facilitate the thought process that the student is expected to emulate for a specific task. The teacher carries out the action as she verbalizes her thoughts. That way, the student is able to hear everything that goes on in the mind of the teacher as she does a particular task. The child is then able to model the same thought processes as he or she carries out similar tasks.

 Check Your Understanding 11.2 Click here to gauge your understanding of the concepts in this section.

SCIENCE INSTRUCTION

General Approaches to Teaching Science

A number of descriptors can be used to capture the essence of science instruction that exists in classrooms in schools today. We begin with an overview of the series of general orientations to science

Orientation	Advantages	Disadvantages
Gee-whiz science	Is engaging.	Gives only isolated bits of information.
	Provides an entry point to more in-depth science.	Should not be the only format for teaching science.
Learn-the-facts science	Gives students information with which to work.	Can lead to the presentation of meaningless and useless pieces of information.
	Allows students to formulate questions and initiate investigations.	
	Minimizes the need to look up information.	
Theoretical science	Provides students with frameworks for organizing and categorizing: what they encounter.	Can be a turnoff for students if this is the only way science is taught.
	Is not only for the brighter students.	May exceed the conceptual levels of some students.
Hands-on science	Is activity/experiment oriented.	Is more difficult to provided—many materials may be needed.
	Provides students with experience working with the materials of science.	May not dispel naive misconceptions.
	Calls for exploration.	Requires different type of teaching behavior.
	Promotes the idea that science can be done by everyone.	
	Is fun.	
Real-life science	Provides a functional orientation to science and applies skills and concepts to actual real-life experiences. Can have a strong career-based orientation.	May not meet science standards.
		Would need to be developed as relevant to particular environments in which students will live as adults.
Big ideas	Focuses on essential concepts that undergird science content areas. Enables emphasis on core considerations rather than extraneous detail. (see also Chapter 10)	Requires effort to identify major concepts and ensure that those become the focus of instruction.
		May be challenging for sequencing units and deriving lessons.

instruction. The information is adapted and summarized from the earlier work by Saul and Newman (1986) and includes their categorical system as well as the advantages and disadvantages of each approach (see Table 11-5). The information provided in the table can provide a strategy for anticipating some of the issues that will arise for students who are in these settings.

The remainder of this section discusses approaches to providing science instruction from the perspective of how content is typically presented. The major approaches covered include the so-called textbook approach, hands-on or activities programs that emphasize inquiry in science, and integrated curriculum that illustrates the ways in which science can be tied to other subject areas.

Textbook Approach.   This traditional approach is used frequently, especially at the upper elementary and secondary levels. As Scruggs, Mastropieri, and Marshak (2011) suggested, "Textbook, or content-based science learning, involves high levels of content coverage, with very substantial amounts of vocabulary learning . . . and factual learning" (p. 445).

Teachers can use commercially published textbooks in various ways. For many, a textbook is the primary vehicle of the science program, with students regularly reading and consulting it. Class lectures and discussions often accompany the textbook approach. Another feature is regular tests. Most textbook series also now include activities for students to perform and an assortment of laboratory materials to assist them in doing so.

Textbook use has both advantages and disadvantages. They can serve as excellent teacher resources, can be of great assistance to the beginning teacher, can help organize a science program, are durable, and should be aligned with state content standards. On the other hand, they require complex literacy and study skills competence, are often abstract, typically have readability levels above the reading levels of students, and may be the only source of science information.

Mason and Hedin (2011) pointed out that science textbooks are informational texts or expository texts in that they explain information (i.e., facts, procedures). As noted earlier, students are required to engage these texts on an independent basis, which can be problematic for those students who have difficulties in reading or studying independently. Four characteristics of expository text are particularly troublesome for many students: unfamiliar text structure, the density with which concepts are introduced, complexity of the vocabulary that is covered in science texts, and assumption that students have adequate prior knowledge (Saenz & Fuchs, 2002).

Hands-On/Activity-Based Approach. Hands-on approaches to science stress the use of process and inquiry skills. They underscore doing and discovery. The National Research Council (NRC, 2000, cited by Miller & Taber-Doughty, 2014) defined inquiry as "a set of interrelated processes by which scientists and students pose questions about the natural world and investigate phenomenon; in doing so, students acquire knowledge and develop a rich understanding of concepts, principles, models, and theories" (p. 556). The NRC (2012, in Therrien et al., 2014) defined core components within activities-oriented or inquiry-based instruction as including "an emphasis on data, evidence as a foundation for claims, and the use of argumentation and analysis about evidence to develop ideas about science" (p. 16).

An initial guideline for an inquiry approach is to use a structured learning cycle when introducing activity-oriented lessons. A common inquiry model is the five E's: engagement, exploration, explanation, elaboration, and evaluation (Miller & Taber-Doughty, 2014). The engagement phase is designed so that real-life activities or problems are used to motivate the students to want to learn the content area and to assess prior knowledge of the topic. The exploration phase involves the development of hypotheses. Students generate ideas and ask questions concerning the real-life problem. Once these ideas and questions are formulated, the students explore and manipulate the contents and equipment of the problem to predict how the

problem might be addressed. The third phase of teaching is the development phase. In this phase, students gather information and make conclusions. The resources the students use to gather information are usually multimedia sources as well as qualified professionals. The final phase involves the extension phase of the students learning by applying their acquired knowledge to new or similar situations (Guillaume, Yopp, & Yopp, 1996).

Scruggs et al. (2008) noted a number of positive features for inquiry approaches including student engagement in hands-on activities, the impact on motivation, and the prospects for increased achievement. On the other hand, possible negative features include the difficulty some students have from learning from "discovery" approaches and the students' continued need for explicit instruction on concepts and vocabulary in science. In a meta-analysis of activity-based instruction with students with learning disabilities, Scruggs, Mastropieri, Berkeley, and Graetz (2010) found that an inquiry approach is generally effective for the students with disabilities.

ENHANCEDetext
video example 11.2
Watch this video to learn more about inquiry methods in science instruction.

Therrien et al. (2014) noted that inquiry approaches can be seen on a continuum from such strategies that are entirely student directed to those that are reflective of guided inquiry to structured inquiry. Some (e.g., Therrien et al., 2011) have noted that, for some students to be successful in science programs that are inquiry based, a certain degree of structure must be present. Miller and Taber-Doughty (2014) noted that guided inquiry methods are student driven but include greater emphasis on structure provided to students. In general, consistent with research on effective instruction for students with special needs, the argument can be made that structured inquiry would best address the needs of students with special needs.

Table 11-6 provides a graphic organizer contrasting these three types of inquiry programs, based on Jarrett (1999), Miller and Taber-Doughty (2014), and Therrien et al. (2011, 2014).

TABLE 11–6   Three inquiry models

Considerations	Student Centered	Guided Inquiry	Structured Inquiry
Key features	Hands-on activities Use of inquiry skills Independent work	Hands-on activities Use of inquiry skills Semi-dependent work	Hands-on activities Use of inquiry skills Teacher-directed process
Student role	Students controlling key questions to explore and decisions regarding procedures	Students controlling some key aspects, such as procedures to follow	Students respond to teacher instruction in implementation of process of inquiry
Teacher role	Teachers select overall topic for focus Provide general guidance regarding implementation	Teachers select topic, guide materials and procedures, cue students to questions for investigation and observations to be made, use prompting to lead to logical explanations	Directives from teacher regarding tasks and processes to be followed Close monitoring of implementation
Use with learners with special needs	Limited (or no) explicit instruction	May be accompanied by some explicit instruction	Explicit instruction for students to understand key vocabulary and concepts

Integrated Curriculum.   Science is an ideal subject for integration with other subject areas. Integrated programming is a powerful teaching strategy that engages students in many different ways. Some schools have fashioned entire basic skills programs around the theme of science. With reasonable effort, science can be incorporated into most curricular areas.

Interdisciplinary themes are good ways to develop *big ideas*—a concept discussed earlier in the chapter. For example, science, music, art, literature, and social science can be integrated under a common theme that will motivate students, provide opportunities to teach high-level content, and relate content to real life (Savage & Armstrong, 1996). The major objective of this type of programming is to integrate science and other subject and skill areas.

This curricular option focuses on working other subjects and skills areas into science. One example of how this can be done involves an integrated science unit of study, as depicted in Table 11-7. This unit on marine biology utilizes many different activities from other areas. Science serves as the backdrop, but much of the school day is devoted to the integration of other subject and skills areas into ongoing science-themed instruction.

Several areas merit further note. The relationship of mathematics to science is apparent, as exemplified by the availability of commercial materials that link these two areas: *Activities for Integrating Math and Science*, *Great Expectations in Math and Science*, and *Teaching Integrated Mathematics and Science*. However, other areas relate well too.

Many science topics involve art-related activities or can be followed up by art activities. For example, in a unit titled "Life of Beans and Peas" (from Elementary Science Study materials), students typically keep regular drawings of plant development. They also might use non-sprouted beans in an art project.

In addition, language arts can be worked into science very easily. In the integrated study of marine biology (in Table 11-7), students might be asked to produce various types of creative writing products (e.g., cinquains, haikus, acrostic poems, limericks), or they might give oral and written reports as an ongoing part of the program. Figure 11-1 is an example of a cinquain that was developed within a unit on insects. Science eventually engages most students in some type of research endeavor, which typically requires reading, vocabulary development, note taking, and outlining.

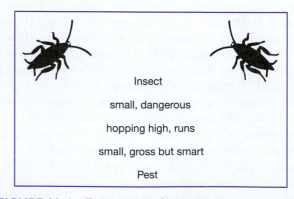

Insect

small, dangerous

hopping high, runs

small, gross but smart

Pest

FIGURE 11–1   Example of a Cinquain

TABLE 11–7 Integrated programming: marine biology example

Disciplines				
Reading	**Research**	**Written Expression**	**Oral Expression**	**Spelling**
Research/gain/locate information on individual marine animals	Brainstorming questions of interest	Whale short story	Group discussions	Functional spelling
Teacher-made handouts specific to area of study: narratives poetry	Classifying questions to five categories	Note taking	Brainstorming	Dictionary, thesaurus skills
In-class writing	Outlining	Outlining	Oral reading stories/poetry	New vocabulary
Story combining "It was a hot summer day . . ."	Drafts	Researching paper drafts editing	Oral presentations	
Class poetry book	Table of contents	Poetry, traditional, cinquain, limerick	Responses to teacher inquires	
	Referencing		Oral sharing of observations	
	Introduction/body/conclusion			

Disciplines				
Math Application	**Science**	**Social Studies**	**Visual/ Performing Arts**	**Tech Skills**
Averaging hermit crab race times	Inquiry skills	Careers related to marine biology	Rap song	Word processing
Graphing shell preferences of hermit crabs	Observation of hermit crabs	Endangered species	Individual lyrics	Marine organism database information sheet
Animal measurement	Comparisons		Class song	Printout of database
Counting of syllables/words for poetry	Classifications of species		Rhythm	Information on marine animals
Problem solving	Hypothesizing		Performance	Graphics (cross section of shoreline and ocean)
	Collecting, recording data		Seaweed pressing	
	Description		Fish printing	
	Inferencing		Rubber stamp art	
	Experimenting		Illustrations to accompany poetry/research project/stories	
	Dissection		Marine animal world/picture art	
	Research		True coloration of student-selected Hawaiian reef fish	
	Database entries			
	Fieldwork			

Many career and life skill topics can be worked into science lessons. For example, in a unit titled "Clay Boats" (from Elementary Science Study materials), a number of careers (e.g., merchant marine, stevedore) and hobbies (e.g., sailing, fishing) can be linked to the theme of the lesson and can be explored. A more extensive list of careers or hobbies that were generated for this lesson can be seen in Figure 11-2. As this lesson is typically presented to students in the elementary grades, the discussion of these careers is at the awareness level only.

Science Instructional Strategies

The focus of this section is on instructional strategies that are relevant to science instruction. Included are strategies that are appropriate practices and science education in general as well as those that are specifically apt for science instruction for students with special needs.

"Clay Boats" — Related Occupations

Boat-related	Water-related	Land-related
• Ship builder	• Fisherman	• Stevedore
• Barge pilot	• Marine biologist	• Truck driver
• Ship captain	• Oceanographer	• Fish market
• Surfboard builder	• Diver	• Grocer
• Navy/coast guard	• Scuba instructor	• Pool maintenance
• Merchant marines	• Raft guide	
• Engineer (design)	• Underwater welder	
	• Ferry driver	
	• Swimming instructor	
	• Lifeguard	

FIGURE 11-2 Sample Career Directions

Tweed (2005) identified five features of effective science instruction based on her review of research in this field. These included emphases on the motivation of students, the importance of assessing students' prior knowledge in science in order to determine their understanding of the concepts and topics studied, ensuring that they are engaged actively and intellectually in terms of the content, helping students think in a scientific fashion and helping them be more metacognitive in terms of learning science concepts, and including opportunities so that they are able to "make sense" of science information and can compare their own ideas to those of their teacher.

Universal Design for Learning. We begin with a brief reprise of the concept of universal design for learning (UDL), which was fully addressed and reiterated earlier, so it is sufficient to just note that in science, instructional practices that reflect universal design principles will be important foundation for effective programs for students with special needs. As noted previously, UDL is based on the philosophy of designing curriculum, materials and equipment, and instruction in such a way that all students with diverse needs can be included appropriately is strongly recommended. Bouck, Courtad, Heutsche, Okolo, and Englert (2009) noted that "universal design for learning focuses on creating curricular content accessible to all students . . . it is intended to remove [learning] barriers and make learning accessible" (p. 14). In science classes, tactics such as advanced organizers, study questions and guides, and graphic organizers will prove valuable to students who need such supports. Other students in the class will benefit from these materials as well. The tenets of UDL align with the underlying theme presented in McGinnis (2013) as it relates to the suitability and usability of educational facilities for all students, stating that "educational facilities must be accessible and usable by all students" (p. 47). This may be demonstrated in various forms (e.g., modifications of assessment materials, adjustment of equipment, time, provision of readers and interpreters).

Strategies for Science Lessons. Effective teaching practice incorporates variety and explicit instruction of material. Some science lessons might be devoted to discussing a topic of current interest, using educational media, reading science materials, listening to a guest speaker, going on a field trip, or carrying out activities in the classroom. However, all science lessons should be planned to accommodate individual differences and follow an organizational schema that provides a certain structure that is helpful to teachers and students.

Tweed (2005) summarized the characteristics of effective science lessons as including the quality of the *lesson design* (such as resources, planning, time, structure, and attention to student needs), the *content* (content that is significant, accurate, and appropriate for student needs; that promotes student engagement; and that reflects teacher understanding of concepts taught), *related components* (confidence of teachers, classroom management, appropriate pace, adjustment of instruction to student understanding, and questioning that enhances the ability of students to understand and solve problems), and the *classroom culture* (respect for students ideas and questions, active participation encouraged, good working relationships between teacher and students and students and students, and positive climate for encouraging ideas and questions). The nearby Teacher Tip further expands on her recommendations, addressing the content–understanding–environment framework.

The actual format of the instructional period depends to a great degree on the nature of the lesson. For most lessons, the class session can be organized into five major components: introduction, attention getting and motivation, data gathering, data processing, and closure (Cain & Evans, 1990):

- **Introduction**—The first component of a lesson should be an introduction to the day and an update on what was done previously. The primary purpose of this part of the lesson is administrative and management related. The teacher's goal should be to get the students settled, prepared, and focused. If done properly, it will serve as a nice transition to the beginning phase of the actual science lesson.
- **Attention-getting and motivating techniques**— Attention-getting and motivating techniques attempt to engage students in the lesson. They set the tone for the day's activities and should make clear to students what they are to do. The key is to activate student interest, get students to ask questions, and initiate discussion.
- **Data-gathering techniques**—This stage typically involves hands-on activities. For many special learners, some explicit instruction and supports

Content–Understanding–Environment Framework

Tweed (2005) discussed the value of the use of a *content–understanding–environment* (CUE) framework within science education. CUE is "designed to improve teachers' abilities to deliver effective instruction to diverse student learners" (p. 9). The subsequent assumption is that this model influences planning units in science and the delivery of individual lessons. Key components of the model as they relate in particular to instructional lessons in science are discussed below:

- **Content**—Effective lessons in science are able to occur only when it is clear what the "big ideas" are concerning conceptual understandings and the concepts to be included. The key is identifying important content, which includes "identifying big ideas and key concepts, unburdening the curriculum (e.g., extraneous subjects), engaging students with content, identifying preconceptions and prior knowledge,

developing assessments (how do you know that they learned), and sequencing the learning targets into a progression" (p. 14).
- **Student understanding**—This consideration focuses on "engaging students in science inquiry, implementing formative assessments, addressing preconceptions and prior knowledge, providing wrap-up and sense-making opportunities, planning for collaborative science discourse, and providing opportunities for practice, review, and revision" (p. 15).
- **Positive learning environment**—The environmental component relates to "believing all students can learn, thinking scientifically, developing positive attitudes and motivation, providing feedback, reinforcing progress and effort, and teaching students to be metacognitive" (p. 16).

---

may be needed. In an inquiry-based program, structured inquiry or guided inquiry is useful (Jarrett, 1999a). However, the emphasis is on students working individually or cooperatively in small groups and performing tasks related to the topic under study. Students should record their observations and collect data in logs or journals. Logs, which work best if they are in binders, can be enhanced by using pre-punched teacher-produced materials that help structure the assignment. Students should make entries in their logs regularly, and the logs should not be graded for handwriting, spelling, or syntactic correctness.

- **Data-processing techniques**—This part of the lesson asks students to try to make sense of the data they have collected or the activity they have performed. They must organize the data to explain the results. Data can be analyzed individually or pooled and examined on a classwide basis. This part of the lesson is an excellent time for discussion of observations, trends, and outcomes. Students can now begin to draw conclusions, make predictions, and suggest additional activities and experimentation.
- **Closure**—Allocating time to close out the lesson is important to ensure that students understand what they have been doing. This is a good time

to review the day's activities, evaluate performance, emphasize major conclusions, and relate the lesson to the real world. This time might also be used to lead into the next day's activity or other future lessons. From a classroom management perspective, it is also important to use this time to clean up by having the students take responsibility for assisting in making sure the classroom is organized.

**ENHANCEDetext
video example 11.3**
Watch this video to learn more about the importance of students understanding procedures in science lessons.

Inquiry Skills. One of the goals of science instruction is skill development, and specific inquiry-oriented skills are the heart and soul of science instruction. These skills are not only extremely useful in science but also beneficial in other areas of school and life as well. They include the following (as adapted from Cain & Evans, 1984, pp. 8–9):

- Observation: using the senses to find out about subjects and events
- Measurement: making quantitative observations

Adapting Inquiry Lesson through Self-Monitoring

An inquiry approach is commonly and effectively used in science instruction for students including those with disabilities. Miller and Taber-Doughty (2014) developed a self-monitoring strategy to assist with problem solving within an inquiry model. Students are instructed to pose the following self-questions as they monitored their own problem-solving process. The steps included having students pose the following:

- Did I ask the key question?
- Did I observe?

- Did I develop a plan?
- Did I conduct the investigation?
- Did I explain the results?

The process is assisted by an inquiry checklist provided to students so that they could self-monitor the completion of the subtasks in the process.

- Classification: grouping things according to similarities or differences
- Communication: using the written and spoken word, drawings, diagrams, or tables to transmit information and ideas to others
- Data collection, organization, and graphing: making quantitative data sensible, primarily through graphic techniques
- Inference: explaining an observation or set of observations
- Prediction: making forecasts of future events or conditions, based on observations or inferences
- Data interpretation: finding patterns among sets of data that lead to the construction of inferences, predictions, or hypotheses
- Formulation of hypotheses: making educated guesses based on evidence that can be tested

- Experimentation: investigating, manipulating, and testing to determine a result

These inquiry skills should be included regularly in science activities. Most activities require some of these skills; however, the goal is to get students to use many of them as often as possible. These skills have important immediate in-school applications and critical career and real-life implications in the future.

An example of each inquiry skill can be demonstrated from one of the subtopics from the marine biology unit of study introduced earlier in the chapter. In this unit, students worked regularly with a ready supply of hermit crabs. As can be seen in Table 11-8, all of the inquiry skills noted earlier are addressed in the lesson.

TABLE 11–8   Examples of inquiry skills

Inquiry Skill	Hermit Crab Activity
Observation	Identification of body parts
Measurement	Timing of crab races
Classification	Species identification
Communication	Description of habitat poetry
Data collection, organization, and graphing	Shells preferred by crabs
Inference	How crab attaches to inside of shell
Prediction	Location/movement of crabs as a function of time of day and tides
Data interpretation	Conclusions derived from information collected (e.g., species data)
Hypothesis generation	Generation of ideas about how often crabs change shells based on growth patterns
Experimentation	How crabs react to changes in their habitats

In addition to the challenges of teaching science to children with disabilities, a special challenge involves teaching science to such children who also come from culturally and linguistically different backgrounds. Although some studies have been devoted to the teaching of science to diverse learners, more are needed. Raborn and Daniel (1999) indicated that these children learn best when science lessons include inquiry-based and hands-on activities that provide high-context and meaningful opportunities. These types of lessons promote the reciprocal interactions necessary for second-language acquisition with Spanish–English bilingual students with disabilities.

Instructional Management. Teachers must be able to manage their classrooms. In science, this includes establishing *systematic procedures for teachers* for distributing and collecting materials before, during, and after an activity or class period. One method, particularly at the elementary level, is to designate part of the room as the science area and to conduct most science instruction in this area. Within this area or wherever science instruction occurs, tables should be used as much as possible. Scheduling time at the end of class to clean up and organize all of the materials used is essential.

Science also requires *students to follow sets of procedures*. For example, all hands-on science involves a sequence of activities that students have to follow. Some students have difficulty remembering or following a sequence of steps. Teachers may need to take extra time to ensure that the directions are understood and may need to provide supplemental prompts (e.g., visual aids) to help students follow the directions that have been given.

A third aspect of instructional management is safety. Safety is a primary concern in science. Teachers should anticipate and prepare for potential problems. All planned science activities should be performed ahead of time, and equipment should be checked to ensure that it is in proper working condition. Students' eyes should be protected, fire extinguishers should be readily available, and safety instructions should be demonstrated and practiced regularly. Dangerous or potentially dangerous materials should be secured and off-limits signs posted to protect students from injury and the teacher from liability. It is also advisable to consult the safety guidelines of the school district.

Graphic Organizers. Graphic organizers are pictorial representations or diagrams that represent students' understanding of a concept. These mental maps allow students to utilize their higher-order thinking skills of comparing, synthesizing, classifying, and sequencing as they characterize a concept or process.

Graphic organizers facilitate the understanding of intricate interrelationships among concepts that are sometimes difficult for students. They can help to inform the learner regarding the purpose of topics to learn, clarify the big idea or question, provide an organizational structure, support curriculum adaptation and augmentation, identify and build vocabulary, facilitate student engagement through group formats, and then lead to a conclusion with a summary (Ciullo, Falcomata, & Vaughn, 2015). They have been found to be an effective strategy for teaching science content, vocabulary, and comprehension to students with learning disabilities (Dexter, Park, & Hughes, 2011).

Earlier, Table 1-1 illustrated a graphic organizer focused on alternatives in the implementation of an inquiry approach. Figure 11-3 (developed as a class assignment by Lynchburg College graduate students) illustrates the use of a graphic organizer that visually depicts the phases of the water cycle.

Table 11-9 provides another example of a graphic organizer focused on evolution versus creationism. This topic continues to be one of some public controversy in spite of the preponderance of scientific evidence.

ENHANCEDetext
video example 11.4
Watch this video to learn more about concept mapping in science.

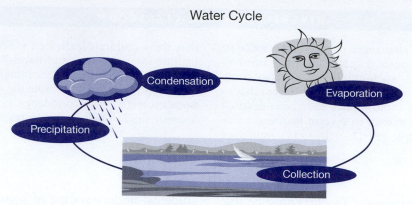

Water Cycle

FIGURE 11–3   Graphic Organizer

Source: Humphrey, E. (n.d.). Water cycle. Unpublished manuscript, Lynchburg College, VA. Used with permission.

Mnemonic Strategies.   Mnemonic instruction is a highly effective strategy to assist students with special needs in their ability to retain and recall science facts (Brigham, Scruggs, & Mastropieri 2011; Therrien et al., 2011). Mnemonic strategies are useful for helping students deal with vocabulary, terminology, and other tasks that are associated with science instruction.

Therrien et al. (2014) reported "consistently positive and strong results for mnemonic instruction (note, in this instance with students with EBD) . . . [with the] solid and extensive evidence needed to recommend the use of mnemonic instruction to increase students' factual knowledge" (p. 24). "Evidence is strongest for the use of mnemonics to increase the acquisition and retention of science factual knowledge" (p. 25). Similarly, Lubin and Polloway (2016) noted that "research has consistently

demonstrated that mnemonic instruction is effective in increasing recall and retention of science concepts with students with disabilities. Science teachers can use these techniques to help students retain difficult-to-remember concepts. Students reported enjoying the use of mnemonic strategies and . . . stated that they would use the technique again. This finding highlights a strong association between mnemonic instruction and intrinsic motivation and makes mnemonic instruction an ideal technique to counter students' possible frustration and limited interest in science classes" (p. 12).

A variety of mnemonic strategies and social studies were discussed earlier. Consistent with the findings of Lubin and Polloway (2016), students tend to be most familiar with the use of acronyms and acrostics and found them to be most helpful (McCabe, Osha, & Roche, 2013), while keywords are the most

TABLE 11–9   Graphic organizer: two variant models

Considerations	Evolution	Creationism (Intelligent Design)
Core Focus	Explains variety and complexity of life forms on Earth	Explains origins of earth and life forms
Source of Position	Evidence gleaned from scientific research	Biblical interpretation based on Book of Genesis
Life on Earth	More than 3.5 billion years old	Approximately 6000–10,000 years old based on literal reading of Genesis
Belief system	Scientific method: testable theories supported by multiple lines of evidence	Faith in strict Biblical interpretation and believe in its inerrancy
Implication	Teach scientific method as best means of understanding natural world	Teach creationism as reflection of belief via Biblical interpretation

Source: Graphic Models and Instructional Tools for Students with Special Needs (p. 50), by E. A. Polloway & J. Lubin, 2016, Lynchburg College Journal of Special Education, Lynchburg College, Lynchburg, VA. Used with permission.

TABLE 11–10   Sample science acrostics

Category	Data to Be Learned	Sample Acrostic(s)
Colors of Rainbow	red, orange, yellow, green, blue, indigo, violet	Riding on your grandmothers' bike (that) is violet.
Layers of the Earth	Crust, Mantle, Core (inner), Core (outer)	CMC^2
Lifecycle of Cells	interphase, prophase, metaphase, anaphase, telophase, cytokinesis	Icy penguins make Antarctica too cold.
Metrics	Metric prefixes: kilo-, hecto-, deca-, (base), deci-, centi-, milli-	King Henry's deeds brought deep cheers to many.
Order of Mohs Hardness Scale	talc, gypsum, calcite, fluoride, apatite, orthoclase feldspar, quartz, topaz, corundum, diamond	Texas girls can fly and other quiet things can do.
Parts of the Flower	stamen, pistil, receptacle, sepal, petal	Sister Paula received six prizes.
Plant Life Cycle	seed, seedling, flower, mature plant	Some singers frequent music places.
Properties of Matter	Mass, density, volume, weight	Monkeys dance very well
Scientific Method (a) (Humphrey, 2006)	Problem, Research, Form a hypothesis, Test hypothesis, Observations, Conclusion	People run faster than old chimps!
Scientific Method (b)	Observe, Inquire, Hypothesize, Experiment, Conclude	Only Ivan has eight cats.
Simple Machines	Pulley, gear, wheel, inclined plane, lever	Poor Gary wants ice-cream lowfat.
Solar System (planets by size)	Mercury, Mars, Venus, Earth, Neptune, Uranus, Saturn, Jupiter	Men March to VENUS Joyfully.
Solar System Planets in Sequence (after Pluto's demise)	Mercury, Venus, Earth, Mars, Jupiter, Saturn, Uranus, Neptune (Pluto)	My Very Eager Mother Just Served Us Nachos (but not Peanuts)
Taxonomic Classification	kingdom, phylum, class, order, family, genus, species	King Phillip came over for great soup.
Types of Environmental Pollution	Air, Thermal, Water, Visual, Land, Noise, Light	Altogether, Tom's wife, Victoria, learned nine languages.

Source: Graphic Models and Instructional Tools for Students with Special Needs (p. 52), by E. A. Polloway & J. Lubin, 2016, *Lynchburg College Journal of Special Education*, Lynchburg College, Lynchburg, VA. Used with permission.

frequently cited strategy used in educational research with students with disabilities. Common and effective mnemonic strategies are discussed below.

First-Letter Mnemonics   First-letter mnemonics include acronyms and acrostics. They are particularly useful for associating various lists of terms that need to be recalled and retained. Table 11-10 and Table 11-11 present sample acrostics and acronyms, respectively, that can be used to assist students in remembering core facts and concepts in science.

Linguistic   Linguistic mnemonics, as discussed earlier, include the use of keywords in order to assist students in associating the new concept with familiar words and/or phrases to help remember the item. As Mastropieri and Scruggs (2010) noted, the keyword method provides a strategy for creating connections between a new term or word to be learned and the information to which it is to be associated.

Possible keyword uses in the subject area of science include vocabulary words and definitions, concepts and meanings, and technical terms and definitions. In their review of the literature on mnemonic instruction in science, Lubin and Polloway (2016) reported on examples of keywords being used successfully to assist students in recalling scientific facts and concepts, such as the hardness level of metals, the names and characteristics of minerals, food chains, vertebrates and invertebrates, animal and plant life, earth science facts, body parts, and weather and astronomy.

One example of the use of the keyword would be in teaching blood vessels. In teaching the word *vein*, the keyword could be *in* with the linkage being that the blood flows into the heart. Similarly, to teach the word *artery*, the keyword could be *a* with the linkage being that the blood flows away from the heart. Accompanying these keywords with a picture to serve as a visual cue completes

TABLE 11–11 Sample science acronyms

Category	Data to Be Learned	Sample Acronym
Characteristics of Living Animals	Movement, Reproduction, sensation, Growth, Respiration, Excretion, Environmental Sensitivity, Nutrition	MRS GREEN
Colors of Rainbow	red, orange, yellow, green, blue, indigo, violet	ROYGBIV
Diet for Diarrhea	Bananas, rice, apples, toast	BRAT
Endocrine Glands	pancreas, pituitary, hypothalamus, adrenal, ovaries, testes, thyroid	TOPP HAT
Invertebrate Classes	Cnidarians, Annelids, Mollusks, Sponges, Echinoderms, Arthropods	CAM SEA ("calm sea")
Life Cycle of a Butterfly	Egg, Larva, Pupa, Adult	EL PA ("the father")
Main Insect Body Parts	head, abdomen, thorax	HAT
Newborn Vital Signs (after Virginia Apgar)	Activity, Pulse, Grimace, Appearance, Respiration	APGAR
Parts of Atom	protons, electrons, neutrons	PEN
Parts of the Pistil	Stigma, Ovule, Ovary, Style	SO²S
Plane Take-Off Preparation	Controls, Instruments, Gas, Altitude indicator, Radio	CIGAR
Primary Parts of Seed	Seed Coat, Embryo, Endosperm	SCEE ("see")
Simple Machines	Pulley, gear, jackscrew, axle and wheel, inclined plane, lever	PG JAIL
Stroke Warning	Face: does one side droop? Arm: does one drift downward, cannot be raised? Speech: sound slurred or strange? Time: identify time of symptom *Call 911 immediately*	FAST.... as in Think FAST
Vertebrate Classes	Fish, amphibians, reptiles, mammals, birds	FARM-B

Source: Graphic Models and Instructional Tools for Students with Special Needs (p. 51), by E. A. Polloway & J. Lubin, 2016, *Lynchburg College Journal of Special Education*, Lynchburg College, Lynchburg, VA. Used with permission.

the process and assists the student with imagery (American Institute for Research, 2016).

Another example was illustrated earlier in Figure 7-2. It shows how a visual image and keyword provide the acoustical link (keyword *meat-eater*) and picture to teach the term *meteorologist*.

Visual Mnemonics Visual mnemonics are strategies that make use of pictures or visualizations in order to create associations with a particular target concept to be learned. As Mastropieri and Scruggs (2010) noted, "Mnemonic pictures are not difficult to create and, once created, can be used again and again to improve students' memory of important content" (p. 244). Figure 11-4 provides a sample visual mnemonic to accompany an acronym.

Adapting Instruction and Differentiation. The concept of differentiating instruction was introduced earlier in the book. A model was discussed that contained six dimensions: setting, content, materials, instruction/intervention, management, and affect. It is important to understand how adjustments in these areas can be very beneficial to students who are struggling in some way in the area of science.

There are multiple adaptations of instruction to meet the needs of students with special needs. Adaptation in instruction carries the idea of a "change in some aspect of instructional delivery that allows students with disabilities to demonstrate competence in achieving the same educational goal that is expected of students who do not have disabilities" (McGinnis, 2013, p. 46). Some examples in science instruction are adjusting the length of assignment, using positive and multisensory techniques, using alternative forms of classroom management, and a variety of materials and instructional strategies (i.e., activity-oriented inquiry approach, tape lectures for playback, peer coaching). Practical ideas for key areas of differentiation or adaptation that are directly

FIGURE 11–4 Visual Mnemonic

CAM SEA (pronounced "calm sea") represents the six classes of invertebrate animals: Cnidarians, Annelids, Mollusks, Sponges, Echinoderms, and Arthropods.

Source: Lubin, J., & Polloway, E. A. (2016). Mnemonic instruction in science and social studies for students with learning disabilities: A review. *Learning Disabilities: A Contemporary Journal, 14* (2), pg. 210.

relevant to science instruction are summarized in Table 11-12 and then discussed further below.

Several of these areas for adaptations are further highlighted below.

Materials Adaptation As noted throughout this chapter, most published science materials used in general education settings are not designed for the diverse learning needs of certain students and must be adapted to be effective. Special education teachers must develop the ability to adapt materials and instruction for students to be successful in inclusive environments. Without question, the most notable barrier for most students with special needs in the area of science will be their ability to negotiate the text-heavy nature of this subject (Mason & Hedin, 2011). As a result, teachers will need to make *text adaptations* to help students deal successfully with the textual materials that they will encounter. In general, the fewer adaptations required, the better, and the modifications (i.e., changes to the content) should not change the core concepts being addressed.

Lenz and Schumaker (1999) pointed out that two types of adaptations exist: content adaptations (i.e., changing the nature or the amount of information to be learned) and format adaptations (i.e., changing the way in which information is presented to students). Content adaptations must be done in light of the requirement that students with disabilities must have access to the general curriculum. The more likely type of adaptation for those students who are following the general curriculum involves format adaptations. Lenz and Schumaker subdivide format adaptations into three categories: altering existing materials, mediating existing materials, and selecting alternative materials.

Another consideration is the *adaptation of laboratory materials*. To be able to perform hands-on activities, it is essential that the appropriate equipment and materials be available when students perform an assigned activity. Furthermore, special educators who are working cooperatively with general education science teachers need to anticipate potential problems that might arise when using certain equipment/materials, thus necessitating various adaptations.

Many elements of an activity-oriented general education program may need to be adapted. Science materials at the secondary level, even if they include hands-on activities through laboratory experiences, often require some reading and the understanding of more complex vocabulary and advanced concepts. Sasaki and Serna (1995) demonstrated how a middle school science program developed for general education, the *Foundational*

TABLE 11–12 Adapting instruction in science

Area	Tactics and Strategies
Setting	• Assign student a seat that accommodates a particular characteristic of concern (e.g., attention, behavior, hearing ability). • Keep distractions to a minimum (e.g., keep science materials out of sight of students when engaged in non-laboratory activities).
Content	• Be prepared to teach certain skills, such as social skills and study skills/learning strategies, to students that impact science learning. • Evaluate skimming and scanning skills and teach these skills as necessary. • Evaluate note-taking skills and teach a system for science lectures if needed. • Provide opportunities to infuse "real-life" topics/applications into existing content. • Cover essential science content, incorporating key accommodations, such as amended homework assignments.
Materials: Textbooks	• Identify and use science textbooks that cover the key content but are written at a lower readability level. • Use audio versions of textual material. • Develop science glossaries that are more appropriate for struggling students. • Review science textbook content with students—go over terms/vocabulary and all graphically presented material in a chapter. • Provide reading-related enhancements, such as advanced organizers, reading guides, semantic maps, and other graphic organizers.
Media	• Introduce all media (e.g., videos) clearly and provide overviews of what to expect and what outcomes are desired. • Provide enhancements, such as graphic organizers or other materials, that will assist the student in gaining meaning from any type of media used. • Discuss major points after viewing.
Instruction: Lecture	• Introduce and explain adequately any new science vocabulary or terms that will be covered. • Limit the length of teacher presentations/lectures. • Provide lecture-related enhancements, such as copies of PowerPoints, advanced notes, and graphic organizers that students have to fill in. • Teach self-monitoring techniques and require aids (e.g., checklists) to engage lectures more successfully.
Class activities	• Ensure that students understand what they are being asked to do. • Use peer-directed grouping.
Lab activities	• Ensure that students understand how to use science lab materials and equipment. • Provide specially designed forms for collecting data and reporting results that offer a framework for completing lab activities.
Projects	• Offer a range of science project options for students with varying academic strengths and limitations to demonstrate mastery. • Consider group projects in which a student with special challenges can contribute. • Ensure that students understand the directions for completing all long-term science projects. • Provide all directions and evaluation criteria in writing as well as explaining them orally. • Set up intermediate deadlines at which time students submit partially completed work on a long-term project. • Have students submit drafts of projects for ongoing feedback from the teacher.
Homework	• Ensure that students understand the directions for completing all science homework assignments. • Use a homework assignment book if needed. • Assign homework that students can reasonably complete given their current level of understanding and skill levels. • Adjust the amount of homework to fit the amount of time that a student typically devotes to homework assignments.

Approach to Science Teaching I (*FAST I*), could be adapted for use with students with disabilities. Through the use of techniques such as notebooks, direct vocabulary development, and thorough introduction to laboratory procedures, students were able to perform successfully in these general education materials.

Instructional Adaptations This dimension refers to those activities that a teacher does in the course of instruction and those activities that students have to do as a result of this instruction. In other words, this dimension has implications for the way a teacher presents information to students and the various ways that a student demonstrates his or her learning of subject matter.

Given the difficulties in accessing information from challenging *science textual material*, teachers can support students by fostering their prior knowledge of the content to be learned, providing enhancements to text as mentioned previously and including graphic organizers, and teaching reading comprehension strategies (see Chapter 7) within the context of this content area (Mason & Hedin, 2011).

A special consideration relates to *science vocabulary*. The reality is that many students have trouble mastering the large amount of new and often complex vocabulary. Teachers must take time to identify the words and concepts that students do not know prior to actual class presentation or text coverage. To facilitate learning, this vocabulary will need to be taught explicitly, and students need to be provided opportunities to gain mastery (e.g., vocabulary drills). Introducing lessons using everyday language before teaching scientific terminology is a promising approach (Brown & Ryoo, 2008).

Another key area is *adaptations associated with lectures and classroom presentations*. One of the presenting problems that some students with special needs bring to inclusive classroom settings is their inability to engage the information being presented by their teacher or the discussions that are part of science classes. Some effective techniques involve ideas as simple as where students sit in class and the dynamics of lessons where lecturing and discussion are common. Others include teaching note taking, using guided notes, and providing advance organizers.

Peer-Mediated Strategies. Peer-mediated learning strategies, such as cooperative learning arrangements, are important to consider for their possible impact on student engagement, learner motivation, and ultimately achievement. Consequently, they are often recommended for use with students with special needs working with their peers within the general education classroom (Carin, Bass, & Contant, 2005). Science can utilize activities that are ideal for creating opportunities for students to work together cooperatively. Sunal and Sunal (2003) noted that "when students work together to achieve a science objective, the potential or positive interactions within the group is enhanced" (p. 264).

Another strategy is peer tutoring. Although there are limited studies, there is some evidence of the possible effectiveness of the peer tutoring in science with students with disabilities (e.g., Therrien et al., 2014). This evidence points to improvement in achievement tests taken by students at the end of the year and also improvement in student behavior.

Technology in Science Instruction. Technology is used extensively in education and is particularly important for students with disabilities, It also reflects universal design principles . The growing amount of innovative media and online resources offers intriguing interactive possibilities for engaging science topics. The possibilities of using the Internet for instructional purposes are almost endless. It is now possible to find websites that address any topic, thus providing a way to enrich ongoing instruction.

It should also be noted that computer technology has distinct advantages for use with special populations. The advent of tablets offers students tools and access to resources in amazing ways.

Some examples of technology applications are outlined in Table 11-13.

Specially Designed Science Curricular Programs. Although not plentiful, instructional programs developed specifically with special populations in mind are available. One of the first comprehensive efforts to develop curricula for students with disabilities was the publication of the *Me Now, Me and My Environment*, and *Me in the Future* programs. Developed by the Biological Sciences Curriculum Study (BSCS), these programs were originally designed for students with varying levels of intellectual disabilities. The programs were multicomponent kits for conducting science activities. Arguably, their most attractive feature was that they did not require reading, thus avoiding this major barrier for some students. Moreover, the curricula focused on topics

TABLE 11–13   Technology applications in science

- Simulations: This type of software can substitute for certain dangerous situations (e.g., chemistry experiments) or can provide wonderful interactive experiences for students.

- Databases: Different types of science databases are available. Some commercially produced software contains already-established databases on topics such as animals; teachers can also create customized databases for their own needs.

- Probeware: Hardware devices (probes) and software that can be used to analyze information that is collected are now available that can be used as laboratory tools. Instruments that connect to the microcomputer can measure light intensity, voltage, temperature of liquids, and time. The measurements can be displayed on the monitor and recorded for future reference.

- Content enrichment: An array of software and online resources are available that can enhance the science topics that are being covered in class.

- Presentation: It is hard to find a school where students are not required to develop presentations on various topics using presentation software. Much instruction is also presented via this style.

- Graphing/charting: Data in science that are collected can easily be graphed for visual analysis using software such as Excel or other programs that are specifically designed for this purpose.

---

that were relevant to students. Another feature was that the teacher manuals provided precise directions for carrying out the activities. Several other specially designed programs are briefly discussed below.

Science for All Children (SAC).   SAC (Cawley, Miller, Sentman, & Bennett, 1993) is a theme-based elementary level program that includes a multiple-option curriculum that is characterized by the design feature referred to as the interactive unit. The four interrelated themes are systems, change, structure, and relationship. The four most essential features of SAC are the following:

- All teachers have all the materials for all the grades.
- There are multiple means of representation, expression, and engagement.
- There are no significant demands for proficiency in reading and writing.
- There is an unlimited number of material formats and supplemental activities that can be incorporated into the program. (p. 164)

Applications in Biology/Chemistry (ABC).   ABC is a secondary level program that targets students who are performing in the middle 50% in academic areas. It is real-life oriented and achieves this goal by linking science topics to a student's personal world.

You, Me, and Others.   This K–6 program designed for students with intellectual disabilities was developed by the BSCS (Carin et al., 2005). Its focus is

in the area of biology generally and genetics specifically. The curriculum includes three units: variety (grades K–2), change (grades 3–4), and the chain of life (grades 5–6).

 Check Your Understanding 11.3 Click here to gauge your understanding of the concepts in this section.

ACTIVITIES

1. Study anatomy by examining the parts of a chicken. This is an easy animal to get, and it lends itself well to study because students are familiar with it.

2. Have students collect plant seeds or small plants: Ask them to describe what they see when the seeds are planted or the plants are small. Have them make periodic written observations to demonstrate that plants do change. Have them place the plants under different conditions—no water, no sun, too much water—and observe the results.

3. So that students can better understand weather changes, have them keep weather charts that record temperature on different days, rain or snow accumulation, and other data students may want to collect. Questions to ask are the following: Does it rain when the sun shines? What happens to water when you freeze it? What does snow look like close up?

4. Science in the home provides a wealth of opportunities for a science unit: What makes an iron work? What causes cakes to rise? What causes bread to mildew?

5. Depending on students' ages and the area in which the school is located, take students to farms where food is grown or animals are raised. Older students or students who live in farming regions can actually grow food products or raise farm animals.

6. Build small models of simple machines, such as a pulley, wheel and axle, wedge, screw, and inclined plane. Use a spring scale to measure the amount of energy saved by using the machines to move and raise books or other heavy objects.

7. A study of different types of plants and flowers can be aided by keeping a log of the plants for the project. The log can be most effective if the plants are sketched or pressed. (To press, put the plant in a catalog with heavy objects on top and leave it for approximately four to six days.)

8. Allow students to catch a caterpillar and place it in a glass jar with holes in the lid. Have students make daily observations of the caterpillar as it passes through metamorphosis. Make daily written reflections or oral recordings of these observations.

CHAPTER 12

Study Skills

John J. Hoover

LEARNING OUTCOMES

Upon completion of this chapter, the reader should be able to:

12.1 Understand the importance of teaching study skills as a critical component of the curriculum.

12.2 Identify and discuss the types of study skills and discussed study skills instruction within a multi-tiered educational program.

12.3 Identify and apply assessment strategies for study skills and demonstrate the ability to use that information in instructional planning.

12.4 Discuss instructional strategies for teaching study skills.

Study skills are essential for students across all grade levels. For students with disabilities, learning and using these skills may be particularly problematic and hence the need for effective instruction. The chapter provides background on the importance of why study skills should be taught, identifies those skills that are most relevant and valuable for students to acquire, and identifies assessment and instructional strategies within this domain.

WHY USE STUDY SKILLS?

Use of effective study skills is essential to help all learners achieve in school, particularly students who struggle and those with mild to moderate disabilities (Hoover, Betty, & Patton, 2015). Student use of various study skills is essential to success in learning and completion of tasks (Deschler & Cornett, 2012; Hoover & Patton, 2007). Learners in today's classrooms must complete an increasing number of assigned tasks along with various assessments to demonstrate knowledge and skills, such as (a) generate more complete and properly edited written assignments, (b) develop and implement an organized schedule for task completion, (c) break down complex tasks into more manageable components, (d) complete homework assignments efficiently and effectively, (e) work cooperatively with classmates, (f) self-manage behavior, or (g) generalize learning to new and different situations.

Study skills are tools employed when the learner wishes to apply useful hints, tips, or strategies to complete specific or assigned tasks more effectively (Hoover & Patton, 2007) (e.g., taking notes, completing a multiple-choice test, making an oral presentation). Once the study skill is used in a specific situation, it is generally not used again until a similar task is completed (e.g., the next time note taking is necessary, taking the next test). Although the appropriate use of study skills is particularly essential at the upper elementary, middle, and secondary levels, acquisition of study skills should begin early in the educational career. Hoover and Patton (2007) emphasized the need for integrated study skills programs throughout one's schooling and as lifelong skills.

Historically, literature about student use of study skills has shown the need for their increased development in students with learning problems (Cohen & Spenciner, 2008; Hoover, 2011; Vaughn & Bos, 2015). For example, unless provided direct instruction, students who experience challenges in learning or managing behavior often develop a limited set of skills for study and tend to use these skills less frequently in instructional situations (Reid, Leinemann, & Hagaman, 2013). In addition, Wolfolk (2012) stressed that teachers need to provide opportunities for students to use study skills and that some students with learning problems often do not possess adequate study skills. Unfortunately, adolescent students with learning disabilities generally have not been taught study skills during elementary education, and as secondary students they often lack sufficient skills to meet their various educational demands. Deficiencies are often found in listening, note taking, test taking, time management, using appropriate rates of reading, locating useful information, and organizational abilities. Additionally, Hoover (2004, 2013) and Brown (2004) discussed students' lack of self-management abilities and effects on learning. Hoover (2011) and Mercer, Mercer, and Pullen (2010) noted deficient test-taking skills in students with high-incidence disabilities. Overall, evidence continues to suggest the need for an increased emphasis on effective study skills for students with special learning needs at both the elementary and the secondary level of education.

Study Skills Research

Much of the need to acquire and use study skills in learning is intuitive, based on their connections to various educational tasks:

- Knowing how to take tests contributes to better test taking.
- Effective note taking facilitates greater understating of lecture content.
- Efficient use of time contributes to more effectively completing tasks.
- Ability to accurately interpret graphic aids is necessary to effectively use picture clues.
- Self-management facilitates efficiency in task completion.
- Using current online technology facilitates efficient gathering and storing of resources and information.
- Using advance organizers facilitates acquisition of new knowledge and skills.

These and other examples strongly imply the necessity for developing study skills, beginning in early elementary school and continuing into and beyond secondary education.

Though intuitive, various researchers and experts in the field of study skills have documented research results or other evidence highlighting the significance of study skills development and usage. For example, Hamblet (2014) found that students with disabilities experience increase success when using various study skills, including time management, organization, and test taking. Hoover et al. (2015) reported that research shows that study strategies instruction (a) supports content learning, (b) enables students to better demonstrate content knowledge, and (c) increases student independence and affect toward learning. Hoover and Patton (2007) also noted that educators must build the use of study skills into daily instruction. Lerner (2008) wrote that listening abilities can be strengthened through direct teaching, and Strichart and Mangrum (2002) found that instruction in study skills improves learner performance on tasks that require use of those skills. Cockrum and Shanker (2013) indicated that note taking becomes easier for students once outlining skills have been mastered.

In addition, Brown (2004) documented that strengthening self-management skills facilitates greater responsibility for students' own learning. Also, Vaughn and Bos (2015) reported that research indicates that lectures in the secondary levels are infrequently preceded by advance organizers needed to facilitate effective and attentive listening. Though important and integral to effective learning, Hoover et al. (2015) found that

TABLE 12–1 Study skill competencies and significance in learning

Competency	Description
Acquisition	Crucial first step involved in learning; the first experiences encountered by learners
Recording	Any activity in the classroom that requires the learner to record responses, answers, or ideas, including both written and verbal forms of communication
Location	Seeking and finding necessary information to complete tasks
Organization	Arranging, managing, and completing learning activities effectively
Synthesis	Integrating elements or parts to form a whole, creating something that was not clearly evident prior to beginning a new task
Memorization	Remembering learned material for both the short and the long term; storing and recalling or retrieving information

students' individualized education programs (IEPs) typically do not include or reference study skills in present levels of performance or objectives. These and related research findings further support evidence that the development and implementation of an ongoing study skills program for students with special needs requires increased attention in today's teaching and learning.

As far back as 1986, Hoover framed the use of study skills within a "big ideas" perspective, reflecting important component competencies still appropriate in today's teaching and learning environment, as shown in Table 12-1.

Many learning tasks and life skills are directly connected to successful application of the above competences; developing study skills usage in K–12 classrooms creates an environment to help students effectively apply these essential competencies, and such skills assist students in confronting the educational tasks associated with the learning process. Thus, study skills facilitate mastery of a number of learning competencies, such as those identified above, necessary for effective and efficient learning to occur.

 Check Your Understanding 12.1 Click here to gauge your understanding of the concepts in this section.

TYPES OF STUDY SKILLS

Various study skills exist, including reading at different rates, listening, note taking/outlining, report writing, making oral presentations, using graphic aids, test taking, using the library, locating and using reference materials, managing time, using organizational skills, and managing behavior. Table 12-2 briefly identifies the importance of each of these skills, which are discussed in the following sections.

Reading at Different Rates

The ability to use different reading rates is an important study skill (Harris & Sipay, 1990) that is most evident as students progress through the grades. Teachers at the elementary and secondary levels must often teach their students how to develop **reading rate** skills. Hoover (2011) and Hoover and Patton (2007) emphasized the importance of reading with purpose and that reading rates must vary to meet different purposes. Although various terms are used to describe the different rates, reading rates include skimming, scanning, rapid reading, normal reading, and careful, or study-type, reading.

Skimming refers to a fast-paced reading rate used to grasp the general idea of material. As students quickly skim materials, they may deliberately skip over different sections. *Scanning* is also a fast-paced reading rate that is used to identify specific items or pieces of information. Students might scan material to search for a name or a telephone number. *Rapid reading* is used to review familiar material or grasp main ideas. In rapid reading, some details may be identified, especially if the reader needs the information only temporarily.

Normal rate is used when students must identify details or relationships, solve a problem, or find answers to specific questions. *Careful*, or study-type, reading is a slow rate used to master details,

TABLE 12–2   Study skills for effective and efficient learning

Study Skill	Significance for Learning
Reading rate	Reading rates should vary with type and length of reading assignments.
Listening	Listening skills are necessary to complete most educational tasks or requirements.
Note taking and outlining	Effective note-taking/outlining skills allow students to document key points or topics for future study.
Report writing	Report writing is a widely used method of documenting information and expressing ideas.
Oral presentations	Oral presentations provide students an alternative method to express themselves and report information.
Graphic aids	Graphic aids may visually depict complex or cumbersome material in a meaningful format.
Test taking	Effective test-taking abilities help ensure more accurate assessment of student abilities.
Library usage	Library usage skills facilitate easy access to much information.
Reference materials usage	Independent learning may be greatly improved through effective use of reference materials and dictionaries.
Time management	Time management assists in reducing the number of unfinished assignments and facilitates more effective use of time.
Self-management	Self-management assists students to assume responsibility for their own behaviors.
Organizational skills	Effective organizational skills assist learners to more effectively complete multiple tasks.

Source: Table 1.1 From *Teaching Study Skills to Students with Learning Problems: A Teacher's Guide for Meeting Diverse Needs*, 2nd Ed. (p. 3), by J. J. Hoover and J. R. Patton, 2007, Austin, TX: PRO-ED. Copyright 2007 by PRO-ED, Inc. Reprinted with permission.

retain or evaluate information, follow directions, or perform other similar tasks (Harris & Sipay, 1990).

The nature of the material being read helps determine the need for varied reading rates; different activities also require different reading rates. In many reading situations, two or more rates must be employed. For example, a student may scan several pages to locate a name and then use normal or study-type reading to learn the details surrounding that name. Varied reading rates, when used appropriately, can be highly effective and important study skills for students with learning problems.

Listening

Listening also is involved in many different activities, as much instruction in elementary and secondary school relies heavily on the listening abilities of students. Listening includes both hearing and comprehending a spoken message. As was noted earlier in this text, listening involves the ability to receive information, apply meaning, and provide evidence of understanding what was heard. **Effective listening** is required in formal presentations, conversations, exposure to auditory environmental stimuli, and attending to various audio and audio-visual materials (Hoover, 2011; Hoover & Patton,

2007). Lerner (2008) suggested that listening skills can be improved through teaching and practice. Since students spend more time listening than in other types of learning (i.e., reading, writing; Vaughn & Bos, 2015), teachers must ensure that classroom conditions facilitate effective listening. Meese (2001) suggested that learners who struggle in school often experience problems with listening and, as described earlier, may be improved through direct instruction and practice.

Taking Notes or Outlining

Taking notes or **outlining** requires students to document major ideas and relevant topics for later use to classify and organize information. Note taking is a skill that requires students to determine the most essential information on the topic and record that content (Dean, Hubbell, Pitler, & Stone, 2014). Outlining is necessary to structure notes into main headings and subheadings for effective study (Coman & Heavers, 2001), and note taking becomes less difficult once outlining skills have been acquired (Cockrum & Shanker, 2013). Furthermore, study skills associated with reading, listening, thinking, and using vocabulary may improve significantly as students develop effective note-taking abilities. These involve summarizing ideas and organizing information into a useful format for future use. Instruction in this study skill area is particularly appropriate for students with learning problems, as they often experience difficulties with organizing and recording information. With sufficient practice and systematic instruction, these students are capable of acquiring note-taking or outlining skills, even though they tend to exhibit some difficulty in the process. Boyle (2013) emphasized the importance of strategically taking notes to best deal with lecture material, teacher cues, and necessary vocabulary.

ENHANCEDetext
video example 12.1
Watch this video to learn more about note-taking strategies.

Writing Reports

Report writing involves the various skills necessary to organize and present ideas on paper, PowerPoint presentations, or other documents in a meaningful and appropriate way. Included are topic selection, note taking, organization of ideas, outlining, spelling and punctuation, and sentence structure. Since a direct connection exists between reading comprehension and writing (Graham & Harris, 2005), educators cognizant of this linkage may assist learners with writing while also addressing other related study skills, such as reading rate. Vaughn and Bos (2015) noted that students with special needs often require more time devoted to writing than typically spent in classrooms.

Making Oral Presentations

Many skills necessary for report writing are also important in oral presentations of various types—interviews, poster presentations, debates, group discussions, and individual or group presentations. Caution should be used to ensure that oral presentations occur in a nonthreatening environment to minimize student anxiety. **Oral presentation** tasks should be clearly defined, and students need preparation time, guidance, and structure in planning their oral presentations. On occasion, oral reports can be an effective supplement to or substitute for written assignments.

Using Graphic Aids

Graphic aids—materials such as charts, graphs, maps, models, pictures, or photographs—can be an effective tool to facilitate learning. Graphic aids may (a) assist students in more easily comprehending complex material, (b) facilitate the presentation of large amounts of information into small, more manageable pieces, and (c) assist students in ascertaining similarities within and differences among cultural, geographic, and economic situations. Thus, numerous important concepts or events can be addressed through visual materials. Students with disabilities can benefit from graphic aids if they are taught what to look for and attend to while reading and interpreting visual material.

Taking Tests

Students in any grade are frequently subjected to various forms of assessment and evaluation. Even though tests are one of the primary means of assessing students in school, many students do not possess sufficient test-taking skills (Hoover & Patton, 2007). **Test-taking** skills are those abilities necessary to (a) prepare and study for tests, (b) take tests, and (c) review completed and graded test results. They are important to ensure that tests accurately measure students' knowledge rather than their poor test-taking abilities. Test-taking skills include reading and following directions, thinking through questions prior to recording responses, and proofreading and checking answers. Though many students with disabilities may lack effective test preparation and test-taking strategies (Kirby, Silvestri, Allingham, Parrila, & La Fave, 2008), researchers at the University of Kansas (Center for Research on Learning, 2014) found that students who used test-taking strategies improved their performance on classroom tests. Conderman and Pedersen (2010) reported that students were able to improve and generalize their test-taking abilities when modeled by the teacher. Thus, students who lack test-taking abilities can learn them through instruction and practice (Hoover & Patton, 2007).

Using the Library

Both virtual and onsite library activities are periodically required of students at every grade level. **Library use** requires skills in locating library materials, including using computerized systems;

locating films, filmstrips, resource guides, and curriculum materials; and understanding the general layout and organization of the library. Darling-Hammond, Zielezinski, and Goldman (2014) stressed the importance of technology to increase access to available resources to support teaching and learning, such as those typically found in libraries. Knowledge of the role of the media specialist is also important. Although library use becomes especially important at the secondary level of education, it should be taught gradually and systematically throughout a student's schooling.

Using Reference Materials

Other study skills become important when students locate materials within the virtual classroom or school libraries. Students must be knowledgeable about the uses and functions of dictionaries and various other **reference materials** and must be familiar with various aspects of their design. They must be able to use a table of contents and an index, to alphabetize and use chapter headings, and to understand how content is arranged in dictionaries, encyclopedias, and other reference sources. Mastery of the use of computerized or online encyclopedias and reference materials is necessary in today's classrooms due to the contemporary emphasis on virtual and online learning within many grade levels. Also, students with disabilities are capable of acquiring these skills if they receive guided instruction and practice (Lerner, 2008).

Managing Time

Time management involves using time effectively to complete daily assignments and carry out responsibilities. It includes allocating time and organizing the environment to study, complete projects, and balance various aspects of individual schedules efficiently. Kuo (2010) found that long-term success with learning outcomes improved for students who planned out their use of time over those who did not efficiently plan time management. In support, Deshler and Cornett (2012) wrote that time on task improves with effective time management in learning. However, should problems with time management skill development persist in early schooling, problems with learning may extend into secondary education and even adulthood (Gore, 2010). In addition, Lewis and Doorlag (2010) indicated that some students have difficulty with the organization and management of time, which may lead to incorrect or unfinished assignments. As students enter secondary school and workloads increase, effective time management becomes increasingly important. In summary, effective time management is an important feature for success, and this skill can be improved with proper supports (Hellsten, 2012). Therefore, teachers of learners with special needs should structure learning situations to encourage students to manage their time responsibly throughout elementary and secondary schooling.

Developing Self-Management Skills

Another important tool necessary for learning is the ability to manage one's own behavior, especially during independent work time. Inappropriate behavior can seriously interfere with task completion. Wehby and Kern (2014) suggested that students who exhibit behavior problems frequently require direct instruction to improve self-management skills to support development of self-control necessary for academic success. Students learn to assume responsibility for their own behavior only when educational programs emphasize self-management and behavior control (Brown, 2004). **Self-management** assists students to be more productive in the classroom (Hoover, 2011) and resolve social problems (Vaughn & Bos, 2015). In addition, self-monitoring is effective in increasing time on task and reducing time required to complete tasks while reducing the demands on teachers for data collection (Lewis & Doorlag, 2010). The act of self-monitoring a behavior also encourages learners to maintain appropriate behaviors during school (Hallahan, Kauffman, & Pullen, 2015). Additionally, Asaro-Saddler (2014) found that teaching self-regulation assisted students with autism with self-management. Various models and programs concerned with self-control and self-management currently exist (Brown, 2004; National Association of School Psychologists, 2002). The nearby Teacher Tips provides a few strategies for helping elementary level students acquire self-management abilities.

Using Organizational Skills

Increased demands being placed on students requires them to better organize and manage their learning. Today, learners are expected to complete

Teaching Self-Management Strategies at the Elementary Level

- Assists learners to acquire useful self-monitoring abilities early in schooling

- Provides learners with skills that support success in the inclusive general education classroom

- Promotes the significance of applying self-regulatory behaviors in teaching and learning

- Should include use of self-monitoring checklists for easy recording of the occurrences of targeted behaviors

more work within shorter time frames and achieve higher standards. Keeping organizational charts or guides will help students with the organization and maintenance of daily or weekly tasks (Cohen & Spenciner, 2008). The ability to effectively organize and manage classroom learning is essential to meet the pressures and expectations found in today's classrooms. **Organizational skills** also assist learners to arrange information so it is easier to remember (Vaughn & Bos, 2015). Similar to other study skills, development of effective organizational abilities requires direct instruction and

systematic support for students with special needs (Hamblet, 2014).

Early Development of Study Skills

A common misperception about study skills is that these are needed only at and beyond the upper elementary grades. For example, as educators, do we not conduct some form of student testing (both formal and informal) in each grade in elementary school? Or, do we not have students in all grades use the classroom or school library? Although the

Teaching Use of Study Skills at the Secondary Level Facilitates Life Skills Usage

Study Skill	Life Skills Application
Reading rate	Reading weekly magazines, technical reports, or legal documents
Listening	Understanding verbal directions; following emergency instructions
Graphic aids	GPS or map reading; locating specific store on shopping mall map
Library usage	Gathering library materials for travel, leisure reading, or home repairs
Reference materials	Consulting phone books, websites, or automobile manuals
Test taking	Completing successfully trade certification or driver's license tests
Note taking/outlining	Documenting directions or generating a shopping list
Report writing	Completing job/college application essays and workplace reports
Oral presentations	Describing problem to repair person or providing oral directions
Time management	Balancing work, leisure, personal, and family time expectations
Self-management	Dealing with own temper/disposition/personal reactions to events
Organization	Prioritizing personal, professional, or family tasks and responsibilities

use of study skills is most reflected in upper elementary and secondary education literature and textbooks, many students will experience difficulty with study skills at the upper grades unless a basic study skills foundation is laid in early elementary school. In addition, it is misguided to believe that only students in upper elementary and secondary education are capable of learning study skills. Further, educators should not ignore the fact that students in lower elementary grades are required to engage in many of the identical activities as students in upper elementary and secondary schooling. For example, students in lower elementary grades also do the following:

- Complete tests
- Do homework
- Write reports
- Listen to the teacher instruct
- Use a library
- Locate and use reference materials
- Manage and organize time
- Manage their own behaviors
- Use contemporary online technology

These are just a few of the tasks that students in lower elementary grades engage in on a regular, daily basis. Study skills are "tools" that any learner may use to complete tasks and assignments. Although some of the structured study strategies discussed in this chapter may be too complex for students in the lower elementary grades, appropriate modifications of these can easily be made to facilitate the development of a sound study skills base in the lower grades. In regard to secondary level learners, teaching and using study skills provides a solid foundation for development of life skills, as illustrated in the nearby Teacher Tips for secondary level educators.

Table 12-3 provides examples of early development of study skills to build a solid foundation for later use. Teachers should use these types of activities on a regular basis to best help students in the lower grades develop a solid foundation for study skills from which to build on as they move into the upper elementary and secondary grades.

Study Skills in Multi-Tiered System of Supports

The contemporary framework for instructing students in school is multi-tiered system of supports (MTSS), which represents a significant shift in how we view teaching and learning and the needs of learners at risk or those with disabilities (Hoover, 2013). The structure of MTSS in K–12 schools includes several tiers or layers of instruction (usually three tiers), in which the duration and intensity level of instruction increases based on student progress toward academic and behavioral benchmarks. Within any effective K–12 MTSS model, student use of study skills is essential to (a) achieving adequate rates of progress, (b) maintaining acceptable levels of academic proficiency, and (c) building the foundational base for further developing social-emotional skills (Hoover, 2011).

As specific progress monitoring data are gathered for struggling students, educators should also consider the learner's abilities to apply and generalize the various study skills discussed in this chapter. This includes the use of different formal and informal assessment devices, including the classroom-based Study Skills Inventory (SSI) (see Figure 12-1). Specifically, the value of efficient and effective uses of study skills within tiers of instruction in MTSS is seen in their application to instructional and assessment tasks in which accurate determination of acquired knowledge and skills is the overall outcome. Table 12-4, developed from information found in Hoover (2011), Hoover, Klingner, Baca, and Patton (2008), and Hoover et al. (2015) provides an overview of key contributions of effective study skill usage in MTSS, thereby empowering both students and educators to provide high-quality instruction and associated assessments.

As shown, a variety of applications of study skills exist within MTSS. Adherence to these helps provide all learners, especially those who struggle, with the highest-quality instruction possible within tiered learning. Since MTSS is concerned primarily with the delivery of effective instruction, development and use of study skills programs in each tier of instruction provides both students and educators with improved opportunities to learn and teach.

 Check Your Understanding 12.2 Click here to gauge your understanding of the concepts in this section.

TABLE 12–3 Developing foundation for study skills in early elementary grades

Study Skills	Early Development Suggestions
Reading rate	Rates of reading relate specifically to reading purposes. As students begin to read or are read to, help them listen or read for different purposes (pleasure, identifying main character, locating a detail, etc.).
Listening	List and post *Good Listener Skills* in the classroom. Be certain to include and discuss the difference between *hearing* something and *understanding* what is heard. Periodically stop verbal discussions or instruction and ask students to state what is being talked about and how it relates to the topic at hand.
Note taking/outlining	Critical to effective note taking/outlining is the ability to recognize and record essential information in an organized manner. In early elementary school, use of semantic webs or other graphic organizers helps students acquire a foundation for more complex note-taking/outlining tasks in the future.
Report writing	Written reports provide students opportunities to discuss, evaluate, or explore a topic in writing. A variety of tasks help students in early elementary grades begin to develop these skills, including use of the cloze procedures, sentence completion activities, or language experience tasks.
Oral presentations	An underlying skill needed to successfully give oral presentations is the ability to speak in front of others to formally share ideas or information. A variety of tasks in early elementary school facilitate initial development of this study skill, including reporting orally about lessons learned on a field trip, experiences during summer vacation, or briefly sharing a talent or hobby.
Graphic aids	Studying pictures is one of the first ways children learn about different topics (e.g., items in a forest) as well as to support written text (i.e., picture clues). Activities that combine pictures with simple text help students in early grades develop an appreciation for use of graphic material, not only in reading but also in making oral presentations as discussed previously.
Test taking	Students in any grade are subjected to some form of testing in the classroom. Early support for test-taking skills in the early elementary grades should include the development and posting of three graphic aids: (a) how to study for a test, (b) how to take at test, (c) how to review a graded test. Each poster should depict (in written and/or graphic form) two or three main items associated with each of the three poster topics so all students in the class understand the items.
Library usage	Most, although not all, students have some experience with the elementary school's library. The foundation for library usage can easily be strengthened in early elementary school through simple tasks that require students to use the library to locate a book, resource, map, or other library material. These types of activities should be encouraged to begin early the process of using a library effectively.
Reference materials	As discussed, teachers should provide students in early elementary school with tasks that require locating and using simple reference materials. Completing activities that require use of dictionaries and encyclopedias written for lower elementary grades assists in building a solid foundation for more complex uses of reference materials in later grades.
Time management	Effective use of time becomes more important as learners experience increased workloads and responsibilities. However, simple yet effective time-management skills can be acquired in lower elementary grades. Examples include development of brief daily schedules with associated times, posting and periodically reviewing a time-management poster with two or three easy-to-understand tips, posting the daily tasks along with beginning and ending times, or providing students with two tasks that must be completed within a specified time.
Self-management	"Behaving" or keeping one's behavior under control is an expectation of all students beginning with the first day they enter a formal school setting. A most effective strategy for helping early elementary students with self-management is through the use of self-monitoring techniques. This method is easily adapted to meet younger student needs and helps learners become more aware of their own behaviors.
Organizational skills	Similar to time management, organizing one's learning becomes more important as workloads and responsibilities increase. Helping students develop and use a simple organization chart documenting daily tasks helps younger students begin the process of developing effective organizational skills.

Source: Table 3.1 From *Teaching Study Skills to Students with Learning Problems: A Teacher's Guide for Meeting Diverse Needs*, 2nd Ed. (p. 28-29), by John J. Hoover, James R. Patton, 2007, Austin, TX: PRO-ED. Copyright 2007 by PRO-ED, Inc. Reprinted with permission.

Study Skills	Pre	Post	Study Skills	Pre	Post
Reading Rates Scanning			Uses organized note card format		
Skimming			**Report Writing** Organizes thoughts		
Normal rate			Uses proper punctuation		
Rapid reading			Uses proper spelling		
Careful reading			Uses proper grammar		
Listening Attends to listening tasks			**Oral Presentations** Participates freely		
Applies meaning to verbal messages			Organizes presentation		
Filters out auditory distractions			Uses gestures		
Note Taking/Outlining Appropriately uses headings			Speaks clearly		
Takes brief and clear notes			**Use of Graphic Aids** Attends to relevant elements		
Records important information			Understands purposes		
Uses for report writing			Incorporates in presentations		
Uses during lectures			Develops own visuals		
Test Taking Organizes answers			Uses guide words		
Proofreads			Understands uses of each		
Reads and understands directions			Uses for written assignments		
Identifies clue words			Identifies different reference materials		
Properly records responses			**Time Management** Organizes daily activities		
Answers difficult questions last			Completes tasks on time		
Narrows possible correct answers			Organizes weekly/monthly schedules		
Corrects previous test-taking errors			Understands time management		
Library Usage Use of card catalog			Reorganizes time when necessary		
Ability to locate materials			Prioritizes activities		
Organization of library			**Self-Management of Behavior** Monitors own behavior		
Role of media specialist			Changes own behavior		
Reference/Dictionary Usage Identifies components			Thinks before acting		
Makes well-organized outlines			Is responsible for own behavior		

FIGURE 12–1 Study Skills Inventory

Source: Table 4.1 From *Teaching Study Skills to Students with Learning Problems: A Teacher's Guide for Meeting Diverse Needs*, 2nd Ed. (p.50-53), by John J. Hoover, James R. Patton, 2007, Austin, TX: PRO-ED. Copyright 2007 by PRO-ED, Inc. Reprinted with permission.

ASSESSMENT OF STUDY SKILLS

Numerous instruments exist for assessing study skills; they include norm-referenced, criterion-referenced, and standardized devices as well as informal and teacher-made checklists. Table 12-5 and Table 12-6 identify a variety of such devices. The appropriate use of the various types of instruments is discussed here; selected devices are presented to familiarize the reader with existing instruments, not to provide evaluative judgments. The reader should

TABLE 12–4 Study skills and the implementation of MTSS for struggling learners

Study Skill	Significant Applications in MTSS
Reading rate	Adequate use of different reading rates is essential for students to accurately demonstrate academic progress; lack of properly applied reading rates may assist to explain insufficient progress in various content areas where reading is central to the assessment tasks.
Listening	Many of the research-based interventions used to deliver tiered instruction in MTSS models are grounded in direct instruction, which frequently requires extended periods of time with listening tasks; some students who struggle may demonstrate difficulty maintaining attention to task due to concerns with extended listening time and may need more active, cooperative methods to make adequate progress.
Note taking/outlining	Students who lack the ability to take notes and outline material that is read or heard, often find themselves lagging behind peers in academics; MTSS include a continuous development process to help learners effectively take notes and outline material since lack of these skills will directly affect progress monitoring results.
Report writing	Ability to generate acceptable written reports or other material in writing often challenges students who struggle in school; MTSS that contain a structured process for teaching students proper strategies for report writing facilitate greater success with academic progress.
Oral presentations	Although much of what occurs in school is based on students' abilities to verbally share or present information, some students are more proficient at demonstrating acquired knowledge and skills through tasks that are less reliant on oral communication abilities; MTSS that contain opportunities for students to share their knowledge in a variety of ways facilitate more effective learning and associated progress.
Graphic aids	Ability to use and interpret visual material, either while presenting acquired learning or when consuming information, is necessary for academic success in any tier of instruction in MTSS.
Test taking	A cornerstone of response to intervention is universal screening and progress monitoring both of which require sufficient test-taking skills; lack of student test-taking abilities may inadvertently lead educators to conclude that the learner lacks knowledge or skills when in reality screening or monitoring results reflect poor test-taking abilities and not lack of knowledge; MTSS that provide struggling learners with multiple means to demonstrate acquired knowledge and skills as well as manage any test anxiety produce more accurate progress results.
Library usage	Possessing effective library usage abilities is essential at any grade level and tier of instruction; MTSS that integrate the development and use of library materials in teaching and learning within each tier of instruction provide all students greater opportunities to learn and succeed.
Reference materials usage	Integrated within several of the above study skills is the need to be able to access and use reference materials on a daily basis; MTSS facilitate learner development in acquiring this important skill given the tremendous amount of information that is easily accessible to students in today's classrooms.
Time management	The ability to manage time effectively is essential to completing tasks, demonstrating progress and maintaining sufficient growth toward academic benchmarks; structures within MTSS should provide educators with accurate information about how well a learner manages time and how to hold realistic expectations about how long a task should take if insufficient learner progress is evident.
Self-management	Similar to time management, one's ability to self-manage behavior is essential to making adequate progress in any tier of instruction within MTSS; inability to manage own behavior is often reflected in poor academic progress, and adjustments in self-management programs may be needed rather than a change in content or intervention.
Organizational skills	Multiple tasks within different tiers of instruction in MTSS require learners to be highly organized, or they run the risk of incomplete assignments, lack of in-depth demonstration of knowledge, insufficient time to complete all tasks, or other related outcomes resulting from ineffective organizational management skills; RtI models that facilitate development and application of effective organizational skills assist students to adequately progress in school in any tier of instruction.

consult each instrument's manual or cited references for additional information and evaluative reviews. The tables provide titles and summary information about selected norm- and criterion-referenced instruments. Each is based on information provided by Cohen and Spenciner (2014), Harris and Sipay (1990), McLoughlin and Lewis (2007), and Salvia, Ysseldyke, and Bolt (2009).

TABLE 12–5 Study skills assessment instruments

Norm-Referenced General Achievement Tests
California Achievement Tests (CTB/McGraw-Hill)
Comprehensive Test of Basic Skills (CTB/McGraw-Hill)
Iowa Silent Reading Tests (Harcourt Brace Jovanovich)
Iowa Tests of Basic Skills (Riverside)
SRA Achievement Series—Reading (Science Research Associates)
Stanford Achievement Test Series (Pearson/PsychCorp)

Standardized Study Skill Instrument
LASSI (Learning and Study Strategies Inventory) (H & H Publishing)

Criterion-Referenced Instrument
BRIGANCE Diagnostic Inventories (Curriculum Associates)
Study Skills Inventory (SSI) (Hoover and Patton, 2007)

Although norm-referenced general achievement tests may be used in schools, these measures tend to produce a low estimate of students' performance (McLoughlin & Lewis, 2007). In addition, this type of test may pose particular problems to students with disabilities because such instruments are often timed and require students to record their own answers.

Norm-referenced tests attempt to separate student results into a distribution of scores (Salvia et al., 2013). Such tests assume that students have sufficient independent work habits to monitor their own time and behavior and to sustain attention to the various tasks presented by the tests (McLoughlin & Lewis, 2007). Furthermore, these tests frequently include only a small number of items to assess study skills and thus may not adequately assess student abilities. Nonetheless, group tests are often appropriate as screening devices to identify students who require additional assistance (Salvia et al., 2013). When study skill assessment does include use of group-administered, norm-referenced general achievements tests, results must be interpreted carefully. Salvia et al. (2013) noted that **criterion-referenced tests** measure one's development of skills in terms of absolute levels of mastery. They suggest that criterion-referenced tests be used to assist classroom teachers in program planning. The norm- and criterion-referenced tests listed in Table 12-6 may assist in identifying specific grade levels for determining study skills that students have or have not mastered.

Despite the availability of the previously mentioned commercial instruments, many teachers find themselves needing to develop their own informal checklists to assess study skills efficiently as areas requiring further assistance are identified (McLoughlin & Lewis, 2007). Informal analysis of students' study skills may be the easiest aspect of diagnosis for helping students improve learning abilities. Hoover and Patton (2007) identified several steps that should be followed in an informal assessment of study skills. These are summarized as follows:

1. Identify study skills necessary to complete various tasks.
2. Construct a teacher checklist to assess study skills.
3. Construct a student self-analysis scale similar to the teacher's checklist.

TABLE 12–6 Norm-referenced (NR) and criterion-referenced (CR) assessments

Test	Type	Subtest	Grade Level
Brigance Diagnostic Inventories	CR	Reference Skills/ Graphs and Maps	K–12
California Achievement Tests	NR	Reference Skills	3.6–12.9
Comprehensive Test of Basic Skills (CTBS)	NR	Reference Skills	1–6
Iowa Silent Reading Tests	NR	Directed Reading	6–14
Iowa Tests of Basic Skills	NR	Reference Materials	1.7–9
LASSI (Learning and Study Strategies Inventory)	NR	Study Skills	Postsecondary

4. Develop and implement learning tasks that require students to employ needed study skills and observe students engaged in those tasks.
5. Complete teacher and student checklists documenting student uses of the study skill and compare results.

If commercial study skill devices are inappropriate for a particular situation or student, teachers may want to develop an inventory like the one provided in Figure 12-1.

Incorporating Study Skills in IEPs

Assessment data provide the basis for instructional planning. For students with special needs, this includes the IEP, which, as noted previously, is a required document for all learners receiving special education services (IDEA of 2004) that provides a road map for appropriate instruction (Diliberto & Brewer, 2012a, 2012b). Overall, student use of various study skills and strategies is foundational to successful completion of most academic and behavioral tasks (Deschler & Cornett, 2012; Hoover & Patton, 2007), including those documented on an IEP. As previously discussed, though important, unless incorporated in the delivery of classroom instruction, study skill usage often becomes lost or secondary to task completion, thereby affecting progress toward achievement of IEP objectives. *That is, ineffective uses of study skills may contribute to the lack of progress toward IEP benchmark achievement.* Additionally, student study strategies usage assists teachers with instructional efficiency in classroom management (Konrad, Helf, & Joseph, 2011).

An introductory overview of examples of how an IEP may incorporate study skills into its development provides a foundation that readers may bring to their teaching situations, as illustrated in Table 12-7.

As illustrated, the table includes examples of five IEP objectives along with indication of the study skills most needed to master the objectives (i.e., left column). The center column provides a brief description of the significance of the relevant study strategy to assist with effective mastery of the associated IEP objective. The far right, third column illustrates one example of the original IEP objective (left column) revised to form an objective that blends the use of select study abilities to support mastery of the academic or behavioral IEP objective. Classroom teachers who emphasize study strategies that most connect with IEP achievement outcomes provide students with increased opportunities to learn, thereby facilitating greater success.

Student use of study skills relevant to work associated with IEP objectives strengthens potential outcome progress. Given that research supports the value of student use of study skills, addressing these on a regular basis will assist students to successfully master IEP objectives. To this end, the following are five recommendations for practitioners to consider in the delivery of IEP tasks and activities within the structure of incorporating select study skills addressed in this chapter.

Time Management. Educators should make certain that when an IEP objective requires a student to manage time to more efficiently complete required tasks, the learner should be provided time management supports and subskill development sufficient to independently keep track of and maintain one's own learning within specified time frames. It is essential to make certain that effective time management exists in order to best interpret progress scores and other curriculum-based data associated with IEP progress monitoring.

Using Reference Materials. IEP objectives often require learners to locate and use appropriate resources to successfully complete required tasks. Educators should avoid assuming that learners know and understand what to select and how to apply the selected resources in the many tasks required to master IEP achievement objectives. Rather, each IEP objective should be analyzed to determine needed resources and, using the SSI, identify learner strengths and needs in this area, followed by necessary supports to ensure that proper resource usage occurs for each IEP objective.

Self-Management. Though managing one's own behavior is necessary for most effective learning to occur, some IEP objectives require more concentrated amounts of learner self-management than others. Once developed, the IEP outcome should be analyzed to determine the level of student self-management required, followed by an analysis of how well the learner exhibits the needed management skills using the SSI. Finding the correct balance between teacher direction and learner self-management is essential to providing students with disabilities sufficient opportunities to master IEP objectives while simultaneously becoming independent learners.

Test Taking. As previously emphasized, students are regularly assessed to determine progress toward

TABLE 12–7   IEP objectives blended with study skills

IEP Objective	Study Skill–IEP Objective Linkage	Revised Objective with Study Skill
1. Student will demonstrate grade-appropriate non-fiction reading comprehension by accurately answering 16 out of 20 multiple-choice questions on a fifth-grade-level reading passage within three minutes. *(Relevant Study Skill: Test Taking)*	Proper multiple-choice test-taking skills are needed to ensure that the student accurately demonstrates responses to 16 items; lack of these skills may lead to inaccurate results (i.e., learner appears to incorrectly respond though actually knows correct answers).	Using the multiple-choice test-taking skills of (a) *eliminating obvious wrong answers* and (b) *using proper clue words*, student will demonstrate grade-appropriate non-fiction reading comprehension by accurately answering 16 out of 20 multiple choice questions on a fifth-grade-level reading passage within three minutes.
2. Student will effectively manage writing time, as evidenced by ability to complete 75% of writing tasks within the given time frame, neatly and legibly. *(Relevant Study Skill: Time Management)*	Assisting the learner to employ simple time management techniques will help the learner remain on task 75% of the time while reducing writing errors.	Using the time management skills of (a) *adjusting to time allotment* and (b) *accurately perceiving required time needed*, student will complete 75% of writing tasks within the given time frame, neatly and legibly.
3. Student will independently complete class work with limited prompting and redirection by requiring no more than two teacher prompts or redirections per period. *(Relevant Study Skill: Self-Management)*	Independent work requires self-management, and providing this student supports with this strategy will impact task completion with reduced prompting.	Using the self-management skill of *self-monitoring*, student will complete class work with limited prompting and redirection requiring no more than two teacher prompts per period.
4. Student will increase accuracy in math by self-checking math work (multiple math calculations and applied problem solving) with fewer than three adult prompts per session. *(Relevant Study Skill: Organization)*	Learner is required to manage multiple math tasks using different types of calculations, requiring an organized approach to increase accuracy with limited teacher prompting.	Applying the organizational skill of *using a process to self-check completion of tasks*, student will self-check math work (multiple math calculations and applied problem solving) with fewer than three adult prompts per session.
5. Student will increase time on task as evidenced by ability to get the proper reference materials and begin work within two minutes of receiving independent work directions in four out of five independent work times. *(Relevant Study Skill: Reference Materials)*	Locating and using proper resources in a timely manner once instructions have been provided contributes to increased time on task, leading to more accurate independent work.	Applying the *using resources skill* of *using a checklist for selecting proper resources*, student will locate the proper materials/resources and begin work within two minutes of receiving independent work directions in four out of five independent work times.

Source: Adapted from J. J. Hoover, M. Betty, & J. R. Patton (2015). *Assessing study strategies to inform IEP development & implementation.* Unpublished manuscript. Presented at the San Diego CA Council for Exceptional Children Convention (April, 2015). Used with permission of the authors.

and mastery of IEP outcomes. Therefore, any IEP objective that specifically states that a student will demonstrate growth through use of a test, CBM, or other classroom assessment requires supports provided to the student sufficient to make certain the assessment reflects learner's true IEP knowledge and skills rather than the inability to accurately take and understand the testing process.

Organizational Skills.   The complexities associated with delivering and monitoring IEP tasks and objectives require significant skills in organizing one's learning. Multiple tasks and multiple components within tasks continue to challenge students with disabilities to make efficient and effective decisions about their learning. Providing supports to complete tasks in an organized manner is often an ongoing need to help learners master IEP objectives.

ENHANCEDetext
video example 12.2
Watch this video to learn more about test taking. https://www.youtube.com/watch?v=hF1lowm60Hk

Check Your Understanding 12.3   Click here to gauge your understanding of the concepts in this section.

IEPs and Study Skills

IEP objectives directly or indirectly require students to apply needed study skills for successful completion leading to instructional efficiency in the classroom.

Today's educational system places significant emphasis on assessment to measure IEP progress, highlighting the need for learners to possess effective *test-taking* skills.

The tremendous amount of information currently available to students, along with multiple ways of learning, requires students to acquire highly efficient *resource selection and usage* skills.

Increased class sizes and expectations placed on classroom teachers necessitate more effective and productive student *self-management* to ensure that all IEP objectives are satisfactorily taught and mastered.

The combined issues associated with the above items require effective *organizational skills*, along with efficient *time management skills*, to allow students with IEPs to meet and master each important academic and behavioral objective.

TEACHING STUDY SKILLS

Students best apply study skills when learned and used within the actual context of completing meaningful academic tasks (Hoover, 2011) and, when used strategically, increase class participation (Vaughn & Bos, 2015). This section presents numerous study skill strategies and teaching suggestions; however, these must be used within the overall classroom structure as well as within specific teaching practices. As with any area of education, the teaching and learning of study skills must be individualized to meet unique learning needs. Though the development and application of each study skill is specific to that study skill, a general process may be followed for learning and using study skills in the classroom to assist students in their development. One such process is presented next, followed by a discussion of two effective classroom practices for facilitating additional study skills use for students with learning problems.

Steps to Teaching Study Skills

The classroom development and use of study skills should follow a circular process that begins with assessment and is refined through ongoing evaluation.

Assessment.   The initial step in teaching study skills to learners is to assess particular need areas within the classroom to determine the study skills the student must acquire. During this assessment stage, specific study skill areas requiring some development or refinement are determined (e.g., time management,

report writing, listening during lectures). This process is specific to individual learners as unique classroom needs often arise. The process for assessing needed study skills was discussed in a previous section in this chapter, and the reader is referred to those procedures. The steps for informally assessing study skills are most appropriate in this process, although general information may be obtained through standardized measures. Once the specific study skill areas requiring development have been determined through assessment, the second step begins.

Selection.   In this second step, two major decisions must be made: (a) which study skill area(s) will be initially addressed and (b) which methods or strategies will be selected to help the student learn the identified study skill(s). The selection of the study skill(s) to initially address should be determined based on classroom needs, immediate academic needs, and student motivation. Once the study skill to address has been selected, one or more methods or strategies for developing the skill must be determined. Numerous strategies for assisting students with the different study skills are presented in this chapter. Some of these are individual teaching strategies (e.g., follow a consistent form of note taking, ensure proper reading rates are used, reward effective use of time, review test-taking errors); others are fully developed student strategies that contain procedures where a specific process is outlined and followed (e.g., SQ3R, Guided Lecture Procedure [GLP], COPS, TOWER, ReQuest). In the selection step, the teacher and student must identify the study skill area to address (e.g., reading rate, time management) and then select teaching and student strategies that will assist the learner to develop and use the targeted study skill more successfully. Once this process has been completed, the third step begins.

Implementation.   During the implementation step, the study skill teaching strategies and student strategies are reviewed and applied within actual classroom situations whenever the targeted study skill is needed. Teaching suggestions can easily be incorporated into various lessons and activities to help the student focus on the appropriate use of the study skill. The use of selected student strategies (e.g., ReQuest) requires some preparation and training on the part of the teacher. These student strategies (see Table 12-8) each contain specific steps to follow to be properly used in the classroom and learning situation. Initial development of these student strategies should include time for practicing and learning the steps. Most of these strategies contain a few simple steps through which students may easily progress. Once the learner is familiar with and has practiced the steps within the selected strategy, its use should be applied on a regular basis when needing the targeted study skill; for example, if COPS is selected, it should be used regularly when completing written reports. The use of selected teaching suggestions and student study strategies should be continued for a specified amount of time (e.g., two school weeks, next five written reports), and the impact on the targeted study skill should be documented. For example, if COPS is used for five consecutive written reports, the students should document how their reports have improved in punctuation and capitalization. Once the targeted study skill has been determined and implementation of relevant teaching and student study strategies has begun, the final step occurs. For further information on these strategies and their sources, see Hoover and Patton (2007).

Evaluation.   As discussed in the preceding step, the teacher should determine the specific amount of time that each strategy will be used. The evaluation of the effectiveness of the strategy used on the targeted study skill must also be determined. That is, how you will know if the strategy is working must be determined. Use of simple checklists or anecdotal logs will facilitate regular and easy documentation

of the effectiveness of the strategy on the student's use of the targeted study skill (e.g., better written reports, more effective use of time, more organized lecture notes). As the study skill strategies are used by the learner, the effects on student use of the study skill will become apparent and should be documented. Use of the strategies should continue for the specified amount of time. Using the ongoing documentation as a guide, the use of the strategy to assist with the targeted study skill should be evaluated. If sufficient progress has been made, its use should continue. If not, other strategies should be tried following the procedures outlined in the second and third steps of the process.

In addition to the four-step process for teaching study skills, other popular and widely used classroom practices facilitate study skills development. Two of these are semantic webbing and cooperative learning. Both of these teaching practices facilitate the development, maintenance, and generalization of study skills while also assisting students with learning problems with various academic tasks. When used in conjunction with the preceding steps, varied experiences and opportunities are provided for students to develop and use the study skills discussed in this chapter.

 LEARNING MODULE 12.1 Click here to learn more about effectively teaching study skills (part 1). http://iris .peabody.vanderbilt.edu/module/ss1

Semantic Webbing and Study Skills

Semantic webs (or maps) are frequently discussed as an effective teaching practice to assist with vocabulary, reading comprehension, and related areas of learning (Bender, 2008). Use of semantic webs provides students the opportunity to collectively relate new and existing knowledge. **Semantic mapping** helps students acquire and apply study skills within the context of classroom tasks or situations. Semantic webbing or mapping was also discussed earlier; refer to that earlier discussion or to Hoover and Patton (2007) for an overview of this teaching practice. As students use semantic webs they elaborate on what they know and graphically organize that knowledge. In addition, Dean et al. (2014) wrote that visual representation of information (i.e., semantic web, graphic organizer) often facilitates knowledge development.

TABLE 12–8 Study skill strategies

Strategy	Task Areas	Process	Description
CAN-DO	Acquiring content	Create list of items to learn Ask self if list is complete Note details and main ideas Describe components and their relationships Overlearn main items followed by learning details	This strategy may assist with memorization of lists of items through rehearsal techniques.
COPS	Written reports	Capitalization correct Overall appearance Punctuation correct Spelling correct	This strategy provides a structure for proofreading written work prior to submitting it to the teacher.
DEFENDS	Written expression	Decide on a specific position Examine own reasons for this position Figure order for main topic and details and expose position in first sentence of written task Note each reason and associated points Drive home position in last sentence and search for and correct any errors	This strategy assists learners to defend a particular position in a written assignment.
FIST	Reading comprehension	First sentence is read Indicate a question based on material in first sentence Search for answer to question Tie question and answer together through paraphrasing	This questioning strategy assists students to actively pursue responses to questions related directly to material being read.
GLP	Note taking	Guided Lecture Procedure	GLP provides students with a structure for taking notes during lectures. Group activity is involved to facilitate effective note taking.
PANORAMA	Reading	Preparatory stage—identify purpose Intermediate stage—survey and read Concluding stage—memorize material	This strategy includes a three-stage process to assist with reading comprehension.
PARS	Reading	Preview Ask questions Read Summarize	PARS is recommended for use with younger students and with those who have limited experiences with study strategies.
PENS	Sentence writing	Pick a formula Explore different words to fit into the formula Note the words selected Subject and verb selections follow	PENS is appropriate for developing basic sentence structure and assists students to write different types of sentences by following formulas for sentence construction.
PIRATES	Test taking	Prepare to succeed Inspect instructions carefully Read entire question, remember memory strategies, and reduce choices Answer question or leave until later Turn back to the abandoned items Estimate unknown answers by avoiding absolutes and eliminating similar choices Survey to ensure that all items have a response	PIRATES may assist learners to more carefully and successfully complete tests.
PQ4R	Reading	Preview Question Read Reflect Recite Review	PQ4R may assist students to become more discriminating readers.

TABLE 12–8 *(continued)*

Strategy	Task Areas	Process	Description
RARE	Reading	Review selection questions Answer all questions known Read the selection Express answers to remaining questions	RARE emphasizes reading for a specific purpose while focusing on acquiring answers to selection questions initially not known.
REAP	Reading writing, thinking	Read Encode Annotate Ponder	REAP is a method that assists students to combine several skills to facilitate discussion about reading material.
ReQuest	Reading, questioning	Reciprocal questioning	Teacher and student ask each other questions about a selection. Student modeling of teacher questions and teacher feedback are emphasized as the learner explores the meaning of the reading material.
RIDER	Reading comprehension	Read sentence Image (form mental picture) Describe how new image differs from previous sentence Evaluate image to ensure that it contains all necessary elements Repeat process with subsequent sentences	This visual imagery strategy cues the learner to form a mental image of what was previously learned from a sentence just read.
SCORER	Test taking	Schedule time effectively Identify clue words Omit difficult items until end Read carefully Estimate answers requiring calculations Review work and responses	This test-taking strategy provides a structure for completing various tests by assisting students to carefully and systematically complete test items.
SQRQCQ	Math word problems	Survey word problem Identify question asked Read more carefully Question process required to solve problem Compute the answer Question self to ensure that the answer solves the problem	This strategy provides a systematic structure for identifying the question being asked in a math word problem, computing the response, and ensuring that the question in the problem was answered.
SQ3R	Reading	Survey Question Read Recite Review	SQ3R provides a systematic approach to improve reading comprehension.
TOWER	Written reports	Think Order ideas Write Edit Rewrite	TOWER provides a structure for completing initial and final drafts of written reports. It may be used effectively with COPS.
TQLR	Listening	Tuning in Questioning Listening Reviewing	This strategy assists with listening comprehension. Students generate questions and listen for specific statements related to these questions.

Source: Table 6.1 From *Teaching Study Skills to Students with Learning Problems: A Teacher's Guide for Meeting Diverse Needs*, 2nd Ed. (p. 3), by J. J. Hoover and J. R. Patton, 2007, Austin, TX: PRO-ED. Copyright 2007 by PRO-ED, Inc. Reprinted with permission.

Through semantic webbing, students build on previous study skill knowledge and experiences, no matter how inexperienced they may be in using study skills (Hoover & Patton, 2007). Table 12-9, developed from information found in Hoover and Patton (2007) and Hoover et al. (2008), lists study skills discussed in this chapter, along with several suggested semantic web topics for which subordinate ideas may be generated by the students.

As shown, different semantic web topics and subtopics exist to help learners use their study skills. These may easily be adapted and expanded for classroom application in any grade level.

Figure 12-2 provides an example of a completed semantic web for helping students learn the important study skill of note taking or outlining. In this example, the teacher identifies the main topic (note taking/outlining) and the subtopics (i.e., headings and subheading, recording information from printed material, recording information from oral presentations and lectures). The items surrounding subtopics are examples of student-generated ideas for using the study skill and applying the subtopics to their note taking and outlining. Once the web has been completed by an individual or a small group of students, all learners should receive copies of the semantic web and select one or two ideas from the web to begin to apply in their learning. Students may draw on this example to guide themselves in their documenting of activities related to lectures or other oral presentations as well as printed material. After students complete a note-taking or outlining task, they should analyze why and in what ways the web ideas helped them and what they can do in the future to produce more effective notes or outlines. This note-taking and outlining example is only one of many that teachers can model and adapt as they use semantic mapping to help students use study skills in the classroom. Procedures for their development are similar to those described for the note-taking and outlining web.

Students who have learning problems may require specific training or coaching to successfully

TABLE 12–9 Study skills semantic web topics

Study Skill	Suggested Semantic Web Topics
Reading rate	Understanding reading purpose; fast, slow, and normal reading rates—*finding the main idea; locating primary and secondary details; generating proper sequence of ideas; using strategies for retaining and recalling read material based on purpose*
Library usage	Online cataloging system; layout and structure of a school or classroom library; role of library specialist
Reference materials usage	Thesaurus, dictionary, encyclopedia, atlas, online sources—*determining purpose for needing the reference material; locating information; using key or guide words, table of contents, index, glossary*
Information presentations (*graphic aids, oral presentations, written reports*)	Written and oral reporting and papers; visuals and graphics in presentations—*selecting the topic; gathering and organizing thoughts; using proper grammar, sentence structure, and punctuation; using proper oral delivery and presentation mechanics*
Instructional listening	Attending during formal lectures; engaging in small-group discussions; interpreting audiovisual material—*attending to message heard; clarifying speaker's ideas and intentions; applying relevant meaning to message; applying strategies to recall message*
Task organization	Determining tasks to be completed and how to complete larger tasks within shorter time frame; achieving greater proficiency with multiple tasks
Effective note taking and outlining	Research papers, draft versions, group projects—*organizing and managing notes; including sufficient details; using proper headings and subheadings; using effective organizational format*
Test taking: *preparing, taking, reviewing*	Short or long answer essay tests; true–false tests; multiple-choice exams—*using test studying skills, skills for taking the test, reviewing the test results*
Behavior self-management	Monitoring behavior; assuming personal responsibility for behavior; charting, changing, and owning personal behaviors
Effective time management	Identifying required tasks; prioritizing tasks; completing and recording tasks; generating daily, weekly, monthly task schedules

Note: Main semantic web topics appear in roman type; suggested subtopics appear in italics.

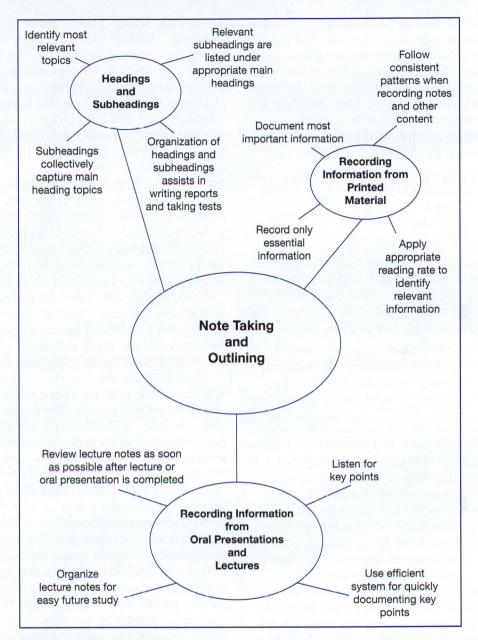

FIGURE 12–2 Semantic Web

complete semantic webs for study skills development. A critical follow-up in the use of semantic webs is to develop and use study skills in actual classroom situations. As students share their successes with their study skill webs, they will assist others to become more proficient in that study skill. Use of the various study strategies and teaching suggestions discussed in this chapter will help students apply the study skills they have identified through semantic webbing.

Study Skills and Cooperative Learning

A classroom structure built on **cooperative learning,** and its principles may also teach essential study skills. Dean et al. (2014) suggested that a structure that organizes students into cooperative groups facilitates highly effective learning. The use of cooperative learning on a regular basis in the classroom is a decision left to each individual teacher. However, should cooperative learning be used, study skills education should be an integral part of each student's academic and social growth. The following discussion provides a general overview of cooperative learning, along with consideration of ways to teach study skills through this method. Although researchers in this area have identified various ways of implementing cooperative learning, several common elements are frequently discussed. These include (Hoover et al., 2008) the following:

- Positive interdependence
- Individual accountability
- Positive interactions
- Interpersonal training
- Group processing

Through cooperative learning, students learn that their individual goals are best achieved through shared work and cooperation with others. Each of the five elements is briefly summarized (Cohen & Spenciner, 2008; Hallahan et al., 2015; Hoover et al., 2008):

- **Positive interdependence**—refers to a shared sense of mutual goals and tasks. All members complete their assignments and draw on the knowledge and skills of other group members in their own learning.
- **Individual accountability**—allows each student to individually acquire the knowledge and skills and also requires individual demonstration of mastery while learning in a group situation.
- **Positive interactions**—is the element that supports sharing ideas and assisting others in their learning. As students interact in meaningful ways, important individual and group learning occurs.
- **Interpersonal training**—is necessary to prepare students, especially those unfamiliar with cooperative learning, to successfully and fully participate in the process. This is an important element in the strategy as the success of cooperative learning in the classroom depends on how well prepared students are to take on group work and group functioning.
- **Group processing**—is the culminating task where the cooperative group members evaluate their own contributions to the task. Through this culminating task, group members discuss their contributions, identify ways to improve overall member interactions, and suggest recommendations for future efforts. Documented student or teacher observations of the group's functioning may facilitate the debriefing of the group by providing objective data for members to discuss.

Effectively Using Study Skills in Cooperative Learning. Within the parameters of cooperative learning, a direct relationship exists between effective use of study skills and the efficient implementation of cooperative learning. As previously discussed, study skills were identified as tools that learners use to more effectively and efficiently acquire, record, organize, synthesize, and remember tasks and skills (i.e., competencies presented in Table 12-1). To best learn in school, regular and consistent use of study skills is necessary, especially in an era when increased workloads and expectations exist for all learners. In addition, as tasks become more complex, such as what is seen in Common Core, use of study skills becomes even more critical. Therefore, whether working cooperatively or independently, students must develop, maintain, and generalize the use of various study skills.

Table 12-10, developed from discussion about cooperative learning found in Hoover and Patton (2007) and Cohen and Spenciner (2008), provides examples of how study skill development and use are integral to cooperative learning structures.

Illustrated are the five elements of cooperative learning along with suggested connections to students' use of study skills. The degree to which students use study skills effectively can affect the overall performance of other group members. This includes student development and use of study skills, group sharing of study strategies for effective use of study skills, or the reflection of study skills used by group members during the group processing stage. Conversely, students' inefficient use of time, inappropriate behavioral self-management, inefficient library or reference materials usage, ineffective test-taking abilities, or inability to select and use appropriate reading rates may significantly interfere with the success of the cooperative group. However, when used appropriately in cooperative groups, more effective group interactions and learning can occur.

LEARNING MODULE 12.2 Click here to learn more about study skills strategies for improving students' academic performance. http://iris.peabody.vanderbilt.edu/module/ss2

Implementing a Study Skills Program

Study skills programs should introduce simple variations of study skills in lower elementary grades and gradually increase in complexity as students progress through the grades (Hoover & Patton, 2007). The

TABLE 12–10 Enhancing study skills development through cooperative learning

Cooperative Learning Component	Study Skills Development through Cooperative Interactions and Team Support
Positive interdependence	As cooperative team members use study skills, others are affected in positive ways, contributing to the study skill development of all members within a cooperative learning group or pair.
Individual accountability	Within a cooperative group structure, individuals are still responsible and accountable for demonstrating acquired knowledge and skills; being able to recognize and use own study skill strengths is important to achieve this outcome. Through this process, individual cooperative team members are able to identify ways to best contribute to the group and how others on the team may best assist them with their study skill development. Informal pre- and post-assessment of individual study skill abilities through use of the Study Skills Inventory (SSI) ensures that individual accountability is developed and maintained.
Positive interactions	Students more proficient with study skills usage are better prepared to help others with their study skills development in cooperative learning team structures. Sharing of study skills relevant to completion of the cooperative learning task helps learners strengthen each other's study skill abilities.
Interpersonal training	A key component of classroom instruction is the inclusion of a comprehensive study skills program to facilitate greater independence in learning that is strengthened through cooperative interactions. The need to engage students in interpersonal training activities to effectively develop study skills should be integral to cooperative learning preparation and application in the classroom. As students become proficient with each of the study skills (e.g., time management, self-management, outlining, organization, library usage), they become empowered to engage in interpersonal interactions necessary for successful cooperative learning to occur.
Group processing	As students reflect on the effectiveness and results of their cooperative interactions, attention to specific study skills used may provide insight into strategies to improve future cooperative teamwork and individual accountability.

age, ability, and individual needs of special learners must determine the extent of that complexity; however, early efforts may prove beneficial throughout the entire educational program. The following list outlines several guidelines for teachers to follow in developing and/or improving their study skills programs. These are adapted from Hoover and Patton (2007) and can be applied to all students; however, they are of particular significance for teachers of students who have special learning needs:

1. Introduce simple variations of the different study skills in the early grades.
2. Gradually increase to the more complex elements associated with each study skill as the students progress through the grades.
3. Identify specific goals and objectives for a study skills program prior to program implementation.
4. Let students' individual strengths and weaknesses guide decision making concerning which study skills to emphasize at any particular time.
5. Know what motivates students to use different study skills and emphasize these motivations in program implementation.
6. Explain, model, and demonstrate the proper use of each study skill.
7. Expect students to use different study skills appropriately through guided practice and planned learning experiences.
8. Provide continued opportunity for practicing study skill use to assist students in acquiring and maintaining mastery of the skills.
9. Facilitate the use of study skills in natural classroom settings and on a regular basis as the need arises in different subject areas and learning activities.
10. Assist students in generalizing acquired study skills through an emphasis on more complex use of the skills once initial mastery of the basic study skills has been achieved.

Students at any grade level, especially students with disabilities, require direct teacher guidance in study skill areas.

In addition to the general guidelines just presented, teachers may find more specific instructional strategies useful in implementing a study skills program. For each study skill, a brief vignette is presented to illustrate an example of learner needs associated with the skill. Selected suggested best practices for improving the targeted study skill needs illustrated are provided subsequent to each vignette.

Reading Rates Vignette. Peter is a fourth grader who experiences difficulty reading different types of material. Although he eventually acquires the needed information, it often takes him unusually long periods of time to read for different types of assignments. After observing and reading with Paul, it became obvious that he applies the same slower-type reading rate no matter what the assignment requires (e.g., some tasks ask only for the name of a person, others require finding the detailed main idea, and others require getting the gist of a paragraph). Helping Peter acquire and apply the most appropriate reading rate based on reading purpose is needed to help him use his reading time more efficiently.

Suggested Best Practices Attempt one or more of these reading rate suggestions:

1. Ensure that proper reading rates are used for different reading activities.
2. Establish clear purposes for each reading assignment.
3. Ensure that each student is familiar with each type of reading rate.
4. Provide opportunities for the appropriate use of each reading rate.

Listening Skills Vignette. Martha is a second grader in a classroom with 24 students. Although students frequently work in learning centers or stations where she is attentive and completes her work, during whole-class direct instruction led by the classroom teacher, Martha is often off task, inattentive, and appears to not be listening to what is being said. Her desk during these times is situated near the classroom door, which is usually open during class times. She infrequently is able to respond to questions asked of her during whole-class instruction and regularly loses her place in materials used during the instruction. Providing Martha a whole-class situation to help her remain on task during listening direct instruction activities and to better attend to the class activities is necessary.

Suggested Best Practices Attempt one or more of these listening suggestions:

1. Reduce distractions and deal quickly with classroom disruptions.
2. Encourage each student to speak loudly enough so that all can hear.
3. Repeat and emphasize important items in the verbal message.
4. Summarize the verbal message at strategic points in the lecture.
5. Use visual materials to support oral presentations.
6. Situate the learner who is distracted by outside noise away from entrances or windows when appropriate.

Note Taking or Outlining Vignette. Francisco is a fifth grader who likes to read and is an average writer. However, he exhibits significant difficulties summarizing what he has read and struggles with producing an outline of his work. After reading a several-paragraph passage, Francisco is unable to generate relevant notes on what he has read, making it difficult for him to explain main ideas, sequence story events, or draw conclusions about author intent. When asked to outline material prior to completing a writing task, he often neglects to include key main ideas or relevant supporting details. Although Francisco is an average writer, his written expression skills would improve significantly if he developed a more organized and complete outline reflecting his notes taken during a lecture or reading activity prior to engaging in the writing task.

Suggested Best Practices Attempt one or more of these note-taking/outlining suggestions:

1. Encourage students to follow a consistent note-taking/outlining format.
2. Teach students to identify and focus on key topics and ideas.
3. Discuss with students the uses and advantages of making outlines and taking notes.
4. Model different note-taking/outlining formats for students.
5. Begin with simple note-taking/outlining activities and gradually introduce more complex types of activities.

Report Writing Vignette. Alicia is a 10th-grade student who struggles with writing assignments, specifically with tasks that lead to final written reports, such as literacy analyses, research papers, or summaries of interviews. Although Alicia is capable of producing written assignments possessing effective note-taking and outlining skills, she exhibits problems in organizing her thoughts and explaining the main ideas in a coherent manner. She demonstrates the most proficiency when completing short written assignments and shows the most need when writing longer papers or reports. In discussing her writing with Alicia, it became apparent the she lacked knowledge of an overall writing process and is often unclear as to the purpose of various assigned written tasks, both of which are required to best succeed with the study skill of report writing.

Suggested Best Practices   Attempt one or more of these report writing suggestions:

1. Clarify the purpose for each writing assignment with the students.
2. Provide guided instruction in the use of an organized writing process, ensuring that the students understand the steps and procedures and apply them when writing.
3. Begin writing activities with simple, less complex written assignments and gradually introduce more difficult types of written reports.
4. Facilitate students' use a dictionary and other reference materials when necessary and that they proofread their written work.
5. Work with students as they complete different stages of writing assignments.
6. Provide periodic review and encouragement to students as they complete writing reports, making certain that they continue to understand the purpose for the assignment and apply the writing process.

Oral Presentations Vignette.   Juliana is an eighth-grade student who has a learning disability in reading, exhibiting academic problems with higher-level comprehension questions. She also has difficulty expressing herself orally both when called on to respond to a question and if asked to share her work with her classmates. In small-group or peer situations, Juliana freely participates and is able to verbally respond to questions and makes attempts at sharing her ideas with her peers. Building on her strength of being able to complete oral presentations and responses in smaller instructional settings, Juliana may be able to experience greater success sharing with the whole class if she

is provided a few differentiations being guided to make certain that she comprehends material she is expected to share.

Suggested Best Practices   Attempt one or more of these oral presentation suggestions:

1. Allow sufficient time for students to prepare for oral presentations.
2. Conduct oral presentations in a nonthreatening environment to minimize peer criticism.
3. Provide different situations for oral presentations (e.g., with students seated or standing by their desks, standing in front of a small group, addressing the whole class).
4. Ensure that students know and understand the purposes for oral presentations.
5. Make certain that students sufficiently understand the material they are presenting in their oral presentation preparations.

Use of Graphic Aids Vignette.   Juan is a second-grade student who has limited experiences with formal schooling and academic materials. However, he possesses sufficient experiential background to be moderately successful with academic work in school. Through classroom observations of Juan, it became apparent that he becomes confused with illustrations, captions, and other visuals, particularly in reading and mathematics materials. Juan is capable of learning and using reading and math vocabulary yet is often unable to fully comprehend the material due to an inability to properly use and interpret graphic aids. Juan seems to be a student who would benefit from direct teaching in the usage of graphic aids, both when sharing his learning in the classroom and when using reading and math materials to complete assigned tasks.

Suggested Best Practices   Attempt one or more of these graphic aids suggestions:

1. Allow students to use graphic aids with or as alternatives to oral and written reports.
2. Ensure that students know why specific material is presented in graphic form by discussing with students their interpretations of the graphic material.
3. Provide specific time for learners to study the visual material incorporated into oral presentations or written materials.

4. Assist students in focusing on important aspects of graphic aids, linking these to the text or other aspects of a task or problem.
5. Provide sufficient time for students to read and interpret graphic aids presented during lectures.
6. Assist learners to understand how graphic aids assume an important role in helping them understand material or in getting key points across when sharing with others.

Test-Taking Vignette. Sharon is sixth-grade student who experiences difficulty completing tests to demonstrate her knowledge and skills. She experiences most difficulty with objective test questions (e.g., true or false, multiple choice), while she exhibits greater success with test questions that require short responses or explanations of answers. After discussing Sharon's completed test with her, she shared that she often is confused as to what a test question may be asking or what to do when she is uncertain of the correct response. She also said that she seems to study the "wrong information" for tests. Assisting Sharon with a few key test-studying and test-taking skills will help her address these particular needs.

Suggested Best Practices Attempt one or more of these test-taking suggestions:

1. Discuss with students the purposes of tests and show them how to complete different types of tests items.
2. Provide students opportunities to practice completing different types of test questions to become more familiar with: (a) how items tend to be structure, (b) how to determine exactly what is being asked in the item, and (c) ways to narrow down response options should uncertainty exist with the correct response.
3. Explain the different methods of study necessary to prepare for various types of tests (e.g., objective, essay) and provide opportunity to practice in the classroom prior to tests.
4. Review completed and graded tests with the students, identifying test-taking errors. Discuss options for correcting the errors on future tests.
5. Ensure that students know the time allotted for completion of each test.
6. Explore test directions with students to ensure that they are familiar with different types of test instructions connected to various testing items.

Library Use Vignette. Mica is a seventh-grade student who likes to write and share information about his experiences and learning. However, he lacks the ability to gather and use information that he reads on topics written by others. Although Mica is able to locate information on the Internet, his difficulties in using the school and community libraries severely interfere with his use of credible and reliable sources to complete research papers or other related assignments. In order for Mica to continue to make progress academically, he needs to acquire more effective library usage skills for gathering and using needed resources to complete written papers or related writing projects.

Suggested Best Practices Attempt one or more of these library usage suggestions:

1. Review the uses and importance of a library and familiarize students with its organizational layout.
2. Discuss with students the similarities and differences between information found over the Internet and in library materials, examining how they can be certain the information is credible and reliable.
3. Structure assignments so that students must use a library to complete them.
4. Be sure that students know the purpose of using the library in any library activity.
5. Teach students to consult media specialists and other library personnel as necessary.
6. Provide students guidance to help them understand the differences between firsthand and secondhand sources when considering library materials for their assignments.

Reference Materials Usage Vignette. Nubia is fourth-grade student who experiences difficulty using reference materials to complete various assigned classroom tasks. She understands the importance of consulting different reference materials to complete written assignments yet lacks sufficient experience directly using these types of materials. One result of her inability to effectively use reference materials is the need to provide extended periods of time to complete assigned tasks. Unless she obtains more effective reference materials usage skills, she will continue to experience problems completing tasks, which will become even more significant as she progresses into the secondary grades.

Suggested Best Practices Attempt one or more of these reference usage suggestions:

1. Ensure that dictionaries, thesauri, and so on are readily available to all students.
2. Structure various assignments to require students to use different reference materials located in the classroom and school library.
3. Be sure that each student possesses sufficient skills to successfully use general reference and dictionary materials when these are required.
4. Create situations that help students understand the proper uses of reference materials.
5. Familiarize students with the different components of general reference materials and dictionaries prior to requiring their use in assignments (e.g., guide words, index, table of contents).

Time-Management Vignette.
Roberto is a fifth-grade student who experiences difficulty completing multiple assignments on time. He tends to spend too much time on those tasks that he likes and an insufficient amount of time on those in which he is less interested. This inefficient management of time leads to some assignments being completed in depth, while others are submitted in an incomplete manner by containing minimal or superficial responses and information. Roberto would benefit from greater time-management strategies along with increased understanding of why it is necessary to distribute use of time in more effective ways.

Suggested Best Practices Attempt one or more of these time-management suggestions:

1. Reward students' effective use of time when completing tasks or making daily learning decisions.
2. Provide students a model to follow to effectively manage time, especially completing several tasks within a defined block of time; provide opportunities to learn and practice model.
3. Structure classroom activities so that students are required to budget their own time, adhering to steps or a process selected to help with development of time management.

4. Praise on-task behaviors, especially during independent work times.
5. Ensure that students know the amount of time allotted for completion of each activity or set of activities.
6. Periodically discuss with students their time-management strategies and their effects on task completion within allotted time frame.

ENHANCEDetext
video example 12.3
Watch this video to learn more about time management.
http://goo.gl/hC9Q72

Self-Management of Behavior Vignette.
Russell is a sixth-grade student who has a learning disability in reading and exhibits frequent off-task and out-of-seat behaviors. He is easily distracted, especially during large-group direct instruction activities. Based on a series of classroom observations and discussions with several of his teachers, it appears that Russell lacks self-control. During one-to-one instruction with Russell, his off-task behaviors diminish, yet his impulsive tendencies continue to be evident. Russell could benefit from increased self-management, which provides him a structure to assume greater responsibility for his own behaviors as well as complete more academic work in a timely manner.

Suggested Best Practices Attempt one or more of these self-management suggestions:

1. Be sure that students know specific classroom and instructional behavioral expectations.
2. Establish with students a self-monitoring program to help them become more aware of their behaviors and how frequently these are exhibited.
3. Assist students in setting realistic and attainable goals in a self-management program.
4. Be consistent in enforcing behavioral expectations of students.
5. Allow sufficient time for a self-monitoring program to be implemented before the effects of the program are interpreted.
6. Periodically discuss with students their self-monitoring programs, being certain to help them realize the connections between self-control of one's behavior and completion of assignments.

Organizational Skills Vignette. Amanda is a ninth-grade student who always attends school and participates in various school activities. She is very busy during and after the school day, frequently forgetting to complete some of her assigned tasks or homework. As a result, her grades are beginning to suffer, and she is becoming frustrated with her daily schedules. Amanda is very capable of successfully completing multiple tasks if only she would be more organized. Some direct instruction and guidance on ways to become more organized would benefit Amanda, thereby allowing her to more efficiently and effectively balance her tasks both during and after the school day.

Suggested Best Practices Attempt one or more of these organizational suggestions:

1. Emphasize to students the need and benefits of organizing one's own learning by discussing and illustrating strengths of being organized in school routines.
2. Provide students time and opportunity to develop their own organizational skills personalized to their particular needs.
3. Periodically discuss with students their organizational plans and how they assist in helping them more effectively keep themselves organized.
4. Provide students with several daily assignments and instruct them to create a chart illustrating the order they will follow to

complete the tasks; debrief with them to discuss adherence to the selected order.
5. Encourage students to share their organizational strategies with others, especially when cooperative learning is used in the classroom.
6. Assist students to develop related learning strategies connected to acquiring effective organizational abilities.

**ENHANCEDetext
video example 12.4**
Watch this video to learn more about organization skills.
http://goo.gl/bQMl19

Learning Strategies

This chapter concludes with a general overview of six learning strategies that are appropriate for use with students who experience learning or behavior problems. Learning strategies are methods that help learners solve problems, achieve goals independently, become more efficient learners, and evaluate their own learning (Vaughn & Bos, 2015). Although related, study skills and learning strategies are different approaches to meeting similar learning needs. Bender (2008) described a primary difference between study skills and learning strategies as one emphasizing the cognitive aspects associated with learning (i.e., learning

---

CULTURALLY RESPONSIVE CLASSROOMS

An essential tool that must be developed by culturally and linguistically diverse students is their ability to effectively employ study skills in the classroom. I acquired this important knowledge through many years of teaching and research with K–12 students (and their teachers) in special education multicultural classrooms and school environments. Development and use of effective study skills becomes most critical to avoid misinterpreting diverse students' learning differences as somehow being synonymous with learning disabilities. To the contrary, learning differences represent strengths that need to be valued to best instruct diverse students. One of the more effective ways to ensure that diverse student learning is properly delivered and assessed is to include a structured program designed to integrate the development and use of study skills in K–12 instruction. Proper use of study

skills allows diverse students to contextualize learning relative to cultural background and language development. Often, the inability of diverse students to adequately demonstrate progress more accurately reflects unfamiliarity with expected tasks or assessments rather than lack of knowledge and skills. Study skill usage allows learners to put instructional tasks into a more relevant cultural context and provides educators more accurate assessment results. Cultural responsive teaching includes classrooms that consider and value cultural and linguistic diversity; proper use of study skills increases diverse students' opportunities to learn while providing teachers more reliable and accurate instructional progress monitoring results.

John J. Hoover is associate professor of research at the University of Colorado, Boulder.

strategies), whereas the other (i.e., study skills) emphasizes the actual task itself (e.g., writing the report, taking the test, being organized). Although different in scope and/or purpose, when used collectively, the study skills discussed in this chapter and the learning strategies presented next facilitate improved teaching and learning. The six learning strategies are not all-inclusive; rather, they represent additional types of study strategies effective in meeting academic and educational needs. Learning strategies emphasize learning how to learn and complement use of existing study skills known to the student (Hoover, 2011). As such, they are excellent ways in which teachers can make study skills instruction work more effectively.

Active Processing. Active processing involves the use of self-talk or self-questioning in order to activate knowledge. Self-talk or verbalization supports student learning by allowing students to say to themselves what they have just learned or heard (Hoover, 2011). This strategy also assists students to elaborate on a particular content area in order to complete a task. Skills such as summarizing, scanning, questioning, and predicting may be used. When using this strategy, teachers must make certain that students know that self-talk is appropriate and acceptable to help them define, evaluate, monitor, and complete a task.

Analogy. Analogy allows an individual to recall previously acquired learning and knowledge and relate these to a new topic or experience. In addition, use of analogy assists leaners to see that material or items that initially appear dissimilar may contain similar features, thereby increasing understanding of that new material (Dean et al., 2014). This strategy may use schema, metaphor, or cloze procedures as students learn new material. The effective use of analogy in the classroom requires that teachers help students to recall and access prior learning and then compare, contrast, substitute, or elaborate on that knowledge to learn and retain new information. Use of analogy also helps students increase their confidence in learning (Cottrell, 2001).

Coping. Coping is a problem-solving learning strategy that enables students to confront issues and tasks systematically and objectively. A variety of problems may be addressed as the learner confronts issues, develops solutions, identifies necessary assistance, attempts solutions, persists with a task, and eventually generates successful resolution to the problem or learning task. Students with learning problems benefit from problem-solving or coping tasks by helping them relate solutions to learning outcomes and social needs (Vaughn & Bos, 2015). Teachers should be sensitive to students' values and problem-solving preferences when assisting them to develop this learning strategy.

Evaluation. Evaluation helps students become aware of what is needed to successfully complete a task and monitor whether that task has been completed. Self-monitoring, reflection, prediction, generalization, and feedback skills are all used with this strategy. Independent work skills of students may improve through this strategy. Teachers should demonstrate to students how to check answers, monitor progress toward task completion, reflect on procedures and results of the completed task, and transfer skills to new tasks or situations. Self-evaluation is also important as this facilitates students' judgments of the quality of their work (Vaughn & Bos, 2015). Successful mastery of these and similar skills will facilitate effective use of the evaluation strategy.

Organization. The strategy of organization emphasizes student abilities to group or cluster items, tasks, ideas, and skills. Classifying items includes knowing the rules that guide the groupings (e.g., color, function; Dean et al., 2014). A variety of organizational patterns may exist for specific items or skills, and specific instructional situations may dictate the use of different organizations (e.g., broad versus narrow groupings). Students may initially experience problems with knowing what types of categories or clusters are acceptable or appropriate for different learning situations. Teachers should employ direct teaching to help learners explore possible ways to categorize and then evaluate effectiveness.

Rehearsal. Rehearsal helps students think about a task prior to beginning the task, while working at it, and upon its completion. Elements such as reviewing, reciting, and recalling different aspects related to an assignment are important in rehearsal. This strategy allows students to think through what they are doing as they proceed in task completion (Hoover, 2011). This, in turn, minimizes problems and facilitates more effective use of time. Pausing, questioning, visualizing, and summarizing are important features of this strategy, and teachers should help students practice these as tasks are completed.

Classroom Activities—Learning Strategies

The six strategies just discussed will help students in their overall study skill development. In actual practice, study skills and learning strategies are frequently used in combination. Table 12-11 illustrates examples of the integrated uses of study skills

TABLE 12–11   Integrating study skills and learning strategies

Learning Strategy	Overview	Integrated Study Skills
Active processing	Use of self-talk/questioning to activate and recall prior knowledge	*Self-management*—Managing self is necessary to successfully using self-questioning.
		Test taking—Various test-taking strategies help students recall knowledge and skills.
		Library usage—Effective use of library resources supports further development of activated knowledge.
Analogy	Relating new knowledge with previously acquired knowledge/skills	*Note taking/outlining*—These skills help learners integrate new/existing knowledge.
		Reference materials—Reference materials provide access to new knowledge.
		Reading rates—Various rates are used to acquire new knowledge building on existing skills.
Coping	Use of problem-solving techniques in learning to address needs, issues	*Test taking*—Test-taking strategies help students break down test items and problem solve to identify solutions to correct test-taking errors.
		Organizational skills—Effective organizational skills are needed to help students cope with learning new skills/knowledge.
		Time management—Effective time management helps students persevere and persist with learning setbacks.
Evaluation	Use of self-monitoring to check work and reflect on solutions	*Self-management*—Self-management facilitates effective evaluation of students' own learning.
		Organizational skills—Students must work in an organized manner to best check and reflect on their own learning.
		Note taking/outlining—Skills associated with taking notes and creating outlines help with documenting self-monitored progress.
Organization	Unique ways that students organize learning and group concepts and skills	*Note taking/outlining*—These abilities contribute to better organized and grouped ideas, concepts, and skills.
		Test taking—Test-taking abilities assist learners to organize and group acquired learning while preparing for tests.
		Graphic aids—Graphic aids assist learners to better understand and group complex material.
Rehearsal	Reflecting on tasks; thinking through issues prior to beginning assignment	*Listening*—Listening to others' views helps learners better reflect on assignments prior to starting tasks.
		Self-management—Skills provide a structure to help students reflect on their own learning.
		Organizational skills—Organizational skills help learners organize thoughts to think through steps necessary to complete tasks.

Source: Hoover, J. J., Klingner, J. K., Baca, L.M., and Patton, J. M., *Methods for Teaching Culturally and Linguistically Diverse Exceptional Learners*, © 2008, Table 12-7. Reprinted by permission of Pearson Education, Inc., Upper Saddle River, NJ.

Student: _____ Date: _____

Task/Goal to which Active Processing is applied: _____

Instructions: Respond to each step in the application of Active Processing to the identified task/goal. Refer to the completed guide during task completion to ensure effective use of Active Processing.

Step 1: Definition

What is the purpose of completing the task or goal?

What do I already know about this topic or subject?

Step 2: Specification

What steps will I follow to complete the task/achieve the goal?

Step 3: Evaluation

Am I following my steps?

Does my answer/outcome appear correct?

Did I achieve my task/goal?

Step 4: Monitoring

What might be an alternative approach if my first attempt does not work?

Did my first approach work or do I need to try another? Do I need to make a change?

What did I learn from my first attempt(s) or from any mistake(s) I made?

Step 5: Completion

How will I know that I have completed my task or achieved my goal?

Did I complete my task or achieve my goal?

How will I congratulate myself for my accomplishment?

FIGURE 12–3 Student Application Guide: Active Processing

Source: John J. Hoover (2011). *Response to intervention models: Curricular implications and interventions* (p. 255). Pearson/Allyn & Bacon. Reprinted with permission.

and learning strategies. As shown in the table, for each learning strategy, several relevant study skills are identified along with potential interrelationships among each.

In addition, Figure 12-3, Figure 12-4, and Figure 12-5 provide sample student guides for using selected learning strategies in the classroom. The items in each guide reflect important skills

Student: _____ Date: _____

Task/Goal to which Analogy is applied: _____

Instructions: Respond to each step in the application of Analogy to the identified task/goal. Refer to the completed guide during task completion to ensure effective use of Analogy.

Step 1: Prior Knowledge

What do I already know that is similar to this new content or skill?

When did I previously need to use this knowledge or skill?

Step 2: Comparison

How does this new content or skill compare to what I already know?

Does it seem to have similar applications or uses?

How is it different from what I currently know?

Step 3: Substitution

How can I use some of what I already know about a similar topic or skill to help me learn the new task or concept?

Step 4: Elaboration

How might my prior experiences in learning the new task/skill help me to learn the new task, material, or skill?

FIGURE 12–4 Student Application Guide: Analogy

Source: John J. Hoover (2011). *Response to intervention models: Curricular implications and interventions* (p. 256). Pearson/Allyn & Bacon. Reprinted with permission.

Student: _____ Date: _____

Task/Goal to which Evaluation is applied: _____

Instructions: Respond to each step in the application of Evaluation to the identified task/goal. Refer to the completed guide during task completion to ensure effective use of Evaluation.

Step 1: Analysis

What steps do I need to follow to complete my task?

Do I have all the necessary materials, and how much time do I need to complete the task?

What task have I recently completed successfully? Can I use some of what I did in that task to help complete this task?

Step 2: Strategy Identification

What strategies might I use to help me complete my task or achieve my goal?

Why do I think these might be good strategies to use in this situation?

How will I prioritize the selection and use of my selected strategies, beginning with the one I think will be most effective?

Step 3: Strategy Implementation

Do I understand how to use the strategy?

Am I using the strategy for the reasons for which I thought it should be used in this situation or task?

Can I use this same strategy in different situations?

Is more than one strategy necessary to complete the task or accomplish my goal?

Step 4: Feedback/Reflection

Is the selected strategy working?

Am I making steady progress toward my goal or task?

Do I think I may need to try to use an alternative strategy? If so, which other strategy might I try?

Did I continue using this strategy until I achieved my goal or accomplished my task?

Step 5: Elaboration/Generalization

Did I achieve my goal to the level I originally hoped for?

Did I become upset if I achieved my goal but it fell short of my expectations?

Why do I think that the strategy I used helped me to meet my goal or accomplish my task?

Did I evaluate the implementation of my plan sufficiently to know how well I was progressing toward my goal or task completion in order to make needed adjustments?

In what other situations might I be able to use the same strategy?

FIGURE 12–5 Student Application Guide: Evaluation

Source: John J. Hoover (2011). *Response to intervention models: Curricular implications and interventions* (pp. 260–261). Pearson/Allyn & Bacon. Reprinted with permission.

needed to successfully use the strategy and offer a structure to assist learners apply the strategy to specific tasks. These also provide a quick way for the teacher to determine student uses of the strategies. Additional guides for student use of the other learning strategies discussed in this section can be found in Hoover (2011).

Teacher Study Skills Applications

1. Identify a specific academic or behavioral task and describe one study skill (i.e., Table 12-3) that can be used to support students in the elementary grades to learn and use that skill for the task.

2. Select two study skill strategies (i.e., Table 12-8) and develop a process for teaching them to

students, helping them learn how to incorporate into task completion.

3. Complete the Study Skills Inventory (SSI) for an elementary or secondary learner and summarize results by identifying study skills in most need of further development.

4. Examine an IEP and determine which study skills are most necessary to help the student master each objective listed.

 Check Your Understanding 12.4 Click here to gauge your understanding of the concepts in this section.

ACTIVITIES

1. Students can be asked to look for ways that the items of information to be remembered can be placed into two or more categories. They then write and underline the name of each category. Under the name of each category, students write each item of information that is associated with that category. To remember the items, students think of the first category and the items that are associated with it. Students repeat this for each of the other categories. Students can use the categorization strategy to memorize, for example, the names of countries by sorting them into two or more categories.

2. Students can use the acronym strategy when trying to remember information that does not have to be recalled in order. Students write each item they need to remember. They underline the first letter of each one. If there is more than one word in an item, underline the first letter of only the first word in that item of information. Students then arrange the underlined letters to form an acronym that is a real word or that is not a real word but that can be easily pronounced (e.g., remembering the names of the five Great Lakes with HOMES: Huron, Ontario, Michigan, Erie, Superior).

3. Students can use an abbreviation strategy where they write the names of information they must remember in the order in which they must remember them. They underline the first letter of each item. If there is more than one word in an item, underline the first letter of only the first word in that item of information. Students write the underlined letters in order to form the abbreviation.

4. Students think of a place they know well and picture that place. They visualize each item they want to remember and associate it with one of the features of that place. To remember the information, they visualize each feature selected and the item associated with it.

5. Have students use repetition to learn important facts, poems, or songs taught in different subject areas.

6. After students have completed actively reading, have them reflect on what they read. They should look over their highlights, notes, and pictures and headings in the text again. They can make flash cards or note cards for the important ideas, using their own words.

Social Competence and Self-Determination Skills

LEARNING OUTCOMES

Upon completion of this chapter, the reader should be able to:

13.1 Understand the history and terminology related to social and self-determination skills instruction.

13.2 Demonstrate knowledge of assessment procedures in the area of social skills, self-determination training, and social-emotional learning.

13.3 Demonstrate knowledge of curricular and instructional strategies for social, self-determination skills, and social-emotional learning programs.

This chapter provides information for teachers who are seeking to establish a social and self-determination skills program for students who are exhibiting failure in the classroom and community. The chapter provides information about historical precedents, definition of terms, assessment procedures, curriculum, and teaching strategies.

HISTORY AND TERMINOLOGY

Historical Overview

Although recent historical reviews have been published (e.g., Hupp, LeBlanc, Jewell, & Warnes, 2009; Weissberg, Durlak, Domitrovich, & Gullotta, 2015; Wiley & Siperstein, 2015), a complete history of social and self-determination skills teaching has not been written. The work of Wolpe (1958) is often singled out as the most influential antecedent to the development of these respective fields. Initially, he emphasized the use of behavioral principles and techniques to ameliorate adult psychiatric patients' problems with interpersonal interaction. He and his colleagues introduced the idea of teaching assertive and self-advocacy behaviors to people who were experiencing such problems due to stressful life events.

Behavioral principles of shaping and chaining were then applied to the teaching of many new behaviors (Bandura, 1977). Simultaneously, Argyle (1967; Argyle & Kendon, 1967) was developing a body of knowledge that attempted to explain appropriate social interactions between two or more individuals. Argyle noted that several skills were necessary, including the ability to accurately (a) determine social goals (e.g., the need to make friends); (b) perceive, interpret, and act upon cues in the environment (e.g., determine which peers would be most receptive to becoming a friend, determine whether a peer would be an appropriate friend, and introduce oneself to the peer); and (c) understand and respond to the feedback given (e.g., interpret whether the peer positively responds to the initiation of friendship). Once these models were established, several researchers from that era (Argyle, 1967; Bellack & Hersen, 1979; Liberman, King, DeRisi, & McCann, 1975) developed social skills teaching programs for various populations. The positive results achieved sparked the enthusiasm of professionals in special education.

As researchers worked to promote the success of children and adolescents, they realized that certain personal or self-determination skills were not being addressed within curricula and consequently not being learned. In addition, many children with disabilities were not well accepted by peers without disabilities or by teachers (Bryan, 1983). Reports concerning adolescents with various disabling conditions indicated a rise in the number of students dropping out of school, having difficulties establishing relationships, and deciding on inappropriate life goals and a decrease in those exhibiting independent behaviors and maintaining long-term jobs (e.g., Williamson, Modecki, & Guerra, 2015). Many self-determination skills were lacking, and students were not being taught to develop goals for themselves, collaborate with others to attain goals (e.g., seek out mentors), and solve problems that present barriers to goal attainment (Serna & Lau-Smith, 1994–1995).

Adding to this growing body of research, investigators (e.g., Bauminger & Kimhi-Kind, 2008; Cook, Gresham, et al., 2008; Milsom & Glanville, 2010) gathered data indicating that the social competence of children with learning disabilities and behavioral disorders is rated lower than peers or siblings without disabilities. These researchers noted that environmental and contextual variables play a large role in the social and self-determined behavior of these children and adolescents. Further, Wong (2003) proposed that educators consider the need for a resilience and empowerment framework that promotes social and self-determined behavior if students are to succeed. Therefore, teachers have the responsibility of ameliorating behavioral problems as well as developing appropriate social

interactions and personal competence skills (i.e., social-emotional and self-determination skills) among children and adolescents with special needs.

In response to this need, professionals in special education and psychology developed promising and evidence-based programs and procedures to teach social skills (e.g., Campbell & Siperstein, 1994; McGinnis, Goldstein, Sprafkin, & Gershaw, 2005; Odom et al., 1997; Serna, Nielsen, & Forness, 2007), self-determination skills programs (e.g., Gibbons, 2002; Hoffman & Field, 1995; Serna & Lau-Smith, 1995; Wehmeyer, 1995), and social-emotional learning (SEL) programs for children and adolescents with disabilities. The following discussion introduces the concepts of social and personal competence by defining the three dimensions of social skills, social problem-solving skills, and self-determination skills.

Social and Personal Competence

Professionals historically have defined the constructs of **social and personal competence** as a person's overall ability to achieve his or her goals and desires in the personal and social aspects of life (Ford, 1985). Ford elaborated by identifying three components that interact to make up social and personal competence: self-perception (i.e., an individual's ability to recognize and set goals for oneself), behavioral repertoire (i.e., a person's ability to effectively perform social skills, problem-solving skills, role-taking abilities, assertive skills, and language/communication skills), and effectiveness (i.e., a person's ability to determine whether set goals and desires are achieved).

Ford (1985) outlined three additional factors that interact with the components of social and personal competence: (a) motivation, (b) development, and (c) environment. Motivation is a factor that interacts with social and personal competence in that an individual may have the desired skills (i.e., setting goals, behaving appropriately, and evaluating achievement) in his or her behavioral repertoire but may not be motivated to use these skills. Development, on the other hand, interacts with social and personal competence in that a person's age or developmental growth may influence the type of goals set and achieved by an individual. Finally, environment pertains to the culture, society, or family expectations that influence the social and personal behavior of an individual (e.g., some Native American populations do not believe in long-term goal setting). A competent person is able to move from one environment to another, recognizing the social rules of each setting and acting accordingly. The individual who consistently demonstrates the ability to shift from one environment to another and exhibit appropriate social behavior in each setting is considered a socially competent person. The person who demonstrates the ability to set and achieve goals, make appropriate decisions, and persist through difficult times by using problem-solving skills is considered a personally competent individual.

Social Skills. The definition of **social skills** reflects the knowledge that researchers have acquired concerning social behavior. For example, Schumaker and Hazel's (1984) behavioral definition of social skills included overt behaviors as skill components necessary in the interactions between two or more people and also cognitive functions (i.e., covert behavior). Overt behaviors include observable non-verbal behaviors (e.g., eye contact and facial expression) and verbal behavior (what words are used and how the person communicates a message). Covert behaviors consist of a person's ability to empathize with another person and discriminate social cues. The appropriate and fluent use of these behaviors is rewarded by the attainment of the person's goal.

Other researchers have classified social competence and social skills with regard to the social validity of the behavior (e.g., Gresham, 2002). Cook, Gresham, et al. (2008) explained that social skills depict individual performances of social tasks (e.g., eye contact or following instructions). On the other hand, the construct of social competence is used as an evaluative term whereby individuals judge the performance of an individual as acceptable to others in the environment or within the context in which the skill was observed.

Taking into account Gresham's (2002) analysis, the following classic definition of social skills has addressed the social validity view and broadened the term to eliminate the possibility that an individual would use specific social skills to manipulate, intimidate, or violate a person's rights. Phillips (1978) defined a socially skilled person according to "the extent to which he or she can communicate with others in a manner that fulfills one's rights, requirements, satisfactions, or obligations to a reasonable degree without damaging the other person's similar rights, requirements, satisfactions,

or obligations, and shares these rights, etc., with others in free and open exchange" (p. 13). This definition is quite encompassing in that it includes the reciprocal interactions of both individuals involved in the social exchange. Social skills should be proactive, prosocial, and reciprocal in nature. In this way, the participants of the interaction share in a mutually rewarding experience.

The nearby Teacher Tip provides a complementary focus on resiliency in children.

Social Problem Solving. Behavioral pioneers Bijou and Baer (1978) defined problem solving as a sequence or an algorithm of behaviors. When we are able to identify this sequence or algorithm of behaviors, we are able to teach it to others. Because problem solving is a covert or cognitive behavior, much of its analysis must be done through language. **Social problem solving**, therefore, is the sequence of behaviors developed to ameliorate a particular social interaction problem. We are able to identify the social problem-solving process through the analysis of a person's language about a particular social event. Researchers in the area of cognitive-behavioral interventions (e.g., Mayer, Van Acker, Lochman, & Gresham, 2009) have promoted the use of social problem solving as well as other cognitive interventions for students with learning and behavioral issues in the school environment.

Over the years, several researchers proposed an algorithm for teaching social problem solving (Kazdin, 2001; O'Donohue & Fisher, 2012; Shure, 1999). These authors outlined five components to be used in a social problem-solving algorithm: (a) problem orientation, (b) problem definition and formulation, (c) generation of solutions, (d) decision making, and (e) implementation of plan and evaluation and verification of the outcome. This algorithm may include other covert behaviors that influence the effectiveness of the problem solving. These additional covert behaviors include empathy, moral judgment, the ability to process non-verbal cues, and the ability to make inferences (e.g., Jennings, Mitchell, & Hannah, 2015).

 ENHANCEDetext video example 13.1
Watch this video to learn more about social problem solving.

Fostering Resiliency in Children

Teachers who wish to profile resilient children as socially competent or self-determined may look for their ability to problem solve, think critically, and take initiative. These children foresee a positive future for themselves as they set goals for themselves and are motivated to achieve in school and life situations. Interestingly, many resiliency skills identified by researchers (e.g., O'Dougherty Wright & Masten, 2015; Wright, 2013) can be categorized into the domains of social skills and community skills, cognitive social behavior, self-determination skills, and motivational theory. The following table depicts the resiliency skills with regard to these categories:

Social Skills and Community Involvement	Cognitive Social Skills	Self-Determination Skills	Motivational Theory
Donate time and service	Problem-solving skills	Exhibit decision-making skills	Can generalize learned information and skills
Exhibit assertiveness skills	Positive attribution thinking with positive futuristic view	Exhibit self-management and self-control skills	Exhibit motivation in personal and professional life
Establish friendships and positive relationships	Ability to adapt to challenging situations	Exhibit independent thinking and behavior	
Exhibit sense of humor			
Engage in extracurricular activities			
Exhibit confidence			

Self-Determination Skills. The area of **self-determination** skills for students with disabilities was built on federally funded projects initiated in the early 1990s in which self-determination was researched, skills were identified, and curricula were developed for adolescents with disabilities and for those who are at risk for failure in their communities and schools. The definition of self-determination continually evolves as the research in this area continues to develop (e.g., Wehmeyer, 2015). All of the definitions in the current literature, however, are similar in considering that goal-setting skills, self-regulation skills, decision-making skills, problem-solving skills, social skills, and self-evaluation skills are among the behaviors needed to identify a self-determined person (e.g., Palmer & Wehmeyer, 2003). Serna and Lau-Smith (1995) noted that self-determination can be defined as the awareness by individuals of their weaknesses and strengths, their ability to establish personal goals, the opportunity and right to make personal choices. If a person is self-determined, then he or she can make his/her own decisions independently taking advantage of the supports and resources that may be available.

Shogren et al. (2015) further noted that self-determination refers to determining one's own fate or to determining one's own course of action. Essential characteristics of self-determination include autonomy, self-regulation, self-realization, and empowerment.

Individuals who are self-determined also exhibit the skill of persistence through problem solving. In meeting one's goals, everyone is faced with barriers or problems. To succeed in accomplishing these goals, the ability to overcome barriers is needed. Usually, this is done through continuous use of the skill of problem solving. With all of this in mind, the individual pursues his or her goals through ethical and appropriate strategies.

Expanding with Social-Emotional Learning. Mayer, DiPaolo, and Salovey (1990) and others introduced the term *emotional intelligence*, which refers to a student's ability to recognize emotions and their meaning as they relate to other people or situations. Eventually, Goleman (1998) took the vague constructs of emotional recognition, management, motivating oneself, and handling relationships and included the more teachable skills of self-awareness, self-regulation, motivation (e.g., goal setting), empathy, and social skills. The specification of these skills gives educators more realistic and data-based programs from which to draw and closely aligned with evidence-based social skills and self-determination skills programs.

Emanating from the emotional intelligence movement are the terms *emotional literacy* (Joseph & Strain, 2003) and *social-emotional learning* (Durlak, Domitrovich, Weissberg, & Gullotta, 2015). These two developments continue to promote the social and self-determination skills of self-awareness, self-regulation, communication, problem solving, decision making, and collaboration (Wiley & Siperstein, 2015). Additionally, new research on *mindfulness* or self-awareness (e.g., Brown, Creswell, & Ryan, 2015; Singh et al., 2007) and the need for goal setting as well as developing lasting relationships (Rimm-Kaufman & Hulleman, 2015) are on the horizon for students with disabilities. Although the terms and theories may differ in these recent additions to the literature, the skills for teaching social or self-determination skills remain the same. This chapter includes examples of how these new additions intersect with social or self-determination skills.

 Check Your Understanding 13.1 Click here to gauge your understanding of the concepts in this section.

ASSESSMENT

The discussion of the definitions of social competence, social skills, social problem solving, and self-determination skills is important because it relates to the assessment of student behaviors. For example, the construct of social competence introduces global behaviors as well as several dimensions of social behaviors. The assessment instruments for social competence, therefore, are usually global in nature, addressing many behaviors that contribute to a student's total behavior in school and community environments. The instruments designed for the assessment of social skills and social problem solving, however, are more specific in nature. They identify specific non-verbal and verbal behaviors that are required to complete a successful social interaction with another person. The assessment measures for self-determined behaviors are still developing and are in the initial stages of validation on a large population of students.

In the discussion below, each assessment category is discussed by presenting brief descriptions of the assessment instruments, how they are implemented, and the advantages and disadvantages of using each assessment category. Attention is given to the assessment of specific social (and social-emotional), problem-solving skills, and self-determination skills. These assessments are most accessible to teachers and most relevant in establishing social skills and self-determination programs for students in any type of classroom environment.

Assessment of Social Competence

Numerous assessment instruments relate to social competence. They typically collect global information and are particularly useful when screening a student for a certain program. Measures under this category include sociometric ratings, ratings by teachers and other adults, and self-report measures.

Sociometric Ratings. Sociometric ratings typically have an adult or peer evaluate the student according to some designated dimension (e.g., best friend, most popular). The most common procedures used with students are nominations by peers with regard to who is liked or disliked and peer ratings of each student in the classroom (usually on a Likert-type scale) according to how much the student is liked. For example, a teacher may gather information from peer ratings by giving students a list of their peers (or by displaying snapshots of peers) and asking them to identify their best friend or with whom they would most like to play or work. Scores taken from peer nominations and peer rating scales are compiled to determine the students who are most liked or most disliked.

Sociometric measures generally exhibit reliability and validity in predicting the student who is at risk for behavior problems. A disadvantage or limitation of the sociometric procedures is that they often do not provide teachers with information concerning specific behaviors that must be taught or ameliorated. At most, teachers know that a student receiving votes in the "dislike" category is in need of intervention.

Ratings by Teachers. A number of standardized adaptive behavior and social skills rating scales

TABLE 13–1 Behavior rating scales commonly used in social skills assessments

Assessment Skills	Age Ranges	Publisher
Conners Rating Scales—Third Edition (Conners, 2008)	2–adulthood	Pearson
Revised Behavior Problem Checklist (Quay and Peterson, 1996)	5–18	Children's Research Center
Social Skills Improvement System Rating Scales (Gresham & Elliott, 2008)	3–18	Pearson
Social Skills Rating System (Gresham & Elliott, 1990)	3–18	American Guidance Service
Vineland Adaptive Behavior Scales—Second Edition (Sparrow, Balla, & Cicchetti, 2005)	Birth–90	American Guidance Service

have been developed as screening instruments for identifying students at risk for behavior problems. Some common, well-validated scales are presented in Table 13-1. (For a detailed listing and discussion of adaptive behavior scales, see also Olley, 2015.)

A classic example is the *Social Skills Rating System* (Gresham & Elliott, 1990). This adaptive scale not only identifies students at risk for behavior problems but also provides teachers with information concerning specific social skill deficits. Parents, teachers, and students are asked to rate a student's behavior on the following dimensions: cooperation (e.g., helping others, sharing), assertion (e.g., asking for information), responsibility (e.g., ability to communicate about property and work), empathy (e.g., behaviors showing concern or respect), and self-control (e.g., behaviors that emerge during conflict situations). Ratings are based on the memory of parents, teachers, and students with regard to the frequency (i.e., never, sometimes, very often) that a specific behavior occurs. Additionally, a second assessment requires the teachers, parents, and students to rate the importance of each behavior.

Perhaps the most valuable aspect of the *Social Skills Rating System* is that the authors provide several examples that illustrate how to use the results of the assessment to target specific social skills and develop an intervention program for a student. Teachers should remember, however, that the assessment relies on the memory of the rater and does not indicate the exact frequency with which the behaviors occur (i.e., we don't know what "sometimes" means). Finally, unless several raters fill out the assessment on each child, the teacher cannot be sure if the problem behaviors are due to

social deficits or motivation problems within the classroom environment.

Assessment of Social and Problem-Solving Skills

Rating scales, as noted above, have been criticized for their reliance on the memory of the rater or on subjective interpretations. Consequently, direct observation assessment procedures have been developed that require a student to respond to specific instructions or stimuli and then allow observers to rate the performance of the student in that particular situation. These assessments are usually related to specific social skills and can help the teacher or tester identify specific non-verbal and verbal behavioral component deficits of a particular skill. For example, a teacher can assess a student's non-verbal skills of eye contact, facing a person, and facial expression while a student is trying to ask for help. Similarly, a teacher can assess the verbal components (e.g., verbal statements as well as voice tone, interrupting) a student exhibits while trying to ask for help. This direct observation procedure provides information concerning performance of the specific skill components (e.g., eye contact) of a particular social skill and in a specific situation. Additionally, the observation can determine whether the social skill is absent due to skill deficits or lack of motivation to use the social skill. Teachers wanting to pursue this form of assessment may want to initiate the following procedures when developing an assessment instrument for their particular classroom of students (see Table 13-2). The discussion after the table elaborates on procedures.

TABLE 13-2 Procedures for direct observation assessments of specific social skills

Procedural Steps

1. Task analyze the social skill.
   - Identify the skill that addresses the problem behavior.
   - Consider non-verbal behaviors required of the skill.
   - Consider the verbal and paraverbal behaviors required of the skill.
   - Place the non-verbal and verbal behaviors in sequence.

2. Develop definitions for each behavioral component of the skill.
   - Develop a definition that explicitly describes each step of the skill sequence.
   - Develop a definition that describes an approximation of the explicit definition of each step of the skill sequence.
   - Develop a definition that describes an inappropriate demonstration of each skill step.

3. Implement a rating scale to assess the defined behavioral components.
   - A score of 2 indicates the skill step was performed according to the explicit definition.
   - A score of 1 indicates the skill step was performed according to the definition regarding the approximated performance of the skill step.
   - A score of 0 indicates the skill step was performed inappropriately or did not perform the skill step at all.

4. Secure a reliability observer.
   - After identifying another observer, explain each definition for each skill step.
   - Demonstrate the desired, approximated, or inappropriate behavior of each skill step.
   - Practice the scoring procedure with the observer by independently observing a student's skill performance.
   - Practice the interrater reliability until the observers agree on 80% or more of the skills steps performed.

5. Generate real-life situations that require the student to use the targeted social skills.
   - Generate real-life home situations that require the student to use the skill.
   - Generate real-life school situations that require the student to use the skill.
   - Generate real-life community situations that require the student to use the skill.

6. Plan for individual test sessions.
   - Determine which method of assessment is most appropriate.
   - Implement procedures for the desired method of assessment.
   - Rate the student according to the 2-1-0 rating system.
   - Conduct multiple assessments (3).
   - Calculate and graph the score(s).

Step 1: Task Analyze the Skill. After the teacher identifies a problem area (e.g., student is unable to attend to and follow instructions), the teacher can develop a social skill that meets the needs of the student (e.g., following instructions skill). The teacher should consider the non-verbal and verbal components of the social skill. In most social skills, four non-verbal behaviors can be identified: facing the person, eye contact, facial expression (e.g., serious or smiling), and posture (e.g., straight or relaxed). The paraverbal behaviors of voice tone (e.g., pleasant or serious) and volume are also considered during the observation of the social skill. The teacher can then task analyze the verbal components of the "asking for help" skill. For example, after the

student gets the attention of the teacher, he or she will ask for the help needed. The task analysis will require a step-by-step sequence of behaviors that must be executed when asking for help. Table 13-3 exhibits a task analysis of one example of a skill. Notice how the verbal components of the skill are labeled and followed by a verbal example.

Step 2: Develop Definitions for Each Behavioral Component of the Skill. This step requires that the teacher develop a definition of each component of the skill. For example, the non-verbal behavioral component of "face the person" may be defined as "the student's shoulders are positioned parallel to the person giving the instruction, with face and eyes

TABLE 13–3 Task analysis of the "asking for help" skill

Asking for Help

1. Look at the person.
2. Have a neutral face.
3. Speak in a neutral tone of voice.
4. Keep a relaxed posture.
5. Ask yourself
   - *"Do I need help?"* or *"Can I do this task on my own?"*
6. If you think you need help, get the person's attention (e.g., a teacher). You can say *"Excuse me"* or raise your hand in class.
7. Quietly wait for the person to acknowledge you.
8. When you have the person's attention, ask for help. Say *"I need help with _____."* or *"I don't understand _____."*
9. If the person can help you, listen to the instruction.
   - If you don't understand, ask more questions or say, *"I'm still confused."*
   - If the person cannot help you, find someone who can. (Repeat steps 6–9.)
10. Thank the person for helping you.

---

directed toward the person." An approximation of this non-verbal behavioral component may be defined as the "student's shoulders are positioned at a 45-degree angle away from the person giving the instructions, but the face and eyes are still directed toward the person." A definition that describes an inappropriate use of this component may state that the "student turns the whole body away from the person giving the instructions."

Step 3: Implement a Rating Scale to Assess the Defined Behavioral Components. Although a variety of rating scales exist, an efficient scale (i.e., Hazel, Schumaker, Sherman, & Sheldon-Wildgen, 1981b) used a 2-1-0 rating scale for each behavioral component of a skill. For example, the score of 2 is recorded when the student is performing the behavioral component exactly as defined. A score of 1 is recorded when the student approximates the defined behavior (see step 2). A score of 0 is recorded if the student exhibits the behavioral component inappropriately or does not perform the behavior at all. When the rating scale is applied to the definition of each behavioral component of a skill, the teacher can determine what behavioral components need intervention and can secure a mean score for the student's performance.

Step 4: Secure a Reliability Observer. Next, the teacher can seek another individual to observe the student's performance and reliably score the behaviors according to the definition criteria developed in step 3 of these procedures. The teacher should instruct the observer by explaining the definitions of the behavioral components in each skill step and demonstrating the desired behaviors. The teacher and observer should practice the scoring procedures by independently observing a student performing a skill (e.g., following instructions) and then comparing their scores. When the teacher's and observer's scores agree on 80% or more of the behavioral components, the teacher can feel confident that the scoring of the behavioral components (according to the stated definitions) is accurate.

Step 5: Generate Real-Life Situations That Require the Use of the Targeted Social Skills. The teacher then generates several situations that require the student to use the targeted skills. These situations are used during role-play test sessions (i.e., the teacher and student act out the situation so that the student's performance can be evaluated). The situations should be based on real-life incidences that occur in many different settings (home, school, community). For example, a situation that is common to most children and adolescents takes place at home when the parent asks the youth to take out the trash. The situation may read as follows: "You are in the kitchen when your mother asks you to take out the trash. I'll be your mother and let's act out the situation. '———,' would you take the garbage out to the trash bin?" This particular situation is used during a role-play test session that assesses the student's performance for the "following instructions" skill.

Finally, in order that students practice novel role-play situations, teachers should generate many realistic situations for students to practice the skills. The situations can range from easy to difficult and cover an array of people, events, and opportunities. By employing these varied situations, teachers are using the "multiple exemplar" strategy that can promote generalization of the skill.

Step 6: Plan for Individual Test Sessions.

The final step is to plan individual test sessions for each student. There are three methods of collecting the assessment information. First, the teacher can wait for naturally occurring interactions to take place in the classroom and then score the behavior. Although this is the most preferable method to use, it can be problematic if there are few opportunities for the behavior to occur or if the behavior does not occur at all. A second method, the use of confederates, can also be employed if the teacher desires to obtain information in the natural setting. With this method, the teacher must secure the cooperation of other peers or teachers to set up situations so that the student can respond to the peer's (or teacher's) initiations. This method is advantageous if the peers are cooperative; do not prompt the student to use certain behaviors and do not tell the student that they were asked to participate in this endeavor.

Another, third method of assessing social skill behavior is during a simulated role-play situation. The teacher should begin a test session by securing a private room for the student, teacher, and reliability observer. Once the teacher has eliminated as many distractions and interruptions as possible, the student is told that he or she will be role-playing (acting out) several situations with the teacher. Because pre-teaching assessments do not require the student to act in accordance with the targeted social skill, the student is instructed to be himself or herself and respond as normally as possible. The teacher then reads the situation (developed in step 5) to the student, making sure that the student understands the scenario before beginning. Once the student understands the situation, the role-play interaction begins. During the interaction, the teacher must not prompt the student and must observe the student's behavior carefully (in addition to acting out the role designated in the situation). After this brief role-play interaction (it should not last more than two or three minutes), the teacher

and reliability observer should score each non-verbal and verbal behavior of the social skill according to the designated definitions rating scale (steps 2 and 3). This procedure continues until all the targeted social skills are assessed.

Regardless of the test method used, the teacher can assess the student's behavior on specific social skills. Multiple assessments (at least three), using different situations and different methods, should be gathered to obtain an overall performance score. With this information, a student's mean scores (or cluster of scores) can be graphed or recorded so that pre-test and after-teaching scores can be compared.

Assessment of Self-Determination Skills

Assessment tools for self-determination skills reflect the work of early researchers who developed self-determination skills curricula (e.g., Hoffman & Field, 1995; Serna & Lau-Smith, 1995). The following description outlines criterion-referenced and curriculum-based assessment tools, as well as behavioral checklists, that accompany self-determination curricula described later in this chapter.

Assessment Tools for the Steps to Self-Determination Curriculum.

Field, Hoffman, and Sawilousky (2004) described two assessment tools that were developed to accompany their curriculum. The first tool, the Self-Determination Observation Checklist (SDOC), is a teacher-administered behavioral observation checklist that identifies 38 behaviors correlated with self-determination skills found in the classroom. The second tool is the Self-Determination Knowledge Scale (SDKS), a 30-item structured response test designed to assess cognitive knowledge of different self-determination skills.

Assessment Tools for the Learning with PURPOSE Curriculum.

Three assessment tools were developed to complement the Learning with PURPOSE Curriculum (Serna & Lau-Smith, 1995). The first involves a behavioral checklist for each self-determination skill covered in the seven-domain curriculum. The second is a teacher and parent general report in which the individual is required to rate the student's skill competency on a 7-point Likert scale for each of the seven skill areas. The third assessment tool is a 75-item report filled out by the teacher, parent, and student.

TABLE 13–4   Suggested social emotional learning skills assessments

Assessment	Age Ranges	Publisher
Behavioral and Emotional Rating Scale (BERS-2) (Epstein & Sharma, 1998)	K–12	PRO-ED
Comprehensive School Climate Inventory (National School Climate Center)	K–12	National School Climate Center
Devereaux Early Childhood Assessment (DECA-P2) Preschool Program (Devereux Center for Resilient Children, n.d.)	2–5	Kaplan Early Learning Co.
Devereaux Student Strength Assessment (DESSA) (LeBuffe, Shapiro, & Naglieri, 2009)	K–12	Apperson, Inc.
Social-Emotional Assets and Resilience Scales (SEARS) (Merrill, 2008)	Preschool–high school	Brookes Publishing
Social Skills Improvement System Rating Scales (SSIS-RS) (Gresham & Elliot, 2008)	Pre-K–12	Pearson

Assessment Tool for the ChoiceMaker Curriculum. A criterion-referenced tool, developed by Martin and Huber-Marshall (1995), is used in conjunction with their curriculum that emphasizes self-determination skills to be used during individualized education program (IEP) meetings. The teacher is required to rate the student's self-determination skills and whether opportunities to use the skills occur in the school settings.

Assessment Tools for Social-Emotional Learning (SEL) Skills

Over 70 assessment tools have been identified in the area of Social-Emotional Learning (SEL) (Haggerty, Elgin, & Woolley, 2010). Although many of these assessments are quite reputable, not all are appropriate for the school environment. Based on researchers' analysis of these assessments (e.g., Denham, 2015; Haggerty et al., 2010) approximately 14 have been recommend for use with students in the school environment. Of these 14 assessments, six were chosen to showcase, as they are closely mapped to the SEL constructs of self-awareness, self-management/regulation, social awareness, relationship skills, and responsible decision making (see Table 13-4).

Each of these tools has been evaluated for its reliability and validity and proves to meet the standards of acceptability. Except for the CSCI, all of the tools closely align with the skills in SEL curricula. The CSCI was included because it is an assessment that focuses on how the school and community environment can support student needs with regard to SEL skills. It is designed to assess the constructs of risk and protective factors in the community, family, and school and with peers (Haggerty et al., 2010). Table 13-4 identifies specific information regarding each of these assessment tools.

Final Note on Assessment. As with all assessment instruments, we must be aware of cultural differences that children might be exhibiting when they interact with others. The way teachers perceive these interactions may affect their ratings of children's behaviors. In response to any bias, teachers should strive to create a positive culture in their classroom. This culture is created with all the students working together to develop verbal and nonverbal social behaviors that are acceptable in the classroom culture. In this way, behaviors may be predictable in a safe, social environment.

Check Your Understanding 13.2 Click here to gauge your understanding of the concepts in this section.

SOCIAL, SELF-DETERMINATION, AND SOCIAL-EMOTIONAL SKILLS: CURRICULA AND INSTRUCTION

Social Skills Curricula

Commercially produced social skills curricula are available to teachers of students with special needs. The following discussion will briefly describe each of the social skills curricula mentioned with regard to the assessment procedures recommended, skill content, instructional material, and instructions to the teacher. (Table 13-5 summarizes this discussion.) Whether teachers decide to use any one of these programs depends on their preferences, the adaptability of the program to the students' needs, and the teachers' familiarity with social skills instruction.

Skillstreaming the Elementary Student. Skillstreaming the Elementary School Child (McGinnis et al., 2005) is one of the most popular social skills programs for students in the elementary grades. It provides the teacher with different assessment options from direct observation to sociometric ratings. Particular emphasis is placed on teacher frequency ratings of the students' skill performances. The authors recommend this assessment when deciding on the social skills to be targeted for teaching. The social skills presented in this program are divided into five groups: (a) surviving in the classroom, (b) friendship making, (c) dealing with feelings,

TABLE 13–5 Social skills curricula

Social Curricula	Assessment Procedures	Skill Content	Instructional Materials	Instruction to Teacher
1. Skillstreaming the Elementary School Child (McGinnis et al., 2005)	Student skill checklist Teachers skill checklist Group chart	Classroom survival Friendship making Dealing with feelings Alternatives to aggression Dealing with stress	Samples of homework reports Contingency contracts Self-monitoring Home journals	Beginning a group Constructing a structured learning group Suggestions Managing behavior problems
2. ACCEPTS Program (Walker et al., 1983)	Teacher questionnaire Screening checklist Observation forms Placement test Recess rating form Behavior rating form	Classroom skills Basic instructions Getting along Making friends Coping skills	Videotapes	Direct instruction Teaching scripts for each skill Behavior management procedures
3. Skillstreaming the Adolescent (Goldstein, Sprafkin, Gershaw, & Klein, 2006)	Skill checklist Group chart Master record	Beginning skills Advanced skills Dealing with feelings Alternatives to aggression Dealing with stress Planning skills	Videotapes	Structured learning procedures Selection and grouping Managing behavior problems
4. The ASSET Program: A Social Skills Program for Adolescents (Hazel, Schumaker, Sherman, & Sheldon-Wildgen, 1981a)	Criterion checklist Pre- and post-training checklist Parent questionnaire Parent satisfaction Participant satisfaction	Giving positive feedback Giving negative feedback Accepting negative feedback Negotiation Following instruction Problem solving Resisting peer pressure Conversation	Skill sheets Videotapes Home notes Sample parent letter Sample telephone conversation with parent	Starting a group Basic teaching steps Group leader steps Conducting group meetings Group rules and behavior problems Maintaining skills Quick-reference guide
5. Social Storytelling Curriculum (Serna, Nielsen, & Forness, 2007)	Student skill checklist Direct observation	Listening and following instructions Problem solving Self-management of behavior sharing	Storybook Coloring book Songs	Instructor's manual for each skill area

(d) using alternatives to aggression, and (e) dealing with stress. The skills are task analyzed so that each has up to six general steps outlined for the student. Through modeling, discussion, and prompting, teachers must extend the teaching of each step in the social skill. Finally, a social learning approach/direct instructional procedure is outlined for teachers to use when teaching the skill.

ACCEPTS Program. The Walker Social Skills Curriculum: ACCEPTS Program (Walker et al., 1983) was developed to promote teacher–student and peer-to-peer interaction skills. It includes a placement test, direct instructional procedures, guidelines for teaching, scripts for teaching skills, and activities that enhance skill learning. A behavior management procedure and videotape are also available with the program. Five areas are emphasized: (a) classroom skills (e.g., listening, following rules), (b) basic interaction skills (e.g., eye contact, starting, taking turns), (c) getting-along skills (e.g., sharing, assisting others), (d) making-friends skills (e.g., smiling, complimenting), and (e) coping skills (e.g., when to say "no").

Skillstreaming the Adolescent. Skillstreaming the Adolescent (Goldstein et al., 2006) initially presents the teacher with a rating scale for evaluating the social behavior of their students. Like the rating scales described earlier, the authors list the target skill (e.g., saying "thank you"), give an example of the skill (e.g., "Does the student let others know that he or she is grateful for favors etc.?"), and then provide a frequency rating scale of 1 to 5 (i.e., a rating of 1 would indicate "never," and a rating of 5 would indicate "always"). The assessment of these 50 skills allows the teacher to target the most deficient skills in the student's repertoire.

Once the deficient skills have been targeted, the authors present the 50 skills under six groups: (a) beginning social skills (e.g., listening, starting a conversation), (b) advanced social skills (e.g., asking for help, joining in), (c) skills for dealing with feelings (e.g., knowing your feelings, dealing with fear), (d) skill alternatives to aggression (e.g., asking permission, sharing something), (e) skills for dealing with stress (e.g., making a complaint, dealing with embarrassment, responding to persuasion), and (f) planning skills (e.g., deciding on something to do, setting a goal). Each is then task analyzed for the student. The authors then instruct the teacher by providing transcripts of social skills instruction groups, which provide examples of the direct instructional

procedures and how to prompt a student to use each step of the targeted skill. A videotape instructing teachers how to conduct a social skills group is available.

ASSET Program. The ASSET Program is for adolescents (Hazel et al., 1981a) and consists of a leader's guide manual and skill sheets that are used during the skill-teaching sessions. The authors socially validated the eight skills presented in the curriculum. Teachers, court officers, and professionals working with adolescents identified eight skills that were the most beneficial for adolescents to learn and be successful in the academic, home, and community environments, including giving positive feedback, giving negative feedback, accepting negative feedback, resisting peer pressure, problem solving, negotiating, following instructions, and having conversations.

A feature of this program is the skill sheets that are provided for the teacher and students. Each involves a step-by-step task analysis of each skill. The task analysis is divided into non-verbal, verbal, and some covert skill components (e.g., listening). Each verbal step of the skill is accompanied by a verbal example of what an adolescent might say in a certain situation. This feature is advantageous for those students who require verbal prompts and possess limited English/verbal skills. The skill sheets are also adaptable to all grade levels by modifying the number of skill steps and the difficulty of the language used. The final section of the leader's guide includes sociometric measures for teachers, parents, and students. Instructional videotapes are also available separately but are not necessary to conduct an effective social skills program.

Social and Self-Determination Curricula for Young Children

The majority of the social and self-determination curricula have been developed for adolescents with disabilities. Ultimately, however, skill building in this area should begin as early as possible. If children are taught following-instruction, self-evaluation, self-advocacy, self-regulation, problem-solving, and decision-making skills at an early age, numerous social and mental health issues that plague young children can be prevented (Serna, Forness, & Nielsen, 1998).

One curriculum for young children is the Social Storytelling Curriculum (Serna et al., 2007). After socially validating four social and self-determination skills for young children (i.e., following instructions, sharing, self-regulations, and problem solving), a curriculum based on storytelling was initiated. This storytelling process involves the orchestration of carefully developed stories with direct instructional procedures embedded throughout the introduction, plot, and resolution of the story. The teacher can begin by (a) introducing the person or animal in the story, (b) reading the story, (c) talking about each section of the story that emphasizes a directional step, (d) modeling the skill steps introduced in the story, and (e) requiring each child to practice the steps.

Once the children learn the self-determination/social skill in the story-time portion of the day, a learning center is available for the children to practice their newly acquired skill. The practice is monitored by the teacher and feedback is given to each child. Generalization of the skill is prompted and reinforced at other learning centers and during outside play time. Preliminary observations indicate that very young children can learn these social or self-determination skills through a story format.

ENHANCEDetext
video example 13.2
Watch this video to learn more about social skills an instruction.

Self-Determination Curricula

As noted above, the federal Office of Special Education and Rehabilitative Service initiated a series of grants (1990–1993) for demonstration projects in self-determination. The charge given to these researchers was to investigate and develop determination programs that taught youth to become more independent and future oriented. Of these projects, five socially validated programs are outlined as follows. Table 13-6 provides a self-determination curricula at a glance.

Steps to Self-Determination Curriculum. This program (Field & Hoffman, 1992) consists of six

TABLE I3–6 Self-determination curricula at a glance

Self-Determination Curricula	Assessment Procedures	Skill Content	Instructional Materials	Target Audience
Steps to Self-Determination: A curriculum to help adolescents learn to achieve their goals	Self-Determination Knowledge scale	Relationships Self-advocacy Leadership Transition	Curriculum DVD Reproducible forms Trainer's guide Student activity book	Adolescent students with developmental disabilities
Learning with PURPOSE (Serna & Lau-Smith, 1995)	Skills checklist pre/post	Seven domains with a total of 34 skills (social skills, self-evaluation skills, self-direction skills, networking skills, collaboration skills, persistence and risk-taking skills, stress management)	Instructor's manual Skill manual Materials	Adolescent students at risk for failure/EBD
Choice Maker: a comprehensive self-determination transition program (Martin & Marshall, 1995)	Criterion referenced self-determination transition assessment tool designed for the program	Choosing and expressing goals Taking action	Lesson packages infused in schoolwork and programs	Adolescent students with learning disabilities
Life-Centered Career Education (Brolin, 1995)	Knowledge and performance battery Transition assessment	Daily living skills Personal-social skills Occupation guidance	Lesson plans for teaching transition IEP planning	Adolescent students with disabilities
Classroom Competency-Building Program (Abery, Rudrud, Arndt, Schauben, & Eggebeen, 1995)	*Self-Determination Skills Evaluation Scale (SDSES)* (Abery & Eggebeen, 1992) Behavior Rating Scale	10 modules (self-awareness, self-esteem, perceptions of personal control, personal values, goal setting, assertive communication, choice making, self-regulation, problem solving, personal advocacy)	Curriculum with activities and homework	Adolescent students with mild to moderate developmental disabilities and their families

steps to independence and self-determination, including (a) knowing yourself, (b) valuing yourself, (c) planning, (d) acting, (e) experiencing outcomes, and (f) learning. Each of these steps is divided into 16 class sessions where the students are taught specific skills of self-evaluation, goal setting and planning, risk taking, decision making, independent performance, and adjustment. The program is designed to be implemented in a one-semester period and involves the parents and community members as support people during the program.

Learning with PURPOSE. This program (Serna & Lau-Smith, 1995) is a curriculum developed for use by teachers who work in inclusive settings with students who have mild to moderate disabilities and are at risk for failure in their school and community. The teaching model of the curriculum was piloted with students who were high, regular, and at-risk achievers as well as students receiving special education services.

The curriculum contains seven domain areas with a total of 34 skills and three guideline areas. The domain areas consist of (a) prerequisite social skills, (b) self-evaluation skills, (c) self-direction skills, (d) networking skills, (e) collaboration skills, (f) persistence and risk-taking skills, and (g) stress management. The program is designed to be used during a five-year period (grades 8 through 12). For example, eighth-grade students could begin learning the skills of communication and assertiveness (social skills) as well as self-direction skills. By the time they are in the 12th grade, they should be learning the skills of collaboration and formal networking to prepare them for their transition into the community and workplace.

TEACHER *Tips*   **Secondary Level**

Fostering Informed Risk Taking through Responsible Decision Making

Decision making is a skill that is found in social skills, self-determination skills, and SEL skills curricula. It is of particular interest as it relates to the problem-solving skill. If the skill of problem solving is task analyzed, a common format consists of (a) determining the problem, (b) brainstorming multiple solutions, (c) evaluating the consequences of each solution, (d) deciding on the most appropriate solution, and (e) determining how the chosen solution will be executed and then executing the solution. It is the fourth step in this skill that requires a student to execute with proficiency the decision-making skill. Unfortunately, many teachers and researchers do not recognize the importance of this particular component. For example, let's say a student who has experienced an altercation with his peers is asked to problem solve his dilemma. When he comes to the brainstorming of solutions, he is able to generate productive and nonproductive solutions. He then is able to determine the consequences of each solution. Next comes the decision of choosing the solution that will solve the problem. He chooses an inappropriate solution (e.g., go punch the other person). If he acts on this decision, he will ultimately get into trouble and make his situation worse.

The student did not choose wisely for a variety of reasons: (a) anger, (b) revenge, (c) will feel better, (d) save face, (e) easiest to implement, and (f) most expedient solution in the eyes of the student. The list goes on. What is a teacher to do when the values and the cognitive maturity of the student contradict the appropriate thing to do? Perhaps teaching the skill of moral decision making will help.

Often, making a choice or decision that can impact your future is called risk taking. Decision making, in a sense, can be considered informed risk taking. Informed risk taking is seeking information about the consequences of one's options (not just generating consequences). If the information indicates that details related to the consequence hold far more weight than first suspected (e.g., punching a person not only can get you suspended but may involve the law, court expenses, a lawsuit, a hospital stay, medical bills, etc.), it might cause a person to pause rather than take the risk of engaging in a nonproductive (dangerous) choice. The skill of risk taking through decision making is important because it allows students to make the most logical and rational decision possible. Many times, students are forced into decisions under unreasonable circumstances or when the decision is based on irrational emotions (e.g., based on fear and anger). If students base their decision on a logical and structured process, they can think through all aspects of the decision to choose the best option for themselves, their future, and their family. By teaching students to evaluate their options based on personal benefits or losses, family or friends' benefits or losses, and social considerations, the outcome may be advantageous to the student.

ChoiceMakers. ChoiceMakers (Martin & Huber-Marshall, 1995) specifically focuses on the leadership of students during their IEP meetings. This curriculum contains three basic sections: choosing goals, expressing goals, and taking action. Within these three sections, seven concepts are taught in the form of skills areas. These areas include (a) self-awareness, (b) self-advocacy, (c) self-efficacy, (d) decision making, (e) independent performance, (f) self-evaluation, and (g) adjustment. All skills taught in the curriculum address transition areas and student attainment during their high school years. The goal is to plan and prepare students for a successful transition into the working world and the community outside of school.

ENHANCEDetext
video example 13.3
One key component of self-determination is self-advocacy, a key consideration for students with disabilities. Watch this video to learn more about self-advocacy.

Life-Centered Career Education Curriculum. This curriculum was developed by Brolin (2004) for youth with developmental disabilities. As part of the federally funded self-determination projects, Wehmeyer (1995) adapted and field-tested the curriculum to promote self-determination skills for adolescents with disabilities. The curriculum includes 350 lesson plans for students who are 12 to 18 years of age. Self-determination lessons are intended to be used sequentially beginning with lesson 10 (goal setting), yet all lessons enhance the learning of independence among adolescents.

Classroom Competency-Building Program. Abery et al. (1995) developed a 10-module curriculum that includes the following skill areas: (a) self-awareness, (b) self-esteem, (c) perceptions of personal control, (d) personal values, (e) goal setting, (f) assertive communication, (g) choice making, (h) self-regulation, (i) problem solving, and (j) personal advocacy. The curriculum is designed for students with mild to moderate developmental disabilities and is, for the most part, experiential in nature to encourage active learning among the students. A parent program also was incorporated along with this curriculum.

Direct Instruction of Social and Self-Determination Skills

The teaching process typically employed in social skills instruction is structured learning or direct instruction. This behavioral approach to teaching consists of modeling, role-playing, corrective feedback, and planning for generalization (Goldstein et al., 2006). Historically, the most celebrated structured learning model is a teaching interaction procedure, perfected by Phillips, Phillips, Fixsen, and Wolf (1974), which requires the teacher to engage in specific steps that can be used with an individual and in a group situation. The steps include the following: (a) begin with a positive statement about the student, (b) define the social skill to be learned, (c) give a rationale regarding the importance of the skill, (d) give an example of when the skill could be used, (e) introduce and explain each non-verbal and verbal component of the targeted social skill, (f) model how the skill should be used, (g) rehearse the social skill with the student using real-life situations, (h) provide corrective feedback regarding the student's performance, (i) practice the social skill until the student is able to perform it exactly as described, and (j) plan when the skill could be used. See Table 13-7 for a detailed breakdown of the teaching behaviors (adapted from Hazel et al., 1981a; Phillips et al., 1974).

In addition to being an effective instructional procedure, the teaching procedure provides additional advantages because it (a) follows a structured format for teachers and students, (b) minimizes emotional reactions from teacher and students, (c) encourages incidental teaching, and (d) encourages preventive teaching. The key to successful implementation of the teaching interaction is to involve the student in the teaching procedure. For example, before defining the targeted social skill, the teacher should ask the students if they know what the skill means. Likewise, asking the students to provide rationales for why the skill is important to learn allows the student to think of how the skill can be integrated into everyday social interactions. By personalizing the social skill, the teacher may find that students are more willing to use the skill.

Within the direct instructional model, the teacher demonstrates how the skills should be used. Usually, a role-play situation is delineated, and the teacher models how the skill is to be performed. It is during this time that teachers should give a flawless performance of the skill. The rationale behind

TABLE 13–7 Teaching interaction

Nonverbal Behavior

1. Face the student.
2. Maintain eye contact.
3. Maintain a neutral or pleasant facial expression.

Paraverbal Behavior

4. Maintain a neutral tone of voice.
5. Speak at a moderate volume.

Verbal Teaching Behavior

6. Begin with a compliment related to the student's efforts and achievements.
7. Introduce the social skill and define what the social skill means.
8. Give a rationale for learning the skill and for using the skill with others.
9. Share an experience when you used the social skill or could have used the social skill.
10. Specify each behavior (e.g., non-verbal and verbal behavior) to be considered when exhibiting the skill.
11. Demonstrate or model the use of the skill.
12. Have the student rehearse the social skill. (Observe the student's behavior.)
13. Provide positive corrective feedback. State what the student did correctly. Provide suggestions for improvement. Demonstrate the corrective suggestions.
14. Practice the social skill with the student. (Make sure you do not prompt.)
15. Continue to provide corrective feedback to practice until the student masters (100%) the social skill in a novel situation.
16. Plan, with the student, when and where to use the social skill.

Note: Make sure the student participates throughout the lesson. Ask questions and let the student share ideas and thoughts. Praise the student for participating and rehearsing the social skill.

this suggestion is that the students will perform the skill exactly how it was demonstrated. Therefore, if the teacher leaves out one or two skill steps during the modeling of the skill, the students are likely to leave out those same skill steps. Students usually perform what they see—even if the skill is not modeled correctly. Practice modeling the skill to perfection so that students will follow suit.

Once the skill has been modeled and the students have practiced the skill, they must develop some degree of fluency if the execution of a skill is to be successful. Three areas have been identified as needing fluency in order to be successful in the execution of a skill. First, students must be able to recognize when a specific skill should be used. Many times, students learn five to eight skills and become confused when to use each skill in different situations. Often they try to use the wrong skill to accommodate a particular situation because they do not recognize the characteristics of the situation and how to match it with the specific learned skills. Teachers can build fluency in this area by playing games that require a student to recognize which skill should be used. For example, call out

a situation (e.g., your friends are trying to get you to cheat on a test) and see if they can come up with the correct skill to use (i.e., resisting peer pressure).

A second area of fluency is the knowledge of the skill and skill steps. When teaching the skill steps to the students, develop some strategy that students can use to remember all the skill steps of the skill. Some devices that have been used are memorization strategies or mnemonic strategies that facilitate the learning of the skill steps. If students know all the skill steps, their speech will flow from one step to the next when interacting with others. In this way, the student will not hesitate and will seem more confident in executing the skill.

A final area of fluency is the performance of the skill. Teachers plan that the students will try to meet a goal of 100% accuracy when performing a skill. If a student can reach a 100% accuracy rate during the acquisition stage of learning the skill, that same student will probably maintain the skill at 80% over time. This maintenance score will ensure that the student is performing the skill at a fairly fluent level and can be successful in his or her interactions with others.

ENHANCEDetext
video example 13.4
Watch this video to learn more
about teaching a social skills
lesson.

Social-Emotional Learning (SEL) Curricula

The expansion of social skills and self-determination skills curricula, through the efforts of social-emotional learning (SEL) researchers, has taken place over a period of 25 years. The skills of self-awareness, self-regulation, communication, problem solving, decision making, and collaboration (Wiley & Siperstein, 2015) are the primary skills found in SEL curricula. These skills are direct complements to skills found in social and self-determination skills curricula. To further expand these skills, researchers in the area of *mindfulness* have focused on using self-awareness and emotional self-regulation skills for the purpose of reducing the anxiety of children (Semple, Reid, & Miller, 2005) as well as increasing

their self-awareness and self-regulated behaviors when interacting with peers and performing academic work more proficiently (Maynard, Solis, & Miller, 2015). In this section, five evidence-based elementary SEL curricula are briefly presented with further detail on each curricula found in Table 13-8.

In general, the five identified evidence-based curricula (i.e., Caring School Community, Promoting Alternative Thinking Strategies, Positive Action, The Responsive Classroom, and Second Step) have targeted three categories of skills: (a) social or interpersonal skills, (b) self skills (e.g., self-regulation, self-talk, academic skills), and (c) social problem-solving skills. One curriculum, the Positive Action curriculum, also identified positive (a) self-concept, (b) action toward body, and (c) thoughts and behaviors. In each case, the authors of the curricula have established goals that will enhance the social and emotional boding of children with their teachers, schools, peers, and families as well as the integration of cognitive skills to enhance their academic performance. The

TABLE 13–8 Elementary SEL curricula at a glance

SEL Curricula	Goals of Curricula	Target Skills	Curricula Components
Caring School Community (CSC) (Development Studies Center, 2006)	Increase connections and bonding toward students and schools	Interpersonal problem solving and self skills (social and academic)	Class meetings Cross-age buddy activities Home activities Schoolwide activities
Promoting Alternative Thinking Strategies (Kusche & Greenberg, 1994)	Enhance emotional, interpersonal, and cognitive skills	Self-regulation, understanding emotions, social relationships, and social problem solving	Units to recognize and label social cues, friendship skills, feelings and behaviors, good manners
Positive Action (Positive Action, 1979–1982)	Build positive self-worth, thoughts, and behaviors	Self-concept, positive action toward body, responsible management of social interactions, emotional responses, and relationships Honesty	Schoolwide program, family involvement, and classroom instruction (small groups, role-play, skill practice, games)
The Responsive Classroom (RC) (Northeast Foundation for Children, 2011)	Improve classroom and social environment Create a caring classroom Classroom management Improve interpersonal cognitive skills	Social skills Community building Academic learning Choice making Self-regulation	Ten teaching practices: Morning meetings Classroom community Learn and practice social skills Create interest in academic and social learning
Second Step (Committee for Children, 2011)	Improve emotional, interpersonal, and cognitive skills of students	Problem solving Focused attention Listening Assertiveness Self-talk to manage attention Conflict resolution Empathy Management of emotions	Lessons and activities to enhance SEL skills in the classroom Explicit instruction, prepared scripts, stories with discussion, practice of skills, selected books Home component

rationale for these goals determines that if students are able to identify and bond with a positive community that values them, they are more likely to succeed socially, academically, and in life. These, too, are the goals of social and self-determination skills curricula and research.

LEARNING MODULE 13.1 Click here to learn more about helping students become independent learners via self-determination and self-regulated behaviors. http://iris .peabody.vanderbilt.edu/module/sr

Generalization of Skills

With social, problem-solving, and self-determination skills instruction assuming increasing importance in the promotion of competent behaviors, the effectiveness of direct instructional procedures is well noted in the literature. Yet the success of acquiring these skills in the instructional setting is only half the journey toward fluency of skills and eventual social and personal competence. Skill generalization is the other key factor in promoting social and personal competence.

Haring and Liberty (1990) defined the generalization of social or self-determination skills as the use of acquired skills (a) with people other than the social or self-determination skills instructor, (b) across environments other than the instructional settings, and (c) applied to situations other than those experienced during instruction of the social or self-determination skill.

In the past, the generalization of any skill was thought to be a phenomenon that just happened. Teachers were accustomed to the idea that once a skill was taught, a student could naturally perform the skill when needed. Generalization, though, was quickly recognized as the performance of acquired skills through the use of procedures specific to the skill (Stokes & Baer, 1977).

Acknowledging the problems with generalization of social and self-determination skills, researchers are currently investigating the use of different generalization strategies. A majority of these strategies are the outcome of the work by Stokes and Baer (1977). In their classic article, the authors outlined a technology of generalization that can be used to facilitate the use of any acquired skill with different people, in different settings, and in varied situations. The following discussion outlines strategies

that are based on their work and provides examples of the identified strategies. The strategies are presented under four categories.

Antecedent Strategies. Haring and Liberty (1990) suggested that two generalization strategies can be categorized as antecedent strategies, or strategies introduced during the teaching of the social skill. By using antecedent strategies during instruction of the social skill, teachers are incorporating environmental factors that may prompt or maintain the use of the social skill outside the teaching setting. The use of antecedent strategies may accomplish the goal of acquisition and generalization through one intervention. The first antecedent strategy, program common stimuli, uses a predominant factor or a salient stimulus that is common to both the instructional setting and a generalization setting. A teacher, therefore, should consider what stimuli are present in both settings and then employ the salient stimulus (or stimuli) during the instruction of the social skill. Classroom peers exemplify a very obvious salient stimulus. Using peers (especially peers from general education classes) to participate in the teaching, learning, or monitoring of social skills can facilitate the use of social skills. The second antecedent strategy used to facilitate generalization is sufficient exemplars. This strategy incorporates the teaching of several examples using the same direct teaching procedures, so generalization of social skills to new settings and new situations and responses can occur. An example of teaching sufficient exemplars can be seen in the study by Hazel et al. (1981b). These authors taught sufficient exemplars during the rehearsal portion of their teaching interaction. A new situation was used each time a student rehearsed the social skill. This continued until the student rehearsed the skill to 100% criteria in a novel role-playing situation. The outcome was generalization to hypothetical situations presented during post-testing of the social skills.

Setting Strategies. The second category of generalization strategies involves an intervention that is implemented whenever the social skills behavior is desired. This strategy, sequential modification, is a tactic of planning a social skills program in every condition (i.e., across people, setting, or situation) in which generalization is desired. For example, a teacher might develop a program of study in social skills instruction whereby the teaching was provided in one classroom and the generalization of the acquired skills was assessed in different desired settings (other classrooms, cafeteria, and playground). If the generalization of the skills did not occur in the different settings, the teacher must teach the social skills, sequentially, in each setting until generalization occurs over all the desired settings.

Consequence Strategies. Haring and Liberty (1990) proposed that a third category of generalization strategies dealing with the reinforcement of social skill behaviors in the natural setting (outside the instructional setting). The reinforcement or punishment (i.e., consequences) of the social skill directly relates to the continued use of the social skill and, therefore, directly relates to the generalization of the behavior. Three consequence strategies are identified below (Stokes & Baer, 1977).

The first generalization strategy under the category of consequences is to introduce natural, maintaining contingencies. This strategy deals with the use of people (or outcomes) who may reinforce the student for appropriate use of the social skill in the natural environment. Teaching the social skill to fluency can facilitate this strategy as well as make sure that the student experiences reinforcement for social skill performances. Although empirically based studies demonstrating the effectiveness of this strategy are not found in the social skills literature, teachers employ this strategy throughout the school year when they inform teachers and parents that a student has learned a particular skill and should be praised for the use of the skill in their classrooms or at home.

The use of reinforcement is highly desirable when one wishes to maintain a skill in any environment. The use of intermittent reinforcement can maintain a behavior for long periods of time (Kazdin, 2001). The use of indiscriminable contingencies, therefore, becomes another generalization strategy under the category of consequent strategies. This strategy is recognized when a student is unable to determine when reinforcement is going to occur for a desired behavior. Not knowing when reinforcement will occur makes students more likely to engage in the behavior in hope that a positive outcome will emerge.

The last strategy under this category is the train-to-generalize strategy. This strategy can be described as a systematic use of instruction to facilitate generalization. A teacher can tell the student about generalization, model the generalized use of the social skill, and ask the student to use the skill.

Other Strategies. Haring and Liberty (1990) created a fourth category of other strategies, including train loosely, mediate generalization, and train and hope. The strategy of train loosely is described as teaching social skills during every appropriate opportunity during the school day. This means that a teacher may elect to teach social skills using the context of the presenting classroom or school environment. By doing so, the teacher can enhance the possibility that students will begin to use their social skills in a variety of settings, with other people, and in different situations. This strategy has not been investigated through experimental procedures but can be demonstrated when teachers and parents use every opportunity to teach social skills to a student (e.g., parents often teach their children to say "please" and "thank you" at every available opportunity).

The second strategy in this category is the mediate generalization strategy. Using this generalization strategy, a teacher will instruct a student in the use of covert or overt behaviors that will facilitate remembering how and when to use a social skill. Most exemplified in the literature on social skill generalization for adolescents is the self-monitoring or self-control procedures. Self-monitoring procedures are taught to students so that they can remember to use the learned social skills in settings outside the teaching environment (e.g., Kiburtz, Miller, & Morrow, 1984).

Finally, Haring and Liberty (1990) (based on Stokes & Baer, 1977) identified the "train and hope" practice. Train and hope signifies the nonexistence of any generalization strategy. Providing social skills instruction, therefore, and then "hoping" the skills will occur across different settings, people, or situations exemplify this aspect of generalization. Train and hope strategies are not recommended; they rarely produce generalization effects.

Using Technology in a Social or Self-Determination Skills Program

While technology programs and information are growing, we do not have a substantial amount of data to support the use of technology in the area of social skills. Nevertheless, the use of computer technology is an important form of learning, teaching, and communicating.

Because technology has the potential to isolate children and impede their face-to-face social interactions with others, teachers must carefully plan the use of technology. The following discussion begins with the use of simple technological interventions and proceeds with more sophisticated uses of technology with social and self-determination skills.

Teachers might start out using simple tools such as cell phones, digital cameras, and video cameras. By employing cell phones in the classroom, teachers might show students proper etiquette when using this technology. A discussion of cell phone rules and when to use the cell phone is important. How to talk to authority figures (e.g., employers) over the phone can be useful as well as how to leave a message that is meaningful to friends and authority figures.

Another useful classroom tool is the digital camera or a video camera. Teachers can use these tools to capture interactions between individuals and give appropriate feedback on the social behavior. Videotaping role-play situations and discussing the interactions can have great learning potential as well as being useful for the generalization of the skills.

Skouge, Kelly, O'Brien, and Thomas (2003) reported on the use of video cameras by students to create video stories about themselves. The student (and parents) can produce a self-advocacy film by initiating a story about his or her life and how others can help him or her reach the goals they have developed. Video stories can be used to promote "visualization" and self-modeling to create plays or stories to explore alternative futures and act out dreams. In this way, students are developing social and self-determination skills as well as learning how to communicate their goals and action plans to others.

Many education-oriented publishing companies are marketing social skills programs on computer disks. For the most part, these programs offer knowledge-based information about social situations and interactions. Students are able to view the programs on CDs (and sometimes videotapes). There are limited data to substantiate whether children benefit from these programs. One recommendation is that teachers use these programs as an initial introduction to the skills. Role-playing and practice must follow in order that students demonstrate knowledge *and* performance of the skill.

Establishing a Social or Self-Determination Skills Program

After a teacher decides that a social or self-determination skills program should be made part of the school curricula, preparation for implementing the program can follow this sequence: (a) identify students through observation and assessment, (b) develop students' social skills profiles, (c) consider the grouping of the students, (d) prepare for program implementation, (e) implement social skills teaching procedures, (f) evaluate student performances after each skill is taught, and (g) program for generalization of the learned social skills to the natural environment.

Identify Students. The initial step is to identify the students who are exhibiting interpersonal and personal problems in or outside the classroom environment. This may be done by observing student behaviors during classroom activities, using standardized adaptive behavior scales, and surveying significant other people (i.e., other teachers, parents, and peers) concerning the students' social behaviors. Once the teacher has gathered this firsthand and secondhand information, an analysis of the data may reveal that specific social skills are needed. At this point, the teacher will broaden the scope of information by isolating a set of specific social or self-determination skills and assessing the student's performance of each skill during simulated situations. From this information, the teacher can identify whether skill components (e.g., recognizing that a skill should be used, non-verbal behaviors, verbal behaviors) of each skill are present in the student's repertoire and whether students are choosing not to use social skills that are in their repertoire (motivation problem). From this analysis, a final set of social or self-determination skills can be targeted for the overall needs of the students.

Develop Student Profiles. After the teacher compiles a set of targeted skills for each student, a skills profile may be developed. The profile will illustrate the competency level of each skill and indicate which skills need to be taught. When a profile is constructed for each student, the teacher may wish to identify a group of social skills that seem to be common across all the students.

Group Students. If a teacher plans to implement a social or self-determination skills program with a select number of students (rather than the entire class), it is wise to identify several aspects of the group's composition (Goldstein et al., 2006). An important consideration may be grouping students who are friends and would enjoy learning the social skills together. Although this may work well for the students, a teacher also must consider if a group of this composition would exhibit unmanageable behaviors; if so, a different grouping may be considered. Authors of social skills curricula suggest that teachers compose a group that is heterogeneous (males and females) in nature. Also, a group of students with varying intelligence is beneficial because students needing help can be paired with a peer who already knows the skill. The two students can work together in a tutor–tutee relationship.

Finally, a teacher may wish to consider the size of the skills instruction group. Although an entire class (15 or more) can engage in the skills program, teachers might find the behavioral rehearsal of the skills (role-playing) difficult to manage. This monitoring is especially crucial when establishing mastery performance criteria. On the other hand, more student participants can add to the diversity of the shared problems so that everyone can learn that other students have similar or worse problems. Sharing these experiences, coupled with learning how to deal with situations through the use of social and self-determination skills, may facilitate the generalization of the social skills among peers.

Prepare for Program Implementation. Once the assessment and student groupings are established, preparation for the social skills teaching includes deciding when and where the teaching will take place (e.g., three times a week), making sure the teaching procedures are well understood (refer to the skill teaching section of this chapter), and explaining the program to the students (e.g., describing the social skills that will be learned, explaining the benefits of learning the social skills, enlisting their cooperation, and creating enthusiasm for learning the social skills).

CULTURALLY RESPONSIVE CLASSROOMS

Social competence is a critical life skill needed by all students. Social skills correlate positively with school success and must be taught formally and informally throughout the curriculum. Students with and without disabilities or cultural differences who misperceive the social situation and choose the wrong option may find themselves rejected by peers, continuously being the recipients of harsh discipline consequences, or isolated from peers, family, and authority figures because of undesirable behaviors. All too often, the behaviors of children from diverse populations are misunderstood and devalued, and a level of disconnectedness occurs in the teaching and learning process.

- **Building relationships is a must**—Know the value orientation standards for achievement, social taboos, relational patterns, communication styles, and motivational systems of diverse learners. Be personally inviting and create a family-type learning community in the classroom. When it is necessary to reject specific behaviors, respect, relate, and communicate acceptance of students. Manage classrooms with firm, consistent, and loving control.

- **Accommodating culture is essential to learning—** Social skills instruction is an integral part of the daily curriculum and should be taught explicitly as an academic content subject weekly/daily. After skills have been learned, use cooperative learning and peer and cross-age learning strategies as a means to encourage and reinforce development and positive peer interactions.

- **Empowering diverse parents in the teaching and learning process**—Create a welcoming environment for divers parents by building relationships and providing information and resources to parents on an ongoing basis. All parents want their children to succeed; some need additional support.

Remember, classrooms and teachers must be personally and physically inviting. Diverse learners in need of social skill instruction can develop social competence if taught and affirmed in a caring, connected, culturally relevant learning school community.

Cathy Kea is a professor of special education at North Carolina State University. Her current research focuses on preparing teachers to design and deliver culturally responsive instruction.

Implement the Program. The direct instructional procedures outlined in this chapter and in social and self-determination skills curricula have been experimentally evaluated to be some of the most effective methods for teaching skills to children and adolescents. In addition to these procedures, though, Hazel et al. (1981a) stressed that teachers must exhibit other teaching behaviors, including (a) controlling off-task behavior, (b) using students' names, (c) programming for student participation throughout the teaching process, (d) teaching at a lively pace to avoid boredom, (e) using praise continuously, (f) exhibiting enthusiasm during the teaching of social skills, (g) using humor whenever possible, (h) being sincere and interested in the successful acquisition and mastery of the social skills, (i) displaying a pleasant manner, and (j) being empathetic with the students.

Another aspect of teaching social skills that is not usually emphasized is teaching to mastery. Teachers should make sure that the students have learned the components of each social skill (e.g., use a learning strategy or memorize the skill for long-term retention) without hesitation and can then exhibit the skill at a 100% mastery in a novel role-playing situation during the social skills teaching sessions.

Evaluate Student Performance. Once the students have reached a 100% mastery level in the social skill teaching setting, the teacher should evaluate the students' performances in the test setting or in the natural environment. Assessments that take place in the test setting allow the teacher to evaluate the student's individual performance on novel, simulated situations in a setting outside the teaching environment. Assessing the students' social skill performances in the natural environment may involve using confederate peers or teachers or arranging the environment so that the teacher can observe whether a student recognizes the need for the social skill and then engages in that particular social or self-determination skill. In either case, teachers are assessing some aspect of skill generalization and should use the information to program for further teaching of the social skill or to progress to the teaching of a new skill.

Program for Generalization. Once the teacher determines that the students have acquired the targeted social skills, an analysis of whether the social skills are generalizing to the natural environment must be made. If students are not using their newly acquired skills, teachers should plan for and employ the generalization strategies (discussed earlier). Additionally, classroom activities may be planned so that students have opportunities to use their learned social and self-determination skills and teachers have opportunities to reinforce the students' use of their social and self-determination skills.

Check Your Understanding 13.3 Click here to gauge your understanding of the concepts in this section.

ACTIVITIES

Elementary Level

1. Institute a regular "Friday Shakes" activity in which students line up at the door before Friday dismissal and the teacher shakes the hand of each student and gives him or her some personalized compliment or praise.
2. As students learn appropriate behaviors and social skills in the classroom, they should start identifying these behaviors in other students. Place a box with a slot in a prominent location and label it the "Praise Box" (or whatever creative title is desired). As you and the students (stress student participation) observe someone doing acts of kindness, consideration, encouragement, and learning social skills in and out of the classroom, have them write a note (or write a note yourself) telling of the appropriate activity, noting the time, the place, and the name of the person doing the behavior. At the end of the day or week, open the box and give all praise notes to the named students. Be sure that each student gets at least one "praise" note per time (Hayden, 1980).
3. In class, during a specified time, have each student find and say one thing he or she likes about two classmates.
4. Develop specific routines to welcome new students to the classroom. During class meetings, ask the students, "What things would you want to know if you were new in this school?" Make a list of informational facts about the

school so that the students can answer any questions a new student might have.

5. Assign "buddies" to new students in your classroom. The buddy is responsible for introducing the new student to peers and other teachers as well as for asking the new student to participate in different social situations (e.g., eat lunch together, play games, sit together at school assemblies).

Middle School Level

1. Develop a specific skill for welcoming visitors to the classroom. Each week, assign a student to greet visitors, ask them to sit down, and perform any other task that may make the visitors more comfortable in the classroom.

2. Read a story involving a particular social interaction problem or issue. Through a class discussion, let the students identify the problem, list possible solutions and the outcomes of each solution, and decide which solution would be most beneficial to all involved.

3. Instead of just playing team sports, have students work together to decide the best offensive and defensive strategies to use during a game. The position of each team member can be discussed and agreed upon by the team as a whole instead of being assigned by the coach.

4. During the morning class meeting, have students talk about personal or interpersonal problems around school and the community. Conduct a problem-solving session where peers provide possible solutions to the problems. Then, as a class, decide on the best solution for all involved and how the solution will be implemented. Role-play the implementation of the solution, as it often requires the use of many social skills. Always follow up to see if the implemented solution worked.

5. Each time a group of students seems to be disagreeing, have them resolve the conflict by each "giving and taking" a little through the skill of negotiation. Make sure you foster a "win–win" situation.

Secondary Level

1. Teach students the skill of negotiation. Each week, select a student to be the peer mediator who will facilitate a conflict resolution when it occurs between two or more persons. Make sure the peer mediator is well liked and respected among the peers.

2. Have students develop goals that relate to their learned social skills. For example, one goal may be this: "I will use my skill of problem solving three times this week." Have students monitor their achievements with goal accomplishment sheets and graphs.

3. Have each student think of a social skill upon which he or she would like to improve and write this goal on a card (e.g., "I will use my Accepting Criticism skill with Mr. P——"). The students check off each time they used or did not use the skill on the card (which is filed in a box in the classroom) every day for two weeks. At the end of one week and at the end of two weeks, have the students discuss their progress and any changes they recognize.

4. Arrange for professionals from the community to come visit your class. People involved in real estate, dentists, telephone operators, and so forth can provide information that students can seek out. As a follow-up, have the professional agree to mentor a student at the work cite for one day. The student can list the professional behavior, social skills, and self-determination skills that are expected and required at the professionals' work situation.

5. Keep a problem box in your classroom. Students may write down problems and put them in the box. Once a week, take time to discuss the problems in a group. Have students generate solutions to the problems and discuss the possible outcomes to each problem. Emphasize that problem solving is a way to persist toward a certain goal or to overcome a barrier.

Applied Academics

LEARNING OUTCOMES

Upon completion of this chapter, the reader should be able to:

14.1 Understand the concept of functional competence.

14.2 Identify the areas of applied academics within the curriculum.

14.3 Identify strategies for the assessment of functional competence.

14.4 Provide examples of general curricular and instructional approaches and specific teaching strategies for each applied academics curricular area.

Regardless of the goals of education that one advocates, the ability to function in society is certainly on the list of such goals. We want our students to become productive and contributing citizens. The skill- and content-related topics that have been covered in this book contribute in various ways to this goal.

Effective functioning, either in the home, in postsecondary education settings, in the workplace, or in any number of community settings, requires many skills. These skills, of course, range from the simple to the far more complex. Unfortunately, most students who have struggled in school are directly taught very few of the requisite skills needed to deal with the demands of adulthood that we all face on a daily basis. The assumptions that students automatically adjust to community living after exiting formal schooling and that they will demonstrate proficiency with a wide range of everyday challenges are erroneous, as the evidence from the many follow-up studies has shown (see, e.g., Newman, Wagner, Cameto, & Knokey, 2009; Wagner, Newman, Cameto, Garza, & Levine, 2005).

This chapter explores a variety of applied or functional topics that relate to dealing successfully with the many demands of adulthood that await *all* students who are moving into a new stage of life when high school ends. The first section of the chapter discusses the concepts of personal and functional competence, provides a framework for conceptualizing and operationalizing the specific demands of adulthood, and describes how functional topics relate to scholastic areas of the general education curriculum. The second section discusses the functional implications of the four key subject areas (language arts [reading and writing], math, science, and social studies) around which applied academic curricula are designed. The next section of the chapter covers formal and informal ways to assess functional competence. The last major section focuses on how to teach functional content, with an emphasis on how to integrate real-life topics into the general education curriculum and how to align this content with state content and performance standards.

FUNCTIONAL COMPETENCE

This initial discussion of functional competence is intended to provide basic information about functional knowledge and skills. The section has four major objectives: to discuss the general meaning of the concepts of functional competence, to introduce typical terminology that is used in school settings in reference to personal and functional competence, to identify the major demands associated with functioning in adulthood, and to demonstrate the relationship of functional topics to the general education curriculum.

Functional Competence as Everyday or Applied Intelligence

The ability to deal effectively with the demands of everyday life at any stage of adulthood—functional competence—requires three key components: knowledge acquisition, the development of relevant skill sets, and the intelligent application of knowledge and skills to specific situations within certain settings. Individuals need to acquire knowledge about the various real-life demands that they face now and in the future. Ultimately, they must be able to apply the knowledge and skills that have been learned to new and novel situations that will inevitably occur and when other supports may not be present.

As an example, learning how to take public transportation from home to work requires knowledge of the route, schedule, amount of time it will take to get to work, and the skills associated with accessing the bus or metro system and navigating the route that is required. The essence of whether someone has developed the required competencies associated with using public transportation is demonstrated when an individual must use his or her knowledge of the system and associated skills when taking a new route that has never been experienced previously.

The notion of "personal competence," as discussed initially by Greenspan and Driscoll (1997), suggests that a person must be competent in four areas:

- Physical competence: organ competence; motor competence
- Affective competence: temperament; character
- Everyday competence: practical intelligence; social intelligence
- Academic competence: conceptual intelligence; language

This model recognizes that many factors contribute to achieving personal competence. Of particular relevance to this chapter is the notion of everyday competence. Greenspan and Driscoll (1997) suggest that "everyday competence" is a function of one's practical and social intelligence and define it in the following way:

> one's ability to think about and understand problems found in such real-world settings as work, play, social relationships, and home. . . . Practical intelligence refers to the ability to think about and understand mechanical, technical, or physical problems in everyday settings. . . . Social intelligence refers to the ability to think about and understand problems found in relationships with other people. (p. 134)

The concepts of practical and social intelligence relate directly to the intelligent application of knowledge and skills to new situations or settings. The concept of applied intelligence also has relevance to the notion of functional competence. Sternberg, Kaufman, and Grigorenko (2008) noted that "being intelligent is more than being book-smart; it is knowing how to apply it" (p. 1). They identified three parts to the theory: what goes on inside the person, the person's past experience in dealing with various situations, and the person's ability to adapt to, change, or find new environments in which one has to exist.

Terminology

Functional as a term is used in varying ways, and its meaning is very much determined by context. A wide range of terms have been used to convey the concept of functional skills. Some of the most frequently used terms to describe those skills that are needed to "function" in everyday life include

- activities of daily living,
- applied academics,
- daily living skills,
- everyday intelligence,
- functional academics,
- functional literacy,
- independent living skills,
- life skills, and
- survival skills.

Cronin, Patton, and Wood (2007) explained nuances of different terminology:

> At times, the meaning associated with the terms is interchangeable; however, at other times, differences in meaning are apparent. For instance, the term *applied academics* suggests skills that are clearly different from self-care skills of toileting and grooming that are associated with *daily living skills*. (p. 2)

Functionality is also determined by context. The term *functional* typically refers to practical types of everyday living skills. However, certain higher-order skills involving complex math calculations have "functionality" in the field of engineering. Nevertheless, the notion of functionality used in this chapter will follow the more common application to everyday living situations.

This chapter focuses on the topic of applied academics. However, applied academics are also real-life skills. For purposes of this chapter, these terms are defined as follows:

- **Applied academics**—the real-world application of core academic content and related skills that are meaningful and relevant to an individual's life now and in the future. (Table 14-1 lists some examples of functional academic content.)
- **Real-life skills**—specific competencies (i.e., knowledge, skills, intelligent application) of local and cultural relevance needed to perform everyday activities across a variety of settings.

Functional curriculum should be distinguished from the terms presented previously, as it is used frequently in the field of special education. It refers to a specifically designed scope and sequence of content coverage (i.e., curriculum) that is completely focused on functional topics. Clark, Field, Patton, Brolin, and Sitlington (1994) have defined functional curriculum as "a way of delivering instructional content that focuses on the concepts

TABLE 14–1 Traditional academic content areas and examples of functional activities

Content Area	Functional Activities
Reading	Read a newspaper article
	Read a recipe
	Read the signs on restroom doors
	Read instructions for video game
	Read a job application
	Read a course schedule of classes for college
Math	Add sales tax to purchase order
	Use calculator to add grocery item totals
	Compare prices at a local movie rental store
	Calculate income tax return
	Compute square footage for a carpentry task
Science	Calculate boiling point for candy recipe
	Use medication chart
	Plant and harvest vegetable garden
	Identify weather to select appropriate clothing
Social studies	Register to vote
	Identify cultural holidays and customs
	Identify headlines in newspapers
	Determine bus route in the community
Health	Brush teeth and practice oral hygiene
	Plan balanced meals
	Identify and purchase items for class first aid kit
	Identify health services in the community
	Label sexual feelings and attitudes
Expressive writing	Write a thank-you note
	Dictate a personal story
	Write a biography for college entrance application

Source: Table 6.1 From *Functional Curriculum for Elementary and Secondary Student with Special Needs*, 3rd Ed. (p. 165), by Paul Wehman, John Kregel, 2012, Austin, TX: PRO-ED. Copyright 2012 by PRO-ED, Inc. Reprinted with permission.

and skills needed by all students with disabilities in the areas of personal-social, daily living, and occupational adjustment" (p. 37). Valletutti, Bender, and Baglin (2008) simply stated that "life is the curriculum" (p. 1).

Demands of Adulthood

Young adults with special needs face an array of challenges when they move from high school to community living. The identification of critical functional knowledge and skills needed in adulthood should be based on the behaviors that will be demanded of those individuals in the community settings in which they will live, learn, and work.

Results from the National Longitudinal Transition Study—2 (Newman et al., 2009; Wagner et al., 2005) indicated that the functional skill levels

TABLE 14–2   Functional skills and out-of-school youth, by disability category

	Learning Disability	Intellectual Disability	Emotional Disturbance
Percentage rated by parents "high" on:			
Self-care skills	98.5	84.2	97.7
Functional cognitive skills	80.4	42.3	83.6
Percentage with social skills rated[a]			
High	19.1	7.3	5.4
Low	17.4	26.0	45.8
Percentage communicating with no trouble	83.3	55.2	80.4
Percentage with health Reported to be[b]			
Excellent	41.2	30.4	36.0
Fair or poor	8.1	12.1	13.5

Source: NLTS2 (p. 2–5). Wave 2 parent/youth interviews.
[a]The category "medium" is omitted from the exhibit.
[b]The categories "very good" and "good" are omitted from the exhibit.

of many students, as reported by their parents, remained deficient after students left school. Data for three student groups (learning disability, intellectual disability, and emotional disturbance) are provided in Table 14-2. The data do not cover all areas where functional competence is needed, but they do provide insights in the areas of self-care, functional cognitive skills (e.g., making change), social skills, communication skills, and health status. These findings underscore the importance of addressing functional skill areas prior to students leaving school, as these areas create barriers to functioning competently later in life.

The identification of the major demands of life after high school provides the foundation for local school systems to address the need to ensure competency across a range of everyday living areas. A number of taxonomies exist depicting the **demands of adulthood** (see Cronin et al., 2007, p. 16).

Two curricular sources that provide a useful framework for understanding the demands of everyday adult life and that are highlighted in this chapter include Cronin et al.'s (2007) Major Life Demands model and Brolin's (2004) Life-Centered Career Education (LCCE) model. Table 14-3 provides an overview of these two models.

As can be seen, the Major Life Demands model is organized according to six adult domains and 23 subdomains. These subdomains are further subdivided into 136 major life demands. The LCCE model includes three major domains and 22 competencies that are further subdivided into

97 subcompetencies. Many of the domains and subcategories require functional competence in an array of applied academic areas.

Both lists provide a comprehensive reference of the most demands that most adults in the United States are likely to face. It is important to recognize that some individuals will not need to become functionally competent on some of the knowledge or skill areas, as the specific area will not apply to them. For example, a person who lives in a rural area of the country will not need to be competent in the use of a public transportation system, as long as he or she does not move to any area where one might be needed.

The subcompetencies used by Brolin (2004), the major life demands developed by Cronin et al. (2007), or other lists of functional competencies tend to correlate highly with one another. They all represent reasoned efforts to help practitioners develop meaningful programs for students.

Relationship of Applied Academics to the General Education Curriculum

Understanding the relationship between knowledge and skills associated with the general education curriculum and applied academic is important. The merging of scholastic instruction and instruction on functional topics provides a likely solution to the balance between addressing content and performance standards and meeting the functional needs of students, as is addressed later in the chapter. Table 14-4 provides selected secondary

TABLE 14–3   Models of adult functioning

Model	Adult Domain/Curriculum Area	Subdomains/Competency Areas
Major Life Demands (Cronin, Patton, & Wood 2007)	Employment/education	General job skills General education/training considerations Employment setting Career refinement and reevaluation
	Home and family	Home management Financial management Family life Childrearing
	Leisure pursuits	Indoor activities Outdoor activities Community/neighborhood activities Travel Entertainment
	Community involvement	Citizenship Community awareness Services/resources
	Physical/emotional health	Physical health Emotional health
	Personal responsibility and relationships	Personal confidence/understanding Goal setting Self-improvement Relationships Personal expression
Life-Centered Career Education (Brolin, 2004)	Daily living skills	Managing personal finances Selecting and managing a household Caring for personal needs Raising children and meeting marriage responsibilities Buying, preparing, and consuming food Buying and caring for clothing Exhibiting responsible citizenship Utilizing recreational facilities and engaging in leisure Getting around the community
	Personal-social skills	Achieving self-awareness Acquiring self-confidence Achieving socially responsible behavior Maintaining good interpersonal skills Achieving independence Making adequate decisions Communicating with others
	Occupational guidance and preparation	Knowing and exploring occupational possibilities Selecting and planning occupational choices Exhibiting appropriate work habits and behavior Seeking, securing, and maintaining employment Exhibiting sufficient physical-manual skills Obtaining specific occupational skills

Source: Table 1.1 From *Infusing Real-Life Topics into Existing Curricula: Recommended Procedures and Instructional Examples for the Elementary, Middle, and High School Levels* (p. 3), by James R. Patton, Mary E. Cronin, Susan J. Wood, 1999, Austin, TX: PRO-ED. Copyright 1999 by PRO-ED, Inc. Reprinted with permission.

level examples of how functional topics relate to scholastic areas. Activities emphasizing functional application of scholastic skills can—and should—be developed at the elementary level as well (for elementary examples, see Cronin et al., 2007).

 Check Your Understanding 14.1   Click here to gauge your understanding of the concepts in this section.

TABLE 14–4 Secondary matrix: Relationship of scholastic skills to functional topics

	Employment/ Education	Home and Family	Leisure Pursuits	Community Involvement	Emotional/ Physical Health	Personal Responsibility and Relationships
Reading	Read classified ads for jobs.	Interpret bills.	Locate and understand movie information in a newspaper.	Follow directions on tax forms.	Comprehend directions on medication.	Read letters from friends.
Writing	Write a letter of application for a job.	Write checks.	Write for information on a city to visit.	Fill in a voter registration form.	Fill in your medical history on forms.	Send thank-you notes.
Listening	Understand oral directions of a procedure change.	Comprehend oral directions for making dinner.	Listen to a weather forecast to plan outdoor activity.	Understand campaign ads.	Attend lectures on stress.	Take turns in a conversation.
Speaking	Ask your boss for a raise.	Discuss morning routines with your family.	Inquire about tickets for a concert.	State your opinion at a school board meeting.	Describe symptoms to a doctor.	Give feedback to a friend about the purchase of a CD or DVD.
Math Applications	Understand the difference between net and gross pay.	Compute the cost of doing laundry in a laundromat versus at home.	Calculate the cost of a dinner out versus eating at home.	Obtain information for a building permit.	Use a thermometer.	Plan the costs of a date.
Problem Solving	Settle a dispute with a coworker.	Decide how much to budget for rent.	Role-play appropriate behaviors for various plates.	Know what to do if you are the victim of fraud.	Select a donor.	Decide how to ask someone for a date.
Survival Skills	Use a prepared career planning packet.	List emergency phone numbers.	Use a shopping center directory.	Mark a calendar for important dates (e.g., recycling, garbage collection).	Use a system to remember to take vitamins.	Develop a system to remember birthdays.
Personal/ Social	Apply appropriate interview skills.	Help a child with homework.	Know the rules of a neighborhood pool.	Locate self-improvement classes.	Get a yearly physical exam.	Discuss how to negotiate a price at a flea market.

Source: Figure 3.5 From *Life Skills Instructions: A Practical Guide for Integrating Real-Life Content into the Curriculum at the Elementary and Secondary Levels for Students with Special Needs or Who are Placed at Risk*, 2nd Ed. (p. 62), by Mary E. Cronin, James R. Patton, Susan J. Wood, 2007, Austin, TX: PRO-ED. Copyright 2007 by PRO-ED, Inc. Reprinted with permission.

APPLIED ACADEMICS

Applied academics is used within this chapter to refer to the real-world application of content and skills that are associated with the core academic subject areas. Traditionally, applied academics have been restricted to three areas: reading, writing, and math. We have expanded the view of applied academics to include the other subjects of science and social studies. Throughout this section of the chapter, we also use the term *functional* (e.g., functional reading) in the description of each area.

A key distinction needs to be made in regard to the areas included under the term *applied academics*. Functional reading and functional writing really refer to skills, whereas functional math, science, and social studies refer to knowledge acquisition and skill performance associated with subject area content (see Figure 14-1). Functional reading and writing are essential tool skills that are

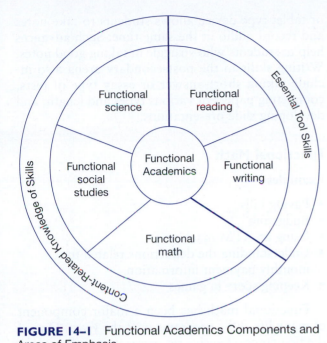

FIGURE 14–1 Functional Academics Components and Areas of Emphasis

not content specific; they are used in a variety of ways and across many different settings (e.g., reading as an academic area does not have content; the content comes from other areas such as literature, science, or social studies). Functional math, science, and social studies are content laden, and as a result, a significant amount of information (facts, concepts) is considered part of the discipline. Of course, in addition to the knowledge that is imparted in these subjects, certain specific skills are typically developed in these subject areas as well (e.g., inquiry skills in science, problem-solving skills in math, research skills in social studies).

The general education curriculum is composed of four major subject areas for which content and performance standards have been created and on which students are tested regularly throughout their school careers.

The subject area of language arts, at the elementary level, is dedicated to the development of critical tool skills in reading and writing that will be needed in school, at home, in the community, and in the workplace. As students move to the secondary level, critical reading and writing skills are emphasized, and students engage various types of literature in their coursework, exposing students to a variety of different types of narrative and expository material and the need to be able to write coherently about what they have read.

As indicated at the beginning of this section and to remain in line with the organization of the general education curriculum, we have conceptualized applied academics in the following way:

- **Functional reading**—includes areas of reading that are used in everyday situations by most individuals
- **Functional writing**—focuses on the writing demands needed in everyday life situations
- **Functional math**—focuses on math content in the areas of money management and other measurement applications (volumetric, linear, temporal, temperature, weight)
- **Functional science**—focuses on science content as it relates to life (especially health), physical, and environmental science in the everyday world
- **Functional social studies**—focuses on social studies content that relates to community involvement and citizenship

Real-life applications for the functional areas are discussed in the following sections and examples are presented in two locations. A few examples are provided at the beginning of each of the following sections. A comprehensive listing of applied examples, organized around the five subcategories (everyday living, school, community, work, and leisure), can be found in Appendices 14-A to 14-E. Although the appendices are comprehensive, they do not include every possible situation where functional competence is needed.

Functional Reading

Examples:

- Reading tax-related documents
- Understanding a menu in a restaurant
- Reading a policy manual at work
- Reading an online newspaper

The functional application of reading includes a number of areas that individuals encounter every day. An extensive list of areas in which reading is needed in the real world is provided in Appendix 14-A. As can be seen in this appendix, various types of reading skills are used regularly in everyday life from reading notes left by other family members to reading instruction manuals for new electronic games and equipment. Accordingly, the reading skill level required varies according to the textual material. As an example of the demands of varying levels of reading competence, the readability of a car owner's manual can range from fourth-grade to over 10th-grade reading levels.

In addition to developing competence in comprehending a vast array of textual material, as highlighted in Appendix 14-A, students must also achieve mastery of other types of reading skills. For example, the ability to scan and skim textual material (see also Chapter 12) has high functional value in higher education settings. Interestingly and often overlooked is the reality that we use these skills regularly in our everyday lives as well. Hoover and Patton (2007) provided more detailed coverage on what these skills are and how to teach them.

Functional Writing

Examples:

- Taking a phone message
- Writing the directions to a location in the community
- Responding to an email from a coworker
- Maintaining a personal journal/blog

Although not as extensive and arguably not as limiting as problems in reading, if one has problems in this area, the need to be able to write in everyday life occurs in many different ways, as suggested in Appendix 14-B. Writing skills involve the ability to generate written products both by hand and by using a keyboard. As noted earlier, the associated skills of handwriting and spelling also play important roles in this process.

Except in instances in which one chooses a career in which large amounts of writing are required (e.g., journalism, author), most of the everyday writing demands for adults involve relatively short writing tasks (writing notes, email or text messages, phone messages). Frequently, writing tasks are coupled with the need to read materials as well (e.g., completing an application, responding to someone else's letter or email).

On the other hand, for those who pursue further education after high school, writing becomes a crucial tool skill for the successful completion of course requirements. A particular example is the importance of adequate writing skills that are needed in the taking of good notes during class. Technology in the form of apps for one's computer

or tablet-type device allows students to take notes and record audio at the same time. Such advances help to students who struggle in taking good notes. Writing skills in the postsecondary arena also include taking short-answer or essay type of tests, completing papers of various types and length, and developing slide presentations.

Functional Math

Examples:

- Paying bills
- Budgeting
- Using an ATM machine
- Understanding the deductions related to monthly payment information
- Keeping score in games

Functional math has been a major component of many life skills programs over the years. One of the first comprehensive resources written for teachers to use with learners with special needs was the classic *Functional Mathematics for the Mentally Retarded* (Peterson, 1972). Curricular materials such as *Real Life Math* (Glisan, 2001) were developed with a functional orientation to them.

In more recent years, the general education version of what could be referred to as "functional" math was a course that typically was called "practical math" or "consumer math." The usual content of practical math courses has included units on topics such as the following (Staudacher & Turner, 1990):

- Budgeting
- Earning a paycheck
- Banking and saving (using a checking account)
- Selecting housing
- Buying and preparing food
- Buying personal items
- Owning a vehicle
- Cash or credit
- Recreation, travel, and entertainment

Educational reforms have shifted the curricular landscape, resulting in different emphases and requirements, such as the need to have more than one algebra course. As a result, courses such as consumer math or practical math have been dropped from the curriculum in many school districts and have virtually disappeared. This is too bad because no other course that was part of the general education curriculum had more "functional" face value than this type of course.

There is no question that all of the broad topics typically covered in practical math courses have importance in contributing to functional competence. Students have to acquire the knowledge and develop the skill sets to be able to accomplish the specific math situations that are associated with these topical areas. Coursework that was available in schools used to provide this opportunity; however, for most students, these opportunities no longer exist. The need to teach key functional math skills remains high; however, the means to do so remain elusive.

The number of subskills that are associated with many math tasks can be substantial. For example, consider the skills that are involved with using an ATM machine. Kregel (2012), in his task analysis of using an ATM machine, lists 17 different steps, as shown in Figure 14-2. The point here is that many of these everyday math skills will require explicit instruction for a number of students in order for them to master this particular skill.

---

1. Approach ATM.
2. Remove ATM card from purse, wallet, or pocket.
3. Insert card into machine, orienting the card as necessary.
4. Select language to be used to display directions.
5. Enter Personal Identification Number (PIN).
6. Accept or decline additional transaction fees as necessary.
7. Select type of transaction.
8. Select specific account (i.e., checking) to be used for transaction.
9. Select "receipt requested" when prompted by ATM.
10. Enter amount of transaction.
11. Remain at ATM while processing occurs.
12. Collect money when dispensed.
13. Place money in purse, wallet, or pocket.
14. Select "transaction complete" when prompted by ATM.
15. Collect receipt when dispensed.
16. Collect ATM card when dispensed.
17. Place receipt and ATM card in purse, wallet, or pocket.

FIGURE 14–2 Task Analysis of Using an ATM to Make a Cash Withdrawal from a Checking Account

Source: Kregel, J. (2004). Designing instructional programs. In P. Wehman & J. Kregel (Eds.), *Functional curriculum for elementary, middle, and secondary age students with special needs* (2nd ed.). Austin, TX: PRO-ED, p. 76.

Everyday life is full of situations where math knowledge and skills are needed. What might be surprising is that a great deal of the math that we use on a daily basis involves estimation and approximations—not precise math. example, most of us estimate how long it will take to get to work or we have a general idea of how much money is in our checking account. Appendix 14-C provides a comprehensive list of essential math skills where some degree of competence is needed to deal successfully with the everyday demands of adulthood.

ENHANCEDetext
video example 14.1
Watch this video to learn more about applied, real-world math instruction.

Functional Science

Examples:

- Knowing first aid procedures
- Recognizing dangerous materials in the home
- Knowing to stay hydrated when doing summertime activities
- Treating illness

Functional science is not a term or a concept that has been used often in school discussions. However, the implication that certain topics in science have functional utility is no different than making the same claim in math. The functional linkage of science facts, concepts, and skills to everyday lives of people is straightforward. Many topics covered in life, physical, and environmental science have real-world applications, as documented in Appendix 14-D.

Functional science extends beyond basic, simple science knowledge and skills competence; it also involves being scientifically literate. This notion is embodied in the idea that "scientifically literate people are able to use thought processes and the scientific knowledge they have acquired to think about and make sense of many ideas, claims, and events they encounter in their everyday lives" (American Association for the Advancement of Science, cited in Sunal & Sunal, 2003).

Science is an easy subject to relate to the everyday world, as it is all around us. Probably the most important functional application of science relates to personal life science. Examples include being able to plan a healthy diet, exercising regularly, and treating minor injuries. However, science is all around us at home and in the community. Being able to fix a toilet (really a simple appliance) or keeping pipes from freezing in the winter involve actions that are grounded in everyday science.

Beyond the benefit of having access to functional content that students need to know, another key reason exists for linking science topics covered in textbooks and in class to real-world situations to which students can relate: Doing so increases the chance that they will retain what is being presented.

Functional Social Studies

Examples:

- Knowing one's legal rights (e.g., Miranda warning)
- Responding to a call for and serving on jury duty
- Using community services
- Understanding the need for accommodations in the workplace

If *functional science* as a term seems unusual at first, then *functional social studies* may seem equally atypical. However, like science and math, social studies includes many topics that have relevance to everyday life. Using the same rationale that was used with functional science, one could argue that every student should leave school being literate in a range of functional social studies topics, as identified in Appendix 14-E.

In social studies, functional topics include important considerations associated with one's legal rights across a range of areas, as provided in the following three examples. Students need to know what a contract (i.e., renting furniture for an apartment) is and what it means for them if they sign it. Students with disabilities who go on to further education need to know what their rights are within this system (ADA and Section 504) and understand that the system operates very differently from the one they are leaving. Students also need to understand what their rights are if they encounter the criminal justice system (Miranda warning and its implications).

One other area in social studies that has important functional value is the topic of transportation. Although a discussion on transportation in a world geography course may be more on the economic need for and relevance of various types of transportation systems, a functional application of this topic is also warranted for those settings where this knowledge and skill set will be needed.

 Check Your Understanding 14.2 Click here to gauge your understanding of the concepts in this section.

ASSESSING FUNCTIONAL COMPETENCE

To address the functional needs of students with special needs, teachers need to use appropriate functional assessments for the following four reasons. First, they must determine a student's present levels of functioning. IDEA requires that the IEP contain a statement of present levels of academic achievement and functional performance (PLAAFP) in all areas that are needed. The 2004 reauthorization of the law emphasized that functional areas must be considered as much as academic areas have been focused on in the past. In addition, the IEP must include measurable annual goals that are based on the PLAAFPs. Second, teachers must monitor the progress of students over time as instruction is provided. Third, teachers, particularly when a student approaches age 16, must engage in the process of identifying the transition needs of students and plan for their post-school life. This planning must, according to IDEA, be based on a student's strengths, preferences, and interests, as is discussed at length in the next chapter. Fourth, as a result of the 2004 reauthorization of IDEA, students must be provided with a summary of their functional performance and academic achievement prior to their exit from high school. The very intent of this mandate involves assembling all pertinent information for determining the functional impact of a student's disability in terms of living, working, and learning.

Teachers have a variety of instruments and techniques from which to choose in order to address these goals. Some are formal instruments and may be standardized or non-standardized. Others are informal in nature and usually include observation, recollection methods (interviews, checklists, rating scales), curriculum-based assessment, and performance-based procedures. This section examines formal and informal techniques for obtaining information about personal and functional competence

TABLE 14–5   Formal instruments for assessing functional competence

Type of Assessment	Specific Instruments
Adaptive behavior	• Adaptive Behavior Assessment System—Third Edition (ABAS-3) • Adaptive Behavior Diagnostic Scale (ABDS) • Adaptive Behavior Evaluation Scale—Revised Second Edition (ABES-2) • Adaptive Behavior Inventory (ABI) • Adaptive Behavior Planning Inventory (ABPI) • Brigance Transition Skills Inventory • Diagnostic Adaptive Behavior Scale (DABS) • Scales of Independent Behavior–R (SIB-R) • Vineland-II Adaptive Behavior Scales (VABS-II)
Life skills instruments	• Kauffman Functional Academic Skills Test (K-FAST) • Life Centered Career Education Knowledge Battery • Life Centered Career Education Performance Battery

and considers the importance of the summary of performance procedures as a way of operationalizing data regarding functional performance.

Formal Instruments

Two types of formal measures that provide information about functional competence (adaptive behavior instruments and life/functional skills instruments) are discussed in this section. Measures related to occupational interest and transition needs/strengths can also provide useful information; however, these measures are discussed in some detail in the next chapter. Table 14-5 is a list of representative instruments in the areas of adaptive functioning and life/functional skills. For detailed information on these instruments, readers are encouraged to consult professional resources on assessment (e.g., Cohen & Spenciner, 2007; Olley, 2015; Power, 2006).

Adaptive Behavior/Adaptive Functioning Measures.

As Cronin et al. (2007) noted, "more than any other measure used in schools—excluding specific transition instruments—adaptive behavior measures provide the most extensive set of information about real-world functioning" (p. 30). These measures examine the following areas: self-care/daily living skills, home living skills, social behavior, communication skills, leisure skills, community use skills, health/safety skills, functional academic skills, self-direction, and work-related skills.

Adaptive behavior/functioning refers to the ability to cope with the demands of everyday life. The assessment of adaptive functioning focuses on the measurement of typical behavior over time—the fact that an individual was able to perform the behavior on some isolated occasion does not matter; what matters is the consistent trend of the behavior over time.

Three cautions need to be mentioned in relation to the assessment of adaptive functioning. First, consideration of age and cultural context is an essential when conducting this type of assessment. Second, the assessment of adaptive functioning must be current for it to be useful. The essence of adaptive functioning is that, with proper instruction, competence can improve. Therefore, when looking at adaptive functioning, it is important that we look at it in a current context. Third, most of the formal instruments that measure adaptive functioning include only a sample of behaviors in each of the adaptive areas. As a result, most instruments have limited use for curriculum planning purposes.

Most adaptive behavior measures listed in Table 14-5 use a structured-interview format whereby information is obtained through the information provided by respondents who know about the performance of the individual on which the assessment is being conducted. For the most part, adaptive behavior measures do not use direct observation to generate data; the information is obtained indirectly through interviews with persons who have observed and are familiar with the individual.

The results of most formal adaptive behavior assessments provide quantitative (i.e., scores) and, in a limited way, qualitative data. However, for data from these types of measures to be useful, the information collected needs to be analyzed and typically additional information may be needed. One instrument, the *Adaptive Behavior Planning Inventory* (ABPI) (Patton, Mruzek, & Pearson, in press), is designed to provide and exhaustive list of adaptive behaviors that can be used for planning and progress monitoring purposes. The instrument includes over 900 items organized according to various adaptive domains. The user of this instrument does not have to engage all of these items, only those that are pertinent to the student with whom he or she is working.

Life Skills Instruments. Certain instruments measure only functional areas and do so primarily by directly assessing whether the person has the knowledge or can perform a particular skill or set of skills related to a functional area. In other words, life skill measures "typically involve the student in some observable activity—answering questions (knowledge-related) or performing activities (skill-related)" (Cronin et al., 2007, p. 30). Some of the more frequently used measures are listed in Table 14-5.

These types of instruments take more time to administer, as they require the administration of items to which a student responds. In addition, these instruments can measure only a limited number of knowledge and skill areas from a vast domain of possible questions. Often, teachers who work with students on a regular basis will know the levels of performance of their students, thus reducing the necessity of administering these types of measure.

Transition Instruments. The topic of transition is covered in detail in the next chapter and attention is given to assessment in that chapter. As Cronin et al. (2007) pointed out, "Transition instruments, while related in some ways to adaptive behavior and life skills measures, focus on the perceived competence levels of students. Most instruments seek the perspective of different parties—student, family, and school personnel. The main intent of these instruments is ultimately to guide programming and contribute to transition planning" (p. 30).

Transition measures do yield important information about functioning—much like that of adaptive behavior measures; however, as stated, the purpose of the assessment is to identify needs (and strengths) on which one develops transition-related goals to assist the student's move from school to whatever environments he or she will be in when school is over.

Informal Techniques

Information about the functional competence and career interests of students can be obtained through informal measures. These techniques can be used to complement, supplement, or replace the data generated through formal techniques. The key variable is that, whatever the technique that is selected, it should be age appropriate and effective for the purpose of the assessment.

Two of the most popular informal techniques that teachers like to use are checklists and rating scales. Many instruments have been developed and can generate information that is useful for determining levels of personal and functional competence. Three "Informal Assessments for Transition" resources—each of which includes more than 50 informal instruments—cover the areas of living, working, and learning: Independent Living and Community Participation (Synatschk, Clark, & Patton, 2008), Employment and Career Planning (Synatschk, Clark, Patton, & Copeland, 2007), and Postsecondary Education and Training (Sitlington, Clark, & Patton, 2008).

One of the most useful techniques for assessing functional competence is **performance assessment**. Wolfe and Kubina (2004) described performance assessment as "concerned with how a student applies knowledge" (p. 122) as opposed to whether he or she knows something or not. In this type of assessment, the individual must "produce or perform a response" (Wolfe & Kubina, 2004, p. 122). **Authentic assessment** is a form of performance assessment that requires the individual to produce or perform certain behaviors in the natural context where these behaviors should be performed. For example, to determine whether a student can use a microwave oven, the assessment would occur in the kitchen, and the person would have to perform the appropriate sequence of behaviors to cook an item in this device.

Ultimately, the method of assessing functional competence will be predicated on the following variables: the purpose of the assessment (i.e., the information that is needed), the amount of time available for performing the assessment (e.g., performance assessment takes much more time than a recollective technique), the availability of certain instruments, and the comfort level (i.e., the competence level) of the personnel doing the assessment with a specific instrument or technique.

Functional Impact and the Summary of Performance

IDEA 2004 introduced a new requirement when a student graduates from school or reaches the age of 22. The reauthorization required that "a summary of the child's academic achievement and functional performance" that includes recommendations on how to help the student in meeting his or her postsecondary goals be developed. This document, typically referred to as a summary of performance (SOP), has the potential to be one of the most important activities that the school can do in assisting the student to get ready for the life that will follow school.

The law and accompanying regulations specify only that the SOP contain three pieces (postsecondary goals, present levels, and recommendations). If sufficient work is put into developing quality SOPs that contain information in these three areas, the SOP can be a useful tool for students and their families as they embark into the world of young adulthood. This document could have been enriched if one other requirement had been included in the law. Descriptions of the functional impact of the person's disability in terms of work, education and training, and living make this document a very powerful tool. As Patton, Clark, and Trainor (2009) noted, a functional impact statement "provides a realistic picture of how the areas of concern are likely to impact the functional performance of the student in various future situations" (p. 10). As Patton and colleagues stressed, the development of quality SOPs is a type of preventive problem-solving process.

 Check Your Understanding 14.3 Click here to gauge your understanding of the concepts in this section.

TEACHING APPLIED ACADEMICS

This section focuses on the instructional dimensions of teaching functional topics. Seven topics are addressed and include general approaches to teaching applied academics, curricular considerations and challenges related to teaching functional skills, real-life coursework, integration of real-life topics into existing content, aligning applied academics with the general education curriculum, instructional relevancy, use of assistive technology to enhance functional competence, and instructional materials that might be useful.

General Approaches for Teaching Applied Academics

Three options are available for developing the requisite knowledge and skills needed to function successfully with the demands of adulthood: school-based instruction, community-based instruction, and home-based instruction.

School-based instruction includes all of the activities that are typically associated with providing and appropriate education to students. The knowledge and skills associated with applied academics need to be included within the curricular structure and ongoing instructional activities that occur in a classroom. For students who are in a parallel, life skills–oriented class, doing this is more straightforward and easily accomplished. For students who are in inclusive settings, the coverage of applied academics is more complicated and depends, in great part, on the skills of the general education teacher to make the content that is being covered more relevant to students.

Community-based action includes a number of situations where students are gaining real-world experience from actual paid or non-paid placements in settings within the community. Examples of some of the types of experiences students might get include internships for apprenticeships. Without question, students will have opportunities and be required to use various applied academics in the settings. Instruction would include on-site applications. Of course, the types of skills that might be learned or potentially reinforced from school-based instruction would be limited to the types of skills needed in a particular situation.

Home-based instruction is very much an ongoing, natural process that occurs outside of formal schooling as the student grows up typically in a home environment. Many topics that are related to real-life skills and applied academics can be and are learned at home. An example would include task such as preparing meals where applied academic skills such as reading a recipe and measuring ingredients associated with the recipe are used regularly. The extent and depth associated with the number of applied academic skills learned in a home environment will vary from family to family.

Creating Communities of Caring and Learning

Preparing students for everyday life at school, home, and the future is a task that can far exceed the classroom and the classroom teacher. Using school resources as well as family and community involvement can help students with disabilities from diverse backgrounds gain resources that can help them secure a better future.

Epstein and Salinas (2004) recommended that teachers involve six communities of caring (or learning) for students. These include partnership involvement with (a) parents of diverse families; (b) volunteers from the community or different family members; (c) child and family learning projects at home; (d) school, family, and student decision-making groups, (e) school, family, and community communication systems; and (f) community collaborations. Each area can take on as many forms as needed by diverse populations and disabilities in the school. Here are six examples for teachers on how they can enhance the development of student skills and future prospects:

1. Create a parent–student reading club. Teaching parents how to foster recreational reading together can enhance the reading skills of the student (and, in some cases, the parents).

2. Collaborate with the health care community to create a health fair at the school. Many students are not aware of the community services they can access to help enhance their health and well-being as well as deal with health-related problems.

3. Organize a spaghetti dinner night so parents can come with their children and socialize in a non-threatening environment. This can build community as well as the social skills of the students. Perhaps the students can help cook the meal.

4. Collaborate with families on cultivating a family/school vegetable garden to teach children how to grow nourishing, organic food. Many students are not aware that they can have fresh produce at home if they are able to grow certain vegetables. The cultivation of a garden can teach many life skills as well as promote a healthy lifestyle.

5. Organize a career/vocational night for parents and students in high school. Booths with different community professionals can (a) talk to families about jobs and careers, (b) show them what makes a good job application, and (c) show parents how to apply for financial aid for college. Often, students and parents are not aware that certain opportunities are available within the community. Helping parents and students plan for the future through networking is important.

6. Sponsor a math night where parents are taught how math is being taught and how they might tutor their child with math homework. Teaching parents about math can help promote the development of math skills of their children.

The ability for teachers to think outside the box is vital in these endeavors. Securing funds to promote the communities of care can present challenges. Applying for community grants may offset the costs of the projects.

Curricular Orientations and Challenges

A great need exists to teach students with special needs a comprehensive set of functional skills within a framework of providing these students with access to the general education curriculum. The need to make the general education curriculum more relevant to students has been underscored for years by secondary level teachers (e.g., Halpern & Benz, 1987).

Once a comprehensive list of functional skills has been identified at a local level, the next important task is to organize these topics so that they can be presented to students in their programs. Instruction of applied academics involves different things for different students. For example, students for whom higher education is a possibility should have access to academically oriented programs in general education. However, in our opinion, these students will need to have their academic coursework balanced with exposure to other important adult outcome areas. Other students, for whom high school may be the termination of formal schooling, are likely to be in different courses of study.

The challenge for school administrators, curriculum development specialists, and teachers is how to cover important life skills topics within existing curricular structures. Figure 14-3 depicts a continuum of options for teaching functional knowledge and skills. The reality of schools today is that more students with special needs are pursuing more traditional diploma routes and are receiving much of their education in inclusive settings. Given this scenario, along with the IDEA mandate of access to the general education curriculum, the options at the right of the figure are the more likely avenues for covering applied academics/functional topics.

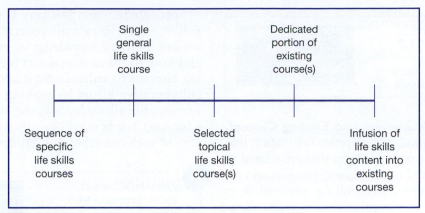

FIGURE 14–3 Options for Organizing Life Skills Content for Formal Instruction

Coursework with a Functional Orientation

Three of the options depicted in Figure 14-3 involve teaching functional topics through the development of *life skills coursework*. The intent of this option is to offer coursework that is clearly adulthood referenced but still academic in nature. The coursework could be either non-credit or credit; however, most often it will be the former. Moreover, this type of coursework is likely to be implemented in non-diploma-track programs that exist in most schools.

The advantage of dedicating coursework to functional topics is that the likelihood of covering topics more comprehensively and in more depth is increased. Moreover, the courses have a direct bearing on a person's immediate (relevancy) and later (meaningfulness) life. Courses with more functional characteristics are now being offered in college programs (Hart, Grigal, & Weir, 2010) and as adult education programs for students with developmental disabilities in various locations. For more detailed coverage of life skill course development, see Cronin et al. (2007).

Integrating Real-Life Topics into Existing Content

The more realistic option for covering functional topics, given the nature and structure of current school programs, involves the *integration of life skills topics* into the predetermined content of existing coursework. This approach is important and has received acceptance because it can be used in any type of educational setting in which many students with special needs receive their education

and is inherently consistent with access to the general curriculum. Two variations of the integration technique exist: augmentation and infusion.

Augmenting Existing Content. Augmentation implies extending the coverage of what is being taught as part of the explicit curriculum into more meaningful, functional areas. This can be accomplished by dedicating a portion of a course to "applied" topics. Teachers could set aside a day or two during each grading period or part of class each week to cover important functional topics that are related to the content of the course being provided.

The key features of this approach include the fact that covering functional topics has appeal and value for all students in the class. In addition, specific functional topics can be selected and planned for ahead of time, thereby allowing for adequate coverage of the topic. Another feature of the augmentation approach is that the functional topics covered will not take much of class time that has to be spent covering the explicit content of the course. A few examples follow:

- **Math or economics course:** Dedicate instructional time to addressing topics such as the economics of dating or the real-life skills associated with maintaining an apartment.
- **Physical science course:** Add a component called "appliance science" to the course and cover how everyday appliances found at home actually work (e.g., toilets, coffeemaker).
- **U.S. history course:** Include a session on state, regional, and local parks in relation to the establishment of the National Park system that is typically covered in this class.

ENHANCEDetext
video example 14.2
Watch this video to learn more
about a classroom lesson
teaching functional skills.

Infusing Applied Academics into Existing Content.
In the infusion method, the objective is to infuse into
the existing content real-life topics that are related to
a topic being covered in the natural progression of a
class. Two key features distinguish this approach from
that of augmentation. First, the infusion approach relies on content that is "naturally" encountered as the
course is being taught (e.g., topics that are mentioned in
a textbook). Second, coverage is momentary—more of
a "hit and run"—in that only a relatively brief amount
of time is dedicated to talking about functional topics.

The infusion approach is typically characterized by
some degree of advanced planning, although it does
not require the same amount of planning that the augmentation approach requires. With this technique, the
teacher needs to examine course content and identify
"points" where functional topics can be infused. It is
also important to recognize the age or grade level of
the students with whom one is teaching to determine
the nature of the functional topics to be covered.

Patton, Cronin, and Wood (1999) suggested that
the functional content that is infused can be restricted
to topics that relate to the subject matter that is being
taught. For example, if the word *battery* is mentioned
in a science textbook and therefore identified as the
"infusion point," then discussion of how to maintain
battery charge could be discussed. Such a discussion
certainly relates to the science of batteries. However,
Patton and colleagues also recommended infusing
topics that go beyond the content area of the course.
For example, in the previous example, discussion
could focus on where is the best place to buy batteries. This discussion has functional value but is more
about consumer economics than science.

Since functional coverage is brief—what Patton
et al. (1999) referred to as "infusion bursts"—the
amount of planning and preparation is not as detailed or extensive as is required in an augmentation
approach. However, the number of opportunities
is more common. As a matter of fact, the number
of "infusion points" (reference points that relate to
functional topics) that exist in the content of most
courses is plentiful. As a result, it is not possible to
cover all potential "functional" topics and decisions
about which topics to cover must be made.

Special education teachers who are working in
collaborative roles with general education teachers can use their knowledge of major life demands
and how to infuse functional topics into the existing content to enhance their contributions to the
collaborative effort by making instruction more
relevant for all students in the class. Most general
education teachers will greatly appreciate the benefits of such contributions. Students certainly will.

ENHANCEDetext
video example 14.3
Watch this video to learn more
about the life skills instruction.

Aligning Applied Academics with General Education Content

Teachers can easily apply skills associated with
reading, speaking, listening, writing, computing, and problem solving to the context of adult
situations (i.e., applied academics) and relate these
functional topics to content and performance standards. Patton and Trainor (2002) analyzed the
content and performance standards from a number
of states to determine how "functional" standards
were—as written. The analysis found that most
standards are either straight-on functional or have
some element of functionality to them.

Table 14-6 reflects that much of what is taught
in general education can have some level of functional value. Wolfe and Ostryn (2012) illustrated
the functional implications of two objectives in social studies. These two objectives exemplify the different levels of functionality of general education
content, as written, and how this content relates to
practical knowledge and skill areas. Note that the
first objective in Table 14-6 does not seem, on face
value, as functional as the second standard. Nevertheless, a number of functional activities can be
conducted in relation to this first objective.

Instructional Relevancy

The importance of applying various academic
skills to and demonstrating competence in real-life
situations cannot be overemphasized. The intent
of teaching life skills is to prepare individuals to
use foundational, basic tool skills in ways that will
make their lives more productive and meaningful,
leading to some sense of personal fulfillment.

TABLE 14–6 Examples of how to make general education content functional

Social Studies

Identify and participate in discussions about local, national, and world current event topics from newspapers, television, and current periodicals.	• Use newspapers to identify current event topics. • Discuss current event issues with regular education peers. • Watch news and discuss events with parent, peers, and teacher. • Read and recall current event articles from periodicals (e.g., *Newsweek*). • Participate in current event games.
Use a map to plan a trip, calculating number of miles for the trip, identifying restaurants and hotels, and estimating the total cost for the trip.	• Choose a rental car from a local dealership. Call or visit dealerships and compare prices, miles per gallon, safety features, and available options. • Determine items needed for trip location, planned activities, and season of the year and write a detailed packing list. • Plan route using map, including miles, cities, routes to follow, time required for trip, and when to stop for gas. • Call travel agencies (e.g., AAA) for literature on hotels, restaurants, leisure activities, and local tourist attractions. • Estimate costs of trip.

Source: Wolfe, P. S., & Ostryn, C. (2012). *Functional academics.* In P. Wehman and J. Kregel, *Functional curriculum for elementary, middle, and secondary age students with special needs,* 3e (p. 191), Austin, TX: Pro-Ed.

When teaching functional topics, it is crucial to recognize the difference between two seemingly similar terms: *meaningful* and *relevant*. These terms are also used interchangeably, but they have different meanings. Patton et al. (1999) distinguished the terms in the following way:

- Meaningfulness—implies that a given topic has some degree of impact on one's life, perhaps in some future sense or context.
- Relevance—implies that content is not only meaningful but also timely in that it has impact on one's life now. (p. 5)

Teaching content that is relevant is far easier than teaching content that is meaningful.

An instructional technique that teachers should adopt as a way of regularly self-assessing the importance of what they are teaching-and really what students are learning-is the set of "So What?" questions. The questions can and should be incorporated into almost any lesson that is being taught. Their value is that they get the students to apply what they have learned. The questions are the following:

- So who else might use this _____?
- So what kinds of job, activities, etc., might use this _____?
- So when might you use this _____?
- So where might you use this _____?
- So how could you use this _____ in a job, with your friends, etc.?
- So why is this important?

The questions may have to be adapted somewhat depending on the topic(s) being discussed. However, the fundamental notion is that teachers should provide students with a rationale for why anything that is being taught is important. The intent of asking these questions relates to the suggestion that Wehman and Kregel (2012) made about considering the conditions under which a functional behavior may occur.

Assistive Technology

Some students will benefit from the support that comes with the use of various types of assistive technology. Assistive technology devices and services are mandated by IDEA to assist a student obtaining an appropriate education. Another perspective on the use of assistive technology is to consider its use in helping a student deal with the "functional" demands of everyday living outside of school.

Often, in the context of dealing successfully with the demands of the real world, simple, low-tech supports can make a big difference in the lives of individuals with learning-related challenges. Table 14-7 provides a few examples of how low-tech solutions can supplement attempts to develop competence in the functional academic areas described earlier in the chapter.

Instructional Resources

To teach functional content, teachers need to have access to instructional materials and resources in all of the areas of interest. Cronin et al. (2007)

TABLE 14–7 Assistive technology strategies

Functional Area	Assistive Technology Suggestion
Functional reading	Text-to-speech capabilities (e.g., Word)
	Pen that reads words aloud and provides definitions of words
	e-Books
Functional writing	Voice recognition software
	Note-taking apps that record audio while taking notes
	Small, portable voice recorder/tape player to record notes instead of having to write them
	Various input devices for keying in information
	Specially designed writing instruments
	Spell-checker as part of word processing software
	Outlining and concept mapping software
Functional math	Calculators on smartphones
	Specialized calculators
	Personal finance software
	Prepaid tag—express lane of toll roads
Functional science	Digital devices for taking temperature
	Daily/weekly pillboxes
	Weather alert radios
	Insulin-level monitors
	Digital thermometers for outside temperature
Functional social studies	GPS navigation systems for getting around in the community—on smartphones
	Jury duty summons online
	Online reservation systems
	Apps for identifying resources in community—Yelp
	Other online services—Craigslist, Angie's list

dedicated over 60 pages of their book to a listing of materials that can be used to teach real-life topics. This resource focused mainly on instructional materials that can be used directly with students.

The major features that should characterize innovative instruction of functional topics for most students with learning-related problems include the following: adult referenced, comprehensive, relevant to students, empirically and socially valid (i.e., appropriate to one's specific situation), flexible, community based when possible, and sensitive to cultural and family values. Appendix 14-F provides a list of selected resources that teachers should find helpful for teaching functional topics. This list includes the type of resource, the title of the special product, the name of the publisher, and a brief description of the features of the material.

 Check Your Understanding 14.4 Click here to gauge your understanding of the concepts in this section.

ACTIVITIES

1. Applied social studies: Have students conduct opinion polls on several topics. This exercise requires students to use various data-gathering and interpretative skills.

2. Applied writing: Direct students to write responsible letters to elected officials. Help students express their opinions on various political or social issues.

3. Applied mathematics: Real Life Math: Living on a Paycheck is a consumer simulation program. Students move out of their parents' homes, get jobs, hunt for and choose apartments, sign leases, pay deposits, pay rent, and buy starter furniture and basic household needs. They budget their money to rent and furnish their apartments, buy cars and gas fill-ups, pay bills, buy groceries, buy clothes, and pay for medical care.

4. Applied science: So students better understand weather changes, have them keep weather charts that record temperature on different days, rain or snow accumulation, and other data students may want to collect.

5. Applied reading: Obtain menus from local restaurants and fast-food chains. Give students specific assignments to compare prices and develop lists of meals. Students may also construct a composite menu to be printed and used for review.

6. Applied mathematics and social studies: Have students conduct interviews with and observe various households for a period of time. Students must pay close attention to the responsibilities of the renter with regard to maintaining the house/apartment.

7. Applied writing and communication: Have each student to develop a catalog of possible careers of interest. Create a folder to browse through and explain any to others. Students must be able to give a brief 30-second pitch or brief written essay for wanting to choose this career.

8. Applied mathematics: Create a grocery store in the classroom. Use play money as students interact with the grocery store buying and selling everyday items and then move on to using real money in the grocery store. Take students out on a field trip to an actual grocery store where they can buy and sell using real money as they interact with store attendants.

APPENDICES

APPENDIX 14–A Functional reading: Real-life applications

Functional Setting	Specific Skills
	Individual can read:

Everyday Living	• personal information (name, address, phone number)
	• important documents:
	  • contracts (e.g., leases)
	  • policies (e.g., insurance)
	  • warranty information
	  • terms of agreement (e.g., purchase of software)
	• tax-related documents
	• mail:
	  • personal mail
	  • bills
	  • advertisements
	• manuals:
	  • appliances
	  • equipment
	  • car/truck
	  • technology
	  • driver's license materials
	• various print materials:
	  • catalogs
	  • telephone books
	• directions:
	  • recipes
	  • food preparation
	  • taking medicine
	  • laundry recommendations
	  • assembling materials
	• documents from service providers (e.g., plumber, vet)
	• shopping-related materials:
	  • receipts for items purchased
	  • return policy information
	• warning labels
	• applications (e.g., credit cards)
	• charts and tables

School	• course schedules
	• syllabi
	• textual materials:
	  • textbooks
	  • required readings
	  • printed class materials (e.g., handouts)
	• in-class materials:
	  • exam materials
	  • slides shown in class
	  • materials written on board
	• internet materials:
	  • searches
	  • websites
	• menus—cafeteria
	• materials posted on bulletin boards
	• policies, rules, regulations of the school, dorm

(continued)

Functional Setting	Specific Skills
	Individual can read:

Community	• functional signage:
	  • restroom designations (men, women)
	  • warnings (e.g., "danger")
	  • directives (e.g., "keep off the grass")
	  • informational (e.g., "men working")
	• descriptive signage:
	  • road/street
	  • business names
	  • advertisements/billboards
	  • notices, announcements, directives
	  • posters
	• procedural signage:
	  • directions on how to use (e.g., gas pump)
	  • directions on where to go
	• menus in restaurants
	• shopping-related materials:
	  • hours of operation information
	  • unit price data
	• schedules (e.g., bus)
	• maps/other visual materials:
	  • directory of businesses (e.g., at a mall)
	  • room location in a building (e.g., courthouse)
	  • park
	  • campus

Workplace	• applications
	• policy manuals
	• notices, memos (print or electronic)
	• job-related manuals
	• reports and other documents
	• internet materials:
	  • searches
	  • websites

Leisure	• newspaper(s):
	  • front page
	  • local/state news
	  • weather information
	  • sports
	  • business section
	  • everyday section
	  • classified ads
	  • special advertisements
	• local entertainment periodicals
	• magazines
	• expository/narrative materials:
	  • books—fiction
	  • books—nonfiction
	  • short stories
	  • poetry
	• comic books
	• directions to boardgames, card activities, etc.
	• travel brochures

APPENDIX 14–B Functional writing: Real-life applications

Functional Setting	Specific Skills	
	Individual can write:	**Individual can complete:**

Everyday Living	• personal information (name, address, phone number)
	• letters:
	  • personal
	  • business
	  • action (e.g., complaint)
	• notes:
	  • to others
	  • on behalf of others (e.g., notes to school for children)
	• phone messages
	• information from other sources (e.g., telephone book)
	• greeting cards (e.g., birthday)
		• bills
		• legal documents:
		  • leases
		  • contracts
		• tax forms
		• order forms
		• product registration forms (print or Internet)

School	• in-class products:
	  • activities that are part of the class session
	  • assignments/information given in class
	• course requirements:
	  • papers
	  • reports
	  • other projects involving writing
	• exams/quizzes:
	  • essay
	  • short-answer
	• notes from:
	  • in-class lectures/presentations
	  • PowerPoint slides/board
	  • assigned readings
	  • materials from researching a topic (e.g., searchers)
	• messages to fellow students, instructor, or others (print or e-mail)
		• course registration materials
		• school-related forms:
		  • housing
		  • health services

Community	• directions for locating a street address	• bank (e.g., deposit/withdrawal/transfer slip) • surveys
Workplace	• memos/e-mail messages • reports	• job applications • job-related forms (e.g., W-4) • grievance forms • quality control materials
Leisure	• personal journal/diary • E-mails, text messages, instant messages with friends • creative writing products	• puzzles involving writing (e.g., crosswords)

Functional Setting	Specific Skills
	Individual can use math skills in the following areas:
Everyday Living	*Money management:*

Money management:
- budgeting income and expenses
- banking-related services:
  - checking and savings accounts
  - online banking
  - credit card use:
    - APR
    - credit limits
    - payment cycles
  - monitor investments
  - retirement planning
  - credit rating status
- paying bills:
  - due dates
  - payment options
  - late fees, penalties
- insurance:
  - life
  - disability
  - home/rental
  - long-term care
- paying fines/penalties
- paying taxes
- making and receiving change

Living arrangements:
- locating a place to live
- comparison shopping
- costs and affordability:
  - rent or mortgage
  - initial closing costs
  - ongoing fees
  - taxes
  - insurance
  - moving costs
  - utilities

Home management:
- food preparation:
  - scheduling meals throughout week
  - measuring amounts for recipes
  - cooking times
- appliances/equipment usage around the home:
  - phone
  - clocks (digital and analog)
  - timer (for cooking)
  - microwave
  - stove/oven/crockpot
  - washer/dryer
  - thermostat
- home repair and maintenance:
  - seasonal needs
  - repairs and upgrades:
    - linear measurement
  - yard maintenance
  - contrast for services

Functional Setting	Specific Skills
	Individual can use math skills in the following areas:

Automobile/truck:
- comparison shopping
- costs and affordability:
  - price
  - insurance
  - maintenance costs
  - fuel costs
  - depreciation
- payment options
- scheduling:
  - routine maintenance
  - repairs

Heath-related:
- health management:
  - caloric intake
  - nutritional content of food
  - exercise schedule
  - measure weight of self and others
- budgeting medical/dental costs:
  - regular checkups
  - treating problems
- illness identification and treatment:
  - taking temperature
  - monitoring conditions (e.g., blood pressure, sugar levels, weight)

School
- budgeting:
  - finances
  - meal account
- purchasing, school-related materials (books, equipment)
- time management:
  - hours needed to graduate
  - scheduling of courses
  - scheduling of time for:
    - study, test preparation, projects
    - extracurricular activities
    - work responsibilities
    - meetings
    - rest and relaxation

Community
- paying for various transportation services
- shopping/purchasing:
  - personal items
  - groceries
  - services (e.g., cell phone)
  - commodities (e.g., gas)
- banking services:
  - ATM
  - walk-in services
  - drive-through services
- restaurants:
  - menu use
  - payment
  - tipping
- using specific devices:
  - vending machines
  - stamp machines

(continued)

Functional Setting	Specific Skills
	Individual can use math skills in the following areas:

Workplace	• pay/salary:
	  • wages/income
	  • deductions (taxes, social security, retirement, insurance)
	  • commission
	• hours worked (including overtime)
	• benefits (number of personal/sick days, vacation)
	• scheduled holidays
	• time management (quotas, deadlines)
	• specific math skills related to a particular job (e.g., truck driver—miles driven, amount of gas used, etc.)
	• dues

Leisure	• home entertainment (costs— purchase/rental, math needed to use):
	  • TV
	  • VCR, DVD player, TiVo
	  • electronic devices
	• games/sports:
	  • keeping score
	• membership fees—clubs, organizations
	• subscription costs (newspaper, magazines, online services)
	• hobbies:
	  • measurement skills
	  • costs of equipment, supplies, etc.
	• entertainment costs
	• vacation/travel:
	  • scheduling
	  • budgeting
	• playing the lottery

APPENDIX 14–D Functional science: Real-life applications

Functional Setting	Specific Knowledge	Specific Skills
Everyday Living Health:	*Maintenance:* • healthy lifestyle • personal care and hygiene	• identifying and maintaining healthy diet • exercising regularly • dressing appropriately for situations • maintaining good self-care skills
	Prevention of problems: • food tolerance	• avoiding certain foods
	Treatment: • first aid/emergency procedures • illness identification and treatment	• taking care of minor cuts, bites, allergic reactions • recognizing when someone is sick • using appropriate treatment for the illness • knowing when to consult professional help (doctor, ER, etc.)
Physical/Environmental:	• tool identification • home maintenance and repair	• using tools appropriately • performing simple home repairs (e.g., toilet repair, screen door) • performing seasonal home maintenance • fertilizing lawn

	• Safety at home:
	  • fire
	  • electricity
	  • poisonous materials
	  • bathroom
		• implementing a home evacuation plan
		• safeguarding outlets
		• keeping dangerous material in protected location
		• safeguarding bathrooms

Functional Setting	Specific Knowledge	Specific Skills
School Health:	• unsafe conditions • possible activities: • tattoo/piercing	• avoiding situation where one's health is in jeopardy • getting safe procedure

Community Health:	• safety concerns:
	  • playgrounds
	  • bicycles
	  • skateboards
	  • animals	

Physical/Environmental:	• weather-related:
	  • severe storm:
	    • lightning
	    • flooding
	    • hurricanes
	• brush fire
	• drought
		• taking protective action
		• avoiding low water crossings
		
		• implementing an evacuation plan
		• protecting one's house
		• implementing a mandated/volunteer watering schedule

Workplace Health:	• protection from contagious conditions • safe behaviors	• implementing protective measures (e.g., hand washing) • following work safety procedures • wearing protective gear as directed • lifting heavy items appropriately
Physical/Environmental:	• office machinery maintenance and repair • hazardous materials • operation of machinery, equipment, tools	• making simple repairs (e.g., jammed copy machine) • avoiding dangerous areas • initiating emergency procedures • using machines, equipment, and tools as directed in the operation guidelines

Leisure Health:	• preventing illness when traveling
	
	• sports-related injuries:
	  • prevention
	  • treatment
		• keeping hydrated
		• washing hands regularly
		• stretching before activity
		
		• wrapping ankles, using braces

Physical/Environmental:	• hobbies (select examples):
	  • gardening
	
	  • astronomy
	  • hiking
	
	  • bicycling
		• choosing plants
		• using nutrients
		• using telescope
		• selecting equipment
		• protecting environment
		• repairing flat tire

Functional Setting	Specific Knowledge	Specific Skills

Everyday Living	• contributing citizen:
	  • awareness of current events
	• personal legal information:
	  • rights
	  • procedural safeguards
	
	• home ownership:
	  • deed restrictions
	  • tax liability
	  • personal liabilities
	• personal grooming:
	  • stylish dress
	  • good appearance
		• keeping up with local news and issues
		
		• explaining and reacting to Miranda warning
		• filing a small claims complaint
		
		• consulting with key individuals who provide insurance

School	• legal rights as a student:
	  • confidentiality
	  • harassment
	  • protections
	• participation in various groups and organizations
	• participation in student governance
	• advocate for issues of concern to students
		• filing a grievance
		• taking action to join
		• running for office or voting for candidates
		• attending rallies, meetings, presentations

Community	• citizen responsibilities/choices:
	  • voting
	
	  • jury duty
	  • neighborhood activities (e.g., crime watch)
	  • volunteer opportunities
	• awareness of local community
	• governmental services:
	  • health
	  • social
	  • housing
	  • employment
	• community services:
	  • transportation:
	    • bus
	    • taxi
	    • train
	    • plane
	• post office
	• recreation
	• retail businesses:
	  • department store
	  • specialty store
	  • drug store
	  • grocery store
	  • convenience store/gas
	• specialized service:
	  • lawn
	  • cleaning
	  • repair
	  • maintenance
	• professional services:
		• registering
		• participating in elections
		• responding to call for jury duty
		
		• using map skills to identify locations in the community
		• locating and contacting appropriate office
		
		• locating, contacting, going to appropriate service
		• acquiring bus pass
		• contacting airlines
		• purchasing tickets
		• navigating an airport
		• distinguishing different types of mail service

Workplace	• legal rights as an employee:
	  • discrimination
	  • harassment
	  • protections/safeguards
	• participation in a union
		• filing a grievance
		• joining and maintaining membership

Functional Setting	Specific Knowledge	Specific Skills
Leisure	• vacation planning	• contacting travel agent
		• making reservations
	• city, public, state, national parks	• locating and finding transportation
	• local hiking/biking trails	• locating and finding transportation
	• free, public entertainment:	• scheduling, planning, arranging transportation
	• cultural events	
	• outdoor concerts	
	• local entertainment venues:	• scheduling, planning, arranging transportation
	• sporting events	
	• nightclubs	
	• visual and performing arts:	• scheduling, planning, arranging transportation
	• theater	
	• concerts	
	• museums	

APPENDIX 14–F   Curricular and instructional materials in the life skills area

Type of Resource	Title	Publisher	Feature(s)
Comprehensive Curricula	• Life-Centered Career Education (LCCE)	Council for Exceptional Children	• 3 major areas: Daily Living Skills, Personal-Social Skills, Occupational Guidance & Preparation
	• The Transitions Curriculum	Stanfield House	• 3 modules: Get a Plan, Get a Job, Get a Life
	• Daily Experiences and Activities of Living (DEAL)	PRO-ED	• 6 areas: Working, Consumer Buying, Information Sources, Nutrition & Health, Housing, Transportation
	• The Syracuse Community-Referenced Curriculum		• 3 major domains: Community Living; Functional Paul Brooks Academic Communication, and Motor Skills
Activity Resources	• Life Skills Activities for Special Children	Center for Applied Research in Educ.	• 145 ready-to-use activities
	• Life Skills Activities for Secondary Students with Special Needs	Center for Applied Research in Educ.	• 190 ready-to-use activities
	• Finding Wheels	PRO-ED	• Transportation/mobility
	• Language for Living Series	PRO-ED	• Manuals on Practical Time, Out in the World, The Newspaper
Professional Resources	• Functional Curriculum for Elementary, Meddle, and Secondary Age Students with Special Needs (2nd ed.)	PRO-ED	• Includes ideas for self-determination, activities of daily living, community living, social skills, transportation, work, home living, money management

Career Development and Transition across School Levels

LEARNING OUTCOMES

Upon completion of this chapter, the reader should be able to:

15.1 Explore the important aspects of career education and development most beneficial to students with special needs and provide tactics for preparing for them for future careers.

15.2 Identify key transitions that occur beginning in the early childhood years and leading to the important transition from secondary education.

15.3 Explore the basic components related to the transition planning process for students who are exiting school.

This final chapter of the text focuses on the articulation that should exist throughout the schooling process that assists a student and his or her family with the key transitions that will occur during the early years, when the individual is in school, and ultimately throughout one's life—beyond high school. Although the chapter provides closure to many topics covered in previous chapters, the content of this chapter highlights the need to support a student and his or her family in paving the way to a fulfilling life as an adult.

CAREER EDUCATION AND DEVELOPMENT

This section addresses critical topics related to the preparation of students for life after high school. It covers the following topics: the concept of career development and its relationship to students with special needs; the importance of assessing career interests, preferences, and strengths; ways to explore potential careers; the need to ensure that students have an understanding of the occupational vocabulary that they will encounter in the work world; the need to develop a positive work attitude; and the array of vocational training options that may be available at the secondary level.

Career Development and Students with Special Needs

The concept of career development is akin to the idea of instruction in functional areas. It was used often in the early 1970s and intermittently since that time. Career development suggests that individuals should be presented with information that is related to a variety of situations (i.e., careers) associated with community living. The term *career* can be misleading because it is often viewed solely from an occupational perspective. However, the broader notion of career can include a variety of adult roles (e.g., in the home and community).

Career development should be viewed as a lifelong process that begins at the preschool level and continues past retirement. This view has been espoused by the Division on Career Development and Transition (DCDT) of the Council for Exceptional Children. The view of the DCDT is reflected in the following principles (Clark, Carlson, Fisher, Cook, & D'Alonzo, 1991):

- Education for career development and transition is for individuals with disabilities at all ages.
- Career development is a process that begins at birth and continues throughout life.
- Early career development is essential for making satisfactory choices later.
- Significant gaps or periods of neglect in any area of basic human development affect career development and the transition from one stage of life to another.
- Career development is responsive to intervention and programming when the programming involves direct instruction for individual needs.
- Guided by these principles, schools and adult services should strive to provide mechanisms for facilitating lifelong career development.

Career development has typically been described as a set of stages or phases that increase in complexity and involvement, as the individual gets older.

Wehman, Targett, and Richardson (2012) provided a conceptualization of the typical stages of career education: career awareness, career exploration, career preparation, and job placement (see Figure 15-1):

- **Career awareness:** This phase is focused on making students aware of various careers and occupations. Activities should begin during the elementary years, although a strong argument can be made that such activities may begin at the preschool level. Examples of infusing career development topics into the curriculum were shown in the previous chapter.
- **Career exploration:** This key phase typically occurs during the later elementary or middle school or junior high school years when an emphasis is placed on "exploring" careers, occupations, and specific jobs in more detail. Exploration activities provide students with a more enriched picture of specific jobs.
- **Career preparation:** This phase is dedicated to preparing a student for a job in which he or she has demonstrated interest. Activities involve instruction that related to the specific requirements of a job. It is important to recognize that, for some careers, post-secondary education and training will be needed (e.g., engineering, teaching, etc.).
- **Job placement:** This phase involves all of the efforts associated with locating a job for which a person has been prepared and assisting the person in obtaining this job.

Professionals in the field of education have consistently endorsed starting this process early. It is critical that career awareness activities begin at the elementary level. The following ideas are suggestions that, in our opinion, should be part of an elementary

	Career Awareness	Career Exploration	Career Preparation	Job Placement
Elementary	■	■		
Junior High		■	■	
Senior High			■	
At graduation				■

FIGURE 15–1 Stages of Career Development during the School Years

Source: Table 1.1 From *Functional Curriculum for Elementary and Secondary Student with Special Needs,* 3rd Ed. (p. 11), by Paul Wehman, John Kregel, Austin, TX: PRO-ED. Copyright 2012 by PRO-ED, Inc. Reprinted with permission.

level career education program. Some of the recommendations presented were initially introduced by Clark (1979) in his classic work on career education:

- Provide instruction and guidance for developing positive habits, attitudes, and values toward work and daily living.
- Provide instruction and guidance for establishing and maintaining positive human relationships at home, at school, and at work.
- Provide instruction and guidance for developing awareness of occupational alternatives.
- Provide instruction for an orientation to the realities of the world of work, as a producer and as a consumer.
- Provide instruction for acquiring actual job.
- Explore the variety of leisure activities, including hobbies and recreational activities.
- Discuss what is expected of and required from a contributing member of the community.
- Examine the responsibilities of maintaining a house or an apartment, assuming both an owner's and a renter's perspective.

As students move through school and develop the need for exploration and as more specific occupational preparation becomes evident, other program goals arise. These include the following:

- Enhance the occupational awareness and aspirations of students through career counseling.
- Conduct an assessment of each student's occupational interests and aptitudes.
- Integrate the assessment findings into the individualized education program.
- Provide students with community-based training opportunities.
- Ensure the development of entry-level job skills.
- Provide job placement for and work supports to students as needed.

Given especially that the unemployment rate for adults with disabilities is higher than it is for other individuals who do not have disabilities, efforts to develop careers must continue. Many persons with disabilities will obtain jobs, continue their education and training, and begin to assume their roles in the community and/or within their families. However, changes often occur in jobs (e.g., layoffs, promotions) and in families (e.g., offspring, divorce), requiring a reeducation process for many people. As a result, some of the early phases just described may have to be repeated at a later point in life.

Assessing Career Interests and Preferences

Many instruments have been developed for a variety of purposes related to career interests, job preparation, and employment. In this section, we focus the discussion on the area of career interests, strengths, and preferences. Students with special needs must be provided with opportunities to become aware of and *explore* various occupational options that are potentially available to students. More formalized assessment in this area is often conducted by guidance and counseling staff or by vocational assessment personnel. However, it is important for teachers to be aware of the instruments that are typically used with students and be able to use some of them during the initial stages of career development process.

The assessment of career interests and strengths should be undertaken earlier rather than later. While the process of acquainting students with various careers (career awareness) should begin at the elementary level, a more systematic assessment of interests, preferences, and strengths should occur during the middle school years. Formal measures, such as the *Kuder Navigator* and the *Strong Interest Inventory*, can be used to generate useful information about career interests.

Many informal resources also exist for accomplishing this task. One resource that can be used to ascertain this information is the *Informal Assessments for Transition: Employment and Career Planning* (Synatschk, Clark, Patton, & Copeland, 2007). This resource contains 62 informal instruments that cover four areas: interests and preferences, abilities and skills, career exploration, and job searching and securing. Other examples of informal instruments include Reach for the Stars; More Information from You, About You; Skills You Are Good At; Job Readiness Checklist; Job Analysis Short Form; and Interview Simulation.

It is important for teachers at the middle school level to be able to initiate the career exploration process. A computer-based instrument called the *Career Interest, Preferences and Strengths Inventory* (CIPSI; Clark, Synatschk, Patton, & Steel, 2012) allows school-based personnel to obtain enough information from a student to be able to explore career clusters and therefore specific occupations. The CIPSI has four surveys that are used for obtaining information from the student: General Preferences, Personal Interests, Strengths, and Careers. The career clusters or occupations that are identified for exploration are based on information that the student provides from these four surveys. The results from two of the surveys (Personal Interests and Strengths) are directly linked to the O*NET online database (see the next section) so that further investigation of careers and occupations can be conducted. A sample results screen from the Strength survey is illustrated in Figure 15-2.

Exploring Potential Careers

To accomplish reasonable exploration of careers and occupations, efforts must be made to provide teachers with appropriate information, resources, and techniques for teaching about careers. Accentuating the importance of career education, demonstrating its educational and personal relevance, and providing ways for incorporating it into the existing curriculum will assist in its successful implementation. Two examples of excellent resources that teachers can access and that are now available online are O*NET Online (http://online.onetcenter.org) and the *Occupational Outlook Handbook* (http://www.bls.gov/oco/home.htm). Both resources provide detailed information about occupations that are extremely useful during the exploration phase.

A technique for assisting with the process of career exploration that is recommended for upper elementary or middle school students is maintaining a portfolio that includes information related to occupations. Students should be engaged in activities that lead to acquiring information that will answer some of the following questions: What occupations interest me? Who works in these

Strengths
Student: Pat Jameson
Date: 6/2/2017

The following career clusters are sorted based on your strengths from highest to lowest. The percentage listed by each career cluster shows the number of strengths you indicated were like you out of the total number possible for that cluster. To see some careers associated with a selected career cluster, click the **View** button. To print your results, click the **Print Report** button.

Career Cluster	Average	View Related Careers
Government & Public Administration	80%	View
Human Services	80%	View
Marketing, Sales & Service	78%	View
Education & Training	76%	View
Law, Public Safety, Corrections, & Security	75%	View
Business, Management & Administration	73%	View
Health Science	72%	View
Hospitality & Tourism	64%	View
Transportation, Distribution & Logistics	57%	View
Agriculture, Foods & Natural Resources	50%	View
Finance	45%	View
Science, Technology, Engineering, & Mathematics	38%	View
Architecture & Construction	24%	View
Arts, A/V Technology & Communication	19%	View
Information Technology	14%	View
Manufacturing	10%	View

FIGURE 15–2 Sample Screenshot from Strengths Survey

Source: From *Career Interest, Preferences, and Strengths Inventory*, by Gary M. Clark, Katherine O. Synatschk, Lawrence E. Steel 2012, Austin, TX: PRO-ED. Copyright 2012 by PRO-ED, Inc. Reprinted with permission.

Career Cluster _____

Career _____

SOC Code _____ Salary Range _____

Job Requirements _____

Education Required _____

Jobs in My Community:

Name _____

Address _____

Phone _____ Email/Website _____

FIGURE 15–3 Career Exploration Form

Source: From *Career Interest, Preferences, and Strengths*, by Gary M. Clark, Katherine O. Synatschk, James R. Patton, Lawrence E. Steel, 2012, Austin, TX: PRO-ED. Copyright 2012 by PRO-ED, Inc. Reprinted with permission.

occupations? What is the lifestyle of the workers? Whom do they work with? Where are their jobs? How do the workers accomplish their jobs? What type of education and training is necessary? What is the typical salary for this job? Activities such as these expose students to the different roles of different workers and also aid students in clarifying alternatives for future study and consideration. An example of a form that can be used for exploration purposes is shown in Figure 15-3.

Developing a Usable Vocational Vocabulary

To be proficient in the job-seeking process (school, vocational rehabilitation, vocational training) or the world of work, individuals must understand the vocabulary of jobs and the workplace. Figure 15-4 provides a list of the 52 most frequently used occupational vocabulary terms. It will be important to assess a student's understanding of these terms and to teach their meaning, if the student does not understand it.

ability	eligible	job description	responsibility
accommodation	employment	layoff	safety
apply	experience	merchandise	satisfactory
benefits	fired	occupation	schedule
break	first aid	on time	shift
breakage	full time	overtime	signature
checklist	harassment	part time	skill
competent	hazardous	paycheck	supervisor
cooperation	hire	policy	transportation
deduction	hours	preferences	union
department	income	promotion	vacation
dependable	interests	qualification	wages
directions	interview	raise	warning

FIGURE 15–4 Essential Occupational Vocabulary

Source: Table 1.1 From *Understanding Occupational Vocabulary* (p. 4), by Sherrilyn K. Fisher, Gary M. Clark, James R. Patton, 2004, Austin, TX: PRO-ED. Copyright 2004 by PRO-ED, Inc. Reprinted with permission.

Developing a Positive Work Attitude

U.S. culture is result oriented, and the definition of transition services, as stated in the 2004 reauthorization of IDEA, affirmed this notion. Many of the results that are usually accorded positive treatment in our society are work related (i.e., those who hold a job are held in higher esteem than those who do not hold a job). The individual with a results or work-oriented attitude is in a better position to obtain a job than the individual who is negative or naïve about work, so it is clear that education should assist students in developing strong positive work personalities with habits and attitudes that will ultimately lead them to become what they are interested in and capable of becoming. Ways to assess work attitudes can be found in *Informal Assessment of Transition Planning* (Gaumer Erickson, Patton, & Clark, 2012).

During the preschool stage, youngsters observe the daily living and working habits of those around them. Their observations, as well as interactions with older persons in their environment, begin to yield the perceptions of life that will ultimately cause these individuals to develop a particular type of work personality. The family has a tremendous influence on the child. Families who are consistent in meeting family members' needs or who are work oriented tend to produce persons who behave in the same fashion. Families who are not consistent in meeting family members' needs or who are not work oriented tend to produce young adults who exhibit these latter types of behaviors. Certainly, there are exceptions to this generalization, but it depicts the importance of the family to the preschool child.

During elementary school, students form a clearer, more precise perception of the world and their immediate surroundings. As students engage in academic and non-academic endeavors, teachers need to be aware of the importance of their developing behaviors that will lead to positive work habits and positive work personalities—for example, starting a task on time, cooperating with others, or cleaning up and putting things away. As children get older and can accept more responsibilities, they should be given more important responsibilities in classrooms and in school. Students should also be given tasks that require them to express their ideas and understanding about different occupations. For example, students might be asked to write a composition or tell a story about a certain job, such as being a plumber, or students might role-play the actions of different persons, such as a park ranger or travel agent.

The secondary school period is a crucial stage in the life of the potential worker. Most adolescents with learning-related problems require a curriculum that is responsive to their transitional needs across the life span. Some facet of their secondary programming should include attention to the development of occupational knowledge and the acquisition of some specific vocational skill.

Developing Employment Skills

A number of school-based and community-based options for preparing students for employment may be available in a school system. Mazzotti and Test (2016, p. 523-524) identified examples of both school-based instruction (SBI) and community-based instruction (CBI) that can be found in schools through the country. As they noted, examples of school-based instruction include jobs in the school setting, student organizations focused on vocational emphases, enterprises located in school settings, and career and technical education. Examples of community-based instruction include apprenticeships, internships and local businesses and agencies, service-learning programs, volunteering within the community, job shadowing, employment for pay, and other forms of supported work. Mazzotti and Test (2016) also provided an in-depth discussion of these various instructional options.

Although vocational training is often offered at the post-secondary level (community colleges, community training programs), students with special needs can benefit from receiving some form of employment preparation and skill development prior to exiting from secondary school. This is critical because too often these students will not access such training at a later time.

Unfortunately, many students with special needs leave school without any usable employment skills, often because they are in academically oriented programs that do not allow time for employment training. Also, not all of the options are available to students with special needs in many school districts.

 Check Your Understanding 15.1 Click here to gauge your understanding of the concepts in this section.

TRANSITIONS ALONG AND ACROSS THE SCHOOL YEARS

Transitions are part of all person's lives. Some are predictable from afar, while others occur more spontaneously. Although the focus of this chapter is on those transitions that occur during school years, it is worthwhile to think about transitions as a lifelong reality (Price & Patton, 2003), as dramatic transitions will occur later in life as well.

Types of Transitions

As mentioned, throughout life, we all experience many different transitions. Some transitions are minor (e.g., changing moving from one cubicle to another at work), and others are major life events (e.g., getting married). If we consider that transitions typically imply change and movement from one situation to another, then it is not difficult to think that people handle these changes differently. Most individuals will enjoy more successful transitions if these events are approached more systematically.

Two general types of transitions that we experience in life are vertical and horizontal transition. Examples of both types are shown in Figure 15-5. This chapter focuses on preschool and school transitions:

- **Vertical transitions** (e.g., beginning kindergarten, moving from elementary to middle school) are predictable—or normative—and most people experience them. These types of transitions have also been referred to as *developmental* or *age-based* (Wolery, 1989) and *chronological* (Lazzari, 1991).

- **Horizontal transitions** (e.g., frequent changes in living situations, recovery from a major illness or accident, returning to public school from a juvenile correctional facility) are non-normative—more individual specific—and not as predictable. Some people experience them whereas many others will not. Wolery (1989) described these as *non-developmental* in nature and Lazzari (1991) as *ongoing*. The horizontal transitions highlighted in Figure 15-5 represent only some of many different changes that can occur.

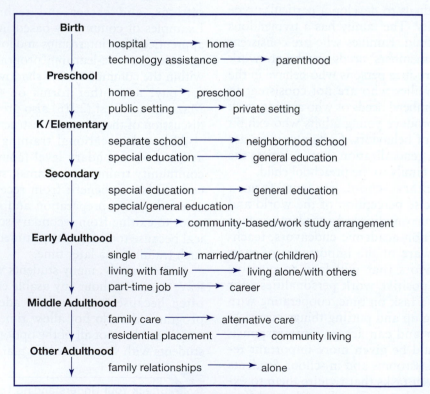

FIGURE 15–5 Vertical and Selected Horizontal Transitions

Source: Transition from school to young adulthood for students with special needs: Basic concepts and recommended practices, by J. R. Patton and C. Dunn, 1996, Unpublished manuscript. Copyright 1996 by J. R. Patton. Adapted with permission.

The school years include many of these normative and non-normative transitions. Most vertical transitions are common to all students, whereas many of the horizontal transitions are person specific and are relevant only to certain students and often relate to students with special needs (e.g., moving from a self-contained special education setting to a more inclusive environment).

Most of the transitions depicted in Figure 15-5 are handled by the individual or his or her family without any particular assistance from others. However, two of the transitions have legal mandates for action that must be taken. First, IDEA mandates that transition activities occur for young children who are moving from early intervention services (i.e., birth to 3 years of age—Part C of IDEA) to a range of options during the preschool years. For infants and toddlers who qualify and are served through early intervention programs, the transition from early intervention programs to any number of possible preschool settings (e.g., early childhood special education—Part B, private day care) is extraordinarily important and is a key component of the individualized family service plan (IFSP).

Second, the other mandated transition is to living in the community as a young adult. The focus of this transition is on students who are 16 years of age (in some states, 14 years of age) and who are preparing to move on from high school to the community. This transition should be a focal point of the special education process for students who have reached the age of 16. As the major school-level transition, emphasis in this chapter has been given to this important transition.

A number of other key school transitions (e.g., preschool to kindergarten, elementary to middle school, middle school to high school) exist and warrant attention. Many other important transitions may be encountered; however, only these two require transition-related activity. Teachers should have knowledge of and skills for handling the various transitions that students with special needs will experience as they move through various levels of schooling.

Critical Elements of Successful Transitions

Certain important elements are associated with increasing the chances of any transition being successful (Patton & Dunn, 1998). The point that should be noted is that, regardless of the transition that an individual is moving through, certain activities will make the transition smoother and what is referred to often as "more seamless." The three key elements originally identified by Patton and Dunn are discussed below.

Systematic and comprehensive planning involves two major activities: needs assessment and individual planning. The assessment phase should address two separate but related elements: (a) the evaluation of the demands and requirements of the setting(s) to which the person is likely to go next and (b) the evaluation of the individual's competence (i.e., knowledge and skill levels) associated with handling these impending demands. In assessing a student's levels of competence, attention should be directed to both areas of strength and areas of need. Another key point that IDEA requires is that the assessment tools used must be age appropriate. Individual planning is the formal or informal process of formulating an action plan to address areas of concern and to capitalize on areas of strength. The plan could be a document that is mandated by law, such as an IEP, or something much less formal; however, developing some type of plan of action is needed.

The second element, the *action phase*, refers to the follow-through on the planning that was previously done. Well-executed needs assessment and the resulting comprehensive planning are meaningless if the plans that have been generated are not carried out in an efficient, effective, and timely way. Some of the action items that are part of the plan may be simple activities that are achieved in a relatively short time; however, other planning areas may require more elaborate activities and larger investment of time and effort.

Coordination, cooperation, communication, and collaboration refers to the various relationships and ongoing efforts between the sending environment (early intervention services, preschool, elementary school, high school) and any number of receiving settings. Ideally, representatives from specific receiving settings would participate actively in the individual planning phase; however, regular participation of these individuals is infrequent or not possible. As a result, at the very least some level of cooperation and communication must exist between sending agencies and receiving agencies.

If transition planning (regardless of the transition of interest) is not conducted at all, is conducted in minimal fashion, or is conducted ineffectively, several problems are likely to arise. They may include the interruption of important services, the termination of needed services through oversight or lack of information, inadequate preparation of the student in the sending environment, or inadequate preparation of the receiving environment. For most students with special needs and their families, these can contribute to a host of problems in the environments to which they have transitioned.

Key Transitions Before and During the School Years

Students experience many transitions during their school careers. For some students, the process of receiving special services started early (i.e., right after birth). As noted in Figure 15-5, students will experience certain vertical transitions as well as some horizontal ones depending on their specific life situation. This section focuses on some key transitions that have particular interest to school-based personnel.

Although special education professionals focusing on secondary students' transition from school to adult living like to think they "invented" the notion of transition planning and transition services, early childhood educators began thinking about this at about the same time in the mid-1980s. Both groups of educators had different outcomes in mind for their groups, but much of the conceptual base was the same. Repetto and Correa (1996) pointed out the common features of the delivery of transition services for both early and secondary levels. For example, in comparing definitions applied to both age-level groups, the following commonalities are seen: curriculum, location of services, futures planning, multiagency collaboration, and family and student focus.

Transition from Early Intervention. Part C of the IDEA provides federal resources to designated state agencies to provide initial services to infants and toddlers with disabilities. Through Part C, usually referred to as early intervention, states receive funds to plan, develop, and implement services, supports, and information systems for children with disabilities, birth to age 3, and their families.

Early intervention services provide a range of supports to families and their very young child. The key document for guiding early intervention services is the IFSP. As a toddler approaches age 3, specific activities must occur to determine whether this young child qualifies for special education under Part B of IDEA. It should be noted that not all young children receive services under Part C will qualify for services under Part B.

An important requirement of early intervention services is the development of a transition plan for the child and his or her family to assist them in moving from early intervention services to whatever services might be used during the preschool years. Specifically, the law "establishes a transition plan in the IFSP not fewer than 90 days—and, at the discretion of all parties, not more than nine months—before the toddler's third birthday" (IDEA, §303,209[d][2]). Furthermore, the transition plan must include the following:

- Steps for the toddler with a disability and his or her family to exit from the Part C program
- Any transition services that the IFSP team identifies as needed by that toddler and his or her family (IDEA, §303,209[d][3])

Preschool to Kindergarten. Through a formula based on census counts and poverty levels, states and local school systems receive federal resources to provide special education and related services to preschool-age children with disabilities under Part B, Section 619, of IDEA. Moving into kindergarten from some type of preschool environment is a key transition and is a challenging adjustment (e.g., Pianta & Kraft-Sayre, 2003). This challenging transition was noted early on after the federal initiatives for establishing preschool programs for children with disabilities. Instruction in transition skills for making the move to kindergarten became recommended practice with "survival skills" curricula appearing in the literature (Rule, Fiechtl, & Innocenti, 1990). Rule et al. (1990) stated, "One rationale for teaching survival skills to preschoolers with [disabilities] is that they will encounter different learning conditions when they graduate into kindergarten or first grade" (p. 79). This same statement could be made for high school to postsecondary education settings, underscoring again the conceptual similarities in planning for life transitions.

Teachers often find it more helpful to have a set of specific skills in mind when starting to think more specifically about transition planning from preschool to kindergarten. Chandler (1993) provided some of examples of various social skills and other classroom behaviors that are typically required for successful experiences in a kindergarten classroom, organizing them around four groups of transitional skills and including behaviors in these respective domains: social (such as positive social interactions, cooperative work and play, following classroom rules, respecting others), communication (such as responding to feedback, answering questions, communicating interests and needs, following teacher directions), task -related (such as using materials, seeking attention in appropriate ways, responding to instructions, completing work), and self-help (such as staying away from danger, feeding, toileting). Attention to these skills and behaviors can assist with preparing for the transition to kindergarten by virtue of knowing what the expectations are of the receiving environment.

Regardless of the type or location of early intervention services, there is strong support for a "seamless system" of services for birth through kindergarten (Campbell & Halbert, 2002). Transitions are more likely to be successful when young children are taught survival skills for entering new environments through systematic instruction. These young children are also more likely to succeed after this transition process occurs when there is a clear policy on interagency collaborations, specific guidelines for sending and receiving programs for planning and implementing children's movement from program to program, and a commitment to include parents in the process.

The involvement of family in the transition process is a fundamental component of this process of moving from preschool years to formal schooling. As a result, efforts need to be made to involve parents by informing them of the changes that will be occurring when their child enters kindergarten. There is no question that doing this is easier when the child has been in a special education preschool program where the teachers should be familiar with the demands of the receiving environment—in this case, kindergarten.

Elementary to Middle School. One of the most overlooked vertical transitions that all students experience during the school years is from elementary to middle school. Although middle schools typically have an orientation for fifth-grade students

and their parents, these events occur close to the start of the school year and may not be sufficient to make this transition as seamless as possible for students with special needs. The unique challenges that exist as a student moves from elementary to middle school (Robinson, Braxdale, & Colson, 1985) or from middle to a ninth-grade center or high school setting (Wells, 1996) have been recognized for a long time. Moreover, the time when a student leaves the elementary setting and moves on to middle school is a time of many critical changes, such as an increasing importance of friendships and relationships. In addition, this time period is also one of major biological change in the students.

Difference between Elementary and Middle School. The nature of the school experience and structure changes when a student moves to the middle school level. For many students with special needs, the experience can be like being an English-speaking traveler in a non–English-speaking country. Given the significant differences that exist between elementary and secondary schooling, it is important that systematic transition planning occur, especially for those who will be in inclusive settings.

Certain features of the secondary school setting may make it particularly alien to the new arrivals. Some of the most obvious differences include a larger student population, a different type of class scheduling that implies more teachers to deal with each day, heavy curricular emphasis on content areas, increased homework, need for more self-regulated behavior, and different in-school procedures (e.g., use of lockers, physical education).

**ENHANCEDetext
video example 15.1**
Watch this video to learn more about transitioning from elementary to middle school.

Demands of the Middle School and Secondary Setting. In addition to the obvious distinctions just noted, major demands are placed on students that affect their academic success and social acceptance. Robinson et al. (1985) noted three areas that are crucial to success: academic demands, self-management/study skills demands, and social/adaptive demands.

Based in part on this conceptualization, the following organizational system includes six areas.

- **Academic demands**—behaviors or competencies that relate to the application of basic skills to the demands of the classroom setting. These skills include reading, listening, speaking, and writing and, when successfully used, result in successful performance as evidenced by being able to complete assignments or activities and receiving passing grades (at a minimum). This area does not include mastery of content.
- **Content demands**—behaviors or competencies, based primarily on previous knowledge acquisition, that relate to current knowledge and skill levels in specific subject areas that the student has to take as part of his or her course of study.
- **Academic support skills demands**—behaviors or competencies associated with the acquisition, recording, remembering, and use of information. The majority of these skills are typically associated with study skills and include skills such as organizational skills, note-taking skills, the ability to use reference materials, and test taking (see Chapter 11 on study skills).
- **Technical skill demands**—competencies associated with the use of various technologies (e.g., use of computers, tablet, Internet). This is now a necessity at the secondary level. The development of these skills are likely to have occurred at the elementary level. Students are expected to be able to access the Internet in meaningful ways to participate in class, complete assignments, and generate projects.
- **Social/adaptive demands**—behaviors or competencies that lead to acceptance by peers, balanced by compliance with school-based and classroom-based rules and procedures. As Robinson et al. (1985) pointed out, this latter point is particularly problematic for some students, as explicit and implicit classroom-specific rules and procedures vary from one teacher to another and are often difficult for students with special needs to recognize.
- **Nonacademic demands**—behaviors or competencies that do not relate directly to scholastic success but are required to be successful at the middle school level. Some examples of demands in these areas are using a locker, changing clothes or showering for physical education class, and bringing appropriate materials (books, notebooks, calculators) to specific classes. This dimension also taps the "informal" demand of participating in an assortment of extracurricular activities that become available at the middle school level.

To help identify areas in which students are strong as well as where possible challenges may occur, we have developed the *Middle School Transition Inventory* (*MSTI*). This instrument, provided in Appendix 15-A, is organized according to the six areas noted above. The instrument includes items that are rated both by the student (when appropriate) and by his or her teacher(s). As indicated, the intent of the instrument is to identify areas of strength as well as areas that might become barriers to success at the middle school level. Ideally, the instrument should be implemented at the beginning of fifth grade so that instruction can be provided for to address those areas of need and/or to establish supports systems that might be useful in the next year of schooling. Ratings are based on three levels of proficiency (not proficient, partially proficient, proficient). The results of performing this informal assessment should lead to appropriate instruction that will assist in making this transition more successful.

Enhancing Transition from Elementary to Middle School.   Like all other transitions, the successful movement from the sending school to the receiving school depends on the identification of the skills required in the receiving environment, the assessment of student competence in relation to these demands, and then addressing the areas that need attention. This sequence of activities must be accomplished before students arrive at the secondary level by maximizing communication, cooperation, coordination, and collaboration between the elementary staff and those at the secondary level.

Carter, Cushing, Clark, and Kennedy (2005) recommended that students, their families, and school-based personnel incorporate strategies into the planning process for moving from elementary to middle school. Although their suggestions were developed with students with more significant disabilities as the focal group, their recommendations have merit for other students as well and align with the themes offered in this chapter. Incorporating many of their strategies, we recommend the following actions:

- Start planning early.
- Assess the transition needs of students.
- Collaborate and communicate across schools.
- Prepare students early.
- Encourage and support family involvement.
- Develop peer support programs.
- Foster independence.

To help organize the information provided in this section, a checklist for planning for this transition is provided in Appendix 15-B. The checklist is an adaptation of a timeline developed by Carter et al. (2005). The checklist is organized along four time frames: during the final years of elementary school, during the months prior to entering middle school, during the first few weeks of middle school, and throughout middle school. It can contribute to establishing a framework for thinking through this process and making sure that essential activities are accomplished. It, too, can be the impetus for establishing ongoing collaborative efforts between school personnel.

Transition from High School

The transition from high school to whatever happens after high school is most often the subject of policy, research, and practice. The concept of formally planning for the transition of students with disabilities was first developed in the 1980s in response to the difficulty adolescents with disabilities often experienced after leaving high school. At that time, family members, teachers, researchers, and policy makers focused on how to help youth with disabilities find employment. The federal government emphasized this focus on employment in the initial formal discussions on transition in the early 1980s. Professionals came to realize, however, that finding fulfilling and gainful employment was only one component of adult life. The model produced by Halpern (1985) was an integral first step in expanding the notion that transition planning needed to involve more than just a focus on employment.

Focus in the area of transition planning quickly expanded to include the much broader concept of community involvement. This expanded focus included independent living skills and social networks for people with disabilities—in addition to the important area of employment. Now, a wide range of transition planning domains is commonly identified as in need of attention. Patton and Clark (2014) have identified the following major transition domains: career choice and planning, employment knowledge and skills, further education/training, functional communication, self-determination, independent living, personal money management, community involvement and usage, leisure activities, health, and interpersonal relationships.

IDEA, as amended in 2004, defined "transition services" as

> a coordinated set of activities for a child with a disability that is designed within an results-oriented process that is focused on improving the academic and functional achievement of a child with a disability to facilitate movement from school to post-school activities including post-secondary education, vocational training, integrated employment, continuing adult education, adult service, independent living, or community participation. (§300.42[a][1])

Other notable elements associates with transition services that were part of the mandates in the 2004 reauthorization include the following:

- Transition services, now defined as "a coordinated set of activities for a student, designed within a results-oriented process," indicated a change from the previous wording of "outcome-oriented process."
- The IEP for students 16 and older—and younger when appropriate (some states use 14 and older as their guideline)—must contain certain elements: Appropriate measurable post-secondary goals based upon age-appropriate transition assessments related to training, education, employment, and, where appropriate, independent living skills. (§300.320([b][1])
- Transition services should be based on the individual student's needs, taking into account the student's strengths, preferences, and interests (§300.42[a][2])
- Services that are needed to attain post-secondary goals should be specified (this would include courses of study).
- Documentation that the student is informed of his or her rights as an adult no later than one year before age of legal adulthood (according to state law)—which is age 18 in most states—should be provided.

- For students graduating or exiting school due to aging out, the law now requires local school districts to provide a student with a summary of his or her academic achievement and functional performance that includes recommendations on how to assist the student in meeting his or her post-secondary goals.

Adult Outcomes. While the addition of transition services to secondary special education programs has been a significant boon, post-secondary outcomes for youth with disabilities continue to generate concern. One important measurement of post-secondary success is obtaining a high school diploma. This remains a challenge for adolescents with disabilities. Only 65.1% of students in special education received a regular diploma during the 2012–2013 school year (U.S. Department of Education, 2015). While that percentage of students in special education who received a diploma increased significantly since 1996, when the percentage was only 42.4, it is clear that many students still do not receive a diploma. In a related matter in terms of academic success, the overall dropout rate for youth served under IDEA was 18.8% of all students in special education during the 2012-2013 school year (U.S. Department of Education, 2015). Although the number of students with disabilities who drop out has decreased over the years (note that the figure was 31.1% in 2003–2004), many students, particularly those with emotional and behavioral disorders (35.4%; U.S. Department of Education, 2015), do not complete high school. Certainly, educational attainment is relevant to other indicators of post-secondary success, such as employment and enrollment in training programs and institutions of higher education.

The National Longitudinal Transition Study—2 (NLTS-2; Newman, Wagner, Cameto, & Knokey, 2009; Wagner, Newman, Cameto, Garza, & Levine, 2005), a 10-year study that followed youth with disabilities throughout their transition into young adulthood, was conducted by SRI. The results of this ongoing study provided a detailed picture of experiences across multiple transition domains, including education, employment, and community involvement, to name only a few. Data also provide information about transition experiences across groups of youth by disability category, race/ethnicity, age, and gender.

Although the first National Longitudinal Transition Study (NLTS-1) documented gaps in both types of employment (full and part time) and wages earned between transition-aged youth with disabilities and youth without disabilities, NLTS-2 has provided evidence that employment and wage gaps are narrowing for youth with disabilities when compared to their age peers without disabilities (Newman et al., 2009; Wagner et al., 2005). About 55% of youth with disabilities in NLTS-1 gained paid work experiences after high school, whereas nearly 71% of youth with disabilities in NLTS-2 had done so. Further, youth with disabilities in the second study were more likely to earn more than the federal minimum wage; however, this gain is mitigated by the fact that youth from NLTS-2 were actually *less* likely to be employed full time (Wagner et al., 2005). Also, gaps in employment and wages between these two groups may increase as youth age because youth with disabilities are less likely to obtain the benefits that are associated with college degrees. Table 15-1 provides an example of the range of outcomes for students identified as having intellectual disabilities, as reported in the Wagner et al. (2005) report.

Postsecondary Options for Students with Special Needs. Today, the options for students with special needs when they leave high school are greater than they ever have been. While much work still needs to be done, many noteworthy efforts have occurred in recent years. This section explores the post-secondary options in three main areas: employment, further education, and living arrangements.

Young adults with disabilities are capable of working successfully in a number of different types of jobs. First and foremost, efforts need to be made to identify full-time, competitive employment settings for these individuals. For many of them, part-time work opportunities may be available. Another option that might be desirable in some cases is voluntary work opportunities. This last situation may be a viable option for some individuals as a way of spending most of their work time or as a way to supplement other work opportunities.

Further education can imply a number of various settings. Some individuals with special needs can and should pursue higher education opportunities. Students with high-incidence disabilities can achieve success in higher education when the proper supports are in place. This group, however,

TABLE 15–1   Summary of NLTS-2 findings of students with intellectual disabilities

Area	Findings
Transition services	• Many students (60%) had transition planning begun by age 14.
	• 48.7% did not provide input in discussing their transition plans.
	• Very few individuals (3.3%) took leadership role during transition process.
	• General educators' involvement in the transition process was minimal.
	• Few individuals (9.8%) chose postsecondary education as transition goal.
	• 51.4% of the students chose living independently as a transition goal.
	• 75.8% received instruction specifically focused on transition-related topics.
	• The program provided for most students (79.5%) was identified as "very or fairly well suited" for preparing them to achieve transition goals.
Outcomes	Postsecondary school enrollment (percentage):
	• Any postsecondary school (15.4)
	• Postsecondary vocational, business, or technical school (11)
	• Two-year/community college (5.1)
	Current employment (24.8)
	Living arrangements
	• With parents (72.2)
	• On own, with spouse, roommate, or in dorm (16.3)
	Postschool independence: have a . . .
	• Driver's license/permit (20.7)
	• Checking account (10.1)
	• Charge account or credit care (6.9)
	Leisure time:
	• Watching television/videos (41)
	• Using a computer (13.5)
	• Listening to music (18.7)
	• Doing hobbies, reading for pleasure (4.7)
	• Talking on the phone with friends (9.2)
	• Playing sports (16.3)
	Friendship interactions in past year:
	• Saw friends outside of school or work at least weekly (46.3)
	• Communicating by computer at least daily (21.9)
	Participation in community activities in the past year: took part in . . .
	• Community group (e.g., sports team, club, religious group) (23.8)
	• Volunteer or community service activity (22.7)

Source: Wagner et al. (2005).

must wrestle with the issue of whether they are comfortable disclosing their disability to the college's office of disability services that is typically on campus and serves this population. If a student decides not to disclose their disability, then it is essential for that student to be prepared to be a good self-advocate for their needs. It should be pointed out that higher education is not only intended for students with high-incidence disabilities. In recent times, a number of programs have been established on the campuses of various colleges for students with more significant support needs.

In terms of living arrangements, young adults with disabilities can be found in a number of different settings. Many individuals in their young adult years will live at home. Others, as a function of any number of reasons, may move to supported living environments. Examples of this arrangement include living in an apartment by oneself or with a roommate while receiving varying levels of support services. Group homes and other community-based residential settings are also possible. It should be noted also that a number of communities exist that are made up of individuals with disabilities.

ENHANCEDetext
video example 15.2
Watch this video for a discussion of the IEP and transition planning.

Transition and the IEP

An individualized transition plan is one part of a student's IEP, and typically a series of IEP meetings will be dedicated to the topic of transition. The plan, which is part of the IEP, must be a formal, written plan that includes specific learning objectives relative to the transition goals of the student. Although recommended practices in transition suggest that domains other than education and employment, as discussed previously, should be addressed in individual transition plans, a review of existing transition plans revealed that other domains, such as health care and transportation, were far less likely to be addressed (Everson, Zhang, & Guillory, 2001).

Because transition is results based, the IEP must contain a statement of expected outcomes in each post-school domain that the plan addresses. For example, in the domain of post-secondary education, is the expected outcome to attend college? If so, will the individual attend a community college, four-year university, or some other learning institution? Clearly, the learning objectives addressed in each major domain of the transition plan, as well as the plan to access the general education curriculum, must address the expected outcome in that domain (Wehmeyer, 2002). This is important so that the educational goals in the IEP align with the measurable post-secondary goals that have been identified by the student.

For example, if a student states that he wants to attend a four-year university, his IEP must reflect assessment that has examined all aspects of future need in this setting and contain learning objectives that contribute to making this goal become a reality. In this example, objectives would include necessary academic skills to prepare the student for a university setting (addressing strengths and needs in study skills as well as core academic subjects, such as reading and language arts). Furthermore, in this example, access to the general curriculum and statewide assessments, whether stated in the IEP or in the transition component, must align with the goal of attending university.

Guiding Principles Related to Transition

This section discusses principles that should guide the transition process. These principles are critical for maximizing the effectiveness of transition-related activities when the student is still in school and for increasing the probability that the student will be successful in a range of post-school environments.

Comprehensive Planning. Although the actual transition domains used in a given state or local school district may vary, it is essential that the assessment and planning process cover critical areas in which one must show some levels of competence in order to be successful. Table 15-2, based on the domains used in the *Transition Planning Inventory* (2nd ed.), lists 11 transition domains that show the type of comprehensiveness that should be used when providing transition planning and services. The table also provides a few examples of what each domain covers. It is important to be reminded that students do not have needs in all of the domains; they have transition needs in only some of the areas. Nevertheless, all areas should be examined for needs and strengths during this process.

Assessment of Transition Needs. A required activity in developing effective transition plans based on individualized post-school goals is to collect data regarding the present level of functioning, as well as ongoing assessments of needs and strengths (Sitlington, Neubert, & Clark, 2010). For example, subject-specific, criterion-referenced tests provide a snapshot of students' academic abilities. Norm-referenced instruments can be used to assess career aptitudes or establish college entrance criteria. Less formal instruments, such as the CIPSI, mentioned earlier, can provide entry points for exploration. Certain assessment techniques, both formal and informal, measure transition-related competencies and may include functional and ecological assessments (Sitlington, Neubert, Begun, Lombard, & Leconte, 2007).

TABLE 15–2   Transition domains

Domain	Description
Working	
Career Choice & Planning	• Knows about jobs
	• Knows how to get a job
Employment Knowledge & Skills	• Acquires and performs general and specific skills related to a job or jobs
	• Knows how to change jobs
Learning	
Further Education/Training	• Knows about options for further development beyond high school
	• Has the skills to be successful
	• Knows how to use support services
Functional Communication	• Is able to read, write, listen, and speak in applied settings
Living	
Self-Determination	• Understands his or her strengths and weaknesses
	• Is able to plan, set goals, make decisions
	• Is able to be in charge of his or her own life
Independent Living	• Has skills related to a variety of everyday demands such as cooking, cleaning, making simple repairs
	• Is able to solve everyday problems that arise
	• Has skills to use current technology
Personal Money Management	• Has skills associated with buying everyday items
	• Is able to pay bills, maintain checking and savings accounts, budget
Community Involvement & Usage	• Has skills associated with being a capable citizen
	• Is able to use services and resources in the community
	• Is able to use local public transportation
Leisure Activities	• Is aware of range of leisure activities
	• Participates in indoor and outdoor activities
	• Engages in various types of entertainment
Health	• Has knowledge and skills associated with staying physically healthy
	• Has knowledge and skills associated with staying emotionally and mentally healthy
	• Has knowledge of appropriate sexual behavior
Interpersonal Relationships	• Has skills to interact appropriately with a range of other people
	• Is able to make and keep friends
	• Is able to deal with conflict
	• Has knowledge and skills to be a good parent

A number of age-appropriate assessment procedures have been developed to assess directly various transition domains. Some of the instruments are comprehensive in nature, while others focus on a specific topic. Informal techniques can include observations and interviews of students and important adults (e.g., parent[s] or a supervisor at a part-time job setting). Informal assessment can also involve the administration of checklists and rating scales. One resource that includes good examples of these types of instruments is *the Informal Assessments for Transition Planning* (2nd ed.; Gaumer Erickson et al., 2012).

In addition to many informal techniques that are available to school personnel for assessing needs, strengths, preferences, and interests, a few formal transition instruments exist as well. These assessments, while meeting the requirement of being age appropriate, provide results that span a range of transition domains. They can serve as effective tools for conducting a comprehensive assessment of transition needs on which individualized planning can be based. They include the following:

- *Brigance Transition Skills Inventory* (Brigance, 2010)
- *Enderle-Severson Transition Rating Scales* (Enderle & Severson, 2003)
- *Transition Skills Inventory* (Halpern, Herr, Doren, & Wolf, 2000)
- *Transition Planning Inventory* (2nd ed.) (Patton & Clark, 2012)

Student Involvement. Individualization is an essential element of any comprehensive transition component, yet this practice has not been implemented with widespread success. Many studies that have included reviews of transition components of IEPs have revealed that individualization was not occurring. At times, this lack of individualization resulted from the use of disability-based expected outcomes rather than the preferences of the student (Grigal, Test, Beattie, & Wood, 1997). More frequently, however, has been the documentation of a lack of student involvement in developing transition plans (Williams & O'Leary, 2001). One way to increase the individualization—and therefore the usefulness—of transition components is to increase the participation of the student in the plan's creation.

Increasing the active involvement of students with disabilities in the development and implementation of their transition component has the potential to increase the individualized nature of the document. In addition, incorporating students' perspectives (as required by IDEA 2004) fosters a sense of student ownership, increasing the active involvement of students in the implementation of plans that reflect their goals for the future (Bassett & Lehmann, 2002). When planning and providing services related to post-secondary transition, incorporating the preferences of students with disabilities makes sense.

Students must actively participate in their transition planning and instructional activities so that teachers, family members, and personnel from outside agencies are able to understand his or her short-term as well as post-secondary goals and are able to facilitate goal attainment. Although students with and without disabilities may display a wide variety of preferences and maturity levels when invited to participate in formal meetings with adults, skills such as self-advocacy, goal setting, and problem solving can be taught (Powers et al., 2001).

To capitalize on this active involvement, teachers and other adults must consistently promote student **self-determination** skills (see also Chapter 13) as well as listen to the decisions young adults with disabilities make about their own lives and support them while they work to make their dreams become realities. Shogren et al. (2015) noted that self-determination refers to determining one's own fate or one's own course of action. Essential characteristics of self-determination include autonomy, self-regulation, self-realization, and empowerment. The literature is replete with evidence concerning the benefits of self-determination skills in students with ID. For example, Lee, Wehmeyer, and Shogren (2015), in a meta-analysis of studies on the self-determined learning model of instruction, reported that such a focus had a positive impact on both academic and functional outcomes and successful adult transition.

Parent/Family Involvement. The involvement of family members is also an essential element in transition planning. Parent participation throughout all special education processes is mandated by IDEA 2004. Additionally, parents and siblings and, in many cases, extended family members play important roles as advocates for and role models to their children. More important, parents and other family members will likely continue to be critical supports to their children as they become young adults. When educators and other school personnel invite family members to actively participate in transition planning, the end result is a meaningful, individualized plan that addresses post-secondary transition goals that are specific to the person with a disability (Hanley-Maxwell, Pogoloff, & Whitney-Thomas, 1998).

Collaboration between families and schools during the transition process does occur. Families have expressed that professionals who listen carefully to their needs while arranging connections between them and community resources are highly valued (deFur, Todd-Allen, & Getzel, 2001). The creation of a trusting relationship between home and school, as well as effective communication and logistics that favor parents' schedule constraints, have the potential to facilitate parent involvement (Salembier & Furney, 1997).

Barriers to the active involvement of family members have also been identified in research. Some concerns family members have shared about the successful transition of their children with disabilities include a sense that partnerships between school and home were limited (Schuster, Timmons, & Moloney, 2003) and that family-identified transition needs and goals are not consistently represented on transition plans (Thompson, Fulk, & Piercy, 2000). Another reality is that some parents will not participate as fully as school-based professionals would like. Transition personnel must be sensitive to family values and resources in terms of how much and the type of involvement parents are able to give to this process.

Diversity Considerations. As the U.S. student population becomes more racially/ethnically diverse, educators must learn to respond to this diversity in ways that engage members of culturally and linguistically diverse subpopulations. Cause for concern about the efficacy of transition planning and instruction and diverse groups of young adults stem from evidence illustrating that youth of color, English language learners, and youth from low socioeconomic backgrounds all face challenges to successful post-secondary transition in employment and post-secondary education. Outcomes for many adolescents in these groups are less positive than outcomes for adolescents without disabilities or European American adolescents with disabilities.

Surveys of diverse groups of parents indicate that collaborative experiences with schools have the potential to be negative in which the cultural identity of families has been disregarded (Geenen, Powers, Lopez-Vasquez, & Bersani, 2003). The concept of transition is built upon ideals of independence and equity, which means that the preferred practices in transition planning and implementation support increasing students' abilities to become self-determining as well as obtaining the same opportunities as their peers without disabilities. These values and beliefs, however, may be interpreted differently by people, in part based on their cultural identities (deFur & Williams, 2002). Additional surveys of parents' perspectives provide evidence that the type of disability also influences parents' expectations for transition planning and instruction (Grigal & Neubert, 2004). The nearby Diversity in the Classroom box explores transition considerations further.

Interagency Cooperation. Whereas educational and related services are guaranteed to youth with disabilities in the public schools, adult agencies provide services based on eligibility rather than entitlement (Cozzens, Dowdy, & Smith, 1999). This means that post-secondary transition involves a shifting of shared responsibility and that an adult with a disability—and, in some cases, with the assistance of his or her family members—must learn to disclose disability status, access adult agencies, and participate in eligibility determination activities.

Some examples of adult agencies are the following:

- Social Security Administration
- Federal employment programs
- Vocational rehabilitation agencies
- State, local, and private service providers for people with disabilities
- Post-secondary educational institutions
- Disability advocacy groups

Connecting students with disabilities to programs and agencies they will need to access once they have exited high school is one way to increase the potential for post-secondary success. These connections, like all other aspects of transition planning, must be individualized. Some young adults with disabilities may need to establish connections to independent living facilities, such as supported living settings, whereas others may need to contact offices for student services at colleges and universities to determine available academic supports.

Key to establishing these relationships is to formalize the connection within the transition component, including inviting adult agency representatives to transition planning meetings as well as incorporating related transition linkage goals that establish contact between the student and the agency representative. For a student who has an interest in pursuing a career in photography, for example, linking her to adult service providers might involve arranging a visit to the local community college where she would meet with a student services provider or counselor to determine how the college could accommodate her needs. In addition, subsequent visits could be arranged where she could meet other students with similar interests, perhaps sit in on a class, and/or participate in a tour of the

Considerations for Transition Planning with English Learners with Disabilities

Increasingly, diverse groups of students now receive transition services, and these groups experience different post-school outcomes in terms of graduation, employment, education, independent living, and community integration. English learners with disabilities (ELSWDs) are one such group.

ELSWDs are a heterogeneous group with diverse circumstances impacting their achievement including language proficiency, disabilities status, family income status, immigration or refugee status, and access to social and cultural capital in their communities. Mismatches in cultural assumptions and value systems between students/families and educators/schools can exacerbate the impact of these circumstances and hinder both in-school and post-school achievements. Some considerations for planning warrant attention:

Recognize barriers to access. Individualization of transition services based on disability classification alone is insufficient because of their cultural and linguistic backgrounds, which influence post-secondary outcomes in employment, education, and independent living. Transition planning for them should create opportunities where biliteracy or multiliteracy is an asset for future education and employment and allows them to function effectively across multiple cultural milieus. This process involves (a) examining how student background affects their current and future goals, (b) recognizing cultural and linguistic diversity as strengths in multiple settings (e.g., employment, education, community), and (c) finding ways to highlight the opportunities that biliteracy or multiliteracy may bring these students.

Develop cultural competencies. Transition educators bring their own values into the planning process that can affect their work with students and families on issues such as family involvement, post-school expectations, work ethics, and self-determination. These beliefs are not culturally neutral and might cause counterproductive interactions with students and families. Seemingly universal values about post-school expectations in education, employment, and independent living may not be universal, and one's good intentions based on erroneous assumptions could lead to discriminatory practices.

Assess social validity. Social validity considers whether those receiving services believe the services to be useful. Understanding whether ELSWDs and their families are satisfied with the transition process can help educators to be more effective in facilitating post-school outcomes. Transition planning and services must therefore be evaluated in neutral ways so that students and parents can express their level of satisfaction and provide redirection if appropriate.

In addition to the above considerations, the following three assumptions should be avoided when working with ELSWDs:

1. Their needs are adequately addressed by focusing on Latino communities. ELs speak over 400 different languages including Arabic, Chinese, Hmong, Vietnamese, and Somali. About one in five ELs does not speak Spanish. Needs fluctuate depending as demographics shift and new arrivals.
2. The needs of ELSWDs are adequately addressed by focusing on low achievers. ELSWDs have needs that are different from ELs or SWDs due to the intersection of disabilities and second- or third-language learning processes. Their needs differ from other low achievers.
3. Their needs are adequately addressed by focusing on economically disadvantaged students. While many ELSWDs come from low-income families, other factors, such as cultural norms, eligibility for services, and job opportunities, differ across families.

Transition professionals who participate in the continuous process of developing cultural competencies to effectively broker resources and support ELSWDs in transition can (a) have greater awareness of their own assumptions and values about post-school achievement, (b) develop more effective relationships with students and families, (c) provide more relevant and useful information for ELSWDs, and (d) recognize assets serving ELSWDs rather than focusing on their deficits.

Yen K. Pham is an assistant professor of special education at the University of New Mexico. Her research examines transitioning adolescents impacted by disabilities and poverty.

TABLE 15–3   Indicator 13: Improving Transition Services (Items)

1. Is there an appropriate measurable post-secondary goal or goals in this area?
2. Is (are) the post-secondary goal(s) updated annually?
3. Is there evidence that the measurable post-secondary goal(s) were based on age appropriate transition assessment?
4. Are there transition services in the IEP that will reasonably enable the student to meet his or her post-secondary goal(s)?
5. Do the transition services include courses of study that will reasonably enable the student to meet his or her post-secondary goal(s)?
6. Is (are) there annual IEP goal(s) related to the student's transition services needs?
7. Is there evidence that the student was invited to the IEP team meeting where transition services were discussed?
8. If appropriate, is there evidence that a representative of any participating agency was invited to the IEP team meeting with the prior consent of the parent or student who has reached the age of majority?

photography facilities. The point is to establish a multiyear, outcomes-based goal (e.g., pursue an associate's degree in photography) and develop short-term goals that both align with the long-term goal and create connections to adult agencies.

Although linking students to adult services providers is a recommended practice, Agran, Cain, and Cavin (2002) surveyed rehabilitation counselors and teachers and found that counselors were rarely invited to transition planning meetings and that a lack of collaboration between adult vocational rehabilitation agencies and schools characterized the process. A lack of connections to other adult services, such as Social Security administrators and representatives from work incentive programs, has also been documented (Schuster et al., 2003). Weak or non-existent connections to adult service providers may also serve as additional barriers for culturally and linguistically diverse families. Geenen et al. (2003) found that language barriers and unfamiliarity with adult agencies contributed to diverse family members' decisions to *not* pursue services for their young adult children with disabilities.

Accountability. It is critically important for schools to conduct transition services in the best possible manner. To ensure that schools (i.e., states) comply with the regulations across all areas stipulated in IDEA, the Office of Special Education Programs issued a set of 20 State Performance Plan/Annual Performance Report (SPP/APR) performance indicators. Four of the *indicators* relate to keeping students in school and improving the probability of a more successful life when school is over: indicator 1, improving graduation rates; indicator 2,

decreasing dropout rates; indicator 13, improving transition services; and indicator 14, improving outcomes for students moving from secondary to post-secondary activities. A list of the eight components of indicator 13—the indicator most closely related to this chapter—is provided in Table 15-3.

 Check Your Understanding 15.2 Click here to gauge your understanding of the concepts in this section.

TRANSITION PLANNING PROCESS

Although the transition provisions in IDEA 2004 provide specific information regarding the age of the child and the types of documents that must be in place to meet the letter of the law (policy compliance), they do little to describe the range of transition services that best meet the spirit of the law (alignment with preferred practices). In other words, what do effective transition services for adolescents with disabilities *actually* look like?

Key elements of the transition process are depicted in Figure 15-6 (developed by Patton & Dunn, 1998; revised by Patton & Clark, 2014). This model conveys the importance of a broad range of planning activities that include the following features:

- The transition process starts very early and can be accomplished by addressing post-school topics when opportunities arise in the curriculum or during instruction.
- It is essential to expose students to a range of post-secondary issues early enough so that they can "dream" about their futures.

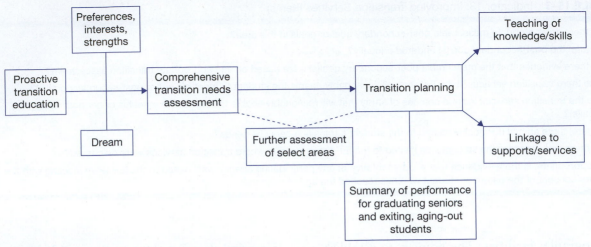

FIGURE 15–6 Transition Planning Process

Source: From Informal Assessments for Transition Planning, Second Edition Manual (p. 8-9), by A. S. Gaumer Erickson, G. M. Clark and J. R. Patton, 2013, Austin, TX: PRO-ED. Copyright 2013 by PRO-ED, Inc. Reprinted with permission.

- This dream phase needs to be followed by a realistic exploration of careers and other post-school topics such as where one wants to live and play.
- Prior to age 16, a comprehensive assessment of needs, preferences, interests, and strengths must occur using age-appropriate instruments or techniques.
- Sometimes more in-depth assessment may be needed to determine the specific transition needs of a student.
- Measurable post-secondary goals that are student-driven need to be identified and clarified.
- Specific transition goals and activities need to be developed that address the "transition needs" of the students. As Scanlon, Patton, and Raskind (2011) noted, "there are two types of goals that should result from transition planning: *Instructional*—which addresses academic, behavioral, and social outcomes, and *Linkage*—which concerns connections among services and agencies" (p. 600).
- Prior to a student leaving school through graduation or reaching the age of 22, a student-oriented summary of performance must be developed to assist the student with certain aspects of his or her life after high school.
- The model implies that collaboration among home, school, and adult agencies, occurs simultaneously with the purpose of increasing a student's ability to respond with knowledge, skills, experience, and supports to be able to deal with the array of demands of adulthood.

Transition services vary widely among states, districts, and even schools. Some elements of transition planning may vary according to the needs and strengths associated with specific disabilities. For example, transition-related needs of young adults with high-incidence disabilities, such as learning disabilities, may differ from the needs of young adults with low-incidence disabilities, such as students who are deaf or blind. Yet several decades of practicing and researching transition services have resulted in a wide range of recommended transition practices. Three key recommended practices are individualization of transition components, active student and family involvement, and interagency collaboration.

Key Components of the Transition Model

The model of transition assessment and planning depicted in Figure 15-6 shows a process that begins in the early years of school and continues up until the time when a student graduates or leaves school. We feel that each component of the model is essential for ensuring that a comprehensive transition process is provided to students. A strong argument can be made that this process is valuable for all students who are in school—not only for those students have an IEP. The following discussion provides an insight to the various components of the model.

Proactive Transition Education. This component refers to activities that typically occur in the elementary grades that relate to later adult outcomes. This phase includes the beginning stages talking about real-life topics and includes the first stage of the career education process, as discussed earlier in this chapter. This component relates to topics covered in the previous chapter suggesting ways to infuse real-life topics into the existing content that is covered in language arts, math, science, and social studies.

Dream.   This component of the model refers to providing students with the opportunities to "dream" about their futures. It is extremely important for students to have the chance to think openly—and sometimes crazily—about what they want to do in the future and where they want to do it. An important point, however, is that we must provide these opportunities early enough so that students have an opportunity to recognize whether their dreams are realistic.

Determination of Preferences, Interests, and Strengths.   As a beginning step in the "formal" transition planning process, we need to develop ways to find out the preferences and interests of students in regard to careers and other life-related areas. A simple form that is part of the transition planning inventory and that was designed to obtain information about preferences and interests is shown in Figure 15-7. It is also essential that we capitalize on student strengths, and as a result, we need to have tools for identifying the strengths. As mentioned earlier in the chapter, CIPSI includes a way of identifying students.

Transition Needs Assessment.   At the centerpiece of this process is the compilation of activities that determine the transition needs that a student has. It is important to do this early in the process so that there is sufficient time, knowledge, and skills for that person in order that transition plans are developed, instruction is provided and linkage activities established when needed. An important point that needs to be understood about this component of the process is that, whatever tools are used to determine needs, these tools need to be comprehensive so that all of the areas of transition are considered. Furthermore, the tools that are utilized must be efficient so that the determination of need can be done in a reasonable amount of time. A number of instruments that can be used to accomplish this task were listed earlier in the chapter.

Further Assessment of Select Areas.   Often, there is a need to obtain more detailed information about certain transition domains. When this is necessary, we need to have an array of additional assessment tools available to be able to establish more in depth information about certain areas. The need for further assessment occurs when we have utilized tools in the comprehensive assessment stage that include items that are broad in nature due to the fact that those instruments are designed so that school personnel can use them efficiently and effectively.

The *Transition Planning Inventory* (2nd ed.) (TPI-2), is an example of an assessment will that provides multiple levels for determining transition needs. Level 1 of this instrument consists of 57 items that cover 11 transition domains. Level 2 of the instrument contains over 800 items that are related to each of the 57 items in level 1. The assessment also provides informal instruments that are related to the 57 items as well (level 3). Figure 15-8 illustrates the three levels for the transition domain of self-determination.

Transition Planning.   Upon completion of the assessment phase, actual transition planning should commence. As noted in the model, two forms of planning can and should be considered: instructional goals that are associated with the "teaching of knowledge/skills" and linkage goals that are associated with "linkage to support/services."

Instructional goals are related to the knowledge and skills associated with transition skill areas that still need development. In all likelihood, new measurable annual goals should be created to address these areas of need. It is certainly possible that some areas may already be represented by measurable annual goals that are in the IEP.

Linkage goals refer to the connections that need to be made to those supports and services that are available in the community and will be useful and, most of the time essential for success in the future. The important point here is that action has to be taken when the student is still in school to ensure that the supports and services are available during the seamless transition to life after high school.

ENHANCEDetext
video example 15.3
Watch this video for an example of transition planning in action.

Transition Planning Inventory–Second Edition
Student Preferences and Interests Form–Basic

Student Name: _____   Date: _____

Directions: For each question, explain what you are thinking at this time based on your interests and preferences. If you do not have an answer to a question, leave it blank. Start at the top of each column and read downward. Begin with **1**, then proceed to **2a** through **2e**, then move on to columns 3 and 4.

1 General

1. What do you plan on doing after high school?

2 Working	3 Learning	4 Living
2a. What jobs are you considering?	**3a.** What would you like to study or get training in after high school?	**4a.** What do you like to do during your leisure time?
2b. What type of setting would you prefer to work in (for example, indoor versus outdoor, office versus factory, etc.)?	**3b.** How do you prefer to get information—by reading or asking questions?	**4b.** What type of friendships do you enjoy having?
2c. How would you find out more about the jobs you are interested in?	**3c.** How do you prefer to share information—by speaking, writing, or signing?	**4c.** How do you prefer to make decisions that affect your life?
2d. In the next 2–3 years, how would you like the school to help you get ready for getting a job?	**3d.** In the next 2–3 years, how would you like the school to help you get ready for going to college or entering a training program?	**4d.** In the next 2–3 years, how would you like the school to help you get ready for being able to deal with everyday life in the community?
2e. How will your disability affect you when you get a job?	**3e.** How will your disability affect you when you go to college or go into a training program?	**4e.** How will your disability affect you when you live in the community?

© 2014, 2006, 1997 by PRO-ED, Inc.
1 2 3 4 5 6 7 8 9 10   22 21 20 19 18 17 16 15 14 13

Additional copies of this form (#14172) may be purchased from
PRO-ED, 8700 Shoal Creek Blvd., Austin, TX 78757-6897
800/897-3202, Fax 800/397-7633, www.proedinc.com

FIGURE 15–7 Transition Planning Inventory (2nd ed.)

Source: From *Transition Planning Inventory - Second Edition (TPI-2) Preferences & Interest - Basic Form* by Patton, Clark, Austin: PRO-ED., Austin, TX: PRO-ED. Copyright 2014 by PRO-ED, Inc. Reprinted with permission.

Level 1: TPI-2 1tem	Level 2: Comprehensive Informal Inventory	Level 3: Aligned Informal Assessments
18. Understands his/her strengths and limitations.	10 indicators (pp. 25–26)	3. Job Interview: Are You Ready to Answer Questions? 4. Job Interview Skills 9. Personal Strengths 18. Challenges in the Classroom 21. Study and Learning Skills Inventory 23. Disability and Me 26. Self-Determination/Self-Advocacy Checklist
19. Explains the impact of his/her disability on various life situations.	11 indicators (p. 26)	23. Disability and Me 26. Self-Determination/Self-Advocacy Checklist
20. Advocates for self-interests and needs.	19 indicators (pp. 26–27)	15. Informal Supports for College and Training Programs 25. Self-Advocacy Scenarios 26. Self-Determination/Self-Advocacy Checklist
21. Makes personal decisions.	17 indicators (p. 27)	1. Job-Related Preferences Checklist 6. Reflecting on My Interests 24. How Do You Know You're Successful? Goal Attainment Scale 25. Self-Advocacy Scenarios 47. Health Quiz
22. Sets goals based on personal preferences, interests, strengths, and needs.	9 indicators (p. 27)	24. How Do You Know You're Successful? Goal Attainment Scale 26. Self-Determination/Self-Advocacy Checklist
23. Plans for reaching goals and making plans work.	10 indicators (p. 28)	24. How Do You Know You're Successful? Goal Attainment Scale 26. Self-Determination/Self-Advocacy Checklist
24. Knows his/her basic legal rights.	15 indicators (p. 28)	22. Americans With Disabilities Act (ADA) Quiz 34. Citizenship and Legal Skills 35. Citizenship Scenarios
25. Knows how to make legal decisions affecting his/her life.	14 indicators (pp. 28–29)	34. Citizenship and Legal Skills 35. Citizenship Scenarios

FIGURE 15–8 Levels of Assessment for Self Determination

Source: From *Informal Assessments for Transition Planning, Second Edition Manual* (p. 8-9), by A. S. Gaumer Erickson, G. M. Clark and J. R. Patton, 2013, Austin, TX: PRO-ED. Copyright 2013 by PRO-ED, Inc. Reprinted with permission.

Summary of Performance. IDEA mandates that a summary of the student's academic achievement and functional performance, along with recommendations on how to help the student in meeting his or her post-secondary goals, be developed prior to the student's leaving school. The summary of performance provision is not part of the transition services section of the IDEA; however, this provision is clearly part of the transition process. As Patton, Clark, and Trainor (2009) suggest, "The *summary of performance* provision is focused on providing the student, as well as his or her family, with information that will be useful in the future across a range of settings" (p. 5).

LEARNING MODULE 15.1 Click here to learn more about helping students with disabilities plans for the post–high school setting. http://iris.peabody.vanderbilt.edu/module/tran

CONCLUDING THOUGHTS

The preceding discussion has not exhaustively covered all transition issues. The transition needs of youth in special education are being addressed in both general and special education, by transition specialists within special education, and by researchers who specialize in studying how adolescents with disabilities move from high school to the demands of adult living. Additionally, most parents and families engage children with disabilities in transition-related issues in an ongoing manner.

Considering the breadth of transition within the field of special education, many important discussions are beyond the scope of this chapter. Additional concerns include access to the general curriculum and graduation requirements and high-stakes assessment outcomes. Each of these issues intersects with the aforementioned foci in this field.

Students with disabilities—and their family members—are key players in participating actively in the transition process and ultimately in navigating the sometimes rough waters of life in the community for their sons and daughters. Additionally, questions about linguistic and cultural diversity must be recognized and considered in problem-solving efforts around access and accountability. Finally, each of these issues must be considered in the context of the individual, with a particular focus on related strengths, needs, and preferences.

 Check Your Understanding 15.3 Click here to gauge your understanding of the concepts in this section.

ACTIVITIES

1. A positive attitude and enthusiasm are key characteristics for success in the workplace. Discuss with students what constitutes a positive and negative attitude and the importance of having a positive attitude instead of a negative one. Have students understand that having high self-esteem is important to the development of a positive attitude. The dice game below can be used to help students develop a positive attitude toward them. In groups, students will take turns rolling the dice twice or three times and will complete the given statement on each turn (roll).

> Roll 1: I am thankful for . . .
>
> Roll 2: Other people compliment me on my ability to . . .
>
> Roll 3: Something I would like other people to know about me is . . .
>
> Roll 4: I feel really good about myself when . . .
>
> Roll 5: I am proud of my ability to . . .
>
> Roll 6: Something nice I recently did for someone else was . . .

2. Have students record in their journals the positive things they see happening throughout their day, such as at school, in the supermarket, on the road, at home, and so on. They can also focus on one of their personal failures and explain how they used this failure to help them become a better, more successful individual and decision maker. In their journals, students can also explain whether they believe/think failure is important and why.

3. Engage students in role-play activities that will enable them to practice in verbal and non-verbal communication skills needed in the workplace The role-plays will also engage students in using the essential vocabulary words that are commonly used in the workplace, such as hours, income, and responsibility.

4. Students can be engaged in completing career worksheets online that can help them get to know themselves better in terms of their likes/dislikes, interests, and so on and then receive a list of careers that match their personalities and characteristics.

5. Students can be taken out to spend the day at various business establishments of their interest where they will gain opportunities to interact with workers and other personnel so that they can receive firsthand information of what the job entails. They will also be able to discover whether the job fulfills their expectations and whether they have the necessary skills to be successful in this chosen career.

6. Students can be placed in various business establishments which relate to their areas of interest at least once or twice a week on a voluntary basis. Doing this will help students receive the necessary training in order to acquire the skills that they need for a field of work, such as in communication, social interaction, problem solving, and responsibility.

7. Create a rating scale of appropriate communication behaviors that may be observed at school and at home. Observe the student communicating with others. Rate the student as you observe his or her strengths and weaknesses. Provide intervention to develop the student's weak areas. Parental involvement is important in this activity.

8. Students will choose a career, research it, and present all they know about this particular career. Students may choose to use actual professionals in the field or videos of such or lead the information session through. This activity may work much like a show and tell.

APPENDIX 15–A   Middle school transition inventory

Secondary Demands	Specific Areas of Focus	Level of Proficiency			
		Not Proficient	Partially Proficient	Proficient	Highly Proficient
Academic Skill Demands	• Reading rate—flexibility in using different types of reading skills such as reading for meaning, skimming, and scanning	0	1	2	3
	• Listening skills—primarily for lecture-type classes; following directions	0	1	2	3
	• Writing skills—to complete in-class assignments, homework, report writing, and other course requirements that involve writing	0	1	2	3
	• Speaking skills—for oral presentations in class, communication with classmates/teacher, negotiation, persuasion	0	1	2	3
Content/Performance Demands	• Adequate knowledge base in foundational content areas:				
	• language arts	0	1	2	3
	• math	0	1	2	3
	• science	0	1	2	3
	• social studies	0	1	2	3
	• Adequate levels of skill competence in performing certain activities related to foundational content areas (e.g., lab skills, manipulating materials)	0	1	2	3
Academic Support Demands	• Technological competence	0	1	2	3
	• Homework skills (school and home)	0	1	2	3
	• Research skills (papers, projects)	0	1	2	3
	• Note taking/outlining/paraphrasing	0	1	2	3
	• Use of graphic aids	0	1	2	3
	• Test preparation/test taking	0	1	2	3
	• Library usage	0	1	2	3
	• Use of reference materials—print and online	0	1	2	3
	• Organizational strategies	0	1	2	3
	• Scheduling and time management	0	1	2	3
	• Self-management (e.g., goal setting)	0	1	2	3
Social/Personal/ Adaptive Demands	• Interpersonal skills:				
	• Collaborative competence (i.e., ability to learn with peers)	0	1	2	3
	• Cooperating with others in group situations	0	1	2	3
	• Perspective taking (i.e., ability to appreciate others' points of view)	0	1	2	3
	• Negotiation (e.g., ability to resolve different points of view)	0	1	2	3
	• Making and maintaining friendships	0	1	2	3

Secondary Demands	Specific Areas of Focus	Level of Proficiency			
		Not Proficient	**Partially Proficient**	**Proficient**	**Highly Proficient**
	• Initiating conversation	0	1	2	3
	• Getting along with classmates	0	1	2	3
	• Respecting the rights of others	0	1	2	3
	• Personal skills:				
	• Having self-advocacy skills	0	1	2	3
	• Being aware of one's strengths and weaknesses (e.g., academic, social, behavioral)	0	1	2	3
	• Accepting feedback/criticism	0	1	2	3
	• Accepting praise/compliments	0	1	2	3
	• Managing stress	0	1	2	3
	• Handling failure/rejection/disappointments	0	1	2	3
	• Managing anger	0	1	2	3
	• Disagreeing appropriately	0	1	2	3
	• Giving critical feedback	0	1	2	3
	• Giving praise/compliments	0	1	2	3
	• Being aware of and understanding classmates' behavior	0	1	2	3
	• Expressing appreciation	0	1	2	3
	• Encouraging classmates	0	1	2	3
	• Classroom survival skills:				
	• Following classroom rules and procedures	0	1	2	3
	• Respecting authority	0	1	2	3
	• Obtaining teacher attention appropriately	0	1	2	3
	• Seeking assistance appropriately	0	1	2	3
Nonacademic Demands	• Logical demands:				
	• Locker usage	0	1	2	3
	• Lunch	0	1	2	3
	• Managing daily class schedule	0	1	2	3
	• Movement from classroom to classroom	0	1	2	3
	• Transportation (e.g., bus identification)	0	1	2	3
	• Personal safety (i.e., how to take protective measures to ensure safety)	0	1	2	3
	• Readiness for extracurricular opportunities:				
	• Clubs and organizations	0	1	2	3
	• Sports	0	1	2	3
	• Social events	0	1	2	3

APPENDIX 15–B   Checklist for transition to middle school

During the final year of elementary school:
— Administer some type of needs assessment such as the Middle School Transition Inventory
— Address areas identified through the needs assessment through instruction
— Identify supports and services that will be needed when the student gets to middle school
— Determine concerns that the student might have in regard to going to middle school
— Determine concerns of parents/guardians regarding the middle school experience
— Ensure that student demonstrates self-management/self-advocacy skills, especially if the student will be in general education classes
— Connect parents/guardians with other parents who have had children attend middle school

During the months prior to entering middle school:
— Visit the middle school on more than one occasion and at different times of day, especially at the beginning and end of the school day
— Check out the website of the middle school to get a feel for what is going on
— Identify key individuals at the middle school who can be contacted for information and guidance
— Request meeting that includes student, parents/guardians, current school personnel (elementary level), and future school personnel (middle school) to increase the probability of a seamless transition to middle school
— Become acquainted with course offerings, extracurricular options, and other features of the middle school experience
— Attend ALL orientation events (typically there will be only one) that are provided to students and their families who will be moving from the elementary level to the middle school level
— Provide opportunities for students to practice using lockers, moving quickly from one class to another, getting from and to transportation

During the first few weeks of middle school:
— Identify/locate a peer or peers who can act as supports for the students across all areas of need
— Assess how well the student is handling the routines/procedures of middle school
— Modify routines/procedures that have become problems for the student (e.g., tardiness to getting to classes on time)
— Assess how well the student is handling the academic demands of middle school
— Assess how well the student is handling the social aspects of middle school
— Encourage students to get involved in extracurricular activities

Throughout middle school:
— Monitor areas of problem as identified prior to going to middle school as well as any problems that arose after arrival
— Monitor student's academic and social/behavioral performance on an ongoing basis
— Continue to assess any concerns that parents/guardians might have
— Create opportunities for families to talk with each other about a wide range of issues and concerns that arise
— Begin to prepare for the next transition: moving from middle school to high school

A to Z Teacher Stuff. (2015). *Grades 6 to 8 lesson plans*. Retrieved from http://atozteacherstuff.com/Lesson_Plans/Language_Arts/_Grades_6-8/index.shtml

Abery, B., Rudrud, L., Arndt, K., Schauben, L., & Eggebeen, A. (1995). Evaluating a multicomponent program for enhancing the self-determination of youth with disabilities. *Intervention in School and Clinic, 30*, 170–179.

Ae-Hwa Kim, B., Vaughn, S., Wanzek, J., & Shangjin Wei, J. (2004). Graphic organizers and their effects on the reading comprehension of students with LD: A synthesis of research. *Journal of Learning Disabilities, 37*, 105–118.

Agran, M., Cain, H. M., & Cavin, M. D. (2002). Enhancing the involvement of rehabilitation counselors in the transition process. *Career Development for Exceptional Individuals, 25*, 141–155.

Airasian, P. W., & Russell, M. K. (2008). *Classroom assessment: Concepts and applications* (6th ed.). New York: McGraw-Hill.

Alberto, P. A., & Troutman, A. C. (2006). *Applied behavior analysis for teachers* (7th ed.). Upper Saddle River, NJ: Merrill/Pearson.

Allison, N. (2015). *Curriculum-based language assessments*. Retrieved from http://southeastareacoop.org/wp-content/uploads/2014/09/Curriculum-Based-Language-Assessment.pdf

Allor, J. H., Gifford, D. B., Al Otaiba, S., Miller, S. J., & Cheatham, J. P. (2013). Teaching students with intellectual disability to integrate reading skills: Effects of text and text-based lessons. *Remedial and Special Education, 34*(6), 346–356.

Allor, J. H., Mathes, P. G., Jones, F. G., Champlin, T. M., & Cheatham, J. P. (2010). Individualized research-based reading instruction for students with intellectual disabilities: Success stories. *Teaching Exceptional Children, 42*(3), 6–12.

Allor, J. H., Mathes, P. G., Roberts, J. K., Jones, F. G., & Champlin, T. M. (2010). Teaching students with moderate intellectual disabilities to read: An experimental examination of a comprehensive reading intervention. *Education and Training in Autism and Developmental Disabilities, 45*, 3–22.

Allor, J. H., Mathes, P. G., Roberts, J. K., Cheatham, J. P., & Otaiba, S. A. (2014). Is scientifically based reading instruction effective for students with below-average IQs? *Exceptional Children, 80*(3), 287–306. doi:10.1177/0014402914522208

Alston, J., & Taylor, J. (1987). *Handwriting: Theory, research and practice*. Beckenham: Croom Helm.

American Institute for Research. (2016). *The Access Center: Improving Outcomes for All Students K–8*. Retrieved from http://www.k8accesscenter.org

American Speech-Language-Hearing Association. (2012). *2012 schools survey*. Retrieved from http://www.asha.org/uploadedFiles/Schools-2012-Caseload.pdf

American Speech-Language-Hearing Association (2015). *Late blooming or language problem?* Retrieved from http://www.asha.org/public/speech/disorders/LateBlooming.htm

American Speech-Language-Hearing Association (2015a). *Augmentative and alternative communication*. Retrieved from http://www.asha.org/public/speech/disorders/AAC

American Speech-Language-Hearing Association. (2015b). *Dynamic assessment*. Retrieved from http://www.asha.org/practice/multicultural/issues/Dynamic-Assessment.htm

American Speech-Language-Hearing Association. (2015c). *Language based learning disabilities*. Retrieved from http://www.asha.org/public/speech/disorders/LBLD.htm

American Speech-Language-Hearing Association. (2015d). *Late blooming or language problem?* Retrieved from http://www.asha.org/public/speech/disorders/LateBlooming.htm

Andrade, H., & Valtcheva, A. (2009). Promoting learning and achievement through self-assessment. *Theory into Practice, 48*, 12–19.

Argyle, M. (1967). *The psychology of interpersonal behavior*. London: Penguin.

Argyle, M., & Kendon, A. (1967). The experimental analysis of social performance. *Advances in Experimental Social Psychology, 3*, 55–97.

Armbruster, B., Lehr, F., & Osborn, J. (2001). *Put reading first: The research building blocks for teaching children to read. Kindergarten through Grade 3*. Washington, DC: National Institute of Child Health and Human Development. (ERIC Document Reproduction Service No. ED458 536)

Asaro-Saddler, K. (2014). Self-regulated strategy development: Effects on writers with autism spectrum disorders. *Education and Training in Autism and Developmental Disabilities, 49*(1), 78–91.

Asaro, K., & Saddler, B. (2009). Effects of planning instruction on a young writer with Asperger's syndrome. *Intervention in School and Clinic, 44*, 268–275.

Athanases, S., & Achinstein, B. (2003). Focusing new instructors on individual and low performing students: The centrality of formative assessment in students: A pilot study. *Computers and Education*, 54, 1248–1253.

Bailey, G., Shaw, E. L., & Hollifield, D. (2006). The devaluation of social studies in the elementary grades. *Journal of Social Studies Research*, 30(2), 18–30.

Baker, S. K., Chard, D. J., Ketterlin-Geller, L. R., Apichatabutra, C., & Doabler, C. (2009). Teaching writing to at-risk students: The quality of evidence for self-regulated strategy development. *Exceptional Children*, 75(3), 303–318.

Balu, R., Zhu, P., Doolittle, F., Schiller, E., Jenkins, J., Gersten, R., et al. (2015). *Evaluation of response to intervention practices for elementary school reading executive summary* (NCEE 2016-4000). Washington, DC: National Center for Education Evaluation and Regional Assistance.

Bambara, L. M., & Kern, L. *Individualized supports for students with problem behaviors: Designing positive behavior plans.* New York: Guilford Press.

Bandura, A. (1977). Self-efficacy: Toward a unifying theory of behavior change. *Psychological Review*, 84, 191–215.

Baroody, A. J. (1987). Children's mathematical thinking: *A developmental framework for preschool, primary, and special education teachers.* New York: Teachers College Press.

Barrera, I., Corso, R., & Macpherson, D. (2003). *Skilled dialogue: Strategies for responding to cultural diversity in early childhood.* Baltimore: Brookes.

Barrish, H. H., Saunders, M., & Wolf, M. M. (1969). Good behavior game: Effects of individual contingencies for group consequences on disruptive behavior in a classroom. *Journal of Applied Behavior Analysis*, 2, 119–124.

Bassett, D. S., & Lehmann, J. (2002). *Student-focused conferencing and planning.* Austin, TX: PRO-ED.

Bateman, B. D. (1971). *The essentials of teaching.* Sioux Falls, SD: Dimensions.

Bates, E. (1976). *Language and context: The acquisition of pragmatics.* New York: Academic Press.

Bauminger, N., & Kimhi-Kind, I. (2008). Social information processing, security of attachment, and emotional regulation in children with learning disabilities. *Journal of Learning Disabilities*, 41(4), 315–332. doi:10.1177/0022219408316095

Bauwens, J., & Hourcade, J. (1995). *Cooperative teaching.* Austin, TX: PRO-ED.

Beatty, L. S., Gardner, E. G., Madden, R., & Karlsen, B. (2002). *Stanford Diagnostic Mathematics Test—Fourth Edition.* San Antonio, TX: Psychological Assessment Resources.

Beirne-Smith, M. (2012). Spelling assessment and instruction. In E. A. Polloway, L. Miller, & T. E. C.

Smith (Eds.), *Language instruction for students with special needs* (4th ed., pp. 373–406). Denver, CO: Love.

Beirne-Smith, M., Patton, J. R., & Kim, S. H. (2006). *Mental retardation: An introduction to intellectual disabilities* (7th ed.). Upper Saddle River, NJ: Pearson Merrill Prentice Hall.

Bellack, A. S., & Hersen, M. (1979). *Research and practice in social skills.* New York: Plenum Press.

Bender, W. N. (2005). *Differentiating math instruction: Strategies that work for K–8 classrooms.* Thousand Oaks, CA: Corwin Press.

Bender, W. N. (2008). *Differentiating instruction for students with learning disabilities: Best teaching practices for general and special educators.* Thousand Oaks, CA: Corwin Press.

Bereiter, C., & Engelmann, S. (1966). *Teaching disadvantaged children in the preschool.* Upper Saddle River, NJ: Prentice Hall.

Berkeley, S., Scruggs, T. E., & Mastropieri, M. A. (2010). Reading comprehension instruction for students with learning disabilities, 1995–2006: A meta-analysis. *Remedial and Special Education*, 31, 423–436.

Berliner, D. C. (1988). The half-full glass: A review of research on teaching. In E. L. Meyen, G. A. Vergason, & R. J. Whelan (Eds.), *Effective instructional strategies for exceptional children* (pp. 7–31). Denver, CO: Love.

Bertin, P., & Perlman, E. (2000). After your students write: What's next? *Teaching Exceptional Children*, 20, 4–9.

Betty, M. (in press). IEPs and the development of measurable goals using SMART principles. In J. J. Hoover & J. R. Patton (Eds.), *IEPs for English language and other diverse learners.* Thousand Oaks, CA: Corwin Press.

Bialas, J. B., & Boon, R. (2010). Effects of self-monitoring on the classroom preparedness skills of kindergarten students at risk for developmental disabilities. *Australian Journal of Early Childhood*, 35(4), 40–52.

Bickel, W. E., & Bickel, D. D. (1986). Effective schools, classrooms, and instruction: Implications for special education. *Exceptional Children*, 52, 489–500.

Bijou, S. W., & Baer, D. M. (1978). *Behavior analysis of child development.* Upper Saddle River, NJ: Prentice Hall.

Birchell, G. R., & Taylor, B. L. (1986). Is the elementary social studies curriculum headed back-to-basics? *The Social Studies*, 77, 80–82.

Blachowicz, C., & Ogle, D. (2001). *Reading comprehension: Strategies for independent learners.* New York: Guilford Press.

Black, D. S. (2015). Mindfulness training for children and adolescents: A state-of-the-art review. In K. W. Brown, J. D. Creswell, & R. M. Ryan (Eds.), *Handbook of mindfulness: Theory, research, and practice.* New York: Guilford Press.

Blackbourn, J. M., Patton, J. R., & Trainor, A. (2004). *Exceptional individuals in focus*. Upper Saddle River, NJ: Pearson/Prentice Hall.

Blackwell, R., & Laman, S. (2013). Strategies to teach sight words in an elementary classroom. *International Journal of Education*, 5(4), 37–47. doi:10.5296/ije.v5i4.4024

Bley, N. S., & Thornton, C. A. (2011) *Teaching mathematics to students with learning disabilities* (5th ed.). Austin, TX: PRO-ED.

Boaler, J. (2016). *Mathematical mindsets: Unleashing students' potential through creative math, inspiring messages and innovative teaching*. San Francisco: Jossey-Bass.

Boardman, A. G., Arguelles, M. E., Vaughn, S., Hughes, M. T., & Klingner, J. (2005). Special education teachers' views of research-based practices. *Journal of Special Education*, 39, 168–180.

Bouck, E. C., Courtad, C. A., Heutsche, A., Okolo, C. M., & Englert, C. S. (2009). The virtual history museum: A universally designed approach to social studies instruction. *Teaching Exceptional Children*, 42(2), 14–20.

Bouck, E. C., & Satsangi, R. (2015). Is there really a difference? Distinguishing mild intellectual disability from similar disability categories. *Education and Training in Autism and Developmental Disabilities*, 50, 186–198.

Bowers, L., Huisingh, R., Loguidice, C., & Orman, J. (2005). *The WORD Test 2: Adolescent*. Austin, TX: PRO-ED.

Boyle, J. R. (2013). Strategic note-taking for inclusive middle school science classrooms. *Remedial and Special Education*, 34(2), 78–90.

Boyle, J. R., & Rivera, T. Z. (2012). Note-taking techniques for students with disabilities: A systematic review of the research. *Learning Disability Quarterly*, 35(3), 131–143. doi:10.1177/0731948711435794

Bradshaw, C. P., Zmuda, J. H., Kellam, S. C., & Ialango, N. S. (2009). Longitudinal impact of two universal preventative interventions in first grade on educational outcomes in high school. *Journal of Educational Psychology*, 10(1), 926–937.

Brigance, A. H. (1990). *Brigance Diagnostic Inventory of Essential Skills*. North Billerica, MA: Curriculum Associates.

Brigance, A. H. (2010). *Brigance Transition Skills Inventory*. North Billerica, MA: Curriculum Associates.

Brigham, F. J., Berkeley, S., Simpkins, P., & Brigham, M. S. P. (2007). A focus on reading comprehension strategy instruction. *Current Practice Alerts*, no. 12, 1–4.

Brigham, R., & Brigham, M. (2001) Mnemonic instruction. *Current Practice Alerts*, 5 (1), 1–4.

Brigham, F. J., Scruggs, T. E., & Mastropieri, M. A. (2011). Science education and students with learning disabilities. *Learning Disabilities Research and Practice*, 26(4), 223–232. doi:10.1111/j.1540-5826.2011.00343.x

Brolin, D. (1995). *Life centered career education: A competency based approach*. Reston, VA: Council for Exceptional Children.

Brolin, D. E. (2004). *Life-centered career education: A competency-based approach* (4th ed.). Reston, VA: Council for Exceptional Children.

Brophy, J., Alleman, J., & Knighton, B. (2009). *Inside the social studies in the classroom*. New York: Routledge.

Browder, D. M., Trela, K., Gibbs, S. L., Wakeman, S., & Harris, A. A. (2007). Academic skills: Reading and mathematics. In S. L. Odom, R. Horner, M. E. Snell, & J. B. Blacher (Eds.), *Handbook of developmental disabilities* (pp. 292–309). New York: Guilford Press.

Brown University Education Alliance. (2015). *Teaching diverse learners*. Retrieved from http://www.brown.edu/academics/education-alliance/teaching-diverse-learners

Brown, A. L., & Palincsar, A. (1982). Inducing strategic learning from texts by means of informed, self-control training. *Topics in Learning and Learning Disabilities*, 2(1), 1–17.

Brown, B. A., & Ryoo, K. (2008). Teaching science as a language: A content-first approach to science teaching. *Journal of Research in Science Teaching*, 45(5), 529–553.

Brown, K. W., Creswell, J. D., & Ryan, R. M. (2015). *Handbook of mindfulness: Theory, research, and practice*. New York: Guilford Press.

Brown, L. (2004). Evaluating and managing classroom behavior. In D. D. Hammill & N. R. Bartel (Eds.), *Teaching students with learning and behavior problems* (7th ed.). Austin, TX: PRO-ED.

Brown, V., Cronin, M., & Bryant, D. (2012). *Test of mathematical abilities—Third Edition*. Austin, TX: PRO-ED.

Brown, V. L., Weiderholt, J. L., & Hammill, D. D. (2009). *Test of Reading Comprehension—Fourth Edition*. Austin, TX: PRO-ED.

Bruce, A. (2015). *Cognitive factors' influence on fraction development in students of varying ability levels*. Unpublished dissertation, University of Virginia, Charlottesville.

Brueckner, L. J., & Bond, G. L. (1967). Diagnosis and treatment of learning difficulties. In E. C. Frierson & W. B. Barbe (Eds.), *Educating children with learning disabilities*. New York: Appleton-Century-Crofts.

Bryan, T. (1983, October). *The hidden curriculum: Social and communication skills*. Paper presented at Lynchburg College, Lynchburg, VA.

Bryant, B., & Blalock, G. (2000). *Gray Silent Reading Tests*. Austin, TX: PRO-ED.

Bryant, B. R., & Bryant, D. P. (2008). Introduction to the special series: Mathematics and learning disabilities. *Learning Disability Quarterly*, *31*(1), 3–8.

Bryant, B. R., Pedrotty Bryant, D., Kethley, C., Kim, S. A., Pool, C., & Seo, Y. J. (2008, Winter). Preventing mathematics difficulties in the primary grade: The critical features of instruction in textbooks as part of the equation. *Learning Disability Quarterly*, *31*(1), 21–35.

Bryant, B. R., Wiederholt, J. L., & Bryant, P. B. (2004). *Gray Diagnostic Reading Tests—Second Edition*. Austin, TX: PRO-ED.

Bryant, D. P., Bryant, B. R., Gersten, R., Scammacca, N., & Chavez, M. M. (2008). Mathematics intervention for first- and second-grade students with mathematics difficulties: The effects of tier 2 intervention delivered as booster lessons. *Remedial and Special Education*, *29*(1), 20–32. doi:10.1177/0741932507309712

Bryant, M. T. (2001). *School district reorganization on the Great Plains. The Rural Educator*. Fort Collins, CO: National Rural School Association.

Buck, G. H. (2008). Creative arts: Visual arts, music, dance and drama. In E. A. Polloway, J. R. Patton, & L. Serna (Eds.), *Strategies for teaching learners with special needs* (pp. 347–369). Upper Saddle River, NJ: Pearson.

Bulgren, J. (2004). Effective content-area instruction for all students. In T. E. Scruggs & M. A. Mastropieri (Eds.), *Advances in learning and behavioral disabilities: Vol. 17. Research in secondary schools* (pp. 147–174). San Diego, CA: Elsevier.

Bulgren, J., Deshler, D., & Lenz, K. (2007). Engaging adolescents with LD in higher order thinking about history concepts using integrated content enhancement routines. *Journal of Learning Disabilities*, *40*, 97–192.

Bulgren, J. A., Sampson Graner, P., & Deshler, D. D. (2013). Literacy challenges and opportunities for students with learning disabilities in social studies and history. *Learning Disabilities Research and Practice*, *28*(1), 17–27. doi:10.1111/ldrp.12003

Bulgren, J. A., Schumaker, J. B., & Deshler, D. D. (1988). Effectiveness of a concept teaching routine in enhancing the performance of LD students in secondary-level mainstream classes. *Learning Disability Quarterly*, *11*(1), 3–17.

Bullock, J., Pierce, S., & McClellan, L. (1989). *TouchMath*. Colorado Springs, CO: Innovative Learning Systems.

Burns, M. K., Walick, C., Simonson, G. R., Dominguez, L., Harelstad, L., Kincaid, A., et al. (2015). Using a conceptual understanding and procedural fluency heuristic to target math interventions with students in early elementary. *Learning Disabilities Research and Practice*, *30*(2), 52–60.

Burns, M. K., & Ysseldyke, J. E. (2009). Reported prevalence of evidence-based instructional practices in special education. *Journal of Special Education*, *43*, 3–11.

Bursuck, W., & Damer, M. (2007). *Reading instruction for students who are at risk or have disabilities*. Boston: Allyn & Bacon.

Business Insider. (2015). *Chart of the day: Kids send a mind boggling number of texts every month*. Retrieved from http://www.businessinsider.com/chart-of-the-day-number-of-texts-sent-2013-3?op=1

Butler, D. L., Elaschuk, C. L., & Poole, S. (2000). Promoting strategic writing by postsecondary students with learning disabilities: A report of three case studies. *Learning Disability Quarterly*, *23*, 196–213.

Butler, D. N. (2005). Promoting strategic learning by eighth-grade students struggling in mathematics: A report of three case studies. *Learning Disabilities Research and Practice*, *20*(3), 156–174.

Cahill, S. M. (2009). Where does handwriting fit in? Strategies to support academic achievement. *Intervention in School and Clinic*, *44*(4), 223–228. Retrieved from http://search.ebscohost.com/login.aspx?direct=true&db=eric&AN=EJ830745&site=eds-live&scope=site; http://dx.doi.org/10.1177/1053451208328826

Cain, S. E., & Evans, J. M. (1984). *Sciencing: An involvement approach to elementary science methods* (2nd ed.). Columbus, OH: Merrill.

Cain, S. E., & Evans, J. M. (1990). *Sciencing: An involvement approach to elementary science methods* (3rd ed.). Upper Saddle River, NJ: Prentice Hall.

Calhoon, M. B., Al Otaiba, S. A., & Greenberg, D. (2010). Introduction to special issue, spelling knowledge: Implications for instruction and intervention. *Learning Disability Quarterly*, *33*, 145–147.

Calhoon, M. B., Greenberg, D., & Hunter, C. V. (2010). A comparison of standardized spelling assessments: Do they measure similar orthographic qualities? *Learning Disability Quarterly*, *33*, 159–170.

Campbell, P. H., & Halbert, J. (2002). Between research and practice: Provider perspectives on early intervention. *Topics in Early Childhood Special Education*, *22*, 213–226.

Campbell, P., & Siperstein, G. (1994). *Improving social competence: A resource for elementary school teachers*. Needham Heights, MA: Allyn & Bacon, Simon & Schuster Education Group.

Carin, A. A., Bass, J. E., & Contant, T. L. (2005). *Methods for teaching science as inquiry* (9th ed.). Upper Saddle River, NJ: Pearson.

Carnine, D. (1995, April). *The BIG accommodation for the middle grades*. Presentation at the annual meeting of the Council for Exceptional Children, Indianapolis, IN.

Carnine, D., Crawford, D., Harniss, M., & Hollenbeck, K. (1995). *Understanding U.S. history* (Vol. 1), Eugene, OR: Considerate Publishing.

Carnine, D. W., Silbert, J., Kame'enui, E. J., & Tarver, S. (2004). *Direct instruction reading* (4th ed.). Upper Saddle River, NJ: Merrill/Pearson.

Carrow-Woolfolk, E. (2011). *Oral and Written Language Scale—Second Edition*. Austin, TX: PRO-ED.

Carter, E. W., Cushing, L. S., Clark, N. M., & Kennedy, C. H. (2005). Moving from elementary to middle school: Supporting a smooth transition for students with severe disabilities. *Teaching Exceptional Children*, 37(6), 15–25.

Cartledge, G., Lo, Y., Vincent, C. A., & Robinson-Ervin, P. (2015). Culturally responsive classroom management. In E. T. Emmer & E. J. Sabornie (Eds.), *Handbook of classroom management* (2nd ed., pp. 205–219). New York: Routledge, Taylor & Francis Group.

Cash, D. (2011). *The 3-2-1 strategy*. Unpublished manuscript.

Cawley, J. F. (Ed.). (1984). *Developmental teaching of mathematics for the learning disabled*. Austin, TX: PRO-ED.

Cawley, J. F. (1994). Science for students with disabilities. *Remedial and Special Education*, 15, 67–71.

Cawley, J. F. (2002). Mathematics interventions and students with high-incidence disabilities. *Remedial and Special Education*, 23, 2–6.

Cawley, J. F., Fitzmaurice-Hayes, A. M., & Shaw, R. A. (1988). *Mathematics for the mildly handicapped: A guide to curriculum and instruction*. Boston: Allyn & Bacon.

Cawley, J. F., Foley, T. E., & Miller, J. (2003). Science and students with mild disabilities: Principles of universal design. *Intervention in School and Clinic*, 38(3), 160–171. doi:10.1177/10534512030380030501

Cawley, J. F., Goodstein, H. A., Fitzmaurice, A. M., Lepore, A., Sedlak, R. A., & Althaus, V. (1976, 1977). *Project MATH: Mathematics activities for teaching the handicapped: Levels I–V*. Tulsa, OK: Educational Progress Corporation.

Cawley, J. F., Miller, D., & Carr, S. (1989). Arithmetic. In G. A. Robinson, J. R. Patton, E. A. Polloway, & L. R. Sargent (Eds.), *Best practices in mental retardation* (pp. 67–86). Reston, VA: Division on Mental Retardation, Council for Exceptional Children.

Cawley, J. F., Miller, J., & School, B. (1987). A brief inquiry of arithmetic word-problem solving among learning disabled secondary students. *Learning Disabilities Focus*, 2(2), 87–93.

Cawley, J. F., Miller, J., Sentman, J. R., & Bennett, S. (1993). *Science for all (SAC)*. Buffalo: State University of New York Press.

Center on Education Policy. (2006). *From the capital to the classroom: Year 4 of the NCLBA*. Washington, DC: Author.

Chalk, J. C., Hagan-Burke, S., & Burke, M. D. (2005). The effects of self-regulated strategy development on the writing process for high school students with learning disabilities. *Learning Disability Quarterly*, 28, 75–87.

Chandler, L. K. (1993). Steps in preparing for transition: Preschool to kindergarten. *Teaching Exceptional Children*, 25, 52–55.

Ciullo, S., Falcomata, T., & Vaughn, S. (2015). Teaching social studies to upper elementary students with learning disabilities: Graphic organizers and explicit instruction. *Learning Disability Quarterly*, 38(1), 15–26.

Clark, G. M. (1979). *Career education for the handicapped child in the elementary classroom*. Denver, CO: Love.

Clark, G. M., Carlson, B. C., Fisher, S., Cook, I. D., & D'Alonzo, B. J. (1991). *Career development for students with disabilities in elementary schools: A position statement of the Division on Career Development*. Reston, VA: Division on Career Development, Council for Exceptional Children.

Clark, G. M., Field, S., Patton, J. R., Brolin, D. E., & Sitlington, P. L. (1994). Life skills instruction: A necessary component for all students with disabilities: A position statement of the Division on Career Development and Transition. *Career Development for Exceptional Individuals*, 17(2), 125–133. doi:10.1177/088572889401700202

Clark, G. M., Synatschk, K., Patton, J. R., & Steel, E. (2012). *Career interests, preferences and strengths inventory*. Austin, TX: PRO-ED.

Cockrum, W., & Shanker, J. L. (2013). *Locating and correcting reading difficulties*, (10th ed.). Columbus, OH: Pearson.

Cohen, L. G., & Spenciner, L. J. (2007). The role of extended time and item content on a high-stakes mathematics test. *Learning Disabilities Research and Practice*, 20, 225–233.

Cohen, L., & Spenciner, L. J. (2008). *Teaching students with mild and moderate disabilities: Research-based practices*. Upper Saddle River, NJ: Merrill/Pearson.

Cohen, L. G., & Spenciner, L. J. (2014). *Assessment of children and youth with special needs. Pearson eText with Loose-Leaf Version* (5th ed.). Boston: Pearson.

Coker, D. L., & Ritchey, K. D. (2010). Curriculum based measurement of writing in kindergarten and first grade: An investigation of production and qualitative scores. *Exceptional Children*, 76, 175–193.

Coman, M., & Heavers, K. (2001). *How to improve your study skills*. New York: Glencoe McGraw-Hill.

Committee for Children. (2011). *Second Step*. Seattle: Second Step Suites.

Common Core State Standards Initiative. (2010). *Common core standards*. Retrieved from http://www.corestandards.org/wp-content/uploads/ELA_Standards1.pdf

Conderman, G., & Pedersen, T. (2010). Preparing students with mild disabilities for state and district tests. *Intervention in School and Clinic, 45*(4), 232–241.

Conners, C. K. (2008). *Conners Rating Scales—Third Edition*. San Antonio, TX: Pearson.

Connolly, A. J. (2007). *KeyMath3 Diagnostic Assessment*. Minneapolis: NSC Pearson.

Cook, B. G., Buysse, V., Klingner, J., Landrum, T. J., McWilliam, R. A., Tankersley, M., et al. (2015). CEC's standards for classifying the evidence base of practices in special education. *Remedial and Special Education, 36*(4), 220–234. doi:10.1177/0741932514557271

Cook, B. G., Tankersley, M., & Landrum, T. J. (2009). Determining evidence-based practices in special education. *Exceptional Children, 75*, 365–383.

Cook, C. R., Gresham, F. M., Kern, L., Barreras, R. B., Thornton, S., & Crews, S. D. (2008). Social skills training for secondary students with emotional and/or behavioral disorders. *Journal of Emotional and Behavioral Disorders, 16*(3), 131–144. doi:10.1177/10663426608314541

Cooke, N. L., Heron, T. E., & Heward, W. L. (1983). *Peer tutoring: Implementing classwide programs in the primary grades*. Columbus, OH: Special Press.

Cooper-Duffy, K., Szedia, P., & Hyer, G. (2010). Teaching literacy to students with significant cognitive disabilities. *Teaching Exceptional Children, 42*(3), 30–39.

Cottrell, S. (2001). *Teaching study skills and supporting learning*. New York: Palgrave Macmillan.

Council for Exceptional Children. (2015). *What every special education teacher must know: Professional ethics and standards*. Reston, VA: Author.

Coyne, M. D., Kame'enui, E. J., & Carnine, D. W. (2007). *Effective teaching strategies that accommodate diverse learners* (3rd ed.). Upper Saddle River, NJ: Merrill/Pearson.

Cozzens, G., Dowdy, C., & Smith, T. E. C. (1999). *Adult agencies: Linkages for adolescents in transition*. Austin, TX: PRO-ED.

Crabtree, T., Alber-Morgan, S. R., & Konrad, M. (2010). The effects of self-monitoring of story elements on the reading comprehension of high school seniors with learning disabilities. *Education and Treatment of Children, 33*(2), 187–203.

Crescimbeni, J. (1965). *Arithmetic enrichment activities for elementary school children*. West Nyack, NY: Parker.

Cronin, M. E., & Patton, J. R. (2007). *Life skills for students with special needs: A practical guide for developing real-life programs* (2nd ed.). Austin, TX: PRO-ED.

Cronin, M., Patton, J. R., & Wood, S. J. (2007). *Life skills instruction: A practical guide for integrating real-life content into the curriculum at the elementary and secondary levels for students with special needs or who are placed at risk* (2nd ed.). Austin, TX: PRO-ED.

Damico, J. S., Smith, M., & Augustine, L. E. (1996). Multicultural populations and language disorders. In M. D. Smith & J. S. Damico (Eds.), *Childhood language disorders* (pp. 272–299). New York: Thieme Medical.

Darling-Hammond, L., Zielezinski, M. B., & Goldman, S. (2014). *Using technology to support at-risk students' learning*. Washington, DC: Alliance for Excellent Education.

Datchuk, S. M., Kubina, R. M., & Mason, L. H. (2015). Effects of sentence instruction and frequency building to a performance criterion on elementary-aged students with behavioral concerns and EBD. *Exceptionality, 23*(1), 34–53. Retrieved from http://search.ebscohost.com/login.aspx?direct=true&db=eric&AN=EJ1051341&site=eds-live&scope=site; http://dx.doi.org/10.1080/09362835.2014.986604

Dawson, J., & Stoute, C. (2013). *Structured Photographic Expressive Language Test—Third Edition*. Austin, TX: PRO-ED.

De la Paz, S., Morales, P., & Winston, P. (2007). Source interpretations: Teaching students with and without LD to read and write historically. *Journal of Learning Disabilities, 40*, 97–192.

Dean, C. B., Hubbell, E. R., Pitler, H., & Stone, B. J. (2014). *Classroom instruction that works: Research-based strategies for increasing student achievement* (2nd ed.). Boston: Pearson.

deFur, S. H., Todd-Allen, M., & Getzel, E. E. (2001). Parent participation in the transition planning process. *Career Development for Exceptional Individuals, 24*, 19–35.

deFur, S., & Williams, B. T. (2002). Cultural considerations in the transition process and standards-based education. In C. A. Kochhar-Bryant & D. S. Bassett (Eds.), *Aligning transition and standards-based education: Issues and strategies* (pp. 105–123). Arlington, VA: Council for Exceptional Children.

Denham, S. A. (2015). Assessment of SEL in educational contexts. In J. A. Durlak, C. E. Domitrovich, R. P. Weissberg, & T. P. Gullotta (Eds.), *Handbook of social and emotional learning: Research and practice* (pp. 285–300). New York: Guilford Press.

Dennis, M. S., Bryant, B. R., & Drogan, R. (2015). The impact of tier 2 mathematics instruction on second graders with mathematics difficulties. *Exceptionality*, 23(2), 124–145.

Deshler, D. D. (2005). Adolescents with learning disabilities: Unique challenges and reasons for hope. *Learning Disability Quarterly*, 28, 122–124.

Deshler, D. D., & Schumaker, J. B. (1986). Learning strategies: An instructional alternative for low-achieving adolescents. *Exceptional Children*, 52, 583–590.

Deshler, D.D., & Cornett, J. (2012). Leading to improve teacher effectiveness: Implications for practice, reform, research, and policy. In J. B. Crockett, B. S. Billingsley, & M. L. Boscardin (Eds.), *Handbook of leadership and administration for special education* (pp. 239–259). New York: Routledge.

Development Studies Center. (2006). *Caring School Community (CSC)*. Oakland, CA: Author.

Devereux Center for Resilient Children. (n.d.). *Devereux early childhood assessment preschool program*. Villanova, PA: Author.

Dewey, J. (1902). *The child and the curriculum*. Chicago: University of Chicago Press.

Dewey, J. (1938). *Experience and education*. New York: Collier Books.

Dexter, D. D., & Hughes, C. A. (2011). Graphic organizers and students with learning disabilities: A meta-analysis. *Learning Disability Quarterly*, 34, 51–72. Retrieved from http://ezproxy.lynchburg.edu/login?url=http://search.ebscohost.com/login.aspx?direct=true&db=edsjsr&AN=edsjsr.23053296&site=eds-live&scope=site

Dexter, D. D., Park, Y. J., & Hughes, C. A. (2011). A meta-analytic review of graphic organizers and science instruction for adolescents with learning disabilities: Implications for the intermediate and secondary science classroom. *Learning Disabilities Research and Practice*, 26(4), 204–213. doi:10.1111/j.1540-5826.2011.00341.x

Diliberto, J. A., & Brewer, D. (2012a). Six tips for successful IEP meetings. *Teaching Exceptional Children*, 44(4), 30–37.

Diliberto, J. A., & Brewer, D. (2012b). Six tips for successful IEP meetings. *Teaching Exceptional Disabilities*, 49(1), 78–91.

Doabler, C. T., Fien, H., Nelson-Walker, N., & Baker, S. K. (2012). Evaluating three elementary mathematics programs for presence of eight research-based instructional design principles. *Learning Disability Quarterly*, 35(4), 200–211.

Dodge, B. (2005). *WebQuest vs. Kleenex. WebQuest News*. Retrieved from http://webquest.org/news/index.html

Doyle, W. (2006). Ecological approaches to classroom management. In C. M. Evertson & C. S. Weinstein (Eds.), *Handbook of classroom management: Research, practice, and contemporary issues* (pp. 97–125). Mahwah, NJ: Lawrence Erlbaum Associates.

Dunlap, G., Kincaid, D., Horner, R. H., Knoster, T., & Bradshaw, C. P. (2014). A comment on the term "positive behavior support." *Journal of Positive Behavior Interventions*, 16(3), 133–136.

Durlak, J. A., Domitrovich, C. E., Weissberg, R. P., & Gullotta, T. P. (2015). *Handbook of social and emotional learning: Research and practice*. New York: Guilford Press.

Edgar, E. (1988). Employment as an outcome for mildly handicapped students: Current status and future directions. *Focus on Exceptional Children*, 21(1), 1–8.

Edgar, E., & Polloway, E. A. (1994). Education for adolescents with disabilities: Curriculum and placement issues. *Journal of Special Education*, 27, 438–452.

Edmark Associates. (2002). *Edmark Reading Program*. Seattle: Riverdeep Interactive Learning. http://itc.gsu.edu/academymodules/a304/support/xpages/a304b020600.html

Elias, M. J., & Schwab, Y. (2006). From compliance to responsibility: Social and emotional learning and classroom management. In C. M. Evertson & C. S. Weinstein (Eds.), *Handbook of classroom management: Research, practice, and contemporary issues* (pp. 309–342). Mahwah, NJ: Lawrence Erlbaum Associates.

Elksnin, C. K., & Elksnin, N. (2006). *Teaching social-emotional skills at school and home*. Denver, CO: Love.

Ellis, E. S., & Sabornie, E. J. (1986). *Teaching learning strategies to learning-disabled students in post-secondary settings*. Unpublished manuscript.

Embry, D. D., & Flannery, D. J. (1994). *Peacebuilders—Reducing youth violence: A working application of cognitive-social-imitative competence research*. Tucson, AZ: Heartsprings.

Enderle, J., & Severson, S. (2003). *Enderle-Severson Transition Rating Scales*. Moorhead, MN: ETRS.

Engelmann, S. (1999). *SRA Corrective Reading Program*. Chicago: Science Research Associates.

Engelmann, S. (2003). *Reading Mastery Program*. Chicago: Science Research Associates.

Engelmann, S., & Bruner, E. (1988). *DISTAR Reading*. Chicago: Science Research Associates.

Engelmann, S., & Carnine, D. (1981). *Corrective Mathematics*. Chicago: Science Research Associates.

Englert, C. S. (1983). Measuring special education teacher effectiveness. *Exceptional Children*, 50(3), 247–254.

Englert, C. S., & Mariage, T. V. (1991). Shared understandings: Structuring the writing experience through dialogue. *Journal of Learning Disabilities*, 24, 330–343.

Englert, C. S., Mariage, T. V., Garmon, M. A., & Tarrant, K. L. (1998). Accelerating reading progress in early literacy project classrooms: Three exploratory studies. *Remedial and Special Education*, *19*, 142–159, 180.

Englert, C. S., Tarrant, K. L., & Mariage, T. V. (1992). Defining and redefining instructional practice in special education: Perspectives on good teaching. *Teacher Education and Special Education*, *15*, 62–86.

Englert, C. S., Wu, X., & Zhao, Y. (2005). Cognitive tools for writing: Scaffolding the performance of students through technology. *Learning Disabilities Research and Practice*, *20*, 184–198.

English Linx. (2015). *Metaphors worksheets*. Retrieved from http://englishlinx.com/metaphors

Epstein, J. L., & Salinas, K. C. (2004). Partnering with families and communities. *Educational Leadership*, *61*(8), 12–18.

Epstein, M. H., & Sharma, H. M. (1998). *The Behavioral and Emotional Rating Scale: A strength based approach to assessment*. Austin, TX: PRO-ED.

Epstein, M. H., Polloway, E. A., Foley, R. M., & Patton, J. R. (1993). Homework: A comparison of teachers, and parents, perceptions of the problems experienced by students identified as having behavioral disorders, learning disabilities, and no disabilities. *Remedial and Special Education*, *14*(5), 40–50.

ESL Gold Net. (2015). *Idiom links*. Retrieved from http://www.eslgold.com/idioms/idioms_links.html

ESLprintables.com. (2016). *Slang language worksheets*. Retrieved from http://www.eslprintables.com/vocabulary_worksheets/idioms/slang_language

Esmode, I. (2009). Ideas and identities: Supporting equity in cooperative mathematics learning. *Review of Education Research*, *79*(2), 1008–1043.

Everson, J. M., Zhang, D., & Guillory, J. D. (2001). A statewide investigation of individualized transition plans in Louisiana. *Career Development for Exceptional Individuals*, *24*, 37–49.

Evertson, C. M., & Weinstein, C. S. (2006). *Handbook of classroom management: Research, practice, and contemporary issues*. Mahwah, NJ: Lawrence Erlbaum Associates.

Fallon, L. M., O'Keefe, B, V., Gage, N. A., & Sugai, G. (2015). Assessing attitudes toward culturally, and contextually relevant schoolwide positive behavior support strategies. *Behavioral Disorders*, *40*(4), 251–260.

Fallon, L. M., O'Keeffe, B. V., & Sugai, G. (2012). Consideration of culture and context in school-wide positive behavior support: A review of current literature. *Journal of Positive Behavior Interventions*, *14*(4), 209–219.

Farkas, S., & Duffett, A. M. (2010). *High schools, civics and citizenship: What social studies teachers think and do*. American Enterprise Institute Program on American Citizenship. Retrieved from http://www.aei.org/paper/100145

Feil, E. G., Severson, H. H., & Walker, H. M. (1998). Screening for emotional and behavioral delays: The Early Screening Project. *Journal of Early Intervention*, *21*(3), 252–266.

Fernald, G. (1943). *Remedial techniques in basic school subjects*. New York: McGraw-Hill.

Field, S., & Hoffman, A. (1992). *Steps to self-determination* (Field-Test Version). Detroit: Wayne State University, College of Education, Developmental Disabilities Institute.

Field, S., Hoffman, A., & Sawilowsky, S. (2004). *Self-Determination Assessment Battery*. Detroit: Wayne State University Press.

Finson, K. D., & Ormsbee, C. K. (1998). Rubrics and their use in inclusive science. *Intervention in School and Clinic*, *34*, 79–88.

Fitch, W. T. (2010). *The evolution of language*. Cambridge: Cambridge University Press.

Fletcher, D., Boon, R. T., & Cihak, D. F. (2010). Effects of the TOUCHMATH program compared to a number line strategy to teach addition facts to middle school students with moderate intellectual disabilities. *Education and Training in Autism and Developmental Disabilities*, *45*(3), 449–458.

Flores, M. M. (2010). Using the concrete–representational–abstract sequence to teach subtraction with regrouping to students at risk for failure. *Remedial and Special Education*, *31*(3), 195.

Flores, M. M., Hinton, V., & Strozier, S. D. (2014). Teaching subtraction and multiplication with regrouping using the concrete-representational-abstract sequence and strategic instruction model. *Learning Disabilities Research and Practice*, *29*(2), 75–88. doi:10.1111/ldrp.12032

Fontana, J. L., Scruggs, T., & Mastropieri, M. A. (2007). Mnemonic strategy instruction in inclusive secondary social studies classes. *Remedial and Special Education*, *28*(6), 345. Retrieved from http://ezproxy.lynchburg.edu/login?url=http://search.ebscohost.com/login.aspx?direct=true&db=f5h&AN=27616050&site=eds-live&scope=site

Ford, M. E. (1985). The concept of competence: Themes and variations. In H. A. Marlow & R. B. Weinberg (Eds.), *Competence development: Theory and practice in special populations* (pp. 3–38). Springfield, IL: Charles C. Thomas.

Freeman-Green, S. M., O'Brien, C., Wood, C. L., & Hitt, S. B. (2015). Effects of the SOLVE strategy on the mathematical problem solving skills of secondary students with learning disabilities. *Learning Disabilities Research and Practice*, *30*, 76–90. doi:10.1111/ldrp.12054

Fuchs, D., & Deshler, D. D. (2007). What we need to know about responsiveness to intervention (and shouldn't be afraid to ask). *Learning Disabilities Research and Practice*, 22(2), 129–136. doi:10.1111/j.1540-5826.2007.00237.x

Fuchs, D., Fuchs, L. S., Mathes, P. G., & Martinez, E. A. (2002). Preliminary evidence on the social standing of students with learning disabilities in PALS and NO-PALS classrooms. *Learning Disabilities Research and Practice*, 17, 205–215.

Fuchs, L. S., & Fuchs, D. (2005). Peer-assisted learning strategies: Promoting word recognition, fluency, and comprehension in young children. *Journal of Special Education*, 39, 34–44.

Fuchs, L., Powell, S. R., Seethaler, P. M., Cirino, P. T., Fletcher, J. M, Fuchs, D., et al. (2011). The development of arithmetic and word-problem skills among students with mathematics disability. In J. M. Kauffman & D. P. Hallahan (Eds.), *Handbook of special education* (pp. 434–444). New York: Routledge.

Gardner, N. A., & Brownell, L. (2011). *Expressive One-Word Picture Vocabulary Test—Fourth Edition* Austin, TX: PRO-ED.

Garwood, J. D., Brunsting, N. C., & Fox, L. C. (2014). Improving reading comprehension and fluency outcomes for adolescents with emotional-behavioral disorders: Recent research synthesized. *Remedial and Special Education*, 35(3), 181–194. Retrieved from http://search.ebscohost.com/login.aspx?direct=true&db=eric&AN=EJ1024610&site=eds-live&scope=site; http://dx.doi.org/10.1177/0741932513514856

Gast, D. L., & Nelson, C. M. (1977). Legal and ethical considerations for the use of timeout procedures in special education settings. *Journal of Special Education*, 11, 457–467.

Gaumer Erickson, A., Patton, J. R., & Clark, G. M. (2012). *Informal assessments for transition planning* (2nd ed.). Austin, TX: PRO-ED.

Geenen, S., Powers, L. E., Lopez-Vasquez A., & Bersani, H. (2003). Understanding and promoting the transition of minority adolescents. *Career Development for Exceptional Individuals*, 26, 27–46.

Gentry, J. R. (2000). A retrospective on invented spelling and a look forward. *Reading Teacher*, 54, 318–333.

Georgia Department of Education. (2015). *AAC in the classroom for students with autism*. Retrieved from http://www.pbs.org/parents/education/learning-disabilities/strategies-for-learning-disabilities/communication-strategies/aac

Gerlach, K. (2015). *Let's team up! A checklist for teachers, paraeducators, and principals*. Port Chester, NY: NEA Professional Library Publication.

German, D. J. (2014). *Test of Word Finding—Third Edition*. Austin, TX: PRO-ED.

Gersten, R., Baker, S. K., Smith-Johnson, J., Dimino, J., & Peterson, A. (2006). Eyes on the prize: Teaching complex historical content to middle school students with learning disabilities. *Exceptional Children*, 72, 264–280.

Gersten, R., & Dimino, J. (1990). *Reading instruction for at-risk students: Implications of current research*. Eugene: Oregon School Study Council, University of Oregon.

Gibb, G. S., & Dyches, T. T. (2000). *Guide to writing quality individualized education programs: What's best for students with disabilities?* Boston: Allyn & Bacon.

Gibb, G. S., & Dyches, T. T. (2007). *Guide to writing quality individualized education programs* (2nd ed.). Needham Heights, MA: Allyn & Bacon.

Gibb, G. S., & Dyches, T. T. (2014). *Guide to writing quality individualized education programs* (2nd ed.). Columbus, OH: Pearson.

Gibb, G. S., & Dyches, T. T. (2016). *Guide to writing quality individualized education programs* (3rd ed.). Columbus, OH: Pearson.

Gibbons, M. (2002). *Self-directed learning handbook: Challenging adolescent students to excel*. San Francisco: Jossey-Bass.

Gillam, R. B., & Pearson, N. A. (2004). *Test of Narrative Language*. Austin, TX: PRO-ED.

Gillespie, A., & Graham, S. (2014). A meta-analysis of writing interventions for students with learning disabilities. *Exceptional Children*, 80(4), 454–473. Retrieved from http://search.ebscohost.com/login.aspx?direct=true&db=eric&AN=EJ1048526&site=eds-live&scope=site; http://dx.doi.org/10.1177/0014402914527238

Gilliam, J. E., & Miller, L. (2006). *Pragmatic Language Skills Inventory*. Austin, TX: PRO-ED.

Gillon, G. (2004). *Phonological awareness: From research to practice*. New York: Guilford Press.

Glisan, E. (2001). *Real life math: Living on a paycheck*. Austin, TX: PRO-ED.

Goldstein, A. P., Sprafkin, R. P., Gershaw, N. J., & Klein, P. (2006). *Skillstreaming the adolescent: A structured learning approach to teaching prosocial skills* (2nd ed.). Champaign, IL: Research Press.

Goleman, D. (1998). *Working with emotional intelligence*. New York: Bateman Books.

Gore, M. C. (2010). *Inclusion strategies for secondary classrooms: Keys for struggling learners*. Thousand Oaks, CA: Corwin Press.

Graham, S. (1992). Helping students with LD progress as writers. *Intervention in School and Clinic*, 27, 134–144.

Graham, S. (2000). Should the natural learning approach replace traditional spelling instruction? *Journal of Educational Psychology*, 92, 235–247.

Graham, S., & Harris, K. R. (2005). Improving the writing performance of young struggling writers: Theoretical and programmatic research from the Center on Accelerating Student Learning. *Journal of Special Education, 39*, 19–33.

Graham, S., & Harris, K. R. (2006). Preventing writing difficulties: Providing additional handwriting and spelling instruction to at-risk children in first grade. *Teaching Exceptional Children, 38*, 64–66.

Graham, S., & Harris, K. R. (2009). Almost 30 years of writing research: Making sense of it all with the wrath of Khan. *Learning Disabilities Research and Practice, 24*, 58–68.

Graham, S., Harris, K. R., & Fink, B. (2000). Is handwriting causally related to learning to write? Treatment of handwriting problems in beginning writers. *Journal of Educational Psychology, 92*, 620–633.

Graham, S., Harris, K. R., & Larsen, L. (2001). Prevention and intervention of writing difficulties for students with learning disabilities. *Learning Disabilities Research and Practice, 16*, 74–84.

Graham, S., & Miller, L. (1980). Handwriting research and practice: A unified approach. *Focus on Exceptional Children, 13*(2), 1–16.

Greenland, R., & Polloway, E. A. (1995). *Handwriting and students with disabilities: Overcoming first impressions.* (ERIC Document Reproduction Service No. ED378754)

Greenspan, S., & Driscoll, J. (1997). The role of intelligence in a broad model of personal competence. In D. P. Flanagan, J. Genshaft, & P. L. Harrison (Eds.), *Contemporary intellectual assessment: Theories, tests, and issues* (pp. 131–150). New York: Guilford Press.

Gregg, N., Coleman, C., Davis, M., & Chalk, J. C. (2007). Timed essay writing: Implications for high-stakes tests. *Journal of Learning Disabilities, 40*, 306–318.

Gresham, F. M. (2002). Best practices in social skills training. In A. Thomas & J. Grimes (Eds.), *Best practices in school psychology IV.* Washington, DC: National Association of School Psychologists.

Gresham, F. M. (2004). Current status and future directions of school-based behavioral interventions. *School Psychology Review, 33*(3), 326–343.

Gresham, F. M., & Elliott, S. N. (1990). *Social Skills Rating System.* Circle Pines, MN: American Guidance Service.

Gresham, F. M., & Elliott, S. N. (2008). *Social Skills Improvement System Rating Scales.* Minneapolis: Pearson.

Grigal, M., & Neubert, D. A. (2004). Parents' in-school values and post-school expectations for transition-aged youth with disabilities. *Career Development for Exceptional Individuals, 27*, 65–85.

Grigal, M., Test, D. W., Beattie, J., & Wood, W. (1997). An evaluation of transition components of individualized education programs. *Exceptional Children, 63*, 357–372.

Grossen, B. (n.d.). *The research base for corrective reading SRA—University of Oregon.* Retrieved from https://www.sraonline.com/di_home_research.html?PHPSESSID=784bb902f57458c78e92c9bae162569f

Guillaume, A. M., Yopp, R. H., & Yopp, H. K. (1996). Accessible science. *Journal of Educational Issues of Language Minority Students, 17*, 67–85.

Gurganus, S., Janas, M., & Schmitt, L. (1995). Science instruction: What special education teachers need to know and what roles they need to play. *Teaching Exceptional Children, 27*(4), 7–9.

Hagaman, J. L., Luschen, K., & Reid, R. (2010). The "RAP" on reading comprehension. *Teaching Exceptional Children, 43*(1), 22–29.

Hagaman, J. L., & Reid, R. (2008). The effects of the paraphrasing strategy on the reading of middle school students at risk for failure in reading. *Remedial and Special Education, 29*, 222–234.

Haggerty, K., Elgin, J., & Woolley (2010). *Social-emotional learning assessment measures for middle school youth.* Seattle: RAIKES Foundation.

Hagood, B. F. (1997). Reading and writing with help from story grammar. *Teaching Exceptional Children, 29*(4), 10–14.

Hall, C. Kent, S. C., McCulley, L., Davis, A., & Wanzek, J. (2013). A new look at mnemonic and graphic organizes in the secondary social studies classroom. *Teaching Exceptional Children, 46*(1), 47–55.

Hallahan, D. P., Kauffman, J. M., & Pullen, P. C. (2015). *Exceptional learners: An introduction to special education* (13th ed.). Boston: Pearson.

Hallahan, D. P., Lloyd, J. W., & Stoller, L. (1982). *Improving attention with self-monitoring: A manual for teachers.* Charlottesville: University of Virginia Learning Disabilities Research Institute.

Halpern, A. S. (1985). Transition: A look at the foundation. *Exceptional Children, 51*, 479–486.

Halpern, A., & Benz, M. (1987). A statewide examination of secondary special education for students with mild disabilities: Implications for the high school curriculum. *Exceptional Children, 54*, 122–129.

Halpern, A. S., Herr, C. M., Doren, D., & Wolf, N. K. (2000). *Transition Skills Inventory [NEXT S.T.E.P.]* (2nd ed.). Austin, TX: PRO-ED.

Hamblet, E. C. (2014). Nine strategies to improve college transition planning for students with disabilities. *Teaching Exceptional Children, 46*(3), 53–59.

Hammill, D. D., Brown, V. L., Larsen, S. C., & Weiderholt, J. L. (2007). *Test of Adolescent and Adult Language—Fourth Edition.* Austin, TX: PRO-ED.

Hammill, D. D., & Larsen, S. C. (2009). *Test of Written Language—Fourth Edition*. Austin, TX: PRO-ED.

Hanley-Maxwell, C., Pogoloff, S. M., & Whitney-Thomas, J. (1998). Families: The heart of transition. In F. Rusch & J. Chadsey (Eds.), *Beyond high school: Transition from school to work* (pp. 234–264). Belmont, CA: Wadsworth.

Hardman, M. L., & Drew, C. J. (2005). *Human exceptionality: Society, school, and family* (8th ed.). Boston: Allyn & Bacon.

Haring, N., & Liberty, K. A. (1990). Matching strategies with performance in facilitating generalization. *Focus on Exceptional Children*, 22(8), 1–16.

Harniss, M., Caros, J., & Gersten, R. (2007). Impact of the design of U.S. history textbooks on content acquisition and academic engagement of special education students: An experimental investigation. *Journal of Learning Disabilities*, 40, 97–192.

Harris, A. J., & Sipay, E. R. (1990). *How to increase reading ability*. New York: Longman.

Harris, K. (2010, December). *Self-regulated strategy development*. Reston, VA: CEC Webinar.

Harris, K. R., Friedlander, B. D., Saddler, B., Frizzelle, R., & Graham, S. (2005). Self-monitoring of attention versus self-monitoring of academic performance: Effects among students with ADHD in the general education classroom. *Journal of Special Education*, 39(3), 145–156.

Harnis, M. K., Carnine, D. W., Silbert, J., & Dixon, R. C. (2007). Effective strategies for teaching mathematics. In M. D. Coyne, E. J. Kame'enui, & D. W. Carnine (Eds.), *Effective teaching strategies that accommodate diverse learners* (3rd ed.). Upper Saddle River, NJ: Merrill/Pearson.

Harris, M. L., Schumaker, J. B., & Deshler, D. D. (2011). The effects of strategic morphological analysis instruction on the vocabulary performance of secondary students with and without disabilities. *Learning Disability Quarterly*, 34(1), 17–33.

Harris, R. E., Marchand-Martella, N., & Martella, R. C. (2000). Effects of a peer-delivered corrective reading program. *Journal of Behavioral Education*, 10, 21–36.

Hart, D., Grigal, M., & Weir, C. (2010). Expanding the paradigm: Postsecondary education options for individuals with autism spectrum disorder and intellectual disabilities. *Focus on Autism and Other Developmental Disabilities*, 25(3), 134–150. doi:10.1177/1088357610373759

Hayden, T. (1980). *One child*. New York: Avon Books.

Hayes, D. (1988). Toward students learning through the social studies text. *The Social Studies*, 79, 266–270.

Hazel, J. S., Schumaker, J. B., Sherman, J. A., & Sheldon-Wildgen, J. B. (1981a). *ASSET: A social skills program for adolescents*. Champaign, IL: Research Press.

Hazel, J. S., Schumaker, J. B., Sherman, J. A., & Sheldon-Wildgen, J. B. (1981b). Group social skills: A program for court-adjudicated probationary youth. *Criminal Justice and Behavior*, 9, 35–52.

Hedeen, D. L., & Ayres, B. J. (2002). "You want me to teach him to read?" Fulfilling the intent of IDEA. *Journal of Disability Policy Studies*, 13, 180–189.

Hellsten, L. M. (2012). *What do we know about time management? A review of the literature and a psychometric critique of instruments assessing time management*. Retrieved from http://www.intechopen.com/books/time-management/what-do-we-know-about-time-management-a-review-of-the-literature-and-a-psychometric-critique-of-inst

Henk, W. A., Helfeldt, J. P., & Platt, J. M. (1986). Developing reading fluency in learning disabled students. *Teaching Exceptional Children*, 18, 202–206.

Heward, W. L. (2003a). *Exceptional children: An introductory survey of special education* (7th ed.). Upper Saddle River, NJ: Merrill/Pearson.

Heward, W. L. (2003b). Ten faulty notions about teaching and learning that hinder the effectiveness of special education. *Journal of Special Education*, 36, 186–205.

Higgins, J., McConnell, K., Patton, J. R., & Ryser, G. R. (2003). *Practical ideas that really work for students with dyslexia and other reading disorders*. Austin, TX: PRO-ED.

Hock, M., Brasseur, I., Deshler, D., Catts, H., Marquis, J., Mark, C., et al. (2009). What is the reading component skill profile of adolescent struggling readers in urban schools? *Learning Disability Quarterly*, 32, 21–38.

Hoffman, A., & Field, S. (1995). Promoting self-determination through effective curriculum development. *Intervention in School and Clinic*, 30, 134–142.

Hogan, T., & Catts, H. W. (2004). *Phonological awareness test items: Lexical and phonological characteristics affect performance*. Paper presented at the annual convention of the American Speech-Language-Hearing Association, Philadelphia.

Holifield, C., Goodman, J., Hazelkorn, M., & Heflin, L. J. (2010). Using self-monitoring to increase attending to task and academic accuracy in children with autism. *Focus on Autism and Other Developmental Disabilities*, 25(4), 230–238.

Homme, L. (1969). *How to use contingency contracting in the classroom*. Champaign, IL: Research Press.

Hoover, J. J. (2004). Teaching students to use study skills. In D. D. Hammill & N. R. Bartel (Eds.), *Teaching students with learning problems* (7th ed., pp. 347–380). Austin, TX: PRO-ED.

Hoover, J. J. (2011). *Response to intervention models: Curricular implications and interventions*. Upper Saddle River, NJ: Pearson/Allyn & Bacon.

Hoover, J. J. (2013). *Linking assessment to instruction in multi-tiered models: A teacher's guide to selecting reading, writing and mathematics interventions.* Boston: Pearson/Allyn & Bacon.

Hoover, J. J., Betty, M., & Patton, J. R. (2015, April). *Assessing study strategies to inform IEP development and implementation.* San Diego, CA: Council for Exceptional Children Convention Presentation.

Hoover, J. J., Klingner, J. K., Baca, L. M., & Patton, J. M. (2008). *Methods for teaching culturally and linguistically diverse exceptional learners.* Upper Saddle River, NJ: Merrill/Pearson.

Hoover, J. J., & Love, E. (2011). Supporting school-based response to intervention: Practitioner's model. *Teaching Exceptional Children, 43*(3), 40–48.

Hoover, J. J., & Patton, J. R. (2005). *Curriculum adaptations for students with learning and behavior problems: Differentiating instruction to meet diverse needs* (3rd ed.). Austin, TX: PRO-ED.

Hoover, J. J., & Patton, J. R. (2007). *Teaching study skills to students with learning problems: A teacher's guide for meeting diverse needs* (2nd ed.). Austin, TX: PRO-ED.

Hoover J. J., & Patton J. R. (2008). The role of special educators in a multi-tiered instructional system. *Intervention in School and Clinic, 43,* 195–202.

Hoover, J. J., & Patton, J. R. (in press). *IEPs for English language and other diverse learners.* Thousand Oaks, CA: Corwin Press.

Horner, R. H., Sugai, G., Todd, A. W., & Lewis-Palmer, T. (2005). Schoolwide positive behavior support. In L. M. Barmbara & L. Kern (Eds.), *Individualized supports for students with problem behaviors: Designing positive behavior support plans* (pp. 359–390). New York: Guilford Press.

Hourcade, J. J., & Bauwens, J. (2003). *Cooperative teaching: Rebuilding and sharing the schoolhouse* (2nd ed.). Austin, TX: PRO-ED.

Hresko, W. P., Herron, S. R., Peak, P. K., & Hicks, D. L. (2012). *Test of Early Written Language 3.* Austin, TX: PRO-ED.

Hughes, C. A., Schumaker, J. B., & Deshler, D. D. (2005). *The essay test-taking strategy.* Lawrence, KS: Edge Enterprises, Inc.

Hulit, L. M., & Howard, M. R. (2011). *Born to talk: An introduction to speech and language development* (5th ed.). Upper Saddle River, NJ: Pearson/Allyn & Bacon.

Humphrey, E. (2006). *Scaffolding.* Unpublished manuscript.

Hupp, S. D. A., LeBlanc, M., Jewell, J. D., & Warnes, E. (2009). History and overview. In J. Matson (Ed.), *Social behavior and skills in children* (pp. 1–21). New York: Springer.

Identifying mechanisms that matter. (2015). In J. A. Durlak, C. E. Domitrovich, R. P. Weissberg, & T. P. Gullotta (Eds.), *Handbook of social and emotional learning: Research and practice* (pp. 151–166). New York: Guilford Press.

Idiom Connection. (2015). *English idioms and quizzes.* Retrieved from http://www.idiomconnection.com

Indiana Department of Education (2015). *Indiana academic standards: English/language arts.* Retrieved from http://www.doe.in.gov/standards/englishlanguage-arts

Individuals with Disabilities Education Act Amendments of 1991, 20 U.S.C.§1400–1485.

Individuals with Disabilities Education Act Amendments of 1997, 20 U.S.C.§140.

Individuals with Disabilities Education Act, Pub. L. No. 105–117, 20 U.S.C. § 1401 *et seq.* (1997).

Individuals with Disabilities Education Improvement Act of 2004, HB 1350.

Info Net. (2015). *Teen internet usage.* Retrieved from http://www.infoplease.com/science/computers/teen-internet-usage.html

Infoplease.com. (2015). *Teen internet usage.* Retrieved from http://www.infoplease.com/science/computers/teen-internet-usage.html

Institute for Education Sciences (2013). What Works Clearinghouse Review of the Report "Improving Reading Comprehension and Social Studies Knowledge in Middle School." http://ies.ed.gov/ncee/wwc/Docs/SingleStudyReviews/wwc_readingcomp_082713.pdf

International Business Times. (2014). *Millennials are on Instagram, their parents play Words with Friends, and everyone is on Facebook.* Retrieved from http://www.ibtimes.com/millennials-are-instagram-their-parents-play-words-friends-everyone-facebook-1666440

Internet TESL Project. (2015). *Self-study homonym quizzes.* Retrieved from http://a4esl.org/q/h/homonyms.html

Isaacson, S. L. (1989). Role of secretary vs. author in resolving the conflict in writing instruction. *Learning Disability Quarterly, 12,* 200–217.

Isenbarger, L. M. & Barrody, A. (2001). Fostering the mathematical power of children with behavioral difficulties: The case of Carter. *Teaching Children Mathematics, 7*(8), 468–471.

Jacobson, L. T., & Reid, R. (2010). Improving the persuasive essay writing of high school students with ADHD. *Exceptional Children, 76,* 157–174.

Jarrett, D. (1999a). *The inclusive classroom: Mathematics and science instruction for students with learning disabilities.* Portland, OR: Northwest Regional Educational Laboratory.

Jarrett, D. (1999b). *Teaching mathematics and science to English-language learners.* Portland, OR: Northwest Regional Educational Laboratory.

Jennings, P. L., Mitchell, M. S., & Hannah, S. T. (2015). The moral self: A review and integration of the literature. *Journal of Organizational Behavior, 36,* S104–S168.

Jitendra, A. K. (2013). Understanding and accessing standards-based mathematics for students with mathematics difficulties. *Learning Disability Quarterly, 36*(1), 4–8. doi:10.1177/0731948712455337

Jitendra, A. K., & Gajria, M. (2011). Reading comprehension instruction for students with learning disabilities. *Focus on Exceptional Children, 43*(8), 1–16

Jitendra, A. K., Hoppes, M. K., & Xin, Y. P. (2000). Enhancing main idea comprehension for students with learning problems: The role of a summarization strategy and self-monitoring instruction. *Journal of Special Education, 34,* 127–139.

Jitendra, A. K., & Star, J. R. (2011). Meeting the needs of students with learning disabilities in inclusive mathematics classrooms: The role of schema-based instruction (SBI) on mathematical problem-solving. *Theory into Practice, 50*(1), 12–19, doi:10.1080/00405841.2011.534912

Johnson, D. R., & Johnson, F. P. (2009). *Joining together: Group theory and group skills* (10th ed.). Upper Saddle River, NJ: Merrill/Pearson Education.

Joseph, G. E., & Strain, P. S. (2003). Enhancing emotional vocabulary in young children. *Young Exceptional Children, 6*(4), 18–26.

Joseph, L. M. E., & Eveleigh, L. (2011). A review of the effects of self-monitoring on reading performance of students with disabilities. *Journal of Special Education, 45*(1), 43–53. doi:10.1177/0022466909349145

Joseph, L. M., & Seery, M. E. (2004). Where is the phonics? A review of the literature on the use of phonetic analysis with students with mental retardation. *Remedial and Special Education, 25,* 88–94.

K12 Reader. (2015). *Homophone worksheets.* Retrieved from http://www.k12reader.com/subject/vocabulary/homophone-worksheets

Kauffman, J. M. (2002). *Education reform: Bright people sometimes say stupid things about education.* Lanham, MD: Scarecrow Press.

Kauffman, J. M., & Hallahan, D. P. (1995). *The illusion of full inclusion.* Austin, TX: PRO-ED.

Kaye, C. B. (2010). *The complete guide to service learning: Proven, practical ways to engage students in civic responsibilities, academic curriculum, and social action.* Minneapolis: Free Spirit.

Kazdin, A. E. (2001). *Behavior modification in applied settings* (6th ed.). Belmont, CA: Wadsworth/Thomson.

Kellough, R. D. (2005). *Your first year of teaching: Guidelines for success.* Upper Saddle River, NJ: Merrill/Pearson.

Kerr, M. M., & Nelson, C. M. (2009). *Strategies for addressing behavior problems in the classroom* (6th ed.). Upper Saddle River, NJ: Pearson Prentice Hall.

Kerr, M. M., & Nelson, C. M. (2010). *Strategies for addressing behavioral problems in the classroom.* Upper Saddle River, NJ: Pearson Education.

Kiburtz, C. S., Miller, S. R., & Morrow, L. W. (1984). Structured learning using self-monitoring to promote maintenance and generalization of social skills across settings for a behaviorally disordered adolescent. *Behavior Disorders, 4,* 47–55.

Kim, A., Vaughn, S., Wanzek, J., & Wei, S. (2004). Graphic organizers and their effects on the reading comprehension of students with LD: A synthesis of research. *Journal of Learning Disabilities, 37,* 105–118.

Kinder, D., Bursuck, W., & Epstein, M. (1992). An evaluation of history textbooks. *Journal of Special Education, 25,* 472–491.

Kingsdorf, S., & Krawec, J. (2014). Error analysis of mathematical word problem solving across students with and without learning disabilities. *Learning Disabilities Research and Practice, 29*(2), 66–74. doi:10.1111/ldrp.12029

King-Sears, M. (2015). An exploratory study of universal design for teaching chemistry to students with and without disabilities. *Learning Disability Quarterly, 38*(2), 84–96. doi:10.1177/0731948714564575

Kirby, J. R., Silvestri, R., Allingham, B. H., Parrila, R., & La Fave, C. B. (2008). Learning strategies and study approaches of postsecondary students with dyslexia. *Journal of Learning Disabilities, 41*(1), 85–96.

Kirk, S. A., & Johnson, G. O. (1951). *Educating the retarded child.* Cambridge, MA: Houghton Mifflin.

Kirk, S., Kirk, W., & Minskoff, E. (1986). *Phonic remedial reading lessons.* Novato, CA: Academic Therapy.

Kirk, S. A., Kliebhan, J. M., & Lerner, J. (1978). *Teaching reading to slow and disabled learners.* Boston: Houghton Mifflin.

Klein, D. (2003). A brief history of American K–12 mathematics education in the 20th century. In J. M. Royer (Ed.), *Mathematical cognition* (pp. 175–225). Greenwich, CT: Information Age.

Klingner, J. K., Urbach, J., Golos, D., Brownell, M., & Menon, S. (2010). Teaching reading in the 21st century: A glimpse at how special education teachers promote reading comprehension. *Learning Disability Quarterly, 33,* 70–73.

Klingner, J., Vaughn, S., Arguelles, M., Hughes, M., & Leftwich, S. (2004). Collaborative strategic reading: Real-world lessons from classroom teachers. *Remedial and Special Education, 25,* 291–302.

Knight, V., Browder, D., Agnello, B., & Lee, A. (2010). Academic instruction for students with severe disabilities. *Focus on Exceptional Children, 42*(7), 1–14.

Knoff, H. M., & Batsche, G. M. (1995). Project ACHIEVE: Analyzing a school reform process for at-risk and underachieving students. *School Psychology Review, 24*, 579–603.

Kohn, A. (1993). *Punished by rewards: The trouble with gold stars, incentive plans, A's, praise, and other bribes.* Boston: Houghton Mifflin.

Kolstoe, O. P. (1976). *Teaching educable mentally retarded children* (2nd ed.). New York: Holt, Rinehart and Winston.

Konrad, M., Helf, S., & Joseph, L. M. (2011). Evidence-based instruction is not enough: Strategies for increasing instructional efficiency. *Intervention in School and Clinic, 47*(2), 67–74.

Kounin, J. (1970). *Discipline and group management in classrooms.* New York: Holt, Rinehart and Winston.

Krawec, J., Huang, J., Montague, M., Kressler, B., & de Alba, A. M. (2013). The effects of cognitive strategy instruction on knowledge of math problem-solving processes of middle school students with learning disabilities. *Learning Disability Quarterly, 36*(2), 80–92.

Kregel, J. (2004). Designing instructional programs. In P. Wehman & J. Kregel (Eds.), *Functional curriculum for elementary, middle, and secondary age students with special needs* (2nd ed., pp. 37–66). Austin, TX: PRO-ED.

Kregel, J. (2012). Designing instructional programs. In P. Wehman & J. Kregel (Eds.), *Functional curriculum for elementary, middle, and secondary age students with special needs* (3rd ed., pp. 57–92). Austin, TX: PRO-ED.

Kroeger, S. D., & Kouche, B. (2006). Using peer-assisted learning strategies to increase response to intervention in inclusive middle math setting. *Teaching Exceptional Children, 38*, 6–13.

Kubina, R. M., & Hughes, C. A. (2007). Fluency instruction. *DLD Current Practice Alerts,* no. 15, 1–4.

Kuo, Y. H. (2010). *Self-regulated learning: From theory to practice.* Kaohsiung, Taiwan: Wenzao Ursuline College. (ERIC Document Reproduction Service No. 510 995)

Kusche, C., & Greenberg, M. (1994). *The PATHS Curriculum.* South Deerfield, MA: Channing-Bete Co.

Lamberg, T., & Wiest, L. R. (2015). Dividing fractions using an area model: A look at in-service teachers' understanding. *Mathematics Teacher Education and Development, 17*(1), 30–43.

Lane K. L., & Menzies H. M. (2015). Classroom management in inclusive settings. In E. T. Emmer & E. J. Sabornie (Eds.), *Handbook of classroom management* (2nd ed., pp. 205–219). New York: Routledge.

Lannie, A. L., & McCurdy, B. L. (2007). Preventing disruptive behavior in the urban classroom: Effects of the Good Behavior Game on student and teacher behavior. *Education and Treatment of Children, 30*, 85–98.

Larsen, S., Hammill, D., & Moats, L. (2013). *Test of Written Spelling* (TWS-5). Austin, TX: PRO-ED.

Lazzari, A. M. (1991). *The transition sourcebook: A practical guide for early intervention programs.* Tucson, AZ: Communication Skill Builders.

LeBuffe, P. A., Shapiro, V. B., & Naglieri, J. A. (2009). *The Devereaux Student Strengths Assessment (DESSA).* Lewisville, NC: Kaplan Press.

Lee, S.-H., Wehmeyer, M. L., & Shogren, K. A. (2015). Effective instruction with the self-determined learning model of instruction on students with disabilities: A meta-analysis. *Education and Training in Autism and Developmental Disabilities, 50*(2), 237–247.

Leflot, G., van Lier, P., Onglena, P., & Colpin, H. (2010). The role of teacher behavior management in the development of discipline behaviors: An intervention study with the Good Behavior Game. *Journal of Abnormal Child Psychology, 38*, 869–882. doi:10.1007/sl.0802-010-9411-4

Lenz, K., & Schumaker, J. (1999). *Adapting language arts, social studies, and science materials for the inclusive classroom.* Alexandria, VA: Council for Exceptional Children.

Lerner, J. W. (2008). *Learning disabilities and related mild disabilities: Characteristics teaching strategies, and new directions.* Boston: Houghton Mifflin.

Lewis, R. B., & Doorlag, D. H. (2010). *Teaching special students in general education classrooms* (8th ed.). Upper Saddle River, NJ: Merrill/Pearson.

Lewis, T. J., Mitchell, B. S., Trussell, R., & Newcomer, L. (2015). School-wide positive behavior support: Building systems to prevent problem behavior and develop and maintain appropriate social behavior. In E. T. Emmer & E. J. Sabornie (Eds.), *Handbook of classroom management* (2nd ed., pp. 40–59). New York: Routledge, Taylor & Francis Group.

Lewis, T. J., & Sugai, G. (1999). Effective behavior support: A systems approach to proactive school-wide management. *Focus on Exceptional Children, 31*(6), 1–24.

Liaupsin, C. J., Scott, T. M., & Nelson, C. M. (2006). *Functional behavioral assessment: An interactive training and module.* Longmont, CO: Sopris West.

Liberman, R. P., King, L. W., DeRisi, W. J., & McCann, M. (1975). *Personal effectiveness: Guiding people to assert themselves and improve their social skills.* Champaign, IL: Research Press.

Lienemann, T., Graham, S., Leader-Janssen, B., & Reid, R. (2006). Improving the writing performance of struggling writers in second grade. *Journal of Special Education, 40*, 66–78.

Lindamood, C., & Lindamood, P. (1998). *The Lindamood Phoneme Sequencing Program for Reading, Spelling, and Speech*. Austin, TX: PRO-ED.

Lindamood, C., & Lindamood, P. (2004). *Lindamood Auditory Conceptualization Test—Third Edition*. Austin, TX: PRO-ED.

Literary Devices. (2015). *Literary devices*. Retrieved from http://literarydevices.net/discourse

Little, M. E., & Delisio, L. *Explicit instruction in mathematics (Go for it)*. Published by TeachingID © 2015.

Lloyd, J. W., & Hallahan, D. P. (2005). Going forward: How the field of learning disabilities has and will contribute to education. *Learning Disability Quarterly, 28*, 133–136.

Lovitt, T. C. (1975). Applied behavior analysis and learning disabilities: Part 2. *Journal of Learning Disabilities, 8*, 504–518.

Lovitt, T., & Horton, S. (1991). Adapting textbooks for mildly handicapped adolescents. In G. Stoner, M. R. Shinn, & H. M. Walker (Eds.), *Interventions for achievement and behavior problems* (pp. 439–472). Silver Spring, MD: National Association of School Psychologists.

Lubin, J., & Polloway, E.A. (2016). Mnemonic instruction in science and social studies for students with learning disabilities: A review. *Learning Disabilities: A Contemporary Journal, 14*(2), 109–120.

MacArthur, C. A., & Philippakos, Z. (2010). Instruction in a strategy for compare-contrast writing. *Exceptional Children, 76*, 438–456.

Maccini, P., & Gagnon, J. C. (2000). Best practices for teaching mathematics to secondary students with special needs. *Focus on Exceptional Children, 32*(5), 1–16.

Mace, R. L. (1997). *The Center for Universal Design* [Online]. Retrieved from http://www.design.nesu.edu/cud/univ_design/princ_overview.htm

Maheady, L., Harper, G. F., & Mallette, B. (2001). Peer-mediated instruction and interventions and students with mild disabilities. *Remedial and Special Education, 22*, 4–14.

Malmgren, K. W., & Trezek, B. J. (2009). Literacy instruction for secondary students with disabilities. *Focus on Exceptional Children, 41*(6), 1–12.

Mancl, D. B., Miller, S. P., & Kennedy, M. (2012). Using the concrete-representational-abstract sequence with integrated strategy instruction to teach subtraction with regrouping to students with learning disabilities. *Learning Disabilities Research and Practice, 27*(4), 152–166. doi:10.1111/j.1540-5826.2012.00363.x

Manning, M. L., & Lucking, R. (1991). The what, why and how of cooperative learning. *The Social Studies, 80*, 173-175.

Many Things. (2015). *Commonly-used American slang*. Retrieved from http://www.manythings.org/slang

Maroney, S. A., & Searcy, S. (1996). Real teachers don't plan that way. *Exceptionality, 6*, 197–200.

Martella, R. C., Nelson, J. R., & Marchand-Martella, N. E. (2003). *Managing disruptive behaviors in the schools: A schoolwide, classroom, and individualized social learning approach*. Boston: Allyn & Bacon.

Martin, B. (1983). *Brown bear, brown bear, what do you see?* New York: Scholastic.

Martin, G., & Pear, J. (2015). *Behavior modification: What it is and how to do it* (9th ed.). Boston: Pearson Education.

Martin, J. E., & Huber-Marshall L. (1995). ChoiceMaker: A comprehensive self-determination transition program. *Intervention in School and Clinic, 30*, 147–156.

Martin, N., & Brownwell, R. (2010). *Receptive One-Word Picture Vocabulary Test—Fourth Edition*. Austin, TX: PRO-ED.

Martin, N., & Brownwell, R. (2011). *Expressive One-Word Picture Vocabulary Test—Fourth Edition*. Austin, TX: PRO-ED.

Marzano, R. J. (2003). *Translating research into action*. Alexandria, VA: Association for Supervision and Curriculum Development.

Marzano, R. J., Marzano, J. S., & Pickering, D. (2003). *Classroom management that works: Research-based strategies for every teacher*. Alexandria, VA: Association for Supervision and Curriculum Development.

Marzano, R. J., Pickering, D. J., & Pollock, J. E. (2001). *Classroom instruction that works: Research-based strategies for increasing student achievement*. Alexandria, VA: Association for Supervision and Curriculum Development.

Maslin, L. (2011a). *The history of English*. Retrieved from http://thehistoryofenglish.com

Maslin, L. (2011b). *The history of English: Late modern English (c. 1800–present)*. Retrieved from http://thehistoryofenglish.com/history_late_modern.html

Mason, L. H., & Hedin, L. R. (2011). Reading science text: Challenges for students with learning disabilities and considerations for teachers. *Learning Disabilities Research and Practice, 26*(4), 214–222. doi:10.1111/j.1540-5826.2011.00342.x

Mason, L. H., Meadan-Kaplansky, H., Hedin, L., & Taft, R. (2013). Self-regulating informational text reading comprehension: Perceptions of low-achieving students. *Exceptionality, 21*(2), 69–86.

Mastropieri, M. A., & Scruggs, T. E. (1992). Science for students with disabilities: A review of research. *Review of Educational Research, 62*, 377–411.

Mastropieri, M. A., & Scruggs, T. E. (2002). *Overcoming special education's greatest challenge: Motivating students to learn!* Paper presented at the annual meeting of the Council for Exceptional Children, New York.

Mastropieri, M. A., & Scruggs, T. E. (2007). *The inclusive classroom: Strategies for effective instruction* (3rd ed.). Upper Saddle River, NJ: Merrill/Pearson.

Mastropieri, M. A., & Scruggs, T. E. (2010). *The inclusive classroom: Strategies for effective differentiated instruction*. Upper Saddle River, NJ: Merrill/Pearson.

Mastropieri, M. A., Scruggs, T. E., Graetz, J., Norland, J., Gardizi, W., & McDuffie, K. (2005). Case studies in co-teaching in the content areas: Successes, failures and challenges. *Intervention in School and Clinic, 40*, 260–270.

Mastropieri, M. A., Scruggs, T. E., Irby Cerar, N., Guckert, M., Thompson, C., Bronaugh, D. A., et al. (2015). Strategic persuasive writing instruction for students with emotional and behavioral disabilities. *Exceptionality, 23*(3), 147–169. doi:10.1080/0936283 5.2014.986605

Mathes, P., & Torgesen J. (1998). All children can learn to read: Critical care for the prevention of reading failure. *Peabody Journal of Education, 73*, 317–340.

Mathews, S. C., & Miller, L. (2014). *Test of Preschool Vocabulary—Second Edition*. Austin, TX: PRO-ED.

Mayer, J. E., DiPaolo, M. T., & Salovey, P. (1990). Perceiving affective content in ambiguous visual stimuli: A component of emotional intelligence. *Journal of Personality Assessment, 54*, 772–781.

Mayer, M. J., Van Acker, R., Lochman, J. E., & Gresham, F. M. (2009). *Cognitive-behavioral interventions for emotional and behavioral disorders: School-based practices*. New York: Guilford Press.

Maynard, B. R., Solis, M. R., & Miller, V. (2015). Mindfulness-based interventions for improving academic achievement, behavior and socio-emotional functioning of primary and secondary students: A systematic review. *The Campbell Collaboration Library of Systematic Reviews*. Retrieved from http://www.campbellcollaboration.org

Mazzotti, V. L., & Test, D. W. (2016). Transitioning from school to employment. In F. E. Brown, J. J. McDonnell, & M. E. Snell (Eds.), *Instruction of students with severe disabilities* (8th ed., pp. 508–553). Columbus, OH: Pearson.

McCabe, J. A., Osha, K. L., & Roche, J. A. (2013). Psychology students' knowledge and use of mnemonics. *Teaching of Psychology, 40*(3), 183–192. doi:10.1177/0098628313487460

McConnell, K., Patton, J. R., & Polloway, E. A. (2006). *Behavioral intervention planning* (3rd ed.). Austin, TX: PRO-ED.

McCoy, K. (2005). Focus on exceptional children: Strategies for teaching social studies. *Focus on Exceptional Children, 38*(3), 1–16.

McCurdy, B. L., Lonnie, A. L., & Barnabas, E. (2009). Reducing disruptive behavior in an urban school cafeteria: An extension of the Good Behavior Game. *Journal of School Psychology, 47*, 39–54. doi:10.1016/j.jsp.2008.09.003

McDougall, D. (1998). Research on self-management techniques used by students with disabilities in general education settings. *Remedial and Special Education, 19*(5), 310–320.

McGhee, R., Bryant, B. R., Larsen, S. C., & Rivera, D. M. (1995). *Test of Written Expression*. Austin, TX: PRO-ED.

McGinnis, E., Goldstein, A. P., Sprafkin, R. P., & Gershaw, N. J. (2005). *Skillstreaming the elementary school child: A guide for teaching prosocial skills* (2nd ed.). Champaign, IL: Research Press.

McGinnis, J. R. (2013). Teaching science to learners with special needs. *Theory into Practice, 52*(1), 43–50. doi:10.1080/07351690.2013.743776

McGowan, T., & Guzzetti, B. (1991). Promoting social studies understanding through literature-based instruction. *The Social Studies, 82*, 16–21.

McLaughlin, T. F., & Skinner, C. H. (1996). Improving academic performance through self-management: Cover, copy and compare. *Intervention in School and Clinic, 32*, 113–118.

McLeskey, J., & Waldron, L. N. (2011). Educational programs for elementary students with learning disabilities: Can they be both effective and inclusive? *Learning Disabilities Research and Practice, 26*(1), 48–57.

McLoughlin, J. A., & Lewis, R. B. (2007). *Assessing special students: Strategies and procedures* (7th ed.). Upper Saddle River, NJ: Merrill/Pearson.

McLuhan, M. (1964). *Understanding media: The extensions of man*. New York: McGraw-Hill.

McMaster, K. N., & Fuchs, D. (2002). Effects of cooperative learning on the academic achievement of students with learning disabilities: An update of Tateyama-Sniezek's review. *Learning Disabilities Research and Practice, 17*, 107–117.

McTighe, J., & Lyman, F. G., Jr. (1988). Cueing thinking in the classroom: The promise of theory-embedded tools. *Educational Leadership, 47*(7), 18–24.

Meese, R. L. (2001). *Teaching learners with mild disabilities: Integrating research and practice* (2nd ed.). Belmont, CA: Wadsworth/Thompson Learning.

Mercer, C. D. (1979). *Students with learning disabilities*. Columbus, OH: Merrill.

Mercer, C. D., Mercer, A. R., & Pullen, P. C. (2010). *Teaching students with learning problems*. Upper Saddle River, NJ: Pearson.

Merriam-Webster Dictionary. (2015). Retrieved from http://www.merriam-webster.com/dictionary/slang

Merrill, K. W. (2008). *Social-Emotional Assets and Resilience Scale*. Eugene, OR: Strong Kids.

Meyer, A., & Rose, D. H. (2000). Universal design for individual differences. *Educational Leadership*, 58(3), 39–43.

Mihalas, S., Morse, W. C., Allsopp, D. H., & McHatton, P. A. (2009). Cultivating caring relationships between teachers and secondary students with emotional and behavioral disorders: Implications for research and practice. *Remedial and Special Education*, 30(2), 108–125. doi:10.1177/0741932508315950

Miller, B., & Taber-Doughty, T. (2014). Self-monitoring checklists for inquiry problem-solving: Functional problem-solving methods for students with intellectual disability. *Education and Training in Autism and Developmental Disabilities*, 49(4), 555.

Miller, J. C. (2015). *It's raining cats and dogs*. Retrieved from http://www.education-world.com/a_tsl/archives/00-1/lesson0001.shtml

Miller, L., Gillam, R. B., & Peña, E. C. (2001). *Dynamic assessment and intervention: Improving children's narrative skills*. Austin, TX: PRO-ED.

Miller, S. P. (1997). Perspectives on mathematics instruction. In D. D. Deshler, E. S. Ellis, & B. K. Lenz (Eds.), *Teaching adolescence with learning disabilities* (pp. 313– 367). Denver, CO: Love.

Miller, S. P., Stringfellow, J. L., Kaffar, B. J., Ferreira, D., & Mancl, D. B. (2011). Developing computation competence among students who struggle with mathematics. *Teaching Exceptional Children*, 44(2), 38–46.

Milsom, A., & Glanville, J. L. (2010). Factors mediating the relationship between social skills an academic grades in a sample of students diagnosed with learning disabilities or emotional disturbance. *Remedial and Special Education*, 31(4), 241–251. doi:10.1177/0741932508327460

Moats, L. C. (2003). Why have teachers been left unprepared to teach reading? *Phi Delta Kappan*, 84, 679–681.

Mononen, R., Aunio, P., & Koponen, T. (2014). Investigating RightStart mathematics kindergarten instruction in Finland. *Journal of Early Childhood Education Research*, 3(1), 2–26.

Morocco, C. C., Hindin, A., & Mata-Aguilar, C. (2001). Enhancing student comprehension of social studies material. *The Social Studies*, 96, 18–24.

Moyer, S. B. (1982). Repeated reading. *Journal of Learning Disabilities*, 15, 619–624.

Mueller, J. (2011). *Authentic assessment toolbox*. Retrieved from http://jfmueller.faculty.noctrl.edu/toolbox/portfolios.htm

Munk, D. D., Bruckert, J., Call, D. T., Stoehrmann, T., & Radant, E. (1998). Strategies for enhancing the performance of students with LD in inclusive science classes. *Intervention in School and Clinic*, 34, 73–78.

Munk, D. D., & Bursuck, W. D. (2001). Preliminary findings on personalized grading plans for middle school students with learning disabilities. *Exceptional Children*, 67, 211–234.

Munk, D. D., & Bursuck, W. D. (2004). Personalized grading plans: A systematic approach to making the grades of included students more accurate and meaningful. *Focus on Exceptional Children*, 36, 1–11.

Murawski, W. W., & Lochner, W. W. (2011). Observing co-teaching: What to ask for, look for and listen for. *Intervention in School and Clinic*, 46(3), 174–183. doi:10.1177/1053451210378165

Nation, K., & Hulme, C. (1997). Phonemic segmentation, not onset time segmentation, predicts early reading and spelling skills. *Reading Research Quarterly*, 32(2), 154–167.

National Assessment of Educational Progress. (2010). *The nation's report card: Executive summary*. Washington, DC: Author.

National Association of School Psychologists. (2002). *Behavior problems: Teaching young children self-control skills*. Retrieved from http://www.nasponline.org/resources/handouts/revisedPDFs/selfcontrol.pdf

National Center for Education Statistics. (2016). *English language learners*. Retrieved from https://nces.ed.gov/fastfacts/display.asp?id=96

National Center on Universal Design for Learning. (2015a). *The three principles of UDL*. Retrieved from http://www.udlcenter.org/aboutudl/whatisudl/3principles

National Center on Universal Design for Learning. (2015b). *UDL and the common core state standards*. Retrieved from http://www.udlcenter.org/implementation/udl_ccss

National Center on Universal Design for Learning. (2015c). *UDL guidelines—Version 2.0: Examples and resources*. Retrieved from http://www.udlcenter.org/implementation/examples

National Center on Universal Design for Learning. (2016). *The three principles of UDL*. Retrieved from http://www.udlcenter.org/aboutudl/whatisudl/3principles

National Council for the Social Studies. (1994). *Curriculum standards for social studies: Expectations of excellence*. Washington, DC: Author.

National Council of Teachers of Mathematics. (1995). *Professional standards for teaching mathematics*. Reston, VA: Author.

National Council of Teachers of Mathematics. (2006). *Curriculum focal points for prekindergarten through grade 8 mathematics: A quest for coherence*. Reston, VA: Author.

National Endowment for the Humanities. (2015). *Allegory and the art of persuasion*. Retrieved from http://edsitement.neh.gov/lesson-plan/animal-farm-allegory-and-art-persuasion#sect-introduction

National Institute on Deafness and Other Communication Disorders. (2015). *Statistics on voice, speech, and language*. Retrieved from http://www.nidcd.nih.gov/health/statistics/pages/vsl.aspx#3

National Joint Committee on Learning Disabilities. (2008). *Adolescent literacy and older students with learning disabilities*. Retrieved from http://www.ldonline.org/njcld

National Reading Panel. (2000). *Teaching children to read: An evidence-based assessment of the scientific research literature on reading and its implications for reading instruction* (NIH Publication No. 00-4769). Washington, DC: U.S. Government Printing Office.

National Science Teachers Association (2004). *Position statement on students with disabilities*. Retrieved from http://www.nsta.org/about/positions/disabilities.aspx

Nelson, J. R., Benner, G. J., & Gonzalez, J. (2005). An investigation of the effects of a prereading intervention on the early literacy skills of children at risk of emotional disturbance and reading problems. *Journal of Emotional and Behavioral Disorders, 13*, 3–12.

Nelson, J. S., Epstein, M. H. Bursuck, W. D., Jayanthi, M., & Sawyer, V. (1998). The preferences of middle school student for homework adaptations made by general education teachers. *Learning Disabilities Research and Practice, 13*, 109–117.

Nelson, J. S., Jayanthi, M., Epstein, M. H., & Bursuck, W. D. (2000). Students preferences for adaptations in classroom testing. *Remedial and Special Education, 21*, 41–52.

New Mexico Public Education Department. (2010). *Addressing student behavior*. Retrieved from http://www.ped.state.nm.us

Newby, D. E., & Higgs, P. L. (2005). Using inquiry to teach social studies. *The Charter Schools Resources Journal, 9*(1), 20–31.

Newcomer, P. L. (2014). *Diagnostic Achievement Battery—Fourth Edition*. Austin, TX: PRO-ED.

Newcomer, P., & Barenbaum, E. (2003). *Test of Phonological Awareness Skills*. Austin, TX: PRO-ED.

Newcomer, P. L., & Hammill, D. D. (1997). *Test of Language Development—Intermediate—Third Edition*. Austin, TX: PRO-ED.

Newcomer, P., & Hammill, D. D. (2008). *Test of Language Development—Primary—Fourth Edition*. Austin, TX: PRO-ED.

Newman, L., Wagner, M., Cameto, R., & Knokey, A. (2009). *The post-high school outcomes of youth with disabilities up to 4 years after high school: A report from the National Longitudinal Transition Study-2 (NLTS2)* (NCSER 2009-3017). Washington, DC: U.S. Government Printing Office.

Newmeyer, F. J. (2005). *The history of linguistics*. Washington, DC: Linguistic Society of America.

Next Generation Science Standards. (2016). *Get to know the standards*. Retrieved from http://www.nextgenscience.org

Northeast Foundation for Children. (2011). *The Responsive Classroom approach*. Retrieved from http://www.responsiveclassroom.org

Nunes Carraher, T., Carraher, D. W., & Dias Schliemann, A. (2004). Mathematics in the streets and in the schools. In T. P. Carpenter, J. A. Dossey, & J. L. Koehler (Eds.), *Classics in mathematics education research* (pp. 187–193). Reston, VA: National Council of Teachers of Mathematics.

Odom, S., McConnell, S. R., Ostrosky, M., Peterson, C., Skellenger, A., Spicuzza, R., et al. (1997). *Play time/social time: Organizing your classroom to build interaction skills*. Minneapolis: Institute on Community Integration, University of Minnesota.

O'Donohue, W. T., & Fisher, J. E. (2012). *Cognitive behavior therapy: Core principles for practice*. New York: Wiley.

O'Dougherty Wright, M., & Masten, A. S. (2015). Pathways to resilience in context. In L. S. Theron, L. Liebenberg, & M. Ungar (Eds.), *Youth resilience and culture: Commonalities and complexities* (pp. 3–22). New York: Springer.

Okilwa, N. S. A., & Shelby, L. (2010). The effects of peer tutoring on academic performances of students with disabilities in grade 6 through 12: A synthesis of the literature. *Remedial and Special Education, 31*(6), 450–463.

Okolo, C. M., Englert, C. S., Bouck, E. C., Heutsche, A., & Wang, H. (2011). The Virtual History Museum: Learning U.S. history in diverse eighth grade classrooms. *Remedial and Special Education, 32*(5), 417. doi:10.1177/0741932510362241

Olley, J. G. (2015). Adaptive behavior instruments. In E. A. Polloway (Ed.), *The death penalty and intellectual disability* (pp. 187–200). Washington, DC: American Association on Intellectual and Developmental Disabilities.

Olsen, J. Z. (2015). *Handwriting without tears*. Gaithersburg, MD: Handwriting Without Tears.

Olsen, J. Z., & Knapton, E. F. (2008). *Handwriting without tears: Pre-K teacher's guide*. Retrieved from http://www.hwtears.com

Orton, J. L. (1964). *A guide to teaching phonics*. Winston-Salem, NC: Orton Reading Center.

Owens, L. L. (2004). *The effects of handwriting without tears program on the handwriting of students in inclusion classrooms*. Master's thesis. Virginia Commonwealth University, Richmond. Retrieved from http://etd.vcu.edu/theses/available/etd-07192004-152755

Owens, R. E. (2015). *Language development: An introduction* (9th ed.). Boston: Allyn & Bacon.

Pacheco, M. B., & Goodwin, A. P. (2013). Putting two and two together: Middle school students' morphological problem-solving strategies for unknown words. *Journal of Adolescent and Adult Literacy, 56*(7), 541–553. doi:10.1002/JAAL.181

Palincsar, A. S., & Brown, A. L. (1984). Reciprocal teaching of comprehension—Fostering and monitoring activities. *Cognition and Instruction, 1*, 117–175.

Palmer, S., & Wehmeyer, M. (2003). Promoting self-determination in early education. *Remedial and Special Education, 24*, 115–126.

Parish, P. (2012). *Amelia Bedilia*. New York: HarperCollins.

Patton, J. R. (1994). Practical recommendations for using homework with students with learning disabilities. *Journal of Learning Disabilities, 27*, 570–578.

Patton, J. R., Blackbourn, J. M., & Fad, K. (1996). *Exceptional individuals in focus* (2nd ed.). Upper Saddle River, NJ: Merrill/Prentice Hall.

Patton, J. R., & Clark, G. M. (2014). *Transition Planning Inventory* (2nd ed.). Austin, TX: PRO-ED.

Patton, J. R., Clark, G. M., & Trainor, A. A. (2009). *Summary of performance system* [Computer software and manual]. Austin, TX: PRO-ED.

Patton, J. R., Cronin, M. E., & Wood, S. (1999). *Infusing real-life topics into existing curricula at the elementary, middle, and high school levels: Recommended procedures and instructional examples*. Austin, TX: PRO-ED.

Patton, J. R., & Dunn, C. (1998). *Transition from school to young adulthood: Basic concepts and recommended practices*. Austin, TX: PRO-ED.

Patton, J. R., Mruzek, D. W., & Pearson, N. (in press). *Adaptive behavior planning inventory*. Austin, TX: PRO-ED.

Patton, J. R., Polloway, E. A., & Cronin, M. E. (1987). Social studies instruction for handicapped students: A review of current practices. *The Social Studies, 71*, 131–135.

Patton, J. R., Polloway, E. A., & Cronin, M. E. (1994). *Science education for students with mild disabilities: A status report*. Austin, TX: Learning for Living. (ERIC Document Reproduction Service No. ED370329)

Patton, J. R., & Trainor, A. (2002). Using applied academics to enhance curricular reform in secondary education. In C. A. Kochhar-Bryant & D. S. Bassett (Eds.), *Aligning transition and standards-based education: Issues and strategies* (pp. 55–75). Arlington, VA: Council for Exceptional Children.

Paul, R., & Norbury, C. (2012). *Language disorders from infancy through adolescence: Listening, speaking, reading, writing, and communicating*. St. Louis, MO: Elsevier Mosby.

PBS Parents (2015). *Education: Augmentative and alternative communication*. Retrieved from http://www.pbs.org/parents/education/learning-disabilities/strategies-for-learning-disabilities/communication-strategies/aac

Pea, R. (1993). Practices of distributed intelligence and designs for education. In G. Salomon (Ed.), *Distributed cognition: Psychological and educational considerations* (pp. 47–87). New York: Cambridge University Press.

Peña, E., & Bedore, L. (2008). Child language disorders in bilingual contexts. In R. Schwartz (Ed.), *Handbook of child language disorders* (pp. 310–332). New York: Psychology Press.

Peña, E., Summers, C., & Resendiz, M. (2007). Assessment and intervention of children from diverse cultural and linguistic backgrounds. In A. Kamhi, K. Apel, & J. Masterson (Eds.), *Clinical decision making in developmental language disorders* (pp. 99–118) Baltimore: Brookes.

Penner-Williams, J., Smith, T. E. C., & Gartin, B. C. (2009). Written language expression: Assessment instruments and teacher tools. *Assessment for Effective Intervention, 34*, 162–169.

Peterson, D. L. (1972). *Functional mathematics for the mentally retarded*. Columbus, OH: Merrill.

Phelps-Terasaki, D., & Phelps-Gunn, T. (2000). *Teaching competence in written language* (2nd ed.). Austin, TX: PRO-ED.

Phelps-Terasaki, D., & Phelps-Gunn, T. (2007). *Test of Pragmatic Language—Second Edition*. Austin, TX: PRO-ED.

Phillips, E. L. (1978). *The social skills basis of psychopathology: Alternative to abnormal psychology and psychiatry*. New York: Grune & Stratton.

Phillips, E. L., Phillips, E. A., Fixsen, D. L., & Wolf, M. M. (1974). *The teaching-family handbook*. Lawrence, KS: Beach Center on Families and Disability.

Pianta, R. C., & Kraft-Sayre, M. (2003). *Successful kindergarten transition: Your guide to connecting children, families and schools*. Baltimore: Brookes.

Pisha, B., & Coyne, P. (2001). Smart from the start: The promise of universal design for learning. *Remedial and Special Education, 22*(4), 197–203.

Polloway, C. H., & Polloway, E. A. (1978). Expanding reading skills through syllabication. *Academic Therapy, 13,* 455–462.

Polloway, E. A. (2009). Written language assessment: Introduction to the special series. *Assessment for Effective Intervention, 34,* 132–133.

Polloway, E. A., Bursuck, W. D., & Epstein, M. H. (2001). Homework for students with learning disabilities: The challenge of home–school communication. *Reading and Writing Quarterly, 17,* 181–187.

Polloway, E. A., Bursuck, W., Jayanthi, M., Epstein, M., & Nelson, J. (1996). Treatment acceptability: Determining appropriate interventions within inclusive classrooms. *Intervention in School and Clinic, 31,* 133–144.

Polloway, E. A., Epstein, M. H., & Bursuck, W. D. (2003). Testing adaptations in the general education classroom: Challenges and directions. *Reading and Writing Quarterly, 19,* 1–4.

Polloway, E. A., Epstein, M. H., Polloway, C. H., Patton, J. R., & Ball, D. W. (1986). Corrective Reading program: An analysis of effectiveness with learning disabled and mentally retarded students. *Remedial and Special Education, 7,* 41–47.

Polloway, E. A., & Lubin, J. (2016). Graphic models and instructional tools for students with special needs. *Lynchburg College Journal of Special Education,* Lynchburg College, Lynchburg, VA.

Polloway, E. A., Miller, L., & Smith, T. E. C. (2012). *Language instruction for students with disabilities* (4th ed.). Denver, CO: Love.

Polloway, E. A., Patton, J. R., & Serna, L. (2008). *Strategies for teaching learners with special needs* (9th ed.). Upper Saddle River, NJ: Merrill/Pearson.

Polloway, E. A., Patton, J. R., Smith, J. D., & Roderique, T. W. (1992). Issues in program design for elementary students with mild retardation: Emphasis on curriculum development. *Education and Training in Mental Retardation, 26,* 142–150.

Positive Action. (1979–1982). *Positive Action.* Twin Falls, ID: Author.

Powell, S.R., Driver, M.K., & Julian, T.E. (2013). The effect of tutoring with nonstandard equations for students with mathematics difficulty. *Journal of Learning Disabilities, 48*(5), 523–534. doi:10.1177/0022219413512613.

Powell, S. R., & Fuchs, L. S. (2015). Intensive intervention in mathematics. *Learning Disabilities Research and Practice, 30,* 182–192. doi:10.1111/ldrp.12087

Power, P. W. (2006). *A guide to vocational assessment* (4th ed.). Austin, TX: PRO-ED.

Powers, L. E., Turner, A., Westwood, D., Matuszewski, J., Wilson, R., & Phillips, A. (2001). TAKE CHARGE for the future: A controlled field-test of a model to promote student involvement in transition planning. *Career Development for Exceptional Individuals, 24*(1), 89–104. doi:10.1177/088572880102400107

Premack, D. (1959). Toward empirical behavior laws: I. Positive reinforcement. *Psychological Review, 66,* 219–233.

Pressley, M., & Fingeret, L. (2005). *What we have learned since the National Reading Panel: Visions of a next version of Reading First.* Retrieved from http://www.msularc.org/symposium2005/pressley_paper.pdf

Price, L., & Patton, J. R. (2003). A new world order: Connecting adult developmental theory to learning disabilities. *Remedial and Special Education, 24,* 328–338.

PRO-ED. Inc. (2011). *Edmark Reading Program.* Retrieved from http://www.proedinc.com/customer/ProductView.aspx?ID=1068

Przychodzin, A. M., Marchand-Martella, N. E., Martella, R. C., & Azim, D. (2004). Direct instruction mathematics program: An overview and research summary. *Journal of Direct Instruction, 4*(1), 53–84.

Pullen, P. C., & Lloyd, J. W. (2008). A focus on phonics. *Current Practice Alerts,* no. 14, 1–4.

Purdue Online Writing Lab. (2015a). *ESL teacher resources.* Retrieved from https://owl.english.purdue.edu/owl/resource/586/01

Purdue Online Writing Lab. (2015b). *OWL.* Retrieved from https://owl.english.purdue.edu/owl

Quay, H. C., & Peterson, D. R. (1967). *Manual for the behavior problem checklist.* Champaign: University of Illinois, Children's Research Center.

Quay, H. C., & Peterson, D. R. (1996). *Revised Behavior Problem Checklist.* Lutz, FL: Psychological Assessment Resources.

Raborn, D. T., & Daniel, M. J. (1999). Oobleck: A scientific encounter of the special education kind. *Teaching Exceptional Children, 31*(6), 32–40.

Rafdal, B. H., McMaster, K. L., McConnell, S. R., Fuchs, D., & Fuchs, L. S. (2011). The effectiveness of kindergarten peer-assisted learning strategies for students with disabilities. *Exceptional Children, 77*(3), 299–316.

Rafferty, L. A., & Rimondi, S. L. (2009). Self-monitoring of attention versus self-monitoring of performance: Examining the differential effects among students with emotional disturbance engaged in independent math practice. *Journal of Behavioral Education, 18,* 279–299.

Rankin-Erickson, J., & Pressley, M. (2000). A survey of instructional practices of special education teachers nominated as effective teachers of literacy. *Learning Disabilities Research and Practice, 15,* 206–225.

Rao, K., Wook, M., & Bryant, B. R. (2014). A review of research on universal design educational models. *Remedial and Special Education, 35*, 153–166. doi:10.1177/0741932513518980

Reeves, C. K. (1989). *Designing a mainstreamed environment*. In J. W. Wood (Ed.), *Mainstreaming: A practical approach for teachers*. Upper Saddle River, NJ: Merrill/Prentice Hall.

Reid, R., Lienemann, T. O., & Hagaman, J. L. (2013). *Strategy instruction for students with* learning disabilities (2nd ed.). New York: Guilford Press.

Readwritethink.org. (2016). *Using word webs to teach synonyms for commonly used words*. Retrieved from http://www.readwritethink.org/classroom-resources/lesson-plans/using-word-webs-teach-282.html

Rekate, A. C. (2015). *Have a metaphor*. Retrieved from http://www.thirteen.org/edonline/lessons/mlk/index.html

Repetto, J. B., & Correa, V. I. (1996). Expanding views on transition. *Exceptional Children, 62*, 551–563.

Riccomini, P. J. (2011). Teaching mathematics to students with learning disabilities. *New Times for DLD, 29*(1), 1–2.

Rieth, H. J., Bryant, D. P., Kinzer, C. K., Colburn, L., Hur, S., Hartman, P., et al. (2003). An analysis of the impact of anchored instruction on teaching and learning activities in two ninth grade classrooms. *Remedial and Special Education, 24*, 173–184.

Rimm-Kaufman, S. E., & Hulleman, C. S. (2015). Social and emotional learning in elementary school settings: Identifying mechanisms that matter. In J. P. Durlak, C. E. Domitrovich, R. P. Weissberg, & T. P. Gulotta (Eds.), *The handbook of social and emotional learning* (pp. 151–166). New York: Guilford Press.

Rizzo, R. (2015). *What are idioms?* Retrieved from http://k6educators.about.com/cs/lessonplanskin/a/lessonplan46c.htm

Robinson, S. M., Braxdale, C. T., & Colson, S. E. (1985). Preparing dysfunctional learners to enter junior high school: A transition curriculum. *Focus on Exceptional Children, 18*(4), 1–10.

Rock, M. L., Thead, B. K., Gable, R. A., Hardman, M. L., & Acker, R. V. (2006). In pursuit of excellence: The past as prologue to a brighter future for special education. *Focus on Exceptional Children, 38*(8), 1–2. Retrieved from http://search.ebscohost.com/login.aspx?direct=true&db=a9h&AN=22885243&site=eds-live&scope=site

Romero-Little, M.E. (2008). Language socialization of Indigenous children. In J. M. González (Ed.), *Encyclopedia of bilingual education* (pp. 493–497). Thousand Oaks, CA: Sage.

Romero-Little, M. E. (2010). How should young indigenous children be prepared for learning? A vision of early childhood education for indigenous children. *Journal of American Indian Education, 49*(1 & 2), 7–27.

Rooney, K. (1988). *Learning strategies*. Richmond, VA: Learning Resource Center.

Roseberry-McKibbin, C. (2014). *Multicultural students with special language needs: Practical strategies for assessment and intervention* (4th ed.).Oceanside, CA: Academic Communication Associates.

Rosenfield, S., & Berninger, V. (2009). *Implementing evidence-based academic interventions in school settings*. New York: Oxford University Press.

Rosenshine, B., & Stevens, R. (1986). Teaching functions. In M. C. Wittrock (Ed.), *Handbook of research on teaching* (3rd ed., pp. 376–391). Columbus, OH: Merrill.

Rule, S., Fiechtl, B. J., & Innocenti, M. S. (1990). Preparation for transition to mainstreamed post-preschool environments: Development of a survival skills curriculum. *Topics in Early Childhood Special Education, 9*(4), 78–90.

Russell, W. (2007). *Using film in the social studies*. Lanham, MD: University Press of America.

Russell, W. (2009). *Teaching social issue with film*. Charlotte, NC: Information Age.

Ryser, G., Patton, J. R., Polloway, E. A., & McConnell, K. (2006). *Practical ideas that really work for teaching math problem solving*. Austin, TX: PRO-ED.

Sabornie, E. J., & Pennington, M. L. (2015). Classroom and behavior management research in special education environments. In E. T. Emmer & E. J. Sabornie (Eds.). *Handbook of classroom management* (2nd ed., pp. 186–204). New York: Routledge, Taylor & Francis Group.

Saddler, B., & Preschern, J. (2007). Improving sentence writing ability through sentence-combining practice. *Teaching Exceptional Children, 39*(3), 6–11.

Saenz, L. M., & Fuchs, L. S. (2002). Examining the reading difficulty of secondary students with learning disabilities: Expository versus narrative text. *Remedial and Special Education, 23*(1), 31–41. doi:10.1177/074193250202300105

Salembier, G., & Furney, K. S. (1997). Facilitating participation: Parents' perceptions of their involvement in the IEP/transition planning process. *Career Development for Exceptional Individuals, 20*, 29–42.

Salend, S. J. (2005). *Creating inclusive classrooms: Effective and reflective practices* (5th ed.). Upper Saddle River, NJ: Merrill/Pearson.

Salend, S. J. (2011). *Creating inclusive classrooms: Effective and reflective practices*. Upper Saddle River, NJ: Merrill/Pearson.

Salvia, J., Ysseldyke, J. E., & Bolt, S. (2013). *Assessment in special and inclusive education* (12th ed.). Belmont, CA: Wadsworth.

Sample, K. J. (2005). Promoting fluency in adolescents with reading difficulties. *Intervention in School and Clinic, 40*, 243–246.

Sandall, B. R. (2003). Elementary science: Where are we now? *Journal of Elementary Science Education, 15*(2), 13–30.

Sandmel, K. N., Brindle, M., Harris, K. R., Lane, K. L., Graham, S., Nackel, J., et al. (2009). Making it work: Differentiating tier two self-regulated strategies development in writing in tandem with school wide positive behavioral support. *Teaching Exceptional Children, 42*(2), 22–33.

Santangelo, T., & Olinghouse, N. G. (2009). Effective writing instruction for students who have writing difficulties. *Focus on Exceptional Children, 42*(4), 1–20.

Santoro, L. E., Coyne, M. D., & Simmons, D. C. (2006). The reading–spelling connection: Developing and evaluating a beginning spelling intervention for children at risk of reading disability. *Learning Disability Research and Practice, 21*, 122–133.

Sapon-Shevin, M. (2008). Learning in an inclusive community. *Educational Leadership, 66*(1), 49–53.

Sasaki, J., & Serna, L. A. (1995). FAST science: Teaching science to adolescents with mild disabilities. *Teaching Exceptional Children, 27*(4), 14–16.

Sass, E. J. (2015). *Language arts lesson plans and resources.* Retrieved from http://www.cloudnet.com/~edrbsass/edeng.htm#synonyms

Satsangi, R., & Bouck, E. C. (2015). Using virtual manipulative instruction to teach the concepts of area and perimeter to secondary students with learning disabilities. *Learning Disability Quarterly, 38*(3), 174–186.

Saul, W., & Newman, A. R. (1986). *Science fare: An illustrated guide and catalog of toys, books, and activities for kids.* New York: Harper & Row.

Savage, T. V., & Armstrong, D. G. (1996). *Effective teaching in elementary social studies* (3rd ed.). Upper Saddle River, NJ: Merrill/Prentice Hall.

Scanlon, D., Patton, J. R., & Raskind, M. (2011). Transition to daily living for persons with high incidence disabilities. In J. M. Kauffman & D. P. Hallahan (Eds.), *Handbook of special education* (pp. 594–607). New York: Routledge.

Scarmadalia, M., & Bereiter, C. (1986). Research on written composition. In M. C. Wittrock (Ed.), *Handbook of research on teaching* (3rd ed., pp. 778–803). Columbus, OH: Merrill.

Scheuermann, A. M., Deshler, D. D., & Schumaker, J. B. (2009). The effects of the explicit inquiry routine on the performance of students with learning disabilities on one-variable equations. *Learning Disability Quarterly, 32*(2), 103–120. Retrieved from http://ezproxy.lynchburg.edu/login?url=http://search.ebscohost.com/login.aspx?direct=true&db=a9h&AN=40088273&site=eds-live&scope=site

Schewel, R. H. (1989). Semantic mapping: A study skills strategy. *Academic Therapy, 24*, 439–447.

Schewel, R. H., & Waddell, J. G. (1986). Metacognitive skills: Practical strategies. *Academic Therapy, 22*, 19–25.

Schniedewind, N., & Salend, S. (1987). Cooperative learning works. *Teaching Exceptional Children, 19*, 22–25.

Schubert, W. H. (1993). Curriculum reform. In G. Cawelti (Ed.), *ASCD 1993 yearbook: Challenges and achievements of American education* (pp. 80–115). Alexandria, VA: Association for Supervision and Curriculum Development.

Schumaker, J. B., Deshler, D. D., & Denton, P. (1984). *The learning strategies curriculum: The paraphrasing strategy.* Lawrence: University Press of Kansas.

Schumaker, J. B., Deshler, D. D., Nolan, S., Clark, F. L., Alley, G. R., & Warner, M. M. (1981). *Error monitoring: A learning strategy for improving academic performance of LD adolescents* (Research Report No. 32). Lawrence: University of Kansas, Institute for Research on Learning Disabilities.

Schumaker, J. B., & Hazel, J. S. (1984). Social skill assessment and training for the learning disabled: Who's on first and what's on second? Part I. *Journal of Learning Disabilities, 17*, 422–430.

Schumm, J. S., Moody, S. W., & Vaughn, S. (2000). Grouping for reading instruction: Does one size fit all? *Journal of Learning Disabilities, 33*, 477–488.

Schumm, J. S., & Strickler, K. (1991). Guidelines for adapting content area textbooks: Keeping teachers and students content. *Intervention, 27*, 79–84.

Schuster, E. H. (2005). No, Virginia, diagramming will not improve students' writing. *Education Week, 24*(29), 34.

Schuster, J. L., Timmons, J. C., & Moloney, M. (2003). Barriers to successful transition for young adults who receive SSI and their families. *Career Development for Exceptional Individuals, 26*, 47–66.

Scientific Research Institute International. (2004). *National Longitudinal Transition Study—2.* Retrieved from http://www.nlts2.org/nlts2faq.html

Scott, B., & Vitale, M. (2003). Teaching the writing process to students with LD. *Intervention in School and Clinic, 38*, 220.

Scott, C. M. (2012). Learning to write. In A. G. Kamhi & H. W. Catts (Eds.), *Language and reading disabilities* (3rd ed., pp. 233–273). Boston: Allyn & Bacon.

Scott, S. S., McGuire, J. M., & Shaw, S. F. (2003). Universal design for instruction: A new paradigm for adult instruction in postsecondary education. *Remedial and Special Education, 24*, 369–379.

Scruggs, T. E., Mastropieri, M. A., & Marshak, L. (2011). Science and social studies. In J. M. Kauffman & D. P. Hallahan (Eds.), *Handbook of special education* (pp. 445–455). New York: Routledge.

Scruggs, T. E., Mastropieri, M. A., & Okolo, C. M. (2008). Science and social studies for students with disabilities. *Focus on Exceptional Children, 41*(2), 1–24.

Scruggs, T. E., Mastropieri, M. A., Berkeley, M. A., & Graetz, J. (2010). Do special education interventions improve learning of secondary content? A meta analysis. *Remedial and Special Education, 31,* 437–449.

Secondary School Educators. (2015). *Rubrics—Writing and grading rubrics*. Retrieved from http://7-12educators.about.com/cs/rubrics

Seeley, J. R., Small, J. W., Walker, H. M., Feil, E. G., Severson, H. H., Golly, A. M., et al. (2009). Efficacy of the First Step to Success intervention for students with attention-deficit/hyperactivity disorder. *School Mental Health: A Multidisciplinary Research and Practice Journal, 1,* 37–48.

Semple, R. J, Reid, E. F. G., & Miller, L. (2005). Treating anxiety with mindfulness: An open trial of mindfulness training for anxious children. *Journal of Cognitive Psychotherapy: An International Quarterly, 19*(4), 379–392.

Sendak, M. (1962). *Chicken soup with rice*. New York: Harper & Row.

Sensoy, O. (2010). It's all in your name: Seeing ourselves in historical and cultural context. In E. E. Heilman, with R. F. Amthor & M. T. Missias (Eds.), *Social studies and diversity education: What we do and why we do it*. New York: Routledge.

Serna, L. A., Forness, S. R., & Nielsen, M. E. (1998). Intervention versus affirmation: Proposed solutions to the problem of disproportionate minority representation in special education. *Journal of Special Education, 32,* 48–51.

Serna, L. A., & Lau-Smith, J. A. (1994–1995). *Learning with PURPOSE: Instruction manuals for teaching self-determination skills to students who are at risk for failure*. Unpublished manual.

Serna, L. A., & Lau-Smith, J. A. (1995). Learning with PURPOSE: Self-determination skills for students who are at risk for school and community failure. *Intervention in School and Clinic, 30*(3), 142–146.

Serna, L. A., Nielsen, M. E., & Forness, S. R. (1997). *Systematic early detection and self-determination approach for mental health intervention Head Start*. Grant funded by Department of Health and Administration for Children and Families (CDFA: 93.600).

Serna, L. A., Nielsen, M. E., & Forness, S. R. (2007). *Social skills in pictures, stories, and songs: A multisensory program for preschool and early elementary students*. Champaign, IL: Research Press.

Seymour, H. N., Roeper, T. W., & de Villiers, J. (2003). *Diagnostic evaluation of language variance*. San Antonio, TX: Psychological Assessment Resources.

Shannon, T., & Polloway, E. A. (1993). Promoting error monitoring in middle school students with learning disabilities. *Intervention in School and Clinic, 28,* 160–164.

Shapiro, E. S. (2010a). *Academic skills problems: Direct assessment and intervention* (4th ed.). New York: Guilford Press.

Shapiro, E. S. (2010b). *Academic skills problems: Fourth edition workbook*. New York: Guilford Press.

Shaywitz, S. (2003). *Overcoming dyslexia: A new and complete science-based program for reading problems at any level*. New York: Knopf.

Sheehy, K. (2005). Morphing images: A potential tool for teaching word recognition to children with severe learning difficulties. *British Journal of Educational Technology, 36*(2), 293–301. http://dx.doi.org/10.1111/j.1467-8535.2005.00458.x

Shipley, K. G., Stone, A.T., & Sue, M. B. (1983). *Test for Examining Expressive Morphology*. Austin, TX: PRO-ED.

Shippen, M., Houchins, D., Calhoon, M., Furlow, C., & Sartor, D. (2006). The effects of comprehensive school reform models in reading for urban middle school students with disabilities. *Remedial and Special Education, 27,* 322–329.

Shogren, K. A., Wehmeyer, M. L., Palmer, S. B., Forber, A. J., Little, T. J., & Lopez, S. (2015). Causal agency theory: Re-conceptualizing a functional model of self-determination. *Education and Training in Autism and Developmental Disabilities, 50*(3), 251–263.

Shure, M. B. (1999, April 1–11). Preventing violence the problem-solving way. *Juvenile Justice Bulletin*. Publication of the U.S. Department of Justice, Office of Juvenile Justice and Delinquency Prevention.

Siegler, R. S., Duncan, G. J., Davis-Kean, P. E., Duckworth, K., Claessens, A., Engel, M., et al. (2012). Early predictors of high school mathematics achievement. *Psychological Science, 23,* 691–697.

Silbert, J., Carnine, D., & Stein, M. (1990). *Direct instruction mathematics* (2nd ed.). Upper Saddle River, NJ: Merrill/Prentice Hall.

Silverman, F., & Miller, L. (2017). *Introduction to communication sciences and disorders* (5th ed.). Austin, TX: PRO-ED.

Simonsen, B., Fairbanks, S., Briesch, A., Myers, D., & Sugai, G. (2008). Evidence-based practices in classroom management: Considerations for research to practice. *Education and Treatment of Children, 31*(3), 351–380.

Simonsen, B., & Sugai, G. (2009). School-wide positive behavior support: A system-level application of behavioral principles. In A. Akin-Little, S. G. Little, M. A. Bray, & T. J. Kehle (Eds.), *Behavioral interventions in schools: Evidence-based positive strategies* (pp. 125–140). Washington, DC: American Psychological Association.

Singh, N. N., Lancioni, G. E., Singh Joy, S., Winton, A. S. W., Sabaawi, M., Wahler, R. G., et al. (2007). Adolescents with conduct disorder can be mindful of their aggressive behavior. *Journal of Emotional and Behavioral Disorders*, 15(1), 58–63.

Sitlington, P. L., Clark, G. M., & Patton, J. R. (2008). *Informal assessments in transition planning: Postsecondary education and training.* Austin, TX: PRO-ED.

Sitlington, P. L., Neubert, D. A., Begun, W. H., Lombard, R. C., & Leconte, P. J. (2007). *Assess for success: A practitioner's handbook on transition assessment* (2nd ed.). Arlington, VA: Division on Career Development and Transition.

Sitlington, P. L., Neubert, D. A., & Clark, G. M. (2010). *Transition education and services for students with disabilities* (5th ed.). Boston: Pearson.

Skiba, R. J., Simmons, A., Ritter, S., Kohler, K., Henderson, M., & Wu, T. (2006). The context of minority disproportionality: Practitioner perspectives on special education referral. *Teachers College Record*, 108, 1424–1459.

Skouge, J. R., Kelly, M., O'Brien, R., & Thomas, K. (2003). *Creating futures: Video empowerment for self-determination.* Paper included in the 2003 Virtual Reality Conference. Retrieved from http://www.csun.edu/cod/conf/2003/proceedings/Tssts~1.htm

Slosson, R. L., Nicholson, C. L., & Hippsman, T. L. (2002). *Slosson Intelligence Test—Revised—Third Edition.* East Aurora, NY: Slosson Educational Publications.

Smith, D. D., & Tyler, N. C. (2014). *Introduction to contemporary special education: New horizons.* Columbus, OH: Pearson.

Smith, L. J., & Smith, D. L. (1990). *Social studies: Detecting and correcting special needs.* Boston: Allyn & Bacon.

Smith, T. E. C., Polloway, E. A., Doughty, J., Patton, J. R., & Dowdy, C. A. (2016). *Teaching students with special needs in inclusive settings* (7th ed.). Columbus, OH: Pearson.

Smith, T. E. C., Polloway, E. A., Patton, J. R., & Dowdy, C. A. (2008). *Teaching students with special needs in inclusive settings* (5th ed.). Boston: Allyn & Bacon.

Smith, T. E. C., Polloway, E. A., Patton, J. R., & Dowdy, C. A. (2012). *Teaching students with special needs in inclusive settings* (6th ed.). Boston: Pearson.

Soares, D. A., Vannest, K. J., & Harrison, J. (2009). Computer aided self-monitoring to increase academic production and reduce self-injurious behavior in a child with autism. *Behavior Interventions*, 24, 171–183.

Solís, M., Vaughn, S., & Scammacca, N. (2015). The effects of an intensive reading intervention for ninth graders with very low reading comprehension. *Learning Disabilities Research and Practice*, 30(3), 104–113. doi:10.1111/ldrp.12061

Southall, C. M., & Gast, D. L. (2011). Self-management procedures: A comparison across the autism spectrum. *Education and Training in Autism and Developmental Disabilities*, 46(2), 155.

Southern Pueblos Agency. (2002). *Science checklist, building exceptional schools for tomorrow.* Albuquerque, NM: BEST Council. (Retrieved from compact disc).

Spalding Education International. (2000). *Spalding implementation of research findings from the report of the National Reading Panel.* Phoenix, AZ: Author.

Spalding Method Catalog. (2002). Phoenix, AZ: Spalding Education International.

Sparrow, S. S., Balla, D. A., & Cicchetti, D. V. (2005). *Vineland Adaptive Behavior Scales—Second Edition.* Circle Pines, MN: American Guidance Service.

Spencer, M., Quinn, J. M., & Wagner, R. K. (2014). Specific reading comprehension disability: Major problem, myth, or misnomer? *Learning Disabilities Research and Practice*, 29(1), 3–9. Retrieved from http://search.ebscohost.com/login.aspx?direct=true&db=eric&AN=EJ1029983&site=eds-live&scope=site; http://dx.doi.org/10.1111/ldrp.12024

Spinelli, C. G. (2005). *Classroom assessment for students in special and general education* (2nd ed.). Upper Saddle River, NJ: Merrill/Pearson.

Spinelli, C. G. (2012). *Classroom assessment for students in special and general education* (3rd ed.). Upper Saddle River, NJ: Merrill/Pearson.

Spörer, N., & Brunstein, J. C. (2009). Fostering the reading comprehension of secondary school students through peer-assisted learning: Effects on strategy knowledge, strategy use, and task performance. *Contemporary Educational Psychology*, 34, 289–297. doi:10.1016/j.cedpsych.2009.06.004

Sprague, J. R., & Golly, A. (2004). *Best behavior: Building positive behavior supports in schools.* Longmont, CO: Sopris West.

Sprague, J. R., & Walker, H. M. (2005). *Safe and healthy schools: Practical prevention strategies.* New York: Guilford Press.

Stanovich, K. E. (1986). Matthew effects in reading: Some consequences of individual differences in the acquisition of literacy. *Reading Research Quarterly*, 21(4), 360–406.

Stanovich, K. E., & Stanovich, P. J. (1995). How research might inform the debate about early reading acquisition. *Journal of Research in Reading, 18*, 87–105.

Stanovich, P. J., & Stanovich, K. E. (2003). *Using research and reason in education: How teachers can use scientifically based research to make curricular and instructional decisions.* Washington, DC: U.S. Department of Education.

Staudacher, C., & Turner, S. (1990). *Practical mathematics.* Upper Saddle River, NJ: Fearon Education.

Steinbrink, J. E., & Jones, R. M. (1991). Focused test review items: Improving textbook-test alignment in social studies. *The Social Studies, 82*, 72–76.

Stepanek, J., & Jarrett, D. (1997). *Assessment strategies to inform science and mathematics instruction: It's just good teaching.* Portland, OR: Northwest Regional Educational Laboratory. Retrieved from http://www.nwrel.org/msec/book4pdf.pdf

Sternberg, R. J., Kaufman, J. C., & Grigorenko, E. L. (2008). *Applied intelligence.* New York: Cambridge University Press.

Stevens, R., & Rosenshine, B. (1981). Advances in research on teaching. *Exceptional Education Quarterly, 2*, 1–9.

Stoddard, J. D., & Marcus, A. S. (2006). The burden of historical representation: Race, freedom, and "educational" Hollywood film. *Film and History, 36*(1), 26–35.

Stokes, T. F., & Baer, D. M. (1977). An implicit technology of generalization. *Journal of Applied Behavior Analysis, 10*, 349–367.

Stone, C. A. (1998). The metaphor of scaffolding: Its utility for the field of learning disabilities. *Journal of Learning Disabilities, 31*, 344–364.

Strichart, S. S., & Mangrum, C. T., III. (2002). *Teaching learning strategies and study skills to students with learning disabilities, attention deficit disorders, or special needs* (3rd ed.). Boston: Allyn & Bacon.

Strickland, T. K., & Maccini, P. (2012). The effects of the concrete-representational-abstract-integration strategy on the ability of students with learning disabilities to multiply linear expressions within area problems. *Remedial and Special Education, 34*(3), 142–153.

Strong, W. (1983). *Sentence combining: A composing book* (2nd ed.). New York: Random House.

Stull, J., Varnum, S., Ducette, J., & Schiller, J. (2011). The many faces of formative assessment. *International Journal of Teaching and Learning in Higher Education, 23*(1), 30–39.

Sugai, G., & Horner, R. H. (1999). Discipline and behavioral support: Preferred processes and practices. *Effective School Practices, 17*, 10–22.

Sugai, G., & Simonsen, B. (2012). *Positive behavioral interventions and supports: History, defining features, and misconceptions.* Retrieved from http://www.pbis.org/common/cms/files/pbisresources/PBIS_revisited_June19r_2012.pdf

Sunal, C., & Sunal, D. (2003). Teacher candidates' conceptualization of guided inquiry and lesson planning following web-assisted instruction. *Theory and Research in Social Education, 31*(2), 243–264.

Swanson, E. (2008). Observing reading instruction for students with learning disabilities: A synthesis. *Learning Disability Quarterly, 31*, 115–133.

Swanson, H. L., Orosco, M. J., & Lussier, C. M. (2014). The effects of mathematics strategy instruction for children with serious problem-solving difficulties. *Exceptional Children, 80*(2), 149–168.

Synatschk, K. O., Clark, G. M., & Patton, J. R. (2008). *Independent living and community participation.* Austin, TX: PRO-ED.

Synatschk, K. O., Clark, G. M., Patton, J. R., & Copeland, L. R. (2007). *Employment and career planning.* Austin, TX: PRO-ED.

Taft, R., & Mason, L. H. (2011). Examining effect of writing interventions: Spotlighting results for students with primary disabilities other than learning disabilities. *Remedial and Special Education, 32*, 359–370. doi:10.1177/0741932510362242

Tanol, G., Johnson, L., McComas, J., & Cote, E. (2010). Responding to rule violations or rule following: A comparison study of two versions of the good behavior game with kindergarten students. *Journal of School Psychology, 48*, 337–355. doi:10.1016/j.jsp.2010.06.001

Taylor-Green, S., Brown, D., Nelson, L., Longton, J., Gassman, T., Cohen, J., et al. (1997). School-wide behavioral support: Starting the year off right. *Journal of Behavioral Education, 7*, 99–112.

Teacher Vision. (2015). *Metaphor unit poems.* Retrieved from https://www.teachervision.com/poetry/lesson-plan/5454.html

TeachNet.com. (2015). *Synonyms and antonyms.* Retrieved from http://teachnet.com/lessonplans/language-arts/synonyms-and-antonyms

The Next Generation Science Standards (2015). *American Educator, 39*(3), 40–40. Retrieved from http://ezproxy.lynchburg.edu/login?url=http://search.ebscohost.com/login.aspx?direct=true&db=ehh&AN=110194794&site=eds-live&scope=site

Therrien, W. J., Taylor, J. C., Hosp, J. L., Kaldenberg, E. R., & Gorsh, J. (2011). Science instruction for students with learning disabilities: A meta-analysis. *Learning Disabilities Research and Practice, 26*(4), 188–203.

Therrein, W. J., Taylor, J. C., Watt, S., & Kaldenberg, E. R. (2014). Science instruction for students with emotional and behavioral disorders. *Remedial and Special Education, 35*(1), 15–27. doi:10.1177/0741932513503557

Thirteen Ed Online. (2015). *How media shapes perception.* Retrieved from http://www.thirteen.org/edonline/lessons/media/#close

Thoma, C. A., Bartholomew, C. C., & Scott, L. A. (2009). *Universal design for transition: A roadmap for planning and instruction.* Baltimore: Brookes.

Thombs, M. M., Gillis, M. M., & Canestrari, A. S. (2009). *Using WebQuest in the social studies classroom.* Thousand Oaks, CA: Corwin Press.

Thompson, J. R., Fulk, B. M., & Piercy, S. W. (2000). Do individualized transition plans match the postschool projections of students with learning disabilities and their parents? *Career Development for Exceptional Individuals, 23,* 3–26.

Thorndike, R. L., Hagen, E. P., & Sattler, J. M. (1986). *The Stanford-Binet Intelligence Scale—Fourth Edition.* Chicago: Riverside.

Thousand, J. S., Villa, R. A., & Nevin, A. I. (2007). *Differentiated instruction: Collaborative planning and teaching for universally designed learning.* Thousand Oaks, CA: Corwin Press.

Thurber, D. N. (2008). *D'Nealian handwriting: Student edition.* Glenview, IL: Scott Foresman.

Tomlinson, C. A. (2001). *How to differentiate instruction in mixed-ability classrooms* (2nd ed.). Alexandria, VA: Association for Supervision and Curriculum Development.

Tomlinson, C. (2014). *The differentiated classroom: Responding to the needs of all learners.* Alexandria, VA: Association for Supervision and Curriculum Development.

Tompkins, G. E. (2005). *Language arts patterns of practice* (6th ed.). Upper Saddle River, NJ: Merrill/Pearson.

Tompkins, G. E. (2006). *Literacy for the 21st century: A balanced approach* (4th ed.). Upper Saddle River, NJ: Merrill/Pearson.

Torgesen, J. K., & Bryant, B. (2004). *Test of Phonological Awareness—Second Edition: PLUS.* Austin, TX: PRO-ED.

Torgesen, J. K., & Mathes, P. G. (2000). *A basic guide to understanding, assessing, and teaching phonological awareness.* Austin, TX: PRO-ED.

Torres-Velasquez, D., & Lobo, G. (2005). Culturally responsive mathematics teaching and English language learners. *Teaching Children Mathematics, 11*(5), 249–255.

Troia, G. A. (2002). Teaching writing strategies to children with disabilities: Setting generalization as the goal. *Exceptionality, 10,* 249–269.

Troia, G. A. (2004). A focus on phonological awareness acquisition and intervention. *Current Practice Alerts,* no. *10,* 1–4.

Troia, G. A. (2005, October). *The writing instructional research we have, the writing instruction research we need.* Paper presented at the Literacy Achievement Research Center Symposium on Literacy Achievement, Michigan State University, Lansing.

Troia, G. A., & Graham, S. (2002). The effectiveness of a highly explicit, teacher-directed strategy instruction routine: Changing the writing performance of students with learning disabilities. *Journal of Learning Disabilities, 35,* 290–305.

Truch, S. (1998). *Phonological processing, reading and the Lindamood Phoneme Sequencing Program: A review of related research.* Austin, TX: PRO-ED.

Turner, T. N. (1976). Making the social studies textbook a more effective tool for less able readers. *Social Education, 40,* 38–41.

Tweed, A. (2005). *Classroom instruction that works: Facilitators manual.* Aurora, CO: Mid-Continent Research for Education and Learning.

Uberti, H. Z., Scruggs, T. E., & Mastropieri, M. A. (2003). Keywords make the difference! *Teaching Exceptional Children, 35*(3), 56. Retrieved from http://ezproxy.lynchburg.edu/login?url=http://search.ebscohost.com/login.aspx?direct=true&db=a9h&AN=8735233&site=eds-live&scope=site

University of Kansas. (2014). *Center for Research on Learning.* Retrieved from http://www.ku-crl.org/sim/strategies.shtml.

University of Missouri. (2015). *Teaching tips: Phonemic awareness.* Retrieved from https://ethemes.missouri.edu/themes/543

University of Oregon Center on Teaching and Learning. (2015). *Phonemic awareness.* Retrieved from http://reading.uoregon.edu/big_ideas/pa/pa_teach.php

Unrau, N. (2004). *Content area reading and writing: Fostering literacies in middle and high school cultures.* Upper Saddle River, NJ: Pearson.

U.S. Census Bureau. (2013). *Language use in the United States: 2011.* Retrieved from http://www.census.gov/prod/2013pubs/acs-22.pdf

U.S. Department of Education. (2008). *Final report of the National Mathematics Advisory Panel.* Washington, DC: Author.

U.S. Department of Education. (2014). *36th annual report to Congress on the implementation of the Individuals with Disabilities Education Act.* Washington, DC: Author.

U.S. Department of Education. (2015). *37th annual report to Congress on the implementation of the Individuals with Disabilities Education Act.* Washington, DC: Author.

U.S. Department of Education. (2016). *38th annual report to Congress on the implementation of the Individuals with Disabilities Education Act.* Washington, DC: Author.

Valetutti, P. J., Bender, M., & Baglin, C. A. (2008). *A functional assessment and curriculum for teaching students with disabilities: Functional academics* (3rd ed.). Austin, TX: PRO-ED.

Van de Walle, J. A., Karp, K. S., & Bay-Williams, J. M. (2010). *Elementary and middle school mathematics: Teaching developmentally* (7th ed.). Upper Saddle River, NJ: Pearson Education.

Vaughn, S. R., & Bos, C. S. (2015). *Strategies for teaching students with learning and behavior problems* (9th ed.). Boston: Pearson.

Vaughn, S., Bos, C. S., & Schumm, J. (2006). *Teaching exceptional, diverse, and at-risk students in the general education classroom* (4th ed.). Boston: Allyn & Bacon.

Vaughn, S., Gersten, R., & Chard, D. J. (2000). The underlying message in LD intervention research: Findings from research syntheses. *Exceptional Children, 67*, 99–114.

Vaughn, S., & Schumm, J. S. (1997). Are they getting it? How to monitor student understanding in inclusive classrooms. *Intervention in School and Clinic, 32*, 168–172.

Vaughn, S., Swanson, E. A., Roberts, G., Wanzek, J., Stillman-Spisak, S. J., Solis, M., et al. (2013). Improving reading comprehension and social studies knowledge in middle school. *Reading Research Quarterly, 48*(1), 77–93.

Vaughn, S., & Wanzek, J. (2014). Intensive interventions in reading for students with reading disabilities: Meaningful impacts. *Learning Disabilities Research and Practice, 29*(2), 46–53.

Virginia Department of Education. (2016). Universal design for learning. Retrieved from http://www.doe.virginia.gov/special_ed/disabilities/universal_design_learning.shtml

Wagner, M., Newman, L., Cameto, R., Garza, N., & Levine, P. (2005). *After high school: A first look at the post-school experiences of youth with disabilities: A report from the National Longitudinal Transition Study—2 (NTLS-2)*. Menlo Park, CA: SRI International.

Wagner, R. K., & Meros, D. (2010). *Vocabulary and reading comprehension: Direct, indirect, and reciprocal influences*. Denver, CO: Love. Retrieved from http://search.ebscohost.com/login.aspx?direct=true&db=edsgao&AN=edsgcl.245473138&site=eds-live&scope=site

Wagner, R., Torgesen, K., Rashotte, C., & Pearson, N. (2013). *Comprehensive Test of Phonological Processing—Second Edition*. Austin, TX: PRO-ED.

Walker, H. M., Kavanaugh, K., Stiller, B., Golly, A., Serverson, H. M., & Feil, E. G. (1997). First Step to Success: An early intervention approach for preventing school antisocial behavior. *Journal of Emotional and Behavioral Disorders, 6*, 163–172.

Walker, H. M., McConnell, S., Holmes, D., Todis, B., Walker, J., & Golden, N. (1983). *The Walker social skills curriculum: The ACCEPTS program*. Austin, TX: PRO-ED.

Walker, H. M., Ramsey, E., & Gresham, F. M. (2004). *Antisocial behavior in school: Evidence-based practices*. Belmont, CA: Wadsworth/Thomson Learning.

Walker, H. M., & Severson, H. H. (1992). *Systematic screening for behavior disorders*. Longmont, CO: Sopris West.

Wallace, G., & Hammill, D. D. (2013). *Comprehensive Receptive and Expressive Vocabulary Test—Third Edition*. Austin, TX: PRO- ED.

Wallace, G., & Kauffman, J. M. (1986). *Teaching children with learning and behavior problems* (2nd ed.). Columbus, OH: Merrill.

Wanzek, J., Dickson, S., Bursuck, W. D., & White, J. M. (2000). Teaching phonological awareness to students at risk for reading failure: An analysis of four instructional programs. *Learning Disabilities Research and Practice, 15*(4), 226–239.

Waters, H. E., & Boon, R. T. (2011). Teaching money computation skills to high school students with mild intellectual disabilities via the TouchMath[C] program: A multi-sensory approach. *Education and Training in Autism and Developmental Disabilities, 46*(4), 544–555.

Watson, S. M. R., Gable, R. A., Gear, S. B., & Hughes, K. C. (2012). Evidence-based strategies for improving the reading comprehension of secondary students: Implications for students with learning disabilities. *Learning Disabilities Research and Practice, 27*(2), 79–89. doi:10.1111/j.1540-5826.2012.00353.x

Watts, J. (2016). Assessment strategies. In E. A. Polloway & J. Lubin, *Graphic models and instructional tools for students with special needs* (p. 22), *Lynchburg College Journal of Special Education*, Lynchburg College, Lynchburg, VA. Used with permission.

Wehby, J. H., & Kern, L. (2014). Intensive behavior intervention: What is it, what is its evidence base, and why do we need to implement now? *Teaching Exceptional Children, 46*, 38–44.

Wehman, P., & Kregel, J. (Eds.). (2012). *Functional curriculum for elementary, middle, and secondary age students with special needs* (3rd ed.). Austin, TX: PRO-ED.

Wehman, P., Targett, P., & Green, H. (2012). Going to work. In P. Wehman & J. Kregel (Eds.), *Functional curriculum for elementary, middle, and secondary age students with special needs* (3rd ed., pp. 579–602). Austin, TX: PRO-ED.

Wehmeyer, M. L. (1995). A career education approach: Self-determination for youth with mild cognitive disabilities. *Intervention in School and Clinic, 30*(3), 157–163.

Wehmeyer, M. L. (2002). *Teaching students with mental retardation: Providing access to the general curriculum*. Baltimore: Brookes.

Wehmeyer, M. L. (2015). Framing the future: Self-determination. *Remedial and Special Education, 36*(1) 20–23.

Wehmeyer, M. L., Morningstar, M., & Husted, D. (1999). *Family involvement in transition planning and implementation*. Austin, TX: PRO-ED.

Weinstein, C. S. (2007). *Secondary classroom management: Lessons from research and practice*. Boston: McGraw-Hill.

Weissberg, R. P., Durlak, J. A., Domitrovich, C. E., & Gullotta, T. P. (2015). Social and emotional learning: Past, present, and future. In J. A. Durlak, C. E. Domitrovich, R. P. Weissberg, & T. P. Gullotta (Eds.), *Handbook of social and emotional learning: Research and practice* (pp. 3–20). New York: Guilford Press.

Wells, C. (1996). *Literacies lost: When students move from progressive middle school to a traditional high school*. New York: Teachers College Press.

West, G. K. (1986). *Parenting without guilt*. Springfield, IL: Charles C. Thomas.

West, G. K. (1994, November 10). Discipline that works: Part 1. *The News and Daily Advance*, pp. 13–14.

West, P. (n.d.). *Manipulatives in mathematics instruction*. Unpublished manuscript.

Westphal, L. E. (2009). *Differentiating instruction with menus: Social studies*. Waco, TX: Prufrock Press.

Wexler, L. (2009). The importance of identity, history, and culture in the wellbeing of Indigenous youth. *Journal of the History of Childhood and Youth, 2*(2), 267–276.

What Works Clearinghouse. (2012). *Peer-assisted learning/literacy strategies: What works Clearinghouse intervention report*. Retrieved from http://files.eric.ed.gov/fulltext/ED531596.pdf

What Works Clearinghouse. (2014). *Repeated reading: What works Clearinghouse intervention report*. Retrieved from http://files.eric.ed.gov/fulltext/ED545099.pdf

Wiederholt, J. L., & Bryant, B. R. (2012). *Gray Oral Reading Tests—Fifth Edition*. Austin, TX: PRO-ED.

Wiig, E. H., & Secord, W. A. (2014) *Clinical Evaluation of Language Fundamentals—Fifth Edition*. San Antonio, TX: Pearson Education.

Wiley, A. L., & Siperstein, G. N. (2015). SEL for student with high-incidence disabilities. In J. A. Durlak, C. E. Domitrovich, R. P. Weissberg, & T. P. Gullotta (Eds.), *Handbook of social and emotional learning: Research and practice* (pp. 181–197). New York: Guilford Press.

Wilkinson, G. S., & Robertson, G. J. (2006). *Wide Range Achievement Test—Fourth Edition*. Lutz, FL: Psychological Assessment Resources.

Williams, J. M., & O'Leary, E. (2001). What we've learned and where we go from here. *Career Development for Exceptional Individuals, 24*(1), 51–69.

Williams, J. P., Nubla-Kung, A. M., Pollini, S., Stafford, K. B., Garcia, A., & Snyder, A. E. (2007). Teaching cause-effect structure through social studies content to at-risk second graders. *Journal of Learning Disabilities, 40*, 111–120.

Williamson, A. A., Modecki, K. L., & Guerra, N. G. (2015). SEL programs in high school. In J. P. Durlak, C. E. Domitrovich, R. P. Weissberg, & T. P. Gulotta (Eds.), *The handbook of social and emotional learning* (pp. 181–196). New York: Guilford Press.

Wilson, B. A., & O'Connor, J. R. (1995). Effectiveness of the Wilson reading system used in public school training. In C. McIntyre & J. Pickering (Eds.), *Clinical studies of multisensory structured language education* (pp. 247–254). Salem, OR: International Multisensory Structured Language Education Council.

Wilson Language Training Corporation. (2015). *Wilson Reading System*. Retrieved from http://www.wilsonlanguage.com/programs/wilson-reading-system

Winchester, K., Darch, C., Eaves, R. C., Shippen, M. E., Ern, G., & Bell, B. (2009). An evaluation of two methods for teaching united states history to students with learning disabilities. *Journal of Direct Instruction, 9*(1), 57–73.

Wolery, M. (1989). Transitions in early childhood special education: Issues and procedures. *Focus on Exceptional Children, 22*(2), 1–16.

Wolfe, P. S., & Kubina, R. M. (2004). Functional academics. In P. Wehman & J. Kregel (Eds.), *Functional curriculum for elementary, middle, and secondary age students with special needs* (2nd ed., pp. 113–139). Austin, TX: PRO-ED.

Wolfe, P. S., & Ostryn, C. (2012). Functional academics. In P. Wehman & J. Kregel (Eds.), *Functional curriculum for elementary, middle, and secondary age students with special needs* (3rd ed., pp. 159–210). Austin, TX: PRO-ED.

Woolfolk, A. E. (2009). *Educational psychology*. Upper Saddle River, NJ: Merrill/Pearson.

Woolfolk, A. (2012). *Educational psychology* (12th ed.). Boston: Pearson.

Wolford, P. L., Heward, W. L., & Alber, S. R. (2001). Teaching middle school students with learning disabilities to recruit peer assistance during cooperative learning group activities. *Learning Disabilities Research and Practice, 16*, 161–173.

Wolpe, J. (1958). *Psychotherapy by reciprocal inhibition*. Palo Alto, CA: Stanford University Press.

Wong, B. Y. L. (1982). Understanding learning-disabled students' reading problems: Contributions from cognitive psychology. *Topics in Learning and Learning Disabilities, 1*(4), 43–50.

Wong, B. Y. L. (2003). General and specific issues for researchers' consideration in applying the risk and resilience framework to the social domain of learning disabilities. *Learning Disabilities Research and Practice, 18*(2), 68–76.

Woodcock, R. W. (2011). *Woodcock Reading Mastery Test—Third Edition*. Circle Pines, MN: American Guidance Service.

Woods-Groves, S., Hua, Y., Therrien, W. J., Kaldenberg, E. R., Kihura, R. W., & Hendrickson, J. M. (2015). An investigation of the efficacy of an editing strategy with postsecondary individuals with developmental disabilities. *Education and Training in Autism and Developmental Disabilities, 50*(1), 95–108. Retrieved from http://search.ebscohost.com/login .aspx?direct=true&db=eric&AN=EJ1052830&site= eds-live&scope=site; http://daddcec.org/Publications/ ETADDJournal.aspx

Woods-Groves, S., Hughes, C. A., Therrien, W. J., Hua, Y., Hendrickson, J. M., & Shaw, J. W. (2012). *Effectiveness of an essay writing strategy for post-secondary students with developmental disabilities.* Retrieved from http://search.ebscohost.com/login.asp x?direct=true&db=edsjsr&AN=edsjsr.23880101&sit e=eds-live&scope=site

Woodward, A., Elliott, D. L., & Nagel, K. C. (1986). Beyond textbooks in elementary social studies. *Social Education, 50*, 50–53.

Worrall, R. S. (1990). Detecting health fraud in the field of learning disabilities. *Journal of Learning Disabilities, 23*, 207–212.

Wright, T. (2013). "I keep me safe": Risk and resilience in children with messy lives. *Phi Delta Kappan, 95*(2), 39–43.

Yager, R. E. (1989). A rationale for using personal relevance as a science curriculum focus in schools. *School Science and Mathematics, 89*, 144–156.

Yakubova, G., & Bouck, E. C. (2014). Not all created equally: Exploring calculator use by students with mild intellectual disability. *Education and Training in Autism and Developmental Disabilities, 49*, 111–126.

Yell, M., Rozalski, M., & Miller, J. (2015). Classroom management and the law. In E. T. Emmer & E. J. Sabornie (Eds.), *Handbook of classroom management* (2nd ed., pp. 431–445). New York: Routledge, Taylor & Francis Group.

Young, K. R., West, R. P., Li, L., & Peterson, L. (1997). Teaching self-management skills to students with learning and behavior problems. *Reclaiming Children and Youth, 6*, 90–96.

YourDictionary.com. (2015). *Homonym lesson plans.* Retrieved from http://www.yourdictionary.com/ grammar/homonym-lesson-plans.html

Zevin, J. (2010). *Social studies for the twenty-first century: Methods and materials for teaching middle and secondary schools.* New York: Routledge.

Zhang, D., & Xin, Y. P. (2012). A follow-up meta-analysis for word-problem-solving interventions for students with mathematics difficulties. *Journal of Educational Research, 105*(5), 303–318, doi:10 .1080/00220671.2011.627397

Ziegler, J. C., Pech-Georgel, C., George, F., Lorenzi, C., Smith, E. E., & F.-Xavier, A. (2005). Deficits in speech perception predict language learning impairment. *Proceedings of the National Academy of Sciences of the United States of America, 102*(39), 14110–14115.

Ziegler, J. C., Pech-Georgel, C., George, F., Alario, F. X., & Lorenzi, C. (2005). Deficits in speech perception predict language learning impairment. *Proceedings of the National Academy of Sciences of the United States of America, 102*(3a), 14110–14115.

Zimmerman, I., Steiner, V., & Pond, R. (2002). *Preschool Language Scale—Fourth Edition, Spanish.* San Antonio, TX: Psychological Assessment Resources.

Zirkel, P. (2008). A legal roadmap of SBR, PRR and related terms under the IDEA. *Focus on Exceptional Children, 40*(5), 1–4.

Zumeta, R. O. (2015). Implementing intensive intervention: How do we get there from here? *Remedial and Special Education, 36*(2), 83–88.

Content enhancement techniques, 234, 235–237
Content standards, 6
Content–Understanding–Environment (CUE) framework, 259
Contextual analysis, word recognition and, 128
Contingencies
    contingency contracting, 65
    group, 65–66, 68
Continuous monitoring of performance, 196–197
Continuous reinforcement schedule, 64
Contracts, continuous, 56–57
Conversational discourse, 80–81
    adolescents and, 87–88
    school-age children and, 84
Cooperative learning (CL)
    described, 28
    elements in, 28
    for mathematics, 205
    for science, 259, 267
    study skills and, 289–290, 291
Cooperative teaching
    approaches to, 23–24
    key elements of, 24
    principles of, 24
    for science instruction, 252, 265
Coping, 297, 298
COPS strategy, 183–184, 285, 286
Corrective Mathematics, 218–219
Corrective Reading Program (CRP), 131
CRI (culturally responsive instruction), 21
Criterion-referenced tests
    language, 91, 92
    in social skills assessment, 311
    in study skills assessment, 279, 280–281
Critical reading comprehension, 137
CRUSH strategy, 129
Cultural competence, 72
Cultural diversity
    classroom management and, 72–74
    curriculum and, 73–74, 79
    defined, 72
    transition process and, 369–370
Culturally and linguistically diverse (CLD) children
    language abilities in, 90
    language assessment in, 92–93, 94
    language instruction for, 104–106
Culturally responsive classrooms
    characteristics of, 79
    reading instruction in, 121
    social skills, 322
    study skills, 296
    vocabulary knowledge and, 144–145
Culturally responsive instruction (CRI), 21
Culture
    classroom, 258

foreign, immersing students in, 243
    language and, 78–79
Curricular programs, word-recognition phonemic awareness and, 129–131
Curriculum
    comprehensive, 19
    cultural diversity and, 73–74, 79
    functional, 327, 351
    general considerations, 5–6, 17–19
    general education, 328–329
    relationship of standards to, 18
    science, 247–249
    self-determination (See Self-determination curriculum)
    for social-emotional learning, 318–319
    social skills, 311–313
    social studies, 225–226
    types of, 18–19
    written language in, 157–159
Curriculum-based measurement (CBM)
    of reading comprehension, 140
    of reading skills, 117–118
    in science assessment, 252
    for social studies, 229
    of spoken language, 92
    steps in, 117
    of written language, 161
Cursive writing, 164–165

Data-gathering/processing techniques, in science lesson, 258–259
Decision making, 211, 212
    for secondary school students, 315
Declarative knowledge, mathematics instruction and, 189
Decoding-based programs, 114, 129–131
Defective algorithm (DA), in mathematics assessment, 193
DEFENDS strategy, 286
Delivery, in differentiated instruction, 38–39
Delta Science Modules, 248
Developmental scales, language assessment and, 92
Developmental (vertical) transitions, 358–361
Differential reinforcement strategies, 68–69
Differentiated instruction
    adjustments in, 38–41
    content-based, 36
    intervention-based, 32–33, 261–262
    key elements of, 36
    management dimension of, 262
    materials-based, 36–38
    model of, 36
    overview of, 34–35
    in science, 251, 264–267
    setting dimension of, 36

Direct instruction, 21–22
    for mathematics skills, 195
    PURPOSE teaching format and, 22–23
    for reading skills, 123
    of social and self-determination skills, 316–317
Direct observation of social skills, assessment procedures for, 307–310
Direct service projects, 244
Directed reading/thinking activity (DRTA) technique, 146–147
Disabilities. See Students with disabilities; Students with learning disabilities
Discourse
    adolescents and, 88
    classroom, 100
    language use and, 80–82
    types of, 86
Diversity. See also Culturally and linguistically diverse (CLD) children
    classroom challenges and, 79
    classroom management and, 72–74
    mathematics instruction and, 213
    post secondary transitions and, 369–370
    science instruction and, 261
    social studies instruction and, 228–229
    written expression instruction and, 180
Division skills, 203, 207–208
DMSCBA (mnemonic), 208
D'Nealian handwriting program, 165
Drafting, as writing stage, 173–182
Dramatic discourse, 81
Dreams, future, in transition planning process, 373
DRI strategy, differential reinforcement, 68
DRL strategy, differential reinforcement, 68
    good-behavior game, 68–69
DRO strategy, differential reinforcement, 68
Dropout rate, for students with disabilities, 9–10
Dynamic assessment, 92
    mediated teaching and, 96–98

Early intervention, 9
Edit sheets, 191
EDIT strategy, 184
Editing, 183
Edmark Reading Program, 130–131
Education for All Handicapped Children Act (EHA), 1
Educational practices
    cautions regarding, 8–9
    effective (See Effective educational practice)

Interpersonal training, study skill development, 290, 291
Intervention. *See also* Positive behavioral support (PBS)
early, 9
evidence-based practice and, 7
Intonation, 78
Introduction, science lesson, 258
Invented spelling, 171
Invented spellings, 169–170
Irony, 89

Journals
for mathematics assessment, 194
for science assessment, 253
for social studies assessment, 230

Keyboarding, 166
KeyMath3 Diagnostic Assessment, 191–192
Keyword method, 237
Keywords, 143, 239
Kindergarten, transition from preschool, 360–361
Kindergarten Peer-Assisted Learning Strategies (K-PALS), 131
Knowledge
prior, 115, 157
propositional, 233
types of, mathematics instruction and, 189
word comprehension, 137, 141–145

Laboratory materials, adapting, 265
Language. *See also* Spoken language; Written language
content of, 82–83
culture and, 78–79
English, evolution of, 77
figurative, 83
literal, 83
nature of, 76–79
pragmatics and, 80–82
relationship between communication, speech and, 78
structures of, 82
Language arts
functional, 330–332, 342–345
technology resources for, 108
Language assessment, 91–96
in culturally and linguistically diverse children, 92–93, 94
nonstandardized procedures, 91–92
standardized measures, 91, 92
for students who might need AAC, 93
written, 159–162 (*See also* Writing assessment)
Language-based learning disabilities (LLD), 91
Language development
in adolescents, 87–89

figurative language, 102–103
literate language forms, 96–102
in school-age children, 84–86
slow, characteristics of, 90
Language disorders
language differences *vs.*, 79, 89–91
statistics related to, 80, 89–90
Language Experience Approach (LEA), 143–144
stages in, 145
Language instruction
for culturally and linguistically diverse children, 104–107
for expository discourse, 100–102
for figurative language, 102–104
for narrative discourse, 96–100
state learning standards and, 96, 97
Language-literate households, 81
Language sampling, 92
Large-group instruction, 60, 61
Learning. *See also* Cooperative learning (CL)
problem-based, 26
student-directed, 25–26
universal design for, 28–30
Learning disabilities. *See* Students with learning disabilities
Learning logs
for science assessment, 253
for social studies assessment, 230
Learning strategies
coping as, 311, 312
integrating study skills with, 296–300
school-age children and, 87
Learning with PURPOSE curriculum, 315–316
assessment tools for, 310
Least restrictive environment (LRE)
principle, 4–5
Left-handedness, 166
Legibility of handwriting, maintaining, 166–167
Lesson plans/planning
development suggestions, 62
fundamentals of, 62
purpose of, 61
sample format for, 62
science, 258–259
Library use skills, 274–275
best practices, 274
semantic web topics and, 288
vignette, 274
Life-Centered Career Education Curriculum, 316
Life skills coursework, 339
Life skills instruments, 336
Lindamood Program for Reading, Spelling, and Speech, 129
Linguistic mnemonics
science, 263–264
social studies, 237–238, 239

Listening skills, 273
best practices, 292
semantic web topics and, 288
vignette, 292
Literacy development, stages in, 111
Literacy instruction, methods for, 114–115
Literal language, 83
Literal reading comprehension, 137
Literate language
development of, 86–87
forms of, 96–102
Logical consequences, 68
Lowercase letters
cursive writing, 164
manuscript writing, 163

MAD strategy, in mathematics instruction, 209
Main idea, in text comprehension, 148–149
map, 151
prompt card, 148
Maintenance
handwriting legibility, 166
instructional grouping for, 61
Manuscript writing, 163–164, 165
Materials adaptation/differentiation, 36–38, 265–266
Mathematics
corrective, 218–219
functional, 210–211, 331, 332–333, 342, 348
Mathematics, problem solving in, 211–212
practices for, 218
programs for, 217–220
simple matrix for, 217
strategies for, 212–217
word problems, challenges in, 213–217
Mathematics assessment
curriculum-based measures of, 192–193
informal, 193–194
purpose of, 190–191
standardized diagnostic measures and, 191–192
standardized general achievement measures and, 191
Mathematics education
CCSS Initiative for, 189
importance of, 187
NCTM Initiatives on, 188–189
NMAP recommendations for, 189–190
Mathematics instruction
computational math, 202–211
considerations for, 194–195
for elementary school students, 205
within a multi-tiered system, 200–202
NMAP recommendations, 189
problem solving, 211–220
technology use and, 199, 202
(*See also* Calculators, use of)